W9-BZF-040

COLOMBIA

ANDREW DIER

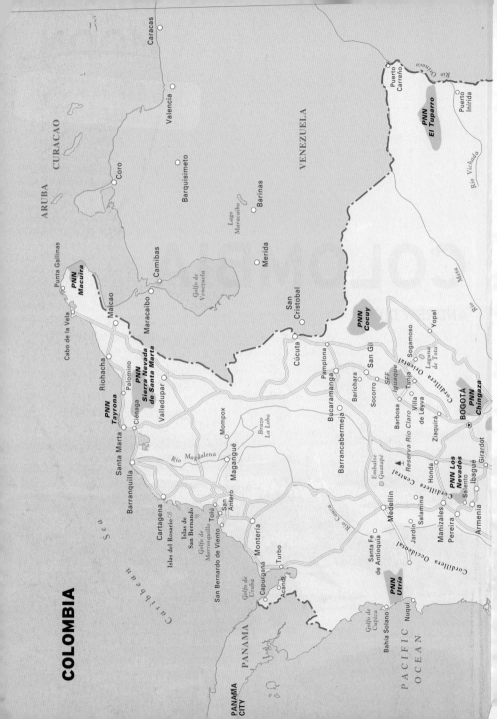

dyllic colonial towns, fast-paced cities, stunning archaeological sites, jaw-dropping scenery, and secluded beaches should be enough to put Colombia on your must-see list. But what really seals the deal is the contagious *alegría* (happiness) of the people you will meet along the way.

Bogotá and Medellín offer all the architecture, culture, restaurants, and nightlife that you would expect in any major world city. For urbanites, these are destinations in their own right. But they are also excellent bases to enjoy creature comforts while organizing trips throughout the country.

Cartagena and the towns of Villa de Leyva and Barichara will transport you back to the 18th century, when citizens were ruled by a king in Madrid. Cartagena never fails to seduce those who stroll along its narrow, cobblestone streets adorned by bougainvillea cascading from balconies above.

The Andes Mountains combined with Colombia's tropical location mean that every possible natural setting is within reach. The Sierra Nevada del Cocuy, virtually unknown outside of Colombia, offers incredible trekking amid glaciers and snowcapped peaks. Coffee farms are nestled in verdant valleys abundant with orchids. Los Llanos, Colombia's eastern

plains, and the Amazon basin are tropical wonderlands, with innumerable opportunities for nature and wildlife viewing.

Even the beaches here are varied. The Caribbean Coast features gems like Parque Nacional Natural Tayrona, where glacier-fed streams flow from snowcapped mountains into the Caribbean Sea. The Pacific Coast offers solitude and a chance to spot humpback whales breaching. And, far from the mainland in the Caribbean, the islands of San Andrés and Providencia are a sultry respite from the rush of city living.

Colombia is one of the most biodiverse countries on the planet. Its people are just as diverse. Beyond differences in language, dialects, and accents, you can tell where someone is from by the songs that they sing, the instruments that they play, and the dances to which they move. In Cali, salsa, with its the fancy footwork, color, and brass instruments, is nothing less than an obsession. In the Llanos, *joropo* is a tribute to Colombian cowboy tradition.

A remarkable transformation has occurred in this corner of South America. And now is a great time to experience this change. Colombia has laid out its welcome mat and beckons: *¡Bienvenidos!*

Planning Your Trip

Where to Go

Bogotá

Against the backdrop of the Andes Mountains, the country's cool capital is a cosmopolitan melting pot. It's a city of stunning colonial and modern architecture, art and culture, glitzy shopping, five-star dining, and euphoric nightlife.

Cartagena and the Caribbean Coast

The Caribbean coastline runs the gamut from the eerie desert landscapes of La Guajira in the far north to the untamed jungles near Capurganá along the Panamanian border. In between are the tropical jungles and mystical Ciudad Perdida of the Sierra Nevada de Santa Marta, as well as Cartagena, the seductive colonial jewel of the Caribbean.

Boyacá and the Santanderes

Cradle of Colombian independence, the departments of Santander and Boyacá are graced with stunning countryside, from the awe-inspiring Cañón del Chicamocha to the snowcapped peaks of the Sierra Nevada del Cocuy. San Gil is the outdoor adventure capital, while nearby Barichara is one of the most beautiful colonial pueblos in the country. The sacred Laguna Iguaque and the nearby town of Villa de Leyva, with its serene white-washed buildings and cobblestone streets, are truly picturesque.

Medellín and the Coffee Region

Ambitious Medellín is known for its temperate climate and fun nightlife. For a break from the city, the Reserva Natural Río Claro makes a fantastic midweek distraction. Photogenic Paisa pueblos abound, with Jardín, Jericó, Salamina, and Salento some of the most colorful. Stay at one of countless coffee haciendas in the lush rolling hills. The landscape is dotted with towering wax palms and brightly colored *barranquero* birds. The snow-covered volcanic peaks of Parque Nacional Natural Los Nevados beckon mountain climbers.

Cali and Southwest Colombia

Colombia's third-largest city is a joyous one of music and dance. When the sun goes down it's hard to resist Cali's hypnotic salsa rhythms. To the west, beyond the endless sugarcane fields of the Valle de Cauca, stands the White City of Popayán, a historic colonial city of presidents and poets. It makes a great base from which to explore the *páramos* of the Parque Nacional Natural Puracé and, beyond that, the mysterious archaeological sites of Tierradentro and San Agustín. Under the looming shadow of Volcán Galeras, Pasto is known for its raucous Carnaval de Negros y Blancos in January. In the bucolic countryside south toward Ecuador are mountains and emerald-green lakes.

IF YOU HAVE...

- **ONE WEEK:** Visit Medellín, stay at a coffee farm, and fly to Cartagena.

- **TWO WEEKS:** Add the Caribbean Coast, then Bogotá and Villa de Leyva.

- **THREE WEEKS:** Add Cali, Popayán, and Parque Nacional Natural Isla Gorgona.

- **FOUR WEEKS:** Add an excursion to the Amazon or Los Llanos.

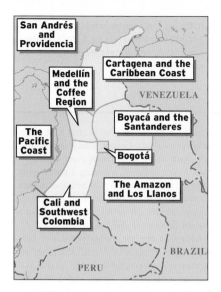

are a playground for humpback whales that spend August through October here. Sea turtles are return visitors, too. Parque Nacional Natural Isla Gorgona is simply spectacular, an island home to endemic species such as the blue anole lizard. Serious divers will want to make the journey to Santuario de Flora y Fauna Malpelo, where schools of hammerhead sharks slowly circle.

San Andrés and Providencia

The paradises of English-speaking San Andrés and Providencia offer everything you'd expect from a Caribbean island vacation. Fantastic diving will keep you occupied for days off of sunny San Andrés. The daily routine of lounging on remote beaches, eating fresh seafood, lazing in hammocks, and stargazing on the beach in perfect Providencia will have you hooked.

The Pacific Coast

The Pacific is Colombia's wild coast, where the thick jungles of Chocó meet the beaches and endless ocean at wonderfully remote Bahía Solano and Nuquí. Warm Pacific waters

The Amazon and Los Llanos

The Amazon rainforest is the lungs of the world. Visit an eco-lodge on the Río Yavarí, where you can take canoe rides above the treetops in the flooded jungle. Observe birds

Iglesia La Ermita, Cali

and pink dolphins by day and look for alligators as darkness falls. Spend a couple of days in the Ticuna village of San Martín and enjoy the blissfully car-free hamlet of Puerto Nariño. In Los Llanos, take in the astonishing wildlife at Hacienda La Aurora. Bathe in the multicolored waters of natural wonder Caño Cristales.

When to Go

Because Colombia straddles the equator, the temperatures and length of days are nearly constant year-round. There are, however, distinct dry and rainy seasons. Throughout most of the country, December through February and July through August are considered *verano* (dry season). *Invierno* (rainy season) is usually between April and May and again between September and November.

In San Andrés and Providencia, June through November is rainy and from February through April it's drier. In the Amazon the drier months are between June and September and the rainy season is December through May. It's worth a visit during either season. In the Pacific coast region, it rains year-round.

High tourist seasons run from mid-December through mid-January, during Easter week (Semana Santa) and, to a lesser extent, school vacations from June to August.

During high season, hotel rates and airline ticket prices soar. Colombians from the interior flock to the Caribbean coast during the New Year's holidays, creating a party atmosphere. In contrast, Bogotá becomes a ghost town during the major holidays. Hotels and flights can also get booked up on the 10 or so *puentes* (long weekends) of the year.

Many of the major festivals and celebrations take place between December and February: the Feria de Cali, the Carnaval de Negros y Blancos in Pasto, Hay Festival in Cartagena, and the Carnaval de Barranquilla. Easter week celebrations are big in colonial cities such as Popayán, Mompóx, Pamplona, and Tunja, while during that time every two years Bogotá puts on the Festival Iberoamericano de Teatro. Humpback whales make their appearance off the Pacific coast from July to October.

the Colombian Amazon

Caño Cristales in Los Llanos

Before You Go

Passports and Visas

Travelers to Colombia who intend to visit as tourists for a period of under 90 days will need only to present a valid passport upon entry in the country. You may be asked to show proof of a return ticket. Tell the immigration officer if you intend to stay up to 90 days, otherwise they will probably give you a stamp permitting a stay of 60 days. Language schools and universities will be able to assist those who may require a year-long student visa.

Vaccinations

There are no obligatory vaccination requirements for visiting Colombia. However, proof of the yellow fever vaccine may be requested upon arrival at the Parque Nacional Natural Tayrona or at the Leticia airport in the Amazon. This vaccination can be obtained at Red Cross clinics throughout the country. If you are traveling onward to countries such as Brazil, Ecuador, or Peru, you may have to provide proof of the vaccine upon entry to those countries.

The Centers for Disease Control and Prevention (CDC) recommends travelers to have all of the basic vaccinations updated. In addition, for most travelers to Colombia, the CDC recommends the hepatitis A and typhoid vaccinations. Hepatitis B, rabies, and yellow fever vaccinations are recommended for some travelers. If you plan to go to the Amazon region, antimalarial drugs may be recommended.

Transportation

Most travelers arrive by plane to Colombia, with the vast majority arriving at the Aeropuerto Internacional El Dorado in Bogotá. There are numerous nonstop international flights into Bogotá from the eastern seaboard of the United States and one flight from Toronto. From Florida and New York there are nonstop flights to Cartagena and Barranquilla. There are flights from Florida to Medellín, Armenia, and Cali.

There are overland border entries from Venezuela (into Cúcuta) and Ecuador (to

Ipiales) and by boat from Peru or Brazil to the Amazonian port of Leticia and from Panama to Capurganá or Cartagena.

Intra-country flights are easy, safe, increasingly more economical, and, above all, quick. Taking the bus to just about anywhere in the country is an inexpensive, popular, and slower option. Renting a car is a viable option in the coffee region where roads are good. In the major cities, there are extensive rapid bus networks, and in Medellín there is a clean and efficient Metro. Private buses and taxis are ubiquitous in cities, although cabs should be ordered by phone. The best way to see the sights of most cities is usually on foot.

What to Take

For those interested in jungle exploration, waterproof hiking boots and possibly some collapsible trekking poles are musts. If going to the Amazon, Capurganá, or to the Pacific coast, a waterproof camera bag and silica gel may prevent the heartache of a ruined camera. For caving, visiting the tombs of Tierradentro, and for finding your way at night, a small flashlight will be of great use and comfort. To spot humpbacks, anacondas, and birds, binoculars will be great to have. If you plan on spending much time on the coast, bringing your own snorkeling gear is a good idea.

To protect against the sun, pack a wide-brimmed hat; against the rain, a lightweight rain jacket and compact umbrella; against the cold, a sweatshirt and lightweight sweaters; against mosquitoes, lightweight and light-colored long-sleeved shirts and some strong repellent. For long bus rides, earplugs, eye masks, and luggage locks will make the trip more relaxing. Finally, a Latin American Spanish dictionary will help you get your point across and make friends.

Casual attire is fine at most restaurants, theaters, and religious venues. Some restaurants in Bogotá and Cartagena may expect more of an effort. In large cities, you'll want to dress to impress in bars and clubs. Shorts are generally frowned upon in interior cities.

sunset in Puerto Nariño, the Amazon

The Best of Colombia

There's not one clear-cut, common way to visit uncommon Colombia. For a first-time visit, a tour of the coffee region and Cartagena on the Caribbean coast will be a beautiful and easy week-long introduction to this fascinating country. In two weeks, you can squeeze in Medellín, a Paisa pueblo or two, the sublime colonial town of Villa de Leyva in Boyacá, and cap it all off with a weekend in fast-paced Bogotá. With a third week, you can explore southwest Colombia and salsa the night away in Cali.

Medellín and the Coffee Region

DAY 1

Arrive in the evening at the Aeropuerto Internacional José María Córdova in Rionegro, outside of Medellín. Make the one-hour trip via cab or bus into town. Get settled at the no-nonsense Hotel Ibis, across from the Museo de Arte Moderno de Medellín, or at the friendly Urban Buddha hostel in the leafy Laureles neighborhood.

Head to the always-lively Parque Lleras area of the Poblado neighborhood. Familiarize yourself with Colombian cuisine at Mondongo's, then have a beer at the coolest corner store in town, El Social Tienda Mixta.

DAY 2

Discover downtown Medellín by taking a ride on the Metro. Here you can check out the finest art museum in the region, the Museo de Antioquia, and have your picture taken in front of your favorite rotund Fernando Botero sculpture in the adjacent plaza.

Hop on the Metro again to see symbols of the new Medellín: the Metrocable gondola network and the Biblioteca España, a boldly designed public library built on the side of a mountain. From there, transfer once more to another Metrocable line to the Parque Arví, a huge recreational area.

Head back to your hotel and freshen up before checking out a salsa or tango bar after dinner.

Medellín at night

DAY 3

Take the three-hour bus ride through the southern Antioquian countryside to the picture-perfect Paisa town of Jardín. Hang out with the locals in the sublime Parque Principal, a park bursting with flowers. Explore the neo-gothic Basílica Menor de la Inmaculada Concepción. Nurse a beer or sip a hot *tinto* at one of the park's *tiendas* (shops).

Relax at the low-key hostel Casa Selva y Café, a pleasant walk away from the town center. Birding and nature enthusiasts will want to stay at La Esperanza.

DAY 4

Set off for the coffee region by heading to Manizales in the morning on a five-hour bus ride. Once in town, have a coffee under the shadow of the remarkable El Cable tower, a gondola system that once transported coffee over the mountains to the Río Magdalena.

Check in to a coffee farm in the valleys near Chinchiná in the late afternoon. The folks from Hacienda Venecia or Hacienda Guayabal, only about a half hour away, can pick you up in town.

DAY 5

Take a tour of a coffee farm today, and admire the orderly rows of deep green coffee plants adorned with bright red beans. Cap it off with a cup of 100 percent Colombian—served black. It's called *tinto*. In the afternoon, take a bus to one of the region's cutest pueblos, Salento, a five-hour trip.

Stay at the bright orange Tralala hostel and have dinner at wonderful La Eliana.

DAY 6

Walk through pasture land and tropical forest of the Valle de Cocora to the Reserva Acaime, where you can watch the hummingbirds flit about at the feeders while you warm up with a *tinto* (coffee). Then head back down through a wonderland of 60-meter-high (200-foot-high) wax palms, Colombia's national tree, in the Valle de Cocora.

Spend the night again in Salento. Before you retire for the night, stroll the atmospheric Calle Real.

verdant valleys in the coffee region

Jet-Setting

Parque Nacional Natural Tayrona

If you don't have the time for a long overland trip, consider flying to these destinations from the major cities.

Getaways close to airports in larger cities such as Santa Marta, Neiva, Montería, and Yopal are served by various major airlines. Check smaller airlines such as **Satena** (Colombian toll-free tel. 01/800-091-2034, www.satena.com) or **Aerolínea de Antioquia** (Colombian toll-free tel. 01/800-051-4232, www.ada-aero.com) for the smaller destinations.

FROM BOGOTÁ

- **Hacienda La Aurora:** See wildlife like never before at this cattle ranch and nature reserve in the Llanos. (Airport: Yopal)
- **Caño Cristales:** Discover the secret of the multicolored waters at this serene national park in the southern Llanos. (Airport: La Macarena)
- **San Agustín:** You'll be blown away by Colombia's best-preserved archaeological site, nestled in the rolling mountains south of Neiva. (Airport: Neiva)
- **Parque Nacional Natural Tayrona:** Enjoy a quick beach break at the spectacular

PNN Tayrona. Be sure to save some time for a jungle hike to **El Pueblito,** remnants of a former Tayrona settlement high in the mountains. (Airport: Santa Marta)

FROM MEDELLÍN

- **Pacific Coast:** Breathtaking sunsets, remote beaches, and the chance to see visiting humpback whales make for a memorable getaway from Medellín. (Airport: Bahía Solano or Nuquí)
- **Capurganá:** On the Panamanian border, Capurganá is a Darien Gap outpost, home to tropical rainforest and wild beach landscapes. (Airport: Acandí or Capurganá)
- **Reserva Natural Viento Solar:** Rejuvenate at this nature reserve set in tropical dry forest along a strip of forgotten coast north of Montería. (Airport: Montería or Tolú)

FROM CALI

- **Parque Nacional Natural Isla Gorgona:** Colombia's version of the Galapagos Islands was also once its Alcatraz. You'll have this incredible island park almost all to yourself. (Airport: Guapi)

Cartagena and the Caribbean Coast

DAY 1

From nearby Pereira, fly to Cartagena, 1.5 hours away. Once you land and change into the airy attire standard for the sultry city, get to know the area by taking a stroll on the massive ramparts protecting the city.

Have dinner at La Vitrola, a Cartagena classic. Spend the night at the Hotel Sofitel Legend Santa Clara or the Blue House hostel, a good budget option.

DAY 2

Walk the Old City streets, getting lost and found again as you amble from the divine Plaza de Bolívar to the Plaza Santo Domingo to Las Murallas, the city's walls. Be sure to check out the impressive Castillo de San Felipe in the late afternoon.

Don't miss out on the old-style fun at Café Havana, and be sure to try one of their famous rum drinks. Go for pizza afterward at nearby Pavia before returning to your hotel for the night.

DAY 3

For a change of pace, take a cab or bus to Bocagrande, Cartagena's version of Miami Beach. A walk along the bay in the Castillo Grande district is a fine way to pass the day.

Spend some time in the hip and happening area of Getsemaní, a neighborhood of tapas bars and watering holes. For inventive local cuisine, try La Cocina de Pepina.

DAYS 4-6

From the Muelle Turístico in town, take a boat to the beaches of Islas del Rosario, the area's finest beaches, and spend a couple of nights at an island hotel. It's worth splurging for the Coralina Isla Boutique.

Return to Cartagena in the late afternoon and take one last walk on the walls, enjoying a cocktail at Café del Mar and dinner at La Cevichería.

EXCURSION TO LA GUAJIRA

If you have 4-5 extra days, consider taking a trip to La Guajira, a desert peninsula that is home to the Wayúu people.

Start at the beach in Palomino or in

Bougainvillea spills onto the streets of Cartagena's Old City.

Riohacha, the departmental capital of La Guajira, and join up with an organized tour group. After a dusty ride past countless cacti and lonely goats, you'll arrive at Cabo de la Vela, where you can take a dip in the Caribbean Sea or try your luck wind- or kite-surfing.

The next stop is Punta Gallinas, the northernmost point of South America. Spend a day or two on a photo safari of the unusual landscape of desert dunes that drop dramatically into the sea.

Take a canoe trip to explore the mangroves, then share a huge, freshly prepared lobster with a friend. If there's time, check out the Santuario de Fauna y Flora Los Flamencos to the southwest for an early morning or late afternoon canoe ride in search of flamingos.

Bogotá and Boyacá
DAY 1
Fly into Bogotá. Set in the Andes at an elevation of 2,625 meters (8,612 feet), the Colombian capital city can be especially cool, so pack some layers and an umbrella. In the late afternoon, wander the historic Candelaria district and visit the world-famous Museo del Oro. Stay at the Casa Platypus downtown.

DAY 2
Take a bus or hire a car for the 3.5-hour trip to the low-key pueblo of Villa de Leyva, one of Colombia's best preserved colonial towns, in the department of Boyacá.

Enjoy the unique atmosphere in Villa de Leyva by walking its stone streets. Check out the woolen *ruanas* (ponchos) at Alieth Tejido Artesanal, and if you have time, check out the Convento del Santo Ecce Homo in the desert nearby.

Stay at the Casa Viena Hostel or splurge at the Hotel Plaza Mayor, where the views are great.

DAY 3
Visit the Santuario Flora y Fauna Iguaque just outside of town and hike to the mist-shrouded Laguna Iguaque for some morning exhilaration. Relax in Villa de Leyva for the evening.

DAYS 4-5
Return to Bogotá and, if it's a weekend day,

the Plaza de Bolívar in Bogotá

Music and Dance Festivals

dancers getting ready for Carnaval in Barranquilla

Get your groove on at these colorful music and dance festivals.

CALI

Caleños boast that their city is the world capital of salsa, and there's no denying that it's an integral part of daily life in Cali. The last week of the year is the **Feria de Cali,** a week-long event of salsa concerts, parties, and pageantry that takes over the city.

Other festivals worth checking out are August's **Festival Mundial de Salsa,** which showcases the glitz and frenetic footwork of the dance, and the **Festival Petronio Álvarez,** a September celebration of Pacific Coast music and culture.

VILLAVICENCIO

On the Llanos, the great eastern plains of Colombia, cowhands work on cattle ranches during the day. At night, they get out their harps and jam a Llanero form of waltz called *joropo*. During the **Torneo Internacional del Joropo** in June, musicians and dancers from across the Llanos converge on Villavicencio, participating in open-air concerts and competitions. Cowboys show their stuff in Llanero rodeos during the week-long festival.

MEDELLÍN

Tango has a long history in Medellín. The **Festival Internacional de Tango** is held each year in June, offering four days of free concerts and dance performances across the city.

BARRANQUILLA

Colombia's favorite festival is the **Carnaval de Barranquilla,** held each year in February. *Cumbia,* an intriguing mix of indigenous, African, and Spanish musical styles, takes center stage at this multi-day event of parades, concerts, and parties.

BOGOTÁ

Typical of the way this metropolis rolls, Bogotá doesn't have just one music celebration. From July to November, the action takes place in the city's largest park, the Parque Simón Bolívar, during the **Festivales al Parque** series of festivals: Salsa al Parque, Jazz al Parque, Opera al Parque, and the thumping Rock al Parque. Best of all, it's free.

go to the top of the Torre Colpatria for an incredible 360-degree view of the massive city. Spend a night in the Zona Rosa and splurge on a meal at Andrés Carne de Res, Colombia's most famous restaurant. Here, the line between dining and rumba gets blurred at around 8 o'clock.

If the next morning is a Sunday, enjoy the city's Ciclovía by renting a bike and joining the thousands of Bogotanos hitting the streets for a little exercise. If it's not a Sunday, you can still stroll the streets.

San Agustín, Popayán, and Cali
DAYS 1-2
Fly into Neiva and immediately head south to San Agustín, the most important archaeological site in Colombia. It's the country's version of Easter Island, set amid lush countryside in the Cordillera Central of the Andes. Take your time visiting the park: Two days should do it.

Stay within walking distance of the park at one of the cute hotels dotting the countryside.

DAY 3
Flag down a bus headed westward and check out the country's other archaeological site. Tierradentro is a series of underground burial tombs spread atop hills in the lush Valle de Cauca countryside. It's a scenic place, and you should take your time and walk the sites at a leisurely pace.

Stay in the village of San Andrés de Pisimbalá at the La Portada hotel.

DAY 4
Take the four-hour scenic bus ride to the historic White City of Popayán. Wander the streets and linger in the beautiful Parque Caldas.

Stay at the Hostel Caracol, where friendly staff will let you take the hostel dog for a late-afternoon walk around town. Before retiring, settle into a booth at El Sotareño and listen to some tango music over a cold beer.

DAY 5
Take the easy two-hour bus ride to Cali. In the late afternoon, enjoy the atmosphere of the

pre-Columbian statue in San Agustín

iguana in San Andrés

Parque San Antonio, the best place for people-watching or enjoying the sunset.

Have dinner in one of the cozy restaurants in the sloping San Antonio neighborhood, and stay there, too, at the Ruta Sur hostel or the San Antonio Hotel Boutique. Later, check out a *salsateca* (dance club) for a truly authentic Cali experience. Get a good night's rest to prepare for your flight home tomorrow.

Excursions and Side Trips

SAN ANDRÉS AND PROVIDENCIA

If you're looking to get away from it all, go to the island of Providencia, part of the San Andrés Archipelago, off the coast of Nicaragua. Allot at least four days for some solid beach relaxation time.

Fly into San Andrés. To get to Providencia from there, it's just a short flight. Once in Providencia, stay at the Hotel Sirius, where dive experts can take you to the reefs for a few underwater adventures. Add 1-2 days in San Andrés if you're into snorkeling, diving, and drinking coco locos.

THE AMAZON

This quick but meaningful Amazon adventure will require at least four days. Leticia is the gateway to the Colombian Amazon. It's a two-hour flight from Bogotá. At the Reserva Natural Tanimboca, you can stay in a tree-house in the jungle, just minutes from town.

For the next couple of days, take a boat up the world's most powerful river and visit the Ticuna community of San Martín. Continue onward to the decidedly eco-friendly Puerto Nariño.

Alternatively, you can head straight to the eco-lodges along the Río Yavarí, in Brazil, where you can take day and nighttime safaris, discovering the abundant life of the Amazonian rainforest and river.

Mountain Highs

Colombia is a great place to conquer the longest continental mountain range in the world, the famed **Andes Mountains.** Extending from Chile and Argentina northward to Colombia and Venezuela, the Andes split into three chains at the Colombia-Ecuador border.

The highest mountains in Colombia are within about 40 kilometers of the palm-lined beaches of the Parque Nacional Natural Tayrona. This is the **Sierra Nevada de Santa Marta,** a mountain chain independent of the Andes, which comprises the world's highest coastal mountains.

- **Ciudad Perdida:** Take the famed multi-day jungle hike to archeological site Ciudad Perdida (Lost City), high in the mountains of the Sierra Nevada de Santa Marta.

- **Sierra Nevada del Cocuy:** Dramatic snow-capped mountains, valleys filled with armies of *frailejón* plants, and crystalline mountain lakes await at the stunning Sierra Nevada del Cocuy. You can spend two or three days day-hiking through the Parque Nacional Natural Cocuy, or the more adventurous can organize a six-day tour.

- **Parque Nacional Natural Los Nevados:** Parque Nacional Natural Los Nevados, in the Cordillera Central, offers hikers of all abilities the opportunity to explore misty cloud forests and get glimpses of snow-covered volcanoes. Take a day tour to the park from Manizales, a one- or three-day trek toward Laguna del Otún from Pereira, or a challenging multi-day trek from Salento to the Nevado del Tolima. Keep your eyes peeled for the iconic Andean condor.

- **Parque Nacional Natural Puracé:** In Parque Nacional Natural Puracé, ambitious hikers can get up at dawn, hike through the tropical forest to the top of Volcán del Puracé, and be back in Popayán for dinner.

- **Parque Municipal Natural Planes de San Rafael and Parque Nacional Natural Tatamá:** In the Cordillera Occidental, check out the lesser-visited

the Ciudad Perdida, in the Sierra Nevada de Santa Marta

Parque Municipal Natural Planes de San Rafael, a former cattle ranch that has been converted into a nature reserve. Beyond that, there's Parque Nacional Natural Tatamá, where you can see the Pacific Ocean beyond the carpet of green of the Chocó rainforest.

- **Parque Natural Chicaque and Parque Nacional Natural Chingaza:** Within minutes of busy Bogotá are various mountain adventures fit for day trips. Parque Natural Chicaque is a private park south of the city. Start your hike in the cold cloud forest, and within minutes the climate and natural surroundings have morphed into tropical hot country. PNN Chingaza is a serene national park of *páramos* and mountain lakes, and is the source of water for eight million thirsty Bogotanos.

The Wild Coasts

If you have the time and an adventurous spirit, check out some of Colombia's wildest stretches of coastline, from the rocky Pacific to the Darien to the dry tropical forests of Córdoba. Try this itinerary in September or October when the whales are frolicking in the Pacific, the waters are calm in the Caribbean, and the tourists have gone back to work and school.

Caribbean Coast

This week-long itinerary takes you to lesser known points along the Caribbean coast. Be prepared to take several modes of transportation in order to get around. If you don't have a full week to spend here, prioritize a visit to Capurganá or Reserva Natural Viento Solar.

DAY 1

From Medellín, take the hour-long flight to the Darien Gap community of Capurganá. On the Caribbean side of the isthmus, a horse-drawn taxi will take you to your jungle lodge. Stay at friendly Cabañas Darius or at the honeymoon-worthy Bahía Lodge.

DAY 2

Walk through the jungle, over the mountain, to the sleepy community of Sapzurro, paying no attention to the cacophony of annoyed howler monkeys. Continue on to Panama if you'd like: It's just a 20-minute hike away, on the other side of a steep and muddy hill. At La Miel on the Panama side of the border, take a dip in the calm waters.

DAY 3

Spend the day diving or snorkeling around the reefs off the coastline of Capurganá. Enjoy dinner on the beach at Donde Josefina.

If you have more time, contact Posada del Gecko to arrange a side trip to Panama's San Blas islands, where you can visit a Guna indigenous village.

poison dart frog, Capurganá

sunset on Playa Almejal, El Valle

DAY 4

Take a boat to the port of Turbo (or fly to Montería) and hop on a bus to Reserva Natural Viento Solar. It's a long day of interesting traveling from the Darien, usually involving several modes of transportation. Expect to be on the road and sea for about eight hours.

This nature reserve is in tropical dry forest on the Córdoba coast. Take a relaxing walk on the beach in the afternoon.

DAY 5

Walk through the forest surrounding Reserva Natural Viento Solar and look for impossibly cute *osos perezosos* (sloths). Snooze in a hammock, then kayak in the calm waters before the sun goes down. Spend your last night at the reserve in an open-air thatched roof hut, lulled to sleep by the gentle breeze and rolling waves in the distance.

DAY 6

Make your way to the beach community of Tolú, with a detour to San Antero. Have a spectacular meal at Pesecar, with an even more spectacular view of Bahía de Cispatá and the mangroves beyond.

Take a mangrove cruise and visit the Asocaiman turtle and alligator nature refuge run by local fishers. Continue onwards to Tolú, where you can take an evening *bici-taxi* (pedicab) tour of this charming fishing town.

DAY 7

If you have more time, set sail to the Islas de San Bernardo and spend a night or two at a rustic or extremely swank hotel—your choice! If you're there during the week, you might have your own private island. Otherwise, catch a flight at the Aeropuerto Golfo de Morrosquillo back to Medellín.

Pacific Coast

The Pacific coast is different from the Caribbean side. There are few roads, and the main mode of transportation is by boat. The best way to visit the Pacific is to pick a spot and limit your time to that area. If you make your accommodations arrangements beforehand, your hostel or lodge will pick you up from the airport. Your lodge can also arrange humpback whale-watching trips from July to October. Seeing these great creatures is a highlight of any visit to the Pacific.

Parque Nacional Natural Utría on the Pacific coast

BAHÍA SOLANO

This town at the fringe of the jungle is a great base for any activity. Go diving or sport-fishing, or hike in the jungle or along the beach to crystal-clear swimming holes and waterfalls like the Cascada Chocolatal. Or hang out in orderly and walkable Bahía Solano and experience city life, Pacific style.

Spend a few nights at one of Bahía Solano's hotels, like Posada Turística Rocas de Cabo Marzo or Posada Turística Hostal del Mar. The flight to Bahía Solano from Medellín takes one hour. You can even walk from the airport to your hotel.

EL VALLE

El Valle boasts broad beaches and the fantastic Estación Septiembre Sea Turtle Hatchery, where newborn sea turtles are born and released into the turbulent waters of the Pacific Ocean, as well as unforgettable sunsets over Playa Almejal.

Stay the night at one of the several fantastic beachside lodges and hostels of El Valle, or get to know the cultural life of the people of the Pacific by staying at one of the *posadas nativas* (guesthouses owned and operated by locals) here, such as Villa Maga or El Nativo.

Get to El Valle by flying into the Bahía Solano airport. El Valle is home to one of the few roads in this area, so you can hop on a *colectivo* to reach your lodge.

NUQUÍ

Five-star eco-lodges, as well as a few economical options, abound on the coastline near Nuquí. If you stay at one of the eco-lodges, like El Cantíl, Morromico, or Luna de Miel, you'll quickly become accustomed to being pampered. Their all-inclusive packages include great seafood dinners, access to remote beaches, guided nature hikes (in search of poisonous frogs!), and day trips to Afro-Colombian villages.

The flight into Nuquí from Medellín takes 45 minutes.

PARQUE NACIONAL NATURAL UTRÍA

This beautiful national park between Nuquí and Bahía Solano is the perfect option for those who want to be surrounded by nature. Take a hike, discover a remote beach, or go swimming. At night, you can hunt for glow-in-the-dark mushrooms, then fall asleep to the sounds of the rainforest.

You can reach PNN Utría from either the Bahía Solano or Nuquí airport. Park staff will pick you up.

Colonial Towns and Countryside

Gorgeous countryside, historic pueblos and cities, and outdoor adventures: Get a taste of what Bogotá, Boyacá, and Santander have to offer.

Days 1-3

Spend a couple of days in Bogotá wandering the Candelaria, the capital city's *centro histórico,* then visit the Quinta de Bolívar, Simón Bolívar's old country home. Don't miss the Cerro de Monserrate, a pilgrimage site with unsurpassed views of the metropolis. Hike up, then take a ride on the gondola or tram back down.

Learn about Colombia's past from the time of the Muiscas to its shaky years as an independent nation in the city's excellent museums, like the extensive art galleries of the Colección de Arte del Banco de la República and the mesmerizing Museo del Oro.

Days 4-5

After setting off from Bogotá, make your way to Tunja, a three-hour bus ride. Tunja is a city of spectacular colonial churches. Spend a few hours checking them out, then head on to the nearby colonial town of Villa de Leyva, one of the country's most beautiful and well-preserved pueblos, just 45 minutes away.

Villa de Leyva's charm is in its quiet atmosphere and lovely whitewashed colonial architecture. The Plaza Mayor is the top place to experience both. In the countryside nearby, check out the Santuario Fauna y Flora Iguaque for a half-day hike to Laguna Iguaque, which was sacred to the Muiscas. In the adjacent arid deserts, visit the lovely Convento del Santo Ecce Homo.

Day 6

Take a bus to Ráquira and spend the day visiting the Convento de la Candelaria, just

Catedral Primada, La Candelaria district of Bogotá

outside of town. Tour the complex, then head back to town to shop for handicrafts, like the city's famous clay pots.

Day 7

Today is a travel day. Return to Tunja to catch a bus bound for Barichara, which is Villa de Leyva's rival for most beautiful pueblo. Judge for yourself as you walk the stone streets of this old tobacco town in the department of Santander.

Stroll the famous Camino Real to the indigenous village of Guane and return to Barichara in time for the spectacular sunset. Stay at the Color de Hormiga Hostel and wake up to the chirping of cheerful, amazingly colorful birds.

Day 8

Barichara makes a great base for all sorts of outdoor adventures in and around San Gil. Spend a day hiking to waterfalls, rafting, splashing in swimming holes, or caving. Have dinner at Gringo Mike's in San Gil. Stay in Barichara unless you want to be in the middle of the action of San Gil.

Days 9-11

Head north to Bucaramanga. On the way there, visit the Cañón del Chicamocha and be blown away by the views. It's a 1.5-hour trip to the canyon.

Once you make it to Bucaramanga, chat up other world travelers in town at the Kasa Guane. If charm is what you seek, head to the colonial district of nearby Girón, checking in at the Girón Chill Out Hotel Boutique and strolling the town's old streets in the evening.

On your last morning in the area, cap things off by paragliding at Mesa de Ruitoque outside of Bucaramanga. If soaring above the green valleys is too much action, visit the beautiful Jardín Botánico Eloy Valenzuela in Floridablanca and munch on a sweet *oblea* (wafer) in the town center afterward.

From the Bucaramanga airport, catch a flight back to Bogotá.

Excursion to El Cocuy

Got more time and need some mountains to conquer? You can get to the Sierra Nevada del Cocuy by land directly from Tunja or from Bucaramanga, going through the highland university town of Pamplona. Add at least four more days for this option.

vivid green hills near Bucaramanga

BOGOTÁ

Busy Bogotá is Colombia's cool capital—and not just in terms of its famously chilly nights. A few years ago, visitors would arrive at the El Dorado airport and spend two days maximum in the Andean metropolis before taking the next flight to Cartagena. Now people are staying awhile, and it's easy to see why.

© ANDREW DIER

HIGHLIGHTS

LOOK FOR ◖ TO FIND RECOMMENDED SIGHTS, ACTIVITIES, DINING, AND LODGING.

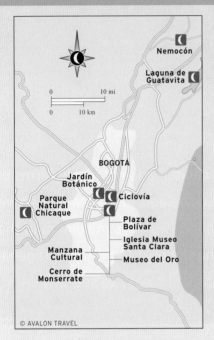

© AVALON TRAVEL

◖ **Iglesia Museo Santa Clara:** This stunning colonial-era church is decorated in the Mudejar style (page 39).

◖ **Manzana Cultural:** Colombia's tumultuous history has given rise to some noteworthy creative expression that is on display in the art museums of the city's cultural block (page 42).

◖ **Museo del Oro:** Anthropology, history, and art combine in this extraordinary presentation of pre-Columbian gold artifacts (page 45).

◖ **Cerro de Monserrate:** The views atop this hill are incredible both by day and by night (page 46).

◖ **Jardín Botánico:** Countless shades of green are on display in this lovely park minutes from downtown (page 51).

◖ **Ciclovía:** When a city can get a quarter of its population to get out and ride a bike on a Sunday, you know it's doing something right (page 61).

◖ **Nemocón:** The plaza and streets of this little-visited salt-mining town are full of charm (page 83).

◖ **Plaza de Bolívar:** Colombia's most important and most photographed plaza is named for Simón Bolívar, the man who gave the country independence (page 36).

◖ **Laguna de Guatavita:** This sacred lake is the source of the El Dorado myth (page 84).

◖ **Parque Natural Chicaque:** Minutes from La Candelaria, the cloud forests of this park seem miles away from everything (page 88).

There is the Museo del Oro, of course, undoubtedly one of the best museums in Latin America. There are precious few reminders of the Muisca settlement of Bacatá in this vast concrete jungle of today, but this museum is a stellar tribute to a people who all but disappeared within decades of the Spanish conquest.

Then there is the living museum that is the historic district, La Candelaria. Every street block has its unique story to tell: the flower vase that changed history, the loyal companion who saved the Liberator's neck, the generosity of a famous painter. Colonial churches surprise with their quiet, steadfast beauty, and grandiose buildings along the Avenida Jiménez stand as testament to the aspirations of the "Athens of South America." Red buses, glitzy shopping areas, and stunning libraries set in manicured parks are proof that Bogotá can, with a little investment and good government, overcome the formidable challenges of its recent past.

A melting pot of nearly eight million, Bogotá

is home to Colombians from every corner of the country who come to study, seek opportunity, or crave the freedom and anonymity that this sprawling city of eight million offers. It shouldn't come as a surprise that it is the country's culinary and cultural capital as well. This is the place to enjoy nouvelle Colombian cuisine, with flavors from the two coasts at a host of innovative restaurants. It's the place where there is always something going on—a massive theater festival, a symphony concert, a dance marathon courtesy of a big-name DJ, a gallery opening—it's just a matter of finding out when and where. Bogotanos' reputation for being gloomy and cerebral is unfair. You only need to experience the sheer *alegría* (joyfulness) of Andrés Carne de Res one weekend night for proof.

When the sensory overload and intensity of this over-caffeinated city becomes too much, the *páramos* (highland moors), cloud forests, and mountain lakes of extraordinary natural parks beckon. Parque Nacional Natural Chingaza, Parque Natural Chicaque, and Laguna de Guatavita are all only about an hour away.

HISTORY

As early as AD 300, the Muisca people settled along the Cordillera Oriental (Eastern Mountain Range) of the Andes Mountains, forming a loose confederation. Bacatá (now Bogotá) was the seat of the Zipa, head of the southern confederation. The Muiscas had an agricultural economy but also extracted salt and emeralds, wove fine textiles, and actively traded for cotton, shells, and gold with other indigenous peoples. The names of many of their settlements—Chía, Suba, Engativá—survive, though no physical traces remain.

Lured by tales of riches, three European armies converged on Muisca territory in 1538. An army headed by Spanish conquistador Gonzalo Jiménez de Quesada arrived from Santa Marta. Another army, headed by Spaniard Sebastián de Belalcázar, arrived from the south. A third army, led by German expeditionary Nikolaus Federmann, arrived from present-day Venezuela.

By the time Federmann and Belalcázar arrived, Jiménez de Quesada had plundered the Muisca lands and had founded, in August 1538, a settlement that he named Santa Fe de Bogotá del Nuevo Reino de Granada de las Indias del Mar. In the late 17th century, the population was less than 15,000 inhabitants. European diseases had almost completely wiped out the Muisca population. Marriages between Muiscas and the Spanish formed the *mestizo* base of the city.

The city was the seat of the first provisional government established after Colombia's declaration of independence in 1810. In 1819, the name of the city was changed to Bogotá, and it became capital of the newly formed Gran Colombia. The city was not connected by railroad to the outside world until the end of the 19th century—and then only to Girardot, a port on the Río Magdalena.

The early decades of the 20th century were a period of growth and prosperity. The post-war period was a time of rapid, haphazard development that saw the establishment of many new industries. Much of the growth was unplanned, and sprawling slums developed, especially in the south of the city.

By the 1990s, Bogotá had become synonymous with poverty, crime, and urban sprawl. A series of mayors, including Enrique Peñalosa and Antanas Mockus, transformed the city. Peñalosa undertook large projects such as the TransMilenio rapid bus system, reclaimed public space, and invested heavily in education and basic services. Mockus worked to improve security and increase civic consciousness. Between 1995 and 2003, the city transformed itself.

Despite all its challenges Bogotá continues to be the economic, cultural, and educational powerhouse of Colombia. The city is a magnet for people from all over Colombia and, in recent years, even from abroad. Today Bogotá ranks as the fifth largest city in South America.

PLANNING YOUR TIME

At the minimum, give Bogotá two days. In that short time span, you can cover La Candelaria, head up to Monserrate, discover the Museo del Oro, and enjoy some good meals in the Zona T, Zona G, or the Macarena.

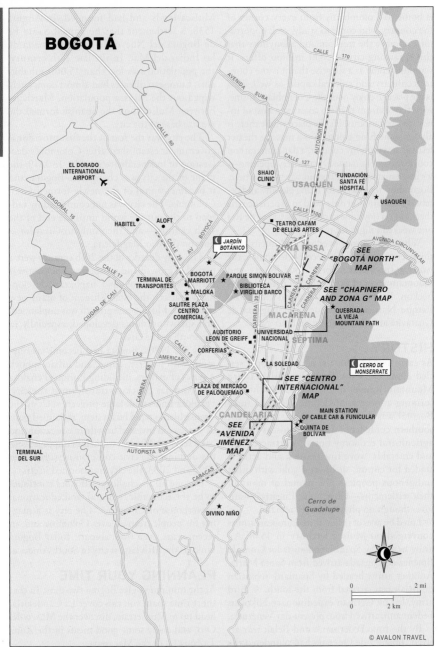

BOGOTÁ

CALLE 170

AVENIDA SUBA

CALLE 80

CALLE 127

AUTONORTE

EL DORADO
INTERNATIONAL
AIRPORT ✈

DIAGONAL 16

CALLE 100

SHAIO
CLINIC ■

FUNDACIÓN
SANTA FÉ
HOSPITAL ■

USAQUÉN

★ USAQUÉN

HABITEL ●   ALOFT ●

CALLE 26

AV. BOYACÁ

TEATRO CAFAM
DE BELLAS ARTES ■

🌙 JARDÍN
BOTÁNICO

ZONA ROSA

AVENIDA CIRCUNVALAR

CALLE 17

★

BOGOTÁ
MARRIOTT ■

PARQUE SIMÓN BOLÍVAR ★

*SEE
"BOGOTÁ NORTH"
MAP*

TERMINAL DE
TRANSPORTES ■

■ MALOKA

BIBLIOTECA
★ VIRGILIO BARCO

CARRERA 15

CARRERA 11

CARRERA 7

*SEE "CHAPINERO
AND ZONA G" MAP*

CIUDAD DE CALI

SALITRE PLAZA
CENTRO
COMERCIAL ■

CARRERA 30

MACARENA

★ QUEBRADA
LA VIEJA
MOUNTAIN PATH

AUDITORIO
LEÓN DE GREIFF ■

UNIVERSIDAD
NACIONAL

SÉPTIMA

CALLE 13

LAS
AMERICAS

CORFERIAS ★

★ LA SOLEDAD

🌙 CERRO DE
MONSERRATE

CARRERA 68

PLAZA DE MERCADO
DE PALOQUEMAO ■

*SEE "CENTRO
INTERNACIONAL"
MAP*

CANDELARIA

MAIN STATION
OF CABLE CAR & FUNICULAR

★ QUINTA DE
BOLÍVAR

AUTOPISTA SUR

*SEE
"AVENIDA
JIMÉNEZ"
MAP*

TERMINAL
DEL SUR ■

CARACAS

★ DIVINO NIÑO

*Cerro de
Guadalupe*

0   2 mi

0   2 km

🌙

With about five days you can explore neighborhoods like the Macarena, check out the botanical gardens, or make a day trip to the Parque Natural Chicaque or to the Laguna de Guatavita. If you're here over a Sunday, you'll absolutely have to head out to the Ciclovía.

If you are staying in Colombia for 10 days, you can try a city-country combo by adding Villa de Leyva. Or make it a city-coast combo, adding a Caribbean Coast destination such as Cartagena or Santa Marta.

Many museums are closed on either Monday or Tuesday. The Museo del Oro is closed Mondays and the art museums of the Manzana Cultural are closed Tuesdays. During the end-of-year holidays and Holy Week (Semana Santa), Bogotá becomes a ghost town as locals head for the countryside, the coast, or abroad. There is very little traffic at those times, but many restaurants are closed and nightspots are empty, especially around Christmas. Bogotá is a particularly dull place to be on New Year's Eve. Semana Santa is perhaps less lonely and can be a good time to visit, especially when the biennial theater festival is on. On long weekends, many Bogotanos skip town; those from the provinces come for a visit.

SAFETY

Bogotá is much safer than it once was, but it is no Copenhagen. The best advice is to, as Colombians would say, *"no dar papaya."* Literally, that translates to "don't give any papayas." Don't hand someone the opportunity to take advantage of you.

While strolling in La Candelaria, keep a watchful eye on cameras and other gadgets. Better yet, leave valuables—including passports—locked away in the hotel safe if possible. Private security guards and police now regularly patrol La Candelaria at night, although it may feel a little spooky after 10 or 11 at night.

You will often come across homeless people or those who claim to be displaced. Most—but not all—of these people are harmless. While ample social services do exist in the city, many of the city's destitute do not have the wherewithal to access them. When street people ask

for money, you may want to have some spare change, a bottle of water, or leftover food to give out (but only if you do not feel threatened in any way).

Traveling by the city's SITP buses is safe and comfortable. The red TransMilenio buses can get crowded, so be aware of pickpockets. Private buses and *colectivos* are less safe and drivers can be reckless.

Bogotá has had a serious problem with taxi crime, commonly known as *paseo milonario.* But recent technological advances have made a noticeable dent in these crimes. Tappsi, a popular and free smartphone app, is indispensable. With this app, you can request a cab, find out the name of the driver, and have your trip tracked by a friend. Alternatively, you can order a cab over the phone. Avoid hailing cabs off the street, particularly when you are alone, when it is late at night, and near nightclubs and upscale dining areas.

If you are heading out for a night on the town, do not accept drinks from strangers. Leave credit/debit cards, your passport, and expensive cell phones at home.

During an emergency, call 123 from any phone.

ORIENTATION

Sprawling Bogotá covers some 1,776 square kilometers (686 square miles), filling a large part of the *altiplano* (high plateau) or savannah of Bogotá. In all likelihood, much of your time will be spent along the corridor that is the **Carrera** or **Avenida 7** (most often called the **Séptima**). The Séptima extends, parallel to the eastern mountains, from the Plaza de Bolívar in La Candelaria through the Centro Internacional, Chapinero, and northern neighborhoods to Usaquén and beyond.

La Candelaria is the oldest part of town, dating to the 16th century. With the Plaza de Bolívar at its heart, it is a neighborhood full of historic buildings, interesting museums, and hostels.

Adjacent to La Candelaria is **Avenida Jiménez,** also known as the "Eje Ambiental." This is a pedestrian street that is shared with

© ANDREW DIER

northern Bogotá

TransMilenio. In addition to being the home of the Museo del Oro, colonial churches, the Quinta de Bolívar, and Monserrate, the area is also known for its grand early-20th-century architecture.

Farther north is the **Centro Internacional.** Major banks have their headquarters in this part of town, and two major museums—the Museo de Arte Moderno de Bogotá and the Museo Nacional—are two of the major tourist attractions in the neighborhood.

Just above the bullfighting ring and the iconic Torres del Parque complex is the quirky neighborhood of the **Macarena,** full of art galleries and cozy restaurants. The popular Parque Nacional marks the end of this area that is often considered **downtown.**

The Distrito Capital of Bogotá comprises 20 *localidades* (official neighborhoods), each with its own local mayor and neighborhood council. **Chapinero** is one of the largest ones along the Carrera 7 (Séptima) corridor. It extends to Calle 100, but most people consider Chapinero to include the neighborhoods from around Calle 45 to about Calle 72. Below the Séptima is a gritty commerce center that is also considered the center of gay nightlife. There are no major sights of interest in Chapinero.

Chauffeured SUVs whizzing by and bodyguards lingering about on the street are telltale signs that you have arrived in the swanky northern neighborhoods. The **Zona G,** between Calles 69 and 70 above the Séptima; the **Zona Rosa,** between Calles 81 and 85 and Carreras 11 and 15; and the **Parque de la 93** area, between Calles 91 and 94 and also between Carreras 11 and 15, are home to excellent restaurants, famous nightspots, glitzy malls, and fancy hotels. It is the center of hedonism in Bogotá. Finally, above the Séptima between Calles 120 and 125 is **Usaquén,** a sleepy pueblo that has been swallowed by big Bogotá. Usaquén is becoming a trendy restaurant area and is also known for its Sunday flea market.

If you look at a map of Bogotá you will realize that this corridor from La Candelaria to Usaquén is a tiny sliver of this massive city. West of the Séptima and in the center of

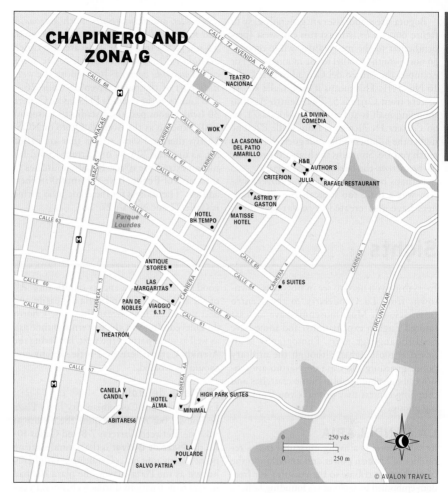

Bogotá is the Parque Simón Bolívar, along with the Jardín Botánico and the Biblioteca Virgilio Barco. These are wonderful green spaces worth checking out on sunny days. These sights are not far from the Avenida El Dorado (Calle 26), which connects the El Dorado airport with downtown. In addition to its new TransMilenio line, this nicely designed thoroughfare is lined with hotels, shopping centers, and the fortress-like U.S. Embassy.

Southern Bogotá includes massive working-class and poor neighborhoods. Sights are few and far between. The Santuario del 20 de Julio and Paloqueamo market are worth visiting and are just a few minutes south of the Plaza de Bolívar. In the huge *localidad* of Kennedy (named in honor of President John F. Kennedy, who visited the area while announcing infrastructure aid in 1961) is the fantastic Biblioteca Tintal public library. The Teatro Mayor Julio Mario Santo Domingo is in the *localidad* of Suba in the northwest of the city. Its stunning theater hosts concerts and dance performances from internationally renowned artists.

Bogotá street addresses are generally easy to figure out. *Calles* (streets) run east-west (perpendicular to the mountains), while *carreras* go north-south (parallel to the mountains). For example, the Museo del Oro address is Calle 16 No. 5-41. This means it is on Calle 16, 41 meters from Carrera 5. The Centro Andino shopping mall is at Carrera 11 No. 82-71, or on Carrera 11, 71 meters from Calle 82. The higher the number of the *calle* goes, the farther north you are. Similarly, the higher the number of the *carrera*, the farther west you go.

Perhaps because the *calle* and *carrera* system was a little too logical, the city planners have also created *avenidas* (avenues), *diagonales,* and *transversales.* Both *diagonales* and *transversales* are streets on the diagonal. To add to the fun, some *calles* are also called *avenida calles,* and likewise there are some called *avenida carrera.* Just ignore the *avenida* part of the name. Avenida Calle 26 is also known as the Avenida El Dorado. Carrera 30 (which goes past the Estadio El Campín) is also known as the Avenida Quito or NQS. Lastly, there are some streets that are called *bis,* as in Calle 70A *bis* or Carrera 13 *bis.* It's like an extra little street. Finally, addresses in the south of Bogotá have *sur* (south) in their address. The address for the 20 de Julio shrine is Calle 27 Sur No. 5A-27.

Sights

Everything you need to see in Bogotá is downtown, from La Candelaria to the Centro Internacional. Most museums have at least limited English explanations, and some have English-language tours. Photography is allowed at most sights, although the military police guarding the Casa de Nariño are sensitive about photography. Some churches and shopping centers may prohibit you from taking photos.

LA CANDELARIA

La Candelaria is a living museum. It is a reminder of Spanish power and ambition in the New World; a tribute to the yearning for freedom embodied by Colombia's founding fathers; and a reflection on the tenacity of the independent Colombian republic to persevere in the face of adversity. La Candelaria is a bustling place and has been for centuries. These days, university students, government bureaucrats, tourists, and old-timers who have lived in the area for decades pass each other along the narrow streets and frequent the same cafés.

You could spend a couple of days admiring the colonial churches and exploring the many museums in the area, but if you don't have that much time, three or four hours will give you a good sense of the area and its significance. All of the sights in La Candelaria are easily and best visited on foot. Areas above the Chorro de Quevedo (toward the eastern mountains), as well as some parts to the west, bordering the Avenida Caracas, can be a little sketchy and should be avoided.

◖ Plaza de Bolívar

Every respectable Colombian city has a Plaza de Bolívar, but none have quite the history as this one. Between Carreras 7-8 and Calles 10-11, the **Plaza de Bolívar** is the natural starting point for any tour of La Candelaria. Originally known as the Plaza Mayor, the plaza has had several reincarnations during its history. In colonial times, it was where the Friday market took place. It was also the setting for executions, including that of independence heroine Policarpa Salavarrieta (whose picture graces the $10,000 peso bill). Following the death of Simón Bolívar, Congress renamed the plaza in his honor in 1846. A diminutive statue of the "Liberator," the first of many Bolívar statues in the world, stands in the middle of the plaza. Today the plaza is home to political demonstrations, inauguration ceremonies for the Bogotá mayor, and concerts.

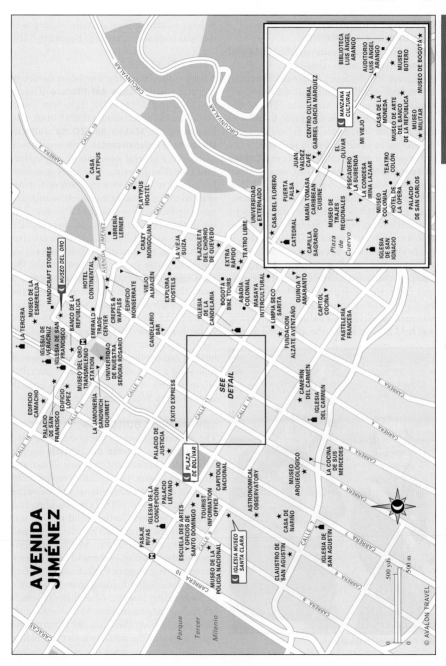

AVENIDA JIMÉNEZ

© AVALON TRAVEL

BOGOTÁ

CATEDRAL PRIMADA AND CAPILLA SAGRARIO

The neoclassical facade of the **Catedral Primada** (mass noon Tues.-Sat., 10:30am, noon, and 1:30pm Sun.) dominates the plaza. It was built in 1807, and this is the fourth cathedral built on that same site. The tombs of Gonzalo Jiménez de Quesada, founder of Bogotá, and independence figure Antonio Nariño are in a side chapel on the right.

Next door to the cathedral is the **Capilla El Sagrario** (Cra. 7 No. 10-40, mass 7:30am and 5pm Mon.-Fri., 5pm Sun.). This chapel was built much earlier than the cathedral, in the 1600s, and is considered to be an excellent example of Santa Fe (as Bogotá was known) architecture. The interior is decorated with a Mudejar or Moorish-style vaulted wooden ceiling. Along the sides of the cross-shaped chapel are several large works depicting biblical scenes by Colombian baroque painter Gregorio Vásquez de Arce y Ceballos. A ceremony was held here to honor the army and Simón

© ANDREW DIER

the Presidential Guard

Bolívar following their decisive victory over the Spaniards at the Battle of Boyacá in 1819.

CASA DEL FLORERO

Across Calle 10 on the northeast corner of the plaza is the **Casa del Florero** (Cra. 7 No. 11-28, tel. 1/334-4150, 9am-5pm Tues.-Fri., 10am-4pm Sat.-Sun, COP$3,000), also known as the **Museo del 20 de Julio** or **Museo de la Independencia.** This small house used to be a general store run by a Spaniard, José González-Llorente. The story goes that his refusal to lend a vase to a pair of Creoles sparked the ire of either incredibly sensitive or cunning locals, who launched a protest during the busy market day against Spanish rule. Historians today dispute much of the tale, but the shattered remains of that colorful vase are exhibited today in the museum. Maybe the most interesting exhibit in the museum is a room that shows the transformation of the Plaza de Bolívar over time, with raw footage of two of the most traumatic events in recent Colombian history: the Bogotazo riots following the assassination of Jorge Eliécer Gaitán in 1948 and the siege of the Palacio de Justicia following a takeover by the M-19 guerrilla group in 1985. A free guided tour in English is given every Wednesday at 3pm.

GOVERNMENT BUILDINGS

The newest building on the plaza, completed in 1991, is the **Palacio de Justicia** on the north side. Housing the Supreme Court and other high courts, this building replaced the previous one, which was destroyed following the tragic events of 1985. (That building had replaced a previous justice building that was burned to the ground during the Bogotazo.) On November 6, 1985, M-19 guerrillas stormed the building, perhaps in cahoots with infamous drug kingpin Pablo Escobar, killing several justices and holding some 350 people in the building hostage. After hours of standoff, the military counterattacked, coordinating their assault from the Casa del Florero. The fight concluded the next day with the building engulfed in flames, result of a military rocket.

More than 100 people were killed. Controversy remains even today about the tragedy and the government's actions. Several victims—mostly workers in the cafeteria—were seen being escorted to safety, never to be found again. Five years later the M-19 demobilized, becoming a political movement. Today, it is telling that there is not even a plaque mentioning the tragedy. Nevertheless, clearly some wounds have healed: former M-19 guerrilla Gustavo Petro was elected mayor in 2011, with his office (*alcaldía*) in the **Palacio Liévano** on the west side of the plaza.

On the south side of the square is the neoclassical **Capitolio Nacional,** home of the bicameral Colombian Congress. Designed by architect Thomas Reed, the Capitolio took over 70 years to build, finally being completed in 1926. Gargoyles keep watch atop the building behind the Ionic columns of the front. For about two months in 2009 the entire facade was covered with 1,300 massive ants, a project of Colombian artist Rafael Gómezbarros. The work was a commentary on forced displacement resulting from Colombia's armed conflict.

West of the Plaza
ESCUELA DE ARTES Y OFICIOS DE SANTO DOMINGO
One of the best trade schools in Latin America for woodworking, embroidery, silversmithing, and leatherworking is the **Escuela de Artes y Oficios de Santo Domingo** (Cl. 10 No. 8-73, tel. 1/282-0534, www.eaosd.org, 9am-5pm Mon.-Fri., free). Attracting students and teachers from around the world, this school is supported by the Fundación Mario Santo Domingo. A brief tour of the school is possible (call ahead to arrange). You will notice a warm and collegial atmosphere at the school, where some 600 students are enrolled. If you are staying in Bogotá for a while, you can inquire about taking a class. The school is housed in two lovely colonial buildings from the 1600s that are connected by a courtyard. A store—which could be mistaken for a small design museum—sells a limited number of items made

by students. Many more are sold at the annual Feria de Artesanías in December.

IGLESIA DE LA CONCEPCIÓN
The **Iglesia de la Concepción** (Cl.10 No. 9-50, 7am-5pm daily) was completed in 1595, making it the second oldest church in the city. Along with a convent, it used to take up an entire block of old Santa Fe. The convent (which no longer exists) was built for the daughters and granddaughters of the conquistadors. The spectacular geometric designs on the ceiling and the polychromatic presbytery are among the most striking aspects of the church. If you pop in, you will no doubt see many faithful—most of humble means—in the pews, in silent meditation. This city block is called the Calle del Divorcio. This refers to a nearby residence for separated or single women who were not allowed into convents and could not live in their family's home.

Farther down the street beyond the Iglesia de la Concepción is the historic labyrinthine artisans market known as the **Pasaje Rivas.**

MUSEO DE LA POLICÍA NACIONAL
The grandiose Palacio de la Policía, built in the early 20th century, was once the headquarters for the national police and today is home to the **Museo de la Policía Nacional** (Cl. 9 No. 9-27, tel. 1/233-5911, 8am-noon and 2pm-5pm Tues.-Sun., free). Obligatory tours are given by knowledgeable and friendly cadets who are fulfilling their one-year public service obligation. The museum does have its fair share of guns, but there are also exhibits on different technologies employed by police in pursuit of the bad guys, along with tributes to police dogs. If you go up to the rooftop, you can get a unique view of the city. In the streets around the museum are dozens of shops selling police and military uniforms. Here you can pick up an official "Policía" baseball cap, but it wouldn't be a good idea to wear it while in Colombia.

◖ IGLESIA MUSEO SANTA CLARA
It is easy to pass by the stone exterior of the **Iglesia Museo Santa Clara** (Cra. 8 No. 8-91,

Golden floral motifs adorn the nave at the Iglesia Museo Santa Clara.

tel. 1/337-6262, www.museoiglesiasantaclara. gov.co, 9am-5pm Tues.-Fri., 10am-4pm Sat.-Sun., adults COP$3,000), but that would be a shame, as this is one of the most beautiful sights in Bogotá. Once part of a convent, the little church is an extraordinary example of Mudejar style in Santa Fe. This convent for barefoot Franciscan nuns known as the Clarisas was completed in 1647. It originally housed 12 nuns, who were descendants of conquistadors, and 12 Creole maidens. Perhaps the most stunning aspect design-wise can be admired by craning your neck and looking up: The single nave is beautifully illuminated by hundreds of golden floral motifs. The church is now strictly a museum; it often hosts edgy contemporary art exhibitions. Admission is free on Sundays.

South of the Plaza
CASA DE NARIÑO

You can have your picture taken with members of the Presidential Guard (they don't mind) at the gates of the neoclassical **Casa de Nariño** (Cra. 8 No. 6-26, www.presidencia. gov.co), home to Colombia's presidents. As is suggested by its name, the presidential palace stands on the site of the birth house of Antonio Nariño, who was one of the early voices for independence in New Granada, which was how the Spaniards named the territory. In 1906 Nariño's house was razed to make way for the first presidential palace, which was designed by the same French architect who designed the Palacio Liévano on the Plaza de Bolívar. The palace has served as home for Colombian presidents off and on since 1886. Minutes after the 2002 inauguration of President Álvaro Uribe, the exterior of the palace was slightly damaged by missiles fired from FARC guerrillas. Several missiles landed on humble homes in slums nearby, killing 13.

Tours are given of the Casa de Nariño, but you must make a reservation several days in advance. For more information on taking the tour visit the website. Even if you don't visit the interior of the palace, you can watch the changing of the Presidential Guard on Wednesday, Friday, and Sunday at 4pm.

Also on the grounds of the Casa de Nariño is the oldest **astronomical observatory** in the New World. This was the initiative of famed botanist and scientist José Celestino Mutis. It was completed in 1803. You can inquire about tours conducted by the Universidad Nacional at the Claustro de San Agustín.

IGLESIA AND CLAUSTRO DE SAN AGUSTÍN

Facing the palace, the **Iglesia de San Agustín** (Cra. 7 No. 7-13, 9am-5pm Mon.-Sun.) was part of the first Augustinian monastery in the Spanish New World, completed in 1668. The Franciscans and Dominicans beat the Augustinians to the punch in Santa Fe, relegating them to the far extremes of Santa Fe. It is a three-nave temple, which distinguished it from other churches at the time. San Agustín has seen its share of drama over the years. An earthquake destroyed the two towers in 1785 (they rebuilt just one). In 1861 in the midst of liberal reforms, the government took control of the church from the Augustinians. The next year the church was the scene of a presidential coup attempt during the Battle of San Agustín, as Conservatives attacked Liberals who were holed up in the church and adjacent monastery (which no longer stands). The church suffered damage yet again during the Bogotazo riots. The **Claustro de San Agustín** (Cra. 8 No. 7-21, tel. 1/342-2340, 9am-5pm Mon.-Sat., 9am-4pm Sun., free) didn't serve long as a seminary, and in fact was used as a garrison in which Antonio Nariño was imprisoned. During the Bogotazo rampage in 1948, international delegates in town for the 9th Pan-American Conference sought shelter from the mayhem there. Today this beautiful cloister is run by the Universidad Nacional, which puts on temporary art exhibits and hosts educational activities.

MUSEO ARQUEOLÓGICO

The **Museo Arqueológico** (Cra. 6 No. 7-43, tel. 1/243-0465, www.musarq.org.co, 8:30am-5pm Mon.-Fri., 9am-4pm Sat., COP$3,000) holds an extensive and nicely presented collection of ceramic work of pre-Columbian indigenous peoples. In addition there is a room on colonial-era decorative arts, in acknowledgement of the history of this 17th-century home of a Spanish marquis. A small café adjoins the museum.

East of the Plaza
MANZANA JESUÍTICA

Three important colonial buildings make up the **Manzana Jesuítica** (Jesuit Block). In the early 17th century, the Compañía de Jesús, a group of Jesuit priests arriving from Cartagena, was given permission by the Spanish ruling authority to build a church and school on the southeastern side of the Plaza Mayor (later to become the Plaza de Bolívar). As part of its commitment to social justice and to education, the cloister of the **Colegio Mayor de San Bartolomé** (Cra. 7 No. 9-96, tel. 1/44-2530, closed to the public) was founded in 1604. The facade of the school was completed in the early 20th century and is considered an excellent example of Republican architecture. It has been in operation continuously since that year and is the oldest school in

Colombia. Important figures in the Colombian independence struggle, such as Antonio Nariño and Francisco de Paula Santander were students at the school. **Iglesia de San Ignacio,** a church dedicated to the founder of the Jesuit order, was completed in 1643. The church has undergone a massive renovation for years, with the large cupola being restored, the roof above the nave being redone (it was on the verge of collapse), and meticulous restoration of the baroque interior, which includes paintings by many famous painters from the colonial era.

Well worth a visit, the **Museo Colonial** (Cra. 6 No. 9-77, tel. 1/341-6017, www.museocolonial.gov.co, 9am-5pm Tues.-Fri., 10am-4pm Sat.-Sun., COP$3,000) showcases a fine collection of art and religious artifacts from the colonial era, including the largest collection of works by Gregorio Vásquez de Arce y Ceballos. On the bottom floor is an exhibit that explores life in colonial times. The museum courtyard is quiet and green. Admission is free on Sundays.

TEATRO COLÓN

Inspired by the Teatro Santi Giovanni e Paolo in Venice, the **Teatro Colón** (Cl. 10 No. 5-62, tel. 1/284-7420) was designed by Pietro Cantini to commemorate the 400th anniversary of Christopher Columbus's 1492 landing in the New World. Tours of the theater have not been offered during the long restoration of the theater, but you can call or stop by and inquire about these. The best way of visiting the theater, of course, is to see a performance there.

PALACIO DE SAN CARLOS

Today housing the Ministry of Foreign Relations, the colonial-era **Palacio de San Carlos** (Cl. 10 No. 5-51, closed to the public) was the home of Colombian presidents from 1825 until 1908. During the Bolívar dictatorship and the turbulent Gran Colombia period, Bolívar's companion Manuela Sáenz earned the nickname "Liberator of the Liberator" for helping him escape through a palace window—saving him from an 1828 assassination attempt. A plaque marking the exact spot draws the curiosity of passersby today.

MUSEUMS

The **Museo de Trajes Regionales** (Cl. 10 No. 6-18, tel. 1/341-0403, www.museodetrajesregionales.com, 9am-4pm Mon.-Fri., 9am-2pm Sat., COP$3,000), which showcases traditional costumes from the different regions of Colombia, is best known for being the home of Manuela Sáenz, Simón Bolívar's companion. The museum is next door to the **Plaza de Cuervo,** a tropical patio in the middle of historic Bogotá. Behind the elegant palm trees is the house where Antonio Nariño is said to have translated the Declaration of the Rights of Man from French into Spanish in 1793. After making about 100 copies of it for distribution to rouse the masses, he became nervous and started to furiously destroy them. (He got busted by the Spanish authorities anyway.)

The **Museo Militar** (Cl. 10 No. 4-92, tel. 1/281-3086, 9am-4pm Tues.-Fri., 10am-4pm Sat.-Sun., free, must present identification) is in a 17th-century house that was home to independence hero Capt. Antonio Ricaurte. Dozens of mannequins dressed in Colombian military uniforms keep you company as you wander the corridors of this museum. One room is dedicated to Colombia's participation in the Korean War. Over 4,300 Colombians fought in the war waged nearly 15,000 kilometers away, with 163 losing their lives. Colombia was the only country in Latin America to send troops in support of the United Nations/United States coalition. Two patios are filled with cannons, tanks, and fighter jets.

The **Museo de Bogotá** (Cra. 4 No. 10-18, tel. 1/352-1864, www.museodebogota.gov.co, 9am-5:30pm Mon.-Fri., 10am-4:30pm Sat.-Sun., free) may be of special interest to city planner types. A permanent exhibition examines the development of Bogotá through the years, and temporary shows have highlighted photography, historic figures in the city, and profiles of neighborhoods in the metropolis.

◖ Manzana Cultural

The **Manzana Cultural** (Cl. 11 No. 4-41) of the Banco de la República is a "Cultural Block" (not Cultural Apple) that comprises the Biblioteca Luis Ángel Arango, the library's concert hall, the Museo Botero, the Museo de Arte, the Colección de Arte del Banco de la República, and the Casa de la Moneda. Without a doubt it is one of the most important addresses for visual arts in Colombia—and a required stop on any visit to Bogotá.

BIBLIOTECA LUIS ÁNGEL ARANGO

The **Biblioteca Luis Ángel Arango** (Cl. 11 No. 4-14, tel. 1/343-1224, www.banrepcultural.org, 8am-8pm Mon.-Sat., 8am-4pm Sun.) is reportedly one of the busiest libraries in the world, with over 5,000 visitors each day. Part of the same complex and located behind the library, the **Casa Republicana** (8am-8pm Mon.-Sat. and 8am-4pm Sun., free) often hosts temporary art exhibits. There is also a beautiful chamber music concert hall in the large complex.

COLECCIÓN DE ARTE DEL BANCO DE LA REPÚBLICA

With 14 galleries highlighting Colombian art from the 17th century to present day, the **Colección de Arte del Banco de la República** (Cl. 11 No. 4-41, tel. 1/343-1316, www.banrepcultural.org, 9am-7pm Mon. and Wed.-Sat., 10am-5pm Sun., free) is an excellent opportunity to discover Colombian art. Look for the series of "dead nuns." It was customary to paint nuns twice in their lifetimes: once when they entered the convent and once more moments after passing away. The nuns from this particular series lived at the nearby convent of the Iglesia de la Concepción.

Another highlight is the spectacular—if a tad on the gaudy side—*La Lechuga* monstrance (a monstrance is a receptacle to hold the Host). It's called *La Lechuga,* meaning lettuce, because of its 1,486 sparkling emeralds, but it is also adorned by hundreds of diamonds, rubies, amethysts, and pearls. The Spaniard who created this extraordinary piece charged the Jesuits the equivalent of a cool US$2 million when he finished it in 1707. Hidden away in a vault for over 200 years, it was acquired by the Banco de la República in 1987 for US$3.5 million.

© ANDREW DIER

courtyard at the Casa de la Moneda

Nineteenth-century landscapes, portraits by impressionist and Bogotá native Andrés Santa María, and works from an array of well-known Colombian artists from the 20th century (including Alejandro Obregón, Eduardo Ramírez, Guillermo Wiedemann, and Luis Caballero) are other museum highlights. Free guided tours in Spanish are offered several times a day.

MUSEO DE ARTE DEL BANCO DE LA REPÚBLICA

Behind the Colección de Arte, in a sleek modern "white box," is the **Museo de Arte del Banco de la República** (Cl. 11 No. 4-21, tel. 1/343-1212, www.banrepcultural.org, 9am-7pm Mon. and Wed.-Sat., 10am-5pm Sun., free), which hosts temporary exhibits and has one floor dedicated to 20th-century Latin American and European art from the Banco de la República collection. On the bottom floor is the **Parqueadero** (2pm-7pm Wed.-Mon.)—the "Parking Lot"—a sort of laboratory on contemporary art.

MUSEO BOTERO

In the **Museo Botero** (Cl. 11 No. 4-41, tel. 1/343-1212, www.banrepcultural.org, 9am-7pm Mon. and Wed.-Sat., 10am-5pm Sun., free) there are still lifes, portrayals of everyday life in Colombian pueblos, and social commentaries by the most accomplished Colombian artist, Medellín-born Fernando Botero. In addition to paintings of corpulent Colombians, there are bronze and marble sculptures of chubby cats and pudgy birds. One side of the lovely colonial house, which surrounds a sublime courtyard, displays the artist's exceptional personal collection of European and American art, including works by Picasso and Dali. All of these were donated by the *maestro* to the Banco de la República so that Colombians of all backgrounds could appreciate and enjoy them without paying a peso—an extraordinary opportunity. Once the home of archbishops during the colonial era, the building was set ablaze during the 1948 disturbances of the Bogotazo. It has been painstakingly recreated.

CASA DE LA MONEDA

Connected to the Museo Botero and the Colección de Arte by patios and a Botero gift shop, the **Casa de la Moneda** (Cl. 11 No. 4-93, tel. 1/343-1212, www.banrepcultural. org, 9am-7pm Mon. and Wed.-Sat., 10am-5pm Sun., free) was where the New World's first gold coins were produced starting in the early 17th century. The museum's **Colección Numismática** shows the history of the Nueva Granada mint.

CENTRO CULTURAL GABRIEL GARCÍA MÁRQUEZ

Designed by Rogelio Salmona, the **Centro Cultural Gabriel García Márquez** (Cl. 11 No. 5-60, tel. 1/283-2200, www.fce.com.co, 9am-7pm Mon.-Sat., 10:30am-5pm Sun., free) was a gift from the Mexican government in honor of the 1982 Nobel Prize winner for literature, Colombian Gabriel García Márquez. Gabo, as he is called, has lived in Mexico since the 1960s. On the main level, where you can enjoy a nice sunset view of the cathedral, is a bookstore with an ample selection of books on Colombia. Next to the Juan Valdez Café below is a space where photography and art exhibits are often shown.

AVENIDA JIMÉNEZ

The Avenida Jiménez used to be the Río San Francisco and the extreme northern boundary of Santa Fe. For the architectural enthusiast, there are several gems on this street that stand in tribute of the city's inflated view of itself during the first half of the 20th century. Most of these historic buildings can only be enjoyed from the exterior. In 2000, in an effort to re-invent the historic Avenida Jiménez, architect Rogelio Salmona created the **Eje Ambiental** (Environmental Corridor), which extends from the Universidad de los Andes campus to the Avenida Caracas. Vehicular traffic is banned from the street except for the red buses of the TransMilenio. Ample pedestrian space has made this a pleasant place for a stroll.

In 2012, the city created a pedestrian zone from the Plaza de Bolívar to the Calle 26. This busy commercial area is now a fun way to check out the city's core, do a little shopping, sightseeing, and people-watching.

Historic Architecture

You don't have to be an expert on architecture to appreciate the many impressive buildings lining the entire length of the Avenida Jiménez. Most of these gems were built in the early 20th century. To the west side of the Séptima (Carrera 7) are: the neoclassical **Palacio de San Francisco** (Av. Jiménez No. 7-56), prior home to the Cundinamarca departmental government; the **Edificio López** (Av. Jiménez No. 7-65), which was built by the same construction firm that built the Chrysler building in New York; and the modernist **Edificio Camacho,** farther down and on the right.

It was on the southwest corner of the Séptima and Avenida Jiménez that populist Liberal Party presidential candidate Jorge Eliécer Gaitán was assassinated on April 9, 1948, which sparked the tragic Bogotazo riots. Up to 3,000 were killed. This precipitated the bloody period of La Violencia that swept the country. At McDonald's, a plaque and flowers mark the spot where the tragedy took place. A young Gabriel García Márquez, then a law student at the Universidad Nacional, lived near the Palacio de San Francisco at that time, and with his building in flames, he and his brother rushed back—to save his typewriter.

On the eastern side of the Séptima, notable buildings include the modernist **Banco de la República** (Cra. 7 No. 14-78); the **Universidad de Nuestra Señora del Rosario** (Cl. 12C No. 6-25), founded in 1653, which is housed in a colonial building that was originally a monastery; the **Edificio Monserrate** (Av. Jiménez No. 4-49), which was home to *El Espectador* newspaper; the fabulous restored **Hotel Continental** (Av. Jiménez No. 4-19), once the most exclusive hotel in town; the neoclassical **Academia Colombiana de Historia** (Cl. 10 No. 9-95); the 17th-century **Iglesia and Convento de las Aguas** (Cra. 2 No. 18A-58), where Artesanías de Colombia has a store; and finally (at the end of the Eje Ambiental) the campus of the

Universidad de Los Andes, one of the top universities in Latin America, with several stunning new buildings. Los Andes has around 25,000 students.

Churches

Typical of most all colonial-era churches, the **Iglesia de San Francisco** (Cl. 16 No. 7-35, 6:30am-8pm Mon.-Fri., 6:30am-12:40pm and 4:30pm-8pm Sat.-Sun.) looks somber from the outside, but inside it's decorated by a fantastic golden altar, considered a masterwork of American baroque. This is the oldest of all the churches in the city, built by the Franciscans in 1557. The church is often full of working-class faithful. Adjacent to the San Francisco is the **Iglesia de Veracruz** (Cl. 16 No. 7-19), which is where several independence figures, executed by the Spaniards, are laid to rest.

The third church in this row is called **Iglesia La Tercera** (Cl. 16 No. 7-35, 7am-6pm Mon.-Fri., 11am-1pm Sat.-Sun.), and it is one of the jewels of colonial churches in Bogotá. It was built in the late 18th century, about 50 years before Colombian independence. Architecturally, the main highlight is its barrel-vaulted ceiling decorated with geometric designs and altarpieces made of cedar and walnut. Unlike other churches, the interior is not covered with gold leaf.

◖ Museo del Oro

Some visitors come to Bogotá specifically to see the world-renowned **Museo del Oro** (Cra. 6 No. 15-88, tel. 1/343-2233, www.banrep. gov.co, 9am-6pm Tues.-Sat., 10am-4pm Sun., COP$3,000). During your museum experience, you will see just a fraction of the thousands of treasures of the Banco de la República, Colombia's central bank, since its first acquisition in 1939. The museum tells the story of how—and why—the native peoples of Colombia created such incredibly detailed and surprisingly modern designs of gold jewelry and religious objects.

What is astonishing about the collection is the sophistication of the work. It is almost all smelted, with Muisca and Sinú peoples

employing a "lost wax" technique, with various metals being purposefully alloyed. Here, rather than large, hammered pieces, as in countries like Peru, you will see intricately crafted and designed jewelry.

One of the highlights, without a doubt, is the golden raft created by local Muisca people. The raft portrays the ritual of El Dorado, "the Golden One." Another piece to look for is the collection's first acquisition, the Quimbaya Póporo. This was used during religious ceremonies. The unforgettable offering room is filled with golden treasures. English explanations are good throughout the museum (so is the audio tour). Just beyond the gift shop is a very popular restaurant that specializes in Colombian and Mediterranean cuisine. If possible try to avoid visiting the museum on weekends, when crowds soar, especially on Sunday, when admission is free.

Museo de la Esmeralda

On the 23rd floor of the Avianca building is the **Museo de la Esmeralda** (Cl. 16 No. 6-66, tel. 1/286-4259, www.museodelaesmeralda. com.co, 10am-6pm Mon.-Sat., COP$5,000). The museum has an impressive recreation of an emerald mine and then several examples of different emeralds from Colombia and elsewhere. Guides, fluent in Spanish and English, will make sure you know that the best emeralds do—without a doubt—come from Colombia, primarily from the Muzo mines in the Boyacá department. Although there is no pressure to do so, you can purchase all different classes of emeralds, and their jewelers can transform the emeralds you choose into rings or earrings within a day. Even if you are not interested in purchasing an emerald it is fun to check out the gems under a magnifying glass, as you learn why some emeralds are much more precious than others. The museum also has a small store on the main floor of the building that sometimes has discounted coupons for museum entry. Security at the Avianca building is stringent, and you will need to bring a photocopy of your passport and produce a telephone number of your hotel for entry.

Quinta de Bolívar

The **Quinta de Bolívar** (Cl. 20 No. 2-91 Este, tel. 1/336-6410/19, 9am-5pm Tues.-Sat., 10am-4pm Sun., COP$3,000) is a lovely country estate that was presented by Francisco de Paula Santander, Vice President of the República de Gran Colombia, as a gift to Simón Bolívar in 1820. El Libertador was president of Colombia from 1819 to 1830. Bolívar stayed there during his brief and sporadic visits to Bogotá, a city he did not like. He spent approximately 432 nights there, give or take. Built in 1800, it is a beautiful example of a late colonial-era house. Furnished with period pieces and set in a beautiful garden under cypress and walnut trees, it is one of the most popular touristic sights in the city. On Wednesdays there are guided tours in English at 11am (if there is a group of at least three). Reserve your spot the day before. Each day there are Spanish-language tours at 11am and 2pm, if you'd like to practice your *español*. An audio tour is available for just COP$1,000, but the narrators are a bit long-winded. Admission is free on Sundays. It is just a five-minute walk uphill from the Quinta to Monserrate.

Cerro de Monserrate

Riding or hiking up to the top of this mountain, the **Cerro de Monserrate,** and taking in the views of the city by day or by night is a memorable one. To get to the top, take a funicular tramway (7:45am-11:45am Mon.-Sat., 6am-6pm Sun., daytime round-trip COP$15,400, nighttime round-trip COP$17,000) or the *teleférico* (cable car, noon-midnight Mon.-Sat., 9:30am-6:30pm Sun., daytime round-trip COP$15,400, nighttime round-trip COP$17,000).

You can also hike to the top, which, due to large crowds on weekends and holidays, is a good plan for a weekday morning. The path is open 5am-4pm Wednesday-Monday. There is no charge to make the somewhat challenging ascent on foot. Those over 75 years old, under a meter tall, or very pregnant are supposedly prohibited from making the climb, but this doesn't appear to be enforced. Going at a fast clip, the

Cerro de Monserrate, as seen from the Quinta de Bolívar

© ANDREW DIER

walk will take under 45 minutes. If you do decide to walk up, bring plenty of sun protection.

In the past there have been reports of bandits lingering in the woods along the path, but the security situation has vastly improved. Bored police cadets are stationed at three or four points along the trail until 4pm, and when there are no police there are plenty of vendors selling refreshments or several others huffing and puffing going up or leisurely coming down. If you feel as if you have done your exercise for the day, you can purchase a one-way ticket at the top to ride the funicular or tramway back down for under COP$8,000.

For the faithful, the white chapel atop, the **Santuario de Monserrate,** may be the goal of this hike. It is not of interest architecturally speaking, and it has been destroyed and rebuilt several times since the 1600s, but it is the highest church around, at about 3,152 (10,341 feet) above sea level. Inside, a 17th-century sculpture of the Fallen Christ of Monserrate attracts many believers. Some pilgrims climb the hill on their knees during Holy Week, believing that the Fallen Christ grants miracles to those who do so.

There are two pricey restaurants on the top of the mountain—a romantic setting for marriage proposals and a favorite spot for locals to bring visitors. These are French-Colombian **Restaurante Casa San Isidro** (tel. 1/281-9270, www.restaurantecasasanisidro.com, noon-midnight Mon.-Sat., COP$30,000) and **Restaurante Casa Santa Clara** (tel. 1/281-9309, www.restaurantecasasantaclara.com, noon-6pm Tues.-Sat., COP$25,000), which serves mostly Colombian fare.

To the south of Monserrate rises the **Cerro de Guadalupe,** with a large statue of the virgin. It can only be accessed by road and was, until recently, unsafe to visit. If you would like to visit (the views are about the same as from Monserrate), take a microbus on Sunday from the intersection of Calle 6 and Avenida Caracas. As you enter the ticket office at the base of Monserrate, you may see an old photograph of a tightrope walker crossing the 890 meters from Monserrate to Guadalupe blindfolded. This stunt was performed by Canadian daredevil Harry Warner in 1895.

CENTRO INTERNACIONAL
Museo de Arte Moderno de Bogotá

Across from the Parque de la Independencia on Avenida 26 is the **Museo de Arte Moderno de Bogotá** (Cl. 24 No. 6-00, tel. 1/286-0466, www.mambogota.com, 10am-6pm Tues.-Sat., noon-5pm Sun., COP$4,000). It often puts on interesting exhibitions highlighting Colombian and Latin American artists. The cinema shows independent films and documentaries. Nicknamed MAMBO, it is another creation by the late architect Rogelio Salmona.

Torre Colpatria Observation Deck

The **Torre Colpatria Observation Deck** (Cra. 7 No. 24-82, tel. 1/283-6665, 6pm-8pm Fri., 11am-8pm Sat., 11am-5pm Sun., COP$4,000) offers unparalleled 360-degree views of Bogotá. The vista of the city from the Colpatria bank tower is arguably superior to that of Monserrate. At 48 floors, the building remains Colombia's tallest. At night the tower goes into disco mode, as it decks out in colorful lights.

Parque de la Independencia

The **Parque de la Independencia,** long a favorite for young lovers and those seeking a pleasant stroll under the towering eucalyptus and wax palm trees, was created in 1910 in celebration of Colombia's 100-year anniversary of independence from Spain. The Quiosco de la Luz houses a tourist information center (Punto de Información Turística, or PIT). The park is undergoing a major expansion with the construction of a **Parque del Bicentenario** (it originally was to be completed in 2010). This exciting project will bring greenspace above the TransMilenio line on Calle 26.

PLANETARIO DE BOGOTÁ

On the north side of the park is the modernist **Planetario de Bogotá** (Cl. 26B No. 5-93, tel. 1/281-4150, www.idartes.gov.co, 10am-5pm

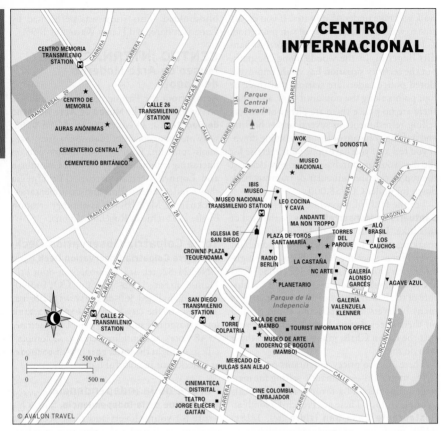

CENTRO INTERNACIONAL

© AVALON TRAVEL

Tues.-Sun., COP$3,000-10,000), which was built in the late 1960s and houses an air and space museum, **Museo del Espacio.** A statue of Copernicus stands outside.

PLAZA DE SANTAMARÍA

Next to the planetarium is the former Plaza de Toros de Santamaría, now renamed **Plaza de Santamaría.** The neo-Mudejar brick arena was built in the 1930s by a Spanish architect and was modeled after bullfighting rings in Madrid. Less messy events such as meditation sessions and even diving exhibitions have taken plaza in the plaza since Mayor Gustavo Petro banned bullfighting in 2012.

TORRES DEL PARQUE

About 100 steps up from the bullfighting ring and planetarium are the iconic **Torres del Parque.** These three brick apartment buildings, running parallel to the eastern mountains, were designed in the 1960s by Rogelio Salmona, the most accomplished architect from Bogotá during the late 20th century. The buildings are perfectly integrated with the Parque de la Independencia and the Plaza de Santamaría. French-born Salmona studied with Le Corbusier and was awarded the Alvar Aalto Prize in 2003 for his lifetime achievements. Public space takes up almost three-fourths of the area in the towers complex, and

© ANDREW DIER

The Torres del Parque were designed by Rogelio Salmona.

art galleries, cafés, and bodegas are nice places to linger on a chilly day.

The Macarena

Just above the Torres del Parque, the laid-back **Macarena neighborhood** (also known as Zona M) is known for its art galleries and cozy restaurants. The adjective "bohemian" is frequently thrown about to characterize the barrio, which steeply slopes up from the Carrera 5 to the Circunvalar ring road. It is indeed an "artsy" place—that is most evident by the handful of galleries lining the east side of Carrera 5. While you may have to ring a doorbell to enter, gallery staff are more than happy for you to come in and check out what's on. The gallery **Valenzuela Kennler** (Cra. 5 No. 26-28, tel. 1/243-7752, www.vkgaleria. com, 10am-6pm Mon.-Fri., 11am-5pm Sat.) features experimental artists and, often, video art. **Alonso Garcés** (Cra. 5 No. 26-92, tel. 1/337-5827, www.alonsogarcesgaleria.com, 10am-1pm and 2pm-6pm Mon.-Fri., 10am-2pm Sat.) features work by major contemporary Colombian artists. It also has a nice bookstore. **NC Arte** (Cra. 5 No. 26-76, tel. 1/282-1474, www.ncearte.org, 10am-6pm Tues.-Sat.) is a newcomer with cool installations. The mix of intellectuals, artists, students, leftists, hipsters, and foreigners makes this neighborhood like no other in Bogotá.

Museo Nacional

The **Museo Nacional** (Cra. 7 No. 28-66, tel. 1/381-6470, www.museonacional.gov.co, 10am-6pm Tues.-Sat., 10am-5pm Sun., free) was designed by English architect Thomas Reed (who also designed the Capitolio Nacional) in the late 1800s to serve as the penitentiary for Cundinamarca, which was at that time one of nine states of the United States of Colombia. This prison was a cross-shaped panopticon, with a central tower from which guards could monitor prisoners housed in the three wings. It was in the late 1940s that the prison was converted into a museum. The permanent collection examines the history of Colombia from pre-Columbian cultures to the 20th century.

On the top floor is a nice introduction to Colombian art. The museum often holds temporary exhibits on the ground floor. There is a pretty good museum store, and Juan Valdez Café brews coffee in the lovely courtyard.

Parque Central Bavaria

Below Carrera 13 is **Parque Central Bavaria** (Cra. 13 No. 28A-21), a large urban renovation project on the first site of the Bavaria brewery. The Bavaria Kopp's Deutsche Bierbrauerei was founded by German immigrant Leo Kopp and his four brothers. Bavaria is one of the few surviving—and thriving—businesses from the 19th century in Colombia. Its beers include Águila, Club Colombia, Costeña, Póker, and Pilsen. The brewery moved from this location in the 1980s and only two of the original brewery's buildings remain today, now home to several restaurants.

Parque Nacional

A center of activity on the weekends, the **Parque Nacional** (between Cras. 5-7 and Clls. 35-39) is the largest park in downtown Bogotá and is the second oldest one in the city. The park is set between a lovely English Tudor-style neighborhood called La Merced and, to the north, the Universidad Javeriana, which was founded by the Jesuits. On Sundays and holidays when there is Ciclovía, free aerobics classes draw huge crowds in the park. In addition there are numerous fields and courts to practice sports, including several clay tennis courts. On the northwest corner of the park is a whimsical sculpture by Enrique Grau called *Rita 5:30.*

Cementerio Central

The most important cemetery in Colombia is the **Cementerio Central** (Cra. 20 No. 24-80, tel. 1/269-3141, 9am-4pm daily), where prominent political, cultural, and business figures rest. Before the cemetery was built in 1830, distinguished persons were buried in churches following Spanish tradition. Francisco de Paula Santander, who is known as Colombia's Thomas Jefferson; Gustavo Rojas Pinilla, a military dictator from the 1950s; Luis Carlos Galán, a liberal presidential candidate who was assassinated under orders of Pablo Escobar in 1989; and Leo Kopp, the German founder of the Bavaria brewery, are all buried here. Some people pray at Kopp's tomb, asking for wishes. There is also a part of the cemetery where thousands of victims from the Bogotazo riots from April 1948 are buried, many of them chillingly listed as "N. N." ("no name").

Immediately west of the cemetery is a remarkable art installation called *Auras Anonimas* by Colombian artist Beatriz González. An abandoned columbarium (structure to keep ashes) is covered with around 9,000 primitive black and white paintings of people carrying away the dead. It is a powerful reflection on the violence and death in Colombia.

CENTRO DE MEMORIA, PAZ Y RECONCILIACIÓN

A memorial to victims of violence associated with the armed conflict is adjacent to the Cementerio Central. The **Centro de Memoria, Paz y Reconciliación** (Cra. 19B No. 24-86, http://centromemoria.gov.co, 11am-1pm and 2pm-4pm Mon., 8am-10am, 11am-1pm, and 2pm-4pm Tues.-Fri., free) is one of the first memorials to victims of violence in Colombia—an important milestone.

CEMENTERIO BRITÁNICO

Neighboring Cementerio Central is the **Cementerio Británico** (English Cemetery, Cl. 26 No. 22-75, tel. 1/334-0057), which was donated by the city to the British government in 1829 in recognition of help provided by the British Foreign Legion during the war of independence. Since then it has been the main burial ground for the city's Protestants. A fence at the back of the cemetery was made with the barrels of the legionnaires' bayonets. It is a green, peaceful place—just knock at the door and the family of caretakers will show you in.

PARQUE RENACAMIENTO

The **Parque Renacamiento,** just west of the cemeteries, opened in 2000 and is noteworthy

© ANDREW DIER

soaring wax palms at the Jardín Botánico

for its bronze sculpture *Man on a Horse,* donated by Fernando Botero.

WESTERN BOGOTÁ
Parque Simón Bolívar

Nicknamed the city's lungs, when it was built in the late 1960s the **Parque Simón Bolívar** (between Clls. 53-63 and Cras. 48-68, 6am-6pm daily) was in the countryside. Now, it's almost exactly in the middle of the city. Two popes have celebrated mass there: Pope Paul VI in 1968 and Pope John Paul II in 1986. The park is an excellent place for watching ordinary Bogotanos at play, especially on the weekends. Numerous festivals and concerts take place here. There are more than 16 kilometers of trails in the park. In August, traditionally the windiest month, thousands of families try their luck catching a breeze for their colorful kites.

Biblioteca Virgilio Barco

Open since 2001, the stunning **Biblioteca Virgilio Barco** (Av. Cra. 60 No. 57-60, tel. 1/315-8890, 2pm-8pm Mon., 8am-8pm Tues.-Sat., 9:30am-5:30pm Sun.), across the street from the Parque Simón Bolívar, is yet another project designed by Rogelio Salmona and is one of four fantastic library-parks in the city created by Mayor Enrique Peñalosa. The purpose of these mega libraries is to provide citizens access to books, Internet, and cultural/educational opportunities in a peaceful environment. While relatively plentiful in northern neighborhoods, green spaces—even trees—are few and far between in the massive lower-income neighborhoods. A bike path (*cicloruta*) surrounds the park and is popular with young inline skaters. The well-maintained grounds are a playground for the young, the old, and the canine.

🄲 Jardín Botánico

Colombia is one of the most biodiverse countries on the planet, and the **Jardín Botánico** (Av. Cl. 63 No. 68-95, tel. 1/437-7060, 8am-5pm Tues.-Fri., 9am-5pm Sat.-Sun., COP$2,700) does an excellent job of showing off that diversity. It won't be hard to find the Colombian national tree, the towering wax palm. And inside the greenhouse, be on the lookout for the Bogotá orchid—yes, Bogotá has its own official orchid! The gardens take you on a tour of the many different climates in the country—from the *páramos* (highland moors) to cloud forests to tropical jungles. Feel free to stray from the paths and get closer. The garden has its own farm and composting station that you can wander about as well. One of the perks of working there is getting fresh organic vegetables! Run by the city, the botanical garden also runs a community garden project in neighborhoods and carries out educational projects across the city.

Other Nearby Attractions

For the romantic ones, a stroll around the **Parque de los Novios** (Lovers Park, Cl. 63 No. 45-10, 6am-6pm daily) might be just the thing for a sunny afternoon. In addition to renting an aquatic bicycle you can also check out the motocross track. The highlight at the **Museo de los Niños Colsubsidio** (Av. Cra. 60 No.

63-27, tel. 1/225-7587, 9am-4pm Mon.-Sat., COP$5,500) is an old Avianca Boeing 727 jet that kids can explore. Also for the kids is the **Salitre Mágico** (www.salitremagico.com.co, 10am-6pm Wed.-Sun., COP$20,000-50,000) amusement park. There you can ride the *rueda de Chicago* (Ferris wheel) or the *montaña rusa* (roller coaster).

NORTHERN BOGOTÁ

Northern Bogotá does not have many tourist sights. But the shopping and restaurant areas might be nice to stroll around on an afternoon.

The **Zona Rosa** (between Clls. 81-85 and Cras. 11-15), an area of shopping, dining, and nightlife, is a tribute to hedonism. Well-known Colombian designers, such as Sylvia Tcherassi, Lina Cantillo, and Ricardo Pava, have boutiques here, catering to the Colombian jet-set. The **Centro Andino, Atlantis Plaza,** and **El Retiro**—the holy trinity of shopping malls— never seem to go out of fashion. On weekend evenings the entire area buzzes with activity and anticipation. Calle 82 and Carrera 13 form a T—hence the moniker **Zona T**—and are pedestrian streets lined with restaurants and happening watering holes. This is where Bogotá comes alive at night.

The **Parque de la 93** (between Cras. 11A-13 and Clls. 93A-B) is a manicured park surrounded by restaurants. Workers from the area stroll the park on their lunch hour. Sometimes there are big screens set up with bean bags strewn about for people to watch soccer matches. At night it is a popular dining area, but not nearly as rowdy as the Zona T.

The **Parque Chicó** (Cra. 7 No. 93-01) is a quiet spot in the north on an old hacienda from the colonial era. The **Museo** (10am-5pm Mon.-Fri., 8am-noon Sat., COP$2,500) has a small collection of pre-Columbian art, religious and decorative objects from around the world.

Once upon a time, charming **Usaquén** was its own distinct pueblo. Now, not even at the fringes of big Bogotá, miraculously somehow Usaquén has retained much of its colonial charm. It has become a dining and drinking hot spot with many restaurants and bars around the main square. On Sundays the neighborhood comes alive during its popular **flea market** (Cra. 5 at Cl. 119B).

SOUTHERN BOGOTÁ

If you mention going to southern Bogotá for sightseeing, Bogotanos may give you a baffled look. El Sur, the South, is synonymous with poverty and violence for many. Barrios lack green spaces, and neighborhoods are almost across the board ugly. This is where the housekeepers and the drivers for wealthy families in the north live. They can earn in a month a little more than what some from Bogotá society spend on a dinner in the Zona G on a Friday night.

But it is not necessarily a place full of despair. The middle class is growing; young people are earning college decrees; the city government is investing in TransMilenio lines, parks, and libraries; and the private sector is building malls. This is evident in all the massive *localidades* (official neighborhoods) in the south: Bosa, Ciudad Bolívar, Kennedy, Los Mártires, and Soacha, which is its own municipality.

Divino Niño

The **Templo del 20 de Julio** (Cl. 27 Sur No. 5A-27, tel. 1/372-5555) is one of the most important pilgrimage sites in Colombia, set in the working class neighborhood of 20 de Julio, just a couple of blocks from the new TransMilenio Portal del 20 de Julio station. July 20, 1810, is the day celebrated as Colombia's independence day. On Sundays and religious holidays, hundreds of thousands of faithful come to pray to the **Divino Niño,** a small statue of a smiling young Jesus in his pink robe, which is kept in a chapel behind the church. Around 30 masses are held between 5am and 7pm on Sundays to meet the extraordinary demand. It is indeed a colorful sight. Built by Salesian priests in 1942, the church provides groceries to poor families in the neighborhood who sign up for it. Nearby the church and plaza are shops selling Divino Niño statues and keychains.

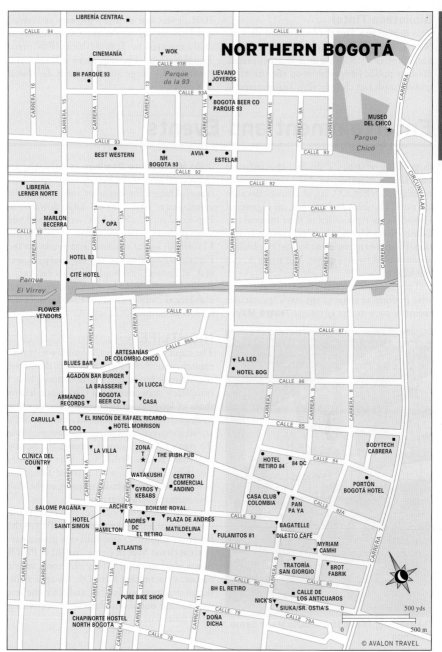

NORTHERN BOGOTÁ

LIBRERÍA CENTRAL

CALLE 94

CALLE 94

CINEMANÍA

WOK

CALLE 93B

BH PARQUE 93

Parque de la 93

LIEVANO JOYEROS

CALLE 93A

BOGOTA BEER CO PARQUE 93

MUSEO DEL CHICÓ

CARRERA 16

CARRERA 15

CARRERA 14

CARRERA 13

CARRERA 11A

CARRERA 10

CARRERA 9A

CARRERA 9

CARRERA 7

Parque Chicó

CALLE 93

BEST WESTERN

NH BOGOTA 93

AVIA

ESTELAR

CALLE 93

CALLE 92

CALLE 92

LIBRERÍA LERNER NORTE

CALLE 91

MARLON BECERRA

OPA

CARRERA 14

13A

13

12

11

CARRERA 10

9A

CALLE 90

7A

CALLE 90

CALLE 90

HOTEL B3

CIRCUNVALAR

CITÉ HOTEL

CARRERA 16

CARRERA

CARRERA 8

CARRERA 7

Parque El Virrey

FLOWER VENDORS

CARRERA 14

CARRERA 13

CALLE 87

CALLE 87

CALLE 86A

ARTESANÍAS DE COLOMBIO CHICÓ

LA LEO

HOTEL BOG

BLUES BAR

ÁGADÓN BAR BURGER

CALLE 86

LA BRASSERIE

DI LUCCA

CARRERA 10

CARRERA 9

CARRERA 8

ARMANDO RECORDS

BOGOTA BEER CO

CASA

CARULLA

EL RINCÓN DE RAFAEL RICARDO

CALLE 85

EL COQ

HOTEL MORRISON

CLÍNICA DEL COUNTRY

LA VILLA

ZONA T

THE IRISH PUB

BODYTECH CABRERA

CARRERA 15

CARRERA 11A

CARRERA 14

CARRERA 13

HOTEL RETIRO 84

84 DC

CALLE 84

CALLE 84

WATAKUSHI

CENTRO COMERCIAL ANDINO

PORTÓN BOGOTÁ HOTEL

GYROS Y KEBABS

CASA CLUB COLOMBIA

PAN PA YA

CALLE 82A

SALOME PAGANA

ARCHIE'S

BOHEME ROYAL

HOTEL SAINT SIMON

ANDRÉS DC

PLAZA DE ANDRÉS

CALLE 82

BAGATELLE

HAMILTON

EL RETIRO

MATILDELINA

FULANITOS 81

DILETTO CAFÉ

CARRERA 7

ATLANTIS

CALLE 81

MYRIAM CAMHI

CARRERA 17

CARRERA 16

CARRERA 14

CARRERA 13A

CARRERA 13

CARRERA 12A

CARRERA 9

TRATORÍA SAN GIORGIO

BROT FABRIK

CALLE 80

CALLE 80

CALLE DE LOS ANTICUAROS

PURE BIKE SHOP

BH EL RETIRO

NICK'S

CARRERA 11

CALLE 79

SIUKA/SR. OSTIA'S

0   500 yds

CHAPINORTE HOSTEL NORTH BOGOTA

DOÑA DICHA

CALLE 79A

0   500 m

CALLE 78

© AVALON TRAVEL

Biblioteca Tintal

The **Biblioteca Tintal** (Av. Ciudad de Cali No. 6C-09, 2pm-8pm Mon., 8am-8pm Tues.-Sat., 9:30am-5:30pm Sun.) is a beautiful, modern public library built on the site of an unused trash recycling facility. Inaugurated in 2001, it was one of many projects conceived and built by Mayor Peñalosa. The library is easily accessed by TransMilenio (Biblioteca Tintal station). The trip there will take you through the large southwestern *localidad* of Kennedy.

Entertainment and Events

Bogotá is, without a doubt, the cultural capital of Colombia. In 2012, the city was named a UNESCO City of Music. Because it's the Colombian melting pot, all regions of Colombia are represented in their musical traditions here. Merengue, salsa, *cumbia* (traditional Caribbean music), *vallenato* (love ballads accompanied by accordion): You name it, you can hear it.

The city also attracts international artists, who perform at some of the city's spectacular theaters, such as the gorgeous **Teatro Mayor Julio Mario Santo Domingo** in Suba, the architectural gem of the Sala de Conciertos Luis Ángel Arango for chamber music, and the iconic Teatro Jorge Eliécer Gaitán downtown. Pop icons such as Paul McCartney and Lady Gaga perform before the masses at the Estadio El Campín soccer stadium, and nearby in the Parque Simón Bolívar, the city puts on several "al Parque" free music festivals each year. Rock al Parque is the best known, but there is also Jazz al Parque, Opera al Parque, and even Gospel al Parque.

NIGHTLIFE

The capital city is also Colombia's nightlife capital. The Zona Rosa may still dominate the nightlife landscape, but downtown hasn't completely surrendered. La Candelaria has its share of long-standing smaller bars, catering to Bogotanos and visitors alike; the non-SUV crowd hangs out in Macarena hideaways; while the party till dawn crowd throngs the nearby nightclub Radio Berlín. Gay bars and cafés thrive in Chapinero, with massive Theatrón, as it has for over a decade, reigning as the club with something for everyone.

Most of the nightspots are, like everything else, located along the Carrera 7. To get the latest on nightlife, and find out about parties, check out Vive In (www.vive.in) or Plan B (www.planb.com.co). Many electronic music parties, attracting big name DJs, take place outside of the city towards Chía, and often the best way to find out about them is by stumbling upon posters on streetlight posts.

© ANDREW DIER

the stunning Teatro Mayor Julio Mario Santo Domingo

Bars and Clubs

Thanks to **Bogota Beer Company** (tel. 1/742-9292, www.bogotabeercompany.com), a successful chain of pubs with several locations throughout the city, sipping on a Candelaria artisan beer has become trendy in Bogotá. They also serve decent burgers. Try one of the northern locations (Cl. 85 No. 13-06 or Cra. 11A No. 93A-94). Sitting on the terrace and listening to rock at the always-packed **Pub Bogotá** (Cra. 12A No. 83-48, tel. 1/691-8711, www.thepub.com.co, noon-close daily, no cover), you're in a strategic position to watch people cruising the Zona T.

Most clubs have a cover between COP$10,000 and 30,000 (rarely). Covers usually include a *consumible* (complimentary drink). You can usually try to negotiate with the bouncer on the cover, especially if you're with a group. Finally, it's always a good idea to head out on the town with lots of smaller bills. Sometimes bartenders suffer from forgetfulness and fail to return your change. Tips are not expected at bars.

It doesn't look like much from the outside, but inside **El Coq** (Cl. 84 No. 14-02, tel. 1/611-2496, hours vary Wed.-Sat., cover COP$20,000), a relaxed and groovy bar in the Zona Rosa, it is pretty stylish. Also in the Zona Rosa, **Armando Records** (Cl. 85 No. 14-46, www.armandorecords.org, hours vary Tues.-Sat., cover COP$15,000) attracts a slightly grungy but cool crowd. The terrace is a fun (but sometimes cold) spot. Live bands and well-known international DJs regularly play at Armando. **La Villa** (Cra. 14A No. 83-56, hours vary Tues.-Sat., cover COP$15,000) hosts the popular Gringo Tuesdays parties, but has all kinds of themed parties catering to locals and visitors alike.

For fans of *vallenato* (love ballads accompanied by accordion), the old-school **Rincón Rafael Ricardo** (Cl. 85 No. 14-55, tel. 1/530-2118, hours vary Thurs.-Sat., no cover) and flashy **Matildelina** (Cl. 81 No. 11-34, tel. 1/805-2933, 9pm-3am Thurs.-Sat., COP$20,000 cover) are the places to go in the Zona Rosa. Live bands from the Caribbean

Coast perform regularly on the big stage at Matildelina, warming up the crowd. **Salomé Pagana** (Cra. 14A No. 82-16, tel. 1/221-1895 or 1/218-4076, 6pm-2:30am Tues. and Thurs.-Sat., cover COP$15,000) is a Zona Rosa staple that is your salsa and *cubana* headquarters, often hosting well-known singers and bands.

Céntrico (Cra. 7 No. 32-16, 41 floor, hours vary Wed.-Sat., cover COP$20,000) is a hot bar-restaurant where you can sip your cocktails while overlooking the city from the 41st floor. It is pretty fancy, so dress to impress.

Trampa de Vallenato Galerías (Cl. 53 No. 27A-31, no phone, 5pm-3am Thurs.-Sat.) may have the warm authenticity that you have been craving. This *vallenato* club is regularly voted as the top in the city. To hear *cubana* and salsa music, you can pop into the charming little downtown bar **Son Salomé** (Cra. 7 No. 40-31, 2nd floor, tel. 1/285-0547, hours vary daily) for a drink or two to unwind.

On Fridays it's often rock that the students, hipsters, and visiting foreigners groove to at classic **Candelario Bar** (Cra. 5 No. 3-14, tel. 1/342-3742, 9pm-3am Fri.-Sat.), but don't be surprised to hear electronic, reggae, or Latin beats. It also serves lunch during the week. **Quiebra de Canto** (Cra. 5 No. 17-76, tel. 1/243-1630, 6:30pm-3am Wed.-Sat., cover COP$10,000) is a classic haunt where jazz, funk, and salsa are often the order of the night. Wednesdays are especially popular in the two-floor joint. A different vibe can be found at the **Viejo Almacén** (Cl. 15 No. 4-30, 6pm-2am Wed.-Sun.), a tango bar named after the famous Viejo Almacén in Buenos Aires.

So, it's 6am and you still need to dance? Near the bullfighting ring and in a basement, **Radio Berlín** (Cra. 6 No. 26-57, 9pm-5am Fri.-Sat., COP$20,000 cover) is almost too cool for school. It's occasionally open on Thursdays. If you're looking for a late-night groove, often featuring international DJs, this is your place.

In the Macarena, cool **Baum** (Cl. 33 No. 6-24, cell tel. 316/494-3799, 10pm-5am Fri.-Sat., COP$15,000) attracts a fun crowd and often hosts international DJs.

LGBT

Bogotá is not lacking in gay nightlife spots. At last count there were over 100 gay establishments in the city. This is the place, after all, where many gay Colombians gravitate to so that they can escape endless questions from relatives about when they are going to get married. This isn't a gay bar town, as most people skip that step and head straight to the clubs.

On Wednesday nights the place to go is **Cavú Club** (Cra. 15 No. 88-71, tel. 1/249-9987, www.cavuclub.com, 9pm-3am Wed. and some weekend nights, cover COP$15,000). Here the music is *música pa' planchar* (music to iron by), and there is usually a performance by a drag queen, such as regular La Lupe. At reliable **Blues Bar** (Cl. 86A No. 13A-30, tel. 1/616-7126, 9pm-3am Thurs.-Sat., cover COP$15,000) you can drink and listen to cool music as you warm up around the bonfire in the patio.

As far as clubbing goes, **Theatrón** (Cl. 58 No. 10-32, tel. 1/235-6879, www.theatrondepelicula.com, 9pm-3am Fri.-Sat., cover COP$20,000) is a humongous disco in Chapinero. Theatrón is one-stop shopping for the gay crowd. It has no fewer than nine dance floors, featuring different types of music, including reggaetón, *vallenato*, pop, house, and trance. In the main room there is usually a drag show or contest at around midnight on Saturdays. There are few bars and clubs specifically for women, although at Theatrón they won't feel like second-class citizens. Theatrón occasionally puts on special parties for women. All the major electronic music clubs are gay-friendly. Salsa and *vallenato* clubs—not so much.

PERFORMING ARTS
Classical Music and Opera

You may not think of classical music when you think Bogotá, or South America for that matter, but the city is home to two excellent orchestras and an opera, and hosts talented performers year round. As is the case for most concerts and events in Bogotá, purchasing tickets in advance from Tu Boleta (tel.

1/593-6300, www.tuboleta.com) is the most convenient option.

The publicly financed **Orquesta Filarmónica de Bogotá** (www.filarmonicabogota.gov.co) and the **Sinfónica Nacional de Colombia** (www.asociacion-sinfonica.org) are the two main orchestras in town and the most important ones in the country. The *filarmónica* performs on the Universidad Nacional campus at the **Auditorio Leon de Greiff** (Cra. 45 No. 26-85, www.divulgacion.unal.edu.co); the **Auditorio Fabio Lozano** (Cra. 4 No. 22-61, tel. 1/242-7030, ext. 1905) at the Universidad Jorge Tadeo; and occasionally at the **Teatro Jorge Eliécer Gaitán** (Cra. 7 No. 22-47, tel. 1/379-5750, www.teatrojorgeeliecer.gov.co). The Auditorio León de Greiff is hard to miss: There is a huge iconic stencil of revolutionary Che Guevara on its exterior. There is often an international guest soloist at these concerts. Although tickets are available at the *taquillas* (ticket offices) at these theaters a few hours before performance time, it is recommended to purchase tickets, which are usually embarrassingly inexpensive (usually COP$20,000-40,000), in advance at a Tu Boleta outlet (such as in Centro Andino or El Retiro).

The *sinfónica* performs at the same theaters, as well as the **Colsubisidio Auditorium** (Cl. 26 No. 25-40, tel. 1/343-2673) and at the spectacular **Teatro Mayor Julio Mario Santo Domingo** (Av. Cl. 170 No. 67-51, tel. 1/377-9840, www.teatromayor.com), which has two concert halls. This theater, public library, and cultural center in the working class *localidad* of Suba is worth a visit regardless of whether there is a performance on. The prominent Santo Domingo family donated nearly US$31 million for the construction of this beautiful center.

At the **Sala de Conciertos Luis Ángel Arango** (Cl. 11 No. 4-14, tel. 1/381-2929, www.banrepcultural.org/musica, ticket office 1pm-8pm Mon.-Fri.) in La Candelaria, chamber music concerts featuring acclaimed international artists are regularly held in its spectacular, modernist theater in the Biblioteca Luis Ángel Arango. An added bonus: free *tinto* or *aromática* (herbal tea) at intermission.

The **Ópera de Colombia** (tel. 1/608-8752 or 1/608-2860, www.operadecolombia.com), one of few opera companies in South America, is highly regarded. They perform classic operas during their season, which usually extends from August to October. The **Teatro Jorge Eliécer Gaitán** (Cra. 7 No. 22-47, tel. 1/379-5750, ext. 213, www.teatrojorgeeliecer.gov.co) and the **Teatro Cafam de Bellas Artes** (Av. Cra. 68 No. 90-88, tel. 1/644-4900, www.teatrodebellasartesdebogota.com) host the soirees.

Theater

The largest theater company, the **Teatro Nacional** (Cl. 71 No. 10-25, tel. 1/217-4577, www.teatronacional.com.co), has three different theaters and performances take place just about every day. Their main theater is named in honor of Fanny Mikey, an Argentinian actress who moved to Bogotá and started its famed theater festival.

Teatro Libre (Cl. 62 No. 9A-65, tel. 1/542-1559, www.teatrolibre.org) has its main location in Chapinero and another in Candelaria (Cl. 12B No. 2-44, tel. 1/281-3516). In its 40-plus years of existence, its repertoire has included mostly classic theater as well as works by Colombian playwrights. **Casa Ensamble** (Cra. 24 No. 41-69, tel. 1/368-9268, www.casaensamble.com), in the cute neighborhood of La Soledad, is an alternative performance space, with avant-garde plays such as *Títeres Pornos (Porno Puppets)*. The theater, which sometimes feels more like a cabaret, is a project of well-known Colombian actress Alejandra Borerro. Source of neighborhood pride, the **Fundación Gilberto Alzate Avendaño** (Cl. 10 No. 3-16, tel. 1/282-9491, www.fgaa.gov.co), in La Candelaria, puts on theater and music performances featuring local talent year round in addition to art exhibits. Many of their events are free of charge.

Film

Most movie theaters in Bogotá, as in the rest of the country, are located inside big shopping malls. In the north that means Centro Andino, Atlantis Plaza, and Centro Comercial Granahorrar, the latter also showing more independent flicks and hosting film festivals. A couple of small cinemas in the north specialize in independent films: **Cinemanía** (Cra. 14 No. 93A-85, tel. 1/621-0122, www.cinemania.com.co), near the Parque de la 93, and **Cinema Paraíso Café + Bar** (Cra. 6 No. 120A-56, tel. 1/215-5316, www.cinemaparaiso.com.co). Downtown, go to Calle 24 at the **Cine Colombia Embajador** (Cl. 24 No. 6-01, tel. 1/404-2463, www.cinecolombia.com) for the usual Hollywood releases. It's across from the **Museo de Arte Moderno de Bogotá** (MAMBO, Cl. 24 No. 6-00, tel. 1/286-0466, www.mambogota.com). The museum often shows foreign, classic, and art films. It's best to go in person to get the schedule.

FESTIVALS AND EVENTS

While Bogotá lacks celebrations that unite the whole city, such as the Carnaval de Barranquilla or the Feria de Cali, a number of annual festivals and events have their followers.

Festival Iberoamericano de Teatro

Every two years during Easter week, theater and dance take over the city during the **Festival Iberoamericano de Teatro** (www.festivaldeteatro.com.co). Attracting more than 100 prestigious international troupes and companies and over 170 representing Colombia, this festival is a living tribute to Fanny Mikey, an Argentinian actress who adopted Colombia as her home. She started the biennial affair in 1988. Known for her bright red hair and distinctive smile, she passed away in 2008. With over 800 performances in the span of two weeks, it is one of the largest such theater festivals in the world. There are always theater groups from English-speaking countries, and there are typically many circus and dance performances. To take a break from the show, you can always hang out at the Carpa Cabaret at night, where you can drink and dance alongside actors from across the globe. Besides performances in theaters, there is an impressive series of free performances in parks and plazas in neighborhoods across the city and workshops for acting students.

ArtBo

More than 50 art galleries representing 400 artists from the Americas converge on Bogotá each November during **ArtBo** (www.artboonline.com), the **Feria Internacional de Arte de Bogotá,** one of the top contemporary art fairs in Latin America. It is held each year at the Corferias fairground (Cra. 40 No. 22C-67, www.corferias.com). One space is dedicated to young, emerging artists.

Feria de Artesanías

In December, and just in time for Christmas, the Corferias fairground (Cra. 40 No. 22C-67, www.corferias.com) is the setting for the fantastic—if overwhelming—**Feria de Artesanías** (www.expoartesanias.com). During two weeks, artisans come from across Colombia to showcase and sell their handicrafts. Many artisans, particularly indigenous peoples and Afro-Colombians from rural areas, have their trip to Bogotá sponsored by Artesanías de Colombia, the event's organizer. You will find that one day will not be enough to see—and buy—everything. The fair is also a great place for yummy Colombian snacks like *patacones* (fried plantains).

Music Festivals

In this city of music, free music festivals take place at the Parque Simón Bolívar during the latter half of the year. The series began in the mid-1990s and has grown in popularity ever since. The most famous outdoor music festival is by far the festival **Rock al Parque** (www.rockalparque.gov.co, July), the largest free outdoor rock festival in Latin America. The 2012 edition attracted 120,000 rockers. Variation include **Salsa al Parque** (Aug.), **Ópera al Parque** (Aug.), **Jazz al Parque** (Sept.), **Hip Hop al Parque** (Oct.) and **Colombia al Parque** (Nov.). Find schedule information online (www.culturarecreacionydeporte.gov.co).

International and national jazz and Latin jazz artists perform annually at the long-running **Festival Internacional de Jazz de Bogotá.** Most concerts are held at the **Teatro Libre** (Cl. 62 No. 9-65, tel. 1/217-1988, www.teatrolibre.org) in Chapinero. This usually takes place in early September, with tickets available at all Tu Boleta stands.

Races

If the altitude doesn't make you huff and puff along the streets of La Candelaria, maybe you would be up for the challenge of a running race in Bogotá. The **Media Maratón** is the city's biggest race, attracting runners from around the world. It usually takes place in August, starting at the Plaza de Bolívar and ending in the Parque Simón Bolívar. Nike sponsors its **We Run 10K** each year in October. The most unusual race of all takes place in December during the **Ascenso Torre Colpatria** race. That's when runners ascend a stairwell 48 floors to the top of the Colpatria building downtown.

Shopping

HANDICRAFTS

Markets selling Colombian handicrafts will likely find you before you find them. The **Pasaje Rivas** (between Cras. 9-10 and Clls. 10-11) dates to the late 19th century. This traditional shopping corridor—one of the few remaining—makes for a fun detour. The passages are so narrow that it is impossible to not interact with the carpenters selling their furniture and women peddling their hand-woven baskets and curios.

The Pasaje Rivas is great for atmosphere, but if you are looking for high quality, visit one of the **Artesanías de Colombia** (www.artesaniasdecolombia.com.co) stores. The same people who put on the amazing Feria

Pasaje Rivas is a traditional shopping corridor.

de Artesanías every December have two stores in Bogotá. The most picturesque, by far, is at a stunningly white colonial church, the **Iglesia Las Aguas** (Cra. 2 No. 18A-58, tel. 1/284-3095, 9am-6pm Mon.-Fri., 10am-noon Sat.). You can also visit the Chicó location (Cl. 86A No. 13A-10, tel. 1/691-7149, 10am-7pm Mon.-Sat.).

El Balay (Cra. 15 No. 75-75, tel. 1/347-1462, 9:30am-7pm Mon.-Sat.) is another option in northern Bogotá. While they have their share of trinkets, you might find a nice hammock or *chamba* (casserole dish).

CLOTHES AND ACCESSORIES

Looking for a cool T-shirt? Check out **America del Sur** (Cl. 85 No. 12-83, www.americadelsur.com.co, 11am-7:30pm Mon.-Sat.), which has mostly Colombia-themed shirts, or **BrincaBrinca** (Cra. 14 No. 85-26, tel. 1/530-1136, www.brincabrinca.com, 10am-7pm Mon.-Sat.). **Cyclus** (Cra. 7 with Cl. 54, east side, tel. 1/249-720, www.cyclus.com.co, 10am-7pm Mon.-Sat.) is a unique store that

makes all sorts of messenger bags, backpacks, and wallets out of recycled tires. The slogan of this environmentally friendly boutique is appropriately "It's a round trip."

ANTIQUES

One street near the Zona Rosa is dedicated almost exclusively to antiques. Nicknamed the **Calle de los Anticuarios** (Cl. 79A between Cras. 7-9), this pleasant one-way street, nice for a mid-morning stroll, is lined by a handful of antique shops as well as some restaurants and, at its top, the Iglesia Santa María de los Ángeles, a popular choice for weekend weddings.

Prominent on the street are: **Cinco en Punto** (Cl. 79B No. 8-31, tel. 1/248-9798, 10am-6pm Mon.-Sat.), offering a range of curios from vases to furniture; **Anticuario Novecento** (Cl. 79B No. 7-60, tel. 1/606-8616, www.anticuarionovecento.com, 10am-6:30pm Mon.-Sat.), with a wide collection that includes religious art from colonial Colombia along with Baccarat crystal from the 1930s; and **Bolívar Old Prints** (Cl. 79B No. 7-46, tel. 1/695-5006, www.bolivaroldprints.com, 10:30am-6pm Mon.-Sat.), which specializes in old maps from Latin America and is owned by a French expat. The website of **Asociación de Anticuarios de Colombia** (Cl. 79B No. 8-49, tel. 1/248-5756, www.asociacionanticuariosde-colombia.com) has a more complete listing of shops as well as an interesting page regarding Colombian heritage pieces that are in peril of disappearing through illegal sales and transport abroad.

A smaller antique area is in Chapinero on the Carrera 9 from Calle 60 to Calle 63. Check out **Librería Errata** (Cra. 9 No. 61-16, tel. 1/249-6234, www.libreriaerrata.com, 10am-6:30pm Mon.-Sat.) for old books and **Ayer & Co.** (Cl. 62 No. 9-11, tel. 1/219-9789, 10am-1:30pm and 2:30pm-6:30pm Mon.-Sat.), which sells *de todo un poco* (a little of everything).

FLOWERS AND MARKETS

The flower market at the **Parque El Virrey** (Cl. 86 at Cra. 15, daily) is always colorful, and, if you are the bargaining type, you might enjoy purchasing some flowers, if only to enjoy for a couple of days. A nearby florist, **Flor Expres** (Cra. 13A No. 86A-49, tel. 1/691-7335, 9am-7pm Mon.-Fri., 9am-5pm Sat.), is also good, with many unusual varieties and orchids, but there's no haggling involved. The king of all flower markets remains **Paloquemao** (Av. 19 No. 25-02, 3am-noon Mon.-Fri.) downtown, but to see it at its most vibrant, you have to get there really early. Best days: Friday and Sunday. Worst day: Monday. There is much more to Paloquemao, with all those exotic Colombian fruits, vegetables, meats, and more. There is a TransMilenio station nearby (Paloquemao station), but it's best to cab it if you go early in the morning.

Two popular flea markets take place every Sunday. The **Mercado de Pulgas San Alejo** (Cra. 7 No. 24-70, 9am-5pm Sun.) takes place in front of the Torre Colpatria. Uptown in Usaquén is the **Mercado De Las Pulgas Toldos De San Pelayo** (Cra. 7B No. 124-77, 8am-5pm Sun.). The crowds that go to these are worlds apart!

JEWELRY

Colombia is one of the top emerald-producing countries in the world, boasting three major mining areas, mostly located in the Boyacá department. Bogotá is probably the best place in the country to pick up one of those gems, but it would be wise to walk into jewelry stores armed with knowledge about how you can tell what is a good gem, an idea about prices, etc. Downtown, check out the **Museo Internacional de la Esmeralda** (Cl. 16 No. 6-66, tel. 1/286-4268, 10am-6pm Mon.-Sat.); **Joyeria Relojeria Museum** (Emerald Trade Center, tel. 1/342-2957, 9am-7pm Mon.-Fri., 9am-5pm Sat.); or the many stores on the block of Carrera 6 between Calles 10 and 13. You can also try your luck wheeling and dealing with the men milling about on the Jiménez just below the Séptima. But there, you're on your own.

Two top-end jewelers at the Centro Andino are **Liévano** (Centro Andino Local 157, tel. 1/616-8608, 10:45am-7:45pm Mon.-Sat.) and **Bauer** (Centro Andino, tel. 1/478-5454, 11am-7pm Mon.-Sat.).

Specializing in Colombian gold is internationally recognized **Galeria & Museo Cano** (Cra. 13 No. 27-97, Torre B, Int. 1-19, tel. 1/336-3255, www.galeriacano.com.co, 9am-7pm Mon.-Fri., 9am-5pm Sat.).

BOOKS

For English books, travel guides, newspapers, and magazines, **Author's** (Cl. 70 No. 5-23, tel. 1/217-7788, 10am-8pm Mon.-Sat., 10am-6pm Sun.) is the best and perhaps only place in town. Author's also has a large selection of children's books. In the north, try **Librería Lerner** (Cl. 92 No. 15-23, tel. 1/636-4295, www.libre-rialerner.com.co, 9am-7pm Mon.-Sat.), a great place to find Colombian literature, or **Librería Central** (Cl. 94 No. 13-92, tel. 1/622-7423, 10am-6pm Mon.-Sat.), which also has some English- and German-language books.

SHOPPING MALLS

Colombia is mall crazy, and Bogotá, with over 20 of them, is the capital of this infatuation. Symbolic of its growing middle class, glitzy shopping malls have popped up literally all across the city. The latest and largest is **Titán Plaza** (Cra. 72 No. 80-94, Cl. 80 at Av. Boyacá, www.titanplaza.com), proudly home of Colombia's first Gap.

In northern Bogotá, **Centro Andino** (Cra. 11 No. 82-71, hours vary daily, www.centroandino.com.co) was a big deal when it opened in 1993, being the first high-end shopping center. The German school, the longstanding Colegio Andino, was razed to make way for it. Colombian men's clothes brand **Arturo Calle, Bosi** for shoes and leather, high-end jeweler **Bauer,** and **L.A. Cano** (specializing in handicrafts) are a few of the many stores in the mall. There is a **Cine Colombia** movie theater as well.

The food court on the top floor provides an unusual vista of the Zona Rosa, and cafés on the terrace below are popular for late afternoon *onces* (tea time).

Next door to Andino is glitzy **El Retiro** (Cl. 81 No. 11-94, www.elretirobogota.com, hours vary daily), home of the **Plaza de Andrés** restaurant; **Mercedes Salazar,** with whimsical jewelry; and **Mundo Único,** which sells skimpy men's underwear. The TurisBog sightseeing bus stops in front of the mall on Calle 81.

Finally, the **Atlantis Plaza** (Cl. 81 No. 13-05, www.atlantisplaza.com, hours vary daily) has a **Cinemark** movie theater, the swimwear shop **Onda de Mar,** and restaurants such as **Crepes & Waffles** and **Hard Rock Café.**

Sports and Recreation

BIKING
◖ Ciclovía

The **Ciclovía** is one of the best things about Bogotá. No wonder it has been copied in cities around the world—from all across Colombia to New York to Brussels. Every Sunday and on holidays (two times at night, even) about 121 kilometers of Bogotá streets are closed to vehicular traffic so that cyclists, joggers, dog walkers, skaters, and people-watchers can claim the streets. The Ciclovía started small in the 1970s as a neighborhood initiative. Today it is an institution, and really one of the few spaces in which people of all classes in Bogotá mix. On particularly sunny days, over two million people have been estimated to have participated in the Ciclovía. That's the equivalent of the entire population of Houston, Texas, out on a bike! Always be prepared for sun, cold, and rain.

While popular with joggers and others, it may be more enjoyable on a bike, especially because you can cover a lot more of the city pedaling rather than walking. The Ciclovía on the Avenida Séptima and on the Carrera 15 are two of the most popular routes, but those are just a fraction of the possibilities. You can go for miles and miles. In fact, this may be a chance to explore parts of the city that you would have never considered before.

There is no need to take a guided group tour, as the Ciclovía is easy to figure out. If you ever get lost, you can always ask the helpful Ciclovía staff, patrolling the routes. Or just ask one of the hundreds of thousands of others out for some fresh air which way to go. Bring money with you so you can grab a freshly squeezed orange juice along the way. Bike repair stations are located on all routes. Keep an eye on the time, as you don't want to be far from your hotel when the cars come roaring back at the strike of 2pm.

Ciclopaseo de los Miércoles

Fast becoming an in-the-know institution is this group of over a hundred cyclists of all ages and abilities that gets together every other Wednesday night for a nighttime ride along the *ciclorutas* (bike paths) and streets of Bogotá. The **Ciclopaseo de los Miércoles** has been going strong for about seven years. The group meets at bike shop **Welcome** (Cl. 96 No. 10-57, tel. 1/256-0915) at 7pm. Find out about the next ride on Twitter (@elciclopaseo) or on Facebook. There is no charge.

© ANDREW DIER

The Sunday Ciclovía is a Bogotá institution.

Bike Rentals

Many bike shops have begun to rent bikes specifically for the Ciclovía. Try **Pure Bike Shop** (Cra. 13 No. 78-47, tel. 1/476-5058, www. purebikeshop.com, daily rental COP$45,000), **Eco Byke** (cell tel. 311/519-2332), or **Bogotá Bike Tours** (Cra. 3 No. 12-72, tel. 1/281-9924, www.bogotabiketours.com). Many shops offer group bike tours.

RUNNING

Traffic in the city makes it tough to find pleasant places to run, but there are a few. The **Parque Nacional** (between Clls. 36-39 and Cras. 7-5), along with the cute English-style Merced neighborhood next to it, is not a bad place for a short morning jog downtown. The **Parkway** (Av. 24 between Clls. 45 and 34) is another option. This is a lovely strip of green in a quiet part of the Teusaquillo neighborhood. Of course the **Parque Bolívar** is also very popular, as is the park of the **Biblioteca Virgilio Barco.** In the north try the **Parque El Virrey** (Cras. 8-15 near Cl. 87). One side of the canal has a bike path, the other a foot path. In this *play* (fashionable) area, you may want to make sure your workout outfit is perfectly color-coordinated. Be careful crossing Carrera 11.

HIKING

The mountains surrounding the city are just too inviting to not explore. There are more mountain paths to conquer besides the one to the top of the **Cerro de Monserrate.**

Another hike in the north that is wildly popular is at the **Quebrada La Vieja,** a path that is operated by the Acueducto. It is open Monday through Saturday 5am-9:30am. On Sundays and holidays it is closed. It may be tricky to find the path at first. It is on the east (mountain side) of the Circunvalar at Calle 71. Most people walk up along the right side of Calle 72 and go through the tunnel under the Circunvalar to reach the path. The hike takes about two hours total.

Amigos de la Montaña (www.amigos-delamontana.org) helps to maintain the Quebrada La Vieja. They also arrange group

flying kites at the Biblioteca Virgilio Barco

© ANDREW DIER

walks. Another group, **Camino Bogotá** (www.caminobogota.wordpress.com), regularly organizes hikes in the mountains around the city. Most of these excursions are accompanied by police officers. A third organization, **Caminar Colombia** (tel. 1/366-3059 or 1/241-0065, www.caminarcolombia.com), offers "ecological walks," usually on Sunday. These are usually outside of, but not far from, Bogotá. These walks cost around COP$40,000 including transportation. On the day of the hike, the group usually meets at 6:30am at the Los Heroes shopping center (Cra. 19A No. 78-85). The TransMilenio station there is called Los Heroes.

SOCCER

There are three professional *fútbol* clubs in Bogotá. **Santa Fe** (www.independientesantafe.com) is known as "Expreso Rojo" (the Red Express). **Millonarios** (www.millonarios.com.co) has, along with América of Cali, won the most national titles. Their color is blue. Both compete at the **Estadio El Campín** (Cra. 30

at Cl. 57). There is a TransMilenio station in front of the stadium (Campín station). The big match in town is Santa Fe versus Millonarios, and it can get quite heated in the stands. Note that you're not allowed to bring in belts or sharp objects to the matches.

The green team, **La Equidad** (www.equidadclubdeportivo.com), is the third club in the city. They are affiliated with La Equidad insurance company. Their modern, covered stadium is in the south of the city.

Tickets for all matches can be purchased at Tu Boleta (www.tuboleta.com, tel. 1/593-6300) or Ticket Express (www.ticketexpress.com, tel. 1/609-1111) outlets. You can also go to each team's ticket offices: **La Tienda Roja** (Cl. 64A No. 50B-08) for Santa Fe or **La Tienda Azul** (Centro Comercial Gran Estación, Local 2-50, Av. Cl. 26 No. 62-47) for Millonarios. The most sought-after seats in the house at the Estadio El Campín are *platea occidental alta* and *baja*. Ticket prices range between COP$20,000 and COP$70,000.

There are two soccer seasons each year. One goes from February to June and the second from June to December. Almost all the matches are on Wednesdays and on weekends.

Colombia hosted the Under 20 Soccer World Cup in 2011, which was a source of pride for the country, with the championship match (Brazil defeated Portugal) played in Bogotá. When the Colombian national team is playing a match, traffic magically disappears on the city's streets!

TOURS
Walking Tours

A free walking tour of La Candelaria is given, in English, every Tuesday and Thursday at 10am and 2pm starting at the tourist information office on the southwest corner of the Plaza de Bolívar. Spanish tours are offered every day. Stop by or call (tel. 1/283-7115) a day before to reserve your place.

Architecture buffs might be interested in taking a Rogelio Salmona walking tour, exploring some of the architect's most celebrated works. These are organized by the

Fundación Rogelio Salmona (Cra. 6 No. 26-85, Piso 20, tel. 1/283-6413, www.fundacionrogeliosalmona.org). There are three different tours: Centro Histórico, the Centro Internacional, and the Biblioteca Virgilio Barco area. Tours last about three hours, each with an expert guide. English-speaking guides can be arranged. The tours are quite pricey, at COP$180,000 for two people. Prices lower substantially if you latch onto a group of at least 12 (COP$45,000).

Bus Tours

TurisBog (Parque Central Bavaria, Local 120, Manzana 2, tel. 1/336-8805, www.turisbog.com, adults COP$63,000) is a hop-on, hop-off bus tour that began operation in late 2012. The green double-decker bus makes seven stops: the Maloka science museum in Salitre, the Jardín Botánico, the Parque de la 93, El Retiro mall, Monserrate, the Parque Central Bavaria in the Centro Internacional, and the Corferias fairgrounds near the Calle 26. Included with the purchase of your ticket is a GPS-activated audio guide in both Spanish and English, a guided walking tour of La Candelaria, and discounts to several restaurants and attractions.

Bike Tours

If you'd like the camaraderie of a group of other visitors as you get to know the city and get in a little exercise, try one of the many excursions offered by **Bogotá Bike Tours** (Cra. 3 No. 12-72, tel. 1/281-9924, www.bogotabiketours.com). They offer bike tours around the city and also many other walking tours, such as an unusual graffiti tour.

Tours Outside of Bogotá

Many hotels can arrange tours to attractions such as Zipaquirá and Laguna de Guatavita, or visits to these can be made via public transportation or by hiring a driver for the day. An agency that specializes in daily Catedral de Sal tours is www.tourcatedraldesal.com. These cost COP$96,000 per person.

There are some extraordinary national natural parks (*parques nacional natural,* or PNN) quite close to Bogotá, making for excellent day hikes. Sometimes these are a bit more difficult to organize without transportation and not being familiar with the area. **Aventureros** (Cra. 15 No.79-70, tel. 1/467-3837, www.aventureros.co) organizes mountain bike trips outside of Bogotá, for instance to the Desierto de Tatacoita near Nemocón. **Ecoglobal Expeditions** (tel. 1/579-3402, www.ecoglobalexpeditions.com) organizes excursions to multiple destinations throughout Colombia, including the famous Caño Cristales and hikes in El Cocuy. They also can organize day trips to parks nearby Bogotá, such as the Parque Natural Nacional Sumapaz, containing the world's largest *páramo* (highland moor), and the PNN Chingaza. **Colombia Oculta** (tel. 1/630-3172, ext. 112, cell tel. 311/239-7809, www.colombiaoculta.org) is a similar organization, with similar destinations.

Accommodations

As tourism has grown in Bogotá, so too have the number of accommodations options. This is evident in the Centro Histórico, with dozens of hostels catering to backpackers, and also in the north, with five-star hotels changing the landscape in upscale shopping and dining areas. Thus room rates tend to climb as you go from south to north, with Chapinero appropriately offering the most in-between options. Weekend rates are often less expensive in the larger hotels that cater to business people.

While it is probably more desirable to stay along the Carrera 7 corridor, other parts of town may be more convenient depending on your length of visit or budget. If you want to be close to the airport, many hotels, several quite new, line Calle 26 (Avenida El Dorado) in western Bogotá. This part of town is known for steel and glass, not colonial charm. There are few interesting restaurant options within walking distance at night; however, it is quite accessible to downtown during the day thanks to the new TransMilenio line (15-20 minutes) and at night by taxi. Besides being close to the airport, hotels in this area are close to the Corferias fairgrounds, the Parque Simón Bolívar area, and the U.S. Embassy.

North of Calle 100 there are many hotel options in what feels like suburbia. You might find some good deals online there, but you will be quite far from downtown attractions.

Hotel rates sometimes automatically include sales tax of 10 percent (IVA). Most hotels include free wireless Internet and breakfast (although the quality of breakfast will vary). While all the fancy hotels and backpacker places have English speaking staff—at least at the front desk—smaller hotels may not. Note that room rates usually depend on the number of persons, not necessarily on the size of the room.

Except for some international chains and upper-end hotels, most hotels will not have heating or air conditioning in their rooms. You'll have to make do with extra blankets and body heat on those chilly Bogotá nights.

A final word: *Moteles* are always, *residencias* are usually, and *hospedajes* are sometimes Colombian love hotels.

LA CANDELARIA

Travelers on a budget will find plentiful, friendly options in La Canderlaria close to all the important sights. Yet it still might feel a little desolate late at night, especially on holidays when the university students are gone and Bogotanos skip town.

Under COP$70,000

Sleek **Explora Hostels** (Cl. 12C No. 3-19, tel. 1/282-9320, www.explorahostels.com, COP$22,000 dorm, COP$50,000 d) is small with minimalist decor. There is not much common space, so you might need earplugs at night if your neighbors are in party mode (unless you join them). **Cranky Croc** (Cl. 12D No. 3-46, tel. 1/342-2438, www.crankycroc.com, COP$23,000 dorms, COP$70,000 d) is big and airy with wood floors throughout, and always has excursions and activities on offer for its guests. Private security guards make this street feel safe after dark.

La Vieja Suiza (Cl. 12 No. 3-07, tel. 1/286-9695, www.laviejasuiza.com, COP$60,000 d) is a cozy and quiet place, run by two Swiss guys, that is connected to their bakery. It's nice to be awoken by the aroma of freshly baked (Swiss) bread.

COP$70,000-200,000

Platypus Hostel (Cl. 12F No. 2-43, tel. 1/352-0127, www.platypusbogota.com, COP$22,000 dorm, COP$100,000 d) is the pioneer backpacker lodge in La Candelaria. Although somewhat worn, it is a welcoming place, where you can mix with other travelers. There are three houses in the Platypus kingdom, all on the same street. The main one, where you check in, is livelier. Platypus is just off the Eje Ambiental (Av. Jiménez).

The folks at Platypus now have gone upscale with the newish ⟨ **Casa Platypus** (Cra. 3 No. 12F-28, tel. 1/281-1801, www.casaplatypus. com, COP$40,000 dorm, COP$150,000 d). It is comfortable, sparkling clean, and friendly. The rooftop terrace is an excellent place to unwind with a glass of wine after a day hitting the streets.

⟨ **Masaya Intercultural** (Cra. 2 No. 12-48, tel. 1/747-1848, www.masaya-experience. com, COP$22,000 dorm, COP$100,000 d) near LaSalle University offers different accommodation options depending on your budget or style, from luxurious private rooms to bunk beds. Tourists stay at this newish hostel range from backpackers to budget travelers. Staff are super friendly. Guests and students conglomerate by the bar/restaurant area in front.

The **Abadía Colonial** (Cl. 11 No. 2-32, tel. 1/341-1884, www.abadiacolonial.com, COP$145,000 s, COP$200,000 d), an Italian-run midrange option, is surprisingly quiet in back around the interior patio. The restaurant specializes in—surprise—Italian cuisine.

Over COP$200,000

⟨ **Hotel de la Ópera** (Cl. 10 No. 5-72, tel. 1/336-2066, www.hotelopera.com.co, COP$330,000 d) still reigns as the luxury place to stay in La Candelaria. One republican-style house and one colonial house have been converted into this hotel. There are two restaurants, including one on the rooftop that has one of the best views downtown. The hotel also offers a spa.

Casa Deco (Cl. 12C No. 2-36 tel. 1/283-7032, www.hotelcasadeco.com, COP$230,000 d) is a nicely refurbished art deco building with 21 well-appointed although somewhat chilly rooms (all named by the color of their interior). The terrace is an excellent place for relaxing on a late afternoon.

CENTRO INTERNACIONAL

This part of town, once a modern and upscale commercial district, is on the rebound. The new TransMilenio line that has opened on the Séptima has been a major factor in transforming the area into a walkable and well-situated place to stay while discovering the city. There are, however, still few hotel options.

COP$70,000-200,000

In the heart of the Centro Internacional, few surprises are in store at **Ibis Museo** (Transversal 6 No. 27-85, tel. 1/381-4666, www.ibishotel. com, COP$120,000). Across from the Museo Nacional, the hotel has 200 smallish rooms and a 24-hour restaurant (breakfast not included). Right on the Séptima, this French economy hotel chain is a nice place to be on Ciclovía Sundays.

The 850-room **Crown Plaza Tequendama** (Cra. 10 No. 27-51, tel. 1/382-0300, www. cptequendama.com.co, COP$180,000 d) was the most exclusive address in Bogotá for many years. Charles de Gaulle even stayed there. It retains its elegance of yesteryear, with shoe-shiners in the lobby, several restaurants and cafés on-site, and smartly dressed bellboys. Rooms are comfortable, and the location is agreeable to taking in the sights downtown. Security is tight here.

WESTERN BOGOTÁ

If you are only passing through and would like to be close to the airport, you may consider staying in one of the many hotels along the Avenida Calle 26 (Avenida El Dorado). With the new TransMilenio line on the El Dorado, it is easy to hop on one of the red buses and spend the day visiting the major sights in the Centro Histórico. There's not much in the way of charm in this part of town. There is, however, a mall: **Gran Estación** (Av. El Dorado No. 62-47). Plus, along the Avenida and the TransMilenio line is a nice bike route and jogging path.

COP$70,000-200,000

Aloft Hotel (Av. Cl. 26 No. 9-32, tel. 1/741-7070, www.starwoodhotels.com/aloft hotels, COP$169,999 d), a member of the Starwood Hotel Group, is smartly decorated, modern, and within five minutes of the airport. There are 142 rooms in this property. It is also within about a five-minute walk of the Portal El Dorado TransMilenio station.

Over COP$200,000

The **Marriott** (Av. Cl. 26 No. 69B-53, tel. 1/485-1111, www.marriott.com, COP$400,000) is luxurious and is close to the Salitre business and shopping area. The two restaurants—one a cool sushi bar and the other serving Italian fare—are excellent. The hotel is within walking distance of a TransMilenio station, and it takes under 12 minutes to get to the airports. Open since in 2009, it is one of the first luxury international hotels to arrive in Bogotá in recent years.

CHAPINERO

Halfway between downtown and the Zona Rosa, the area of Chapinero between Calle 53 and Calle 72 offers quite a few midrange accommodation options. Chapinero Alto, to the east of the Avenida Séptima, is a quiet and leafy middle-class neighborhood. Below the Séptima (to the west), it's gritty. During weekdays Chapinero bustles with merchants and students, and on weekend nights the area is transformed into a mostly gay nightlife area. Hotels in Chapinero are about a 10-minute cab ride from the upscale restaurant areas in the north.

COP$70,000-200,000

The Viaggio chain has nine reasonably priced, furnished apartment buildings in Bogotá. **Viaggio 6.1.7.** (Cl. 61 No. 7-18, tel. 1/744-9999, www.viaggio.com.co, COP$163,000 d) is a high-rise centrally located on the Séptima. Rooms have tiny kitchenettes, but breakfast is included in the price. You can rent rooms on a daily, weekly, or monthly basis.

Classical music fills **6 Suites** (Cra. 3B No. 64A-06, tel. 1/752-9484, www.6suiteshotel. com, COP$150,000 d), which has exactly that in a small house. Some packages include dinner. There is a Saturday vegetable and fruit market in a small park next to the house, as well as a round-the-clock police station.

Moderately priced, clean, and centrally located, the **Abitare 56 Hotel** (Cl. 56 No. 7-79, tel. 1/248-0600, www.abitare56.com, COP$113,000 d) has 28 rooms and is a great deal.

Casona del Patio (Cra. 8 No. 69-24, tel. 1/212-8805, www.lacasonadelpatio.net, COP$135,000 d) is in an English Tudor-style home, and its 24 rooms are reasonably priced despite its location near the Zona G. It has all wood floors, and there is private security on the street at night. With 10 rooms, the **Matisse Hotel** (Cl. 67 No. 6-55, tel. 1/212-0177, www.matissehotel.com, COP$180,000 d) is just minutes away from the Zona G in an English Tudor-style house above the Séptima.

Two hotels in Chapinero exclusively market to gay and lesbian clientele. **High Park Suites** (Cra. 4 No. 58-58, tel. 1/249-5149, contacto@ highparksuites.com, COP$191,000 d) has four spacious rooms and is in Chapinero Alto. If you are planning on taking taxis everywhere you go, the location is perfectly fine. However, if you'd like to walk, it is on the east side of the Carrera 5 speedway—crossing the street there can be like crossing the Indianapolis 500. Warhol-mad **San Sebastian** (Cl. 62 No. 9-49, tel. 1/540-4643, www.hbsansebastian.com, COP$180,000 d) is on the other side of the Séptima, not far from gay mecca Theatrón and the gay-friendly gym and supermarket.

Over COP$200,000

In the leafy Chapinero Alto neighborhood, **The Book Hotel** (Cra. 5 No. 57-79, tel. 1/704-2454, www.thebookhotel.co, COP$273,000 d), which markets itself as gay-friendly, offers very comfortable and modern rooms, and the moderately priced adjacent restaurant with a terrace is popular with locals on their lunch hour.

NORTHERN BOGOTÁ

Uptown is a good option if comfort trumps budget and you want to be close to loads of excellent restaurants.

Under COP$70,000

A good deal within easy walking distance of all the restaurants and stores of the Zona Rosa is **Chapinorte Bogotá Guesthouse** (Cl. 79 No. 14-59, tel. 1/256-2152, www.chapinortehostel-bogota.com, COP$64,000 s with shared bath). It's a real bargain for the north.

COP$70,000-200,000

On a quiet street in a wealthy neighborhood minutes from the Zona Rosa, **Retiro 84** (Cl. 84 No. 9-95, tel. 1/616-1501 www.retiro84.com, COP$173,000 d) has 16 rooms. The breakfast area is not very happening, but the hotel is comfortable and is reasonably priced for this high-rent part of town. It's popular with business travelers in town for longer stays. Near the Atlantis Plaza shopping mall in the Zona Rosa, **Hotel Saint Simon** (Cra. 14 No. 81-34, tel. 1/621-8188, www.hotelsaintsimonbogota.com, COP$180,000 d) is a good value. It is a fairly nondescript brick hotel with about 60 carpeted but well-maintained rooms.

Over COP$200,000

BH (www.bhhoteles.com) is a relatively new Colombian chain of hotels, mostly catering to business travelers. All are comfortable with minimalist design. They operate several hotels in Bogotá. **BH Tempo** (Cra. 7 No. 65-01, tel. 1/742-4095, COP$220,000 d) has 63 rooms and is close to the Zona G. **BH Quinta** (Cra. 5 No. 74-52, tel. 1/742-4908, COP$280,000 d) is in an English Tudor-style house on the busy Carrera Quinta. The most expensive of their hotels is the **BH Retiro** (Cl. 80 No. 10-11, tel. 1/756-3177, COP$370,000), overlooking a park. It's a five-minute walk to the Centro Andino. Farther north still is **BH Parque 93** (Cra. 14 No. 93A-69, tel. 1/743-2820, COP$220,000).

If you'd like to be in the middle of the action in the Zona Rosa, a few comfortable options are around or below the US$150 per night range. Near the Atlantis Plaza shopping mall is the **GHL Hotel Hamilton** (Cra. 14 No. 81-20, tel. 1/621-5455, www.ghlhoteles.com, COP$290,000 d) of the GHL hotel chain.

Cool ◖ **84 DC** (Cl. 84 No. 9-67, tel. 1/487-0909, www.84dc.com.co, COP$248,000 d) blends in well in this upscale neighborhood. It has 24 spacious, modern rooms. Guests have some privileges at the nearby Bodytech gym.

B3 (Cra. 15 No. 88-36, tel. 1/593-4490, www.hotelsb3.com, COP$200,000 d) is one of the most striking hotels in town, due to its wonderful living facade of plants. The lobby area is a lively place in the early evening, when guests munch on tapas and sip cocktails at the bar.

Spanish midrange hotel chain ◖ **NH Bogotá 93** (Cl. 93 No. 12-41, tel. 1/589-7744, COP$240,000) is an unpretentious entry in Bogotá. It offers 137 smart rooms, a nice rooftop terrace, and a small gym.

Finally, the **Hilton** (Cra. 7 No. 72-41, tel. 1/600-6100, www.hilton.com, COP$250,000 d) is back in Bogotá, after having abandoned its location downtown during harsher times. This time the Hilton is in a slick black high-rise on the Séptima near Calle 72. If you book early enough, you can get a good deal on rooms.

Although it's right next door to Andrés D.C. and the rest of the Zona Rosa revelry, you'd never know it in your quiet, comfortable room at the **Bohème Royal** (Cl. 82 No. 12-35, tel. 1/618-0168, www.hotelesroyal.com, COP$310,000 d). You can use the gym at its partner hotel, the Andino Royal on Calle 85. Stately **Hotel Morrison** (Cl. 84 Bis No. 13-54, tel. 1/622-3111, www.morrisonhotel.com, COP$300,000) overlooks a nicely manicured park in the Zona Rosa. It offers spacious rooms and has a "New York style" restaurant. Guests enjoy privileges at the Spinning Center gym across the street. You may want to avoid rooms on the south side of the hotel, where you might feel the pulsating beats from nearby discos.

At **B.O.G.** (Cra. 11 No. 86-74, tel. 1/639-9999, www.boghotel.com, COP$420,000 d), every detail of the hotel has been thought out. An extraordinary giant photograph of an emerald in the gym area downstairs will inspire you to buy one. The most widely heralded chef in Colombia, Leonor Espinosa, has a nouvelle

Colombian cuisine restaurant, and the rooftop pool is luxurious. Just a few blocks away, **Cité** (Cra. 15 No. 88-10, tel. 1/646-7777, www.citehotel.com, COP$400,000 d) may lack some of the finer touches of B.O.G., but its location right on the El Virrey park could not be better. The terrace of the restaurant is a popular place for Sunday brunch. They have a rooftop pool and provide bikes for guests to use on the Ciclovía, which passes by in front every Sunday and holiday.

Estelar (Cl. 93 No. 11-19, tel. 1/511-1555, www.hotelesestelar.com, COP$430,000 d) has a fabulous rooftop bar and pool, and you will be sure to get a good night's sleep thanks in part to the soundproof windows. It's close to the Parque de la 93. The discreet

Hotel Portón Bogotá (Cl. 84 No. 7-55, tel. 1/616-6611, www.hotelportonbogota.com.co, COP$400,000 d) prides itself on its tight security, making it a favorite of visiting diplomats. It has an elegant old-school feel, especially in the restaurant and lounge area, where they light the three fireplaces every evening at 7. Portón guests have unlimited access to the very close Bodytech gym.

If you have real money to burn, try the **JW Marriott Hotel Bogotá** (Cl. 73 No. 8-60, tel. 1/481-6000, www.marriott.com/bogjw, COP$600,000 d). The bar at this 245-room hotel can make more than 70 types of martinis—enough said. Of course, you don't have to shell out 600,000 pesos to saddle up at the bar and sip one of those martinis.

Food

Bogotá is the best city in the country when it comes to dining, with more than its fair share of excellent restaurants. Unfortunately many of these places charge Manhattan prices.

A 10 percent tip is usually included in the price, but it is a requirement for the server to ask you if you'd like the *servicio incluido*. You can say no, but that would be considered harsh. If you are truly impressed with the service, you can always leave a little additional on the table.

The Bogotá dish par excellence is *ajiaco*. This is a hearty potato and chicken soup, seasoned with the secret herb *guascas*. (Oops—there goes the secret.) On some dreary days, there can be nothing better. Heated debate can arise about what else to include in the soup. A small piece of corn on the cob usually goes in, as does a dollop of cream, but capers and avocado slices are controversial additions.

Reservations are helpful on weekend evenings, especially in the Zona G. Restaurant staff will be more than happy to order a cab for you by phone. That is a very good idea, especially at night.

Tap water in Bogotá—*de la llave*—is perfectly fine and good tasting. Besides, if you ever order a fresh lemonade or fruit juice, you're getting *agua de Bogotá* anyhow.

LA CANDELARIA
Cafés, Bakeries, and Quick Bites
Here in coffee country, there is no shortage of tucked away cafés where you can sip a *tinto*, but if you want something more, it's best to stick to the pros. That means **Juan Valdez Café** (Centro Cultural Gabriel García Márquez) and **Oma** (Museo Arqueológico). These chains are all over Bogotá and indeed Colombia, and have a strong following. Their success is one reason perhaps that Starbucks has not yet ventured into Colombia.

If you'd like to stay away from the chains, check out the **Café de la Peña/Pastelería Francesa** (Cra. 3 No. 9-66, tel. 1/336-7488, www.cafepasteleria.com, 8am-8pm Mon.-Sat., 9am-6pm Sun.). This bakery/café is where locals pick up their daily baguette. They serve quiches and light lunches with a few Colombian touches as well. Inside it has a quiet, homey feeling.

The classic place for a *tamal* and a hot chocolate, the **Puerta Falsa** (Cl. 11 No. 6-50, tel.

1/286-5091, 7am-10pm daily) claims to be one of the oldest operating restaurants in Bogotá, having opened in 1816.

Colombian and Fusion

Capital Cocina y Café (Cl. 10 No. 2-99, tel. 1/342-0426, 9:30am-9pm Mon.-Fri., 2pm-9pm Sat., COP$17,000) is your hip little spot on the corner. Hearty lunches are reasonably priced, and the restaurant is vegetarian-friendly. Breakfast is served until noon (just on weekdays), and it's a cozy place for a nightcap. Using Andean ingredients, such as healthy quinoa, one block over is the tiny **(Quinoa y Amaranto** (Cl. 11 No. 2-95, tel. 1/565-9982, 8am-4pm Mon., 8am-9pm Tues.-Fri., 8am-5pm Sat.), a warm little place that is a haven for vegetarians downtown. With lunches for around COP$11,000 it's an herbivore bang for your buck.

An always popular Colombian seafood joint specializing in fried fish and *cazuelas* (seafood stews) is **Pescadero la Subienda** (Cra. 6 No. 10-27, tel. 1/284-9816, noon-6pm Mon.-Sat., COP$20,000). **El Olivar** (Cra. 6 No. 10-40, tel. 1/283-2847, 7:30am-5pm Mon.-Thurs., 7:30am-10pm Fri., 11am-4pm Sat., COP$25,000), across the street, is a more upscale fusion place—and the prices reflect that. Popular at lunchtime with bureaucrats, it serves hearty soups, such as *cazuelas* based in coconut milk, and also Mediterranean cuisine. Finally, **María Tomasa Caribbean Cuisine** (Cra. 6 No. 10-82, tel. 1/744-9097, 9am-4:30pm Mon.-Sat., COP$25,000) is a cheerful place with a Costeño feel. Seafood dishes abound, but there are also the customary *arepa de huevo* (egg fried in corn meal) and juices that you can only get on the coast—like *níspero* (sapodilla) juice.

International

La Manzana (Cl. 11 No. 4-93, tel. 1/284-5335, 9am-7pm Mon. and Wed.-Sat., 10am-5pm Sun.) is inside the Banco de la República art complex. It's a quiet environment, overlooking a modern fountain and magnolia trees in the courtyard between the museums. This restaurant specializes in Mediterranean cuisine

and pastas. They have some pretty good desserts, too.

If mushrooms are your thing, head to **Merlin Café Galería Restaurante** (Cra. 2 No. 12-84, tel. 1/284-9707, noon-1am Mon.-Sat., COP$20,000). They promise the best mushrooms in Bogotá. It's a funky place. Just across the way is candlelit **El Gato Gris** (Cra. 1 No. 13-12, tel. 1/342-1716, www.gatogris.com, 9am-midnight Mon.-Thurs., 9am-3am Fri.-Sat.). The menu has a wide range of fare, including steaks and pastas, and they are proud of their crêpes as well. Both of these are close to the Chorro de Quevedo.

Two classy international cuisine restaurants have been a part of the Candelaria scene for many years now—meaning they are doing something right. **Bonaparte** (Cra. 8 No. 11-19, tel. 1/283-8788, noon-4:30pm Mon.-Sat., COP$30,000) is an authentic French bistro. It's known for its crêpes as well as heartier dishes such as beef Roquefort. Bonaparte remains popular with gossiping politicians and court justices. **Mi Viejo** (Cl. 11 No. 5-41, tel. 1/566-6128, noon-5pm Mon.-Sun., COP$30,000) was the first Argentinian restaurant in La Candelaria, and it has a loyal following. Paradise for beef-eaters, this friendly spot has, as would be expected, an extensive Argentinian wine selection.

Cajun food is the thing at **La Condesa Irina Lazaar** (Cra. 6 No. 10-19, tel. 1/283-1573, lunch Mon.-Sat., COP$35,000). This American-run spot is very easy to miss, but if you are in the mood for pork chops or perhaps crab cakes, this is the place. There are only six tables, so it is best to reserve in advance. If you persuade him, the friendly owner might consider opening the restaurant for you for dinner.

Near loads of backpacker hostels, the **Crazy Mongolian** (Cl. 12D No. 3-77, 12:30pm-9:30pm Mon.-Sat., COP$12,000) lets you choose the ingredients in generous portions of Mongolian barbecue.

The food at the **Mirador** restaurant (Cl. 10 No. 5-22, tel. 1/336-2066, noon-10 pm daily, COP$35,000) on the top of the Hotel de la Ópera may get mixed reviews, but the views?

Above the red roofs and church steeples of La Candelaria, they are incredible.

AVENIDA JIMÉNEZ
Cafés, Bakeries, and Snacks

For a sandwich or coffee on the go check out tiny **La Jamonería Sandwich Gourmet** (Cl. 12C No. 6A-36, tel. 1/283-0361, 7am-6pm Mon.-Fri., 7am-2pm Sat.). If you're in one of those moods, you can order a "Cheese Lonely" sandwich for about COP$7,000.

Brush shoulders with the locals at **La Gran Parilla Santa Fe** (Av. Jiménez No. 5-65, tel. 1/334-4745, 11:30am-5:30pm Mon.-Sat., COP$15,000), a no-surprises and budget-friendly Colombian restaurant downtown. They do the *comida típica* (Colombian fare) thing specializing in grilled meats. **Pastelería La Florida** (Cra. 7 No. 21-46, 8:30am-9pm daily, COP$10,000) is a Cachaco institution, sort of a Colombian greasy spoon diner.

Colombian and Fusion

For a hearty meal of *mamona* (grilled meat), run, don't walk, to **Capachos Asadero** (Cl. 18 No. 4-68, tel. 1/243-4607, www.asadero-capachos.com, 11:30am-3:30pm Tues.-Thurs., 11:30am-5pm Fri.-Sun.), an authentic *llanero* (cowboy) restaurant. For under COP$20,000 you get a healthy portion of grilled meat tenderly cooked for several hours, fried yucca, and a *maduro* (fried plaintain). Goes down well with a beer. On weekends they have live music and dance performances. It's open every day at lunch.

For a taste of the Colombian Pacific, you can't beat the seafood lunch places on Carrera 4 at Calle 20. There are several of them, all serving about the same thing. Try **Sabores del Mar** (corner of Cl. 20 and Cra. 4, lunch Mon.-Sat., COP$15,000) or **Sabores del Pacífico** (Cr. 4 No. 20-29, lunch Mon.-Sat, COP$15,000). If you're looking for cheap fried fish or other typical dishes in a place oozing with character, try the **Mercado de las Nieves** (Cl. 19 No. 8-62, no phone, lunch Mon.-Sat., COP$12,000). The passage that connects Calle 19 with Calle 20 is filled with mom-and-pop restaurants serving mostly fish dishes. (A sign marks the place as Pasaje La Macarena, but few call it that.)

Is it time for a chain? You can't beat always-reliable **Crepes & Waffles** (Av. Jiménez No. 4-55, tel. 1/676-7600, www.crepesywaffles.com.co, noon-8:30pm Mon.-Sat., noon-5pm Sun.), found all over Colombia. Fill up on a *crêpe de sal* (savory crêpe) for around COP$15,000, but save room for the scrumptious deserts (such as a mini-waffle with Nutella and vanilla ice cream). Also, if you have been searching the world over for a crêpe with tofu in it, the crêpe Gandhi awaits. This particular location is in the easy-on-the-eyes Monserrate building on the Eje Ambiental. Other popular locations are on the Zona T, Parque de la 93, and at the airport, where you can get a healthy breakfast before that morning flight.

CENTRO INTERNATIONAL
Cafés and Snacks

Andante Ma Non Troppo (Cra. 5 No. 15-21, tel. 1/341-7658, COP$12,000) is a long-running café that also serves breakfast, sandwiches, and salads.

Colombian and Fusion

In the Centro Tequendama, a popular spot for Cali food is **Fulanitos** (Cra. 13 No. 27-00, Local 101, tel. 1/281-7913, noon-5pm Mon.-Fri, COP$15,000). Another inviting place with a set lunch menu of Colombian favorites is **Ruta** (Cl. 37 No. 13A-26, tel. 1/751-9239, noon-10pm Mon.-Sat., COP$12,000). At **Los Cauchos** (Cl. 26B No. 3A-20, tel. 1/243-4059, noon-10pm Mon.-Sat., COP$25,000), preparing excellent Colombian food is a family affair. They have been around in the Macarena since 1976. Check out their plate of the day: Monday it's *ajiaco* (chicken and potato soup) and on Friday it's *puchero,* a hearty plate of chicken, pork, beef, potatoes, yuca, and corn in a tomato-onion sauce.

Leo Cocina y Cava (Cl. 27B No. 6-75, tel. 1/286-7091, noon-midnight Mon.-Sat., COP$45,000), by internationally acclaimed chef Leonora Espinosa, has been featured by *Condé Nast* magazine as one of the tops—in the world. Her empire has expanded northward with her new sleek and savvy restaurant, **La Leo** (Cra. 11 No. 86-74 at the B.O.G. hotel, tel. 1/639-9999, 6am-10am, noon-3pm, and 7pm-11:30pm Mon.-Sat., COP$40,000), which some say is more style than substance.

International

The Macarena is a veritable United Nations of cuisine. On a quiet street behind the Museo Nacional, **◖ Donostia** (Cl. 29 Bis No. 5-84, tel. 1/287-3943, noon-4pm Mon., noon-4 and 7pm-11pm Tues.-Sat., COP$30,000) is a swanky place for Spanish-Colombian cuisine. You'll want to linger on the colorful sofas. **Alô Brasil** (Cra. 4 No. 26B-88, tel. 1/337-6015, noon-3pm and 6-10pm Tues.-Wed., noon-3pm and 6pm-midnight Thurs.-Fri., noon-midnight Sat., 1pm-5pm Sun., COP$22,000) serves the famous *feijoada brasileira,* a stew of beans with beef and pork. The ladies at **Agave Azul** (Cra. 3A No. 26B-52, tel. 1/560-2702, www.restauranteagaveazul.blogspot.com, 1pm-10pm Sat., noon-3pm Sun., COP$70,000 set menu) have a passion for Mexican food. Tequila is an important part of the equation at this creative place—you were warned. Reservations are necessary.

In the Parque Bavaria the Mexican place **San Lorenzo** (Cra. 13 No. 28A-21, tel. 1/288-8731, noon.-4pm Mon.-Fri., COP$23,000) packs in the banking crowd at lunchtime on the fourth floor of the old Bavaria brewery.

CHAPINERO
Cafés and Snacks

Pan de Nobles (Cra. 9 No. 60-82, tel. 1/606-7262, 7am-8pm Mon.-Sat., 9am-6pm Sun., COP$10,000) started out as a whole-wheat bread bakery. Today it has expanded into a healthy and vegetarian empire. There is a sit-down restaurant upstairs with a set menu. Downstairs on the corner is a "vegetarian express" popular with university students, who chow down on veggie burgers between classes. And the bakery still sells unusual breads, such as feijoa bread and soy arepas (cornmeal cakes).

A typical bakery/café that has packed them in for breakfast and lunchtime since 1943 is **San Marcos** (Cra. 13 No. 40-36, 6am-8:30pm Mon.-Sat., 7:30am-7pm Sun.). They specialize in lasagnas and pastas.

Colombian

It is hard to find a seat, especially on the terrace, at **Canela y Candil** (Cra. 8 No. 56-32, tel. 1/479-3245, lunch Mon.-Fri., COP$12,000). **Las Margaritas** (Cl. 62 No. 7-77, tel. 1/249-9468, noon-4:30pm Mon.-Fri., 8am-6:30pm Sat.-Sun.) has been around for over a century. Try the *puchero,* a meaty stew, on Thursday. The *ajiaco* (chicken and potato soup) is also good. For the best of original coastal cuisine, try friendly **◖ MiniMal** (Cra. 4A No. 57-52, tel. 1/347-5464, www.mini-mal.org, 12:30pm-10pm Mon.-Wed., 12:30pm-11pm Thurs.-Sat., COP$25,000). The stingray *cazuela* (stew) is one of the more exotic items on the menu. There's also a funky gift shop where you can get one-of-a-kind, 100 percent Colombian handicrafts.

International

Hipster-ish **Salvo Patria** (Cra. 54 No. 4A-13, tel. 1/702-6367, noon-10pm Mon.-Sat., COP$22,000) is a happening place. There's a variety of interesting appetizers, sandwiches, meaty main courses, and vegetarian options. You'll be tempted to try a carafe of gin *lulada* (a drink made with the juice of a *lulo,* a type of orange).

To go old school in Chapinero Alto, there are two options. First, **Giuseppe Verdi** (Cl. 58 No. 5-35, tel. 1/211-5508, noon-11pm Mon.-Sat., noon-9pm Sun., COP$20,000) has been around forever, serving typical Italian dishes. They have added a small terrace café for more informal meals or a glass of wine. **La Poularde** (Cra. 4 No. 54-56, tel. 1/249-6156, noon-3pm and 7pm-11pm Mon.-Sat., 12:30pm-4pm Sun., COP$25,000) serves very traditional French dishes, such as escargot and crêpes suzette. There's a 60 percent chance of Edith Piaf songs being played while you're here.

NORTHERN BOGOTÁ
Cafés and Quick Bites

When it comes to *onces* (Colombian tea time), **Myriam Camhi** (Cl. 81 No. 8-08, tel. 1/345-1819, 7am-8pm Mon.-Sun.) takes the cake. Just take a look at the decadent desserts on display. The Napoleon de Arequipe and chocolate flan are favorites. While it is known for sweet indulgence, the extensive lunch menu is also nice, with many lighter dishes such as wraps and a pretty good salad bar. On Fridays Myriam serves *ajiaco* (chicken and potato soup). With a more local feel, **Brot Café** (Cl. 81 No. 7-93, tel. 1/347-6916, 7:30am-7pm daily) has a fiercely loyal following for breakfast and during afternoon *onces.* They are famous for their freshly baked chocolate baguettes. It's also open for lunch. Surrounded by green on their terrace it's easy to forget the chaos of the city.

Siuka (Cl. 79A No. 8-82, tel. 1/248-3765, 9am-7pm Mon.-Sat., 11am-5pm Sun.) has got it all. Well, according to its name at least. *Siuka* means "everything" in Chibcha, the language of the Muiscas. It's hard to find any fault at all with this airy, friendly, and minimalist newcomer. Suika adjoins the good **Los Sánduches de Sr. Ostia** high-class sandwich joint (Cl. 79A No. 8-82, tel. 1/248-3311). Instead of french fries, you can get spicy carrots! (It's by the same people as Donostia downtown.)

Nick's (Cra. 9 No. 79A-28, tel. 1/321-4108, 11am-10pm Mon.-Sat.) is a quaint place specializing in sandwiches that is popular with hipsters and advertising types. If you arrive on bike, Nick will give you a discount. **Doña Dicha** (Cra. 11 No. 78-78, tel. 1/629-7452, 10am-7pm Mon.-Sat.) bakes delicious bread and is a nice place for a cappuccino (always served with a spoon dipped in chocolate). Best to go there during non-rush hour, as the traffic on the Carrera 11 might spoil the mood. **Brown** (Calle 77A No. 12-26, tel. 1/248-0409, www. brownesunareposteria.com, 11am-6pm Mon.-Fri., 11am-4pm Sat.) is cute as a button and has a light lunch menu (half a sandwich, soup, salad, and drink for COP$16,500) and pretty good brownies. It's a nice place to get stuck during the rain. Remember to request your coffee to be strong if that's the way you like it.

Diletto Café (Cra. 9 No. 80-45, tel. 1/317-7383, 7:30am-8:30pm Mon.-Fri., 9am-8pm Sat., 11am-7pm Sun.) often seems to host caffeinated business meetings—and they also can fry eggs. For under COP$10,000 you can have scrambled eggs, a croissant, and a cappuccino for breakfast. **Pan Pa' Ya** (Cl. 82 No. 8-85, www.panpaya.com.co, 7am-9pm daily) is an inexpensive bakery that everyone loves. There are many other locations, even in Weston, Florida! Plan your visit strategically: *Almojabanas* (cheese rolls) come out of the oven at 8:30am and 6:30pm; *palitos de queso* (cheese sticks) at 9:30am and 4:30pm.

Colombian

At **Fulanitos 81** (Cl. 81 No. 10-56, tel. 1/622-2175, lunch daily, COP$20,000) there is always a line at lunchtime. This is Cali cuisine at its best. Try the *chuletas de cerdo* (pork chops) or *sancocho* (soup), and have a refreshing *lulada* (a drink made with the juice of a *lulo*, a type of orange), of course.

If you want a good introduction to Colombian delicacies in an elegant atmosphere that doesn't feel like the Carnaval de Barranquilla, the **Casa Club Colombia** (Cl. 82 No. 9-11, tel. 1/744-9077, 8am-1am, COP$25,000) is an excellent choice. In a lovely house where the fireplace is always lit, *bandeja paisa* (dish of beans, various meats, yuca, and potatoes) and all your favorites from all corners of the country are on the menu.

Andrés Carne de Res is the required stop for all visitors to Colombia. It's sort of like a shrine, but one where you can have mojitos, *patacones* (fried plantains), and a menu full of other typical Colombian dishes. This is one of the first places around that embraced Colombian culture and cuisine with gusto, convinced that it is something to be proud of. And it has worked. The food is good and the atmosphere fantastic. The original, and to many, the best **Andrés** (Cl. 3 No. 11A-56, tel. 1/863-7880, noon-3am Thurs.-Sat., noon-11pm Sun., COP$30,000) is in Chía, about 45 minutes away. This house seems to go on forever, and on weekend nights the slide from dinner to rumba is a slow but definitive one. **Andrés D.C.** (tel. 1/863-7880, noon-midnight Sun.-Wed., noon-3am Thurs.-Sat., COP$35,000) is for an urban Andrés experience—for you and about 1,199 others. Look for the windmills next to the El Retiro mall. **(La Plaza de Andrés** is in the mall itself (8am-10pm daily, COP$25,000). The colorful Plaza is more reasonably priced and is not the full-on rumba experience, although it does have its personality.

Welcome to Santa Marta—in Bogotá, that is. The **(Gaira Cumbia Café** (Cra. 13 No. 96-11A, tel. 1/746-2696, www.gairacafe.com, 9am-10pm Mon.-Wed., 9am-2am Thurs., 9am-3am Fri.-Sat., 9am-6pm Sun., COP$25,000) specializes in Caribbean cuisine. This is a special place, a tribute to music and family. It is run by Guillermo Vives and his mom. Guillo, as he is known, is a talented musician, and is the brother of Carlos Vives, the multiple Grammy Award-winning *vallenato* singer. The food is quite good, and it is popular at lunchtime. At night, Guillo and other musicians regularly perform, to the delight of the whiskey-drinking crowd. On weekends they have special activities for children in the morning. Some just go for the rumba on weekend nights, for which there is a cover.

International

Bagatelle (Cl. 82 No. 9-09, tel. 1/621-2614, 7am-10pm Mon.-Sat., 8am-5pm Sun., COP$20,000) is a long-standing French pâtisserie and restaurant. Their terrace, under the trees, is a nice place for lunch or to sip on a café au lait and nibble at a delicious bread pudding.

French restaurant **Criterión** (Cl. 69A No. 5-75, tel. 1/310-1377, noon-4pm and 7pm-11pm Mon.-Sat., 9am-1pm and 7pm-11pm Sun., COP$40,000) is the standard bearer when it comes to haute cuisine in Bogotá. It is the creation of the Rausch brothers, who are among the top chefs in Bogotá.

Harry's Bakery (Cra. 6 No. 69A-24, tel. 1/321-3940, noon-11pm Mon.-Sat., noon-6pm

Sun., COP$20,000) is headed by another highly regarded chef, Harry Sassón. It serves sandwiches, burgers, popcorn shrimp, and other diner fare. Harry's mom is in charge of the decadent desserts.

Classy **Astrid & Gaston** (Cra. 7 No. 67-64, tel. 1/211-1400, www.astridygastonbogota.com, 12:30pm-3:30pm and 7:30pm-11:30pm Mon.-Sat., bar open until 3am Fri.-Sat., COP$35,000), direct from Lima, and stylish **Rafael** (Cl. 70 No. 4-65, tel. 1/255-4138, 12:30pm-3pm and 7:30pm-11pm Mon.-Sat., COP$30,000) are rivals for the top Peruvian food in town. At Astrid, try an only-in-Colombia coca pisco sour.

The little block of restaurants on Carrera 13 between Calles 85 and 86 has some great options. The vast menu of generous designer burgers at **(Agadón Burger Bar** (Cra. 13 No. 85-75, tel. 1/255-4138, noon-10pm Mon.-Wed., noon-midnight Thurs.-Sat., noon-4:30pm Sun., COP$20,000) will leave you satisfied. It's run by a pair of Israelis, and they even have a couple of vegetarian burgers on the menu. **Casa** (Cra. 13 No. 85-24, tel. 1/236-3755, noon-midnight daily, COP$22,000), in a cozy house with fireplaces and cool artwork on the walls, serves food meant to be shared. You're surrounded by *palma bobas* and other tropical plants in their patio. Across the street is elegant **La Brasserie** (Cra. 13 No. 85-35, tel. 1/257-6402, noon-midnight Mon.-Sat., noon-6pm Sun., COP$32,000). Oh, yes, and the Clintons have dined here.

Opa (Cra. 14 No. 90-80, tel. 1/218-9682, noon-8pm daily, COP$12,000) is a cheap and good gyros joint popular with the work crowd on dull Calle 90. **Gyros y Kebabs** (Cra. 13 No. 82-28, tel. 1/635-9324, noon-11pm daily, COP$15,000) does standard Lebanese food very well. It's cozy to sit by the bread oven and watch the bread guy slide pita bread in and back out, piping hot. Yes, they have an afternoon happy hour.

In Usaquén try **Abasto** (Cra. 6 No. 119B-52, tel. 1/215-1286, http://abasto.com.co, 7am-10pm Mon.-Thurs., 7am-11pm

Fri., 9am-10:30pm Sat., 9am-5pm Sun., COP$22,000), where they use only the freshest and often organic ingredients.

Asian

Having had just a tiny Asian immigration, unlike Peru, Panama, and Brazil, Colombia doesn't have dazzling Asian cuisine, but you'll probably be pleasantly surprised at the offer in Bogotá. The pan-Asian cuisine chain (**Wok** (Quinta Camacho, Cra. 9 No. 69A-63, tel. 1/212-0167, www.wok.com.co, noon-11pm Mon.-Sat., noon-8pm Sun., COP$23,000) is hard to beat. A second location is in the Museo Nacional (Cra. 6 Bis No. 29-07, tel. 1/287-3194). The menu is astoundingly extensive, inventive, and fresh. Hearty fish soups and curries based in coconut milk will warm you up, and there are numerous vegetarian dishes, such as a Vietnamese-inspired grilled tofu sandwich. The quality of their sushi is also good. Wok is an environmentally and socially responsible company, working with family farmers and fishers in small communities throughout Colombia. Don't let the fact that it is a chain dissuade you.

Excellent service awaits at sleek **Watakushi** (Cra. 12 No. 83-17, tel. 1/744-9097, noon-3pm and 6pm-11pm Mon.-Thurs., noon-11pm Fri.-Sat., noon-5pm Sun., COP$35,000), one of the many restaurants operated by local restaurant wizard Leo Katz. It is on the Zona T. **Sushi Gozen** (Cl. 94 No. 14-11, tel. 1/257-0282, noon-3pm and 6:30pm-midnight Mon.-Fri., noon-midnight Sat., COP$25,000) is a Colombian-Japanese restaurant popular with Japanese business people (a good sign) that has much more than just sushi. Finally, **Arigato** (Cl. 76 No. 12-22, tel. 1/248-0764, 11am-9pm Mon.-Sat., COP$20,000) is a family-run

Japanese restaurant. The fresh fish is flown in regularly from the Pacific Coast.

There are few Indian restaurants in Bogotá, but of those, **Flor de Loto** (Cl. 90 No. 17-31, tel. 1/617-0142, noon-3 p.m. and 6pm-9pm Mon.-Sat., COP$24,000) is probably the best. The head chef is originally from the Punjab. The restaurant surrounds a peaceful garden. It's cash-only here.

Italian

Italian restaurants are in abundance in Bogotá. At (**La Divina Comedia** (Cl. 71 No. 5-93, tel. 1/317-6987, noon-4pm and 7pm-11pm Mon.-Sat., COP$25,000) go for the divine *tortellata* (a mix of stuffed pastas). At unpretentious **Trattoría San Giorgio** (Cl. 81 No. 8-81, tel. 1/212-3962, noon-10:30pm Mon.-Sat., noon-6pm Sun., COP$22,000), Italian regulars are often found sipping wine and enjoying a multi-course meal. (**DiLucca** (Cra.13 No. 85-32, tel. 1/257-4269, noon-midnight daily, COP$25,000) is consistently good, with both pastas and pizzas, and they deliver. The atmosphere is rather lively inside.

(**Julia** (Cra. 5 No. 69A-19, tel. 1/348-2835, noon-11pm daily, COP$25,000) serves the best pizza in town. Theirs is the irregular-shaped and paper-thin Roman crust. They also have a couple of non-cheese pizzas, which is unusual for Bogotá. It is astounding to see what the chefs manage to come up with in such a tiny—and infernally hot—kitchen. As no reservations are accepted in this tiny restaurant, it's best to get there on the early side. Second best pizza in town? That would be **Archie's** (Cl. 82 No. 13-07, tel. 1/610-9162, www.archiespizza.com, breakfast to late night daily, COP$22,000). This chain is all over Bogotá and in many cities countrywide. Archie's delivers.

Information and Services

VISITOR INFORMATION

For information on all things Bogotá, go to the **Punto de Información Turística** (PIT). In La Candelaria there is a PIT on the southwest corner of the Plaza de Bolívar (tel. 1/283-7115, daily). Other locations include the Quiosco de la Luz in the Parque de la Independencia (Cra. 7 at Cl. 26, tel. 1/284-2664, 9am-5pm Mon.-Sat., 10am-4pm Sun.), both airport terminals, both main and south bus terminals, and in the north at the Centro Comercial Granahorrar on Calle 72. The attendants will bend over backwards to help you out any way they can, providing maps and tips.

TELEPHONES

The telephone code for Bogotá and many surrounding towns is 1. From abroad, dial 57 for Colombia, then 1 for Bogotá, followed by the 7-digit number. To call a cell phone from a landline, first dial 03 and then the 10-digit number. To do the reverse, call 03-1 (the 1 for Bogotá). Prepaid cell phones or SIM cards can be purchased at any Claro or Movistar store. When in the city, there is no need to dial the 1 before the landline number.

Emergency Numbers

For emergencies, just remember 1-2-3. The single emergency hotline is 123. While some operators may speak English, that is probably unlikely. You should provide the neighborhood you are in and a precise street number.

U.S. citizens who have health, safety, or legal emergencies can contact the **U.S. Embassy** at 1/275-2000.

POST OFFICES AND COURIER SERVICES

Here are some of the main offices of 4-72, the national post office, in Bogotá: Centro Internacional (Cra. 7 No. 27-54, tel. 1/245-4015), Chapinero (Cl. 67 No. 8-39, tel.

1/248-7810), and Chicó (Car. 15 No. 85-61, tel. 1/621-9508). The office hours are the same at all locations (8am-5pm Mon.-Fri., 9am-1pm Sat.). Private courier services are the way most people send correspondence domestically. Two major companies are Servientrega and Deprisa. **Servientrega** is in the Centro Internacional (Mailboxes Cra. 13 No. 32-16) and in Chapinero (Mailboxes Cl. 67 No. 7-28). **Deprisa** is operated by Avianca. There are many offices throughout the city, including in the north at the Centro Comercial Granahorrar (Cl. 73 No. 9-42), near Andino (Cr. 11 No. 81-17), and near the Parque El Virrey (Cra. 15 No. 88-53). Downtown they can be found at Calle 13 No. 7-09. Hours of these offices are typically 8am-5pm Monday-Friday and 9am-1pm Saturday.

INTERNET CAFÉS

Internet cafés are plentiful, especially in La Candelaria area and Chapinero, although you may have some difficulty locating cafés in the wealthier residential neighborhoods of Chicó and Rosales.

NEWSPAPERS AND MAGAZINES

The **City Paper** is a free monthly newspaper in English with information on events, interesting profiles, and essays. It is generally distributed to hotels, restaurants, and cafés during the first two weeks of the month. Two other freebies, **ADN** and **Metro,** both in Spanish, are newspapers that are distributed on street corners in the mornings. Another fun publication is the hip and free bimonthly **Cartel Urbano,** which examines Bogotá cultural life. **GO** is a monthly publication on things going on in the city. **El Tiempo** and **El Espectador** are the two main newspapers in town, and are good sources for information. **Semana** is considered the best news magazine, and is published weekly.

SPANISH LANGUAGE COURSES

The Spanish spoken in Bogotá is considered neutral and clear, compared to accents you may have heard in the Caribbean, Spain, or Argentina. Therefore Bogotá is an excellent place to study Spanish, if you have some time to invest. The best schools are operated by the major universities in town. These include the **Universidad Externado** (Centro de Español para Extranjeros, CEPEX, Cra. 1A No. 12-53, tel. 1/353-7000 or 1/342-0288, www.uexternado.edu.co/cepex), the **Universidad Nacional** (Edificio 229, Torre Sur, Primer Nivel, tel. 1/316-5000), and the **Universidad Javeriana Centro Latinoamericano** (Transv. 4 No. 42-00 Piso 6, tel. 1/320-8320, www.javeriana.edu.co/centrolatino).

MONEY

ATMs are everywhere throughout the city, and this is probably your best option to get Colombian pesos. Transaction fees vary. Some ATMs on the streets are closed at night. Be discreet and cautious when taking out money.

To change money, try **New York Money** at the Centro Andino mall (tel. 1/616-8946), Atlantis Plaza (tel. 1/530-7432), or at the Centro Comercial Granahorrar shopping center (tel. 1/212-2123). They are open also on Sundays and holidays. Note that you'll need to show your passport to change money.

VISAS AND OFFICIALDOM

If you need to stay beyond the 60 or 90 days allowed to visitors from the United States, Canada, Australia, New Zealand, and most European countries, you will need to go to **Migración Colombia** (Cl. 100 No. 11B-27, tel. 1/595-4331). It is best to go there a few days before your current visa expires.

HEALTH
Altitude

At 2,580 meters, Bogotá is the third highest capital city in the world (behind La Paz, Bolivia, and Quito, Ecuador). It is common to feel short of breath and fatigued during the first two days at the higher altitude. Other symptoms of altitude sickness include headache and nausea. Take it easy for those first few days in Bogotá and avoid caffeine and alcohol. If you are sensitive to high altitude, see a doctor, who can prescribe medication to mitigate the effects of high altitude, before your trip. If you feel symptoms such as fever or gradual loss of consciousness, see a doctor immediately.

Also, keep in mind that, being so high up, you are also that much closer to the sun. When it is sunny those rays are deceivingly potent.

Hospitals, Clinics, and Pharmacies

Bogotá has excellent physicians and hospitals. Two of the best hospitals are the **Fundación Santa Fe** (Cl. 119 No. 7-75, www.fsfb.org.co, emergency tel. 1/629-0477, tel. 1/603-0303) and the **Clínica del Country** (Cra. 16 No. 82-57, tel. 1/530-1350, www.clinicadelcountry.com). The **Fundación Shaio** (Diag. 110 No. 53-67, emergency tel. 271-4050, tel. 1/624-3211) hospital specializes in cardiology. For sexual and reproductive health matters, **Profamilia** (Cl. 34 No. 14-52, tel. 1/339-0900, www.profamilia.org.co), a member of the International Planned Parenthood Federation, offers clinical services. It is steps away from the Profamilia TransMilenio station on the Avenida Caracas.

Mom-and-pop pharmacies are all over the city, and sometimes these can be less stringent about requiring physical prescriptions. The Supermarket chain **Carulla** (www.carulla.com) usually has an in-store pharmacy, and the Venezuelan chain **Farmatodo** (tel. 1/743-2100, www.farmatodo.com.co) has around 30 stores in Bogotá; some of them are open 24 hours a day.

Dental Services

Dental care is excellent in Bogotá. Americans are known to come to Colombia specifically for dental treatments and surgeries. **Marlón Becerra** (Cl. 91 No. 15-15, tel. 1/746-1111) has several offices in Bogotá.

LAUNDRY

Wash and dry services that charge by the pound or kilo are plentiful in La Candelaria and in Chapinero. This service is often called *lavandería*, as opposed to dry cleaning (*lavado en seco*). In La Candelaria two such services are: **Limpia Seco Sarita** (Cra. 3 No. 10-69, tel. 1/233-9980) and **Extra-Rápido** (Cl. 12 No. 2-62, tel. 1/282-1002). In Chapinero there is **Lava Seco** (Cra. 9 No. 61-03, tel. 1/255-2582), another **Lava Seco** (Cl. 66 No. 8-20, tel. 1/249-7072), and **Lavandería San Ángel** (Cl. 69 No. 11A-47, tel. 1/255-8116). A good dry cleaning service is **Classic** (Cra. 13A No. 86A-13, tel. 1/622-8759).

Getting There

BY AIR

The **Aeropuerto Internacional El Dorado** (BOG, Cl. 26 No. 103-09. tel. 1/266-2000, www.elnuevodorado.com) is undergoing a massive expansion. The international terminal will finally be connected with the Puente Aereo (Avianca domestic terminal).

You will need to show your luggage receipts before passing through customs. A customs agent will take one copy of the customs declaration and then you may be required to put both checked and carry-on bags through a scanner. They are mostly looking for weapons, cash, and fruits and vegetables.

There are money exchange offices and ATMs just outside of the customs area.

If you are not being picked up by a hotel shuttle or friend, it is imperative to use the official taxi services available outside the arrivals area.

BY BUS

Bogotá has three bus terminals. These are the **Terminal del Sur**, the **Portal del Norte**, and the main bus station, the **Terminal de Transportes** (Diagonal 23 No. 69-60, tel. 1/423-3630, www.terminaldetransporte.gov. co) in Salitre.

You can catch a bus to just about anywhere at the Terminal de Transportes. The terminal is well organized and clean and is divided into three "modules," each generally corresponding to a different direction: Module 1 is south, Module 2 is east/west, and Module 3 is north.

There are two other modules, 4 and 5, corresponding to long-distance taxi services and to arrivals. All modules are located in the same building. Each module has an information booth at the entrance with an attendant who can point you in the right direction.

The terminal has plenty of fast food restaurants, ATMs, a pharmacy, and a Dunkin' Donuts every 50 meters. You can stow your bags in a locker or check them in a storage area. Wireless Internet is available in some areas of the building, and if not, there are Internet and telephone services. To pass the time, you can win big at the many casinos in the terminal or enjoy some peace at the second-floor chapel.

In the arrivals module, there is a tourist information office (PIT), where the helpful attendants can give you a map of the city and assist you in getting to your hotel. There is also an organized and safe taxi service and plenty of public transportation options available.

During the Christmas and Easter holidays, the bus terminal is a busy place with crowds and packed buses. This is also true on *puentes* (long weekends).

The terminal website is not bad, with a map of the modules, information on bus companies with links to their websites, timetables, and price information. Prices listed online are comparable to the prices found at the terminal.

Check prices with a couple of companies, as levels of comfort can vary. Some companies even offer Wi-Fi in their buses, and most show loud, violent movies for your enjoyment.

The **Portal del Norte** (Autopista Norte with Cl. 174), part of the TransMilenio station of the

© ANDREW DIER

TransMilenio bus along Avenida Jiménez

same name, may be more convenient if you are traveling to nearby destinations. As you exit northbound TransMilenio buses, there are well-marked exits to platforms for different nearby destinations. The area for Zipaquirá (shortened to Zipa on signage) and Chía is at the far left of the platform. Destinations such as Laguna de Guatavita (COP$7,400), Sesquilé (COP$5,500), Suesca (COP$6,000), and Tenjo (COP$3,600) are straight ahead. You pay the bus driver directly for these trips.

Meanwhile, in front of the Éxito supermarket/store on the east side of the Autopista is where buses going a little farther on to places such as Nemocón, Villa de Leyva, Tunja, and Bucaramanga pick up passengers. It is not nearly as organized as at the main terminal, but it all somehow manages to work out. It's best to catch these buses during the daytime.

The **Terminal del Sur** (Autopista Sur with Cra. 72D) is near the Portal Sur of TransMilenio. This station serves locations in the south of Cundinamarca, such as Tequendama, and farther south to Girardot, Ibagué, Neiva, Popayán, Armenia, Cali, and all the way to Mocoa in Putumayo.

Getting Around

TRANSMILENIO

While it has become the public transport system that Bogotanos seem to love to hate, the red buses of TransMilenio have clearly transformed the city. This dedicated mass transit system began rolling along the Avenida Caracas in 2000 near the end of the Enrique Peñalosa mayorship. Today, the Caracas line moves more passengers than most subway lines. One of the great characteristics of the TransMilenio project is that, in addition to buses, a requirement has been made to create wide sidewalks, pedestrian bridges, and bike lanes alongside the bus lines. The system has been lauded internationally and copied by several cities as a very cost effective mass transit system. However, lack of investment in new stations and buses has meant that the buses are overcrowded.

How do you determine which bus to take? It's not that easy at first. The stations are divided into 12 zones. For example, the Museo del Oro is classified as Zona J and Calle 85 is Zona B. The first step may be to figure out the zone you are going to and the zone you are starting out from. Because there are many express lines, or lines that skip certain stations, figuring out the system map may give you a migraine. If you are not up for the challenge, just ask one of the attendants at the station.

You are most likely to use the Caracas line to go north and south, with buses that spur off to the Las Aguas station as a convenient way of getting to Centro Histórico attractions. In the opposite direction, that same line—bound for the Portal del Norte—will get you close to the Zona Rosa (Calle 85). The line that goes along the Avenida 30 stops near the Parque Simón Bolívar, the Estadio El Campín, the Universidad Nacional, and Paloquemao. The new line that goes to the Portal Eldorado stops at the cemeteries (Centro Memoria), the fairgrounds (Corferias), and close to the U.S. Embassy (Gobernación). Unfortunately, TransMilenio is not an option to reach the airport.

The system operates 5am-midnight Monday through Saturday and 6am-11pm on Sunday and holidays. Fares are a little more expensive during rush hours (COP$1,700 as opposed to COP$1,400). Also, Bogotanos are usually in a hurry to get where they're going. So the "local" routes—often called "Ruta Fácil"—may be less crowded. Keep your wallet in your front pocket and watch your things, especially during rush hour.

In 2012, Bogotá began replacing private buses with the city SITP buses (www.sitp.gov.co). SITP buses stop only at designated stops. You must purchase a refillable card to ride, which can be found at numerous locations. This is the best way to travel between La Candelaria and the north.

PRIVATE BUSES

They are intimidating at first, but sometimes private buses are the only way to go. The good (and bad) thing about buses is that, although they are not supposed to, they will stop just about anywhere, even in the middle of the street. In both big buses and *colectivos* (minivans), you pay the driver upon entry. It's best to have small bills and change. Exit buses at the back door. You can use the button to alert the driver to stop. Sometimes buses don't come to a complete stop (especially for young men)—they just slow down. Take precautions when exiting any bus that hasn't stopped completely. Heading downtown from the Zona Rosa or Chapinero areas, look for buses that say Normandía on them.

TAXIS

It's estimated that over a million people take a cab each day in the city. There are around 50,000 taxis (mostly yellow Hyundai vehicles) circulating the streets of Bogotá, so you will rarely have a hard time locating one. However, it's important to always order cabs by phone or the smartphone app Tappsi for safety.

A trip from the Zona Rosa area to La Candelaria costs around COP$15,000. A *taxi-metro* calculates units, which determine the price. The rates are listed on a *tarjetón* (large card) with the driver's information. That card is always supposed to be visible. There are special surcharges for cab services ordered by phone, for nighttime, and for going to the airport. Taxi drivers do not expect tips, but you can always round up the fare if you'd like. During the end-of-year holidays, drivers may ask for a holiday tip.

WALKING

You get a real feeling for the city—the good, the bad, and the ugly—by walking its streets. All areas from the historic district through to the Centro Internacional and Macarena are accessible on foot, and walking is often the best way to get around. The same is true for upscale shopping and residential areas to the north. All of these areas are safe to walk around, but it's never a good idea to advertise your tourist status with bulky cameras and backpacks. Old, leafy neighborhoods like Teusaquillo-La Soledad are nice to wander around during the daytime as well. The worst thing about walking in the city is dealing with drivers. Generally speaking, they have very little respect for pedestrians or cyclists. Look for stoplights at intersections to help you safely cross streets. Also, note that when traffic lights turn yellow, that means green. Finally, keep in mind that, when there is no traffic, there are apparently also no speed limits.

BIKING

Bogotá has a huge bike path network, one of the most extensive in Latin America. These are called the *ciclorutas*. For those tired of getting stuck in traffic or dealing with buses, biking it to work has become a nice alternative. But you really have to keep your wits about you. Crossing the street can be tricky, as drivers don't hold a lot of respect for bikers, unfortunately. In addition, most bike paths follow alongside busy thoroughfares like the Carrera 11, so, during rush hours especially, you could be inhaling polluted air. It's nicer on weekends or late at night. If in town for just a limited time, you may prefer to make your bike experience a stress-free Ciclovía one (Sundays and holidays), rather than having to deal with the bike paths. A map of the 344-kilometer bike lane network is available at www.movilidadbogota. gov.co. As part of the public spaces along TransMilenio routes there are always *ciclo-rutas*, such as along Calle 26 (Avenida El Dorado). Another long stretch from downtown to the World Trade Center on Calle 100 goes along the Carrera 11. It's strongly recommended to wear a helmet, and using a bike lock is a good idea.

CAR RENTAL

With more than a million aggressive drivers on the clogged streets of Bogotá, renting a vehicle is a horrible idea for visitors. However, if you are planning to travel to places nearby Bogotá like Villa de Leyva or would like to take your time touring parks or villages, it might be an option. **National** (Cra. 7 No. 145-71, www.na-tionalcolombia.com), **Avis** (Av. 19 No. 123-52 Local 2, tel. 1/629-1722, www.avis.com), and **Hertz** (Av. Caracas No. 28A-17, tel. 1/327-6700, www.rentacarcolombia.co) have offices in Bogotá. Your driver's license is accepted here in Colombia.

Vicinity of Bogotá

TENJO

The town of Tenjo is charming. If you would like to visit a pueblo in the green pastureland outside of Bogotá, this makes a fine day trip. The plaza is shady and compact with a colonial church on one side. People keep warm wrapped in their heavy woolen *ruanas* (ponchos) as they relax on park benches, and people sell *obleas* (wafers) and *almojabanas* (cheese rolls) to passersby.

Just outside of town are two recommended restaurants: **La Granja** (Km. 12 Vía Siberia-Tenjo, tel. 1/864-6148, www.lagranjatenjo. com, COP$25,000), which has a petting farm, and nearby **Viveros Tirrá** (Km. 11 Vía Siberia-Tenjo, cell tel. 312/397-9940, www. restauranteviverostirra.com, COP$25,000). Both of these are popular with families on the weekends.

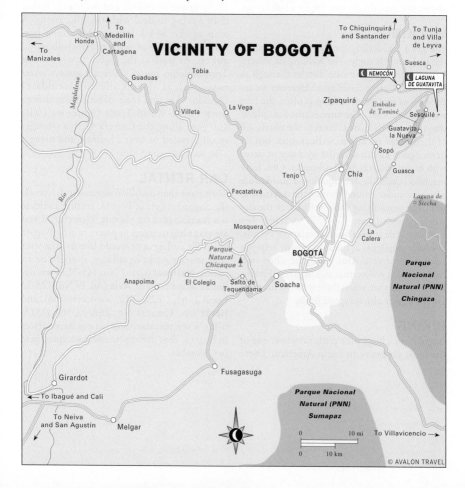

ZIPAQUIRÁ AND VICINITY

A favorite day trip for visitors to Bogotá is the city of **Zipaquirá** (pop. 112,000). About an hour's drive from Bogotá, Zipaquirá is known for its Catedral de Sal—a cathedral built in a salt mine. Zipaquirá is named for the Muisca leader of the Bacatá confederation—the Zipa. The Muisca settlement was very close to the mines, and they traded salt for other commodities with other indigenous groups.

The **Catedral de Sal** (tel. 1/852-3010, www.catedraldesal.gov.co, 9am-5:30pm daily, COP$20,000) is part of the Parque del Sal and the top "Wonders of Colombia" as voted by Colombians. The original cathedral was built by miners in 1951, but due to safety concerns, a new and larger cathedral was built and opened in 1995. The cathedral is indeed an impressive feat of engineering. Tours are obligatory, but you can stray from your group. The tours go past the Stations of the Cross and finally there is a massive cross in the cavernous sanctuary. Masses actually do take place here in the depths on Sundays, and they attract many faithful. Other features include a museum, a rock-climbing wall, and a children's 3-D film, which you could probably skip.

The picturesque main plaza in Zipaquirá, with palm trees rising against a backdrop of green mountains, is always the center of activity in town. Here locals gather to gossip, get their shoes shined, or munch on an *oblea* (wafer) oozing with caramel. Dominating the plaza is a cathedral designed by Friar Domingo de Petrés, who also designed the Bogotá and Santa Fe de Antioquia cathedrals. Construction began in 1805; 111 years later, in 1916, it was completed and dedicated.

On the main road into town from Bogotá, there are several grilled meat-type restaurants, with teenage boys furiously waving red flags to attract customers. A local favorite for a hearty lunch of grilled fish, chicken, or vegetables is **Casa Nnova** (Cra. 10 at Cl. 3), across from the fancy La Cascada restaurant. A good option for overnight accommodations is **Hotel Cacique Real** (Cl. 6 No. 2-36, tel. 1/851-0209, www.hotelcaciquereal.com, COP$88,000 d).

Zipaquirá is an easy day trip. On weekends, families and tourists alike take the Turistren from the Usaquén station. Bands play Colombian *papayera* music as you slowly chug through the savannah of Bogotá on this three-hour trip. The train leaves in the morning and returns in the late afternoon, giving you more than enough time to visit the salt mines. You could also (and probably will want to) just take the train one way, returning by bus or taxi back to Bogotá. Otherwise, buses depart the Portal del Norte TransMilenio station every 10 minutes or so, all day long, and the fare is inexpensive. If arriving via TransMilenio, when exiting the bus take a left and you will see signs pointing the way for "Zipa" buses. The attendants can also direct you. You'll pay the bus driver directly. The trip takes about 45 minutes. You can either walk or take a short taxi ride to the Parque del Sal.

Nemocón

With only 10,000 residents, the sleepy pueblo of **Nemocón** (www.nemocon-cundinamarca.gov.co) is 15 kilometers from Zipaquirá and just 65 kilometers from Bogotá. It is a cute, compact colonial-era town, also home to salt mines, but it does not attract nearly the same number of visitors that Zipaquirá does. That's part of its allure. In pre-Columbian times, this was also a Muisca settlement devoted to salt extraction.

On the plaza, the church is set against a backdrop of eucalyptus-covered hills, obviously some sort of reforestation effort. There is a small salt museum on the corner, and students will be happy to give you a tour in Spanish. About a 10-minute walk toward the hills are the **mines** (9am-5pm daily, COP$17,000). Tours take about 90 minutes. The beautifully renovated section of the mines that you visit is no longer used for salt extraction. In the depths of the mines you will see all types of stalactites and stalagmites. The pools where salt and water were mixed to pump out the salt are a highlight. The reflection of the illuminated vaults on the surface of the pools, combined with the cool lighting, is amazing. You can take some fun photos inside. Once you get back out

© ANDREW DIER

the sleepy pueblo of Nemocón

into daylight, there are simple restaurants with names like the **Venado de Oro** (the Golden Deer) on the plaza or **La Casa de la Gallina** (the Hen House) on Calle 2 (No. 4-24). There's not much in the way of accommodations in Nemocón, but most visitors make it a day trip. Not far from Nemocón is a desert microclimate called the **Desierto de Tatacoita.** It's a popular mountain-biking area.

LAGUNA DE GUATAVITA AND VICINITY
◖ Laguna de Guatavita

The El Dorado myth, which became an obsession for gold-thirsty Europeans in the New World, is based on a Muisca Indian ritual that took place here in this perfectly round mountain lake.

Following the death of the Muisca *cacique* (chief), a nephew would be chosen to succeed him. The day of the ceremony, the nephew would be sequestered in a cave. Then, stripped naked and covered with mud and gold dust, he would be rowed to the center of the sacred lake

with incense and music filling the air. Once there, gold, silver, emeralds, and other tributes were tossed into the cold waters, and the cacique would dive in. Incidentally, the gold used in these ceremonies mostly came from outside Muisca territories. This was an area rich in emeralds, salt, and corn—gold, not so much.

Part of what historians know about the ceremony was confirmed with the finding in 1856 of the miniature golden raft depicting the ceremony. This piece was not found in Guatavita, but rather in a cave close to Bogotá. That raft, of course, is one of the main displays at the Museo del Oro.

From the European perspective, there must have been a profound sense of disappointment once they realized that the "city of gold" just didn't exist. It was the promise of wealth beyond their wildest dreams that had sustained them as they made their arduous trek through the swamps of the muggy Río Magdalena valley, swatting away mosquitoes night after night as they desperately tried to get some rest. When they arrived in Guatavita, they drained

© ANDREW DIER

Laguna de Guatavita

the lake, at least three times, to see what could be found at the bottom. A giant cut in the lake can be still seen today.

After years of neglect, today **Laguna de Guatavita** (9am-4pm Tues.-Sat., COP$13,600) is being given the respect it deserves. An environmental agency maintains the park and, in order to preserve it, has forbidden direct access to the lake. The lake is much better appreciated from above on the well-maintained path along the top of the crater. To reduce the impact on the fragile environment, the path does not go all the way around. On the weekends, you must join a tour group to see the lake. These leave every half hour. Guides are knowledgeable and passionate about their work. English tours are possible, especially for larger groups, but those should be reserved in advance. During the week you can amble along the path at your own pace.

While much of the brick path is flat, there is a fairly steep climb, making it difficult for those with physical limitations. The entire tour takes less than an hour. At the end of the walk, you can walk or hop on a minibus to the entrance of the park. When Monday is a holiday, the park is open Wednesday-Monday.

GETTING THERE

Getting to the Laguna de Guatavita via public transportation is a little tricky, but doable. At the TransMilenio Portal del Norte station, take a bus bound for the town of Sesquilé. On the main square in front of the church you can usually find taxis that will take you to the Laguna de Guatavita and back (one way around COP$25,000). One (and just one) *colectivo* (minivan) by Cootranscovadonga leaves at 8:45am on weekends and holidays for the park, returning at around 4pm, making for a very long day. In addition, several *colectivos* leave all day long from Sesquilé bound for El Hato/Ranchería/El Uval that can drop you off about a two-kilometer hike to the park.

Many visitors opt to hire a driver for the day to make the trip to Guatavita and back. This varies in price and it would be wise to check with a few drivers and bargain. Make sure to specify if there will be additional stops (for a coffee break or for a lakeside lunch). Hotels, hostels and travel agencies in Bogotá can also arrange this trip for you.

Another option is driving. Once you get out of Bogotá, it is fairly stress-free for Colombian standards, as the road is good (mostly four-lane) and with decent signage. Take the Autopista Norte towards Tunja and take the exit to Sesquilé. Past the town a dirt road leads up to the park. If you get lost, locals along the road will help you find your way. You can park right at the park entrance.

An excellent place on the way for a mid-morning coffee and arepa is **Carajillo Restaurante** (Km. 41).

Nueva Guatavita

The actual town of Guatavita no longer exists. Back in the 1960s, when this kind of thing could be done without cries from environmentalists or community activists, the town was flooded in order to build the **Emblase de Tominé,** a large reservoir. They moved the town a little bit inland, calling it Nueva Guatavita. All the buildings here are painted white, as if they were built in the colonial period, but the streets are California-wide. There are two small museums by the water. The **Museo de Arte Religioso de Guatavita La Antigua** (COP$1,000) displays some of the relics from the church salvaged before the great flood. There is a short presentation about the flood and some photos of the submerged town. You used to be able to see the top of an obelisk from the town cemetery, but either a boat ran over it or it just crumbled into the depths. Nearby is a small indigenous culture museum. A few restaurants in town serve fried trout and other local specialties.

Emblase de Tominé

Between Nueva Guatavita and the Laguna de Guatavita alongside the Tominé reservoir are a handful of restaurants, hotels, and marinas.

La Juanita (cell tel. 310/213-5793, felipespath@gmail.com, www.lajuanitaguatavita.com/place) is wonderfully crunchy-granola, in a quiet place within walking distance of the reservoir and about halfway between the Laguna de Guatavita and Nueva Guatavita. They grow their own vegetables, have yoga classes, and offer pottery making and horseback-riding excursions. You can even walk from there to the Laguna de Guatavita.

Overlooking the water, family-run **Los Pinos** (Km. 11 Vía Sesquilé-Guatavita, cell tel. 310/777-6631, www.lospinos.com.co, weekends and holidays only) is a fine place for an afternoon lunch after a day at the lake. Grilled fish and barbecued pork ribs are their specialties, although they can accommodate vegetarians. You can rent a Sunfish sailboat for excursions on the water.

Literally next door to the restaurant, the **Club Marina de Guatavita** (cell tel. 312/592-7468) rents sailboats (Sunfish COP$60,000 per day). You can also rent windsurfing equipment and take classes. You can water-ski for about COP$40,000 for a half-hour trip (including wetsuit). Canoes can be rented for only COP$10,000 per hour. There is also camping available next to the water, which costs COP$25,000. There are five very basic cabins for rent.

PARQUE NACIONAL NATURAL CHINGAZA

The **Parque Nacional Natural Chingaza** extends over 76,000 hectares (188,000 acres) in Cundinamarca and Meta and makes for an excellent day trip of hiking among armies of *frailejones* plants through the melancholy and misty *páramo* (highland moor). One of the better hikes is a 3.5-hour one that takes you to the **Lagunas de Siecha,** which include the three mountain lakes: Suramérica, Siecha, and Guasca. Along with Laguna de Guatavita, these were also sacred Muisca lakes.

The park limits the number of visitors, so it is best to request an entry permit in advance. Hire an experienced guide (COP$50,000/day), as trails are often not obvious. The guides are generally very knowledgeable and friendly. However, they may not speak English. To arrange a visit, call **Parques Nacionales** (tel. 1/353-2400, www.parquesnacionales.gov.co)

© ANDREW DIER

frailejones at the Parque Nacional Natural Chingaza

and request permission to visit PNN Chingaza. They will ask you to send the names of the members of your group in an email and confirm the reservation. They will also provide contact information for the local association of guides. You can save a lot of money, and help the local economy, if you do it this way rather than through an organized private tour.

Packing rubber boots is a must, as you will be hiking along really muddy paths. Sneakers just won't do. A light raincoat or windbreaker and sweatshirt are essential, as well as a packed lunch, snacks, and water. The hike to the *lagunas* takes about 3.5 hours.

Other excursions within the Parque Nacional Natural Chingaza can be made from different entry points.

In the town of **Guasca** you can relax, eat, and stay at the **Posada Café La Huerta** (cell tel. 315/742-0999, www.cafelahuerta.com). They make great American cornbread. If you decide to stay with them for a weekend, they can arrange your transportation and visit to PNN Chingaza.

Down the road a ways from Posada Café La Huerta is the abandoned colonial-era **Capilla de Siecha,** a picturesque white chapel in the middle of farmland. It is guarded by many sheep and some tiny dogs, and you can buy a ticket for entrance from an elderly farmer.

From Bogotá, take a bus to Guasca and from there take a *buseta* (minivan) towards Paso Hondo. The *buseta* will leave you at the intersection of the road that leads to the park. It is about a 90-minute walk to the park entrance from there. These leave at 6:30am, 7:30am, and 9:30am and so forth. You should leave Bogotá by around 7am to make the 9:30am *buseta*. Buses to Guasca leave from the Portal del Norte bus terminal as well as from an informal bus pickup area between Calles 72 and 73 at Carrera 14. It may sound iffy, but if you go there, you can ask any taxi or bus driver where to find the right bus.

If you travel with private transportation, it is possible to drive closer to the park, but only if you have a four-wheel-drive vehicle.

SUESCA

It's all about rock climbing in Suesca. On the weekends, Bogotanos converge on this little Cundinamarca town and head to the *rocas*. Most climbing takes place along cliffs just behind the town—some up to 250 meters high—parallel to some old train tracks and the Río Bogotá. It's a beautiful setting, and the fresh smell of eucalyptus trees and mountain mist add to the feeling of the place.

Several outdoors shops in Suesca rent equipment and organize rock-climbing classes and excursions. **Explora Suesca** (cell tel. 311/249-3491 or 317/516-2414, www.explorasuesca.com) rents out bikes in addition to rock-climbing gear and classes. **Monodedo** (Cra. 16 No. 82-22, tel. 1/616-3467, cell tel. 316/266-9399, www.mondodedo.com) has an office in Bogotá. Expect to pay around COP$60,000 for a three-hour rock-climbing excursion with a guide.

Many folks like making Suesca a camping weekend. The most popular place for this is **Campo Base** (cell tel. 320/241-9976 or 321/415-3930), right across from the rocks. They've got hot water, a place for cooking, and they rent out tents.

At the other end—way other end—of the spectrum is **Casa Lila** (cell tel. 320/204-8262 or 300/835-9472, patriciavalenciaturismo@gmail.com, COP$220,000). This luxurious bed-and-breakfast with nine rooms is so cozy, with fireplaces all around and its own restaurant, that it may be hard to leave. It's right next to an old train station at kilometer 3. In between those two is **El Hostal Vivac** (cell tel. 312/539-5408, www.elvivachostal.com, shared room COP$25,000, private room COP$65,000).

After all that rock climbing, it's time for some Thai food. Check out **Restaurante Vamonos Pa'l Monte** for Phuket vegetables or pad Thai. It's right at the entrance of the *rocas*. The other really popular place is **Rica Pizza** (cell tel. 312/379-3610), on the main road, also near the entrance to the park. They serve more than pizza.

Buses from Bogotá regularly serve Suesca from the Portal del Norte station. You can also contact one of the tour companies based in Bogotá that specialize in rock climbing, who can arrange for transportation for a day trip.

SOUTH AND WEST OF BOGOTÁ

Parque Natural Chicaque

It's hard to believe that such natural beauty is so close and accessible to Bogotá. You can basically take TransMilenio to this natural, private park and be walking amid the cloud forest within an hour.

Parque Natural Chicaque (tel. 1/368-3114/18, www.chicaque.com) is a little-known and underappreciated gem in Bogotá. This private park offers 18 kilometers of excellent paths that meander through virgin cloud forest. It's more than likely that it is only silence that you hear as you explore the park, save for the occasional bird or rustle of leaves. It's got a pretty good website with detailed information on prices and services (in English as well).

Horseback riding is possible, and you can climb a towering oak tree (and spend the night there for COP$110,000). There are two good restaurants, one at the entrance of the park and one below in the lodge. Rooms at the lodge are very simple, designed for families (one adult COP$86,000 including all meals). There are a few cabins with fireplaces for more privacy (COP$250,000 for two people and all meals), and camping (COP$50,000 including all meals) is also available.

Getting to the park is fairly easy. You can take the TransMilenio to the Portal del Sur station and take a park bus from there. This bus leaves at 8am, 10am, 1:30pm, and 4:30pm. There is a fee of COP$6,000 for this trip. The rendezvous point is the fast food **Restaurante Choribroaster** (Cra. 72D No. 57J-03). It is near a large Jumbo store.

Salto del Tequendama

West of Chicaque, on the road towards Mesitas del Colegio, is the **Salto del Tequendama** (Tequendama Waterfall). Back in the early part of the 20th century, this was a lovely place to

vista from the Parque Natural Chicaque

visit, and the falls are certainly dramatic. What was once an elegant hotel overlooks the falls. It has very recently opened its doors once again, this time serving as an exhibition space. The problem with any visit to Tequendama is the horrible stench coming from the Río Bogotá, which you must drive along, into which much of the city's waste is poured. It is a shame.

Parque de Orquideas del Tequendama

The **Parque de Orquideas del Tequendama** (Km. 19 Vía Bogotá-Mesitas del Colegio, cell tel. 300/464-5960, www.orquideasdeltequendama.com, 10am-5pm Sat.-Sun., COP$7,000) has been described as *"un jardín de los dioses"* ("a garden of the gods"). Within minutes of chilly Salto de Tequendama, you descend toward the Río Magdalena valley and it is suddenly—and violently—hot. At this farm, Omar Chaparro has around 6,000 varieties of orchids on display, including delicate miniature orchids, fragrant orchids, and many orchids that are nearly extinct. You'll see the

official orchids of Bogotá and Colombia there, too. A true expert and enthusiast on orchids, Omar has a seed bank with the ultimate goal of propagating orchid species and planting them in their natural habitats throughout Colombia so that they will survive for another generation. Guided tours, unfortunately only in Spanish, are interesting, as Omar and his staff educate guests on the flowers. There is a little open-air restaurant that serves lunch on Sundays, with, of course, colorful views. You can visit during the week if you make a reservation in advance.

Midway between the falls and the orchid farm is the **Zoológico Santa Cruz,** a zoo in which jaguars native to Colombia are sadly confined to small pens.

Public transportation is available from the Portal del Sur bus station to both the Salto del Tequendama and the orchid farm.

Bogotá to Melgar

Heading from Bogotá towards the Río Magdalena valley, you'll pass several *tierra caliente* (hot country) resort towns, such as

© ANDREW DIER

Parque de Orquídeas del Tequendama

Anapoima, Girardot, and—just across the border into the Tolima department—**Melgar** and **Carmen de Apicalá.** Many wealthy Bogotano families have second homes in this part of Cundinamarca, while Melgar, the "city of swimming pools," caters to a more middle-class clientele. These towns are easily reached by bus from Bogotá.

Several websites (www.fincasenarriendo.com or www.alquilerdefincasenmelgar.net) rent houses in this part of the country. Searching under *alquilar* (to rent), *fincas* (farms), and *casas* (houses) will provide you with several options.

During World War II, **Fusagasugá,** between Bogotá and Melgar, had an internment facility for Germans, Japanese, and Italians at the Hotel La Sabaneta. Most of the more than 400 people there had moved to Colombia decades prior to the war and were forced to leave their families and stay in the hotel under the watchful eyes of the Colombian police. There is but a faint reminder of the facility, with just a part of the hotel facade still standing.

A landmark just before Melgar that is an obsession of Colombian kids is the **Nariz del Diablo** (Devil's Nose), a rock formation that juts out along that windy road.

Bogotá to Honda

Guaduas is home to one of the few heroines in the Colombian independence movement, Policarpa (endearingly known as La Pola) Salavarrieta. A thatched roof house, the **Casa de la Pola,** is now a small museum dedicated to her life and is located just off the main plaza. Near a statue of La Pola, vendors at a small outdoor market sell things like hammocks and goat's milk. The surrounding blocks of the town have several colonial buildings set along cobblestone streets. A popular place for pastries is **Nectar,** right on the square, and **La Pesebrera Gourmet** restaurant, in a colonial house nearby the plaza, is a fun place for a hearty lunch; it doubles as a tourist information center.

There is not much in the way of tourist attractions in this hot country town; however,

© ANDREW DIER

Puente Navarro, Honda

Magdalena has shaped its history, and was the reason for its rise to importance. From the 16th century until the mid-20th century, the Río Magdalena was the main transportation route connecting Bogotá to the Caribbean coast and the rest of the world.

Honda was founded in 1539. As a port, Honda was a place where quinine, coffee, lumber, and slaves were loaded and unloaded along the banks of the river.

From this city of 29 bridges, steamships would ply the route toward the coast. In 1919, the Barranquilla-based SCADTA airlines became the very first airline of the Americas, bringing seaplane service to Honda. The river served as an airstrip. It must have been quite a sight to see these planes on the muddy Magdalena. SCADTA would later become Avianca Airlines.

The steamships and seaplanes no longer make their appearances in Honda today. But if you head down to the river's edge, you can ask a local angler to give you a quick jaunt along the river in his boat. Be sure to walk across the bright yellow **Puente Navarro,** a pedestrian bridge built by the San Francisco Bridge Company in 1898. Check out the **Museo del Río Magdalena** (Cl. 10 No. 9-01, tel. 8/251-0129) on the way.

Honda and its sleepy streets makes for a nice stopover en route between Bogotá and Medellín. A popular weekend destination for Bogotanos in need of *tierra caliente* (hot country) relaxation, the town has some good hotel options. For pampering try the **Posada Las Trampas** (Cra. 10A No. 11-05, tel. 8/251-7415, www.posadalastrampas.com). For a friendly welcome, stay at the **Casa Belle Epoque** (Cl. 12 No. 12A-21, tel. 8/251-1176, www.casabelleepoque.com), a moderately priced hotel popular with international travelers.

its plaza is a divine place for a cool beer under the shade of massive ceiba trees. In the town of Villeta, the old two-lane road (through Facatativá) and the newer road (which leads to Calle 80 in Bogotá) meet. Buses from Villeta to Bogotá are frequent and cost around COP$12,500.

In **Sasaima**, towards Facatativá, is a lovely old country farm/vacation home built by a Swiss architect in the 1940s that has been converted into a hotel/spa. It's called **El Refugio** (tel. 1/243-3620/25, www.elrefugiohotelspa.com), and a refuge in the lush Colombian countryside it certainly is. Rooms are comfortable and the restaurant serves nice meals. It's a popular place for city slickers to get away from the honking horns of Bogotá.

Honda

The steamy town of Honda, known as the City of Bridges, rests on the banks of the Río Magdalena, almost exactly halfway between Bogotá and Medellín. It was the country's first and most important interior port city. The Río

Tobia

The one and only game in town in Tobia, about 2.5 hours from Bogotá, is adventure sports Specifically that includes white-water raftin on the **Río Negro,** ziplines, rock climbing, ar horseback riding. The scenery is quite beautif as you enter town through a valley surrounded by cliffs. The town itself is nothing special.

It will not be hard to find tour companies to help you organize your adventures. Touts are everywhere selling packages. Here are some of the prices: rafting (COP$30,000), horseback riding (COP$30,000), and canopy tours (COP$40,000). **EcoAndes** (tel. 1/803-1130 or 1/252-6529, www.ecoandes.net) is a good option for a tour operator. **Los Tobianos** (cell tel. 314/397-0360, www.lostobianos.com) and **Dosis Verde** (tel. 1/232-3735 or 1/492-9329, www.dosisverde.com) are others.

The largest of the basic hotels in town is **La Gaitana** (tel. 1/631-0461, cell tel. 313/466-9092, www.lagaitana.com). On the other side of the river is **Hotel San Juanito.**

Tobia is easily reached by public transportation, costing around COP$16,000 from the Terminal de Buses. It is also a pretty easy drive if you have your own car. There are some expensive tolls, however.

An excellent stop-off between El Vino and La Vega is **La Vara** restaurant, overlooking a verdant valley. You can enjoy an arepa (cornmeal cake) and chocolate or a heartier, meatier lunch.

Buses depart all day long for both of these "hot country" destinations. It takes 2.5-3 hours to get there from the Terminal de Transporte.

CARTAGENA AND THE CARIBBEAN COAST

Colombia's Caribbean coast extends 1,760 kilometers (1,095 miles), from Venezuela to Panama, and is longer than California's coastline. The coastal area varies dramatically, with an astonishing array of landscapes: desolate deserts, snowcapped mountains, lowland swamps, dry savannahs, and rainforest. This region has so much to offer, it could easily be your only destination in Colombia.

© ANDREW DIER

HIGHLIGHTS

LOOK FOR ◖ TO FIND RECOMMENDED SIGHTS, ACTIVITIES, DINING, AND LODGING.

© AVALON TRAVEL

◖ **Cartagena's Old City:** Lose yourself in the romance of Cartagena's narrow streets and plazas, and cap off your day sipping a mojito atop the massive fortified walls (page 100).

◖ **Carnaval de Barranquilla:** Madcap and euphoric, this is Colombia's most famous celebration. Put on a costume and dance your way down the parade route (page 121).

◖ **Minca:** Take a break from the beach and chill in this refreshing town set in the foothills of the spectacular Sierra Nevada de Santa Marta mountains (page 132).

◖ **Parque Nacional Natural Tayrona:** Mountains meet jungles meet beaches at this popular national park near Santa Marta (page 134).

◖ **Ciudad Perdida Trek:** Climb the thousand-plus stone steps through the cloud forest to the mystical Lost City, the most important settlement of the Tayrona civilization (page 140).

◖ **Alta Guajira:** Be mesmerized by the stark beauty of desert landscapes, get to know Wayúu culture, and dine on fresh lobster at the top of South America (page 145).

◖ **Capurganá and Sapzurro:** Walk barefoot along deserted beaches, trek through dense rainforest among colorful frogs and howling monkeys, or cool off in a crystalline brook (page 153).

Cartagena is a majestic walled city full of magnificent churches and palaces, picturesque balcony-lined streets, and romantic plazas. Colombia's colonial past lives on in Mompox, a once-thriving port on the Río Magdalena where it feels as if time has stopped. The old city of Santa Marta has positioned itself as a great base from which to explore the beaches and mountains of the north-central coast.

Beach options abound here. The most famous are at Parque Nacional Natural Tayrona: glimmering golden sand beaches with the jungle backdrop of the Sierra Nevada. Islands in the Parque Nacional Natural Corales del Rosario y San Bernardo, between Tolú and Cartagena, beckon visitors with their white sandy beaches and five-star hotels.

There are many options for nature lovers.

Minca, a small town located on the slopes of the Sierra Nevada not far from Santa Marta, offers unparalleled bird-watching opportunities. In the jungles that envelop Capurganá and Sapzurro, you can go bird-watching, listen to the cries of howler monkeys, and count the colorful frogs you encounter along the many jungle paths in the area. Offshore, dive with the occasional sea turtle and observe myriad marine life in nearby waters.

Adventurous types can hike up to Ciudad Perdida in the Sierra Nevada. The views of the Lost City, with its eerie, beautiful terraces set atop the mountain, are simply unforgettable. Travel up the Guajira Peninsula, home of the Wayúu, Colombia's largest indigenous community. Here you'll find Cabo de la Vela, where the desert meets the sea, and stark, magnificent Punta Gallinas, the northernmost point in South America, where windswept dunes drop dramatically into Caribbean waters.

The Caribbean coast is vibrant with music and dance. It is the birthplace of *vallenato* (love ballads accompanied by accordion), which has European, African, and Amerindian roots. The coast is also home to many musical strains and dances with strong African rhythms, such as *cumbia,* a melodious traditional music once danced by African slaves, and *mapalé* and *champeta,* a more recent urban music born in Cartagena. The Carnaval de Barranquilla, declared a Masterpiece of the Intangible Heritage of Humanity by UNESCO, offers an unparalleled introduction to Caribbean music and folklore. Any time of year, Barranquilla's modern, interactive Museo del Caribe is an excellent overview of the people of the Caribbean and their very vibrant culture.

PLANNING YOUR TIME

There are a lot of sights to see in Cartagena. Take some time to wander the streets of the Old City and soak up the beauty and atmosphere. Two days will suffice, but three days is ideal. The coastal island of Barú or the Islas del Rosario archipelago can be done in an easy day or overnight trip.

From Cartagena, there are many possible excursions. Getting to the riverside town of Mompox involves five hours of travel by road and river, so staying two nights there is necessary. The seaside towns of Coveñas and Tolú are easy excursions with direct bus links from Cartagena. Barranquilla is an easy day or overnight trip.

Santa Marta is an excellent base for exploring the northern coast. If you prefer to be on the sea, the laid-back seaside village of Taganga, only a short ride from Santa Marta, could also be your base for exploration of the north.

Santa Marta offers many excursions. Spending a few days in the tranquil Sierra Nevada town of Minca is a welcome escape from the heat and an excellent base to explore the nearby mountains. The Parque Nacional Natural Tayrona is a possible day trip from Santa Marta or Taganga, but you will probably want to stay at least two nights to explore its beaches and jungles. The seaside resort of Palomino is just a 1.5-hour ride from Santa Marta. All of these towns make fine starting points for the four- to five-day trek to Ciudad Perdida, a must for any backpacker.

Most visitors to the Guajira Peninsula join an organized tour from Riohacha. From Riohacha it is possible to visit Cabo de la Vela via a bus to Uribia and then a ride in the back of a local passenger truck, but it will take several hours. Most tourists visit Cabo de la Vela as part of a tour of La Guajira. There is no transportation north of Cabo de la Vela, so you will need to join a tour to get to magnificent Punta Gallinas or to Parque Nacional Natural Macuira. Do not drive though the Guajira Peninsula without a guide: It is dangerous.

To the southwest of Cartagena, you'll find coastal communities Tolú and Coveñas and the untamed coastline of Córdoba, all easily accessed by bus from Cartagena or Montería. Medellín is the best gateway to the villages of Capurganá and Sapzurro on the Darien Gap. You could happily spend up to five days in this area.

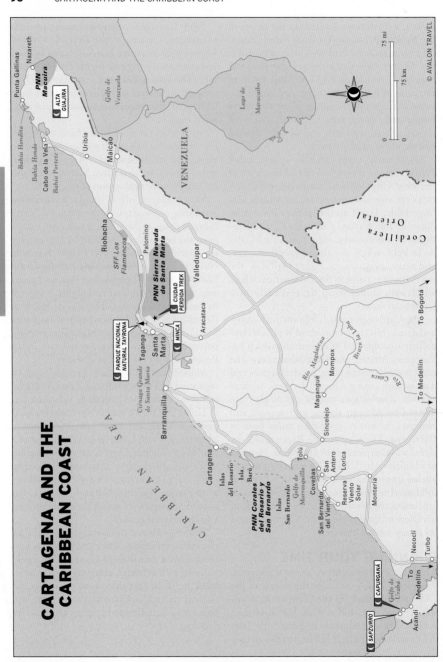

CARTAGENA AND THE CARIBBEAN COAST

© AVALON TRAVEL

75 mi

75 km

0

0

Punta Gallinas
Nazareth
PNN Macuira
ALTA GUAJIRA
Bahía Honda
Bahía Hondita
Cabo de la Vela
Bahía Portete
Golfo de Venezuela
Lago de Maracaibo
Uribia
Maicao
VENEZUELA
Riohacha
Palomino
SFF Los Flamencos
PNN Sierra Nevada de Santa Marta
CIUDAD PERDIDA TREK
Valledupar
Cordillera Oriental
Taganga
PARQUE NACIONAL NATURAL TAYRONA
Santa Marta
MINCA
Aracataca
To Bogotá
Ciénaga Grande de Santa Marta
Barranquilla
Río Magdalena
Brazo de Loba
Mompox
Magangué
To Medellín
Río Cauca
CARIBBEAN SEA
Cartagena
Islas del Rosario
Isla Barú
PNN Corales del Rosario y San Bernardo
Golfo de Morrosquillo
Tolú
Sincelejo
San Antero
Lorica
Islas San Bernardo
Coveñas
San Bernardo del Viento
Reserva Viento Solar
Montería
Golfo de Urabá
CAPURGANÁ
To Medellín
Neocolí
Turbo
SAPZURRO
Acandí

Cartagena

Cartagena is unforgettable and magical, a highlight of any trip to Colombia. The main attraction is the Old City (Cartagena's *centro histórico*), which includes two districts: the Walled City (Ciudad Amurallada) and burgeoning Getsemaní. The magnificent walls of Ciudad Amurallada enclose narrow streets lined with magnificent *casas altas* (two-story houses that were home to wealthy merchants) with bougainvillea spilling out over their balconies. Getsemaní is an old working-class colonial neighborhood (also once enclosed by a wall) that today lures visitors with its many lodging, dining, and nightlife options. Near the Old City is the magnificent Castillo de San Felipe, one of the most impressive Spanish fortifications in the New World.

Outside the Old City, Cartagena is a large, poor, and sprawling city of almost one million people. If you want to get a sense of how big it is, visit La Popa for incredible views of the city and the bay. To get to know the real Cartagena first-hand, visit the frenetic Mercado de Bazurto and then, for contrast, take a stroll through high-end Bocagrande.

If you're looking to play at the beach, escape to the Islas del Rosario, as the beaches of Cartagena are unappealing.

History

Cartagena de Indias was founded in 1533 by Spanish conquistador Pedro de Heredia on a small Carib indigenous settlement. The city owes its glory to its strategic geographic

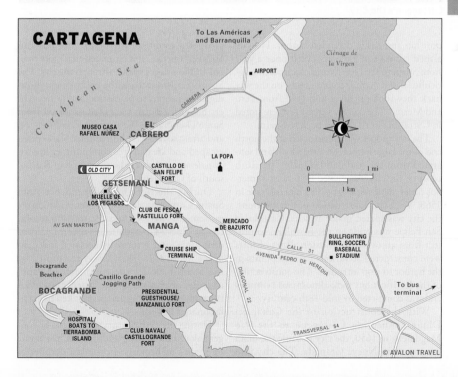

© ANDREW DIER

Cartagena's Old City

position and easily defended harbor. Heavily armed convoys of galleons sailed once a year from Spain to the New World, transporting agricultural and manufactured goods; on the way back they took on silver and gold from Peru and Mexico. The convoy's treasures were stored in Cartagena until the sail back to Spain.

The city proper was constructed at the north end of the large harbor, on a marshy island separated from the mainland. During the 16th century, the city was sacked by pirates numerous times, most notably by Sir Francis Drake in 1568. With the construction of fortifications, the city was spared major attacks. Castillo de San Felipe was built on the mainland to protect from an overland invasion. Pairs of forts were constructed at various passage points in the harbor to stop intruders. The construction of the fortifications took almost two centuries and was completed by mid-18th century.

With the construction of the Canal del Dique connecting Cartagena to the Río Magdalena in 1650, the city became the main entry port to Nueva Granada. The city also

prospered as one of the main slave ports in Spanish America. It is estimated that more than one million slaves passed through the city. The Spanish crown forbade the enslavement of indigenous people, so plantation and mine owners bought African slaves, transported from Santo Domingo or West Africa. Conditions on and after the trip were horrendous. Slaves often escaped and created free communities known as *palenques,* such as the town of San Basilio, south of Cartagena.

During the fight for independence from Spain, Cartagena sided with the revolutionary movement. After Caracas, it was the second city in Nueva Granada to set up an independent junta, and it formally declared independence in 1812. In 1815, it was recaptured by the Spanish under the command of Pablo Murillo, after a siege that lasted more than three months. Cartagena was retaken by revolutionaries in 1821.

During the 19th century, Cartagena no longer enjoyed the activity and status it had as one of Spain's main ports. In the last decades of the century, Barranquilla eclipsed Cartagena as the main center of economic activity on the Caribbean coast. The economic decline had one good side effect: preserving the colonial past. The Old City remained largely intact through the 20th century, prompting UNESCO to declare it a World Heritage Site.

During the 20th century, Cartagena became a major industrial center and domestic tourist destination. In the past two decades, the city has received an estimated 100,000 displaced people, most fleeing violence in the Atlantic coast. The city has been unable to cope with this influx, and the result is a vast belt of shantytowns.

Cartagena remained relatively peaceful even during the worst periods of violence in the 1980s and 1990s, attracting tourists from across Colombia. In the past decade, Cartagena has become a major international tourist destination, with a proliferation of chic hotels in the Old City, glitzy Miami-style condominiums and hotels in Bocagrande, and new resorts along the coast north of the city. It boasts the Hay literary festival, a classical music festival, and an acclaimed film festival that attracts visitors from the world over.

Safety

All in all, the city is a safe place; however, the general precautions for all Colombian cities apply to Cartagena as well. Be careful while walking on the walls after dark. Police have an iffy reputation here, and have been known to stop and frisk young non-Colombian men in the evening, purportedly out of suspicion of drug possession, but in actuality they are looking for money. Some of the poor fishing villages on the islands nearby Cartagena are not safe to visit, at least not alone.

Orientation

Cartagena is located on the Caribbean coast of Colombia about 130 kilometers (80 miles) southwest of Barranquilla and over 1,100 kilometers (680 miles) north of Bogotá. The city is at the north end of a large bay with the same name.

The focal point of Cartagena is the **Old City,** known as the *centro histórico,* or simply El Centro. The Old City is the original Spanish settlement completely enclosed by a massive stone wall. The Walled City is set out in a fairly regular grid with numerous plazas. The streets here have names that change from block to block; no one really knows them or uses them. Find your way by identifying the main squares—Torre de los Coches, Plaza de la Aduana, Plaza de Santo Domingo, Plaza de Bolívar, and Plaza Fernandez de Madrid—and making your way from one to the other. It takes some practice, but walking the charming streets of the Old City is a pleasure.

Historically, the main entrance to the Walled City was the gate where the Torre del Reloj (clock tower) now stands. Just south is the Bahía de las Ánimas and the Muelle de los Pegasos, from which point tourist boats to the Islas del Rosario depart.

During colonial times, the poorer district of **Getsemaní** was a separate island connected by bridge to the Old City. In the late 19th and early 20th centuries, the mangroves and marshes were filled in.

Southeast of Getsemaní is **La Matuna,** a busy commercial center full of 20th-century high-rises. To the east is the massive Castillo de San Felipe and farther on is La Popa, the only significant hill in Cartagena. East of La Popa is Mercado de Bazurto, Cartagena's huge central market, which is on Avenida Pedro de Heredia, the main road that leads to the bus terminal and out of the city.

Just north of the Old City is the 19th-century district of **El Cabrero,** where the villa of former president Rafael Núñez, today the Casa Museo Rafael Núñez, is located. Farther north are the residential neighborhoods of Marbella and Crespo, where the airport is. About two kilometers farther north, next to the fishing village of La Boquilla, is the seaside development of Las Américas.

South of the Old City is **Bocagrande,** with its many high-rise hotels and residential buildings. It was first developed in the 1960s and 1970s as a domestic tourist destination. It is the

typical street in Cartagena

stomping ground of Cartagena's rich residents. Since around 2005, however, there has been a spurt of construction of high-end, Miami Beach-inspired white residential skyscrapers. The main attractions here are the beaches. They are very popular on weekends. (There's even a gay-ish beach at the very end known as Hollywood.) But they're just OK. The sand is gray, and there's a constant stream of persistent vendors and masseuses.

The peninsula of Castillo Grande on the bay side of Bocagrande is an upscale residential neighborhood. The sidewalk that wraps around it makes for a pleasant stroll or place to jog.

SIGHTS
◖ Old City
LAS MURALLAS
Referring to Cartagena's *murallas* (walls), Colombians endearingly call the city "El Corralito de Piedra" (little stone corral). These walls are one of the most salient features of the city. After Drake sacked the city in 1568, the Spanish started fortifying access to the bay and the perimeter wall around the city. The effort took almost two centuries to complete. The walls that can be seen today are mostly from the 17th and 18th centuries.

The most impressive part of the wall is the stretch that runs parallel to the sea. This includes three *baluartes* (bulwarks, or ramparts) where Spaniards stood ready to defend the city from attack. The massive **Baluartes de San Lucas y de Santa Catalina,** built in the very north of the city to repel attacks from land, are known as Las Tenazas because they are shaped like pincers. When the sea started depositing sediments and expanding the seashore, thus enabling the enemy to maneuver south along the wall, the Spanish built a spike to halt them. This defensive structure, known as El Espigón de la Tenaza, is now home to the **Museo de las Fortificaciones** (Baluarte de Santa Catalina, tel. 5/656-0591, www.fortificacionesdecartagena.com, 8am-6pm daily, COP$7,000). At the westernmost tip of the walls, facing the sea, is the equally impressive **Baluarte Santo Domingo,** now home to Café del Mar. At the southern tip of the segment of walls facing the sea, next to the Plaza Santa Teresa, are the **Baluartes de San Ignacio y de San Francisco Javier,** also home to a pleasant outdoor bar.

A *paseo* (walk) on the walls is the quintessential Cartagena late-afternoon experience, enjoyed by international visitors, Colombian honeymooners, and Cartagenan high school students still in their school uniforms. The best time for this promenade is around 5pm. In the evenings, vacationers head to the handful of bars for a pre- or post-dinner drink. Avoid strolling the wall late at night, especially alone.

CLAUSTRO AND IGLESIA SAN PEDRO CLAVER

The **Claustro San Pedro Claver** (Plaza de San Pedro Claver No. 30-01, tel. 5/664-4991, 8am-5:30pm Mon.-Fri., 8am-4:30pm Sat.-Sun., COP$9,000) is an old Jesuit monastery, now museum, where Pedro Claver served as a priest. He is known for his compassion towards newly arrived African slaves, and is said to have baptized thousands of them. For his dedication to slaves, the priest was the first person to be canonized in the New World. The museum has relics and art from the colonial era and sometimes hosts temporary exhibitions. You can visit the small quarters where San Pedro Claver lived and climb up to the choir balcony of the Iglesia de San Pedro Claver. The cloister has a three-story courtyard brimming with flowers and trees.

Adjacent to the monastery is the **Iglesia de San Pedro Claver** (Plaza de San Pedro Claver No. 30-01, tel. 5/664-4991, masses 6:45am and 6pm Mon.-Sat., 7am, 10am, noon, and 6pm Sun.), which is adorned by a beautiful marble altar and is the final resting place for San Pedro Claver.

MUSEO DE ARTE MODERNO DE CARTAGENA DE INDIAS

Cartagena's main art museum, the **Museo de Arte Moderno de Cartagena de Indias** (Cl. 30 No. 4-08, Plaza de San Pedro Claver, tel. 5/664-5815, 9am-noon and 3pm-6pm Mon.-Fri., 10am-1pm Sat., COP$5,000, Tues. free) is

on the square in front of the San Pedro Claver plaza, which is filled with several metallic sculptures by Cartagenero Edgardo Carmona that depict quotidian scenes of Cartagena life. The museum has a small permanent collection of works from 20th-century Colombian artists, including native sons Alejandro Obregón and Enrique Grau. The museum is in the old Customs House.

MUSEO NAVAL DEL CARIBE

Adjoining the rear of the Iglesia de San Pedro Claver is the **Museo Naval del Caribe** (Cl. 31 No. 3-62, Cl. San Juan de Dios, tel. 5/664-2440, www.museonavaldelcaribe.com, 10am-5:30pm daily, COP$7,000). This museum provides a history lesson of the earliest indigenous dwellers who lived in the area, continuing through the Spanish conquest and including a bit about the many (mostly English) pirates who tried to steal the Spaniards' gold loot, which they had absconded with from all across South America. The second floor has a lot of replicas of grand ships from the period and a history of the Colombian navy (you may be surprised to learn of its participation in the Korean War). There are few explanations in English. Part of the building dates to the 17th century and was a Jesuit convent; after they were expelled by the king, it was converted into a hospital.

PLAZA DE BOLÍVAR

One of the city's most pleasant squares is the **Plaza de Bolívar,** once used for bullfights. It was transformed into a park in the late 19th century. With a statue of Simón Bolívar in the center, nearly always with a disrespectful pigeon resting upon his head, this shady spot is very inviting.

CATEDRAL BASÍLICA MENOR

Diagonal to the Plaza de Bolívar is the built-to-last **Catedral Basílica Menor** (tel. 5/664-7283, masses 10am-noon Mon.-Sat., 8am, noon, and 7pm Sun., COP$13,000, free during masses). It was built in the 16th century and doubled as a fortress. It was attacked by Sir Francis Drake

CARTAGENA

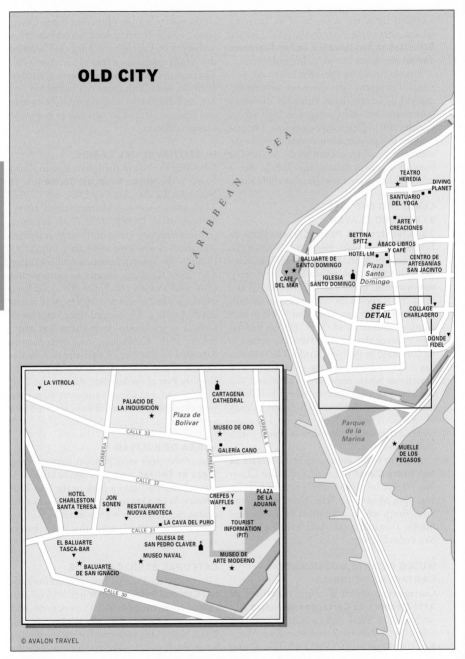

OLD CITY

C A R I B B E A N   S E A

TEATRO HEREDIA ★
DIVING PLANET ■
SANTUARIO DEL YOGA ■
ARTE Y CREACIONES ■
BETTINA SPITZ ■
ÁBACO LIBROS Y CAFÉ ■
HOTEL LM ■
CENTRO DE ARTESANÍAS SAN JACINTO ■
BALUARTE DE SANTO DOMINGO ★
Plaza Santo Domingo
CAFÉ DEL MAR ▼
IGLESIA SANTO DOMINGO ♱

SEE DETAIL

COLLAGE CHARLADERO ▼

DONDE FIDEL ▼

Parque de la Marina

MUELLE DE LOS PEGASOS ★

DETAIL

LA VITROLA ▼

PALACIO DE LA INQUISICIÓN ★

Plaza de Bolívar

CARTAGENA CATHEDRAL ♱

MUSEO DE ORO ★

GALERÍA CANO ★

CALLE 33
CALLE 32
CALLE 31
CALLE 30

CARRERA 3
CARRERA 4
CARRERA 5

HOTEL CHARLESTON SANTA TERESA ●

JON SONEN ■

RESTAURANTE NUOVA ENOTECA ■

LA CAVA DEL PURO ■

CREPES Y WAFFLES ■

PLAZA DE LA ADUANA ★

TOURIST INFORMATION (PIT) ■

EL BALUARTE TASCA-BAR ▼

IGLESIA DE SAN PEDRO CLAVER ♱

MUSEO NAVAL ■

MUSEO DE ARTE MODERNO ★

BALUARTE DE SAN IGNACIO ★

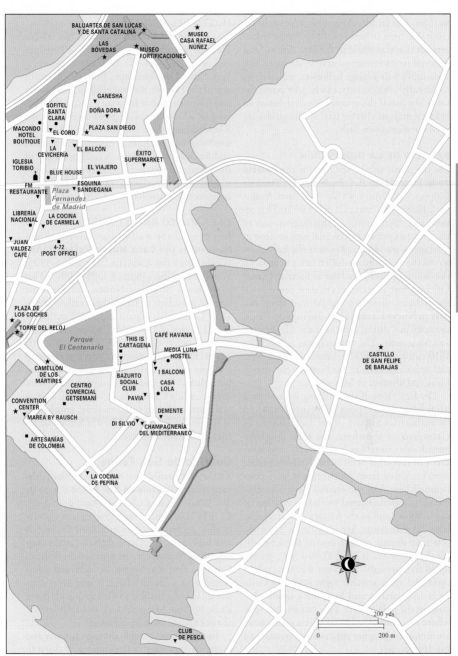

BALUARTES DE SAN LUCAS
Y DE SANTA CATALINA
LAS
BÓVEDAS
MUSEO
FORTIFICACIONES
MUSEO
CASA RAFAEL
NÚÑEZ

GANESHA
SOFITEL
SANTA
CLARA
DOÑA DORA
MACONDO
HOTEL
BOUTIQUE
EL CORO
PLAZA SAN DIEGO
LA
CEVICHERÍA
EL BALCÓN
ÉXITO
SUPERMARKET
IGLESIA
TORIBIO
EL VIAJERO
BLUE HOUSE
FM
RESTAURANTE
ESQUINA
SANDIEGANA
Plaza
Fernandez
de Madrid
LIBRERÍA
NACIONAL
LA COCINA
DE CARMELA
JUAN
VALDEZ
CAFÉ
4-72
(POST OFFICE)

PLAZA DE
LOS COCHES
TORRE DEL RELOJ
Parque
El Centenario
THIS IS
CARTAGENA
CAFÉ HAVANA
MEDIA LUNA
HOSTEL
CASTILLO
DE SAN FELIPE
DE BARAJAS
CAMELLÓN
DE LOS
MÁRTIRES
I BALCONI
BAZURTO
SOCIAL
CLUB
CASA
LOLA
CENTRO
COMERCIAL
GETSEMANÍ
PAVIA
CONVENTION
CENTER
DEMENTE
MAREA BY RAUSCH
DI SILVIO
CHAMPAGNERÍA
DEL MEDITERRANEO
ARTESANÍAS
DE COLOMBIA

LA COCINA
DE PEPINA

0   200 yds

0   200 m

CLUB
DE PESCA

in 1586. The facade, along with most of the interior, has been stripped of the Italianate stucco exterior that was added in the 20th century and restored to its former austere stone look. The cathedral's pale orange belltower, which dates to the early 20th century, can be seen across the Old City. Stroll the ornate cathedral during or before a mass to visit for free. Audio guides are available 8am-6pm daily.

PALACIO DE LA INQUISICIÓN

On the south side of the plaza is the **Palacio de la Inquisición** (Cl. 34 No. 3-11, Plaza de Bolívar, tel. 5/664-4570, 9am-6pm Mon.-Sat., 10am-4pm Sun., COP$15,000). This remarkable 18th-century construction, one of the finest examples of colonial architecture in Cartagena standing today, was the headquarters of the Spanish Inquisition in Cartagena. In this building was housed the Tribunal del Santo Oficio, whose purpose was to exert control over the Indians, mestizos, and African slaves not only in Nueva Granada but also in New World colonies in Central America, the Caribbean, and Venezuela. The tribunal was active from 1610 until the late 17th century. There were two other tribunals in the New World: one in Lima and another in Mexico City.

The first floor of the building is a museum displaying the weapons of torture employed by authorities as part of the Inquisition. In Cartagena as elsewhere, the most common punishable crime was "witchcraft," and hundreds of supposed heretics (indigenous people were excluded from punishment) were condemned here. On the second floor are exhibition spaces dedicated to the restoration of the building and to the history of Cartagena. Most explanations are written in Spanish; you may decide to hire one of the English-speaking guides (COP$35,000 for a group up to five persons). On your way out, take a right and then another right onto the Calle de la Inquisición and look for a small window on the palace wall. This was a secret spot where citizens of colonial Cartagena could anonymously report others for various and sundry heresies.

MUSEO DEL ORO ZENÚ

The **Museo del Oro Zenú** (Cra. 4 No. 33-26, Plaza de Bolívar, tel. 5/660-0778, 10am-1pm and 3pm-7pm Tues.-Fri., 10am-1pm and 2pm-5pm Sat., 11am-4pm Sun., free), on the north side of the Plaza de Bolívar, exhibits gold jewelry and funerary objects from the Zenú indigenous people, who were the original dwellers of the Río Magdalena area and Río Sinú valley, to the southwest of Cartagena. It has excellent Spanish and English explanations. A smaller version of the Museo del Oro in Bogotá, this museum has a regional focus and is one of the few tributes to indigenous culture today in Cartagena.

CASA MUSEO RAFAEL NÚÑEZ

Just beyond the wall in the Cabrero neighborhood is the **Casa Museo Rafael Núñez** (Calle Real del Cabrero, tel. 5/664-5305, 9am-5:30pm Tues.-Sun., COP$10,000). This is the house of Rafael Núñez, the four-time former president of Colombia, author of the 1886 Colombian constitution, and author of the 11 verses of Colombia's national anthem. Núñez governed Colombia from this, his coastal home. The museum, which underwent a renovation in 2013, has memorabilia from his political life and is a beautiful example of 19th-century Cartagena architecture. Núñez was born and died in Cartagena, and he lies at rest in the Ermita de Nuestra Señora de las Mercedes across the street.

Castillo de San Felipe

The largest Spanish fort in the New World, the magnificent **Castillo de San Felipe** (Cerro de San Lázaro, east of Old City, 8am-6pm daily, COP$17,000) must have given pirates pause as they contemplated an attack on the city. It was built atop the Cerro de San Lázaro outside of the Walled City to repel attacks by land. Construction was begun in 1639 and completed over a century later. It was never captured. Tunnels enabled soldiers to quickly move about without being noticed, and cells housed the occasional unlucky prisoner.

Today, visitors ramble through tunnels and secret passageways (a flashlight will come in

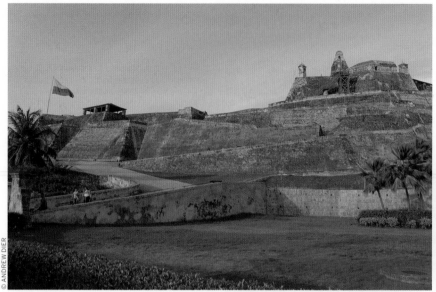

© ANDREW DIER

The monolithic Castillo de San Felipe is one of the most impressive Spanish forts in the New World.

quite handy), and views from the highest points of the fort are magnificent.

The best time to visit the fort is in the late afternoon, when the intense sun abates. Audio tours (COP$10,000) are available. For many, the view of the fort from a distance suffices, especially at nighttime when it is lit up. If you want to do things up for a special celebration, you can rent out the entire *castillo* (fireworks are an additional charge!). Contact the Sociedad de Mejoras Públicas de Cartagena (Castillo de San Felipe de Barajas, tel. 5/656-0590, www.fortificacionesdecartagena.com) for more information.

To get there, take a bus from Avenida Santander (COP$1,500). You can also walk from the Old City, though maneuvering through and around traffic is not fun. A taxi will cost COP$5,000.

La Popa

La Popa is a 150-meter-high (500-foot-high) hill east of the Castillo de San Felipe, so named because of its resemblance to a ship's stern (*popa* in Spanish). La Popa is home to the **Convento Nuestra Señora de la Candelaria** (Cra. 20A 29D-16, tel. 5/666-0976, 9am-5:30pm daily, COP$5,000), which was built by Augustinian monks, reportedly on a pagan site of worship. The monastery has a lovely courtyard, a small chapel where faithful pray to the Virgen de la Candelaria, and memorabilia from Pope John Paul II's visit to the monastery in 1986. Most tourists come here for the views over Cartagena and out to the sea. You can take a taxi there from the Old City for COP$50,000-60,000 round-trip. Arrange the price in advance and make sure the driver will wait for you there.

Sightseeing Tours

The folks at **This Is Cartagena** (Av. Centenario No. 30-42, tel. 5/660-0969, www.ticartagena.com, 9am-6pm Mon.-Fri., COP$115,000) offer two tours of the city. One is a full city tour (about four hours) that hits all the major sights, from La Popa to the beaches of Bocagrande. It's

CARTAGENA

Plaza to Plaza Walking Tour

© ANDREW DIER

the Iglesia Santo Toribio, one of
Cartagena's beautiful colonial churches

The best way to get to know Cartagena is to
go for a morning stroll, finding your way from
plaza to plaza, and even getting lost a couple
of times.

Start at the **Plaza de los Coches** (opposite Getsemaní), once the main entry point to
the city. It is easily identifiable by the iconic
19th-century **Torre del Reloj** (clock tower)
that tops the entrance though the wall. Inside stands a statue of Cartagena's founder
Pedro de Heredia. During the colonial period, this plaza was the site of the city's slave
market. During much of the 20th century it
bustled with commercial activity. Today, the
plaza is filled with watering holes catering
to visitors.

Immediately to the southwest is the large triangular **Plaza de la Aduana,** once the seat of
power in colonial Cartagena. It is surrounded by

stately colonial mansions. A statue of Christopher Columbus presides in the center. It's also
got a fair share of ATMs and is where the main
tourist office is located.

Adjacent to the southeast is the **Plaza de
San Pedro,** a small square located in front of
the towering **Iglesia de San Pedro Claver**
and attached convent where Saint Peter Claver,
a Jesuit monk dedicated to succoring African
slaves, ministered.

Walking two blocks north on Calle de San
Pedro you'll arrive at the city's heart, the leafy
Plaza de Bolívar, a shady park with benches,
fountains, and a statue of Simón Bolívar in the
middle. It is surrounded by some of the most
important buildings of the city, including the
Catedral Basílica Menor and the **Palacio
de la Inquisición.**

On Calle de los Santos de Piedra and Calle
de Nuestra Señora del Rosario is the **Plaza de
Santo Domingo,** heart of the former upper
class quarter. You will notice many superb two-
story *casas altas* built by rich merchants. The
plaza is dominated by the austere Iglesia de
Santo Domingo. A rotund nude bronze sculpture by Fernando Botero, live musical performances, and many outdoor cafés liven up the
popular plaza.

Next is the large, green **Plaza Fernández
de Madrid** in the historic working class San
Diego district. On one side is the charming
Iglesia Santo Toribio with its magnificent
wooden ceiling and cannonball damage (com-
pliments of English pirate Edward Vernon).

On Calle Cochera del Hobo is the tiny **Plaza
San Diego,** which is surrounded by inviting
restaurants. It's also where you can join the
locals who gather around Doña Dora's food
stall. This is the place to sample a *carimañola*
and *arepa de huevo,* two deep-fried and totally
delicious treats.

End your roaming at the **Plaza de las
Bóvedas** at the extreme northwest of the city.
Once the location of a military storehouse, this
is where you can load up on handicrafts at the
Galería de las Bóvedas.

the comfortable way to see the city: in an air-conditioned vehicle. Entries to all the sights are included in the tour price. The second tour is a walking tour of the Old City, in which you'll learn a lot about this fascinating city, its history, architecture, and people. This Is Cartagena offers several other tours, including day trips to the Islas de Rosario, a photography tour, and even a "historic drinking tour."

ENTERTAINMENT AND EVENTS
Nightlife
La Esquina Sandiegana (corner of Cl. del Santísimo and Cl. de los Púntales, 5pm-2am Sun.-Thurs., 5pm-3am Fri.-Sat., no cover) is a locals' place, where the music is salsa and the drink is beer. Its walls are decorated with salsa posters, album covers, and photographs of salsa greats. It's a hole-in-the-wall bar in the San Diego neighborhood.

Bazurto Social Club (Av. del Centenario Cra. 9 No. 30-42, tel. 5/664-3124, www.bazurtosocialclub.com, 7pm-3am Thurs.-Sat., cover varies) is an always-lively restaurant-bar, popular with Colombians and international visitors alike. Get a taste for Afro-Colombian *champeta* beats, as live acts, including the Bazurto All Stars, often perform here. They also serve food, such as shrimp empanadas and paella. The house drink is the fruity rum *machacos*.

The former site of a convent, **El Coro** (Cl. del Torno No. 39-29, tel. 5/650-4700, 5pm-2am Sun.-Thurs., 5pm-3am Fri.-Sat., no cover), at the Hotel Santa Clara, is an inviting, if posh, spot for an after-dinner drink. From Wednesday to Sunday, live music, with a nod to Havana, is on offer until late. How many places can you enjoy Latin jazz while downing mojitos in a former convent?

Café Havana (intersection of Cl. de la Media Luna and Cl. del Guerrero, cell tel. 314/556-3905 or 310/610-2324, www.cafehavanacartagena.com, 8:30pm-4am Thurs.-Sat., cover varies) famously got the endorsement of former Secretary of State Hillary Clinton on her trip to Colombia in 2012. It's a place for rum drinks and dancing. Café Havana is open Sundays when the following Monday is a holiday.

Donde Fidel (Plaza de los Coches, tel. 5/664-3127, noon-2am Sun.-Thurs., noon-3am Fri.-Sat., no cover) is a tiny salsa-lovers' spot where the action spills out onto the plaza in front. Good times and cold beer can be found here.

You've walked atop the massive walls of the Old City, and now it's time for some drinks. A sundown drink, with the Caribbean breeze kissing your face on the *murallas* (walls), is a Cartagena experience that shouldn't be missed. There are three options. First, the **Baluarte Tasca-Bar** (Cl. San Juan de Dios, tel. 5/660-0468, www.baluartesanfranciscojavier.com, 5:30pm-2am daily, no cover) is an open-air restaurant-bar at the northwesternmost corner of the wall, across from the Plaza de Santa Teresa. It's chilled out here, not trendy (but the drink prices are on the steep side: COP$24,000 for a margarita). The most happening spot would be, without a doubt, the **Café del Mar** (tel. 5/664-6513, 5pm-3am daily, no cover), on the wall near the Plaza de Santo Domingo entrance. Here the music is loungey and electronic, and it stays busy until late. It's spread out atop the wall, making it hard to mingle with others or even to carry on much of a conversation. But the drinks will quench your thirst and the music is seductive. The third wall option is to go rogue: hang out on the wall, drink an Águila beer sold by a roaming vendor, and listen to the music emanating from Café del Mar.

Wednesdays are the new Saturdays in Cartagena. In Getsemaní, **Visa por un Sueño** (Media Luna Hostel, Cl. de la Media Luna No. 10-46, tel. 5/664-0639, 9pm-3am Wed., COP$10,000) is a weekly party held on the rooftop of the Media Luna Hostel that has become Cartagena's most famous soiree, when backpackers mix it up with Colombians. Get there early—this party gets packed.

Festivals and Events
Cartagena feels like a celebration all the time, but especially November to February, when an array of cultural events are featured.

HAY FESTIVAL

Hay Festival (www.hayfestival.com) is an important international festival that began in Wales nearly 30 years ago. It celebrates literature, music, environmental awareness, and community and is held in various cities across the world, including in Cartagena in late January. Bill Clinton has called it the "Woodstock of the mind." In addition to talks and concerts, the festival holds educational programs for youth in the neighborhoods of Cartagena. It also provides free or discounted tickets to students. Most of the events take place in the **Teatro Heredia** (Cl. de la Chichería No. 38-10, tel. 5/664-6023 or 5/664-9631). While the festival's name is pronounced as the English "hay," in Colombia it's often pronounced as the Spanish *"hay"* ("ai"). Hay Festival is thus a double entendre: *hay festival* in Spanish means yes, there is a festival!

FESTIVAL INTERNACIONAL DE MÚSICA

Over the course of a week in early to mid-January, the churches, plazas, and theaters of the Walled City become the setting for classical music concerts by musicians from all over the world during the **Festival Internacional de Música** (International Music Festival, www.cartagenamusicfestival.com, tickets www.tuboleta.com). Most concerts sell out far in advance, but if you can't get tickets, you might be able to catch a free performance in one of the churches or plazas in the Old City.

FESTIVAL INTERNACIONAL DE CINE DE CARTAGENA DE INDIAS

If you're in town during late February and are looking for an excuse to escape the heat, here it is: the **Festival Internacional de Cine de Cartagena de Indias** (International Film Festival, tel. 5/664-2345, www.ficcifestival.com). A tradition since the 1960s, this week-long film festival has an interesting program of documentaries, Colombian films, and shorts; a series of roundtable discussions with prominent actors and directors; and educational activities in neighborhoods throughout the city. The venues include historic buildings and plazas.

CONCURSO NACIONAL DE BELLEZA

Beauty contests, and especially the **Concurso Nacional de Belleza** (Miss Colombia Pageant, tel. 5/660-0779, www.srtacolombia.org), are a big deal in Colombia. The coronation of Señorita Colombia takes place every November and is the highlight of Cartagena's Independence Day celebrations. Aspirers for the title represent each of the departments of the country, in addition to some cities. Ladies from the Valle del Cauca and Atlántico have won the most titles (10 each) since the pageant began in the 1930s. In 2001, the first Miss Colombia of Afro-Colombian heritage was chosen: Vanessa Mendoza, who represented the Chocó department. Tickets to the main events—the swimsuit competition at the Cartagena Hilton and the coronation at the Centro de Convenciones—are hard to come by but not impossible to purchase.

ELECTRONIC MUSIC FESTIVALS

In early January every year, especially on the first weekend after New Year's Day, one or two big beachside electronic music festivals take place. The most well-known and regular festival is **Ultra Mar,** but there are others. These parties are often the main reason the under-35 crowd from Bogotá, Medellín, and Cali converges on the city during the New Year's holidays. Tickets and information can be found at Tu Boleta (www.tuboleta.com). Double-check before heading out to one of these events, as sometimes the location changes at the last minute.

SHOPPING
Shopping Centers and Malls

The bazaar-like **Centro Comercial Getsemaní** (Cl. 30 No. 8B-74, tel. 5/664-2508, hours vary daily) shopping center doesn't really cater to tourists. It's made up of hundreds of small mom-and-pop kiosks that sell just about anything: computer supplies, notebooks, beauty supplies, handicrafts, and knickknacks. You can probably get your nails done here as well.

    Centro Comercial Caribe Plaza (Pie de la Popa, Cl. 29D No. 22-108, tel. 5/669-2332,

fresh fish at the Mercado de Bazurto

cuisine special, particularly the seafood and exotic fruits. You'll also meet the vendors who have worked their entire lives behind a stall at the market. Afterwards you'll head to a beach house and have a gourmet lunch featuring lobster and other delicacies prepared by Jorge and his staff.

Handicrafts

The most historic place to pick up some Colombian handicrafts is at **Las Bóvedas** (extreme northeastern corner of the wall, 9am-6pm daily). Once a military storehouse, today it's the place to buy multicolored hammocks and all kinds of Colombian *artesanías* of varying quality.

For high quality handicrafts you're better off going to **Artesanías de Colombia** (Centro de Convenciones, Local 5, tel. 5/660-9615, 10am-7pm Mon.-Sat.). This is a government entity whose mission it is to promote Colombian handicrafts and craftspeople. This store sells handicrafts from across the country but specializes in masks from the Carnaval de Barranquilla, woven *mochilas* (handbags) from indigenous groups in the Sierra Nevada, and the colorful embroidery of *molas* from indigenous groups in the Darien Gap region near Panama.

Jewelry

Colombian emeralds are considered to be some of the finest in the world. Many jewelers in the Centro Histórico sell emerald jewelry and can custom make jewelry for you. One of the most highly regarded jewelers is **Galería Cano** (Plaza Bolívar No. 33-20, Local 679, tel. 5/664-7078, www.galeriacano.com.co, 9am-7pm Mon.-Fri., 10am-7pm Sat.). They specialize in gold, silver, and emerald jewelry. Cano has other locations in the airport and at the Hotel Santa Clara, as well as in Bogotá.

Cigars

In Cartagena, touches of Cuba are found everywhere: mojitos, music, and, too, the cigars. At **La Cava del Puro** (Cl. de las Damas No. 3-106, tel. 5/664-9482, www.lacavadelpuro.

10am-8pm Mon.-Thurs., 10am-9pm Fri.-Sun.) is an upscale modern mall near the Castillo de San Felipe with numerous clothing and shoe stores, movie theaters, and a food court.

MERCADO DE BAZURTO

Definitely not for the faint of heart, a visit to the sprawling, grimy **Mercado de Bazurto** (Av. Pedro Heredia, 5am-4pm daily) is the best way to connect with the real Cartagena. On the periphery of the market be sure to peruse the seafood area, where women sell the catch of the day to restaurant owners. Be amazed at all the different kinds of fruit on offer. To get to the market, take a bus from Avenida Santander (COP$1,500) or a taxi (COP$7,000 from the Old City).

Another way of visiting the market is the **Mercado de Bazurto Tour** (tel. 5/660-1492, cell tel. 315/655-4120, cevicheria@hotmail.com, COP$250,000 pp), organized by Jorge Escandón, the owner of La Cevichería and Bazurto Social Club. On the tour, you'll learn about the ingredients that make Caribbean com, 9am-8pm Mon.-Sat., 10am-8pm Sun.) they don't sell just any old stogie; here the cigars come from Havana and are of the best quality. Smoking is not only permitted here, but in fact promoted. Sometimes a little whiskey is even served to perusing clients. Note that cigars with labels that say "Hecho in Cuba" may be confiscated by customs agents upon arrival in the United States. Cigars that come from the Barichara area in the Colombian department of Santander are quite good and much cheaper, and you can take them across borders with no questions asked.

Clothing

Along Calle Santo Domingo there are several boutiques of top Colombian designers. Bogotana **Bettina Spitz** (Cl. de la Mantilla No. 3-37, tel. 5/660-2160, www.bettinaspitz.com, 11am-1pm and 2pm-8pm daily) sells casual, beach, and formal clothes for women, as well as an array of accessories, shoes, and some men's items. **Jon Sonen** (Cl. Ricaurte No. 31-56, tel. 5/664-1092 or 5/660-4682, www.jonsonen. com, 10am-8pm Sun.-Thurs., 10am-9pm Fri.-Sat.) is a Colombian label specializing in menswear, with stores throughout the country.

You'll notice that guayabera shirts are what men wear around Cartagena, to restaurants and events. It's possible to spend a fortune on them, but if you want to blend in without busting your budget, go to **Arte y Creaciones** (Cl. Don Sancho No. 36-94, cell tel. 320/583-9091, noon-8pm Mon.-Fri., 10am-8pm Sat.-Sun.), where a cotton guayabera will run you about COP$55,000. Another option for cheap guayaberas is **Centro de Artesanías de San Jacinto** (Cl. de la Iglesia No. 35-59, tel. 5/660-1574, 9am-8:30pm daily).

Books

Abaco Libros (Cl. 36 No. 3-86, Cl. de la Mantilla, tel. 5/664-8290, 9am-9pm Mon.-Sat., 3pm-9pm Sun.) is a small book shop/café with a variety of books on Cartagena, top Colombian novels, and a selection of magazines, classics, and best sellers in English. **Librería Nacional** (Cl. Segunda de Badillo No.

36-27, tel. 5/664-1448, 8:30am-12:30pm and 2pm-6:30pm Mon.-Fri., 8:30am-5pm Sat.) is a chain bookstore with shelves full of Colombian and Spanish-language books, but not much in the way of books in English.

SPORTS AND RECREATION

If you're looking for a place to jog or stroll, the bayside path along the peninsula of **Castillo Grande** (Cra. 5 from Clls. 6-10 and along Cl. 6 from Cras. 6-14) in the Bocagrande sector is very nice, particularly in the late afternoon. From here you'll have great views of the Cartagena port and La Popa in the far distance. Forming an L shape, the path is about two kilometers long.

Biking

The best time to explore Cartagena by bike is early on a Sunday morning or on a Sunday or Monday evening when there is little activity and no traffic in the Old City. **Pato Bikes** (Cl. de la Media Luna, Cra. 8B No. 25-110, tel. 5/664-0639, cell tel. 301/423-9996, 9pm-9pm daily, COP$20,000) and **Bike Route** (Callejón de los Estribos No. 2-78, cell tel. 318/456-1392, 10am-11pm daily, COP$5,000/hour, COP$30,000/day) are both located in Getsemaní and rent bikes. In addition to bike rental, **Bicitour Getsemaní** (Cl. Carretero, Getsemaní, cell tel. 300/357-1825, COP$5,000/2-hour rental) offers guided tours of the Old City on two wheels. Many hostels and some hotels also have bicycles for hire.

Diving

Diving Planet (Cl. Estanco del Aguardiente No. 5-94, tel. 5/664-2171, www.divingplanet. org, 8am-7pm Mon.-Sat.) offers classes and diving excursions to some 25 locations throughout the Parque Nacional Natural Corales del Rosario y San Bernardo. A one-day mini-course with two immersions costs COP$305,000. A day trip with two immersions for those who are certified divers costs COP$290,000. If you pay in advance on their webpage or pay in cash once in Cartagena you'll receive a discount. Multiple day PADI certification courses are also available. Some of these plans include an overnight on the white beaches of the Islas del Rosario. Snorkeling excursions are also available (COP$190,000).

Yoga

Santuario del Yoga (Cl. El Estanco del Aguardiente No. 5, tel. 5/668-5338, cell tel. 313/649-3133, 8:30am-5pm daily, COP$15,000 per class) offers yoga classes in a small studio in the Walled City and also classes on the beach on occasion. Some instructors are bilingual.

ACCOMMODATIONS

Cartagena remains the top tourist destination in Colombia (and is second only to Bogotá in terms of international arrivals), and the crowds keep coming. Hotel options have flourished since 2000. The Old City and Getsemaní have become a favorite location for high-end boutique hotels. At the other end of the spectrum, hostels have begun to appear in these same neighborhoods. Finding a good midrange option, however, is a challenge.

A short bus or taxi ride away from colonial Cartagena is its version of Miami Beach: Bocagrande. Large high-rise hotels facing the waters of the Caribbean are the norm. This area is popular with Colombian tourists. There are some midrange and budget options here, though not with a view to the sea.

For those interested in beaches, the Las Américas area two kilometers past the airport is home to many new, large high-rise hotels. Finally, there are lodging options in the Islas de Rosario. Spending a night there may be more satisfying, albeit much more expensive, than a day trip.

Peak tourist seasons in Cartagena are during the last week of November (which is when the city celebrates its independence from Spain and hosts the Miss Colombia beauty pageant), from mid-December to mid-January, Semana Santa (Holy Week) in March or April, June-July during school vacations, and during any of the long weekends when Monday is a holiday (check a Colombian calendar). Cartagena is at its liveliest (and more fun) when the out-of-towners converge on it, particularly during the end-of-year holidays when it's two to three weeks of celebration. But finding a place to stay may be difficult, as room rates spike.

Old City and Getsemaní
UNDER COP$70,000

The Shangri-La of backpacker hostels in Cartagena is the famous **Media Luna** (Cl. de la Media Luna No. 10-46, tel. 5/664-3423, www.medialunahostel.com, COP$37,000 dorm). Located on the edge of Getsemaní, it's a high-energy kind of place with multicultural socializing (and flirting) centered on the small pool in the courtyard. If you're looking to break out of your shell, this may be the place. It has a capacity of over 100 with just a couple of private rooms (book early for those). There's a burrito place attached to the Luna, they organize lots of activities, and bikes are available to rent. Then there's the bar: On Wednesday nights, turn up on the early side (around 9pm) to squeeze in at their famous Visa por un Sueño party. This hostel isn't the best place for travelers over the age of 28.

In the Old City, the Uruguayan hostel chain **El Viajero** (Cl. Siete Infantes No. 9-45, tel. 5/660-2598, www.elviajerohostels.com, COP$30,000 dorm, COP$75,000 pp d) has air-conditioned dorm rooms of various sizes and a handful of private rooms, which are located across the street in a more subdued environment. A decent breakfast is included in the room rate.

Low-key hostel option **◖ Blue House** (Plaza Fernández Madrid, corner of Cl. del Curato and Cra. 7 No. 38-08, tel. 5/668-6501, www.bluehouseht.com, COP$35,000 dorm, COP$150,000 d) is within the Walled City on a relatively quiet side street just a few blocks from the Plaza Santo Domingo. It's got just one dorm room and two private rooms. You'll have no problem finding the hostel—it's true blue.

OVER COP$200,000

The two classic upmarket hotels in the Walled City are the Santa Teresa and the Santa Clara.

The **Hotel Charleston Santa Teresa** (Cra. 3A No. 31-23, tel. 5/664-9494, www.hotel-charlestonsantateresa.com, COP$718,000 d) was originally built as a convent for Clarisa nuns. Post-independence it served many different purposes: headquarters for the police, a jail, a pasta factory. In the 1980s it was finally converted into a hotel. There are two wings to this historic hotel, a colonial one and a modern wing. The two inner courtyards are lovely, and you'll be astounded by the floral displays. Concierges will help arrange any excursion you'd like. Amenities such as four restaurants, a rooftop pool, a spa, and gym ensure a relaxing stay. It's steps away from the wall.

The other old city classic is in San Diego. The **Hotel Sofitel Legend Santa Clara** (Cl. del Torno 39-29, tel. 5/650-4700, www.sofitel.com, COP$747,000 d) is a 122-room hotel synonymous with class and luxury. The stunning colonial courtyard alone is worth taking a peek, even if you're not a guest. The Santa Clara originally served as a convent.

From the rooftop terrace of **C Hotel LM** (Cl. de la Mantilla No. 3-56, tel. 5/664-9100, www.hotel-lm.com, COP$800,000 d) guests enjoy spectacular views of the rooftops of old Cartagena, including the Iglesia San Pedro Claver. This luxury hotel has seven spacious rooms and an "interactive" kitchen where guests order in advance and can even participate in food preparation.

Casa Lola (Cl. del Guerrero No. 29-108, tel. 5/664-1538, www.casalola.com.co, COP$374,000 d) is designed and managed by a Spanish couple who were some of the first hoteliers to take a chance on Getsemaní. The hotel, spread over two buildings (one colonial and one republican-era), has 10 smartly designed rooms.

It's not hard to determine how the owners decided on **Makondo Hotel Boutique** (Cl. del Curato No. 38-161, tel. 5/660-0823, www.hotelmakondo.com, COP$210,000 d) as the name for their small hotel: It's next door to Gabriel García Márquez's house and named for the fictitious Colombian pueblo portrayed in the author's *One Hundred Years of Solitude*. This small hotel is boutique-lite,

with less exorbitant prices. It's got 10 rooms, some rather small. It's within a stone's throw of several good restaurants.

Bocagrande
OVER COP$200,000
Several mediocre hotels along Carrera 3 in Bocagrande fit in the category of economy hotels. For a little more, but for less than most hotels in Cartagena, the **Hotel San Pietro** (Cra. 3 No. 4-101, tel. 5/665-2369, www.pietro.com, COP$228,000 d), located on the same stretch, is more comfortable than its neighbors. It has 35 rooms of different sizes, a cute reading room with books you can check out, and a rooftop terrace with a hot tub (though it can only be used during the day, under the blazing sun). The owners also have an adjacent Italian restaurant.

The old classic in town is the **Hotel Caribe** (Cra. 1 No. 2-87, Bocagrande, tel. 5/650-1160, www.hotelcaribe.com, COP$350,000 d). These swanky digs, comprising three large buildings, are next to the beach (they have a beach club exclusively for guests). Most visitors, however, seem to prefer to lounge by the pools and drink a fruity cocktail.

For a no-surprises brand-name hotel experience, the **Hilton Cartagena** (Av. Almirante Brion, El Laguito, tel. 5/665-0660, www.hilton.com, COP$411,000 d) won't fail you. It's at the tip of Bocagrande, isolated from the crowds, and has multiple pools and restaurants as well as a gym. Guests have to pay extra for wireless Internet access, though.

FOOD
Seafood reigns supreme in Cartagena cuisine. Popular fish are *pargo rojo* (red snapper), *corvina* (sea bass), *dorado* (mahi mahi), and *sierra* (swordfish). Avoid *mero* (grouper) as it is threatened in the Caribbean waters. Shellfish include *langosta* (lobster), *langostinos* (prawns), and *chipi chipis* (tiny clams). These main dishes are often accompanied with delicious coconut rice and *patacones* (fried plantains).

Though many restaurants in the Walled City sport Manhattan prices, an inexpensive meal is not impossible to find. There are still a few mom-and-pop restaurants featuring set (cheap!) lunches for locals who would balk at paying over COP$10,000 for their midday meal.

Old City

Transport yourself to the Havana of yester-year at █ **La Vitrola** (Cl. Baloco No. 2-01, tel. 5/664-8243, noon-3pm and 7pm-midnight daily, COP$35,000), an always elegant, always packed restaurant that specializes in Caribbean seafood, such as their popular tuna steak with avocado and mango, as well as pasta dishes. Immaculately dressed bartenders are a blur of constant motion as they perform their nightly mojito ritual: plucking mint leaves, crushing them with sugar in tall glasses, pouring in soda and rum, squeezing in some fresh lime juice, then giving the concoction a few vigorous shakes. La Vitrola is pricey, but the atmosphere, with live Cuban music in the evenings, makes it worthwhile.

Serving up the best, freshest ceviche in town is **La Cevichería** (Cl. Stuart No. 7-14, tel. 5/660-1492, noon-11pm Mon.-Sat., noon-10pm Sun., COP$28,000). It's got a creative menu, featuring ceviche with mango and ceviche with coconut and lime juice, and outdoor seating on a quiet street.

Tastefully decorated with a lovely garden area, upper-crust **Restaurante FM** (Cl. 2 de Badillo No. 36-151, tel. 5/664-7973, noon-3pm and 7pm-11:30pm daily, COP$38,000) is named for its owner, Francisco Montoya, who has created a menu that features Caribbean and Mediterranean dishes.

El Balcón (Cl. Tumbamuertos No. 38-85, cell tel. 300/336-3876, www.elbalconcartagena.com, noon-midnight daily, COP$22,000) is a friendly place with a view in Plaza San Diego. Get here in the early evening and enjoy a sundowner cocktail as you listen to lounge music or have a light meal like a refreshing gazpacho or their shrimp "sexviche." Casual and cute, **Collage Charladero** (Cl. Roman No. 5-47, tel. 5/660-7626, noon-midnight Mon.-Sat., COP$22,000) serves sandwiches, burgers, falafels, fresh juices (watermelon with lime

and mint), and refreshing sangria in a clean and cool environment close to all the historic sights.

The **Enoteca** (Cl. San Juan de Dios No. 3-39, tel. 5/664-3806, www.enoteca.com.co, noon-11:30pm daily, COP$30,000) never seems to lose its popularity. This institution is best known for its pizzas, professional service, and nice atmosphere, although its pastas are overpriced. While the interior patio decorated with fountains and twinkling lights is certainly atmospheric, you can also dine in their wine cellar room near the front, where the air conditioner always hums.

For a little curry with your shrimp, try **Ganesha** (Cl. de las Bovedas No. 39-91, tel. 5/660-9165, www.ganesharestaurante.com, noon-3pm and 6:30pm-11pm Tues.-Sun., COP$24,000), an authentic Indian restaurant with an extensive menu with many vegetarian options.

La Cocina de Carmela (across from Librería Nacional, Cl. Segunda de Badillo No. 36-50, cell tel. 301/348-7881, 11:30am-11pm Mon.-Sat., COP$12,000) is an unpretentious bargain spot where Colombian and international dishes (served buffet style) are on offer at lunchtime. At night it's à la carte, specializing in seafood and pasta dishes.

Crepes & Waffles (Cl. Baloco Edificio Piñeres, Local 1, tel. 5/664-6062, www.crepesywaffles.com.co, noon-10:30pm Mon.-Thurs., noon-11:30pm Fri.-Sat., 8am-10:30pm Sun.) is a wildly successful and reliable Colombian family-style chain that specializes in savory and sweet crêpes and just sweet waffles. With restaurants as far away as Spain, the restaurant has a progressive policy of hiring women who are heads of their households. Besides healthy and quick meals, Crepes is a good place for an ice cream break on a muggy Cartagena afternoon.

In 1965, Dora Gavíria starting selling her *fritos* (fried snacks) to locals and students in order to support her family of five children. Today she stays in the kitchen mostly, letting her adult children run her stand, but everyone still calls it **Doña Dora** (Plaza San Diego, 4pm-10pm daily). There's always a crowd gathered around the small food stall taking turns dabbing a little more hot sauce on their *arepa de huevo* (egg fried in corn meal), *carimañolas* (meat-stuffed yuca fritters), and empanadas. Beer is the perfect companion for her *fritos*. As you are strolling the narrow streets of the Old City, look for street corner vendors of *agua de coco* (coconut water). This natural sports drink is sold in the actual coconut—just add a straw. It's an unbeatable thirst quencher on hot days. The going price for coconut water is COP$2,000.

Getsemaní and Manga

The Plaza de la Trinidad in Getsemaní is the heart of the neighborhood. It's home to some swanky spots perfect for a couple of drinks or a meal. A little bit of Barcelona can be found there at the **Champagnería del Mediterraneo** (Plaza de la Trinidad, tel. 5/646-3576, 11am-midnight Wed.-Mon., COP$24,000), where Spanish wines accompany Serrano ham sandwiches. **Demente** (Plaza de la Trinidad, cell tel. 311/831-9839, www.demente.com.co, 4pm-2am Mon.-Sat., COP$22,000) is an ultra-cool tapas bar on a competing corner across the plaza that also specializes in cocktails and tapas. It's an open-air spot with a retractable roof, where the music is funky, the cocktails are fine, and the cigars are Cuban. It's a fun place for an evening of tapas and drinks.

Check out **Di Silvio** (Cl. de la Sierpe No. 9A-08, tel. 5/660-2205, 6:30pm-11:30pm Tues.-Sun., COP$24,000), an upscale Italian restaurant just off of the Plaza de la Trinidad. **◖Pavia** (Cl. Guerrero 29-75, tel. 5/664-3308, 6pm-midnight Mon.-Sun., COP$15,000) is a funky little pizza and pasta joint that is run by a musician and artist from Italy.

VIPs such as President Santos have been known to sample the authentic Italian dishes at **I Balconi** (Cl. del Guerrero No. 29-146, cell tel. 311/392-0936, www.ibalconi.com, noon-10pm Sun.-Thurs., noon-midnight Fri.-Sat., COP$18,000). It gets boisterous here as the evenings wear on and the wine flows. It's above Café Havana. Ask for a table on one of the balconies so you can enjoy the street life from on high.

At **◖La Cocina de Pepina** (Callejón Vargas, Cl. 25 No. 9A-06, Local 2, tel. 5/664-2944, noon-4pm and 6pm-10pm Tues.-Sat., noon-4pm Sun.-Mon., COP$25,000), typical dishes from across the Caribbean coast are thoughtfully reinvented. It's a cozy place in an alleyway near the Calle del Arsenal. Make a reservation for dinner.

Marea by Rausch (Centro de Convenciones, Cra. 8, tel. 5/654-4205, www.mareabyrausch.com, noon-3pm and 7pm-10pm Tues.-Sat., 4pm-10pm Sun., COP$45,000) is an ultra-chic seafood restaurant that is the brainchild of the Rausches, two brother chefs from Bogotá. Specialties include a tuna tartar and prawns in a coconut and saffron sauce. This restaurant has excellent views of the bay and the Torre del Reloj.

The food at the **Club de Pesca** (Fuerte San Sebastián del Pastelilo, Manga, tel. 5/660-4594, noon-11pm daily, COP$55,000) is overpriced and overrated, but the view is unsurpassable. This Cartagena classic is in the old San Sebastián del Pastellilo fort with magnificent views to the bay. It's a favorite spot for wedding banquets, and some guests arrive at the fort in yachts. On the menu try the *jaiba gratinada,* which is a crab au gratin.

Bocagrande

Elegant **Arabe Internacional** (Cra. 3 No. 8-83, tel. 5/665-4365, www.restaurantearabeinternacional.com, noon-3:30pm and 7pm-10pm Mon.-Fri., noon-10pm Sat.-Sun., COP$25,000) has been serving authentic Middle Eastern cuisine since 1965. It's a popular place for the Cartagena business crowd.

If you just want a hearty, authentic Colombian meal without the bells and whistles, head to **Mac Dugan's** (Av. San Martín No. 9-42, tel. 5/665-5101, 11am-9pm daily, COP$12,000), a family-run restaurant in Bocagrande.

INFORMATION AND SERVICES

In addition to locations at the airport and at the cruise ship port, there are city-run **tourist information kiosks** near the Torre del Reloj (no phone, 9am-noon and 1pm-6pm Mon.-Sat., 9am-5pm Sun.) and an air-conditioned main office in the historic **Casa de Marquez Plaza de la Aduana** (tel. 5/660-1583, 9am-noon and 1pm-6pm Mon.-Sat., 9am-5pm Sun.). The website for the **Cartagena Tourism Board** is www.cartagenadeindias.travel.

In case of an **emergency**, call the police at 123, 112, or 5/628-4748. For medical emergencies call tel. 5/667-5244.

Although postcards are relatively easy to purchase, sending them is a different matter. Mailing postcards and letters is not common here and not that easy. The post office, **4-72,** has a branch in the Walled City (Cl. de la Moneda No. 7-94, tel. 5/670-0102, 8am-noon and 2pm-5:30pm Mon.-Fri., 9am-12:30pm Sat.). It costs COP$2,000 for postage to the United States and Canada. This branch has a small exhibition space with old postage stamps on display.

Volunteering

The **Fundación Juan Felipe Gómez** (Cl. 31 No. 91-80, Ternera, tel. 5/661-0937, www.juanfe.org) was the inspiration of Catalina Escobar, a Colombian businesswoman. As a volunteer in a maternity clinic in Cartagena, she was holding a tiny infant, born to a teenage mother, who died in her arms, all because the mother didn't have the most basic financial resources to get proper care for her son. Within days, Escobar's own son died in a tragic death. Driven by grief and the desire to help young women to lead healthy and happy lives, she founded this organization. At the Fundación Juan Felipe Gómez, named for the child she lost, young women (often pregnant or new mothers) take classes designed to provide them with workforce skills. Because of Escobar's efforts, she was nominated a CNN Hero of the Year in 2012. Anybody with skill or interest in nutrition, computers, fashion, or teaching English can get involved. Both short- and long-term volunteers are welcomed. If you'd like to visit the center, call in advance to arrange a tour. You can take a public bus or a 20-minute taxi to the *fundación*.

GETTING THERE

Cartagena's **Aeropuerto Internacional Rafael Núñez** (CTG, tel. 5/656-9202, www.sacsa.com.co) is located to the east of the city, about a 12-minute cab ride from Cartagena.

JetBlue (www.jetblue.com) operates three flights a week between New York-JFK and Cartagena. Nonstop from Florida, **Spirit Airlines** (www.spirit.com) has a flight from Fort Lauderdale, and **Avianca** (Col. toll-free tel. 01/800-095-3434, www.avianca.com) has one out of Miami. **Copa** (tel. 5/665-8495, www.copaair.com) serves Cartagena from its hub in Panama City, Panama. The main national carriers, Avianca and **LAN Colombia** (Col. toll-free tel. 01/800-094-9490, www.lan.com), operate many flights each day to Cartagena from various Colombian cities. **Viva Colombia** (tel. 5/642-4989, www.viva-colombia.co) often offers inexpensive fares between Cartagena and Medellín, Bogotá, Cali, and Pereira. **ADA** (Col. toll-free tel. 01/800-051-4232, www.ada-aero.com) serves the city with flights from Medellín, Montería, and Cúcuta. **Easy Fly** (tel. 5/693-0400, www.easyfly.co) has a nonstop from Bucaramanga.

Regular bus service connects Cartagena with all major cities and all coastal cities. The **Terminal de Transportes** (Diag. 56N. 57-236, tel. 5/663-0454) is a long 20- to 30-minute cab ride from the *centro histórico*. Expect to pay about COP$20,000 for the trip.

GETTING AROUND

The Old City, Getsemaní, and Bocagrande are very walkable. For short hops, there are cabs. Taxis here do not have meters, so it's quite possible you won't get the local rate. Before hopping in a cab, ask a local or two how much you should pay. From the Old City to Bocagrande, expect to pay around COP$6,000. A ride to the airport will cost COP$10,000, and a trip to Las Américas will go for COP$12,000. Tipping is not customary for cabbies. Although an additional cost is added if you use a phone service for a cab, added costs for night pickups, air conditioning, and traveling on holidays are not permitted, and you can protest those.

It may seem overwhelming at first, but taking a public bus is a cheap way to get from point A to point B—and you'll hardly ever be overcharged. To hop on a bus to Bocagrande from the Old City, walk down to Avenida Santander along the sea and flag down just about any bus you see (or look for a sign in the window that reads "Bocagrande"). The ride will set you back COP$1,500. When you want out, yell *"¡Parada!"* On the main road just to the east of the walls, you'll see a nonstop parade of buses loading and unloading. From here you can go to the Castillo de San Felipe, to the Mercado de Bazurto, or to the bus terminal, for the same low price of COP$1,500.

BOCACHICA

Bocachica, which means "Small Mouth," is one of two entrances to the Bahía de Cartagena. It is at the southern end of the bay. The other, much wider entrance, is Bocagrande ("Big Mouth"), in the northern part of the bay near Cartagena. In 1640, when three galleons sank at Bocagrande and blocked that passage, the Spaniards decided to fortify the more easily defensible Bocachica.

The **Fuerte de San Fernando** and **Batería de San José** are two forts constructed at either side of Bocachica that were the first line of defense of the bay. The Fuerte de San Fernando, at the southern tip of the island of Tierrabomba, is a particularly impressive example of 18th-century military architecture. It is very well preserved and you can still see the barracks, kitchen, storerooms, and chapel enclosed within the massive fortifications. The low-lying Batería de San José is a much more modest affair. The only way to get to Bocachica is by *lanchas* that depart from the Muelle de los Pegasos, the tourist port in Cartagena near the Torre del Reloj (COP$7,000). The 45-minute trip through the bay provides interesting views of Cartagena and the port. In Bocachica, there are a few small restaurants where you can eat fried fish, coconut rice, and *patacones* (fried plantains) and drink a cold beer.

PLAYA BLANCA AND ISLAS DEL ROSARIO

South of Cartagena is the elongated island of **Barú**, which is separated from the mainland by the Canal del Dique, a manmade waterway built in 1650 to connect Cartagena with the Río Magdalena. On Barú lies **Playa Blanca,** a Caribbean paradise of idyllic, white-sand beaches bordering warm waters of dozens of shades of blue. West of Barú, and about 25 kilometers southwest of Cartagena, is the archipelago **Islas del Rosario,** part of the much larger **Parque Nacional Natural Corales del Rosario y San Bernardo**. On Barú and the Islas del Rosario, traditional Afro-Colombian communities with rich cultural heritages coexist with the vacation houses of Colombia's rich and famous.

Barú is home to several beautiful beaches. With the exception of Playa Blanca, most of these are inaccessible to the general public. The 25 small coral islands of the Islas del Rosario are a marine wonderland. The once-spectacular coral reefs off of Barú and surrounding the archipelago have been badly damaged by the increased flow of fresh water from the Canal del Dique, which has been dredged in recent years.

A trip to Playa Blanca and the Islas del Rosario affords the chance to blissfully bask in the sun and splash about in the ocean. However, be aware that the standard tours, such as those operated by **Optitours** (Av. Santander No. 46-94, Cartagena, tel. 5/666-5957, cell tel. 300/394-4848, www.opitours.com, COP$50,000-70,000) can often be crowded on weekends. Most tours involve cruising down the Bahía de Cartagena, passing through the Strait of Bocachica, and heading to the **Oceanario Islas del Rosario** (www.oceanariocolombia.com, 10am-3pm Tues.-Sun., COP$25,000) on the island of San Martín de Pajarales, part of the Islas del Rosario. Very popular with Colombian families on vacation, the aquarium features a dolphin show. You can swim in the water and rest in the shade if you decide not to patronize the aquarium. Then the boats head off to Playa Blanca, where you can buy lunch. The insistent vendors at Playa

Blanca can make for an unpleasant experience, but you can try telling them *"no, gracias."*

If you are willing to pay more, there are more upscale day tours to the *islas*. One is a day trip (COP$173,000) to the luxurious beachside **Hotel San Pedro de Majagua** (Cartagena office: Cl. del Torno No. 39-29, tel. 5/650-4460, http://nuevo.hotelmajagua. com, COP$400,000 d) on Isla Grande. They take care of transportation from the Muelle de Marina Santa Cruz in Manga (boats leave at 9am daily). The price also includes a seafood lunch and a visit to the Oceanario Islas del Rosario, whether you want to go there or not. You can also spend the night at this comfortable hotel (COP$350,000 d including transportation).

Another recommended day tour is the **This Is Cartagena** (Av. Centenario No. 30-42, tel. 5/660-0969, cell tel. 317/259-3773, www.thisiscartagena.com, 9am-6pm Mon.-Fri., yacht tour COP$200,000) tour to the islands. It's a more relaxed experience, as groups are rarely larger than eight persons.

If you are willing to splurge on an overnight stay, upscale hotel options include **Coralina Isla Boutique** (cell tel. 310/764-8835, COP$577,000 d) or **Agua Azul Beach Resort** (cell tel. 320/680-2134 or 314/504-3540, COP$1,300,000 d high season, COP$700,000 d low season). For a special occasion, you can rent the luxurious houseboat run by the travel agency Aviatur. Their **Casa Navegante** (tel. 1/587-5181, www.aviaturecoturismo.com, COP$1,200,000) is moored on the beautiful Bahía Cholón in the Islas de Rosario.

MOMPOX

This town, founded in 1540 on the eastern edge of a large island between two branches of the Río Magdalena (the Brazo de Loba and the Brazo Mompox), was an opulent center of trade, connecting the interior of the country with Cartagena during the colonial era. But then the mighty river changed its course in the late 18th century. Mompox's importance steadily declined, never to return.

Mompox is what Cartagena looked like

© ANDREW DIER

The Río Magdalena runs through Mompox.

before it became a tourist destination, and it's hard to deny the melancholic charm this oppressively hot town retains even today. The attraction here is strolling the wide streets, admiring the magnificent whitewashed houses decorated with intricate iron latticework, and watching the river flow by. In 1995, because of its architectural importance, it was declared a UNESCO World Heritage Site.

The town is spread out along the river. It does not have a central plaza, but three squares, each with a church, facing the river. It is believed that each of these squares is on the location of a former indigenous settlement. From south to north these are: **Plaza de Santa Bárbara, Plaza de la Concepción** (also known as Plaza Mayor), and **Plaza de San Francisco.** Three main streets run parallel to the river: Calle de la Albarrada (which corresponds to Carrera 1) facing the river; the Calle Real del Medio, Mompox's main street, one block west of the river; and the Calle de Atrás (literally, the "street behind").

There are two historical churches worth visiting in Mompox. However, they are only regularly open during mass times. Nonetheless, the Casa Amarilla can call the church to request that someone open up the doors so that you can take a quick peek. The **Iglesia de Santa Bárbara** (Cl. de la Albarrada and Cl. 14, mass 4pm Sun.), built in 1630, is well worth a visit. The facade is painted a striking yellow, with colorful floral decorations. It has an unusual baroque octagonal tower with a balcony wrapping around it. Inside, it has a magnificent gilded altar. Another noteworthy church is the **Iglesia de San Agustín** (Cl. Real del Medio and Cl. 17, masses 7pm daily, with additional 9am mass on Sun.), which houses the Santo Sepulcro, a gilded reproduction of Christ's tomb, which is carried through the streets during Semana Santa. The only museum in town is the **Museo Cultural de Arte Religioso** (Cl. Real del Medio No. 17-07, tel. 5/685-6074, 9am-noon and 3pm-4pm Tues. and Thurs.-Fri., 9am-noon Sat.-Mon., COP$2,000), which has displays of gold- and silverwork from the colonial era. Mompox silver- and goldsmiths

© ANDREW DIER

the ornate Iglesia de Santa Bárbara, Mompóx

made a name for themselves with their intricate filigree jewelry. Another interesting sight is the **Piedra de Bolívar** (Cl. de la Albarrada and Cl. 17), a monument facing the river with a stone slab that lists all the visits Simón Bolívar made to Mompox. Finally, Mompox's atmospheric 19th-century **Cementerio Municipal** (Cl. 18 and Cra. 4, 8am-noon and 2-5pm daily, free) is well worth a detour.

Festivals and Events

Semana Santa, or Holy Week (Easter), which is held during late March or April, is the most important celebration in Mompox, when visitors from all over Colombia converge on the town to watch its religious processions and attend concerts. You'll have to book months in advance to get a hotel room during that time.

Shopping

Mompox is famous for its intricate gold filigree jewelry. Look for the **Joyería Filimompox** (Cl. 23 No. 3-23, tel. 5/685-6604 or 313/548-2322), where the staff will explain their craft to you during your visit to their workshop. They accept credit cards. At the **Escuela Taller de Artes y Oficios de Santa Cruz de Mompox** (Claustro de San Agustín, Cl. 16 No. 1A-57, tel. 5/685-5204), young people learn traditional handicrafts. Visitors are welcome to drop by and watch these artisans at work. Inside, there's an interior courtyard, an inviting place to linger for a while.

Accommodations and Food

Bioma Hotel Boutique (Cl. Real del Medio No. 18-59, tel. 5/685-6733, cell tel. 315/308-6365, www.bioma.co, COP$190,000 d) may be one of the most comfortable options in town, as it offers 12 air-conditioned rooms, a dipping pool, and good food. The **C Casa Amarilla** (Cl. de la Albarrada No. 13-59, tel. 5/685-6326, cell tel. 301/362-7065, www.lacasaamaraillamompos.com, COP$25,000 dorm, COP$100,000 d), owned by a British travel writer, is another excellent choice, with accommodations for the backpacker as well as private rooms for those seeking more comfort. After a careful restoration, the Casa Amarilla opened a luxury colonial house called the **Casa de la Concepción** (Cl. de la Albarrada No. 13-59, tel. 5/685-6326, cell tel. 301/362-7065, www.lacasaamaraillamompos.com, COP$1,500,000 house rental) in 2013. It has four bedrooms and two interior patio gardens, and the second story balcony has a fine view to the plaza below.

Hotels in Mompox are the best options food-wise, but be sure to confirm with them before arriving. During off-season many do not have cooks on call. Otherwise, the **Comedor Costeño** (Cl. de la Albarrada No. 18-45, tel. 5/685-5263, 7am-5pm daily) is a restaurant that serves *comida típica* (Colombian fare) overlooking the Magdalena. On the renovated Plaza de la Concepción there are some open-air cafés that serve snacks and drinks. This is a nice weekend night gathering area. Plaza Santo Domingo (Cl. 18 and Cra. 3) has **food stalls** serving pizza and other fast food.

Getting There

Most visitors arrive in Mompox from Cartagena, and there are several ways to make the journey.

There is one direct bus that leaves from the Terminal de Transportes in Cartagena (Diagonal 57 No. 24-236, tel. 5/663-0454) at 6:30am. The ride takes eight hours and costs COP$50,000. More comfortable is a door-to-door service (COP$75,000) with a company like **Toto Express** (cell tel. 310/707-0838), which takes six hours. The fastest way involves a van, a boat, and a taxi: take a van (COP$40,000 pp, 3.5 hours) from outside the Terminal de Transportes in Cartagena to Magangué, a port on the Magdalena; there hop on a *chalupa* boat that will take you to a spot called Bodega de Mompox (COP$7,000, 30 mins.); and from there take a shared taxi or *mototaxi* (COP$15,000, 30 minutes) to Mompox.

Barranquilla

Colombia's fourth largest city (pop. 1.6 million) is known for its busy port and for the bacchanalian Carnaval de Barranquilla, designated a World Masterpiece of the Oral and Intangible Heritage of Humanity by UNESCO. This, the most famous celebration in Colombia, is a time of music, dancing in the streets, and revelry. It lasts only about four days, but the city starts readying for it days (if not weeks) in advance.

During the rest of the year there's not a whole lot to lure the visitor to Barranquilla. It is not a colonial city, but vestiges of its early 20th century importance can be seen in its El Prado district.

SIGHTS

Two museums give the visitor a good insight into Barranquilla's people and culture. The first, **Casa del Carnaval** (Cra. 54 No. 49B-39, tel. 5/370-5437 or 5/379-6621,

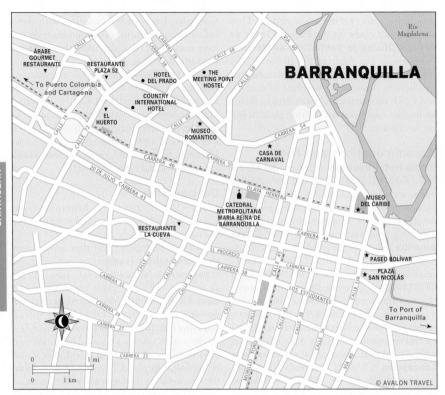

Río Magdalena

ÁRABE GOURMET RESTAURANTE

RESTAURANTE PLAZA 52

HOTEL DEL PRADO

THE MEETING POINT HOSTEL

To Puerto Colombia and Cartagena

BARRANQUILLA

COUNTRY INTERNATIONAL HOTEL

EL HUERTO

MUSEO ROMANTICO

CASA DE CARNAVAL

MUSEO DEL CARIBE

CATEDRAL METROPOLITANA MARÍA REINA DE BARRANQUILLA

RESTAURANTE LA CUEVA

EL PROGRESO

PASEO BOLÍVAR

PLAZA SAN NICOLÁS

LOS ESTUDIANTES

To Port of Barranquilla

CALLE 76 · CALLE 74 · CALLE 72 · CARRERA 59 · CALLE 68 · CALLE 58 · VÍA 40 · CARRERA 54 · CALLE 64 · CARRERA 46 · CARRERA 50 · 20 DE JULIO · CARRERA 43 · OLAYA HERRERA · CARRERA 44 · CARRERA 61 · CARRERA 57 · CALLE 45 · CARRERA 41 · CALLE 50 · CALLE 54 · CARRERA 38 · CARRERA 32 · CARRERA 29 · CARRERA 27 · CARRERA 25 · CALLE 47 · CALLE 43 · LOS ESTUDIANTES · CALLE 38 · CALLE 36 · MURILLO TORO · VÍA 40 · CALLE 33-B

0   1 mi
0   1 km

© AVALON TRAVEL

9am-5pm Tues.-Thurs., 9am-6pm Sat.-Sun., COP$5,000), is *carnaval* headquarters, and its Sala Carnaval Elsa Caridi provides an interactive introduction to the annual event. After a visit here, you'll come to understand the many different components of the celebration, like the different musical styles: *cumbia, mapalé, chandé,* and *son.* While at first blush it may seem that the Carnaval de Baranquilla is just a big party, there is more to it than meets the eye. Behind every costume, parade, and dance there is a story. Knowledgeable guides will share this story and their genuine enthusiasm for the festival at this well-done museum.

The second of Barranquilla's top two museums is **Museo del Caribe** (Cl. 36 No. 46-66, tel. 5/372-0582, www.culturacaribe.org, 8am-5pm Tues.-Fri., 9am-6pm Sat.-Sun., COP$10,000), one of the finest museums in the country, with a focus on Costeño (Caribbean coast) culture. There is a room dedicated to Gabriel García Márquez, which may be hard to understand if you are not familiar with many of his works or if your Spanish isn't perfect; slide shows on ecosystems from the Caribbean region; and exhibits on the people of the Caribbean, including the many different indigenous tribes who live there. Of particular interest is a room that examines immigration to the region, from African slaves to "Turcos," meaning those mostly coming from Syria, Lebanon, and Palestine. The museum has a restaurant with reasonably priced meals and a cute, tiny café on the plaza in front. Both of these keep regular museum hours.

The old downtown of the city is very real, in its rundown and dirty state. The **Paseo Bolívar** (Cl. 34 between Cras. 38-45) is the main drag downtown. It's lined with discount shops and charming used-book stands, where you can often find some Colombian classics—even in English—if you look hard enough. There's always a crowd at the newspaper kiosks, which seems like a scene from a different era. On the restored **Plaza San Nicolás** (between Clls. 32-33 and Cras. 41-42) is the neo-gothic **Iglesia San Nicolás Tolentino** (Cra. 42 No. 33-45, tel. 5/340-2247), which took about 300 years to build.

Not about roses and chocolates, the **Museo Romántico** (Cra. 54 No. 59-199, tel. 5/344-4591, 9am-11:30am and 2:30pm-5:30pm Mon.-Fri., COP$5,000) is really a history museum of Barranquilla with artwork, old *carnaval* costumes, missives signed by Simón Bolívar, and a typewriter used by Gabriel García Márquez. It was once the majestic home of Jewish immigrants who arrived in Colombia at the turn of the 20th century. It is run by an elderly historian and his wife.

Pop singer Shakira has won two Grammys and countless other awards, and is Barranquilla's favorite daughter. To honor her, the people of the city put a statue of her stroking a guitar in a prominent place: in front of the **Estadio Metropolitano Roberto Meléndez** (Aves. Circunvalar Alberto Pumarejo and Murillo).

FESTIVALS AND EVENTS
⟨ Carnaval de Barranquilla

For most Colombians, Barranquilla is synonymous with *carnaval*, and they boast that the Carnaval de Barranquilla is the world's biggest after Rio, although folks from New Orleans may balk at this claim. In Colombia, this is really the only place where the bacchanal is celebrated, although some Caribbean cities and even Bogotá make an effort.

During the four days prior to Ash Wednesday, in late February or early March, the **Carnaval de Barranquilla** (www.carnavaldebarranquilla.org) is full of Costeño pageantry: costumes, music, dance, parades, and whiskey.

Officially, Carnaval gets going on Saturday, but on the Friday night before, **La Guacherna**

is held. One event of the night is the Desfile Gay, which is when outrageously costumed men dressed in drag parade down a street to the hoots and hollers of thousands of bystanders.

Saturday is the main event. That's the day of the **Batalla de las Flores** (Battle of the Flowers) parade. It's when floats carrying beauty queens and dancers and thousands in *comparsas* (groups) in elaborate costumes make their way down the Calle 40 under the sizzling Barranquilla sun. This event dates back to 1903, when the celebration was begun as a celebration of the end of the Guerra de Mil Días (Thousand Days' War). Participation in the parades is serious business here, involving planning, practice, money, and, sometimes, connections. However, there is one *comparsa* during the Batalla de las Flores in which just about anyone can participate, and it's one of the most popular. That's the *comparsa* of "Disfrazate como Quieras"—go however you like. Anybody in a costume, from the silly to the sexy, can join. To participate, visit the web page (www.disfrazatecomoquieras.com).

On Sunday, during the Gran Parada de Tradición y Folclor, groups of dancers perform on the Calle 40 to the typical, hypnotic music of *carnaval*—a mix of African, indigenous, and European sounds. On Monday there is another parade, the Gran Parade de Comparsas, and, starting in the late afternoon, a massive concert attracting more than 30 musical groups. These compete for the award of Congo del Oro. On Tuesday, after four days of music and dancing, things wind down with the parade Joselito Se Va con las Cenizas. This is when Joselito, a fictitious Barranquillero, dies after four days of rumba, and his body is carried through the streets as bystanders weep. On Wednesday, Barranquilleros call in sick.

You can watch all the action of the parades from the *palcos* (bleachers) that line Calle 40. Keep in mind that the parades take place in the middle of the day, meaning lots of sun and heat. Tickets for the *palcos* can be ordered online at Tu Boleta (www.tuboleta.com).

With regard to *carnaval*, it's said that *"quien lo vive, es quien lo goza"* ("whoever experiences

CARTAGENA

it is who enjoys it"). But to do that, it's crucial to get those hotel and flight reservations early.

ACCOMMODATIONS

As a business destination, Barranquilla has a number of hotel options, although hostels are almost nonexistent. Rates significantly drop on weekends.

Meeting Point Hostel (Cra. 61 No. 68-100, tel. 5/318-2599, www.themeetingpoint.hostel. com, COP$60,000 d, COP$25,000 dorm) is the only hostel catering to international backpackers in Barranquilla. It's run by an Italian-Colombian family. If it feels like you're staying in their house, that's because it is their house, down to kids on the sofa playing video games. The neighborhood is quiet and green, and about a 15-minute walk from the El Prado area.

Country International Hotel (Cra. 52 No. 75-30, tel. 5/369-5900, ext. 120, www.countryinthotel.com, COP$238,000 d) has a nice pool and comfortable rooms. It's located in a good area. **Hotel Estelar Alto Prado** (Cl. 76 No. 56-29, tel. 5/336-0000, COP$292,000 d) is a modern, ultra comfortable, and stylish address in Barranquilla.

Ⓒ **Hotel El Prado** (Cra. 54 No. 70-10, tel. 5/369-7777, www.hotelelpradosa.com, COP$236,000 d) debuted in 1930, and for decades, before the relatively recent boom in luxury cookie-cutter hotels, it was the luxury address in town. It's got 200 rooms, a massive boiler room, and a fab pool to lounge around drinking a cocktail. Non-guests can spend an afternoon getting pampered here for only COP$38,000, a price that includes lunch and all the poolside lounging you need.

FOOD

El Huerto (Cra. 52 No. 70-139, tel. 5/368-7171, 8am-7:30pm Mon.-Sat., 10am-3pm Sun., COP$12,000) has been serving the vegetarian minority of Barranquilla since 1986. They have a set lunch menu every day and sell baked goods to go as well.

Barranquilla's many residents of Lebanese and Syrian descent have a few Middle Eastern restaurants to choose from. One of the best is

Arabe Gourmet (Cra. 49C No. 76-181, tel. 5/360-5930, 11am-10pm daily, COP$25,000).

The Ⓒ **Restaurante Bar La Cueva** (Cra. 43 No. 59-03, tel. 5/340-9813, noon-3pm and 6pm-10pm Mon.-Thurs., noon-3pm and 6pm-1am Fri.-Sat., COP$25,000) has history and lots of character. It was the hangout of Gabriel García Márquez and artists such as Alejandro Obregón in the 1960s. Elephant tracks, memorabilia, and photos make it seem like a museum, but it is still a restaurant, and a popular one at that. The specialty here is seafood. There's live music on Friday and Saturday evenings. Be sure to check out the Obregón work *La Mulata de Obregón,* complete with a bullet hole thanks to a drunken friend of the artist.

For steak lovers, the top two options in Barranquilla are **La Bonga del Sinu** (Cra. 53 No. 82-10, tel. 5/358-5035, 11:30am-10pm Mon.-Wed., 11:30am-11pm Thurs.-Sat., 11:30am-9pm Sun., COP$25,000) and **Buffalo Grill** (Cra. 51B No. 79-97, Local 2, tel. 5/378-6519, noon-11pm Mon.-Thurs., noon-midnight Fri.-Sat., noon-10pm Sun., COP$25,000).

Thanks to its location in a strip mall, you may not have soaring expectations for **Restaurante Plaza 52** (Cra. 52 No. 72-114, Local C9, tel. 5/358-1806, 10am-8pm daily, COP$6,500 set lunch). But the lunchtime crowds (and lines) give it away. They serve great down-home food at rock-bottom prices.

Barranquilla's version of street food can be found at the popular, competing **food stands** at the intersection of Carrera 52 and Calle 71. There's always a crowd composed of construction workers and office types hanging out here.

GETTING THERE

From Barranquilla's **Aeropuerto Internacional Ernesto Cortissoz** (Soledad, www.baq.aero), there is excellent air connection with all major cities in Colombia and a handful of nonstop international flights as well. The airport is south of the city in Soledad. Taxis cost about COP$20,000 from downtown to the airport.

Avianca (Centro Comercial Gran Centro Cra. 53 No. 68-242, tel. 5/360-7007, www.avianca.com, 8am-noon and 2pm-6pm Mon.-Fri.,

9am-12:30pm Sat.) flies nonstop from Miami, Bogotá, Cali, and Medellín. **LAN** (Centro Comercial Buenavista Cra. 53 No. 98-99, Col. toll-free tel. 01/800-094-9490, 10am-8pm Mon.-Fri., 10am-noon and 1pm-7pm Sat., 10am-noon and 1pm-5pm Sun.) has flights to Bogotá. On **Copa** (Col. toll-free tel. 01/800-011-2600, www.copair.com) there are nonstop flights to San Andrés and to Panama City.

Viva Colombia (tel. 5/319-7989, www.vivacolombia.com.co) flies from Medellín, **Easy Fly** (tel. 5/385-0676, www.easyfly.com. co) has nonstop flights from Bucaramanga and Valledupar, and **ADA** (Col. toll-free tel. 01/800-051-4232, www.ada-aero.com) flies from Montería.

There is regular bus service to all points in Colombia from the **Terminal Metropolitana de Transportes** (Km. 1.5 Prolongación Cl. Murillo, tel. 5/323-0034, www.ttbag.com.co). Fast van service is also available to Cartagena (COP$17,000) and Santa Marta (COP$17,000) from the **Berlinastur terminal** in town (Cl. 96 No. 46-36, tel. 5/385-0030, www.berlinastur. com).

GETTING AROUND

Barranquilla is not much of a walking city, with taxi cabs the most convenient way to get around. Unfortunately the cabs are not metered, so you might be charged a little more than locals if you're unfamiliar with rates. In town, you should never pay more than COP$13,000 to get from point A to point B. For those with smartphones, the app **Tappsi** enables you to order a cab from anywhere in the city, receive the license plate number and name of the driver, and send this information to a friend, for security purposes.

Transmetro (www.transmetro.gov.co, 5am-11pm Mon.-Sat., 6am-10pm Sun., COP$1,400)

is the Barranquilla version of the TransMilenio rapid bus system in Bogotá, and it runs along two main avenues: Avenida Murillo (also known as Calle 45) and Avenida Olaya Herrera (also known as Carrera 46). There are stations in front of the Museo del Caribe, the cathedral, and the stadium, and you can take the bus downtown from there.

PUERTO COLOMBIA

About a 40-minute bus ride (COP$2,000) outside of Barranquilla is Puerto Colombia, which was once Colombia's most important port.

The pier, the main attraction in town, was built at the turn of the 20th century. At the time, it was one of the longest piers in the world. The pier was severely damaged in major storms in 2009 and 2013, and there are huge gaps in the pier today. Today you can walk the pier and ask local fishers about their catch. Military personnel stand guard, meanwhile, in order to prohibit smuggling of illegal contraband. There are plans to refurbish the pier and to create an artificial beach, in hope of attracting weekend day-trippers and bringing back some of the town's former glory. Part of that effort included the construction of a boardwalk along the water.

The old train station has been converted into a cultural center by the **Fundación Puerto Colombia** (town center, tel. 5/309-6120, fundacionpuertocoombia@gmail.com, 8:30am-12:30pm and 3pm-7pm Mon.-Fri., 9am-1pm Sat., 4pm-6pm Sun., free), and there is often an art exhibit going on here.

There are several seafood restaurants around the pier area. The most famous, perhaps, is **Mi Viejo Muelle** (Cl. 2 No. 3-175, tel. 5/309-6727, noon-8pm daily, COP$22,000). It's got a nice large deck with a view, and old photos of Puerto Colombia decorate the walls.

Santa Marta

Santa Marta is coming into its own as a major tourist destination on the Caribbean coast. In addition to its charming historic district, great hotel options, and restaurants, Santa Marta offers an excellent base from which to explore the Sierra Nevada and the deserts of La Guajira.

Santa Marta was the first permanent Spanish settlement in colonial Colombia, and remained relatively rural until the second half of the 20th century, when it became a major domestic tourist destination. In the mid-1970s, treasure hunters discovered Ciudad Perdida high in the Sierra. Ciudad Perdida was one of the most important settlements of the Tayrona indigenous people. The National Institute of Anthropology carefully excavated the site, opening it to tourism in the 1980s.

In recent years, the old historic downtown, long neglected as development had moved to the Rodadero district, has seen a renaissance. It has become a destination of its own and a staging point for visits to the unspoiled beaches of Parque Nacional Natural Tayrona and hiking trips to Ciudad Perdida.

ORIENTATION

The *centro histórico* extends from the busy Calle 22 (Avenida Santa Rita) in the west to the Avenida del Ferrocarril in the east, toward the seaside village of Taganga. And from south

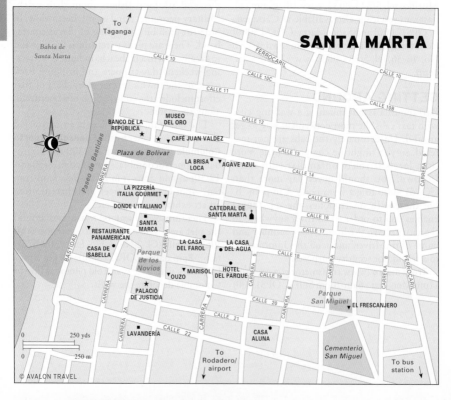

to north, the borders are the same Avenida del Ferrocarril in the south to the *malecón* (Carrera 1C/Avenida Rodrigo de Bastidas). The focal point of the Centro is the Parque de los Novios (Carreras 2A-3 and Calles 19-20). This is a lovely park with pedestrian streets (Calle 19 and Carrera 3) intersecting on its eastern side. Most sights are within a smaller range of streets from Carrera 5 (Camp Serrano) to the water and between Calles 20 and 14.

The Rodadero district is a mini-Miami with condos and hotels lining the beach. It's west of downtown Santa Marta, just around the bend on the main highway. There are constant bus links all day between the two.

SIGHTS
Centro Histórico

The compact *centro histórico* in Santa Marta in itself feels like a living museum, with its mix of colonial and republican-era architecture. All major sights, save for the Quinta de San Pedro Alejandrino, are located here and can be visited in one day.

The **Parque de los Novios** (Cras. 2A-3 and Clls. 19-20) is a symbol of the city's rejuvenation. The pedestrian streets (except for one) around the plaza have a lot to do with it. Today it's a most pleasant place for a stroll and a meal. Restaurants have cropped up along the park's periphery. On the Calle 20 side of the park is the grandiose neoclassical **Palacio de Justicia.** Visitors can only admire it from the outside, as the building is not open to the public.

The **Catedral de Santa Marta** or **Basílica Menor** (Cr. 5 No. 16-30, tel. 5/421-2434, masses at noon and 6pm Mon.-Sat., 7am, 10am, noon, and 6pm Sun.) took around 30 years to build and was completed in 1794, toward the end of Spanish reign in Nueva Granada, as colonial Colombia was called. It is one of the oldest cathedrals in Latin America. The city's founder, Rodrigo de Bastidas, is buried there, and Simón Bolívar laid in rest there before his body was moved to Caracas.

The **Plaza de Bolívar** (Cras. 1-2 and Clls. 14-15) has a statue of Simón Bolívar on horseback, ready to destroy the oppressors. The

Banco de la República (Cl. 14 No. 1C-37, tel. 5/421-0251, www.banrep.gov.co, 8:30am-6pm Mon.-Fri., 9am-1pm Sat., free) often has art exhibits and also has a public library on the third floor (a quiet place to read or work).

The **Museo de Oro Tairona** (Cl. 14 No. 1C-37, tel. 5/421-0251, www.banrepcultural.org, 8:30am-6pm Mon.-Fri., 9am-1pm Sat., free) is in the historic **Casa de la Aduana,** perhaps the oldest customs house in the Americas, dating back to 1531. A smaller version of the famous Museo del Oro in Bogotá, this focuses on the Tayrona people, who were the native settlers of the region and forebears of the Kogis, Arhuacos, Kankuamos, and Wiwas who live in the Sierra Nevada. There are ceramic and gold artifacts on display, and a description of the Ciudad Perdida archaeological site. A visit to this museum may enrich your hike up to the Lost City, as you'll have a better understanding of the people who once inhabited it.

Along the waterfront is the **Paseo de Bastidas** (Cra. 1) boardwalk. A sunset walk along the pier that extends from the boardwalk is a daily Santa Marta ritual. Great views are to be had here of the port on the right, the Isla Morro in the sea, and the gorgeous sailboats on the left docked at the Marina Santa Marta.

Quinta de San Pedro Alejandrino

The Liberator, Simón Bolívar, spent his final days in Santa Marta, passing away at the age of 47 at the **Quinta de San Pedro Alejandrino** (Mamatoco, tel. 5/433-2995, www.museobolivariano.org.co, 9am-6pm daily, COP$12,000). This country estate is now a museum where visitors can see the bedroom in which Bolívar died in 1830. A modern wing houses two art galleries. Young guides will offer to take you around the complex for a small tip of about COP$2,000, but you're probably better off on your own. The *quinta* is set in a manicured botanical garden. There is a small snack bar and gift shop on the grounds.

SHOPPING

The shop **Santa Marca** (Cl. 17 No. 2-45, tel. 5/423-5862, www.santamarca.co, 8am-8pm

© ANDREW DIER

Locals converge on Santa Marta's Paseo de Bastidas to enjoy the sunset.

Mon.-Sat.) has gifts and souvenirs made by local creative types. The **Centro Comercial Arrecife** (Cra. 4 No. 11A-119, tel. 5/422-8873, 9am-9pm daily) is a large shopping mall in the Rodadero area; it has a food court, a Carulla supermarket, a movie theater, and a selection of mostly Colombian brand clothing shops.

RECREATION
Deva Yoga Studio (Cra. 21 No. 15-18, tel. 5/431-0354, www.newfuturesociety.org, classes at 9am and 6:30pm Mon.-Fri., 9am Sat., COP$20,000/class) offers hatha and Tibetan yoga classes and meditation classes. It is affiliated with the New Future Society International, an international yoga organization.

The tour agency **Aventura Sierra Nevada** (Restaurante Marisol, Cra. 3A No. 16-30, cell tel. 311/216-5419, www.aventurasierranevada. com, 10am-9pm daily) organizes activities along the Caribbean coast, from kite surfing courses to bike tours of various lengths, hikes to Tayronaka, a trip to the Yumake nature reserve, and inner tube trips down the Río Don Diego.

ACCOMMODATIONS
The Centro Histórico of Santa Marta was considered to be crumbling, desolate, and even dangerous before the early 2000s, but gentrification has taken hold and today it's gone boutique. In addition to posh boutique hotels, there are comfortable hostels. The Rodadero has plenty of high-rise hotels, most of which are all-inclusive. The village of Taganga is also very close to the city, and some prefer to stay at this relaxed beach village and visit Santa Marta for the day or head to restaurants in the Centro Histórico in the evenings.

Under COP$70,000
◖ **Aluna** (Cl. 21 No. 5-27, tel. 5/432-4916, www.alunahotel.com, COP$30,000 dorm with fan, COP$100,000 d with a/c) gets just about everything right. This hostel has a mix of dorm rooms and private rooms, all immaculate, each with private bath. There's plenty of space to hang out over the three floors of the hostel. There is a small shaded interior courtyard and an excellent top floor terrace that provides

© ANDREW DIER

The Quinta de San Pedro Alejandrino is where Simón Bolívar spent his final days.

vantage points over the city and to the Sierra Nevada in the distance. The hostel restaurant serves gazpacho, falafel, and, for breakfast, those banana pancakes that every traveler craves. It's run by a friendly Dubliner, Patrick.

Fun and high energy: That's **La Brisa Loca** (Cl. 14 No. 3-58, tel. 5/431-6121, www.labrisaloca.com, COP$28,000 dorm, COP$90,000 d), a revamped mansion turned hostel that has earned its spot as a backpacker favorite. There's a small pool in the main courtyard with private rooms and dormitories surrounding it over three floors. On the top floor is an excellent bar that, thanks to its daily drink specials, gets jammed with backpackers and locals alike. On match days, it's soccer enthusiasts who cram the bar. In addition to on-site parties, the hostel organizes a wide array of outdoor adventures to the Sierra Nevada and rents out paddleboards for days at the beach.

Drop Bear Hostel (Cra. 21 No. 20-36, tel. 5/435-8034, www.dropbearhostel.com, COP$18,000 hammock, COP$25,000 dorm, COP$65,000 d) is a funky newcomer to the Santa Marta hostel scene. It's in a huge house that was built by a drug trafficker in the 1980s. Each night the Australian and New Zealander owners give tours of the house, including secret tunnels and nooks where money was stashed away. The bar is aptly named the Cartel Bar. Rooms are massive, and perhaps the nicest feature at Drop Bear is the big pool, which is the main gathering area at this sociable place.

COP$70,000-200,000

The ❰ **Hotel del Parque** (Cl. 19 No. 4-45, tel. 5/420-7508, COP$90,000 d) on the pleasant pedestrian Calle 19 is a gem of a find. Supremely low-key, this hotel has got just a handful of air-conditioned rooms, is very well maintained, and, best of all, it's fairly priced. There's complimentary coffee, but no free breakfast; however, there are many options within walking distance nearby.

Over COP$200,000

A Spanish couple has developed a small empire of boutique lodging and dining options in old Santa Marta. **La Casa del Farol** (Cl. 18 No. 3-115, tel. 5/423-1572, www.lacasadelfarol.com, COP$317,000 d) was their first, and one of the first boutique hotels in the city. It's in an 18th-century house and has six rooms that are named for different cities of the world. From the tiny wading pool on the rooftop you get a nice view of the city.

La Casa del Agua (Cl. 18 No. 4-09, tel. 5/423-1572, www.lacasadelagua.com.co, COP$225,000 d) is across the street from La Casa del Farol. It has four rooms of varying sizes and styles. Try for one with a balcony. The small pool downstairs is a welcome sight after a day out and about in the heat.

For some boutique pampering, try the 10-room **Casa de Isabella** (Callejón del Río, Cra. 2 No. 19-20, tel. 5/431-2082, cell tel. 301/466-5656, www.casaisabella.com, COP$250,000 d). It's a tastefully revamped republican-era house with nods to both colonial and republican styles, and it surrounds a tamarind tree that's over 200 years old. The suites on top have fantastic private terraces and hot tubs.

If you're more interested in a beach holiday, consider the beachfront **Tamacá Beach Resort Hotel** (Cra. 2 No. 11A-98, tel. 5/422-7015, www.tamaca.com.co, COP$315,000 d) in Rodadero. It has 81 rooms with all the usual amenities and a fantastic pool area that overlooks the water. The hotel has two towers, with the beachside tower preferred by most.

FOOD

Foodies from Europe and North America have converged on Santa Marta, making their dreams of opening up a restaurant become reality. And Samarians and travelers alike thank them.

There ought to be more restaurants like **◖ Marisol** (Cl. 19 No. 3-56, tel. 5/420-6511, www.marisolsantamarta.com, 8am-11pm daily, COP$18,000), an unpretentious spot that serves up healthy meals that are not too expensive, as well as deliciously fresh juices. It's run by a man from Cali who ran a successful restaurant in Berlin for many years. The location on the pedestrian Calle 19 is particularly peaceful, and you can grab a seat outside at night if you

want. Sandwiches, pastas, and salads appear on the lunch and dinner menus. You can also grab a late breakfast here and chat with the servers if they're not busy.

For pizza the Sicilian way, look no further than **La Pizzería Italia Gourmet** (Cra. 3A No. 16-24, tel. 5/422-7329, 5pm-11pm Mon.-Sat., COP$30,000) on the cute pedestrian alley, the Callejón del Correo. It's next door to the excellent **Donde L'Italiano** (Cra. 3A No. 16-26, cell tel. 316/429-1131, 5pm-11pm Mon.-Sat., COP$30,000) a cheerful restaurant where even the wallflower *pasta arrabiata* tastes exquisite. Go for a table in the courtyard in back.

An American-run place that delivers quality meals and drinks that will remind you of home is **El Frescanjero** (Cra. 7A No. 19-63, tel. 5/422-0379, 11am-2:30pm and 5:30pm-10:30pm Tues.-Sat., COP$20,000). They've got the most eclectic menu on the coast with Japanese chicken with ginger, vegetarian tacos, po'boys, and a platter of German sausage that automatically comes with a beer. And oh, the cocktail specials!

A locally run spot for a non-fussy, home-cooked meal is **Mandragora** (Cl. 20 No. 6-54, tel. 5/421-9392, cell tel. 301/400-3442, 11:30am-3pm Mon.-Sat., COP$12,000). Each day there is a set menu with fresh fish or typical Colombian dishes, such as *bandeja paisa* (dish of beans, various meats, yuca, and potatoes) on the menu.

For North Americans who've been on the road for a while, it's a treat to stumble upon **◖ Agave Azul** (Cl. 14 No. 3-58, tel. 5/431-6121, noon-10pm Tues.-Fri., 5pm-11pm Sat., COP$25,000). It's a Tex-Mex place, complete with margaritas, burritos, and nachos, in a space awash in warm colors. It's run by the same two American brothers who have **◖ Ouzo** (Cra. 3 No. 19-29, tel. 5/423-0658, 6pm-11pm Mon.-Sat., COP$25,000). Specializing in Mediterranean fare, Ouzo has brought some class to the park. Sizzling seafood or pasta accompanied by a glass of white wine will work out just fine for you. You can dine alfresco by candlelight if you wish, although you may be bothered by street vendors or beggars. It's not uncommon for visitors to hit both of these excellent restaurants in the same day.

The fab **Restaurante Panamerican** (Cl. 18 No. 1C-10, tel. 5/421-2901, noon-3pm and 6pm-10pm Mon.-Sat., noon-4pm Sun., COP$25,000) hasn't changed in decades—and why should it? While its heyday is long past, the Panamerican has an enormous menu specializing in steaks and seafood, but you can also just order a martini and enjoy the retro-chic atmosphere.

The way Samarios talk, it would seem that ◖ **Donde Chucho** (Cl. 6 at Cra. 3, tel. 5/422-1752, 11:30am-10:30pm daily, COP$25,000) is the only restaurant in Santa Marta and that it has been serving its mixed seafood platters since Bolívar was in town. It's in fast-moving Rodadero, and the open-air place is filled with photos of Chucho, the owner and chef, posing with Colombian beauty queens, sports stars, and the odd politician. It's hard to believe that Chucho began this seafood empire (he owns four restaurants now) with a humble wooden ceviche stand in Rodadero in the 1990s.

The terrace of **Pepe Mar** (Cra. 1 No. 6-05, Rodadero, tel. 5/422-2503, noon-10pm Tues.-Thurs. and Sun., until midnight Fri.-Sat., COP$26,000) is the best place for people-watching in all of Rodadero. Try the fried red snapper with coconut rice and, of course, a *patacón* (fried plantain) or two.

INFORMATION AND SERVICES

In addition to a stand at the airport, there is a **PIT** (Punto de Información Turística, Cra. 1 No. 10A-12, tel. 5/438-2587, 9am-noon and 2pm-6pm Mon.-Fri., 9am-1pm Sat.) tourist information booth along the waterfront.

Lavandería Paraíso (Cl. 22 No. 2A-46, tel. 5/431-2466, cell tel. 315/681-1651, 9am-6pm Mon.-Fri., 9am-1pm Sat.) will wash your clothes and have them ready for you to pick up by the next day. With a little charm, you might be able to persuade them to have your things ready before 5pm the same day.

GETTING THERE AND AROUND

Santa Marta is easily accessed by air and by land from all major cities in Colombia.

The **Aeropuerto Internacional Simón Bolívar** (tel. 5/422-4604 or 5/422-4490) is 16 kilometers (10 miles) west of the *centro histórico*. Domestic carriers **Avianca** (www.avianca.com), **LAN Colombia** (www.lan.com), **Viva Colombia** (www.vivacolombia.com.co), and **Easy Fly** (www.easyfly.com.co) connect Santa Marta with the major cities of Colombia. Copa has nonstop flights to its hub in Panama City, Panama.

There is hourly bus service to Cartagena, Barranquilla, and Riohacha. Many buses to nearby coastal destinations leave from the market area in the *centro histórico*. Long-haul buses for destinations such as Bogotá, Medellín, and Bucaramanga depart from the Terminal de Transportes (Cl. 41 No. 31-17, tel. 5/430-2040) outside of town.

Taxis to Taganga cost around COP$8,000, and *colectivo* buses are around COP$1,200. These can be found on the waterfront near the Parque Bolívar, along Carrera 5, or at the market at Carrera 11 and Calle 11.

The best way to get around the *centro histórico* is on foot.

TAGANGA

This popular beachside community is only about a 20-minute ride through the desert to the northeast from Santa Marta and is actually considered part of the city. In the 1970s, this sleepy fishing village was discovered by hippie-types looking for an escape from urban life, and Taganga evolved into a mecca for backpackers. On any given Saturday along the bayside promenade, you'll brush shoulders with a truly mixed lot of humanity: Colombian families, diving fanatics, traveling musicians, and general sunseekers of all ages and nationalities. It's as close as Colombia gets to Venice Beach.

Recreation

DIVING AND SNORKELING

The warm waters (24-28°C/75-82°F) off of Taganga provide some good diving and snorkeling opportunities. Diving excursions take you into the waters off of the Parque Nacional Natural Tayrona to the northeast, the Isla Morro off the coast of Santa Marta, or to a shipwreck near the beaches of Rodadero. The best months for diving here are between July and September.

Run by a Paisa couple, **Tayrona Dive Center** (Cra. 1C No. 18A-22, tel. 5/421-5349, cell tel. 318/305-9589, www.tayronadivecenter.com, 8am-noon and 2pm-6pm daily) is a very organized agency that offers PADI certification courses (COP$650,000) over a period of three days with six dives each day, a one-day mini-course (COP$160,000), and diving excursions for those with experience. They also have a hotel (Cra. 1C No. 18A-22, tel. 5/421-5349, cell tel. 318/305-9589, www.tayronadivecenter.com, COP$40,000 pp) with eight rooms, five with views of the water. Rooms have a safe deposit box and big refrigerators. The hotel is exclusively for divers during high season.

Oceano Scuba (Cra. 2 No. 17-46, tel. 5/421-9004, cell tel. 316/534-1834, www.oceanoscuba.com.co, 8am-noon and 2pm-6pm daily) offers the whole array of diving activities, from one-day dives for certified divers (COP$110,000) to a one-day beginner's course (COP$180,000) to an Open Water PADI certification course (COP$600,000) that lasts three days. Night dives (COP$80,000), during which you might come across eels hunting the waters, and snorkeling (COP$50,000) are also on offer.

BIKING AND TREKKING

Biking and hiking trips are the specialty of **Elemento Outdoor Adventure** (Cl. 18 No. 3-31, tel. 5/421-0870, cell tel. 310/605-0929, www.elementooutdoor.com, 8am-noon and 2pm-6pm Mon.-Fri., 9am-4pm Sat.-Sun.). Elemento offers a range of mountain bike adventures, including a one-day downhill trip

The fishing village of Taganga has become a backpacker mecca.

from Los Pinos to Minca (COP$140,000) with swimming hole stops along the way. There are also multi-day adventures in the area. For less adrenaline-pumping days, Elemento also offers visits to eco-farms, nature reserves, and indigenous communities.

BEACHES

There is a popular beach in front of the La Ballena Azul hotel, but the best beaches are a quick boat ride away. Beaches along the coast from Taganga to the **Parque Nacional Natural Tayrona** can be visited by boat. It costs about COP$40,000 round-trip to go to Tayrona from Taganga, but you can negotiate that price, especially if you are in a group. Although all visitors to the park are supposed to pay an entrance fee (and it is steep for non-Colombians), some boat captains will take you to beaches where no park employees will charge you for park entrance, which park officials rightly do not condone. During the windy months of December-February, boat transportation can be rough and dangerous.

Playa Grande is probably the best beach to visit, and it is one of the closest to Taganga. It costs COP$10,000 round-trip to get there by boat. To arrange for boat transportation to any of these beaches, just head to the beach in front of the promenade or at the La Ballena Azul. There are always boaters hanging about waiting for customers.

Accommodations

Owned by Olga from Bogotá, **Hostal Pelikan** (Cra. 2 No. 17-04, tel. 5/421-9057, cell tel. 316/756-1312, www.hostalpelikan.com, COP$25,000 dorm, COP$65,000 d) is a decent place to stay, with a nice terrace area for your morning coffee. Breakfast (with fruit!) is an additional fee.

The wooden cabins at **La Casa del Profe** (Cl. 21 No. 5A-36, cell tel. 311/882-8912, COP$50,000 pp) dot a mountain's edge and offer great views of the bay. There are eight rooms here, and guests may use the kitchen. It's about a 15-minute hike to the action in Taganga.

La Ballena Azul (Cra. 1 at Cl. 18, tel. 5/421-9009, www.hotelballenaazul.com, COP$173,000 d) is a Taganga classic, started by a Frenchwoman years ago. It's still in the family, and they still serve crêpes in their restaurant. Ballena Azul is on the beach, with the best location in town—in the center of activity.

Probably the most luxurious option in Taganga is the **Hotel Bahía Taganga** (Cl. 4 No. 1B-35, tel. 5/421-0653, cell tel. 310/216-9120, www.hotelbahiataganga.com, COP$235,000 d). It's on the eastern side of the bay. Head to the pool in the late afternoon and watch the sun slip behind the mountains.

Food

On the outdoor terrace of **Bitacora** (Cra. 1 No. 17-13, tel. 5/421-9482, 9am-11:30pm, COP$18,000) diners get front seat views to the boardwalk. Bitacora specializes in fresh, Taganga seafood, but there are also many vegetarian options as well as pastas. If you want to cool off with a coconut lemonade, this is the spot.

Babaganoush Restaurante y Bar (Cra. 1C No. 18-22, 3rd floor above Taganga Dive Center, cell tel. 318/868-1476, 1pm-11:30pm Wed.-Mon., COP$20,000) is an excellent Dutch-run restaurant and bar with amazing views. It's a true crowd pleaser with a diverse menu of falafels, seafood, steak, and even a shout-out to Southeast Asia. But surprisingly, you won't find any babaganoush! Go in the evening for the atmosphere, drinks, and sunsets. The daily happy hour is hard to pass up.

Getting There and Around

Taganga is easily reached from Santa Marta and from points east, such as the Parque Nacional Natural Tayrona and Palomino. Minibuses and buses ply that route daily. Minibuses from the *centro histórico* of Santa Marta depart from the market area on Carrera 5 and also from Carrera 1 near the Parque Simón Bolívar. The trip costs about COP$1,500. Taxis from Santa Marta cost around COP$12,000, more from the bus terminal or airport. Once in Taganga you can walk everywhere you need to go.

◖ MINCA

If you've had your fill of beaches or the seductive Caribbean cities, maybe it's time for an altitude adjustment. Artists, nature lovers, coffee farmers, and transplanted urbanites in the village of Minca (pop. 500) look down upon their neighbors in nearby Santa Marta—literally. At elevation of 660 meters, midway up the Sierra, you get a bird's-eye view of Santa Marta, just 45 minutes away. You also get a great bird's-eye view of birds, especially higher up at the edge of the Parque Nacional Sierra Nevada de Santa Marta. The blissful routine of mountain hikes, dips in invigorating swimming holes, and sunset ogling may make you want to linger here.

Recreation

HIKING

Minca is a paradise for those with a pair of hiking boots and a backpack slung over their shoulder. Hostels and hotels can point you in the right direction to several gentle hikes along tranquil mountain roads and paths to

Peaceful and cool Minca is a nice break from the beach.

© ANDREW DIER

swimming holes of either freezing cold or wonderfully refreshing pure water, depending on the thickness of your skin. Three popular walks with swimming holes are within easy walking distance from Minca: Balneario Las Piedras (45 mins.), Pozo Azul (1 hr.), and the Cascadas Marinka (1 hr.).

For a challenge, try the three-hour hike (one way) to the Los Pinos hostel at an elevation of 1,600 meters (5,250 feet). From there, or nearby, you can often get a fanastic glimpse of the snowcovered Pico Cristóbal Colón and Pico Bolívar, the highest mountain peaks in the country.

The Sierra Nevada de Santa Marta is a renowned coffee-growing region. The **Finca La Victoria** (no phone, 9am-4pm daily, COP$5,000) is a family-run coffee farm that you can visit for a small fee. It is between Pozo Azul and Los Pinos, about a one-hour walk from town.

In and around Minca there are no safety issues, and you can set off and up the mountain on your own without a guide.

BIRD-WATCHING

High into the Sierra Nevada, at an elevation of around 2,400 meters (7,875 feet), the **Reserva El Dorado** (www.proaves.org) is one of the finest bird-watching reserves in the country. For reservations (COP$569,000 3 nights all incl.), contact **EcoTurs** in Bogotá (Cra. 20 No. 36-61, tel. 1/287-6592, info@ecoturs.org) or **Aviatur** (tel. 1/587-5181, www.aviaturecoturismo.com) in Bogotá. The accommodations are excellent, with 10 spacious rooms, great food, and, crucially, hot showers. The area is home to 19 endemic species, including the Santa Marta antpitta, Santa Marta parakeet, Santa Marta bush tyrant, blossom crown, and screech owls. Anybody can stay at El Dorado, even the nonbirding crowd.

Acccommodations

UNDER COP$70,000

◖ **Oscar's Hostal Finca La Fortuna** (400 m from town entrance near casino area, cell tel. 313/534-4500, http://hotelfincalafortuna.

blogspot.com, COP$20,000 hammock, dorm COP$25,000, COP$40,000 d) consists of simple and naturally luxurious cabins for a small capacity of guests dramatically set on a bluff with extraordinary views of Santa Marta and the surrounding countryside. Oscar's is completely off-grid, with solar panels providing electricity and rainwater collection and a well for all water use. Much of the land that you see from here (some 70 acres that is now a sea of trees) is owned by a man named Oscar, who is on a mission to undo some of the damage humans have done to the mountains of the Sierra Nevada through cattle ranching. The sunsets here, particularly from mid-June until mid-December, are "living art," as Oscar puts it. One-to two-day mule tours in the Sierra Nevada, with Oscar, can be arranged for COP$90,000 per day, per person. Reasonably priced breakfasts include homemade granola (COP$4,000), and other meals can be arranged as well.

Rancho de la Luna (300 m from town entrance near casino area, tel. 5/422-3160, cell tel. 317/249-7127, www.ranchodelalunaenminca.com, COP$70,000), in the countryside outside of Minca near Oscar's Hostal, is a guesthouse with two lodges with basic but very comfortable facilities (and great views of Santa Marta). But the real selling point is their wellness program: healthy food, massages, and yoga classes. These have additional costs, although there are packages that include yoga, a massage, meals, and two nights' accommodations for COP$200,000 pp.

El Mirador Hotel (200 m from town entrance, cell tel. 311/671-3456 or 318/368-1611, www.miradorminca.wordpress.com, COP$25,000 dorm, COP$45,000 d) is an enchanting hostel with a great view, warm hosts, and delicious meals. The hostel has three rooms, two private rooms and a dorm room with three beds. It's set in a lush garden, and the lovely dining area is open air. The restaurant is open to the public nightly and meals cost around COP$20,000.

Many travelers head up the mountain to spend some time at sociable **Hostal Los Pinos** (near Campano, cell tel. 313/587-7677 or 321/898-0641, lospinoshostal@yahoo.com, COP$20,000 dorm, COP$60,000 d). Hostal Los Pinos is on a mountain ridge (1,400 meters/4,600 feet) where the views are unbelievable. When it's clear, you can glimpse the snowcapped mountains of the Sierra Nevada. This is a fun spot, with lots of hanging around. There are some nice walks you can take from here, as well as high-adrenaline downhill bike rides, and hikes to waterfalls hidden in the mountains. And occasional paintball duels on-site.

COP$70,000-200,000

Operated by ProAves, the **Hotel Minca** (near town entrance, tel. 5/421-9958, cell tel. 317/437-3078, www.hotelminca.com, COP$135,000 d), once a convent, is one of the first hotels in Minca. There are 13 spacious rooms in this old-fashioned building with broad verandas with hammocks. There's a nature path on the grounds, and numerous hummingbird feeders along the open-air dining area ensure that you'll have a breakfast-time show.

Hostal Casa Loma (50 m uphill from the church, cell tel. 313/808-6134 or 321/224-6632, www.casalomaminca.com, COP$20,000 dorm, COP$80,000 d) is on a hilltop with a truly amazing vantage point over Santa Marta. It's a friendly place, where delicious food (often vegetarian) is served, and you mix and mingle with other travelers. Cabins farther on the hillside are quieter than the rooms near the main social area. Camping (COP$15,000) is also available. To get to Hostal Casa Loma, you must climb up a winding path just behind the town church. Casa Loma offers yoga classes (COP$20,000) on their forest terrace, massages (COP$55,000), and shows two films a week in their outdoor forest cinema.

Hostal Palo Alto (near Reserva El Dorado, cell tel. 300/642-1741 or 312/677-1403, www.tangaratours.co, tangaratours@gmail.com, COP$80,000 pp) is a mountain paradise, up high at an elevation of 1,700 meters, where you don't have to be a bird enthusiast to enjoy the crisp mountain air and natural beauty of the sierra—but if you are, this a great place to be.

It's near the El Dorado bird-watching reserve. Accommodations here are basic, but comfortable.

Food

There are a handful of good eateries in Minca, mostly catering to international travelers. Hotels and hostels are always a reliable and reasonably priced option for guests and non-guests alike. They are open every day with lunch hours generally noon-3pm and dinner 6pm-10pm. Main dishes rarely cost more than COP$20,000. Standouts include **Hostal Casa Loma** (50 m above the church, cell tel. 313/808-6134 or 321/224-6632, www.casalomaminca.com), **El Mirador Hotel** (200 m from town entrance, cell tel. 311/671-3456 or 318/368-1611, www.miradorminca.wordpress.com), and **Rancho de la Luna** (300 m from town entrance near casino area, tel. 5/422-3160, cell tel. 317/249-7127, www.ranchodelalunaenminca.com).

Towards the church from the town entrance is **Hola from La Sierra Café** (town center, cell tel. 310/703-2870, holafromlasierracafe@gmail.com, 9am-9pm Wed.-Sun.). This friendly hippie-ish spot serves light and healthy meals, including breakfasts (pancakes!). They bake bread daily and also sell locally produced organic coffee and other products.

Bururake Fusion (town center, noon-3pm and 7pm-10pm Wed.-Sun., COP$18,000) has a daily menu and offers a little of everything: hamburgers, pastas, vegetarian dishes, and refreshing fruit juices. If you have the munchies after that morning hike, look for **Empanadas Don Luis** (no phone, 9am-7pm daily). They're the best.

Dining at **◖ Ei Mox Muica** (300 m from town entrance, cell tel. 311/699-6718, 10am-9pm daily, COP$18,000) is like being invited to a friend's house. They only have two tables, candlelit at night, and these overlook a lush garden. The menu includes a variety of pastas, salads, crêpes, and wines. Andrea's specialty is cooking while Andrés is a woodcarver. With his father, accomplished painter and sculptor Manuel Bohorquez, he organizes woodcarving and ceramics workshops for visiting artists.

Contact Andrés in advance for information at andresescultor@hotmail.com.

Information and Services

Bring plenty of cash with you to Minca: There are no ATMs here. There is a small **tourist information stand** (near police station, cell tel. 317/308-5270, 10am-6pm daily). It's run by the tour agency **Jungle Joe's** (www.junglejoeminca.com).

Getting There and Around

Minca is easily reached from Santa Marta. *Taxis colectivos* (shared taxis) depart on a regular basis from the market at Calle 11 and Carrera 12. These cost COP$7,000. Private taxis from the airport cost around COP$50,000 and taxis from the Centro cost COP$40,000.

◖ PARQUE NACIONAL NATURAL TAYRONA

Perhaps the best known national park in Colombia, the **Parque Nacional Natural Tayrona** (PNN Tayrona, 34 km northeast of Santa Marta on the Troncal del Caribe highway, tel. 5/421-1732, www.aviaturecoturismo.com or www.parquesnacionales.gov.co, 8am-5pm daily, COP$37,500 non-Colombian, COP$14,000 Colombian resident, COP$7,500 children, COP$7,500 students under age 25 with a valid ID) encompasses gorgeous beaches, tropical rainforests, and archaeological sites.

The park extends over 12,000 hectares (30,000 acres) of land from the edge of Taganga to the southwest to the Río Piedras on the east. The southern border of the park is the Troncal del Caribe highway and to the north is the Caribbean Sea. To the east and south of the PNN Tayrona is the PNN Sierra Nevada de Santa Marta, a much larger national park.

The frequently tempestuous waters of the PNN Tayrona provide dramatic scenery, with palms growing atop massive island boulders, waves crashing up against them. There are more than 30 golden sand beaches in the park that are set dramatically against a seemingly vertical wall of jungle. Although you can't see them from the park, the snow-covered peaks of

© ANDREW DIER

wild horses on the beach at the Parque Nacional Natural Tayrona

the Sierra Nevada de Santa Marta mountains are only 42 kilometers from the coast.

The park includes significant extensions of highly endangered dry tropical forests, mostly in the western section of the park. You will notice that these forests are much less dense than the humid tropical forests. At higher elevations you will see magnificent cloud forests. In addition to beaches, the coast includes marine estuaries and mangroves. The park includes streams with chilly waters that flow from high in the sierra: In the western part of the park, many of these run dry during the dry season, while in the eastern sector they have water year-round.

The forest in Parque Nacional Natural Tayrona is alive with plant and animal life. Over 1,300 plant, 396 bird, and 99 mammal species have been identified here. Four species of monkeys live in the park, and they can often be spotted. Five species of wild cats have been identified in the park. These are the margay, jaguar, ocelot, panther, and jaguarundi. Their numbers are few and these great cats are expert at hiding in the jungle: Don't count on stumbling across them during your visit! Other mammals include sloths, anteaters, armadillos, deer, and 40 types of bats. Birds include migratory and resident species, including the rare blue-billed curassow (locally called El Paujil), a threatened bird that lives in the cloud forest.

PLANNING YOUR TIME

There are two rainy seasons: April-June and September-November, with the latter more intense. During these times, trails can be extremely muddy. If at all possible, avoid visiting the PNN Tayrona during the high seasons mid-December through mid-January and Semana Santa, and to a lesser extent during the Colombian summer school holidays from mid-June until mid-July. During holidays the park is swarmed with visitors. Long holiday weekends (*puentes*) are also quite busy here, regular weekends less so, but during the week is by far the best. While many visit the park on day-trips from Santa Marta, spending one or two nights in the park is recommended, even though accommodations and food are expensive.

Recreation

BEACHES

The beaches in Parque Nacional Natural Tayrona are spectacular, but while the water may appear inviting, currents are deceivingly strong, and, despite the warnings posted on the beach, many people have drowned here. Of the park's 34 beaches, there are only 6 where you are allowed to swim. There are no lifeguards on duty in the park, and no specific hours for swimming. The best swimming beach is **La Piscina,** which is between the beaches of Arrecifes and Cabo San Juan (where you can also take a dip). To the west of Cabo San Juan is a clothing-optional beach. La Piscina is an inviting cove with crystal-clear waters. A natural rock barrier in the water keeps the waters always calm. It's a 20-minute walk west from Arrecifes.

Some of the other beaches open to swimming are in the less-visited western part of the park. **Playa Neguanje** is accessed by car or taxi (COP$15,000 from Santa Marta) through the Zalangana entrance (12 km northeast of Santa Marta). **Playa del Muerto** (Playa Cristal) is another recommended beach in the same area. It is over 20 kilometers from the entrance to the beach. You can visit some of the beaches on the western end of the park all the way to Cabo San Juan by boat from Taganga, but park staff prefer for visitors to enter the park by land. The waters can also be quite rough, especially between December and February.

HIKING

A highlight of any visit to the PNN Tayrona is the trek up to **El Pueblito** (also called Chairama, 3 km, 1.5 hrs. one way), which consists of ruins of what was an important Tayrona settlement. (Unless, that is, you have already visited the more impressive Ciudad Perdida site.) Here there are well-preserved remnants of terraces, and a small Kogi community still lives near the site. The somewhat challenging path through the tropical jungle is steep and the stone steps can be slippery, but it's well worth it. Hikers can go up to El Pueblito without a guide. El Pueblito is usually accessed from within Tayrona by walking west along the beach from the Arrecifes area. It can also be accessed from the main highway, the Troncal del Caribe.

At about 24 kilometers northeast of Santa Marta, ask to be let off at the Calabazo entrance to the park. It's about a 2.5-hour trek from there. It's not necessary, but if you'd like you can hire a guide to lead you to El Pueblito. Inquire about this when you check in.

Accommodations and Food

There are numerous lodging options in the PNN Tayrona for every budget, from the high-end Ecohabs to camping. The travel agency **Aviatur** (Bogotá office Av. 19 No. 4-62, tel. 1/587-5181 or 1/587-5182, www.aviaturecoturismo.com) manages most all lodging facilities in the park. Neither the Ecohabs nor the cabanas could be considered a bargain, but the Ecohabs, where you can awake to a beautiful view of the sea, are indeed special, and worth one or two nights. The cabanas are set back from the beach but are quite comfortable too.

The **Ecohabs** (COP$448,000 pp all meals incl.), in the Cañaveral sector, consist of 14 private *bohíos* (thatched-roof cabins) that, from a distance, look like giant nests amidst the trees. Really they are modeled after the thatched-roof houses of the Tayrona people. They sleep 2-4 persons. There are two floors to the Ecohabs. On the first floor is the bathroom and an open-air social area. On the second floor is the bedroom. A flashlight is necessary if you need to go to the bathroom in the middle of the night, as you have to go outside and downstairs. This is inconvenient for some.

In nearby Arrecifes, there are six two-story **cabanas** (12 rooms, COP$365,650 pp all meals incl.) with a capacity of four persons each. These are like jungle duplexes. The two units are divided by thin walls. There is also a **hammock area** (COP$23,000 pp) in Arrecifes with a capacity of 60 hammocks. For those choosing this option, there are lockers and you can lock things in the safety box at the lobby area.

There are **campgrounds** (COP$15,000 pp) in both Cañaveral and Arrecifes and also at Cabo San Juan, which is a 15-minute walk to the west from the beach at La Piscina. It tends to get very crowded, bordering on unpleasant, during long weekends and holidays.

Safety boxes are included in all rooms, and can be provided to campers as well. That said, some prefer to leave a bag or valuables at a trusted hotel in Santa Marta.

The park has two restaurants in Cañaveral, close to the Ecohabs, and in Arrecifes near the cabanas. They are open every day 7am-9pm, and the specialty here is fresh seafood. Expect to pay around COP$30,000 for a lunch or dinner entrée. There are some snack bars in the park as well.

Getting There and Around

From Santa Marta you can take any bus eastbound along the Troncal del Caribe to the main entrance (Zaino Gate). *Colectivo* buses can be caught at the intersection of Carrera 11 and Calle 11 (the market) in Santa Marta, and the trip takes about an hour and costs under COP$5,000. You can also take a cab for about COP$60,000.

There is usually an extremely thorough inspection of backpacks and bags upon entering the park. Visitors are not allowed to bring in plastic bags (to protect sea turtles) and no alcohol (although it is served at restaurants and snack bars in the park). Be sure to bring bug repellent, a flashlight, and good hiking boots.

At the administrative offices, visitors pay entrance fees. These fees are not included in the Aviatur package prices. Although technically park visitors are supposed to carry proof of a yellow fever vaccination, this is rarely, if ever, checked.

It's about four kilometers from the offices to Cañaveral, and vans make this route on an ongoing basis (COP$2,000). From there it is a sweaty 45 more minutes on foot through the jungle to Arrecifes. Mules can be hired to carry your bags, or you can rent a horse for COP$20,000.

PNN TAYRONA TO PALOMINO

If you prefer less civilization and more tranquility, the coast between PNN Tayrona and Palomino has some interesting places to hang your *sombrero vueltiao* (Colombian hat) for a few days. Between these two very popular tourist destinations, there are beaches that are rather overlooked by the masses. Day trips to PNN Tayrona can be easily coordinated from this area.

Impossibly placed upon giant beach boulders, the guesthouse **Finca Barlovento** (Playa Los Naranjos to the east of PNN Tayrona, Bogotá tel. 1/325-6998, www.fincabarloventosantamarta.com, COP$400,000 d incl. 2 meals) is located between the sea and the Río Piedras. It's an amazing place to stay, and the food's good, too. There are just three rooms and one more luxurious cabin here. Jungle excursions can be arranged by the hotel, but you'll want to enjoy some beachside afternoons. You'll have the beach to yourself.

Self-described as "chilled out," **Costeño Beach Surf Camp and Ecolodge** (Playa Los Naranjos, cell tel. 310/368-1191, www.costenosurf.com, COP$30,000 dorm, COP$80,000 d) gets exceptionally high marks from its guests for its laid-backness. And while you don't have to be a surfer or skater to fit in here, it doesn't hurt either. Boards are rented for COP$30,000 per day, and classes cost COP$25,000. Costeño Beach has both dorm and private accommodations on this former coconut farm. It's also solar powered.

Playa Koralia (48 km east of Santa Marta, cell tel. 310/642-2574 or cell tel. 317/510-2289, www.koralia.com, COP$209,000 d) is a beachchic hotel on the beach just east of the Parque Nacional Natural Tayrona. It's rustic: There is no electricity. Candlelit meals (always vegetarian-friendly), star-gazing, an evening drink by the bonfire, and a little spa time are Playa Koralia's recipe for peace.

PALOMINO

Swaying coconut palms and uncrowded beaches: That's what the Caribbean is all about, isn't it? And at Palomino that's exactly what you get. This town on the Troncal del Caribe is just across the border in the La Guajira department. And it's become quite a popular destination, particularly with backpackers. Caribbean currents can be frustratingly strong here, but the cool waters of the nearby Río Palomino flowing down from the Sierra Nevada de Santa Marta are always refreshing and much more hospitable towards visitors. Palomino is a good stop to make between Santa Marta and desert adventures in the Alta Guajira.

Recreation

Recreational activities in and around Palomino include easy day trip walks to the Río Palomino, about an hour away, where there is also tubing. This river forms the eastern border of the town. Also in the area are the fantastic jungle waterfalls at **Quebrada Valencia** (between PNN Tayrona and Palomino). All hotels and hostels organize these easy excursions. Samarian families visit these swimming holes to cool off on the weekends.

Chajaka (office on the south side of the main coastal highway, cell tel. 313/583-3288) offers interesting day trips or multi-day hiking trips (COP$120,000) into the Sierra Nevada to visit Kogui communities and experience the jungle.

Shivalila Yoga (La Sirena hostel, cell tel. 321/450-7359, yogashivalila@gmail.com, COP$15,000 class) offers yoga classes at the crunchy La Sirena hostel on the beach. Inquire at the hostel for the weekly schedule.

Accommodations and Food

Palomino is well on its way to dethroning Taganga as the deluxe backpacker resort. That's thanks largely to one famous hostel: **The Dreamer** (Palomino, cell tel. 300/609-7229, www.thedreamerhostel.com, COP$29,000 dorm, COP$110,000 d). This is by far the most social option this side of Santa Marta. Dorm and private accommodations are in *malokas* (cabins) surrounding an always-happening pool area and outdoor snack bar.

Next door to The Dreamer is **Cabañas San Sebastián** (Palomino, cell tel. 300/432-7170 or

cell tell. 310/775-4630, www.sansebastianpalomino.com.co, COP$30,000 pp). It consists of two cabins and three rooms for rent, just a few meters from the beach.

Don't miss the excellent juice stand at the beach in front of The Dreamer, where friendly Alejandro even has his own organic chocolate for sale.

At the **Hotel Hukumeizi** (Palomino, cell tel. 315/354-7871 or 317/566-7922, www.turismoguajira.com, info@hukumeizi.com, COP$250,000 pp all meals) there are 16 cute, round *bohíos* (bungalows) with a restaurant in the center. If you go during the week, you'll probably have the place to yourselves, but service may be less attentive. From here it's about a 15-minute walk along the beach to the Río San Salvador and about an hour from the Río Palomino.

El Matuy (Donde Tuchi) (Palomino, cell tel. 315/751-8456, www.elmatuy.com, COP$180,000 pp including meals) is a privately owned nature reserve with 10 cabins amid the palms and no electricity (this means candlelight evenings and no credit card machine). Hotel staff can help organize horseback riding or other activities. Food is varied, yet portions are not extremely generous.

On the Troncal del Caribe, the **Hostal Mochileros Culturart** (Cl. 1B No. 4-25, cell tel. 312/626-6934) is a cultural center for Palomino, where there are often musical performances and other events in the evenings. There is a restaurant here with fine veggie burgers and refreshing juices, and, as the name suggests, there are rooms available at this hostel.

Getting There and Around

There is regular bus transportation along the Troncal del Caribe between Santa Marta and Riohacha. Take a bus bound for Palomino from Santa Marta at the market on Carrera 11 and Calle 11. It's about a two-hour trip. It costs COP$10,000. On the highway where the bus drops you off, there are young men on motorbikes who will take you to your hotel (COP$3,000) on the beach.

PARQUE NACIONAL NATURAL SIERRA NEVADA DE SANTA MARTA

Encompassing almost the entire Sierra Nevada mountain range is the **Parque Nacional Natural Sierra Nevada de Santa Marta** (www. parquesnacionales.gov.co). This park has a total area of 383,000 hectares (945,000 acres), making it one of the larger parks in Colombia.

The main attraction is the **Ciudad Perdida (Lost City)**, the most important archaeological site of the Tayrona, the pre-Columbian civilization that inhabited the Sierra Nevada. The Tayrona had a highly urbanized society, with towns that included temples and ceremonial plazas built on stone terraces. There are an estimated 200 Tayrona sites, but Ciudad Perdida is the largest and best known. Many of these towns, including Pueblito (in the Parque Nacional Natural Tayrona), were occupied at the time of the Spanish conquest. Today, an estimated 30,000 indigenous people who are descendants of the Tayronas, including the Kogis, Arhuacos, Kankuamos, and Wiwas, live on the slopes and valleys of the Sierra Nevada de Santa Marta. These people believe that the Sierra Nevada is the center of the universe and that the mountain's health controls the entire Earth's well-being. Many areas of the sierra are sacred sites to these people and are barred to outsiders.

The Sierra Nevada de Santa Marta mountain range is best described as a giant pyramid, which is bordered on the north by the Caribbean and on the southeast and southwest by the plains of northern Colombia. Although some believe that the range is a distant extension of the Cordillera Oriental (Eastern Mountain Range) of the Andes, most geologists believe it is a completely independent mountain system.

It is the world's highest coastal mountain range, with the twin peaks of **Pico Cristóbal Colón** and **Pico Bolívar** (the two are called **Chinundúa** by indigenous groups in the area) reaching 5,776 meters (18,950 feet; Colón is said to be slightly higher than Bolívar) but located only 42 kilometers from the sea. Pico Cristóbal Colón is the world's fifth most prominent mountain after Mount Everest (Nepal/Tibet, China), Mount Aconcagua (Argentina), Mount McKinley (U.S.), and Mount Kilimanjaro (Tanzania). In addition, there are seven other snow-covered peaks that surpass 5,000 meters: Simonds, La Reina, Ojeda, Los Nevaditos, El Guardián, Tulio Ospina, and Codazzi. Treks to these peaks used to be possible from the northern side of the mountains, starting at the Arhuaco indigenous village of Nabusimake (Cesar), but are no longer permitted by the indigenous communities.

The PNN Sierra Nevada de Santa Marta encompasses the entire mountain range above 600 meters (16,400 feet). In addition, a small segment of the park east of the PNN Tayrona, from the Río Don Diego to the Río Palomino, extends to sea level. This means that the park encompasses the entire range of tropical ecosystems in Colombia, from low-lying tropical forests (sea level to 1,000 meters), cloud forests (1,000-2,300 meters), high mountain Andean forest (2,300-3,500 meters), *páramo* (highland moor, 3,500-4,500 meters), super *páramo* (4,500-5,000 meters), and glaciers (above 5,000 meters). However, because access to the upper reaches of the park is limited, what visitors will most be able to appreciate is low-lying tropical and cloud forest.

The isolation of the range has made it an island of biodiversity, with many plant and animal species found nowhere else. The Sierra Nevada de Santa Marta is home to 187 mammal species, including giant anteaters, spider monkeys, peccaries, tree rats, jaguars, and pumas. There are 46 species of amphibians and reptiles, including several that live above 3,000 meters that are found nowhere else on the planet. There are an astonishing 628 bird species, including the Andean condor, blue-knobbed curassow, sapphire-bellied hummingbird, and black-solitary eagle, as well as many endemic species. There are at least 71 species of migratory birds that travel between Colombia and North America.

the mystical Ciudad Perdida

COURTESY OF JAY SPELLER, CASA LOMA IN MINCA

CARTAGENA

❰ Ciudad Perdida Trek

A highlight for many visitors to Colombia is the four- to six-day, 52-kilometer (32-mile) round-trip trek to the **Ciudad Perdida (Lost City)** in the Sierra Nevada mountains of the Caribbean coast. The Ciudad Perdida is within the confines of the Parque Nacional Natural Sierra Nevada de Santa Marta.

The Ciudad Perdida, called Teyuna by local indigenous tribes and Buritaca 200 by archaeologists, was a settlement of the Tayrona, forebears of the people who inhabit the Sierra Nevada today. It was probably built starting around AD 700, at least 600 years before Machu Picchu. There is some disagreement as to when it was abandoned: There is evidence of human settlement until the 16th century. The site was visited in the early 1970s by *guaqueros* (treasure hunters) who pillaged the site. News of its discovery in 1976 marked one of the most important archaeological events of recent years. From 1976 to 1982, archaeologists from the Colombian National Institute of History and Anthropology painstakingly restored the site.

Spread over some 35 hectares (86 acres), the settlement consists of 169 circular terraces atop a mountain in the middle of dense cloud forest. Archaeologists believe that this sophisticated terrace system was created in part to control the flow of water in this area known for torrential rainfall for much of the year.

Plazas, temples, and dwellings for tribal leaders were built on the terraces in addition to an estimated 1,000 *bohíos* (traditional thatched roof huts), which housed between 1,400 and 3,000 people. A fire was always at the center of the *bohío,* and there was a domestic area where food and water were stored and cooking took place, as well as an artisan area for goldsmithing.

Surrounding the Ciudad Perdida were farms of coca, tobacco, pumpkin, and fruit trees. The city was connected to other settlements via an intricate system of mostly stone paths.

The hike is, by and large, uphill, as you reach an elevation of 1,100 meters (3,600 feet). There are nearly 20 river crossings to be made. Towards the end of the third day, you will climb about 1,200 often treacherously slippery stone steps until you reach the spectacular terraces of Ciudad Perdida. For many this sight makes all the sweat, fatigue, and mosquito bites worthwhile.

There is one set fee (COP$600,000) for the trek. This does not change, no matter if you're making the trek in three, four, or five days. If you are in very good shape and prefer taking the Ciudad Perdida express route, the trek can be done in three nights and four days. This requires six hours hiking per day and rising early. For some, the long nights of card playing at campsites can get old quick; others enjoy the camaraderie with hikers from all over the world. In case of an emergency on the mountain, a burro or helicopter will be sent to retrieve the hiker, for a fee.

It's important to only go with a reputable tour company, such as **Magic Tour** (Cl. 16 No. 4-41, Santa Marta, tel. 5/421-5820; Cl. 14 No. 1B-50, Taganga, tel. 5/421-9429; www.magictourcolombia.com) or **TurCol** (Cl. 13 No. 3-13, Centro Comercial San Francisco Plaza, Local 115, Santa Marta; Cl. 19 No. 5-40, Taganga, tel. 5/421-2556; www.turcol.com or www.buritaca200.com). A third option is **Baquianos Tour** (Cl. 10C No. 1C-59, Santa Marta, tel. 5/431-9667, www.lostcitybaquianos.com). Your tour company will provide food (advise in advance if you have special dietary needs or wants), hammocks or cots with mosquito netting, and mules to carry up supplies.

You'll need to bring a small to medium-sized backpack, enough to carry a few days of clothes, good hiking boots with strong ankle support, sandals for stream crossings (keeping your boots dry), long pants, mosquito repellent, water purifying tablets, sunscreen, cash for refreshments to purchase along the way, a small towel, toilet paper, hand sanitizer, flashlight, sealable bags to keep things dry, light rain jacket, and a water container. If you have them, trekking poles may be a nice addition. Sleeping bags may provide more comfort at night but aren't necessary.

From mid-December through mid-January you'll have plenty of company along the way: It's high tourist season. Other high seasons are during Semana Santa and June-July. The wettest months tend to be April-May and September-November. Expect a daily downpour and doable, but sometimes rather treacherous, river crossings during those times of the year. When it's raining or has been raining, the trek is more challenging. On the plus side, there are usually fewer crowds on the mountain at that time.

Campsites along the way turn into backpacker villages during high seasons, but they never turn in to rowdy scenes by any means. Upon arrival the routine is fairly standard. You'll often be able to cool off in the pristine waters of nearby swimming holes, have dinner, and hit the hammocks. Sleeping in hammocks can be uncomfortable for those not used to them. Earplugs come in handy for light sleepers.

The trek begins at the settlement of Mamey on the Río Buritaca. Along the way you will no doubt come in contact with Kogi people who live in the Sierra Nevada, and will pass through the village of Mutanyi. These lands are theirs and visitors are encouraged to refrain from taking photographs of them without prior permission. One of the most popular tourist activities in Colombia, the trek is considered quite safe.

Estación San Lorenzo

Deeper and higher into the Sierra Nevada de Santa Marta from the town of Minca and set amid pristine cloud forest is the **Estación San Lorenzo** (Santa Marta parks office, Cl. 17 No. 4-06, tel. 5/423-0752 or 5/421-3805, sierranevada@parquesnacionales.gov.co, 8am-noon and 2pm-6pm Mon.-Fri.; Bogotá parks office, tel. 1/353-2400, www.parquesnacionales.gov. co), part of the Parque Nacional Natural Sierra Nevada de Santa Marta. At this spot at 2,200 meters (7,200 feet) in the Sierra Nevada, visitors can make guided walks through the cloud forest to see birds and enjoy views of the snow-covered peaks in the park. The two cabins (COP$25,000-35,000 pp) of San Lorenzo are wonderfully isolated amid the forest.

A stay here can be an inexpensive way to get

to know the Sierra Nevada, but there are many hoops you must go through to arrange it. First you must contact the parks office, preferably in Santa Marta, to inquire about availability. Then you will be required to make a *consignación* (deposit) to their bank account to cover the cost of your stay. This involves filling out a deposit form and standing in line at their bank (Banco de Bogotá).

The easiest way to get to San Lorenzo is by *mototaxi* from Minca, and this can cost around COP$50,000. Alternatively, and if you are traveling in a small group, it may make sense to arrange transportation with an SUV, which can cost up to COP$250,000.

Accommodations are basic here, and there are just two cabins, each with three rooms holding six beds each, for a total capacity of 36. No meals are provided here, but there is a rustic kitchen facility with basic utensils and cooking implements. You will have to provide your own propane gas canister (readily available in Santa Marta) and all your food for cooking. The temperature drops significantly in the evening, thus it is important to bring warm clothes. There is a fireplace in both cabins.

La Guajira

The vast Guajira Peninsula has some of the most rugged, beautiful landscapes in Colombia. It is home to the Wayúu indigenous people, who have maintained their independent way of life through centuries. Though many Wayúu now live in cities and towns, their traditional *rancherías* (settlements) dot the desert. With the growth of tourism, many have set up lodging using traditional *ranchería* houses made out of *yotojoro,* the dried hearts of cactus plants.

The Colombian side of the peninsula (Venezuela shares the other part) can be divided into three sections. The Baja Guajira (Lower Guajira), near the Sierra Nevada de Santa Marta, is fertile agricultural and cattle-ranching land. The much more arid middle swath, with the departmental capital of Riohacha and the unlovely towns of Uribia and Maicao, is home to the majority of the population. The Alta Guajira (Upper Guajira), from Cabo de la Vela to Punta Gallinas, is sparsely populated and has some truly otherworldly landscapes. Focus your visit on this last part.

Lack of infrastructure, especially in the north, makes visiting the Guajira a challenge, so most people opt for organized tours. Though it is possible to get to Cabo de la Vela on public transportation, do not travel elsewhere in the Alta Guajira without a dependable local guide. The roads are unmarked tracks in the sand, and getting lost is inevitable. More urgently, in this somewhat lawless place, where the Colombian government has limited authority, there are unscrupulous people ready to prey on unsuspecting visitors.

During the rainy months September to November, it can be difficult to travel through the desert, which can become muddy to the point of impassable.

History

Spanish navigator Juan de la Cosa, who was a member of Columbus's first three voyages, disembarked in Cabo de la Vela in 1499, making the Guajira Peninsula one of the first places visited by Europeans in South America. It was not until 1535 that explorer Fernando de Enciso founded a settlement near Cabo de la Vela, which became a center of pearl extraction. This early settlement was relocated to Riohacha, which was founded in 1544. The traditional Wayúu inhabitants of the peninsula put up strong resistance to Spanish advances. During the 19th and 20th centuries, the peninsula was used primarily as a smuggling route.

For better or for worse, the fortunes of the Guajira changed in 1975 when the Colombian government entered into an agreement with oil giant Exxon to develop the Cerrejón open-pit coal mine 80 kilometers (50 miles) southeast of

LA GUAJIRA

Riohacha. This project involved the construction of Puerto Bolívar, a coal port located in Bahía Portete, and of a railway to transport the coal. Production started in 1985. Coal has since become one of Colombia's main exports. The mine has generated more than US$2 billion in royalties for the Colombian government. Little of this wealth has trickled down to the people of La Guajira. It is the fourth poorest department in Colombia.

RIOHACHA

Called Süchiimma in the Wayúu language, meaning "city of the river," Riohacha (pop. 231,000) is La Guajira's slow-paced departmental capital. It is one of the oldest cities in Colombia. Not a tourist destination itself, Riohacha is an excellent base from which to launch tours of Alta Guajira.

Sights

Along Calle 1, also known as Avenida Marina,

is the **Paseo de la Playa** boardwalk, where locals and tourists take their evening strolls and take in the sea air. Along the way are kiosks where vendors sell ceviches and Wayúu women set up their brightly colored *mochilas* (traditional woven handbags) on the sidewalk, nonchalantly waiting for customers. The kilometer-long pier known as the **Muelle Turístico** is another favorite place for a walk. There are no railings, so maybe those who have had a couple of drinks should sit this one out.

Parque Padilla (Cl. 2 and Cra. 7), Riohacha's shady main plaza, is named after favorite son Admiral José Prudencio Padilla, who was the most prominent Afro-Colombian commander in the revolutionary wars. To one side of the plaza is the only remnant of colonial Riohacha, the heavily reconstructed **Catedral de Nuestra Señora de los Remedios** (Cl. 2 No. 7-13, tel. 5/727-2442, masses 6:30am and 7pm Mon.-Sat., 7am, 11am, and 7pm Sun.),

the endless deserts of La Guajira

originally erected in the 16th century. The remains of Padilla repose there.

On the Riohacha-Maicao road just outside of town is the **Sendero Eco-Cultural El Riíto** (no phone, 7am-6pm daily), a pleasant nature walk where you can observe birds that was completed in 2013. This is a great place to stretch your legs before or after a long and bumpy ride through the desert.

Accommodations and Food
Riohacha isn't known for fantastic lodging or dining, but then again you will probably be spending limited time here.

The **Hotel Castillo del Mar** (Cra. 9A No. 15-352, tel. 5/727-5043, cell tel. 316/525-1295, hotelcastillodelmar@gmail.com, COP$25,000 dorm, COP$100,000 d) is about a 10-minute walk from the boardwalk in a quiet residential area. It's the choice of backpackers. There are 11 rooms, some with air conditioning, some without. It could be more comfortable, but for the price it's a bargain.

Closer to downtown, the **Hotel Arimaca**

(Cl. 1 Av. La Marina No. 8-75, tel. 5/727-3515, www.hotelarimaca.com, COP$130,000 d) will do for a night. It has 50 rooms and caters to the business crowd during the week. **Oceano** (Cra. 15 No. 9-21, tel. 5/728-1108, www.oceano-hotel.co, COP$140,000 d) has 15 rooms and is a couple of blocks from the boardwalk.

Taroa Lifestyle Hotel (Cl. 1 No. 4-77, tel. 5/729-1122, www.taroahotel.com, COP$200,000) is the first so-called "Wayúu lifestyle hotel" in Colombia, and it opened in July 2013. It is only about half an hour to the northeast. It's on the beach and has 46 rooms.

There are several seafood restaurants along Avenida Marina. Try the **Casa del Marisco** (Cl. 1 4-43, tel. 5/728-3445, 10am-10pm daily, COP$25,000), a restaurant that serves an array of fresh seafood dishes and pastas.

For for a wider range of dishes, try **Sazón Internacional** (Cl. 1 No. 3-57, tel. 5/728-0415, noon-10pm Tues.-Sun.). For something quick go to the food court of the modern **Centro Comercial Suchiimma** (Cl. 15 No. 8-56, 10am-9pm daily). There are some vegetarian options available here, and at the Jumbo store, you can pick up all the provisions you need for a long ride through the desert.

Getting There and Around

Aeropuerto Almirante Padilla (Cl. 29B No. 15-217, tel. 5/727-3854) is five minutes north of town. There are only one or two flights per day from Bogotá to Riohacha on **Avianca** (ticket office Cl. 7 No. 7-04, tel. 5/727-3624, www. avianca.com, 8am-6pm Mon.-Fri., 9am-1pm Sat.). On Tuesdays and Saturdays, **Tiara Air Aruba** (Cl. 2 No. 6-64, Local 2, tel. 5/727-3737, www.tiara-air.com, 8am-noon and 2pm-6pm Mon.-Fri.) operates flights between Riohacha and Aruba, with connections to and from Fort Lauderdale.

The **bus station** (Av. El Progreso and Cl. 11) has frequent services to Maicao, Santa Marta, and Barranquilla. There are also services to Valledupar, Cartagena, and Bogotá. Shared taxis to Uribia, where you can pick up trucks to Cabo de la Vela, leave from Calle 15 and Carrera 1.

The center of town, along the boardwalk, is easily walkable.

BORDER CROSSING

For stays under 90 days, U.S., Canadian, and most European citizens do not require a visa to enter Venezuela. You may be required to show proof of a hotel reservation and proof of an air ticket departing from Venezuela, and your passport must not expire within six months of entry into Venezuela. There is a Venezuelan consulate in Riohacha for further queries: **Consulado de Venezuela** (Cra. 7 No. 3-08, Edificio El Ejecutivo, Piso 2, tel. 5/727-4076, 8am-noon and 2pm-5pm Mon.-Thurs., 8am-1pm Fri.). There is an entry point to Venezuela at the town of Maicao.

SANTUARIO DE FAUNA Y FLORA LOS FLAMENCOS

Any day you see a pink flamingo is a good day. That's enough of a reason to visit the **Santuario de Fauna y Flora Los Flamencos** (Camarones, cell tel. 301/675-3862 or 313/514-0366, ecoturismosantuario@gmail.com, www.parquesnacionales.gov.co, free). This park is 25 kilometers southwest of Riohacha and is home to thousands of *Phoenicopterus ruber ruber* or American flamingos. The 700-hectare sanctuary, which is part of the national park system, encompasses a magnificent coastal estuary where the flamingo fish for shrimp in the shallow waters.

To get there, you can take a bus from Riohacha going towards Camarones or points southwest. From Camarones take a *mototaxi* to the entrance of the park (COP$2,000). To see the flamingos up close, take a *chalupa* (wooden boat) onto the lagoon (COP$15,000 for two people). To avoid the glaring sun, visit the park early in the morning or late in the afternoon.

At the **Centro de Visitantes Los Mangles** (cell tel. 301/675-3862 or 313/514-0366, ecoturismosantuario@gmail.com, COP$100,000 meals and tours) there are five tiny yet spic and span cabins that can be rented, and there is an area for sleeping in *chinchoros* (large hammocks; COP$20,000). These are located between the bay and the sea. In addition to the flamingos, the beach at the park is quite nice and you can take an excursion through the mangroves. It's a charming place, and is a good option if you'd prefer not to stay in Riohacha.

◖ ALTA GUAJIRA

The **Alta Guajira** (Upper Guajira) comprises the entire peninsula east of Cabo de la Vela and Uribia. It is very sparsely populated: The three largest settlements, where most of the tourism infrastructure is located, are Cabo de la Vela, Punta Gallinas at the very northern tip, and Nazareth, in the northeast. The terrain has a striking ochre color, with rocky and sandy patches. The vegetation is mostly shrubs and cacti. The Caribbean coast here is broken by three large bays with stunning turquoise and aquamarine waters: Bahía Portete, Bahía Honda, and Bahía Hondita. The last of these is easily accessible to tourists in day trips from Punta Gallinas. There are a few low mountain ranges, including the Serranía de la Macuira

(864 meters/2,835 feet), located in the extreme northeastern corner of the peninsula, but overall the terrain is low and slightly undulated.

The only destination in the Alta Guajira that is accessible by public transportation is Cabo de la Vela. Though it is possible to contract transportation by land or sea to Punta Gallinas, most visitors opt to visit the region in an easily organized tour.

The sands of Alta Guajira are a favorite location for raucous 4x4 races and competitions. A large annual event is the **Rally Aventura Guajira** (www.ruedalibrexcolombia.net), which takes place in August, when more than 200 vehicles trek across the desert from Riohacha to Cabo de la Vela. If this isn't your bag you may want to double-check your dates of travel to make sure they don't coincide with the event.

Tours

The standard Alta Guajira tour involves going to Cabo de la Vela on day one, with a stop at the now-abandoned salt mines of the Salinas de Manaure (not worth a visit), spending the night at Cabo de la Vela, continuing on the next day to Punta Gallinas, and returning to Riohacha on day three (COP$340,000-380,000 per person, including food and lodging). A longer tour involves two additional nights in Nazareth to visit the Parque Natural Nacional Macuira (COP$800,000-880,000 per person, including food and lodging).

Make sure to check how many people are in your SUV, as there have been reports of tour operators who cram seven people into a vehicle, making for an uncomfortable ride. Tour guides generally have a limited grasp of English.

The most comfortable option by far is to rent an SUV with a driver for your own party. This costs around COP$400,000 per day, not including food and lodging.

The desert countryside seems endless and is beautiful in its own desolate way. You'll be amazed at how these drivers know which way to go, as there are no road signs, only cacti and occasional goats. Every once in a while, you will have to pay "tolls" to Wayúu children who have set up quasi road blocks. To gain their permission to cross, drivers hand over crackers, cookies, or candy.

TOUR COMPANIES

Tour companies offer package tours or private vehicles. A highly recommended tour company is **Expedición Guajira** (Cl. 2 No. 5-06, tel. 5/727-2336, cell tel. 311/439-4677 or 301/464-2758, franklin_penalver@yahoo.com), managed by Franklin Penalver. His guides, of Wayúu origin, know the area like the back of their hands.

Solera Travels (Cra. 9A No. 15-352, cell tel. 316/525-1295, gerenciacomercial@soleratravels.com) has an office at the Castillo de Mar hostel and sells all the regular tour packages. **Kaishi** (Plaza Principal, Uribia, cell tel. 311/429-6315, www.kaishitravel.com) is another agency that has a good reputation.

CABO DE LA VELA

Cabo de la Vela (known as Jepira in the Wayúu language), 180 kilometers north of Riohacha, is a small Wayúu fishing village spread along the Caribbean Sea. It comes as a shock—a pleasant one—after several hours driving through the arid landscape to finally arrive at the waters of the Caribbean. Here the beaches are nice, the views otherworldly, and the atmosphere peaceful. The smooth waters and ample winds provide near perfect conditions for windsurfing and kite surfing, and Cabo de la Vela has become a destination for these sports.

There are several pleasant excursions near town, and if you take an organized package tour, all of these should be included in the price. One is to **El Faro,** a lighthouse on a high promontory with spectacular nearly 360-degree views of the surrounding ocean. Another is to the **Ojo del Agua,** a small but pleasant beach near a freshwater spring. Farther afield is the **Pilón de Azúcar,** a high hill that affords incredible views to the surrounding region. Nearby is the **Playa de Pilón,** a beautiful ochre-colored beach. To the west is the **Jepirachi Wind Farm,** the first of its kind of Colombia; the turbines make for a somewhat surreal sight in the midst of this barren territory. Organized

© ANDREW DIER

Cabo de la Vela, La Guajira

tours include stops at these spots. If you are on your own, hotels can organize these excursions for you. Trips to these sights in SUVs cost around COP$15,000 per person, round-trip, with a minimum of two persons.

Recreation

Cabo de la Vela is an excellent place to practice or learn how to kite or windsurf. **Eoletto** (Ranchería Utta, cell tel. 321/468-0105 or 314/851-6216, www.windsurfingcolombia. com) is a **windsurfing and kitesurfing** school run by Etto from Germany. An eight-hour windsurfing course costs COP$380,000; kitesurfing is COP$900,000. Rentals are available for COP$50,000 per hour.

Accommodations

Family-run guesthouses are plentiful in Cabo de la Vela, and are quite rudimentary. Freshwater is always scarce here in the desert, so long showers are not an option. Floors are usually sandy, and electricity is limited. The street in Cabo de la Vela along the sea is lined with about 15 guesthouses. There are a few lodgings outside of town towards El Faro, such as Rancheria Utta.

The ❮ **Rancheria Utta** (300 m northwest of town, Vía al Faro, cell tel. 312/687-8237 or 313/817-8076, www.rancheriautta.com, COP$15,000 hammock, COP$35,000 bed pp) is a nice place to stay. It is just far enough from the village of Cabo de la Vela that you can experience the magical ambience of being far away from civilization. Cabins are simple with walls made from the hearts of *yotojoro* (cacti). That is a traditional form of construction in the desert. There are 11 *cabañas* with a total of 35 beds and plenty of inviting *chinchorros* (hammocks) for lazing about. Being on the beach at night, looking up at the stars and listening to the sound of gentle waves breaking nearby, is unforgettable. A pleasant restaurant at the hotel serves breakfast (COP$6,000), lunch (COP$15,000), and dinner (COP$15,000). The fare is mostly seafood (lobster is a favorite but will cost extra), but they can accommodate vegetarians.

The **Hospedaje Jarrinapi** (cell tel. 310/366-4245 or 311/683-4281, www.jarrinapi.com, COP$12,000 hammock, COP$35,000 pp) is a large hotel with 19 *yotojoro* cabins for a total capacity of 60 people. This hotel has electricity 24 hours a day and has a nice, orderly kitchen and restaurant. **Posada Pujurú** (cell tel. 300/279-5048, http://posadapujuru.blogspot.com, COP$20,000 hammock, COP$50,000 bed) has 14 rooms and a space for hammocks. Pujurú is next to a kite-surfing school.

Getting There

From Riohacha, shared taxis ply the route to Uribia (COP$15,000, 1 hr.). Catch these at the intersection of Calle 15 and Carrera 5. Ask the driver to drop you off at the spot where passenger trucks depart for Cabo de la Vela and intermediate *rancherías*. Trucks make this route, from Uribia to Cabo de la Vela (COP$15,000, 2 hrs. or more). These trucks depart until 2pm every day. The uncomfortable ride on a bench in the back of the truck can take several hours, depending on how many stops are made, but this is the Guajira way to go.

PUNTA GALLINAS

Punta Gallinas is a settlement on a small peninsula jutting into the Caribbean at the very northernmost tip of the South American continent. It is home to about 100 Wayúu who claim this beautiful spot as their ancestral land. The landscape here is a symphony of oranges, ochres, and browns, dotted with cactus and shrubs. The peninsula is hemmed in to the south by Bahía Hondita, a large bay with bright aquamarine waters and thin clusters of mangroves, and to the north by the deep blue Caribbean.

Activities in and around Punta Gallinas include a visit to the *faro* (lighthouse), which is the northernmost tip of South America; canoe rides in Bahía Hondita to see flamingos and mangroves; or visits to two spectacular beaches. These are the remote and unspoiled beaches at **Dunas de Taroa** (Taroa dunes), where windswept and towering sand dunes drop abruptly some 30 meters into the sea,

and at **Punta Aguja,** at the southwest tip of the peninsula of Punta Gallinas. These excursions are included in tour prices. If you are on your own, hotels charge around COP$20,000 per person to see the dunes (five-person minimum), COP$150,000 for a group boat ride on the Bahía Hondita to spy on flamingos, and COP$20,000 per person to go to Punta Aguja (five-person minimum).

There are two good lodging options in Punta Gallinas, both with splendid views of the Bahía Hondita. ❰ **Hospedaje Luzmila** (Punta Gallinas, cell tel. 312/626-8121 or 312/647-9881, COP$20,000 hammock, COP$30,000 bed pp) has 10 *cabañas* with 20 beds and is spread out alongside the bay. Breakfast (COP$5,000), lunch (COP$15,000), and dinner (COP$15,000) are served in the restaurant. Lobster dishes cost extra.

❰ **Donde Alexandra** (Punta Gallinas, cell tel. 313/512-7830 or 318/760-8501, COP$12,000-20,000 hammock, COP$30,000 bed pp) has 10 rooms and 25 beds. Meals are not included in the prices but are usually around COP$6,000 for breakfast, COP$15,000 for lunch, and COP$15,000 for dinner, unless you order lobster (COP$45,000). Donde Alexandra has sweeping vistas of the bay and beyond from the restaurant area.

Getting There

Although most travelers visit Punta Gallinas on an organized tour, it is possible to travel on your own from the Puerto de Pescadores at Puerto Bolívar on a *lancha* (boat) arranged by Hospedaje Luzmilla or Donde Alexandra (COP$100,000 pp round-trip, minimum 5 passengers). In the rainy season, from September to November, this may be the only option.

PARQUE NACIONAL NATURAL MACUIRA

The remote **Parque Nacional Natural Macuira** (PNN Macuira, 260 km northeast of Riohacha, cell tel. 311/688-2362, macuira@parquesnacionales.gov.co, 8am-6pm, free) covers an area of 25,000 hectares and encompasses the entire Serranía de la Macuira (Macuira Mountain includes 350 species of plants, 140 species of birds (17 endemic), and more than 20 species of mammals. The park is within the large Alta Guajira Wayúu Reservation. In the lower parts of the range, within the park, live many Wayúu families who raise goats and grow corn and other subsistence crops.

The gateway to the park is the Wayúu town of **Nazareth**. Visitors are required to register at the PNN Macuira Park Office, where they must hire an authorized guide (a good idea anyhow, since the trails are not marked). There are various hikes varying 1.5-6 hours, and the cost of a guided walk per group of eight ranges COP$35,000-45,000. Day hikes meander along river beds through tropical dry forest, leading to different destinations. One leads to the **Arewolü Sand Dunes,** which are, surprisingly, located in the midst of the forest. Another takes you to the **Shipanoü pools**. A third hike goes to **Cerro Tojoro,** which affords beautiful views of the coast and the mountain range. There is also a hike along the entire length of the range. If you can, plan to hike early in the morning to increase your chances of seeing birds and other wildlife. Unfortunately for visitors, hiking to the Macuira's unusual cloud forest is not permitted by the Wayúu.

There are bare-bones lodging options in town. One suitable option is **Hospedaje Vía Manaure** (entrance to town, cell tel. 314/552-5513, COP$15,000 hammock), which has a capacity of 50.

There is no public transportation to Nazareth.

© ANDREW DIER

The northernmost point in South America is Punta Gallinas.

Range), an isolated mountainous outcrop at the northeastern tip of the Guajira Peninsula. These mountains are a biological island in the middle of the surrounding desert. The Macuira range, which is 35 kilometers (22 miles) long and 864 meters (2,835 feet) at its highest point (Cerro Palua), captures moisture-laden winds from the sea that nourish a unique low-elevation tropical cloud forest teeming with ferns, orchids, bromeliads, and moss. At lower elevations, there are tropical dry forests. The park

Western Caribbean Coast

The portion of the Caribbean coast that stretches west from Cartagena, down to the Golfo de Urabá, and then juts north through the Darien Gap and the border with Panama is less visited and less familiar than the coastal region to the east. That may be just the ticket for those yearning to explore the undiscovered and escape the crowds.

The Golfo de Morrosquillo is home to the beach towns of Tolú and Coveñas, which have long been popular family getaways. Just north of the gulf, the Islas de San Bernardo are where you'll find the world's most densely populated island, tiny Santa Cruz del Islote. Other nearby attractions include the inland town of San Antero, known throughout Colombia for its Festival del Burro, and, farther southwest, the quiet and peaceful retreat Reserva Natural Viento Solar in the community of Río Cedro. This is a place to truly disconnect from the world, and it's only accessible by motorbike via a dirt path.

Across the Golfo de Urabá, the tropical rainforests of the Darien provide an exuberant backdrop to the seaside towns of Capurganá and Sapzurro, which are accessible only by boat or plane. The diving sites off the coast and toward Panama's San Blas Islands is superb.

However, what most visitors remember and cherish about a visit to this remote part of Colombia is being submerged in truly wild nature.

GOLFO DE MORROSQUILLO

Largely unknown to international visitors, the twin beach communities of **Tolú** and **Coveñas** on the Golfo de Morrosquillo are popular with vacationing Colombian families from Medellín and Montería. If you can afford it, there are several resort islands off the Caribbean coast, such as Tintipán and Múcura, where you can practically have the beach to yourself, especially during the week.

While Coveñas is mostly a long line of beachfront hotels (and an important Ecopetrol oil pipeline), neighboring Tolú to the east has an easy if run-down charm to it. Here you can get around on foot or by *bici-taxi* (bicycle cabs). On weekend evenings, action is centered in the main plaza, but on the weekend, it shifts to the boardwalk, where vendors sell ceviche, bars blast music, and kids play in the water.

One of the main weekend activities here is to take a day-trip tour of the **Islas de San Bernardo**. These always include a look at **Santa Cruz del Islote**, the most densely populated island in the world, with one person for every 10 square meters, and a stop at **Isla Murica** or **Isla Palma** for lunch and a swim. At Isla Palma, a resort run by all-inclusive operator Decameron, international tourists may be put off by the confined dolphins and other animals. Contact **Mundo Mar** (Av. 1 No. 14-40, tel. 5/288-4431, www.mundomar.com.co). Tour operators sell this package for around COP$57,000. They are located in the hotels along the boardwalk. They can also arrange trips to the Islas del Rosario closer to Cartagena.

Beaches in Tolú aren't great; beaches at Playa El Francés or to the west of Coveñas Punta Bolívar are nicer. Before a weekday visit, ask at your hotel about the security situation at these beaches. They are somewhat remote.

Accommodations
[**Villa Babilla** (Cl. 20 No. 3-40, Tolú, tel. 5/288-6124, www.villababillahostel.com, COP$70,000) is the best place to stay in Tolú by a long shot. Rooms have no TV or air conditioning. You can cook your own meals here. There is an Olimpica grocery store a couple blocks away.

The **Camino Verde** (tel. 5/288-5132, www.vacacionescaminoverde.com, COP$160,000 d, COP$240,000 d w/meals) hotel is on the Playa El Francés, a few kilometers east of Tolú, and is a peaceful spot to relax, especially during the week.

(**Punta Norte** (Tintipán, cell tel. 310/655-4851, www.hotelpuntanorte.com, COP$220,000 pp) is run by a friendly Uruguayan (Punta Norte is most often referred to as Donde El Uruguayo, or "Where's the Uruguayan?") and his artist wife. This all-inclusive hotel is on the tiny island of Tintipán. Rooms are simple and the lobsters are huge! Days are spent lounging on beaches or discovering nearby islands. Bring plenty of insect repellent should you decide to go to this remote island paradise.

For white sandy beaches, warm aquamarine waters, and the occasional calorie-loaded cocktail, go to the luxury resort of **Punta Faro** (Bogotá tel. 1/616-3136, www.puntafaro.com, COP$535,000 pp high season), an island resort in the Islas de San Bernardo. High season prices are almost double that of off season rates. There are 45 rooms on the island, ensuring that, while you won't have the island all to yourself, you won't be packed in like sardines. Most guests take a hotel boat from Cartagena, but you can also arrive via Tolú.

Getting There and Around

There is frequent bus service from both Tolú and Coveñas to Cartagena (3 hrs., COP$30,000) and Montería (2.5 hrs., COP$25,000). In addition, the airline **ADA** (Col. toll-free tel. 01/800-051-4232, www.ada-aero.com) flies from Medellín to Tolú, making this a quick, easy, and often inexpensive beach destination. Getting around Tolú? Take a *bici-taxi* (bicycle cab).

SAN ANTERO

This seaside town's claim to fame is the annual **Festival del Burro,** one of those many only-in-Colombia celebrations. There are burro races, burro costume contests (in 2013 the winning burro was dressed as the newly announced pope, who beat out a Shakira burro and a Transmiburro, a four-legged version of Bogotá's TransMilenio bus system), and parades. They even have a modern arena that hosts all the fun. The origin of the festival is

a religious one. During Semana Santa, an effigy of Judas would ride into town on a burro, and would afterwards be burned for having betrayed Christ. The festival evolved over time to be more about burros and less about Judas.

An unexpected find of undisturbed mangroves and forest awaits at the **Bahía Cispatá** nearby. An interesting project by **Asocaiman** (caimanmiranda@hotmail.com) helps in the protection and propagation of alligators and turtles. These creatures were once hunted for their meat and eggs, but today, former local hunters have been trained on the importance of protecting these species. They now work for the animals' protection. You can visit the refuge (tips are encouraged) and take a short tour led by one of the former hunters. They offer different boat tours of the mangroves, which range in cost COP$15,000-45,000. A locally run and quite friendly hotel, the **Mangle Colora'o** (Vereda Amaya, tel. 4/811-0722, cell tel. 301/203-7071, COP$35,000 pp), is just across the street.

San Antero borders the water and has some nice beaches at Playa Blanca. Here there is a long string of waterfront hotels popular with weekenders from Montería and Medellín. During the week, it's very quiet. The **Cispatá Marina Hotel** (tel. 4/811-0197 or 4/811-0887, www.cispata.com, COP$123,000 pp) has an enviable location overlooking the the Bahía Cispatá and, on the other side, the beaches of Playa Blanca. The hotel comprises 16 cute, red-roofed *cabañas* as well as smaller apartments. In addition to the bay and the sea, the hotel also has a large pool.

Go eat at **(** **Pesecar** (Bahía Cispatá, cell tel. 312/651-2651, 7am-9pm daily). It's worth the trip to San Antero just for lunch—fresh, very fresh, seafood, at this restaurant with an unbeatable bayside location.

No trip to the Caribbean coast is complete without a visit to a mud volcano. In San Antero there is a large one, where you'll be able to enjoy the therapeutic properties of the mud without bumping up against anyone. Laugh therapy is one of the many treatments available.

© ANDREW DIER

alligators at the Asocaiman conservation center, Bahía Cispatá

Reserva Natural Viento Solar

It's hard to find a place more peaceful than **Reserva Natural Viento Solar** (village of Río Cedro, cell tel. 311/312-2473, www.vientosolar. org, students and backpackers COP$20,000 no meals, COP$130,000 pp all meals incl.). This private natural reserve composed of tropical dry forest is on a mostly undeveloped Córdoba coastline near the settlement of Río Cedro, southwest of San Antero.

At this reserve extending over 200 hectares (500 acres) along the Caribbean coast, activities include kayaking, nature walks, bird-watching, swimming, and yoga. Gentle *osos perezosos* (sloths) reside in this undisturbed reserve, and you may also see howler monkeys, boa constrictors, and iguanas, as well as many species of birds. The reserve is run by a charismatic Paisa woman, Elena Posada, who is affectionately known as La Mona.

Reserva Natural Viento Solar is accessed through the town of Lorica, a fishing town on the banks of the Río Sinú. It's famous for its waterfront market. From the Tolú-Montería

highway, you can catch a shared taxi (COP$15,000) that will take you to the coastal hamlet of San Bernardo del Viento. From there, Viento Solar will arrange for a *mototaxi* (COP$10,000) to take you the rest of the way to the reserve.

MONTERÍA

The center of Montería, Colombia's cattle-ranching capital (pop. 409,000), has recently been given a facelift, and in the late afternoon or early evening, it's a pleasant place for a stroll. The Plaza de Bolívar is gorgeous and the spectacularly white **Catedral de San Jeronimo** stands prominently facing it. The **Banco de la República** (Cra. 3 No. 28-59, tel. 4/782-3382) may have an art exhibit to check out. For a pleasant walk or jog, head to the **Parque Lineal Ronda del Sinú** between the muddy Río Sinú and the Avenida Primera. This lovely park under the shade of tall trees and with a view to the river has bike and jogging paths, playgrounds, workout stations, an amphitheater, and juice stalls. This is one of the nicest urban parks in the country.

Reserva Natural Viento Solar

© ANDREW DIER

The coolest thing about Montería is the ingenious (and eco-friendly) system to cross the Río Sinú: the *planchones*. These are small ferries attached to a cable that crosses the river as the captain rows passengers across. It only costs COP$400, making it one of the top cheap thrills in all of Colombia. Even though it takes under five minutes to cross, and there's not much need to get to the other side, the *planchones* themselves almost make Montería worth a trip.

Accommodations and Food

Hotels tend to be overpriced in Montería. The **Hotel Casa Real** (Cl. 29 No. 6-26, tel. 4/782-4004, www.hotelcasarealmonteria.net, COP$173,000 d) is a few blocks from the Avenida Primera and is also close to a police station. Many rooms are tiny with no windows.

When in Montería, one eats beef. The famous restaurants are on the outskirts of town and are large outdoor cowboy-ish places. While you could order grilled chicken, when in Montería, order a thick, juicy steak. **Bonga**

del Sinú (Km. 5 Vía Cereté, tel. 5/786-0085, www.labongadelsinu.com, noon-11pm Mon.-Sat. and noon-9pm Sun., COP$22,000) doesn't disappoint its hungry patrons. Along the Avenida Primera are several bars and outdoor restaurants, and the volume kicks up a notch or two on Saturday nights. In a nod to the significant Arab immigration in the area, Montería has a couple of spots where kibbe trumps steaks. Try **Farah Delicias Arabes** (Cra. 6 No. 60-42, tel. 4/789-9680, www.farahdeliciasarabes.com, 4:30pm-10:30pm daily, COP$15,000), an authentic Lebanese restaurant. There is also a **Juan Valdez Café** (Cl. 44 No. 10-139, tel. 4/785-1607) at the Alamedas del Sinú shopping mall. Get your macchiato fix here because you're a long way from another decent cup of joe!

◖ CAPURGANÁ AND SAPZURRO

The sparsely populated **Darien Gap**, a 160-kilometer-long (100-mile-long) and 50-kilometer-wide (30-mile-wide) stretch of mountainous jungle and swamp extending from Panama to Colombia, has long captured the imagination of adventurers. The two crescent-shaped villages of Capurganá and Sapzurro, built between the sea and the interior mountains of the small and low Darien Mountain Range, are within howling distance of the Panamanian border, but they seem far, far away from anything else. Capurganá and Sapzurro are on the eastern edges of the Darien Gap, a stretch of land that connects Central America (via Panama) with South America (via Colombia). The stretch of tropical rainforest here is the only interruption in the famous Pan-American Highway, which extends from Alaska to Patagonia.

With its absence of roads and the cover provided by the jungle's canopy, the entire Darien region has been a major corridor for the trafficking of illegal drugs from Colombia into Central America, which has also meant that there has been a heavy presence of both guerrillas and paramilitaries. Capurganá and Sapzurro suffered greatly from drug-related violence during the 1990s and early 2000s.

the wild, rocky coast of Carpurganá

Thanks in part to a strong military presence, safety in the area has vastly improved. Though drug trafficking continues deep in the jungle, kidnappings and violent skirmishes don't affect locals or visitors.

While much of the Colombian Darien is lowland and swamp, as it is part of the Río Atrato basin, near the border with Panama, the terrain is mountainous and covered in tropical jungle. Within minutes of leaving your hotel you'll be surrounded by the sounds of the jungle, accompanied only by the occasional bright green and black speckled toad and maybe a band of howler monkeys.

Here in the Colombian Darien, the majority of the population is Afro-Colombian. Capurganá is the larger village of the two, though both are tiny. There are no cars in either village. Get around on foot, by bike, or by boat.

To get here, you have to either take a flight from Medellín (to either the Capurganá or Acandí airport) or take a *lancha* (from Turbo or Acandí). Should the seas be too rough or if a general strike shuts down everything (as when we were there), you may just be stuck in the jungle for a couple days more.

Recreation
HIKING
There are several jungle walks to make around Capurganá. These take you through dense jungle overflowing with tropical vegetation and home to howler monkeys, birds, colorful frogs, and snakes. While the walks are short and fairly straightforward, you may want to ask at your hotel or hostel for a guide, especially for the walk between Capurganá and Sapzurro. Guides cost about COP$10,000. Wear hiking boots (waterproof if possible) and a swimsuit underneath your clothes for dips in the water off of Sapzurro or in freshwater swimming holes, and set off in the morning hours to avoid trying to navigate your way in the late afternoon.

An easy walk to make, without the need of a guide, is to **La Coquerita** (20-minute walk north from town, cell tel. 311/824-8022, COP$2,000), a delightfully ramshackle waterside hangout where you can have a refreshing coco-lemonade, maybe some guacamole and *patacones* (fried plantains), and take a dip in the refreshing freshwater or saltwater pools. There are also some handicrafts on sale here. To get there, walk along the Playa Caleta beach just north of the port, passing in front of the Hotel Almar. Continue along the jungle path that hugs the coastline. La Coquerita is under a kilometer from town, and the path is well-marked. Look out for the black and fluorescent green frogs along the way, but don't touch them; they're poisonous.

There are two ways to go to the idyllic hamlet of **Sapzurro:** by boat or on foot. The path to Sapzurro leads you through the exuberant rainforest to a lookout point and then down directly to the Sapzurro beach. The hike takes two hours.

To set off for Sapzurro, start at the soccer field, on the southern end of town, and ask the way. Midway up the uphill path is a shack that is the home of a man who claims to protect the jungle. Once you find him, you know you're

© ANDREW DIER

a frog on the path to Sapzurro

on the right track. He expects those who pass through to pay him about COP$1,000. At the top of the mountain there is a nice overlook with views of Capurganá and the coastline. The hike is not difficult, but the path can get muddy and slippery in places. Wear hiking boots and pick up a walking stick along the way to help you manage on the steep parts.

Once in Sapzurro, you're a short hike (15 minutes) up to the border with **Panama** and the village of **La Miel.** This easy walk begins on the same street as Cabañas Uvali and the Reserva Natural Tacarcuná. The border crossing is at the top of a steep hill with embedded steps. You'll need to show a passport to cross over to Panama. There is not much to the community of La Miel. It has a small military outpost, many young children running around, and a pleasant beach where you can swim and have a seafood lunch or drink.

Another walk to make is to the **El Cielo** waterfall, a 50-minute walk (about 3 km) through the jungle. It's easy to make and is flat, although you'll have to make around a dozen shallow stream crossings. Bring a bathing suit to cool off in the swimming holes you'll encounter. To get to heavenly El Cielo, set out on the road that runs parallel to the airstrip. Ask locals for directions.

It is possible to walk between Capurganá and El Aguacate, but the path, along the shore, is rocky and a bit treacherous.

DIVING AND SNORKELING

As you'd expect, the warm, turquoise waters off the coast of Capurganá and all the way up to San Blas in Panama make for fantastic diving, and there are over 30 diving sites to choose from. The best time for underwater exploration is from May to November. During those months, visibility is exceptional with hardly any waves around the diving spots. There are coral walls, reef rocks, and caves to explore close to the coastline.

Dive and Green Diving Center (facing the port, cell tel. 311/578-4021 or 316/781-6255, www.diveandgreen.com, 7:30am-12:30pm and 2pm-6pm daily) is the best place to organize a diving trip (for certified divers an excursion costs COP$190,000) or to take a PADI certification course (5 days, COP$820,000) with a bilingual instructor. For these packages it is best to pay in cash. Credit card transactions will have an additional fee. For those interested in snorkeling, they can help make arrangements for you, though they don't themselves lead snorkeling trips. Dive and Green offers all the equipment you need. If you are on the fence about whether diving is for you, they offer a Discover Scuba Diving day for COP$150,000. Dive and Green has accommodations: four rooms in a house adjacent to their offices. These cost COP$25,000 per person. Although in town, it's facing the water, guaranteeing a pleasant evening breeze.

Accommodations

There are a surprising number of excellent and inexpensive accommodations options in both Capurganá and Sapzurro. While there are a few large, all-inclusive hotels with welcome drinks and the works, the most interesting and comfortable options are the smaller guesthouses and hostels. Nearly all hotels are owned and operated by out-of-towners.

CAPURGANÁ

Many hotels and hostels are near the *muelle* (port) in Capurganá. Here you have the advantage of being in or near the hub of activity. Many visitors stay at one of the few all-inclusive hotels in Capurganá, but those options have zero charm.

The ◖ **Posada del Gecko** (Centro, cell tel. 314/525-6037, www.posadadelgecko.com, posadadelgecko@hotmail.com, COP$20,000 dorm, COP$35,000 d) is the best place to stay in town. It's run by an Italian-Colombian couple and offers both dorm and private rooms spread over two houses, with a capacity of 28 persons. In between is a spacious open-air garden ideal for lounging in a hammock or the hot tub. Enjoy a good Italian dinner by candlelight from the restaurant (7:30pm-11pm daily). It's open to non-guests as well, but it's best to go by in advance and make a reservation. The hotel

organizes three-day excursions to the San Blas Islands (Panama), in which you visit a Guna indigenous community, frolic on pristine white-sand beaches, and snorkel.

Although there are no sandy beaches there, outside of the center of Capurganá in the Playa Roca area, about a 15-minute walk or horse ride away, are several excellent guesthouses amid the trees. At night you'll need no air conditioner, and in the morning you may awake to birdsong.

One of the perks of staying at welcoming **Cabañas El Tucán** (Playa Roca, www.cabanatucancapurgana.com, COP$65,000), run by a friendly Bogotana-Italian couple, is that they make their own pasta and are good cooks. This house in the jungle is clean and comfortable, and the prices of their two spacious rooms are reasonable. Right across the path from El Tucán is ◖ **Cabañas Darius** (Playa Roca, cell tel. 314/622-5638, www.cdarius.blogspot.com, capurga05@gmail.com, COP$85,000 pp incl. 2 meals), another Colombian-international endeavor. It's a very nice guesthouse in the trees. Rooms are spacious and clean, and it's cool enough at night that you won't miss air conditioning. Balconies and hammocks provide lounging space, but the top selling point is the warm hospitality and Nery's unbelievable cooking. A third option in the same area is **Hotel Los Robles** (Playa Roca, cell tel. 314/632-8408 or 314/632-8428, www.capurganalosrobles.es.tl, COP$85,000 d, COP$70,000 pp). This lodge has quite the entrance—a winding path lined by bright fuchsia ginger flowers. *Caracolí* and *higuerón* trees provide shade and a home for birds. There are 12 rooms in two houses.

The most low-key place to stay in the area is Playa Aguacate. A German has carved a little paradise out of the jungle, and, once there, you won't want to leave. It's popular with honeymooners and those celebrating special occasions. Simple and comfortable cabins, each with a sea view, make up the ◖ **Bahía Lodge** (Playa Aguacate, cell tel. 314/812-2727, www.bahia-lodge.com, COP$190,000 pp 2 meals per day). Over the hill from is the lodge is **Hotel Las Ceibas** (Bahía Aguacate, cell tel.

313/695-6392, Medellín tel. 4/331-7440, www. hotellasceibas.com.co). It has three rooms in two houses set amid gardens, and the rooms have pleasant balconies with hammocks for late afternoon relaxation.

SAPZURRO

In Sapzurro, there are also quite a few options. The only drawback is that there are fewer restaurant options. Most hotels offer meals, though, and are usually the best bet at any rate. **Cabañas Uvali** (cell tel. 314/624-1325, COP$40,000 pp) is a friendly, clean, and straightforward little place in town. It's about a five-minute walk to the beach. **La Posada Hostal & Camping** (www.sapzurrolaposada.com, cell tel. 312/662-7599 or 310/410-2245, COP$65,000 pp d) has one luxury apartment, with a view, a dorm-style room, and a large space for camping under the big mango tree. They have a little tiki bar over the water, which can be set up for your romantic Sapzurro dinner.

The **C Resort Paraíso Sapzurro** (cell tel. 313/685-9862, www.paraiso-sapzurro-colombia.com, COP$10,000 dorm, COP$50,000 pp d) has basic beachfront cabins. Free avocadoes and mangoes is not a bad perk. This hostel is more commonly known as "Donde El Chileno," after the Chilean owner. The hostel can organize oversea journeys directly to Cartagena.

The **C Sapzurro Reserva Natural Tacarcuna** (on the path to La Miel, cell tel. 314/622-3149, COP$40,000 pp) is a special place for anyone interested in the flora and fauna of the region. Owners Martha and Fabio completed a botanical garden of native species with nature trails and a butterfly farm in 2013, and their other passion is birds. Behind their house up the mountain into the jungle, you can grab your binoculars and wait and watch for birds to make their appearances. Four different types of toucans, cuckoos, parakeets, owls, antipittas, tanagers, and many other species can be seen here. Throngs of migratory birds arrive between August and November each year. The two cabins available are cute, spic-and-span,

and of course surrounded by nature. Don't confuse this natural reserve with the all-inclusive Tacurcuna Hotel near the Capurganá airport. They can organize a number of nature hikes in the area and near Acandí.

Food

Hotels are usually the best options for food in the villages. **C Donde Josefina** (Playa Caleta, cell tel. 316/779-7760, COP$30,000, noon-9pm daily) remains the top restaurant for a delicious, gourmet seafood dinner, right on the beach in the heart of Capurganá. Dining on lobster in a coconut and garlic sauce under the swaying branches of a palm tree: That sounds like a vacation! A decent bakery overlooking the soccer field in Capurganá serves breakfast. In Sapzurro, the best place for a meal is at **Doña Triny** (Hostal Doña Triny, cell tel. 312/751-8626 or 313/725-8362, noon-10pm daily).

Information and Services

Bring extra cash to Capurganá: There are no ATMs, and credit cards are not accepted in most establishments. To avoid bringing wads of pesos, many hotels will allow (or require) you to make a *consignación* (deposit) to their bank account in advance. That can usually be done from any city in Colombia. The nearest bank, **Banco Agrario** (Cl. Las Flores with Cl. Consistorial, tel. 4/682-8229, 8am-11:30am and 2pm-4:30pm Mon.-Fri.) is in Acandí, a half-hour boat ride away to the south from Capurganá. To be on the safe side, bring along some extra cash.

Getting There and Around

Aerolínea de Antioquia (ADA, tel. 4/444-4232, www.ada.com.co) serves both Capurganá and Acandí from the Aeropuerto Olaya Herera in Medellín. Acandí is the municipality to which the village of Capurganá is linked. It is south of Capurganá on the Darien. There is one flight per day on ADA Monday through Saturday to Acandí. Direct flights to Capurganá were temporarily suspended at the time of writing.

Boats are a good way to get around Carpurganá.

To get from Acandí to Capurganá, you'll have to take a horse from the airport (seriously) to the docks (a 15-minute trip), at which point you'll take a 30-minute long *lancha* (boat) ride onwards to Capurganá (COP$17,000). There is always a *lancha* at 1pm daily. The seas can be rough at times, so, always try to get a seat in back. You may want to keep your camera or other electronics in their cases so they won't be exposed to seawater. Demand a life vest. The return trip from Capurganá to Acandí leaves at 7:30am daily.

All boats arrive at the *muelle* (docks) in Capurganá, which are in the middle of town. Most hotels are within walking distance, although some, like Cabañas Darius, are a bit of a walk. Try to find someone with a horse to take you there (about COP$10,000). Hotels in Aguacate and Sapzurro are reachable only by taking another *lancha* from the docks in Capurganá, about a 20-minute ride. Those hotels will arrange your transportation from Capurganá in advance.

There are bus links from Medellín (8 hours), Montería (4 hours), and from cities across the Caribbean coast to the rough and tumble coastal port city of Turbo on the Golfo de Urabá. As an alternative to taking a flight to either Capurganá or to Acandí, you can take a 2.5- to 3-hour boat ride from Turbo. These usually depart at 8am, costing about COP$60,000. The early morning departure means that you will probably have to spend the previous night in Turbo. That's not ideal, but if you must, most tourists agree that **Residencias La Florida** (Cra. 13 No. 99A-56, tel. 4/827-3531, COP$30,000 d) is an all right accommodations option, close to the port, and the hotel staff is quite helpful arranging your onward transportation.

Do not plan to take a boat from Turbo to Capurganá from December to March. The 2.5-hour journey can be awful during this time of high winds, and the waves can be unrelenting. If you are unlucky enough to be in the front of the boat, you will step off the boat with, at the very least, a painfully sore back. This is likewise true for the trip from Acandí to Capurganá, although it is a much shorter ride.

Returning to the mainland from Capurganá, it's always best to reserve a day in advance for *lanchas* bound for Acandí or Turbo, especially during peak tourist times. Your hotel should be able to do this for you, but just in case, you can call Sara at the *muelle* (314/614-0704).

From Panama, you can take a flight from Panama City to Puerto Obaldía. From there, boats frequently make the journey onward to Capurganá. It's just a 30-45 minute ride and costs about US$15. You may be required to show proof of yellow fever vaccination to enter Colombia.

If traveling onward to Panama, you must go to the Colombian **Ministerio de Relaciones Exteriores** (Cl. del Comercio, cell tel. 311/746-6234, 8am-5pm Mon.-Fri., 9am-4pm Sat.) the day before for an exit stamp.

CARTAGENA

BOYACÁ AND THE SANTANDERES

Located north of Bogotá, the mountainous departments of Boyacá, Santander, and Norte de Santander (these last two are known collectively as the Santanderes) are rich in history, natural beauty, and outdoor activities. The countryside is dotted with historic colonial towns, including two of the most beautiful and well-preserved in Colombia: Villa de Leyva and Barichara.

© ANDREW DIER

The scenery of the region runs the gamut from the desert landscape near Villa de Leyva to the bucolic rolling hills and pastures of agriculturally rich Boyacá, and from the awe-inspiring Río Chicamocha canyon to the dramatic snow-capped peaks of the Sierra Nevada del Cocuy (Cocuy Range).

Outdoor activities are the draw here, like trekking in the Sierra Nevada del Cocuy and white-water rafting, caving, and paragliding near San Gil. Except for the frenetic and modern Bucaramanga, stoic Tunja, and the border city of Cúcuta, a refreshingly slow pace prevails. The pueblos of Boyacá are easily accessed from Bogotá and can even be visited on a long weekend. It will take a little more time to discover Santander, located between Bogotá and the Caribbean coast. Although most people only stop in the sultry city of Cúcuta on their way to Venezuela or on a visa run, it is a pleasant surprise. The historic pueblo of Pamplona is the most chilled-out place in all of Norte de Santander.

HISTORY

Before the Spanish conquest, Boyacá was part of the Muisca heartland. Hunza, where present day Tunja is located, was the seat of the Zaque, one of the Muisca leaders. The Sun Temple, one of the Muiscas' sacred sites, was in Sogamoso, northeast of Tunja.

Boyacá and the Santanderes played a major role in the struggle for independence. In 1811, Boyacá became the seat of the Provincias Unidas de la Nueva Granada (United Provinces of New Granada), the first republican independent government. It was in Boyacá in 1819 that the two decisive battles of independence were fought: the Batalla del Pantano de Vargas (Battle of the Vargas Swamp) and the Batalla del Puente de Boyacá (Battle of the Bridge of Boyacá). These battles marked the end of Spanish domination in Colombia.

Santander was one of the more dynamic regions in 19th-century Colombia, with an export economy based on the cultivation of quinine, coffee, cocoa, and tobacco. In the early 20th century, Norte de Santander became the first major coffee-producing region in Colombia.

The mid-20th-century fighting between Liberals and Conservatives was particularly acute in Santander and Norte de Santander. In 1960, the Ejercito de Liberación Nacional (National Liberation Army) or ELN guerrilla group was born in rural Santander.

The region has experienced steady economic growth since the early 2000s. Bucaramanga, the capital of Santander, has become a prosperous center of manufacturing and services. Cúcuta, in the neighboring Norte de Santander department, is a center of commerce whose fortunes are linked to Venezuela's.

While poverty is widespread in the Boyacá countryside, the area is an important agricultural center and supplies Bogotá with much of its food. The departmental capital of Tunja has also become a major center of learning: It is home to 10 universities.

PLANNING YOUR TIME

There are three main draws in Boyacá and Santander: the lovely colonial town of Villa de Leyva, the snowcapped wonderland of the Sierra Nevada del Cocuy, and, in Santander, the action-packed area around San Gil, including the nearby town of Barichara.

Villa de Leyva can be visited in a short two-day excursion from Bogotá, but you could easily spend a couple more relaxing days seeing all the sights, including a hike to Laguna Iguaque. Add on a day to visit the churches of Tunja, but be sure to confirm hours beforehand. To further explore Boyacá, extend your visit for a couple of days to the area around Sogamoso, particularly the postcard-perfect towns of Iza and Monguí and Lago de Tota. There are good public transportation links throughout Boyacá, but this is also a fairly easy place to drive.

Getting to the Sierra Nevada del Cocuy is a schlep (11 hours by bus from Bogotá), so a trip there requires a minimum of 4-5 days to make it worthwhile. To just do day hikes into the park, base yourself in either Güicán or El Cocuy, or nearer to the park in one of several lodges. To do the six-day circuit around the park, plan on 10 days so as to include a day or two of acclimatization before you embark. This is a remote

HIGHLIGHTS

LOOK FOR  TO FIND RECOMMENDED SIGHTS, ACTIVITIES, DINING, AND LODGING.

Villa de Leyva is just a couple of hours away from Bogotá (page 164).

Santuario Flora y Fauna Iguaque: Hike through Andean forest and mysterious *páramo* to a sacred Muisca lake (page 172).

Tunja's Historic Churches: Glimpse the splendor of Tunja's colonial past in its beautiful churches (page 176).

Parque Nacional Natural El Cocuy: Stunning scenery greets you at every turn in this remote park of snowcapped peaks (page 190).

Cañón del Chicamocha: Experience the blue skies and deep canyons at this photogenic park not far from Bucaramanga and San Gil (page 201).

Paragliding near San Gil: Soar through the air with the greatest of ease in Colombia's recreational capital (page 204).

Barichara: Decompress and rejuvenate in one of the most beautiful pueblos in the country (page 207).

Villa de Leyva: One of Colombia's most visited and beloved colonial pueblos, relaxed

Camino Real: Follow in the footsteps of native Guane indigenous traders and Spanish colonists on this meandering path through the Santander countryside (page 209).

area and there are fewer public transportation options. Buses depart for the area from Tunja. Roads are for the most part in good shape.

San Gil and Baricabra have a lot to offer, so plan on spending at least three days. Baricabra is a much more beautiful base for exploring the region, but San Gil is home to the main adventure sport tour operators.

There are good public transportation links between Bucaramanga and San Gil and between San Gil and Baricabra. However, getting from Bucaramanga and San Gil to Tunja or Villa de Leyva is not fun, as the highway is

often saturated with big trucks and buses. On holidays it can be difficult to get a seat on a bus out of or to San Gil, an intermediary stop between Bucaramanga and Bogotá.

Between Villa de Leyva and San Gil it is 6-7 hours, with a change of bus in Barbosa and/or Tunja. Even though San Gil and the Sierra Nevada del Cocuy are only 75 kilometers as the crow flies, to get from one to the other, you must transfer buses in Tunja, requiring more than 15 hours on various buses.

There's frequent bus service between Bucaramanga and Pamplona/Cúcuta.

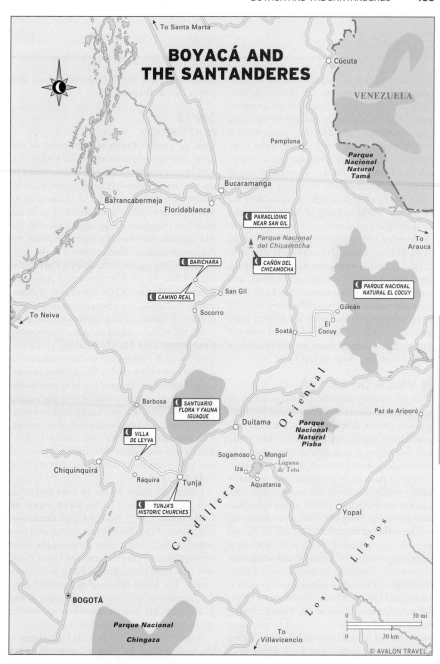

BOYACÁ AND
THE SANTANDERES

To Santa Marta

Cúcuta

VENEZUELA

Pamplona

*Parque
Nacional
Natural
Tamá*

Bucaramanga

Barrancabermeja

Floridablanca

To
Arauca

◖ PARAGLIDING
NEAR SAN GIL

*Parque Nacional
del Chicamocha*

◖ BARICHARA

◖ CAÑÓN DEL
CHICAMOCHA

◖ PARQUE NACIONAL
NATURAL EL COCUY

◖ CAMINO REAL

San Gil

Socorro

Güicán

To Neiva

Soatá

El
Cocuy

O r i e n t a l

Paz de Ariporó

Barbosa

◖ SANTUARIO
FLORA Y FAUNA
IGUAQUE

Duitama

*Parque
Nacional
Natural
Pisba*

◖ VILLA
DE LEYVA

Sogamoso

Monguí

*Laguna
de Tota*

Iza

Chiquinquirá

Ráquira

Tunja

Aquatania

Yopal

◖ TUNJA'S
HISTORIC CHURCHES

C o r d i l l e r a

L o s   L l a n o s

BOGOTÁ

Parque Nacional

Chingaza

To
Villavicencio

0   30 mi

0   30 km

© AVALON TRAVEL

BOYACÁ

Boyacá

To the northeast of Bogotá and the department of Cundinamarca, the Boyacá department is a mostly rural agriculture-oriented area of bucolic highlands, home to campesinos (peasants) often dressed in their warm woolen *ruanas* (capes) as they tend to their dairy cows and potato crops. Boyacá is also known for its role in Colombian history: The capital city of Tunja was effectively the runner-up to Bogotá when the Spaniards sought a capital city for their New World territory of Nueva Granada. Its colonial-era importance can be seen today in the number of impressive churches that stand in its historic center. Nearby, Villa de Leyva has the perfect combination of colonial charm, good hotels and restaurants, attractions, and fantastic weather. Boyacenses are known for their politeness, shyness, and honesty, and will often address you not with the formal *usted* but rather with the super-deferential *sumercé,* a term that is derived from the old Spanish *su merced* (literally, "your mercy").

◖ VILLA DE LEYVA

This enchanting colonial pueblo is set in an arid valley (Valle de Saquencipá) and has been a major tourist destination for decades. The population triples on weekends, when city folk from Bogotá converge on the town. The surrounding desert scenery, a palette of ever-changing pastels, is gorgeous, the typically sunny weather is never too hot nor too cool, and the town's architecture of preserved whitewashed houses along stone streets is charming.

The influx of visitors every weekend doesn't diminish the appeal of VDL, as it's known. A surprising number of activities and attractions are in reach, including paleontological and archaeological sites and outdoor activities such as biking and hiking. The nearby Santuario Flora y Fauna Iguaque is one of the most accessible national parks in the country, and you need only a decent pair of boots to hike to its sacred lakes. Villa de Leyva is also a good base from which to explore the Boyacá countryside and towns such as Ráquira.

Sights
PLAZA MAYOR
Villa de Leyva's **Plaza Mayor** is one of the most photographed locations in Colombia. The town's main square, the largest plaza in the country, is indeed photogenic, but it can be a frustrating task capturing it all in one take: At 14,000 square meters (3.5 acres), it's big. In the middle of the square is a Mudejar-style well, the Ara Sagrada, that was the source of water for the townspeople in colonial times. On the western side of the square is the **Iglesia Parroquial** (Cra. 9 No. 12-68, 8am-noon and 2pm-6pm Tues.-Sat., 8am-noon Sun.), made out of stone, adobe, and wood, which was built in the 17th century. It features a large golden *retablo* altar.

On the western side of the plaza is the quirky **Casa Museo Luis Alberto Acuña** (Cra. 10 No. 12-83, tel. 8/732-0422, www.museoacuna. com.co, 9am-6pm daily). In addition to cubist-influenced paintings of pre-Hispanic indigenous culture, rooms are filled with the artists' private art collection and antiques. The courtyard holds some wood sculptures of the artists. The museum also has a pint-sized gift shop. Acuña was instrumental in the restoration of and preservation of colonial architecture in Villa de Leyva.

One of the oldest houses in Villa de Leyva, and best preserved, is the **Casa Juan de Castellanos** (Cra. 9 No. 13-11) on the northeast corner of the Plaza Mayor. It is so well preserved, in fact, that it today serves as the main office of the city government. The house is not officially open to the public, but you can take a peek. The house belonged to Spaniard Juan de Castellanos, who came to the New World as a soldier. He was an important chronicler of the time.

Across from the Casa Juan de Castellanos is the historic **Casa del Primer Congreso de las**

© ANDREW DIER

a charming cobblestone street in Villa de Leyva

Provincias Unidas de la Nueva Granada (Cra. 9 No. 13-04). Restored by artist Luis Alberto Acuña in the 1950s, this is where the era of the Patria Boba, as it would later (and derisively) be known, was begun. The **Casa Real Fábrica de Licores** (Cl. 13 No. 8-03) was the first official distillery in Nueva Granada. After standing in ruins for decades, the house was restored in the 1950s.

The **Museo El Carmen de Arte Religioso** (Cl. 14 No. 10-04, 10am-1pm and 2pm-5pm Sat., Sun., and holidays, COP$2,500) presents paintings, crucifixes, manuscripts, and religious figures from the colonial era. The museum is on the southwest corner of the grassy **Plazoleta de la Carmen.** The complex (which dates to around 1850) also includes a monastery and convent.

The **Casa Museo Antonio Nariño** (Cra. 9 No. 10-25, 9am-noon and 2pm-5pm Thurs.-Tues., tel. 8/732-0342, free) is a house in which independence figure Antonio Nariño lived and died. It was built in the 17th century, and the museum displays some of his manuscripts as well as items from everyday life in the 19th century, such as a giant mortar used to mill corn. The short and sweet museum often puts on temporary art exhibits, which may have a small admission charge.

OTHER SIGHTS
On the **Plaza Ricaurte,** the 19th-century **Convento de San Agustín** today houses the highly respected **Instituto Humboldt** (Cra. 8 No. 15-98, tel. 8/732-0791, www.humboldt.org.co, free), a research institute dedicated to conservation and environmental education. A small room on threatened animal species in Colombia is open to the public, and a tour is given on Fridays (3pm-5pm). The Humboldt occasionally hosts cultural events.

The **Casa Museo Capitán Antonio Ricaurte** (Cl. 15 No. 8-17, 9am-noon and 2pm-5pm Tues.-Sun., no phone, free) is in the small house where this independence figure was born in 1786. He is a hero of the Colombian air force, and one room is filled with uniforms and memorabilia of that military branch. He died heroically, sacrificing his life by blowing himself up with a cache of gunpowder so that it would not land in the hands of Spaniards.

Entertainment and Events

The most popular place to hang out in the evenings is on the Plaza Mayor, where the thing to do is buy a couple of beers and watch the world go by. But there are other watering holes in town. **La Cava de Don Fernando** (Cra. 10 No. 12-03, tel. 8/732-0073) is a spot for a cocktail where the music is generally, but not always, rock.

For a movie night, head to the **Cine Club Casa Quintero** (Casa Quintero, 2nd fl., tel. 8/732-1801, Thurs.-Sun. evenings).

The dark, crystal-clear skies above Villa de Leyva make for great stargazing. In February each year the town hosts the **Festival de Astronómica de Villa de Leyva** (www.astroasac.com), during which all are invited to view the stars from powerful telescopes in the Plaza Mayor.

BOYACÁ

Shopping

In Villa de Leyva as in the rest of Boyacá, the special handicraft is woolen goods. But the town is home to many creative types, and small jewelers, galleries, and handicraft shops are found on every street.

Alieth Tejido Artesanal (Cl. 13 No. 7-89, tel. 8/732-1672, www.alieth.8m.com) is an association of about 35 women who weave woolen sweaters, *ruanas* (ponchos), *mochilas* (backpacks), gloves, scarves, and some colorful, slightly psychedelic bags. A tour, the "Ruta de la Lana," can be taken to nearby farms to learn about the process from sheep to sweater. It costs COP$48,000 per person, lasts for about five hours, and snacks and a souvenir are included. Alieth Ortíz, the head of this interesting program, requests reservations be made a few days in advance so that they can organize things with the artisans. Another excellent store to browse wool items is **Creaciones Dora** (Cra. 10 No. 10-02, 9am-7pm Mon.-Fri., 9am-9pm Sat.).

© ANDREW DIER

Boyacá is known for its woven woolen scarves and *ruanas*.

La Libelula (Cra. 9 No. 14-35, tel. 8/732-0040, 10am-7pm daily) specializes in leather: handbags, belts, and accessories. The mysterious shop **Misterio** (Cl. 14 No. 9-85, tel. 8/732-0418, 10am-8pm daily) sells colorful scarves, handmade jewelry, and semiprecious stones like quartz, amethyst, and emeralds. Coal mining is a major industry in rugged Boyacá; **Arte al Carbón** (Cl. 15 No. 9-46, www.artealcarbon.galeon.com, 9am-7pm Mon.-Sat.) sells jewelry made out of coal by women from mining communities.

Recreation

HIKING

Close to town, sporty locals regularly take a brisk morning hike up to the **Santo,** a statue on the eastern side of Villa de Leyva. The walk takes about an hour in total, and it is a steep climb. From the statue of the saint you can get a good view of the town and will better appreciate the scale of the fantastic Plaza Mayor. To get to the path, walk east along Calle 11 to the tennis court and track/soccer field. This is to the north of the Hotel Duruelo. The path entrance is marked and it practically leads straight up. The rocks are covered, unfortunately, with religious graffiti. It's best to make the climb early in the morning, before the midday heat envelops the valley. Although the view is nice, you'll be better off leaving your camera at your hotel, not necessarily due to safety reasons, but rather because you may not want to be loaded down with things as you climb. At parts you may be on all fours!

TOURS

Tour companies in Villa de Leyva mostly specialize in adventure activities nearby. The best outfit is **Colombian Highlands** (Renacer, Av. Cra. 10 No. 21, tel. 8/732-1201, www.colombianhighlands.com), the same folks running the Renacer hostel. **Armonita Tours** (Av. Perimetral No. 8-08, tel. 1/643-3883, www.amonitatour.com) can take you to the Santa Sofía area for waterfall rappelling (COP$85,000), caving (COP$75,000), and the Paso de Ángel hike (COP$75,000). They also can arrange horseback riding trips to the Pozos Azules, and they rent bikes. In addition, they have day-trip packages to places like Museo El Fósil de Monquirá and the Convento del Santo Ecce Homo. These cost about COP$60,000 and include transportation and entry to the attractions.

BIKE RENTAL

You'll need plenty of sunscreen and water, but renting a bike to see the sights in the valley near Villa de Leyva is a great way to spend a day and get some good exercise as you huff and puff up that hill to the Convento del Santo Ecce Homo.

Mountain bikes, not necessarily of the highest quality, are readily available for rent in Villa de Leyva. These usually all go for about COP$20,000 for a half day (until 1 or 2pm). **Sentimiento Natura** (Cl. 8 No. 9-47, cell tel. 321/217-2455) rents bikes, usually from a house that is conveniently located near the road through the valley. **Bici Motos** (Transversal 10 No. 7A-10, Barrio Los Olivos, cell tel. 321/225-5769) is also on the way, and the friendly owner lives above the bike shop. That means you can get there on the early side (6am-7am) if you want to pick up a bike. (He doesn't mind.) He charges only COP$10,000 for a five-hour rental.

Accommodations

Villa de Leyva gets hopping on weekends and on holidays, and hotel rates bump up accordingly. Rates are even higher during the Christmas holidays through the second week of January and during Holy Week. During the week you will have your choice of hotels and ought to try to negotiate a better price. Many will provide additional discounts if you pay in cash.

There aren't many midrange hotel options in town, as most hotels target the luxury hotel market. A number of hotels that call themselves boutique have sprung up in recent years just outside of the town or farther in the valley. They may be comfortable but they may lack in the charm department. Hostels in Villa de Leyva are reliably friendly options, and staff are chock full of knowledge and tips on where to go and what to do.

UNDER COP$70,000

◖ **Renacer** (Av. Cra. 10 No. 21, tel. 8/732-1201, www.colombianhighlands.com, COP$35,000 shared room, COP$65,000 d) is the best-known hostel in town and is popular for good reasons. Its location is a hike away from town (about a 15-minute walk), but guests will be reimbursed for their taxi ride upon arrival. It is set amidst green at the foot of a mountain. Facilities are well kept and there is ample open-air common space. There are seven rooms and cabanas for varying numbers of guests, some with private bathrooms. There is also a place for those arriving in campers or vans. The on-site restaurant, **Pekish,** is excellent, with options to please anyone, such as falafels (COP$12,000) and Vietnamese spring rolls (COP$10,000). In addition to the hostel, Renacer, through **Colombian Highlands** (www.colombianhighlands.com), arranges outdoor expeditions to nearby attractions and can even assist in excursions outside of the Villa de Leyva area. They have very good information on how to hike or bike the area solo. This is an excellent place to swap travel tips with backpackers from around the world.

Run by an Austrian-Colombian couple, the ◖ **Casa Viena Hostel** (Cra. 10 No. 19-114, Sector de la Banadera, tel. 8/732-0711, www.hostel-villadeleyva.com, COP$17,000 s, COP$40,000 d) is a quiet and relaxed guesthouse on the same road as Renacer (just before it). It has just three rooms and the owners live in the same house. You may bump into them going to the shared bathrooms. They opened a new farmhouse in 2013 called **Casa Puente Piedra** (COP$25,000 pp) that is even more tranquil. It is within walking distance of the Santuario Flora y Fauna Iguaque. They have excellent mountain bikes for rental. These cost COP$25,000 for a half day.

A low-key and lesser-known hostel option is **Hostal Rana** (Cl. 10A No. 10-31, tel. 8/732-0330, www.hostalrana.com or www.learn-spanishinvilladeleyva.com, COP$20,000 dorm, COP$40,000 d). It opened in 2010 and has one dorm room and four private rooms. Rooms are clean and beds are firm. There is a small kitchen for use. One problem is that the tiny camping area in the courtyard area is sort of icky. They can arrange for Spanish lessons here.

The no-frills **Hospedaje Los Balcones de la Plaza** (Cl. 13 No. 9-94, cell tel. 314/360-8568, COP$45,000 pp w/shared bath) has about four rooms and occupies a corner of real estate overlooking the Plaza Mayor. The views from your balcony can't be beat. They don't provide wireless Internet, but the town government does on the Plaza Mayor. Here there is no common area, but the plaza is as common as it gets.

If you ask locals for a less expensive hotel option, many will tell you to check out **Hospedería Don Paulino** (Cl. 14 No. 7-46, tel. 8/732-1227, COP$35,000 s, COP$65,000 d). It's not a fancy place by any means, but the price can't be beat! The 16 rooms all have wireless Internet and TV, but the ones on the first floor are a little on the stuffy and small side. From the second floor balcony overlooking the outdoor patio you can enjoy the sunset. There's no breakfast included but each morning they do provide coffee.

COP$70,000-200,000

Family-run **Hospedería La Roca** (Cl. 13 No. 9-54, COP$160,000 d) has been a cheapie quietly overlooking the Plaza Mayor for years, but it's no longer a budget option. More than 20 rooms with high ceilings surround two interior courtyards that are filled with greenery. Try for one on the second floor with a squint of a view of the mountains. Around the corner is the welcoming **Posada de Los Ángeles** (Cra. 10 No. 13-94, tel. 8/732-0562, COP$110,000 d), a lovely option overlooking the Plazoleta de Carmen. Some rooms have balconies overlooking the church. Take your American-style breakfast in the cheerfully painted patio filled with potted plants and flowers. No wireless Internet.

Friendly and colorful **Sol de la Villa** (Cra. 8A No. 12-28, tel. 8/732-0224, COP$120,000) has 30-some comfortable rooms and an excellent "in town" location. Walls are a little on the thin side, as are curtains. Rooms towards the back and upstairs are best. A nice service they provide, one that all environmentally aware hotels ought to offer, is free filtered water, so there's no need to buy plastic bottles of water each day. The inviting (**Hospedería El Marqués de San Jorge** (Cl. 14 No. 9-20, tel. 8/732-0240, www.hospederiaelmarquesdesanjorge.com, COP$130,000-200,000 d) is just a block from the Plaza Mayor, has two interior patios that are filled with greenery, and has clean and comfortable modern rooms (despite having been around since 1972). It's a bargain compared to other luxury hotels in town.

OVER COP$200,000

The location of the (**Hotel Plaza Mayor** (Cra. 10 No. 12-31, tel. 8/732-0425, www.hotelplazamayor.com.co, COP$306,000 d), with a bird's-eye view of the Plaza Mayor from its western side, is unrivaled. The hotel's terrace is a great place to watch goings-on in the plaza and to take a photo of the cathedral bathed in a golden light in late afternoon. Rooms are spacious, some have a fireplace, and all are tastefully decorated. Breakfast is served in the pleasant courtyard.

Two other upscale options face parks. On the cute Parque Nariño, the elegant **Hotel La Posada de San Antonio** (Cra. 8 No. 11-80, tel. 8/732-0538, www.hotellaposadadesanantonio.com, COP$295,000 d) is lavishly decorated and has a pleasant restaurant area, a cozy reading room, a pool, an art gallery, a billiards room, and even a small chapel. It was originally a wealthy family's home built in 1845. On the Plaza de Ricaurte, the **Hotel Plazuela de San Agustín** (Cl. 15 No. 8-65, Plaza de Ricaurte, tel. 8/732-2175, www.hotelplazuela.com, COP$300,000 d) is a cozy hotel with enormous (yet carpeted) rooms. Mornings get off to a nice start with breakfast in the courtyard, near a fountain. The hotel is two blocks from the Plaza Mayor. They have another hotel in the countryside towards Santa Sofía.

BOYACÁ

Food

CAFÉS, BAKERIES, AND QUICK BITES

The many cafés and bakeries in town have fiercely loyal clienteles. Bakery **Pan Típica** (Cl. 11 No. 11A-64) is an old local favorite and specializes in *mogolla batida* (whipped bread). **Panadería San Francisco** (Cl. 10, 8am-7pm) is famous for its *galletas de maiz* (corn cookies). The owners of **Pastelería Francesa** (Cl. 10 No. 6-05, 9am-7pm Thurs.-Mon.), a French bakery, often skip town, so don't be disappointed if it is closed, foiling your plan to sip a café au lait accompanied by a *pain au chocolat* (chocolate croissant). **Panadería Doña Aleja** (Cl. 14 No. 9-21, 8am-8pm Mon.-Sat., 9am-4pm Sun.) is known for its *mogollas* (rolls).

At **Sybarita Caffe** (Cra. 9 No. 11-88, cell tel. 316/481-1872, 8am-8pm daily) the owners are on a mission to bring coffee appreciation to the masses. Even if you are one of those "coffee is coffee" people, once you try one of their coffees (from the southern Colombian highland departments of Cauca or Nariño), you may just be jolted out of your slumber. That's some good coffee! If you want your coffee from the Coffee Region, Quindío to be specific, then **Café Los Gallos** (Cra. 8 No. 12-96, cell tel. 300/659-9511, 9am-8pm daily) is your place. This sweet place is filled with rooster paraphernalia; it's named after the family name.

Gelatería Pizzería Santa Lucia (Cra. 10 No. 10-27, cell tel. 314/305-8150, 11am-9:30pm) serves homemade ice cream and yogurts. It's all natural, and the pizza's not bad either. If you just want a thin crust pizza without a big production and expense try **Crepes Pizza y Algo Más** (Cra. 9 11-80, cell tel. 313/854-2051, www.crepespizza.blogspot.com, 6pm-10pm Mon.-Thurs., 1pm-10pm Fri.-Sun., COP$12,000).

Merengues y Besitos (Cra. 9 No. 11-84, cell tel. 312/394-3601, 10am-7pm daily) has very sweet sweets wrapped in colorful packaging.

COLOMBIAN

The **Albahaca Restaurante-Bar Viejoteca** (Cra. 8A No. 13-46, cell tel. 313/844-6613, 10am-9pm daily) is a favorite for visitors for two reasons: the lovely ambience, especially in the evening, and for its non-outrageous prices! Their top dishes include *cuchuco de trigo con espinazo de cerdo* (buckwheat soup with pork back, COP$17,000) and grilled trout in *uchuva* (Peruvian groundcherry) sauce (COP$18,000). Ask for a table in the garden or by the fireplace. The word *viejoteca* is in the name because the owners like oldies music.

MiCocina (Cl. 13 No. 8-45, tel. 8/732-1676, www.restaurantemicocina.com, noon-10pm daily, COP$25,000), where there is a cooking school within the restaurant, has earned a name for itself as an ever-so-slightly upscale restaurant serving the best of Colombian cuisine. After a *calentado bogotano,* a beloved hangover cure made with fried eggs and potatoes, save room for the cheese ice cream from Paipa. It's mostly Colombian meat-based dishes here, but they offer a few vegetarian plates.

Locals tend to steer clear of the overpriced restaurants on the Plaza Mayor. When it comes to *comida,* it's got to be *buena, mucha, y barrata* (good, plentiful, and cheap). Close to the Terminal de Transportes, but not too close, **Los Kioscos de los Caciques** (Cra. 9 No. 9-05, cell tel. 311/475-8681, noon-3pm and 6pm-8pm daily, COP$6,000) specializes in filling local dishes such as *mazamorra chiquita* (beef stew with potatoes, corn, and other vegetables) and *cuchuco con espinazo* (stew with a base of pork spine and potatoes). You can also order from the menu. It's an atmospheric place, where you dine in thatched kiosks. At the Saturday market, those in the know go to **Donde Salvador** (between Clls. 12-13 and Cras. 5-6, Plaza de Mercado) for *mute rostro de cordero,* a hearty corn-based soup with lamb. You can also, of course, pick up plenty of cheap and fresh fruit. **La Parilla** (Cra. 9 No. 9-17, 7am-9pm daily, set lunch COP$5,000) is an everyman kind of place. At the plaza, **Estar de la Villa** (Cl. 13 No. 8-58, tel. 8/732-0251, 10am-9pm daily, COP$8,000) is always packed, often with employees from some of the fancier restaurants nearby.

BOYACÁ

Traveling Taste Buds

Hot, sweet, and gooey—the arepas of Tinjacá are worth both the calories and the trip.

© ANDREW DIER

Forget about counting calories as you try these local specialties near Villa de Leyva.

WINE

Villa de Leyva is one of a handful of areas in Colombia where wine is produced. Take a tour of **Viñedo Aim Karim** (Km. 10 Vía Santa Sofía, cell tel. 317/518-2746, www.marquesvl.com, 10am-5pm, COP$5,000) and try their Marqués de la Villa wine. Their sauvignon blanc won an award in Brussels in 2011.

SAUSAGE

About 25 kilometers west of Villa de Leyva, the town of Sutamarchán is famous for its spicy *longaniza* sausage. The best place to sample this is at **La Fogata** (tel. 8/725-1249, www.longanizasutamarchan.com). It's on the main road on the left as you go toward Ráquira.

AREPAS

Most visitors to Colombia develop a love or hate relationship with arepas, corn-based pancakes that accompany just about every meal. Every region has their own distinct type of arepa, and every Colombian believes that theirs is superior to the rest. It would be hard to find anyone who could resist the famed *arepa quesuda* from the town of **Tinjacá** about 18 kilometers southwest of Villa de Leyva. Meaning "sweating arepa," *arepa quesudas* are two small arepas with sweet, melted cheese in the middle. They're a big mess to eat, but they're so good.

JAM

Tinjacá is also known for its delicious jams made by **El Robledal** (Vereda Santa Bárbara, cell tel. 310/226-5299, www.elrobledal.co). Check out their exotic fruit jams such as *uchuva*, *lulo*, and rhubarb. Their products can also be found in Villa de Leyva at the Savia restaurant in the Casa Quintero on the Plaza Mayor.

BROILED HEN

Sáchica is an orderly, quiet town just outside of Villa de Leyva on the way toward Tunja. Here, the local specialty is broiled hen. Try it at **La Candelaria** (Cl. 3 No. 2-48, cell tel. 311/845-7786).

INTERNATIONAL

Mercado Municipal (Cra. 8 No. 12-25, tel. 8/732-0229, noon-3pm Mon.-Thurs., noon-3pm and 8-midnight Fri.-Sun. and holidays, COP$22,000) has without a doubt one of the coolest settings in VDL. It is in a courtyard (which was once the third patio of a parsonage) filled with herb gardens in which a traditional Mexican barbecue wood-burning oven is built into the ground. In it they cook their famous barbecued goat. International dishes on the menu include pastas and several vegetarian offerings. It's open for breakfast on the weekends and there is a nice bakery in front. The set lunch special is a very good deal.

Authentic French food can be found in Villa de Leyva! That would be at **Chez Remy** (Cra. 9 No. 13-25, tel. 311/848-5000, noon-10pm Fri.-Sat., noon-4pm Sun., COP$24,000). The French-inspired dishes include a *quenelle de mar* (COP$28,000) that combines a myriad of tastes from the faraway sea: salmon, hake, shrimp, and lobster. But on chilly nights, the French onion soup (COP$9,000) really hits the spot.

The **Casa Quintero** on the corner of the Plaza Mayor has several restaurants in a sort of fancy food court setting. There is a little something for everyone here, including a Lebanese restaurant, a surprisingly filling arepa joint, and a pizza place. If you are in the mood for Mexican, try **La Bonita,** run by the same people as the Mercado Municipal, where you can sample delicious dishes such as *lomo a la tampiquena* (COP$33,000), which includes grilled baby beef, a chicken flauta, a quesadilla, and rice with beans. Or go for a barbecued pork taco (COP$26,000).

While you await your rosemary, veggie, *higo* (fig), or barbecue burger (COP$8,500) and refreshing basil lemonade at **Vastago** (Cl. 13 No. 8-43, 9am-8pm daily, COP$17,000), you can check out the little shops and stands in a sort of arcade that has several small shops (ceramics, jewelry) and vendors (old Colombian magazines, antiques). There's a cupcake café in back if you want something sweet afterwards.

La Ricotta (Cra. 10 No. 11-49, tel. 8/732-1042, noon-10pm Fri.-Sun., COP$16,000) makes its own pastas and is a reasonably priced Italian cuisine option.

VEGETARIAN

Casa Salud Natural (Cl. 12 No. 10-74, no phone, noon-9pm daily, COP$14,000) is a mostly lunch place where you get a set meal of a soup and a vegetable protein. A pricey vegetarian/organic restaurant, **Savia** (Casa Quintero, Plaza Mayor, tel. 8/732-1778, noon-9pm Thurs.-Mon., COP$25,000) has an extensive menu and also sells locally produced jams and other items for sale in their *tienda* (store).

Information and Services

The Villa de Leyva **tourist office** (corner Cra. 9 and Cl. 13, off of Plaza Mayor, tel. 8/732-0232, 8am-12:30pm and 2pm-6pm Mon.-Sat., 9am-1pm and 3pm-6pm Sun.) has free tourist maps and brochures. There are several ATMs in Villa de Leyva, particularly along the southern end of the Plaza Mayor. Internet cafés are also numerous.

An efficient and inexpensive laundry service in town near the bus terminal is **Lava Express** (Cra. 8 No. 8-21, cell tel. 320/856-1865, 8am-noon and 2pm-7pm Mon.-Fri., 8am-7pm Sat.). They can provide rush service and pick up and return your items to your hotel.

In case of an emergency contact the **Policía Nacional** (tel. 8/732-1412 or 8/732-0391) or the **Hospital San Francisco** (tel. 8/732-0516 or 8/732-0244).

Getting There and Around

With a recently expanded four-lane highway that bypasses Tunja, Villa de Leyva is easily accessible by private car or by public bus from Bogotá, as well as from Tunja. It isn't a crazy idea to rent a car in Bogotá and drive to Villa de Leyva. That gives you a lot of flexibility to be able to drive around the countryside and visit enchanting pueblos to your heart's content! Nearly all hotels have parking lots.

There are a few direct buses to Villa de Leyva from Bogotá (COP$20,000); however, often it is quicker and easier to take a bus from the Terminal Norte to Tunja and then transfer to a *buseta* (small bus) onward towards Villa de Leyva. These leave around every 15 minutes from the Terminal Villa de Leyva, not the main bus terminal. The last bus leaves Tunja at 7pm. This trip costs just COP$6,000.

Vice versa, the last bus bound for Tunja departs the **Terminal de Transportes** (Cra. 9 between Clls. 11-12) in Villa de Leyva at 6pm. It takes about 45 minutes.

Returning to Bogotá, several companies offer two daily buses that depart between 5 and 6am and again at around 1pm. There are many more options on Saturdays, Sundays, and Monday holidays. These tend to leave in the late afternoon at around 3pm.

To get to Villa de Leyva from Bucaramanga or San Gil in Santander, you'll have to hop on a bus to Tunja. This highway that extends from Bogotá to Venezuela is a busy one, and the journey can take five or six hours.

Once in Villa de Leyva, it is easy (and more importantly, a pleasure) to walk everywhere. A few streets around the Plaza Mayor, including the main drag, the Calle 13, are pedestrian only. Even on non-pedestrian streets it's hard for vehicles to zoom along.

Vicinity of Villa de Leyva
◖ SANTUARIO FLORA Y FAUNA IGUAQUE

One of the country's most accessible national parks is about 13 kilometers from Villa de Leyva. The **Santuario Flora y Fauna Iguaque** (www.parquesnacionales.gov.co, COP$37,500 non-Colombians, COP$14,000 residents in Colombia, COP$7,500 children and students) is an excellent place to experience the unique landscape of the Andean *páramo* (highland moor) as well as dry tropical forest. The protected area extends for some 6,750 hectares. It is also a park of several *lagunas* (mountain lakes). The Laguna Iguaque in particular is known as a sacred lake for the Muisca Indians who predominated in the area. According to their beliefs, the goddess Bachué was born out of the blue-green waters of this lake, giving birth to humanity.

Most day-trippers based in Villa de Leyva visit the park to make the climb up to the Laguna Iguaque. The climb, which takes you through three ecosystems—Andean forest, sub-*páramo*, and *páramo*—begins at the Centro Administrativo Carrizal at an elevation of 2,800 meters (9,185 feet) and ends 4.6 kilometers (2.6 miles) later at the Laguna Iguaque (3,650 meters/11,975 feet). The enjoyable hike takes about 3-4 hours to make. Along the way you may be able to spot different species of birds and perhaps some deer or foxes. At the mist-shrouded Laguna Iguaque, you'll be surrounded by hundreds of *frailejones,* an unusual cactus-like plant found only in this special ecosystem.

It is best to make the hike during the week, as the trails get crowded on weekends. You do not need a guide for the hike to the Laguna Iguaque. During particularly dry spells the threat of forest fires forces the park to forbid entry to visitors. That is most likely to occur in January or August. Ask beforehand at your hostel or hotel to find out if the park is open to visitors.

If you are interested in exploring other paths in the park, consider overnighting at the **Centro de Visitantes Furachiogua,** the park's basic accommodations facilities (catering mostly to student groups). Seven rooms have 6-8 beds each (COP$38,000 pp), and the restaurant is open to day-trippers as well. This is about 700 meters beyond the Centro Administrativo Carrizal. There are camping facilities near the cabins (COP$10,000 pp). To inquire about accommodations or to make a reservation contact the community organization **Naturar-Iguaque** (cell tel. 312/585-9892 or 318/595-5643, naturariguaque@yahoo.es). A guided walk to the Laguna Iguaque costs COP$80,000 for a group of 1-6.

Buses serving the town of Arcabuco from the bus station in Villa de Leyva can stop at the Casa de Piedra (8 km from Villa de Leyva). The first bus leaves at 6am with another departing at 10am. From there it's about three kilometers/two miles (about an hour's walk) to the east to the Centro Administrativo Carrizal visitors center.

PALEONTOLOGICAL SITES

During the Cretaceous period (66-145 million years ago), the area around Villa de Leyva was submerged in an inland sea. Some of the marine species that lived in the area included the pliosaurus, plesiosaurus, and ichthyosaurus.

Towards the end of this period, many species became extinct. Simultaneously the Andes mountains were created when the earth shifted. As the waters gave way to mountains, the bones of these species became imbedded in rock, guaranteeing their preservation. Today there are a handful of paleontological sites worth visiting, where you can view fossils of parts of massive dinosaurs to small ammonites, of which there are thousands. Excavations continue throughout the valley.

In 1977, locals made a fantastic discovery: a distant relative of carnivorous marine reptiles from the pliosaurus family, to be classified as a *Kronosaurus boyacensis Hampe*. It roamed this part of the earth some 110 million years ago. The first ever find of this species in the world can be seen, imbedded in the earth extending for about 10 meters, in the location of its discovery at the **Museo El Fósil de Monquirá** (Km. 4 Vía Santa Sofía, Vereda Monquirá, www.museoelfosil.com, COP$6,000). Guides give a brief tour of the museum, which has hundreds of other animal and plant fossils on display. This is a major tourist sight, and there are souvenir shops and juice stands nearby.

Across the street from Museo El Fósil de Monquirá is the **Centro de Investigaciones Paleontológicas** (cell tel. 314/219-2904, www.centropaleo.com, 9am-noon and 2pm-5pm Mon., Wed., and Thurs., 8am-5pm Fri.-Sun., COP$8,000), which opened in late 2012. On view here are parts of a *Platypterygius boyacensis*, as well as a *Callawayasaurus colombiensis*, which were all found nearby. While the center is a museum as well, the main focus of this nonprofit organization is research. Technicians in lab coats and white gloves carefully work behind the glass preparing and preserving fossils (Fri.-Sun.). An informative 20-minute tour of the center in Spanish is included.

Gondava (Km. 6 Vía Santa Sofía, www.

granvalle.com, 9am-5pm Tues.-Sun., COP$13,000) is more about fun than paleontology. This park is geared toward kids, taking visitors back in time, around 100 million years ago, when Earth was the domain of giant dinosaurs. This park has to-scale replicas of dozens of terrestrial and aquatic dinosaurs. The largest is the *brachiosaurus,* which stands 14 meters (46 feet) high. Other park attractions include a playground, labyrinth, and a 3-D movie theater.

On the northeastern edge of town is the **Museo Paleontológico de Villa de Leyva** (Cra. 9 No. 11-42, tel. 8/732-0466, www.paleontologico.unal.edu.co, 9am-noon and 2pm-5pm Tues.-Sat., 9am-3pm Sun., COP$3,000). Run by the Universidad Nacional, this museum provides an introduction to the fossils that have been found in the area, which date back 110-130 millions of years ago. On display are ammonites, which have become a symbol for the area, and other prehistoric animals that roamed the area. In addition, the museum has an arboretum with gardens of palms, oaks, and an Andean forest. This is behind the museum. It is about a 15-minute walk from the Plaza Mayor to the museum. On weekday mornings it can be a zoo with school groups being herded through.

CONVENTO DEL SANTO ECCE HOMO

Set idyllically atop a hill overlooking the town, the **Convento del Santo Ecce Homo** monastery (Cra. 6A No. 51A-78, tel. 1/288-6373, 9am-5pm Tues.-Sun., COP$5,000) was founded by the Dominicans on Palm Sunday in 1620. The monks were evicted on several occasions from this, their beautiful home. During the struggle for independence it was taken over by rebel troops under the command of a French general in 1816. In a matter of weeks the Spaniards seized it. Following definitive independence, President Santander, not a huge fan of the church, annexed the convent and ordered it to be used as a school. It was finally recuperated by the Dominicans in 1868.

The monastery is a delight to visit. Believers may find inspiration here; non-believers will appreciate the quiet beauty of its setting. In addition to the church, there are two striking small baroque chapels, plus a museum. Part of the museum is dedicated to indigenous cultures in the area. A monk's cell, library, and dining hall area provide a glimpse into monastery life. Surrounded by stone columns, the courtyard is awash in a rainbow of colors, with flowers always in bloom. Across the street from the monastery is a guesthouse and camping area open to the public.

For those feeling energetic, the trip up to the monastery makes for a great bike ride from Villa de Leyva. Be sure to get an early start and stop off at the **Cabanita Roja** (Vereda Barbilla, 1 km before the monastery, cell tel. 321/211-9653) for a pick-me-up snack to give you the stamina to conquer that last long hill.

HIKING

A popular hike for those seeking a thrill is the **Paso de Ángel** near the town of **Santa Sofía.** It's about six kilometers from town. The thrill comes when you walk along a narrow precipice between two canyons. You can take public transportation to Santa Sofía and walk to the Paso de Angel. **Colombian Highlands** (Renacer, Av. Cra. 10 No. 21, tel. 8/732-1201, cell tel. 311/308-3739, www.colombiahighlands.com) offers tours to the area and has maps if you'd like to do this on your own. You can take public transportation to Santa Sofía and walk to the Paso de Angel.

The popular **La Periquera Waterfalls** can be reached by taking a *colectivo* (small bus) bound for Gachantiva and getting off at El Uvalito. There are several falls, but the most impressive has a drop of 15 meters. The entrance to the falls is about 11 kilometers (7 miles) from town. This trip can be easily made on bike as well. A restaurant at the entrance serves snacks.

GETTING THERE AND AROUND

The environs of Villa de Leyva can be visited on bike, by taxi, or by public transportation. **CoomultransVilla** has hourly buses in the mornings, more or less, from the Terminal de Transportes in Villa de Leyva to Santa Sofía

(COP$2,500) departing at 6:45am, 8am, 9am, and 10am. They can let you off within easy walking distance of all the sights (Museo El Fósil de Monquirá, Convento del Santo Ecce Homo, etc.), as well as Santa Sofía if you are interested in the Paso de Ángel walk. Check the opening hours of the sights you'd like to visit so that you won't have to wait around to enter. There are also buses in the afternoon. The last bus departing Santa Sofía bound for Villa de Leyva leaves at around 4. You'll have to be on the lookout for it and flag it down. This company also can take you to the Periquera waterfalls (take the Gachantiva bus), fairly close to Iguaque (Arcabuco bus), and to Ráquira. It's easy and cheap. It's best to confirm all the bus schedules in advance.

RÁQUIRA

This town, 28 kilometers (17 miles) away from Villa de Leyva, is synonymous with *artesanías* (handicrafts). The main drag is lined with colorful shops, where in a one-stop shopping frenzy you can pick up **handicrafts** of every size and shape and from all across the country (and even from China): hammocks, *mochilas* (hats or handbags), and row after row of trinkets.

It's easy to be turned off by the trinket shopping scene, but there is some authenticity to be found in this little town. Ráquira is the capital of Colombian **ceramics** and has been since before the arrival of the Spaniards. In fact, it is said that the name Ráquira means "city of clay pots" in the Chibcha language of the Muiscas, who lived in the area. All of those reddish flower pots and planters you may have seen throughout the country most likely came from here.

Several shops in town specialize in pottery, and behind the shops you will often see trucks being carefully loaded up with pottery as they fulfill orders from across Colombia and beyond. One big shop within two blocks of the pleasant Parque Principal (Cras. 3-4 and Clls. 3-4) where you can peruse aisles upon aisles of the pottery is **Todo Ráquira** (Cra. 5 No. 3A-05, tel. 8/735-7000, www.todoraquira.com,

Ráquira is Colombia's ceramics capital.

9am-6pm daily). The front of the store is filled with a variety of handicrafts, but if you meander to the back, you'll see their pottery factory and can check out bowls, flowerpots, and other items. Many designs are elegant in their simplicity, like the many square planters. It is said that some 500 families in the area make their living harvesting the clay in nearby areas or firing the pottery in their own workshops. A dwindling number of women in the area do things the old-fashioned way—with their hands. They make mostly decorative items like candlestick holders and clay hen piggybanks. These aren't perfect, but they have so much character.

If you'd like to observe the ceramic-making process you can visit the *taller* (workshop) of **Isaias Valero** (cell tel. 310/774-5287, COP$5,000 suggested donation). You can watch him at work, and he can show you the multi-day steps that go into to the process. If he is there, Isaias will gladly welcome your visit. To get to the workshop, walk up about 68 steps on the right just before the Casa de la Cultura.

Convento de la Candelaria

One of the oldest monasteries in Latin America, and one that is still in use today, is the **Convento de la Candelaria** near Ráquira. A pair of Augustinian missionaries arrived in this desert area in 1588 with the mission of bringing Christianity to the native Muisca people. They lived in caves (which you can visit) until the monastery was constructed.

The complex includes two cloisters, which hold a chapel and a museum. The museum is a hodgepodge of religious art and objects, examples of technological advances through the years—from a *reloj borracho* (drunken clock) to an early Apple computer—and a display on the Colombian saint Ezequiel Moreno y Díaz, who is said to have healed cancer victims.

You may see a handful of young soon-to-be priests doing upkeep, often softly singing, in one of the colorful courtyards. They live in one part of the monastery with older monks in another.

Adjacent to the monastery is a modern hotel, **Posada San Agustín** (vocaciones@agustinosrecoletos.com.co, COP$168,000 d), which often hosts yoga and meditation retreats. Rooms are immaculately clean and completely free from clutter. Some even have hot tubs. At nighttime you can sit around a fire in the common area and sip hot, spiced wine. Meals are served in the restaurant, and they can also prepare vegetarian food. It's a quiet and peaceful place and there are some walks you can do nearby, one leading to a waterfall (a 1.5-hour walk).

Getting There

Buses from Villa de Leyva to Ráquira depart from the Terminal de Transportes, leaving between 7am and 8:30am. You may, however, prefer to hire a cab for the day, especially if you're traveling in a small group. Cab drivers typically charge COP$80,000 (for the car) to visit the Convento de la Candelaria and Ráquira, for example, with a couple of stops along the way. They will *esperar* (wait) for you to visit each stop. Be specific about where you want to go and the price at the beginning (put things in writing) to avoid unpleasant surprises later. If you are in a group you may want to upgrade to a minivan. Contact **Transportes G&J** (cell tel. 313/259-0589 or 311/746-8434) for a minivan.

If you'd like to visit the monastery, you can rent a taxi from Ráquira, which will cost about COP$20,000-30,000 round-trip. The trip takes about 15 minutes each way to make. (The taxi driver will wait for you while you visit it.) You can also take public transportation from the Parque Principal, and the bus can leave you at the intersection with a dirt road that leads to the monastery. Buses (COP$2,000) are infrequent, however. You can also walk to the monastery from town. It's a pretty seven-kilometer (four-mile) walk through the hilly countryside to reach the monastery from there.

TUNJA

This university town (pop. 178,000), home to the Universidad de Boyacá, boasts some spectacular churches. Make sure you arrive during church visiting hours, as the city does not have much else to offer. As there are frequent bus connections with Bogotá and Santander, Tunja is a good base from which to explore Boyacá.

Sights

Everything you need to see in Tunja is located in its *centro histórico.*

◖ HISTORIC CHURCHES

Tunja is a city of churches, with over a dozen that date to colonial times. Hours of visitation can be irregular, but they are always open for mass, which is a good time to take a look. Most churches celebrate mass at about 7am and 6pm daily, with more frequent masses on Sundays. There tend to be more churches open for visitation in the mornings (8am-11:30am) than in the afternoons.

On the eastern side of the **Plaza de Bolívar** (Cl. 19 at Cra. 9), **Catedral Santiago de Tunja** (Cra. 9 at Cl. 19) is a 16th-century construction, originally built out of wood and earthen *tapia pisada,* which is an adobe technique. It was the first cathedral to be built in Nueva Granada. It has three naves, four side chapels, and two front chapels.

Santa Clara La Real (Cra. 7 No. 19-58, Cl. 21 No. 11-31, tel. 8/742-5659 or 8/742-3194, 8am-11:30am and 3pm-4:30pm Mon.-Fri., 8am-11:30am Sat., masses 7am and 5pm Mon.-Sat., 7am, 11am, and 5pm Sun.) was built between 1571 and 1574 and was the first Clarisa convent in Nueva Granada. It has one nave with spectacular gold decorations adoring its presbytery with golden garlands, grapes, pineapples (which were a sacred indigenous symbol), pelicans, an anthropomorphic sun, and other symbols of nature. Also look for the seal of Tunja, the double-headed eagle, modeled on the seal of Emperor Charles V, who gave the city its charter. In the choir is the tiny cell where Madre Josefa del Castillo lived for over 50 years in the late 17th and early 18th centuries. From there she wrote two books and several poems, with themes of sexual repression and mystical descriptions of heaven and hell. Near her cell are some frescoes made with coal, an abundant resource in the area. The adjacent Convento Santa Clara La Real was undergoing a painstakingly careful restoration at the time of writing.

The sky-blue interior of the **Iglesia de Santa Bárbara** (Cra. 11 No. 16-62, between Clls. 16-17, tel. 8/742-3021, 8:30am-12:30pm and 2pm-6pm daily, masses 5:30pm and 6pm Mon.-Fri., 7am, 9am, 10am, and 11am Sat., noon, 5pm, 6pm, and 7pm Sun.) and Mudejar ceiling designs make this one of the prettiest churches in Tunja. The single-nave structure, with two chapels making the form of a cross, was completed in 1599. When it was built, it was raised at the edge of Tunja, near an indigenous settlement.

Built in the 1570s, the **Templo de Santo Domingo de Guzmán** (Cra. 11 No. 19-55, tel. 8/742-4725, 8am-11:30am Mon.-Fri., 7am and 6pm masses Mon.-Fri., 7am and 6pm masses Sat., 7am, 10am, noon, and 6pm masses Sun.) is one of the most elaborately decorated churches in Colombia. Visitors have been known to audibly gasp at their first sight of the spectacular Capilla del Rosario, a chapel constructed of wood painted in red and gold-plated floral designs. It's often dubbed the Sistine Chapel

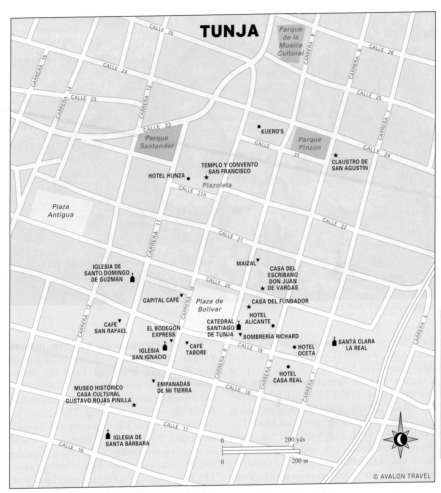

TUNJA

Parque de la Musica Cultural

CALLE 25
CALLE 24
CALLE 23
CALLE 22
CALLE 21A
CALLE 21
CALLE 20
CALLE 19
CALLE 18
CALLE 16
CALLE 12

CALLE 26
CALLE 25
CALLE 24
CALLE 22

CARRERA 15
CARRERA 14
CARRERA 12
CARRERA 11
CARRERA 12
CARRERA 9
CARRERA 8
CARRERA 7
CARRERA 5

Parque Santander

KUERO'S

Parque Pinzón

★ CLAUSTRO DE SAN AGUSTÍN

TEMPLO Y CONVENTO SAN FRANCISCO
HOTEL HUNZA
★ Plazoleta

Plaza Antigua

MAIZAL
CASA DEL ESCRIBANO DON JUAN
★ DE VARGAS

IGLESIA DE SANTO DOMINGO DE GUZMÁN

CAPITAL CAFÉ
Plaza de Bolívar
CASA DEL FUNDADOR

CAFÉ SAN RAFAEL
EL BODEGÓN EXPRESS
CATEDRAL SANTIAGO DE TUNJA
HOTEL ALICANTE
SOMBRERÍA RICHARD

IGLESIA SAN IGNACIO
CAFÉ TABORE
HOTEL OCETA
SANTA CLARA LA REAL

EMPANADAS DE MI TIERRA
HOTEL CASA REAL

MUSEO HISTÓRICO CASA CULTURAL GUSTAVO ROJAS PINILLA ★

IGLESIA DE SANTA BÁRBARA

0   200/yds
0   200 m

© AVALON TRAVEL

BOYACÁ

of baroque art in Latin America. Figures of El Nazareno and El Judío Errante are part of the collection of paintings and woodcarvings in this church with several chapels. If you have time to visit just one church in Tunja, make it this one.

The **Claustro de San Agustín** (Cra. 8 No. 23-08, tel. 8/742-2311, ext. 8306, www.banrepcultural.org/tunja, 8:30am-6pm Mon.-Fri., 9am-1pm Sat., free) dates to the late 16th century. It served as an Augustinian convent until 1821, when it was taken over by the government. The friars were sent to another convent, and the building would become the home of the Colegio de Boyacá and later transferred to the Universidad de Boyacá. Adorning the corridors around the patio are several murals dating back to the colonial era. The *claustro* (cloister) is administered by the Banco de la República, and they often hold cultural events here. You can settle down with a book or work on your computer in the pleasant reading rooms.

Other religious sights worth visiting include

© ANDREW DIER

a decorative church ceiling

the 17th-century **Iglesia San Ignacio** (Cra. 10 No. 18-41, tel. 8/742-6611, 8am-noon and 2pm-5pm Wed.-Sat.), which now serves as a theater, and the **Templo y Convento San Francisco** (Cra. 10 No. 22-32, tel. 8/742-3194, 10:30am-12:30pm and 3pm-5:30pm daily, 7am, 11am, noon, and 7pm mass Mon.-Fri., 11am, noon, 6pm, and 7pm mass Sat., 8am, 10am, 11am, noon, 5pm, 6pm, and 7pm mass Sun.), one of the oldest churches and monasteries in Tunja. It was an important base for evangelization of nearby indigenous communities.

MUSEUMS

The Mudejar-Andalusian style **Casa del Fundador Gonzalo Suárez Rendón** (Cra. 9 No. 19-68, Plaza de Bolívar, tel. 8/742-3272, 8am-noon and 2pm-6pm daily, COP$3,000) was built in the middle of the 16th century. The most remarkable aspects of the house are the frescoes of mythological creatures, human figures, exotic animals, and plants. These whimsical paintings date from the 17th century, although not much else is known about them.

Casa del Escribano del Rey Don Juan de Vargas (Cl. 20 No. 8-52, tel. 8/74-26611, 9am-noon and 2pm-5pm Tues.-Fri., 9am-noon and 2pm-4pm Sat.-Sun., COP$2,000) was owned by an important person in colonial Tunja, the scribe to the king. The scribe's jurisdiction covered all of present-day Boyacá, Santander, Norte de Santander, and parts of Venezuela and Cundinamarca. Student guides will give you a thorough tour of the museum. The house showcases furniture and other examples of colonial life, but the highlight of this Andalusian-style house has to be the unusual painted ceilings portraying exotic animals and mythological creatures, similar to the frescoes that can be found in the Casa del Fundador.

The childhood home of former president Gustavo Rojas Pinilla is now a museum: **Museo Histórico Casa Cultural Gustavo Rojas Pinilla** (Cl. 17 No. 10-63, tel. 8/742-6814, 8:30am-noon and 2pm-6pm Mon.-Fri.). Rojas, after seizing power in 1953, became the only dictator that Colombia has ever had. Upstairs are two exhibition spaces, one with memorabilia of Rojas and the other with portraits of 12 presidents that hailed from Boyacá. Despite his anti-democratic credentials, Rojas is revered in Tunja as the man who brought the mid-20th-century violence between Liberals and Conservatives to an end.

Shopping

Small **7 Kuero's** (Cl. 23 No. 9-90, tel. 8/743-7328, josekueros@hotmail.com, 9am-5pm Mon.-Sat.) is a shop specializing in leather goods. Next to the cathedral, the **Sombrería Richard** (Cr. 9 No. 19-06, tel. 8/747-1276, daily) is an old-school hat shop selling hats that seem to be from the 1950s.

Unicentro (Av. Universitaria No. 39-77, tel. 8/745-4108, 8am-11pm daily) is Tunja's mall, holding a movie theater, food court, and a *plazoleta de cafés,* an area with many different cafés. It is located in the modern neighborhood of La Pradera, to the north of downtown.

Accommodations

Most overnight visitors to Tunja stay in the decent hotels in the *centro histórico* within easy walking distance of the Plaza de Bolívar and sights of interest.

Two blocks from the Plaza de Bolívar is 🌜 **Hotel Casa Real** (Cl. 19 No. 7-65, tel. 8/743-1764, www.hotelcasarealtunja.com, COP$58,000 s, COP$72,000 d), which is a colonial-style house with 10 rooms surrounding a divine courtyard. That's where a very nice breakfast is served for an additional cost in the morning. You can order your breakfast the night before and even request it to be delivered to your room. Rooms are tastefully decorated and comfortable. Prices here are astoundingly low. The courtyard walls are decorated with lovely tile paintings depicting Boyacá country scenes. The artist, **Adriano Guio** (cell tel. 314/319-0822, aguio1@hotmail.com), has a studio near the town of Nobsa.

Across the street from Hotel Casa Real is the **Hotel Ocetá** (Cl. 19 No. 7-64, tel. 8/742-2886, www.hotelocetatunja.com, COP$90,000 d). It opened in 2012 and is clean and functional; beds are firm.

With the same owners as Hotel Casa Real, **Hotel Alicante** (Cra. 8 No. 19-15, tel. 8/744-9967, www.hotelalicantetunja.com, COP$72,000 d) caters to business clientele. This small hotel may not have the charm of Casa Real, but it is clean and matter of fact.

The fancy hotel in town is, as it has been for decades, the **Hotel Hunza** (Cl. 21A No. 10-66, tel. 8/742-4111, www.hotelhunza.com, COP$228,000 d). It's got luxurious king-size beds and card keys to get in. Amenities include a decent sized indoor pool and a steam room. Its neighbor is the Iglesia Santo Domingo, which makes for a strange view. The hotel is a popular place for wedding banquets. There is a lively bar near the entrance, but it shouldn't keep you up at night.

Food

Comida típica (Colombian fare) rules the day in this city lacking in restaurant options. For a really local, greasy-spoon-type experience, try **Restaurante Maizal** (Cra. 9 No. 20-30, tel. 8/742-5876, 7am-8:45pm Mon.-Sat., 9am-4:45pm Sun., COP$12,000). It has been serving *sancocho* (beef stews), *mondongo* (tripe stew), and *ajiaco* (chicken and potato soup) to Tunja for over 50 years. Another old-timer is **El Bodegón Express** (Cra. 10 No. 18-45, cell tel. 321/221-4460, 8am-4pm Mon.-Sat., COP$10,000). It's next to the Iglesia San Ignacio. It specializes in trout dishes and *cocido boyacense* (COP$6,000), which has a variety of meats and some of the unusual tubers from the area, such as *cubios, ibias,* and *rubas.*

🌜 **Empanadas de Mi Tierra** (Cra. 10 No. 17-67, cell tel. 320/414-0857, 10am-7pm daily) is a fast food joint that has 15 types of empanadas, with varieties such as Mexican, Asian, vegetarian, and cheese with quail's eggs. And you can douse them with many types of sauces. The empanadas go down well with a cool *avena cubana,* a creamy and cold oatmeal drink.

Pizza Nostra (Cl. 19 No. 10-63, tel. 8/740-2040, 11am-8pm daily, COP$18,000) has a few locations in and around town. The most famous one is at the Pozo de Donado (tel. 8/740-4200, 11am-11pm daily), a small park and Muisca archaeological site surrounding a lake.

It's a tradition in Tunja to while away the hours in cafés. It must be the chilly weather. While the actual coffee around town may disappoint, the atmosphere, with groups of retirees dressed in suits brushing shoulders with bevies of college students, does not. Put some *aguardiente* (anise-flavored liquor) in your coffee and enjoy the great view from the second floor of **Café Tabore** (Cl. 19 No. 9-57, tel. 8/742-2048, 7am-8pm daily), overlooking the Plaza de Bolívar. The lively Pasaje Vargas on the west side of the plaza is lined with several cafés. Try **Capital Café** (7am-7pm daily), which is at the entrance of the *pasaje* (passage) close to the Plaza de Bolívar. **Café San Rafael** (Cra. 11 No. 18-35, no phone, 8:30am-8pm Mon.-Sat.) is a tad more elegant than the rest.

Getting There and Around

Situated 150 kilometers northeast of Bogotá and 21 kilometers southeast of Villa de Leyva, Tunja is easy to get to by car or by bus. Buses to Bogotá, other towns in Boyacá, and to all major cities in Colombia depart from the **Terminal de Transportes** (Cra. 7 No. 16-40). Buses from Bogotá cost about COP$18,000 and from Villa de Leyva are COP$6,000. The best way to get around the *centro histórico* is on foot.

Puente de Boyacá

This war memorial on the road between Bogotá and Tunja celebrates a decisive battle, the **Batalla del Puente de Boyacá,** that effectively ended Spanish control of Nueva Granada. At this site today there are several memorials and statues, including the Plaza de Banderas, where flags from all the departments of Colombia fly. There is also a sculpture of Gen. Francisco Paula de Santander and a large sculpture of Gen. Simón Bolívar surrounded by angels representing the South American countries that he liberated (Bolivia, Colombia, Ecuador, Peru, and Venezuela). There is a small bridge on the memorial grounds, but this is from the 1930s; the original Puente de Boyacá long gone. Santander and Bolívar achieved immortality

as heroes of Colombian independence for their victory here. After defeating the Spaniards at the Batalla del Pantano de Vargas on July 25, 1819, revolutionary troops under their command marched toward Bogotá. South of Tunja, they engaged with the main Spanish army, defeating it decisively on August 7 at the Batalla del Puente de Boyacá. The engagement was a small affair with fewer than 3,000 men on each side, with about 100 royalists and only 13 rebels losing their lives. Bolívar marched onward to Bogotá, which he took without a fight, ushering in independence.

At 6pm every day there is a short flag-lowering ceremony. You can have your picture taken with Colombian soldiers. Buses passing through between Bogotá and Tunja can drop you off here, or you can contract a taxi from Tunja.

TUNJA TO LAGO TOTA
Paipa

The town of Paipa (pop. 32,000) is known for two things: its thermal baths and the Lanceros monument.

COMPLEJO TERMAL

The **Complejo Termal** (Km. 4 Vía Pantano de Vargas, tel. 8/785-0068, www.termalespaipa.co, 6am-10pm daily), the hot springs, is the biggest attraction in town. There are two parts to the hot springs complex; the **Parque Acuático** (COP$13,000) has three thermal water pools and pools for kids, and the **Centro de Hidroterapia** (COP$41,000) offers six activities for 20 minutes each, including hydro-massage, saunas, and mudbaths. On the weekends the park is packed, especially the Parque Acuático, which teems with families, so it's highly recommended to go on a much calmer weekday. To do the Centro de Hidroterapia circuit, call in advance to make a reservation. Slots are available daily at 7am, 10am, 1pm, 4pm, and 7pm. A limited number of people, around 16, are allowed during each session.

Between Paipa and the Complejo Termal is the manmade **Lago Sochagota.** The pedestrian path around the lake attracts locals and visitors alike, especially in the late afternoon. This is a nice thing to do after a good soak at the baths.

LOS LANCEROS

On the site of the **Batalla del Pantano de Vargas** (Battle of the Vargas Swamp) stands Colombia's largest sculpture, **Los Lanceros** (9 km south of Paipa on Paipa-Pantano de Vargas road, free). The massive monument was designed by Colombian sculptor Rodrigo Arenas Betancourt and built in commemoration of 150 years of Colombian independence. Bronze sculptures show the 14 *lanceros* (lancers on horseback) charging into battle, fists clenched in the air, with fear and defiance depicted on their faces. Above them is an odd triangular concrete slab that points into the heavens. It is 36 steps up to the platform of the monument, the age of Simón Bolívar on that fateful day. The monument generates strong opinions, and there is little gray area: You either love it or detest it.

The Batalla del Pantano de Vargas was a decisive battle during Simón Bolívar's independence march on Bogotá in 1819. After crossing the Llanos from Venezuela and climbing up the Andes via the Páramo de Pisba, the revolutionary army under Bolívar engaged with a contingent of Spanish troops at the Pantano de Vargas on July 25, 1819. Exhausted after their long slog over the Cordillera Oriental mountains, the revolutionary troops were nearly defeated. However, a charge by 14 armed horsemen led by Juan José Rendón saved the day. Soldiers from the British Foreign Legion, under the command of Irishman James Rooke, also played a decisive role in this battle. The royalists lost 500 men in the battle, while 350 revolutionaries perished.

Across from the monument is the **Casa Museo Comunitario Juan Vargas** (COP$1,000), a small museum mostly about the military campaigns of Simón Bolívar. It was in this house that Juan Vargas, his wife, and their 12 children were executed by the Spaniards for supporting the rebel troops. Oddly, there is not much information on the

© ANDREW DIER

the memorial of the Batalla del Pantano de Vargas, *Los Lanceros*

BOYACÁ

battle that occurred in the swamp across the street, but it's worth a quick look anyhow.

ACCOMMODATIONS AND FOOD

While there are some inexpensive hotels in town, it's much more pleasant to stay outside of town near the Complejo Termal, even if it means splurging somewhat. Midweek rates at these fancy hotels drop substantially.

The **Hacienda El Salitre** (Km. 3 Vía Paipa-Toca, tel. 8/785-1510, www.haciendaelsalitre.com, COP$350,000 d) is set in the countryside under towering eucalyptus trees, and you'll pass grazing cows to get there. At the hotel, go for one of the rooms with a thermal bathtub. Each day you'll be treated to a thermal bath three times (staff come in and change the water each time). Rooms are cozy, warm, and spacious, but not quite luxurious. The hotel has a very nice restaurant with outdoor seating, plus a café and a bar. Even if you are just passing through, the restaurant, with its lovely setting, is the best around. Here you can get a massage, and can take a horse out for a trot to a nearby lake. From Sunday to Friday there is a 30 percent discount. It's a big wedding banquet and honeymoon location on the weekends. The hacienda served as a barracks during the Pantano de Vargas battle in 1819.

Overlooking Lago Sochagota is the **Estelar Paipa Hotel y Centro de Convenciones** (tel. 8/785-0944, www.hotelesestelar.com, COP$286,000 d). This upmarket chain hotel is modern, service oriented, and well maintained. On site is a spa with thermal baths, the main attraction, and there are other activities on-site to keep you busy, such as a pool, tennis court, golf course, and horseback riding. With over 100 rooms, it is a popular place for large groups. Rates here don't substantially drop during the week, but it may be worth asking.

GETTING THERE AND AROUND

Paipa is 40 kilometers (25 miles) northeast of Tunja, and frequent buses make this route. The half-hour journey from Tunja costs COP$5,000. From Paipa, taxis to the

Complejo Termal area cost about COP$7,500. Buses from Sogamoso depart from the intersection of Carrera 14 and Calle 16 and cost about COP$4,000. The trip takes about 45 minutes.

Sogamoso

This city of over 100,000 habitants is about 75 kilometers (46 miles) east of Tunja and is known for being an important pre-Hispanic Muisca center. It was known as Suamoxi. It's a city of little charm; however, the Museo Arqueológico de Sogamoso is worth a stop.

SIGHTS

Run by the Universidad Pedagógica y Tecnológica de Colombia (UPTC) university in Tunja, the **Museo Arqueológico de Sogamoso** (Cl. 9A No. 6-45, tel. 8/770-3122, 9am-noon and 2pm-5pm Mon.-Sat., 9am-3pm Sun. and holidays, COP$5,000) has an extensive collection of artifacts of the Muisca civilization, the main indigenous group of Colombia. Muiscas lived in the area that is today the departments Boyacá, Santander, and Cundinamarca. Suamoxi was the seat of power for a confederation led by the Iraca. The Bacatá confederation (near Bogotá) and the Hunza (Tunja) confederation, led by the Zaque, were the most powerful of the Muisca confederations. The most memorable sight on the museum grounds is the fantastic Templo del Sol, a re-creation of a Muisca temple that was burnt to the ground by the Spaniards in the late 16th century. The museum is worth visiting, even though the exhibition spaces are drab and the sequence of exhibits does not flow very lucidly. That is a shame because there is an interesting history to tell and the collection is impressive. If you have the time and speak Spanish, hire a guide. Inquire at the ticket office. Look for the exhibit on *ocarinas,* which are whistles, usually ceramic, that are often zoomorphic in form. Also see the stunning black-and-white geometric designs of *torteros,* which are spindles used in spinning yarn, as well as remarkably well-preserved red-and-white ceramic vessels and urns.

ACCOMMODATIONS AND FOOD

The ◖ **Hotel Finca San Pedro** (Km. 2 Vía Aquitania, tel. 8/770-4222, www.fincasanpedro.galeon.com, COP$25,000 dorm, COP$80,000 d) is a lush hostel set among lovely gardens with fruit trees, vegetables, and flowers. (It's odd that there's no fruit at breakfast!) It's a popular place with international backpackers visiting Boyacá. The owner's son gives yoga classes on occasion. This friendly spot, a five-minute cab ride from Sogamoso (COP$4,000), is the best option in the area.

It is said that Bolívar stayed at the **Hacienda Suescun** (Km. 4 Vía Sogamoso-Tibasosa, tel. 8/779-3333, cell tel. 312/596-4506, www.haciendasuescunhotel.com, COP$164,000 d) before he headed off to face the Spaniards at the decisive Batalla del Puente de Boyacá. This *hacienda,* surrounded by tall trees covered with Spanish moss dangling towards the ground, has 18 rooms. It's north of Sogamoso. They have horses that can be taken out for a ride in the countryside.

GETTING THERE

There are easy bus connections between both Bogotá (3 hrs., COP$23,000) and Tunja to Sogamoso (1 hr., COP$15,000). The **Terminal de Transportes** (Cra. 17 between Clls. 11-11A, tel. 8/770-330) is downtown. Many buses connect Sogamoso with Paipa, Iza, Monguí, and Aquitania. Sogamoso is also a gateway to Los Llanos, with frequent bus service between Sogamoso and Yopal. This is a good, less expensive option for traveling to the Hacienda La Aurora south of Yopal. The trip between Sogamoso and Yopal takes about four hours to make and costs about COP$25,000.

Monguí

The chilly (average temperature is 13°C/55°F) highland colonial town of Monguí was founded in 1601 and was a strategic town for the Spaniards, as it was located between Tunja and the vast Llanos, the eastern plains. It has been designated as one of the most beautiful towns in Boyacá. Its narrow cobblestone streets are lined with white and green houses, many well over a couple of centuries old. It's in a valley below the highland moor of **Páramo de Ocetá,** dubbed the most beautiful *páramo* in the world. You can decide for yourself by hiking among its armies of *frailejón* plants, mountain lakes, and enormous boulders. Hotel staff can contact a knowledgeable local guide (around COP$50,000) to accompany you through this unusual landscape.

SIGHTS

Three colonial constructions in Monguí have been declared national monuments. The stone **Basílica y Convento de Nuestra Señora de Monguí** stand on the Plaza de Bolívar. The Franciscan convent today houses a Museo de Arte Religioso highlighting the work of the famous 17th-century Colombian baroque painter Gregorio Vásquez de Arce y Ceballos. Other historic buildings are the **Capilla de San Antonio de Padua,** which was the town's first church, and the photogenic stone bridge, the **Puente de Calicanto.**

Today Monguí is almost as famous for its soccer ball-making industry as for its colonial beauty. Around 70 percent of the town works in about 20 small factories in this industry, which has been around since the 1950s. They churn out some 30,000 balls each month. (More balls are produced during World Cup years as demand tends to spike.) You can pick up a "Made in Monguí" soccer ball at the shop **Balones Hurtado** (Cl. 7 No. 3-60, tel. 8/778-2021, www.baloneshurtado.com). Their slogan is "more than a ball...inspiration for your feet!"

ACCOMMODATIONS AND FOOD

There are not many accommodations options in and around town, but one of the best is **La Casona de San Francisco de Asis** (Cra. 4A No. 3-41, tel. 8/778-2498, COP$40,000 pp d). Rooms have a view over the Río Morro canyon, and the hotel is quite tidy. The restaurant, which has been in service for over two decades, is also one of the best in town. The restaurant specializes in *cocido boyacense,* which has a variety of meats and some of the unusual tubers from the area, such as *cubios, ibias,* and *rubas.*

The **Calicanto Real** (cell tel. 311/811-1519, juliosaenz66@hotmail.com, COP$25,000 pp) is an old house with five rooms located on the other side of the Puente de Calicanto. It was once owned by a wealthy emerald miner, was abandoned for several years, and now it is has been refurbished as a hotel. Rooms are spacious with nice views and have a lot of character, but the beds are soft. Adjacent to the hotel is a tavern filled with decorations like cowboy hats, animal heads, and an homage to Monguí's most famous poet: Mora Sáenz Rómulo, also known as "El Indio Romulo." Born in the 1930s, the charismatic poet became famous nationwide for defining a genre of campesino poetry, commenting on social ills using the language of rural folk. He recorded several albums of poetry, was awarded dozens of medals for his contributions to cultural life, and even served as mayor of his hometown.

The **Hospedaje el Rincón de Duzgua** (Vereda Duzgua, tel. 8/778-2130) is a cabin outside of town, and it's a good place for exploring the Páramo de Ocetá.

GETTING THERE

There are two roads between Sogamoso and Monguí. The old but scenic route is partly unpaved and winds through eucalyptus forests and the pueblo of Morca. It's about 20 kilometers (12 miles) and makes an excellent bike ride. On the new road, a bus ride to Monguí costs about COP$4,000 and takes about 45 minutes. The bus leaves from the intersection of Carrera 14 and Calle 16.

Iza

Serene and sleepy Iza (pop. 2,081), 14 kilometers (9 miles) southwest of Sogamoso on the way to Lago Tota, is a charming pueblo. There are not heaps of activities to do here, and there is no huge attraction except for possibly nearby hot springs. This well-preserved town, originally a Muisca settlement before the conquest, is nestled in a valley of green pastures and is surrounded by low mountains. Iza's a good place to walk about, take in some fresh air, exchange pleasantries with locals (and cows) surprised by your presence, and escape from the tourist trail.

traffic in Iza

© ANDREW DIER

The thermal baths are just outside of town (you can even walk there) at **Termales Erika** (Vereda Aguacaliente, tel. 8/779-0038, 7am-6pm daily, COP$8,000). They are closed on Mondays for cleaning, thus Tuesday is the best day for a soak!

In Iza, the local specialty is cakes, pies, and other sugary sweets. Bakers constantly swat away bees at their stands on the shady Parque Principal as they await customers on the weekends. A good place to eat something other than sweets is **La Casona Parrilla Bar** (cell tel. 320/222-6293, 1pm-10pm Sat.-Sun., COP$12,000). It specializes in grilled meats.

To get to Iza from Sogamoso, take a bus (COP$3,000) that leaves from the intersection of Carrera 11 with Calle 8. This is known as the Puente de Pesca.

Lago Tota

One of the most popular destinations in Boyacá is the Lago Tota, Colombia's largest lake. The views are spectacular here with mountains, valleys, and fields surrounding the lake. It measures 47 kilometers (29 miles) in perimeter. The main town on the lake is Aquitania; however, most visitors choose to stay at one of the cozy lakeside lodges nearby. A day trip from Sogamoso to Playa Blanca, a chilly lakeside beach, can also be arranged. But to truly relax, plan to stay the night so that you can enjoy watching the sun slowly slip away in the distance at sunset and relax by the fireplace with a glass of wine (bring your own) as the night wears on. Biking, walks, and boat rides to one of the handful of uninhabited islands on the lake are other activities you may enjoy. If you have a mountain bike, a nice ride is along the western side of the lake, along a mostly dirt road.

The lake and surrounding countryside, a patchwork of fields of green onions and potatoes, is beautiful, without a doubt. However, the lake is in peril. The dumping of fertilizers and pesticides from lakeside farms has been the primary reason that the Lago de Tota, a lake that provides drinking water for hundreds of thousands of people, has been declared one of the top five most threatened wetlands in the world by the World Wetlands Network. There are other culprits as well: large caged trout farms, the use of lake water at a nearby steel plant, and the most recent threat, oil exploration in the area by a large French oil company.

RECREATION

Playa Blanca (COP$3,500 entry) is the lake's beach, and a strange scene often awaits you there. Boys playing soccer on the white sand, university students from Bogotá hanging out drinking beer, and teenage boys in swimsuits alongside *abuelas* (grandmothers) bundled up in their wool *ruanas* (ponchos) watching the proceedings. Besides sampling one of 16 fresh trout dishes on offer at the restaurant (open 8am-5pm daily), other activities at the beach include taking a tour of the lake (COP$6,000) and horseback riding.

ACCOMMODATIONS

A handful of inviting lodge-type hotels are around the lake to the north and west of the lakeside town of **Aquitania.** Bargains can be had during the week, when you will have the lodge (if not the lake) blissfully to yourself. The area caters to weekenders from Bogotá.

The Decameron all-inclusive hotel chain has agreements with three hotels in the area. The **Decameron Refugio Santa Inés** (Km. 29 Vía Sogamoso-Aquitania, tel. 8/772-8860, cell tel. 313/261-2429, santaineshotel@gmail.com, COP$99,000 pp d) is a comfortable lodge-type hotel with 13 rooms and two cabins. Wood ceilings and floors add to the atmosphere. Set on the eastern side of the lake, the hotel's terrace is an ideal vantage point to watch the sunset. Beds are very comfortable, there is wireless Internet access, and breakfast is included. The restaurant offers other meals as well. Hotel staff can arrange for walks to a *páramo,* and horseback riding and taking a boat around the lake are other activities on offer. This is the nicest Decameron option. **Hotel El Camino Real** (Km. 20 Vía Sogamoso-Aquitania, tel. 8/770-0684, mauriciofigueroa@yahoo.com,

© ANDREW DIER

serene countryside around Colombia's largest lake, Lago Tota

www.decameron.com, COP$84,000 pp d) and **Refugio Rancho Tota** (Km. 21 Vía Sogamoso-Aquitania, tel. 8/770-8083, www.hotelran-chotota.com, COP$80,000 pp d) are the other two. These have similar pricing and similar facilities, and both have small spas.

For charm, and a room with a view, there are two longstanding stone lodge options. **Rocas Lindas** (cell tel. 310/349-1107, www.hotelrocaslindas.wordpress.com, COP$85,000 pp d) is a cozy lodge with 10 rooms and one cabin. There's no wireless Internet here, and this hotel could use some upgrading. **Pozo Azul** (Bogotá tel. 1/620-6257, cell tel. 320/384-1000, www.hotelrefugiopozoazul.com, COP$196,000 d) was one of the first nice hotels on the lake, and it still oozes charm. When you walk in you'll often see guests gathered by a circular fireplace in the lobby area. The hotel has 15 rooms and two *cabañas*. It is on an inlet of the lake. Some beds are on the soft side, and you have to descend 80 steep steps to get from the parking lot to the lodge. That could be difficult for those with physical limitations, and it

will leave all but Olympic athletes out of breath when they finally reach the hotel.

Getting There
Buses that go directly to Playa Blanca, via Iza, depart Sogamoso from the intersection of Carrera 11 with Calle 8 (Puente de Pesca). Otherwise, take any bus bound for the town of Aquitania (Plaza Principal). From the market, four blocks away, take another bus to Playa Blanca. It takes about an hour to get to the lake, and the bus costs about COP$4,000. Taxis are also available.

SIERRA NEVADA DEL COCUY
The Sierra Nevada del Cocuy, the highest mountains within the Cordillera Oriental (Eastern Range) of the Andes mountain chain, is 260 kilometers (162 miles) northeast of Bogotá in northern Boyacá. The entire mountain range is contained within and protected by the **Parque Nacional Natural El Cocuy,** the country's fifth largest national park. With its 11 jagged snowcapped peaks,

© ANDREW DIER

the beach at Playa Blanca on Lago Tota

massive glacier-formed valleys, extensive *páramos* (highland moors) studded with exotic *frailejón* plants, and stunning crystalline mountain lakes, streams, and waterfalls, it is one of the most beautiful places in Colombia. The sierra appeals to serious mountaineers and rock climbers, but it is also a place that nature-lovers with little experience and no gear can explore by doing easily organized day hikes.

PLANNING YOUR TIME

Getting to the Sierra Nevada del Cocuy entails a long, grueling trip, albeit through the beautiful, verdant countryside of Boyacá. Ideally you would want to spend at least four days there, taking in the spectacular mountain landscapes.

The park has three sectors: the Northern, Central and Southern Sectors, each with many options for day hikes, more strenuous ascents to the snowcapped peaks, or highly technical rock-climbing expeditions. There is also a spectacular six-day trek along a valley between the two main ridges of the sierra. It is not a highly technical trek but requires good high-altitude conditioning. For many visitors, this is the main reason to visit the sierra.

The towns of El Cocuy and Güicán are convenient arrival and departure points to visit the area. In both you can find basic tourist services, tour operators and guides, and stores to stock up on food, though not trekking equipment (though this can be rented from local tour operators). Both have a few interesting sights and are departure points for day hikes. El Cocuy is better located to access the Southern Sector of the park and Güicán the Northern Sector. However, since both of these towns are around 20 kilometers (12 miles) from the park and there is limited public transportation, a good option is to base yourself nearer to the park edge in one of several pleasant lodges or campsites. You could easily spend a few days in each one of the three sectors, setting off on beautiful day hikes.

The only way to do the six-day hike around the park is with an organized tour, as the trails are not marked. If you are planning to do this trek, you may want to arrive a few days earlier to do some high altitude acclimatization hikes. Many peaks are above 5,000 meters (16,000 feet) high.

The only dependable time to visit the Sierra Nevada del Cocuy is from December to March, during the *verano* (main dry season) in the Cordillera Oriental. At other times, there may be permanent cloud cover and much rain. High season, when Colombian visitors flock to the mountains, is from mid-December to mid-January, and again in Holy Week (late March or April). So, if you have the flexibility, visit in early December or from late January through early March.

The best available topographical maps of the Sierra Nevada de Cocuy, which might be helpful in planning your visit, can be viewed and downloaded online (www.nevados.org).

El Cocuy

El Cocuy is a charming colonial town nestled in the lower folds of the Sierra Nevada del Cocuy at an altitude of 2,750 meters. The town is meticulously kept up, with whitewashed houses painted with a band of aquamarine blue. The only real sight to check out is in the Parque Principal, where there is a large diorama of the Sierra Nevada del Cocuy. This will allow you to understand the broken mountain geography, with its multitude of snowcapped peaks, lakes, and valleys. In the town there are decent accommodations, a few tour operators, and some stores to stock up for a visit to the park, though no specialized mountaineering stores.

RECREATION

For a spectacular panoramic view of the entire sierra, take a hike to **Cerro Mahoma** (Mahoma Hill), to the west of the town of El Cocuy. It is a strenuous six- to seven-hour excursion often used by people who are acclimatizing to high altitude before trekking in the Sierra Nevada del Cocuy. The trailhead is outside of town on the road that leads to the town of Chita. As the trail is not marked and splits several times, it is better to go with a guide. For an experienced local guide, contact the local guide association,

ASEGUICOC (Asociación de Prestadores de Servicios Ecoturísticos de Güicán y El Cocuy, cell tel. 311/557-7893, aseguicoc@gmail.com).

ACCOMMODATIONS AND FOOD

Hotel la Posada del Molino (Cra. 3 No. 7-51, tel. 8/789-0377, www.elcocuycasamuseo. blogspot.com, COP$20,000 pp d) is a friendly guesthouse. Rooms in this old house are set around two colorful interior patios. The house has a little history to it, as well. Apparently during the deadly feuds between Güicán and El Cocuy (Güicán was conservative and El Cocuy was liberal), the famous Virgen Morenita image was taken from its shrine in Güicán and hidden away in the house where the hotel is located. You can see the room that hid this secret.

Casa Muñoz (Cra. 5 No. 7-28, tel. 8/789-0328, www.hotelcasamunoz.com, COP$20,000 pp d) has a great location overlooking the main plaza in town. It offers a restaurant in the patio on the main floor. Rooms are fine, though somewhat small, with firm beds and wooden floors.

Hotels, like the Casa Muñoz, generally offer the best food, but don't expect to be gobsmacked come dinnertime. Vegetarians may want to travel with a can of emergency lentils to hand over to kitchen staff to warm up for you.

INFORMATION AND SERVICES

At the offices of the **Parque Nacional Natural El Cocuy** (Cl. 5 No. 4-22, tel. 8/789-0359, 7am-noon and 1pm-4:45pm daily, cocuy@parquesnacionales.gov.co, COP$37,500 non-Colombians, COP$14,000 residents, COP$7,500 children/students), you can obtain a park entry permit and general information.

There is an **ATM** at the Banco Agrario at Carrera 4 and Calle 8.

GETTING THERE

The towns of El Cocuy and Güicán are served from Bogotá by three bus companies. The trip takes 11 hours, stops at El Cocuy, and terminates at Güicán. The most comfortable option is with the bus company **Libertadores** (COP$50,000), which operates a big bus, leaving Bogotá at 8:30pm. The return trip departs El Cocuy at 7:30pm. Bus line **Fundadores** (COP$45,000) has two buses, leaving Bogotá at 5am and 4:30pm, returning from El Cocuy at 7:30am and 8:30pm. **Concord** (COP$45,000) also has two services, leaving Bogotá at 3am and 5pm and leaving El Cocuy for Bogotá at 5:30am and 7:30pm.

Güicán

Long before its foundation in 1822, Güicán was a place of significance for the U'wa indigenous people. The U'wa fiercely resisted the Spanish conquest, and, rather than submit to domination, their chief Güicány led the people to mass suicide off a nearby cliff known as El Peñón de los Muertos. This little-known act of defiance is the New World's equivalent of the Masada mass suicide in ancient Judea.

The town, damaged by fires and civil war, is a mix of modern and old buildings, without much charm. However, it is a convenient starting point to visit the Northern Sector of the park. It has good accommodations, several tour operators, and some interesting sights and is the starting point for numerous beautiful day hikes.

Folks in Güicán resent that the national park carries the "El Cocuy" name. They feel that this natural wonder is just as much theirs as it is their rivals in the town of El Cocuy. You can score points with them by referring to the park as Parque Nacional Natural El Güicán.

SIGHTS

The main sight in town is the image of the Virgen Morenita de Güicán, located in the **Iglesia de Nuestra Señora de la Candelaria** (Parque Principal). This image of the virgin, with strong indigenous traits, appeared to the survivors of the U'wa mass suicide and ushered in their conversion to Christianity.

At the entrance to the town on the road from El Cocuy is the **Monumento a la Dignidad de la Raza U'wa** (Monument to U'Wa Dignity), a large statue that depicts the culture and history of the U'Wa people. It was designed by a local artist with input from the community.

RECREATION

There are several pleasant day hikes to be done from Güicán. A mildly strenuous three-kilometer (two-mile), two-hour round-trip hike takes you to the base of the **Peñón de los Muertos** (3,800 meters/12,500 feet), site of the U'wa mass suicide. The 300-meter cliff is imposing, and the thought of hundreds of people jumping off in defiance will send shivers through your body. From the Parque Principal, follow the road east towards the Vereda San Juan. Several signs indicate the way, so you will not need a guide.

A longer and more strenuous 11-kilometer (7-mile), six-hour hike leads northeast along the **Sendero del Mosco** (Mosco Trail) up the Río Cardenillo, passing sheer cliffs to a spot called Parada de Romero, which is the initial (or ending, depending on which way you go) segment of the six-day circuit around the Sierra Nevada del Cocuy. The hike ends at an altitude of 3,800 meters and is a good acclimatization walk. The trailhead is off the road that leads from El Güicán to the Parque Nacional Natural El Cocuy. As the trail is not marked, it is better to take a guide. Contact the association of local guides, **ASEGUICOC** (Asociación de Prestadores de Servicios Ecoturísticos de Güicán y El Cocuy, cell tel. 311/557-7893, aseguicoc@gmail.com).

ACCOMMODATIONS

The **Brisas del Nevado** (Cra. 5 No. 4-57, cell tel. 310/629-9001, http://brisasdelnevado. com, COP$35,000 pp) has the best accommodations and restaurant in town. Four rooms in the original house sleep 2-4 persons each. Outside is a nicer cabin with two rooms. The only problem is it is located next to a *tejo* bar. *Tejo* is a Colombian sport heavily associated with drinking.

El Eden (Tr. 2 No. 9-58 Urbanización Villa Nevada, cell tel. 311/808-8334, luishernandonc@hotmail.com, COP$30,000 pp) is in a residential neighborhood about 10 minutes up from the main plaza. It's a friendly place with lots of rooms, and you can use their kitchen.

Rabbits and parakeets are caged in the garden below.

Hotel Guaicani (Cl. 5 No. 6-20, cell tel. 312/524-3449, guaicany@hotmail.com, COP$20,000 pp d) is not wonderful, but it does offer trekking services and equipment rental.

Just outside of town is the **Hotel Ecológico El Nevado** (road to El Cocuy, cell tel. 320/808-5256 or 310/806-2149, www.hoteleconevado. jimdo.com, COP$60,000 d), in a spacious and green setting. There are two parts to the hotel: the original quaint farmhouse with an interior patio and a modern wing. The farmhouse has loads more character, but the modern wing is, well, modern.

INFORMATION AND SERVICES

At the offices of the **Parque Natural Nacional El Cocuy** (Tr. 4 No. 6-60, 7am-noon and 1pm-4:45pm daily) you can obtain a park entry permit and general information.

GETTING THERE

Güicán is served from Bogotá by three bus companies. The trip takes 11 hours and terminates at Güicán, with a stop at El Cocuy. The most comfortable option is with company **Libertadores** (COP$50,000), which operates a big bus, leaving Bogotá at 8:30pm and returning from Güicán at 7pm. **Fundadores** (COP$45,000) has two buses, leaving Bogotá at 5am and 4:30pm and departing Güicán at 7am and 8pm. **Concord** (COP$45,000) also has two services, leaving Bogotá at 3am and 5pm and returning to Bogotá from Güicán at 5am and 7pm. If you are in a hurry, you can take **Cootransdatil** to Soatá (COP$15,000) at 7am, 11am, or 2pm. From Soatá there are frequent departures for Duitama and Bogotá.

◖ PARQUE NACIONAL NATURAL EL COCUY

Located about 20 kilometers (12 miles) east of the towns of El Cocuy and Güicán, the **Parque Nacional Natural El Cocuy** (tel. 8/789-0359, cocuy@parquesnacionales.gov.co, COP$37,500 for non-Colombian visitors, COP$14,000

Colombians and residents, COP$7,500 children/students) covers an area of 306,000 hectares (760,000 acres) spanning the departments of Boyacá, Arauca, and Casanare.

The Sierra Nevada del Cocuy, consisting of two parallel ranges 30 kilometers long with 11 peaks higher than 5,000 meters, is the centerpiece of the park. However, the park extends far north and east from the sierra and includes extensive tracts of temperate and tropical forests. It also includes 92,000 hectares (230,000 acres) of U'wa indigenous *resguardos* (reservations), which are not open to tourism.

The Sierra Nevada del Cocuy is home to the largest expanse of glaciers in Colombia, extending 16 square kilometers (6 square miles). What are usually referred to as *nevados* (snow-capped mountains) are in fact glacier-capped mountains. The highest peak is **Ritacuba Blanco** (5,380 meters/17,650 feet). Other notable glacier-capped peaks are **Ritacuba Negro** (5,350 meters, 17,550 feet), **San Pablín Norte** (5,200 meters, 17,060 feet), **Cóncavo** (5,200 meters/17,060 feet), and **Pan de Azúcar** (5,100 meters, 16,730 feet). One of the most striking peaks in the Sierra Nevada del Cocuy is the **Púlpito del Diablo** or Devil's Pulpit (5,100 meters, 16,730 feet), a massive rectangular flat-top rock formation. (A side note: Be sure to refer to it as the Púlpito del Diablo (Devil's Pulpit) and not Pulpíto del Diablo, which means the Devil's Little Octopus.) Of these, Ritacuba Blanco, Cóncavo, and Pan de Azúcar can be ascended by anyone in good physical shape and do not require mountain climbing skills.

Unfortunately, all the glaciers in Colombia, including those of the Sierra Nevada del Cocuy, are rapidly melting due to global warming. A 2013 report by the Colombian Hydrological, Meteorological, and Environmental Studies Institute (IDEAM) forecasts that, by 2030, all the glaciers in Colombia will have disappeared.

At the base of the peaks are numerous glacier-formed valleys supporting *páramos,* unique tropical high altitude ecosystems of the Andes. The *páramos* are covered with beautiful *frailejones,* plants that have imposing tall trunks and thick yellow-greenish leaves. Other *páramo*

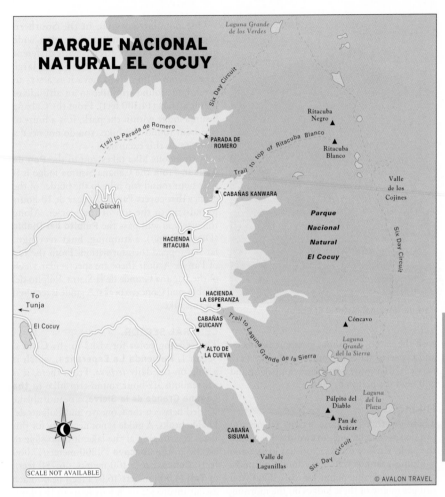

vegetation includes shrubs, grasses and *cojines* (cushion plants).

Erwin Krauss, a Colombian of German descent was the first modern explorer of the sierra in the 1930s. In the 1960s and 1970s, Colombian and European expeditions climbed most of the peaks. During the 1980s and 1990s, there was significant ELN and FARC presence and tourism all but disappeared.

In the past decade, the army has reestablished control of the area around the Sierra Nevada de Cocuy, and tourists have started to come back. In the 2012-2013 season, there were an estimated 9,000 visitors. The Colombian Park Service has been scrambling to deal with the influx of visitors.

Entry permits (which include entry fees) are required and can be easily obtained at the park offices in El Cocuy or Güicán. In peak season from mid-December to mid-January and during Easter week, it is better to obtain the permit several weeks in advance through the Park Service in Bogotá. Call (tel. 1/353-2400) or email (ecoturismo@parquesnacionales.gov.co)

© ANDREW DIER

Parque Nacional Natural El Cocuy

with the names of visitors, passport numbers, and expected dates of your arrival. The Park Service will provide instructions for paying and will send the permit by email.

Hiking

There are three separate sectors where you can do spectacular one- to two-day hikes into the park. Each of these sectors has lodges and camping grounds that serve food and make convenient starting points for these hikes. You can get to any of these lodges on the morning *lechero* (milk truck). Every morning the milk man collects fresh milk from family dairy farms throughout the countryside.

SOUTHERN SECTOR

This sector is accessed by a road from the **Alto de la Cueva,** a stop on the *lechero* route. There are two good lodging options in this area, and they serve as points of reference: **Cabañas Guicany,** a lodge at Alto de la Cueva outside the park, and **Cabaña Sisuma,** a lodge 10 kilometers (6 miles) from Alto de la Cueva inside the park.

One popular day hike in the Southern Sector is up to **Lagunillas** through a wide glacier-formed valley strewn with different types of *frailejones* and passing four large lakes. From Alto de la Cueva it is a six- to seven-hour round-trip hike to an altitude of 4,300 meters (14,100 feet). From the Cabaña Sisuma lodge within the park, it is a four- to five-hour round-trip hike. You do not need a guide to do this excursion.

A strenuous hike takes you to the **Pan de Azúcar.** From the Cabaña Sisuma lodge it is a six-hour round trip hike to the border of the glacier that covers Pan de Azúcar or 10 hours round-trip to the top of the glacier. Along the way you will pass the **Púlpito del Diablo** (Devil's Pulpit), a stunning, huge rectangular flat-topped rock formation. From the top of Pan de Azúcar there are spectacular views of the Laguna Grande de la Sierra, Púlpito del Diablo, and Cóncavo peaks. A guide is required for this hike.

CENTRAL SECTOR

The starting point for visits to the Central Sector is **Hacienda La Esperanza,** which is a stop on the daily *lechero.* From there, it is a strenuous six-hour round-trip hike to **the Laguna Grande de la Sierra,** a beautiful lake nestled between the Cóncavo and Púlpito del Diablo peaks. A guide is not necessary for this hike. By camping at the lake, it is possible to ascend to the **Cóncavo** (5,200 meters/17,060 feet), **Concavito** (5,100 meters, 16,730 feet), or **Toti** (4,900 meters/16,075 feet) peak. Each ascent involves a strenuous four- to five-hour round-trip hike and should be done with a guide. From the Laguna Grande de la Sierra, it is also possible to reach Cabaña Sisuma, in the Southern Sector, in nine hours. A guide is necessary as this trail is not well marked.

NORTHERN SECTOR

The starting point for hikes in the Northern Sector is **Cabañas Kanwara.** A short and mildly strenuous three- to four-hour round-trip hike takes you to the **Alto Cimiento del Padre,** a mountain pass at 4,200 meters (13,800 feet).

This hike offers spectacular views of Ritacuba Negro peak. This hike does not require a guide.

Cabañas Kanwara is also the starting point for hikes to the gently sloping **Ritacuba Blanco,** the highest peak in the Sierra Nevada del Cocuy. The ascent to the top can be done in one grueling 9- to 10-hour excursion, leaving at 2am or 3am in order to reach the peak in the morning when conditions are best for climbing on the glacier. Most people, however, split the trek into two, camping at the Playitas camp spot halfway up. A guide is necessary for this trek.

SIX-DAY CIRCUIT

An unforgettable experience is to do the six-day trek through the glacier-formed valleys lying between the two north-south ranges of mountains. Along the whole trip you will have glacier-capped mountains on both sides. There are a few mountain passes, but generally the altitude is 4,000-4,500 meters (13,100-14,800 feet). You do not need to be an expert mountaineer, but in addition to being in good physical condition, you need to be acclimatized to the altitude. A few days of day treks before doing the circuit may be required. Do not attempt this trek without a knowledgeable guide, as it's easy to get lost in this treacherous landscape. The basic tour, which involves carrying all your own gear, will cost on average COP$700,000 per person. Don't pay less than that because it means the operator is skimping on the guide's salary. High-end tours, with porters and a cook, will cost COP$1,500,000 per person.

TOUR OPERATORS AND GUIDES

Whether you decide to do a couple of day hikes or the six-day trek, securing a reliable, professional guide will greatly increase your enjoyment. For day hikes, contact the local guide association **Asociación de Prestadores de Servicios Ecoturísticos de Güicán y El Cocuy** (ASEGUICOC, cell tel. 311/557-7893, aseguicoc@gmail.com). For day hikes, expect to pay about COP$80,000-100,000. If you ascend to the top of a glacier, the daily rate goes up to

COP$130,000-150,000 and includes necessary gear. One highly knowledgeable guide is **Julio Suárez** (cell tel. 311/509-4413, ucumary13@gmail.com).

One of the leading trekking operators in the Sierra Nevada del Cocuy is **Colombia Trek** (Cra. 4 No. 6-50, Güicán, cell tel. 320/339-3839, www.colombiatrek.com), run by knowledgeable veteran Rodrigo Arias. It is one of the few operators offering English-speaking guides, and it is highly recommended.

Another tour company based in El Cocuy is **Servicios Ecoturísticos Güicány** (Cra. 5 at Cl. 9, El Cocuy, cell tel. 310/566-7554), run by Juan Carlos Carreño, son of the owner of Cabañas Güicány.

Avoid horseback rides through the park. Horses and cattle have caused significant damage to the flora of the park, and both are officially illegal. Unfortunately, many lodge owners do not agree with this environmental policy and refuse to adhere to it.

Accommodations

While not luxurious by any means, the lodging options in and around the park are just what you'd expect and want in this mountain environment. And the owners are all quite attentive and extremely friendly. Plan to spend some time hanging out in and around your hotel. It's nice to explore the countryside and meet locals.

SOUTHERN SECTOR

The best located accommodation in the Southern Sector is ◖**Cabaña Sisuma** (cell tel. 311/236-4275 or 311/255-1034, aseguicoc@gmail.com, COP$35,000 pp), a cozy cabin inside the park in the Lagunillas sector run by the local tour guide association ASEGUICOC. It has six rooms, good food, and fireplaces to keep one warm. It is a two-hour hike into the park from the Alto de la Cueva, a stop on the daily *lechero*.

Another pleasant and comfortable option is ◖**Cabañas Güicány** (Alto de la Cueva, cell tel. 310/566-7554, cab_guaicany@yahoo.es or guaicany@hotmail.com, COP$50,000 pp with meals, COP$30,000 without meals,

COP$10,000 pp camping), owned by old timer Eudoro Carreño. The *lechero* can drop you off at the lodge. It's rustic and the owner is a delight to chat with over a hot *tinto* in his rustic kitchen.

CENTRAL SECTOR

◀ **Hacienda La Esperanza** (cell tel. 310/209-9812, haciendalaesperanza@gmail.com, COP$50,000 d), a working farm on the edge of the park, provides accommodations in a rustic farmhouse oozing with character. The family running the hotel is very hospitable, and the host is a trained chef who enjoys pampering his guests. Nothing beats hanging out by the fireplace in the late afternoon drinking something hot after a day of mountain climbing. The *lechero* makes a stop at this hacienda.

NORTHERN SECTOR

The most conveniently located place to stay in this sector is ◀ **Cabañas Kanwara** (cell tel. 311/231-6004 or 311/237-2260, infokanwara@gmail.com, COP$35,000 pp). This lodge of cute wooden A-frame houses has a great location and serves good food, too.

To get there, you must get off the *lechero* at Hacienda Ritacuba and walk 90 minutes towards the park.

Getting There and Around

From El Cocuy and Güicán to the three park sectors there are three transportation possibilities: hiking 4-5 hours uphill from these towns to the park, taking an express service costing COP$80,000-100,000 (ouch!), or riding an early morning *lechero* (milk truck). This is a working truck that picks up milk along a predetermined route. Merchandise and passengers share the back of the truck, which is covered with canvas. Don't expect any comforts, but expect to have some good tales to tell. The *lechero* leaves Güicán from Carrera 5 and Calle 6 every morning at 5:30am and stops at El Cocuy around 6am. Around 7:30am it arrives at Alto de la Cueva, where you can get off to visit the Southern Sector. Around 9am it pulls right up to Hacienda La Esperanza in the Central Sector. Around 10:30am it reaches Hacienda Ritacuba, from where you can walk up to Cabañas Kanwara in the Northern Sector.

Santander

Beautiful, lush scenery, a delightful climate, well-preserved colonial pueblos, and friendly, outgoing people—this is the Santander department. Located in northeast Colombia, Santander lies to the north of Boyacá and southwest of Norte de Santander. Bucaramanga is the modern capital city, but you'll probably be drawn to the countryside. San Gil and the Cañón del Chicamocha will keep you busy with a smorgasbord of outdoor adventures, while nearby Barichara will seduce you with its tranquil ambiance.

BUCARAMANGA

The Ciudad Bonita (Beautiful City) is the capital of the department of Santander. Bucaramanga is a busy and growing city with a young and vibrant population and an agreeable climate where the flowers are always in bloom. Its central location makes for a strategic launching point for visits to the Santander countryside and is a midway point between Bogotá and Santa Marta on the Caribbean coast as well as Cúcuta in the far east. Including neighborhoods that are an extension of Bucaramanga (Floridablanca, Girón, and Piedecuesta), the population exceeds a million.

ORIENTATION

Most of your time will probably be spent in Cabecera (the upscale shopping and residential area), in the city center (between Cras. 9-17 and Cl. 45 and Av. Quebrada Seca), and in nearby municipalities such as Girón and Floridablanca.

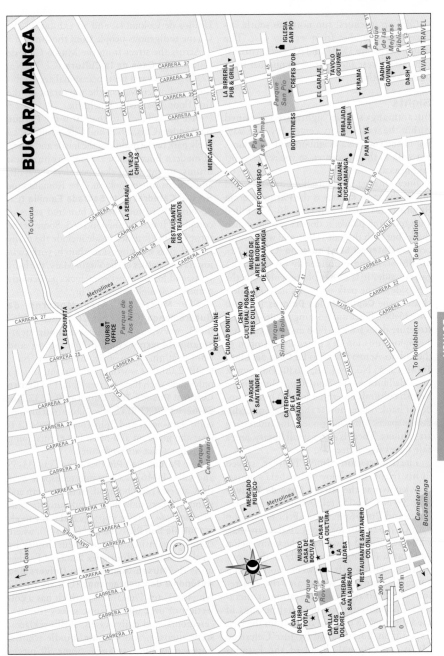

BUCARAMANGA

BOYACÁ

To Cúcuta

To Coast

To Floridablanca

To Bus Station

© AVALON TRAVEL

CARRERA 37
CARRERA 36
CARRERA 35
CARRERA 34
CARRERA 33

CALLE 34
CALLE 35
CALLE 36
CALLE 37
CARRERA 41
CALLE 42
CALLE 44
CALLE 45

IGLESIA SAN PIO
CREPES D'OR
LA BIRRERIA PUB & GRILL
EL GARAJE
TAVOLO GOURMET
KIRAMA
RADHA GOVINDA'S
DASH
CALLE 48
CALLE 51
CALLE 52

Parque de las Mejoras Públicas

Parque San Pio

Parque Los Palmas

BODYFITNESS

EMBAJADA CHINA
PAN PA YA
KASA GUANE BUCARAMANGA

CALLE 50
CALLE 48

MERCAGAN

EL VIEJO CHIFLAS
LA SERRANIA
RESTAURANTE LOS TEJADITOS

CARRERA 30
CARRERA 29
CARRERA 28
CARRERA 27

CAFE CONVERSO
CALLE 43
CALLE 42

MUSEO DE ARTE MODERNO DE BUCARAMANGA

Metrolinea

CARRERA 27
CARRERA 25
CARRERA 24

LA ESQUINTA

Parque de los Niños
TOURIST OFFICE

HOTEL GUANE
CIUDAD BONITA
CENTRO CULTURAL POSADA TRES CULTURAS

Parque Simón Bolívar

CALLE 41

CARRERA 23
CARRERA 22
CARRERA 21

GONZALEZ
ROSITA

CALLE 28A
CARRERA 24
CARRERA 23
CARRERA 22
CARRERA 21
CARRERA 20
CARRERA 19
CARRERA 18

CALLE 35

PARQUE SANTANDER
CATEDRAL DE LA SAGRADA FAMILIA

Parque Centenario

CALLE 34
CALLE 36
CALLE 37
CALLE 45
CALLE 41
CALLE 42
CALLE 46

CALLE 23
CALLE 24
CALLE 28
SANTANDER
CARRERA 22
CARRERA 17
CARRERA 16

CALLE 29A
CALLE 30
CALLE 31
CALLE 33
CALLE 34

MERCADO PUBLICO

Metrolinea

CARRERA 15
CARRERA 14
CARRERA 13
CARRERA 12

CALLE 43
CALLE 44

Cementerio Bucaramanga

Parque García Rovira

CASA DEL LIBRO TOTAL
CAPILLA DE LOS DOLORES
CATEDRAL SAN LAUREANO
MUSEO CASA DE BOLIVAR
CASA DE LA CULTURA
LA ALDABA
RESTAURANTE SANTANERO COLONIAL

0   200 yds
0   200 m

Carreras (avenues) run north to south, increasing in number from west to east. The main *carreras* are 15, 27, and 33. *Calles* (streets) run east to west and increase in number from north to south.

Sights

Bucaramanga's main sights are contained within the walkable city center. If you're staying in the Cabecera neighborhood it's a long, hot walk to the city center, so you're better off taking a cab.

Bucaramanga prides itself on its parks, and one of the most famous is the **Parque García Rovira** (Cras. 10-11 and Clls. 36-37). Filled with towering palms, it doesn't provide much shade, but with the pale yellow and white 19th-century **Catedral San Laureano** (Cra. 12 No. 36-08) standing prominently on the park's eastern side, it is rather photogenic. On the west side of the park is Bucaramanga's oldest church, the **Capilla de los Dolores** (Cra. 10 No. 36-08). This unassuming, white-washed structure dates back to 1748 and no longer has a religious mission. It's generally not open to the public. Across from it is **La Casa del Libro Total** (Cl. 35 No. 9-81, tel. 7/630-3389, www.lacasadellibrotal.com, 8am-10pm Mon.-Fri.), a newish cultural center that (oddly) has a number of bank offices and at the same time exhibition spaces (air-conditioned) for interesting art exhibits. There is also a small library, and a café serves free coffee.

The Libertador, Simón Bolívar, stayed in his friend Juan Eloy Valenzuela's house, now known as the **Museo Casa de Bolívar** (Cl. 37 No. 12-15, tel. 7/630-4258, 8am-noon and 2pm-6pm Mon.-Fri., 8am-noon Sat., COP$2,000) for about 70 days in 1828 while he awaited news from the Convención de Ocaña. (Things went badly at that convention, with a rift between Bolívar and Santander growing wider, and the end result was Bolívar's self-declaration as dictator.) The museum has personal belongs of the Liberator, an original diary from the first Expedición Botánica led by José Celestino Mutis, an original shield of the Estados

Unidos de Colombia, and an exhibit on the Guane indigenous people from the area.

Across the street from the Museo Casa de Bolívar, the **Casa de la Cultura** (Cl. 37 No. 12-46, hours vary) hosts occasional art exhibitions and other events. The restaurant on the first floor is packed at lunchtime.

Five or six blocks to the east is the **Parque Santander** (Cras. 19-20 and Clls. 35-36). It's a lively park in the middle of the hustle and bustle of modern Bucaramanga. Hare Krishnas beat drums, unimpressed skateboarders show off, and dozens others look on. The Romanesque Revival **Catedral de la Sagrada Familia** (Cl. 36 No. 19-56) took over a hundred years to complete. It was finished in 1865. Some of the most striking features inside include the many stained glass windows. The church, with twin towers and statues of the Virgin Mary, the baby Jesus, and Joseph in between, looks particularly grandiose at night when it is lit.

The **Museo de Arte Moderno de Bucaramanga** (Cl. 37 No. 26-16, tel. 7/645-0483, www.museodeartemodernodebucaramanga.blogspot.com, 8:30am-noon and 2pm-5:30pm Mon.-Fri., 8am-noon Sat., COP$2,000) is worth checking out, but it's only open when there is an exhibit. The **Centro Cultural Posada Tres Culturas** (Cl. 37 No. 24-62, tel. 7/683-9142, www.librostresculturas.com, 9am-noon and 2pm-7pm Mon.-Sat.) is near the museum and often has events going on. It has a nice art bookstore.

The **Parque San Pío** (between Cras. 33-35 and Clls. 45-46) is a vibrant greenspace near the Cabecera neighborhood. At the western end stands the Fernando Botero sculpture *Mujer de Pies Desnuda*. On the opposite end is the modern **Iglesia San Pío** (Cra. 36 No. 45-51), where there are paintings on permanent display by local artist Oscar Rodríguez Naranjo. Farther up is the **Museo Guane** at the **Universidad Autónoma de Bucaramanga** (UNAB, Av. 42 No. 48-11, tel. 7/643-6111), which has a collection of over 600 ceramic pieces (figures, ceremonial and daily vessels, shell necklaces, stone utensils, and ceramic spindle whorls) found near Bucaramanga. Some 90 pieces are on display in a small lobby area. Nobody seems to know where the exhibition space is, and you'll have to ask around. You may have to climb around lounging students to even get a look at the collection.

Nightlife

The nightlife scene in Bucaramanga? Maybe exuberant is the right word to describe it. Most bars and clubs are open Thursday through Saturday, closing at 2am or 3am.

Café Con Verso (Cl. 44 No. 28-63, tel. 7/647-1486, 4:30pm-late Mon.-Sat.) is a pleasant café with occasional live music and film nights. **La Birrería Pub & Grill** (Cra. 36 No. 43-46, tel. 7/657-7675, noon-midnight Sun.-Thurs., Fri.-Sat. noon-2am) serves sports bar-type food (although there are some healthy selections) and beer. It's open-air and waitstaff are very attentive. This is the place to watch big *fútbol* matches. **El Garaje** (Cl. 48 No. 33-39, tel. 7/657-4768) is more about burgers and beer.

La Esquinita de los Recuerdos (Cl. 22 No. 25-55, tel. 7/632-0640 or 7/645-6861, hours vary Tues.-Sat.) is a beloved bar and a good place to have a beer while listening to old (Latino style) favorites. The bar itself is an oldie, more or less, having been around since 1965. **Cali Son** (Cl. 33 No. 31-33, no phone) is one of the top salsa bars in Bucaramanga.

As you might imagine from its name, **Dash** (Cl. 52 No. 34-27, cell tel. 315/624-6905) is a high-energy club popular with the college crowd.

Shopping

Bucaramanga is well known in Colombia for its leather shoes, handbags, and wallets. **Nora Lozza First Class** (Centro Comercial El Cacique, Tr. 93 No. 34-99, Local 113, 10am-8pm daily) is a well-known designer of leather bags and accessories made in Bucaramanga. There are stores in El Cacique and several other shopping malls.

Latin Lover (Cra. 35 No. 44-41, tel. 7/695-1369, 9am-noon and 2pm-8pm Mon.-Sat.), created by a pair of Bucaramanga hipsters, sells groovy and original Latino-chic T-shirts. They cost around COP$60,000.

For handicrafts, check out the woven items, including handicrafts made from leaves of the *fique* palm tree, and other accessories at **Luz y Vida** (Centro Comercial Cuarta Etapa, 4th floor, Local 402/9, tel. 7/673-0680, cell tel. 317/316-4487, www.artesaniasluzyvida.web-node.com.co, 10am-8pm Mon.-Sat., 10am-5pm Sun.). This is an association of women heads of household who have been forcibly displaced from their homes.

Accommodations

UNDER COP$70,000

It's not just backpackers who flock to the **Kasa Guane** (Cl. 49 No. 28-1, tel. 7/657-6960, www.kasaguane.com, COP$25,000 dorm, COP$80,000 d). This busy yet friendly place with both dorms and private rooms hosts activities, provides tons of insider information and tips, and is in a great location in Cabecera. The guys here will get you hooked up with paragliding and give you expert insider tips on all the Bucaramanga party spots. On weekends the top floor bar gets lively.

Nest Fly Site Hostel (Km. 2 Vía Mesa de Ruitoque, cell tel. 312/0432-6266, www.co-lombiaparagliding.com, COP$25,000 dorm, COP$60,000 d) is the place to stay if you're interested in paragliding. It's right next door to the fly site. It's a quiet and cute place, 20 minutes away from the bustle of Buca. Nest is run by the same people as Colombia Paragliding and the Kasa Guane hostel. It is near the Ruitoque town next to the Las Águilas launching pad for most paragliding flights near Bucaramanga.

COP$70,000-200,000

Antigua Belén Bed and Breakfast (Cra. 31 No. 17-22, tel. 7/634-9860, www.hotelantigua-belen.com, COP$133,000 d with a/c) has 13 rooms in a modern house full of antiques. It's located in a rather dull part of town not terribly close to nor too far from anything. Breakfast is served in a pleasant patio in the back.

The **Hostal UNAB** (Av. 42 No. 48-160, tel.

BOYACÁ

7/643-6111, ext. 652, COP$154,000 d) has just four comfortable rooms and a restaurant on-site. Right across the street from the university, it might be an odd place to be for a visit to Buca. But it is extremely low-key. It's about a 15-minute walk down to the Parque San Pío from here.

OVER COP$200,000

Hotel Guane (Cl. 34 No. 22-72, tel. 7/634-7014, www.hotelguane.com, COP$206,000 d) is a mid-sized hotel with 40 air-conditioned rooms, a pool, and two restaurants. Cheesy decor. **La Serranía** (Cl. 33 No. 30-26, tel. 7/691-7535, www.laserraniahotel.com, COP$250,000 d) has about 50 new and minimalist-style rooms along with a rooftop pool and restaurant. It's overpriced. **Ciudad Bonita** (Cl. 35 No. 22-01, tel. 7/635-0101, www.hotel-ciudadbonita.com.co, COP$260,000 d) is the fancy hotel in town. It has 70 rooms, two restaurants, a café, a pool, gym, sauna, and there's live music Thursday, Friday, and Saturday evenings. The area it's in is not a pleasant place to walk around day or night.

Food

Want to eat like a local? Look for these Santanderean specialties: *cabrito con pepitoria* (goat fricassee), *carne oreada* (dried meat), and *mute santandereano* (a corn-based meaty stew). And don't forget the ants: fried big bottom ants or *hormigas culonas*. These queen ants are harvested throughout Santander, typically after Semana Santa. After months of hibernation, on one prickly hot day, the queens leave their colony. That's when they are caught. They are later toasted. Eating ants has always been popular and dates back hundreds of years to the Guane culture. Wealthy Santandereanos used to be embarrassed to admit any fondness for the creepy-crawlers, but that's changed, and in fact the ants are showing up more and more on the plates of diners on a quest for the exotic.

◖ Santanero Colonial (Cl. 41 No. 10-54, tel. 7/696-0538, 7:30am-4pm Mon.-Thurs., 7:30am-late Fri., COP$15,000) is one of the top choices for government bureaucrats on lunch break. There is always a set lunch menu (plus à la carte), and frequently you'll have to wait a bit to be seated. Tables are set up around a pleasant sunny patio. It is behind the Gobernación building. **La Aldaba** (Cl. 37 No. 12-32, tel. 7/642-4062, noon-3pm Mon.-Sat.) is a popular place for an inexpensive lunch. They always have a lunch special that features trout, chicken, or beef for under COP$12,000.

One of Bucaramanga's favorite restaurants is **◖ El Viejo Chiflas** (Cra. 33 No. 34-10, tel. 7/632-0640, 9am-midnight Mon.-Wed., Thurs.-Sun. 24 hours, COP$23,000). The atmosphere here is cowboy style with wooden tables and interiors, and the menu features local specialties, such as goat and the Santander classic *carne oreada*. And there's always an arepa (cornmeal cake) with your meal. Portions can be huge. **Los Tejaditos** (Cl. 34 No. 27-82, tel. 7/634-6028, www.restaurantelostejaditos.com, 11am-10pm Tues.-Sat., 11am-5pm Sun., COP$23,000) is an old-style restaurant with a popular special menu at lunchtime. **Mercagán** (Cra. 33 No. 42-12, tel. 7/632-4949, www.mercaganparrilla.com, 11am-6pm Mon. and Thurs., 11am-11pm Tues.-Wed. and Fri.-Sat., 11am-4pm Sun., COP$25,000) is a legendary steakhouse in Bucaramanga that has multiple locations, including in many shopping malls.

For a break from the *comida típica* (Colombian fare) thing, there are a few options in Buca. **Radha Govinda's** (Cra. 34 No. 51-95, tel. 7/643-3382, lunch Mon.-Sat.) is a vegetarian option. It's Hare Krishna-run and is on a quiet street in Cabecera. The **Embajada China** (Cl. 49 No. 32-27, tel. 7/647-1931, 10am-10pm daily, COP$15,000) is run by a Chinese family, and they serve generous portions. It's in Cabecera near the Kasa Guane. Stir-fries, salads, and pastas are on the menu at **Tavolo Gourmet** (Cra. 35 No. 48-84, tel. 7/643-7461, www.tavologourmet.com, 11am-10pm Tues.-Sun., COP$18,000). It's a bright and airy place in a fancy neighborhood. The wildly popular Colombian chain **Crepes & Waffles** (Centro Comercial La Florida, Cl. 31 No. 26A-19, 3rd floor, Local 3090, tel. 7/632-1345,

11:45am-9:30pm Mon.-Sat., 11:45am-8:30pm Sun., COP$17,000) is a welcome sight.

We'll admit that the crêpes at ❰ **Crêpes D'Or** (Cl. 46 No. 34-28, tel. 7/657-4770, 3:30pm-10pm Mon.-Sat., COP$13,000) are nothing to write home about, although they're fine and fairly priced. What makes this unpretentious family-run spot a delight is its setting overlooking the Parque San Pío. Imagine an outdoor terrace where you look out onto park goers, dogwalkers, and joggers and not onto a steady stream of traffic!

Kirama (Cl. 49 No. 33-37, tel. 7/657-6989, 6am-9pm daily) is a wildly popular spot for breakfast on the run, like an *arepa boyacense* (cornmeal cake stuffed with cheese). Do not be confused by Karima, which is immediately next to it. Kirama says Karima came later. **Pan Pa Ya** (Cl. 49 No. 28-38, tel. 7/685-2001, 8am-10pm Mon.-Sat, 9am-noon and 5pm-8pm Sun.) is in all the major cities of Colombia, and it's always a reliable place for a decent cup of coffee, pastries, and inexpensive breakfasts (eggs, fresh fruit).

The **Mercado Público** (between Cras. 15-16 and Clls. 33-34, daily) downtown is a great place to wander about. On multiple floors, you can do some cheap shopping, walking swiftly past the meat section, get a cheap meal on the fourth floor, and enjoy some pretty nice views of the city as well. On the top floor they sell loads of Piedecuesta cigars for cheap as well as baskets, herbs, and *artesanías* (handicrafts). Several stands sell juices and lunches. Some stalls even sell bull's eyes, if you're feeling adventurous.

Information and Services

The **tourist office** (Cl. 30 No. 26-117, tel. 7/634-1132) is parkside at the Parque de los Niños. Police can be reached by dialing 123, the **Hospital Universitario González Valencia** (Cra. 33 No. 28-126) by calling tel. 7/634-6110.

Getting There and Around

The **Aeropuerto Internacional de Palo Negro** (Vía Lebrija), Bucaramanga's airport, is 25 kilometers (15 miles) west of town. **Avianca** (Cl. 52 No. 35A-10, tel. 7/657-3888, www.avianca.com, 8am-6pm Mon.-Fri., 8am-1pm Sat.), **EasyFly** (tel. 7/697-0333, www.easyfly.com.co), **VivaColombia** (tel. 1/489-7989, www.vivacolombia.com.co), and **LAN** (Col. toll-free tel. 01/800-094-9490, www.lan.com) all serve the city. Taxis to and from the airport to Bucaramanga cost COP$32,000.

Frequent bus service is offered between Bucaramanga and all major cities nationwide as well as small locales in Santander. The **Terminal de Transportes** (Km. 2 Tr. Metropolitana, tel. 7/637-1000, www.terminalbucaramanga.com) is modern, clean, and open-air. It is off of Calle 70 on the way towards Girón.

The **MetroLínea** (www.metrolinea.gov.co) is the Bucaramanga version of the Bogotá TransMilenio. These green buses are clean and efficient, and the system covers just about the entire city, although it can be difficult to figure out. Maps of the system are hard to come by, obligating you to ask fellow travelers for information. You can purchase cards for the regular buses (ones that do not have dedicated lanes) at kiosks on the streets.

Taxis are plentiful in Bucaramanga. To order one call **Radio Taxis Libres** (tel. 7/634-8888) or **Taxmovil** (tel. 7/633-9090).

The city center area is easily visited on foot, although there is a lot of traffic. The Cabecera area is also more or less walkable, especially in the evenings when traffic calms down.

Mesa de Ruitoque

A surprisingly quiet and rural area to the southeast of Bucaramanga and Floridablanca, Mesa de Ruitoque sits on a plateau and is perfect for paragliding.

PARAGLIDING

The Bucaramanga area is a great place to get over that fear and fly your first tandem paragliding flight, or to take a 10-day course, and the plateau of Mesa de Ruitoque, just 10 minutes from downtown, is where to go.

The area is blessed with 350 flyable days

per year, meaning more air time and less waiting around. **Colombia Paragliding** (www.colombiaparagliding.com) offers tandem flights of different durations from the **Voladero Las Águilas** (Km. 2 Vía Ruitoque, tel. 7/678-6257, www.voladerolasaguilas.com.co) launch point just outside of town near Ruitoque. The Kasa Guane hostel can arrange transportation for you in their van. Instructors are all certified.

A 10-minute flight costs COP$50,000, 20 minutes is $90,000, and a 30-minute flight costs $120,000. Winds are best at this fly site in the afternoon, from noon until 4pm, and the site itself opens each day at 10am. A 10-day certification course is offered by Colombia Paragliding at the Águilas site with additional flight time in Chicamocha. It costs COP$2,300,000 including transportation, meals, and lodging.

The views are quite spectacular from above Bucaramanga. (Bring your camera!) The best way for pilots to judge the winds is by observing the *chulos* (black vultures) as they fly and glide high above. At the fly site there is also a snack bar. The place gets crazy crowded on weekends and on holidays. For a fee of COP$25,000 you can get a DVD of your flight.

Floridablanca

There aren't loads of reasons to make a special trip to Floridablanca, which has evolved to become essentially a southeastern suburb of Bucaramanga, five kilometers away, but a good one is to take a bite out of one of their famous *obleas*, crisp paper-thin wafers filled with gooey and delicious *arequipe* (caramel spread). **Obleas Floridablanca** (Cra. 7 No. 5-54, tel. 7/648-5819, 10am-8pm daily) is the most famous *oblea* factory of them all. They've been around since 1949 and as you can imagine have their share of loyal customers. There are around 30 types of *obleas* you can order, although there really is no need to go beyond the classic *oblea* with just *arequipe*. The names of the *obleas* are whimsical. Two of the more popular ones are the *amor eterno* (eternal love), which has *arequipe,* cheese, and

a resident yellow-footed tortoise at the Jardín Botánico Eloy Valenzuela

blackberry jam, and the *noviazgo* (courtship), which has *arequipe* and cheese. They also have do-it-yourself *oblea* kits that you can take back home with you.

The **Museo Arqueológico Regional Guane** (Casa de la Cultura, Cra. 7 No. 4-35, tel. 7/619-8181, 8am-noon and 2pm-6pm Mon.-Fri., COP$1,000) is in need of some love, but the collection of ceramics on display is impressive and extensive. In the courtyard are some pre-Hispanic designs that were found on a large boulder.

Along the manicured lawns of the **Jardín Botánico Eloy Valenzuela** (tel. 7/634-6100, 8am-5pm daily, COP$4,000) you can wander along paths (sharing them with turtles) and view enormous ceibas and other trees. If you look closely in the tops of trees you might even see some sloths. The Río Frío (it's a stream, really) flows through the gardens. The gardens were revamped and reloaded in 2012. Security is present in the park, and there are always visitors, but be on your guard at some of the far reaches of the gardens. It's not terribly easy, but you can get to the gardens by way of MetroLínea from Bucaramanga.

Girón

While Bucaramanga is a pulsating tribute to the economic growth of modern Colombia, nearby Girón, under 15 minutes and 12 kilometers (7 miles) away to the west, is a living reminder of the colonial past, at least in the town's historic center: The population of Girón is around 150,000 today! It's somewhat surprising to see, in this age of television, Internet, and shopping malls, how the plaza is still the main meeting place in Girón, as it has been since the 17th century. Locals take pride in their town, and winners of the best facades, doors, and windows contest proudly display their plaques in front of their white-washed *tapia pisada* (adobe) homes.

While it is easy to visit at any time, on weekends Girón has a festive air to it as city folk from Bucaramanga and other day-trip visitors stroll the town's cobblestone streets. There isn't much in the way of tourist sights here, but be sure to visit **Basílica Menor San Juan Bautista** and the **Parque las Nieves,** and walk along the *malecón* (wharf).

You might want to consider making Girón your base, instead of Bucaramanga. It's got charm, it's quiet, and traveling back and forth to the metropolis is not an issue. The trip takes under 15 minutes, and taxis will cost only around COP$10,000. You can also get to Girón on the MetroLínea system.

❰ Girón Chill Out Hotel Boutique (Cra. 25 No. 32-06, tel. 7/646-1119, www.gironn-chillout.com, COP$144,000 d) is run by an Italian couple (hence the Italian flag), and while the name suggests an Ibiza atmosphere, the hotel is in a remodeled colonial house. It's quiet, cute, and homey, and they serve authentic Italian food. **Las Nieves** (Cl. 30 No. 25-71, tel. 7/681-2951, www.hotellasnievesgiron.com, COP$116,000 d with a/c, COP$82,000 d with fan) is right on the plaza, and the best rooms, although at the same time the most used rooms, are the six that have a balcony overlooking the

plaza. The interior of the hotel is full of palm trees and greenery, and the owner's dog will let you pet him/her. There are about 30 rooms, many full of twin beds. It's OK.

La Casona (Cl. 28 No. 28-09, tel. 7/646-7195, www.lacasona-restaurante.com, noon-8pm Tues.-Sun., COP$16,000) is a spiffy old place, and they have a fun *onces* (tea time) menu for late afternoon tea, Colombian style: You get a *tamal* (tamale), cheese, breads, and hot chocolate.

❰ CAÑÓN DEL CHICAMOCHA

With an absolutely spectacular location above the Cañón del Chicamocha, the privately run **Parque Nacional del Chicamocha** (PANACHI, 54 km/34 mi south of Bucaramanga, tel. 7/639-4444, www.parquenacionaldelchicamocha.com, 9am-6pm Tues. and Thurs., 9am-7pm Fri.-Sun., COP$40,000 admission plus round-trip gondola ride) is a mostly cheesy amusement park geared towards Colombian families, but the views? Insert your favorite superlative here. This privately run park has

a gondola ride across the Cañón del Chicamocha

several attractions, like an ostrich farm, areas that celebrate Santander culture and traditions, extreme sports, and soon a water park, but most people opt for the cable car ride (6.3 kilometers/3.9 miles) across the canyon over the Río Chicamocha. For locals and for tourists who are opposed to backtracking, this is not just a nice excursion, it's a means of transportation. On weekends, holidays, and during the Christmas and Easter holidays, from Bucaramanga you can take a PANACHI bus (cell tel. 316/696-3780) to the park, as a day trip. To get there using public transportation, buses leaving from the Bucaramanga bus terminal bound for San Gil can drop you off at the park. (There are always buses passing the park between San Gil and Bucaramanga, and you can flag them down and hop on.) If you happen to be in that part of town, buses also depart for San Gil from the Papi Quiero Piña store in Floridablanca. By the way, the vistas from the road that hugs the canyon high above the Río Chicamocha make that right-hand side window seat from Bucaramanga worth fighting for.

Mesa de los Santos

The village of Los Santos is on the other side of the canyon from the PANACHI. In this area, known as Mesa de los Santos, there are a number of country homes for weekenders from Bogotá, a few places to stay, and numerous outdoorsy things to do, like visit El Duende waterfall. It ranks second in the world for annual number of tremors at 390 per month (a rate of about one every two hours).

The **Refugio La Roca** (Km. 22 in La Mojarra, cell tel. 312/333-1480, www.refugiolaroca.blogspot.com, COP$60,000 d shared bath) is a kind of hippy-ish pad for "rock climbers, walkers, artists, and other dreamers." Their specialty is rock climbing and it's got quite a jaw-dropping view, overlooking the Chicamocha canyon. Here you can camp for COP$10,000 per night (they also have tents and sleeping bags for rent). There is also one dorm room with four beds for COP$80,000.

At the other end of the spectrum is **El Roble**

hotel (after La Mesa toll booth, Mesa de los Santos, tel. 1/232-8595, www.cafemesa.com, COP$398,000 d). The rate includes a tour of the on-site coffee plantation. This lovely getaway is on a large certified organic coffee farm, set underneath towering oak trees, and teeming with over 100 species of birds. **Ecoposada Vina de Aldana** (cell tel. 317/270-5077 or 300/438-5522, ecoposada.dealdana@gmail.com, COP$80,000 d) is a guesthouse with 20 rooms at a vineyard, where you can take walks, view birds, and take a tour of the vineyard.

SAN GIL

Rafting, paragliding, caving, mountain biking, canyoning, hiking, birding, and rappelling are all within reach in San Gil, Colombia's outdoor adventure capital. This spry city (pop. 43,000) on the steep banks of the Río Fonce is 95 kilometers (59 miles) southwest of Bucaramanga. It caters to international tourists. Even if your idea of "adventurous" is merely being in Colombia, the breathtaking Santander scenery of canyons, rivers, waterfalls, and mountains is more than enough reason to warrant a visit.

During the late 19th and early 20th centuries, San Gil and nearby towns built their prosperity on quinine, coffee, cocoa, and tobacco cultivation. Today, old tile-roofed hangars to dry tobacco, known as *caneys,* still dot the landscape. Today it is a peaceful place to visit and a top tourist destination. San Gil can feel claustrophobic, but accommodations in San Gil are plentiful, comfortable, and inexpensive, and it's got Gringo Mike's.

There's no need to stay in bustling San Gil in order to enjoy the many outdoor activities that the area offers. You can easily organize rafting trips or paragliding adventures from quieter and more charming towns such as Barichara (20 kilometers/12 miles north).

Sights

On the Río Fonce about a 15-minute walk from town is the **Jardín Botánico El Gallineral** (8am-5pm daily, COP$8,000). This used to be just a park, but it has been given a fussy makeover to apparently make it more appealing to

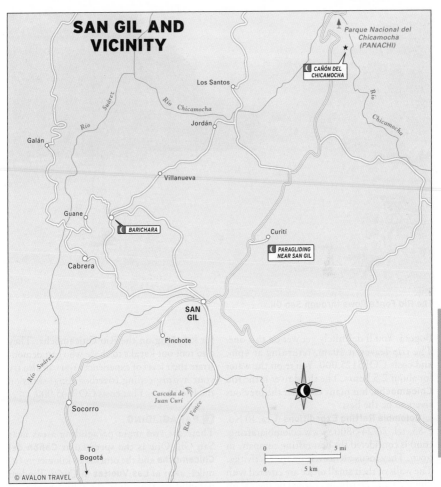

SAN GIL AND VICINITY

Parque Nacional del Chicamocha (PANACHI)

CAÑÓN DEL CHICAMOCHA

Los Santos

Río Chicamocha

Jordán

Galán

Río Suárez

Río Chicamocha

Villanueva

Guane

BARICHARA

Curití

PARAGLIDING NEAR SAN GIL

Cabrera

SAN GIL

Pinchote

Río Suárez

Cascada de Juan Curí

Río Fonce

Socorro

To Bogotá

0   5 mi

0   5 km

© AVALON TRAVEL

tourists, and now it is a botanical garden. There are cute stalls selling handicrafts, sweets, and coffee along the park's orderly paths. It is a pretty place, and a late-afternoon walk among the towering trees is a nice plan. A restaurant on-site is open for lunch.

Shopping

The best place in San Gil to browse handicrafts is at **Corporación Patrimonio Guane, Agata y Yarigui** (Cra. 10 No. 9-67, cell tel. 313/892-9681).

Recreation

RAFTING AND KAYAKING

Three rivers near San Gil offer some excellent rafting adventures. The **Río Fonce,** whose banks the town stands on, is the closest and one of the best suited for rafting. It's a category II-III. It's fine year-round, although in March and April the water level is higher. A rafting trip on the Fonce costs about COP$30,000 for a 90-minute trip. The **Río Suárez** is a category III-V river. The starting point is about an hour's drive towards

The Río Fonce flows through San Gil.

© ANDREW DIER

Bogotá. You'll definitely get wet on this one. The trip leaves at 10am, returning at 4pm, and costs COP$125,000. You're on the water for about 2.5 hours. The third river is the **Río Chicamocha,** but many consider the previous rivers to be the best.

Colombia Rafting Expeditions (Cra. 10 No. 7-83, tel. 7/724-5800, www.colombiarafting.com) is considered the best rafting company in town. They focus exclusively on river activities. The walls of their small office are covered with diplomas and certificates earned by their team of experienced guides. They can organize trips down all the rivers, determining which one is right for you based upon on skill level, your sense of adventure, and water levels. They also do kayak trips. This company takes safety concerns very seriously and conducts safety training exercises in English.

Three-day kayaking courses (four hours per day starting at 8am) are offered by Colombia Rafting. These cost COP$400,000 and take place on the Río Fonce. They can also arrange for kayaking on the Río Chicamocha. They also rent out kayaks to those who can demonstrate their level of experience. You can also try your hydrospeeding (riverboarding) skills on the Río Fonce. That costs COP$45,000.

◖ PARAGLIDING

There are two main paragliding areas near San Gil. One is the spectacular **Cañón del Chicamocha** and the other is 16 kilometers (10 miles) away at **Las Vueltas** in Curití. Tandem paragliding trips over the Chicamocha, of about a 45-minute duration, cost around COP$170,000. That price includes transportation to and from the landing and pickup sites. Chicamocha paragliding flights take place in the mornings. At the windy Las Vueltas location, it will cost you about COP$60,000. Those flights are held in the afternoon. As far as courses go, **Colombian Paragliding** (cell tel. 312/432-6266, www.colombiaparagliding.com) has the best reputation. They are based near Bucaramanga.

WATERFALLS AND RAPPELLING

The **Cascadas de Juan Curí** (road to Charalá, COP$7,000) are quite close to San Gil and easily reached on public transportation or by bike. These falls, about 18 meters high, are privately owned by two neighbors who are fierce rivals! For a more rustic climb through the jungle to reach your refreshing goal, go to the second entrance (Donde Efigenia). It's about a 15-minute hike, and it can be treacherous at points. Wear some shoes you don't mind getting muddy and wet. And bring a bathing suit to cool off in one of the pools. You can camp there as well. It's a nice excursion. If you don't want to sweat and struggle at all, take the first entrance. To test your rappelling skills here, contact **Páramo Extremo** (Cra. 4 No. 4-57, tel. 7/725-8944, www.paramosantanderextremo.com). They can organize an excursion, with all the safety equipment and an experienced guide, for COP$45,000.

© ANDREW DIER

The Cascadas de Juan Curí are a great day trip from San Gil.

CAVING

Several caves around San Gil make for good exploring. The **Cueva Indio** is one of the most popular. It's filled with bats, and you don't really have to do much bending over to explore. It is near the town of Páramo, just beyond the Cascadas de Juan Curí. An excursion including equipment and a guide costs COP$25,000, but that doesn't include transportation. Contact **Páramo Extremo** (Cra. 4 No. 4-57, tel. 7/725-8944, www.paramosantanderextremo.com) in the town of Páramo.

The **Cueva Vaca**, near Curití, is the most challenging of the caves in the area. You will be in water and mud the entire time you are underground, and at one point you'll have to swim underwater to get through to the next cave. It's action packed and there are some tight squeezes as well, but the adventure is worth it. There are lots of stalactites and stalagmites and bats to see. It costs COP$25,000 plus about COP$3,000 in bus transportation. **Colombia Rafting** (Cra. 10 No. 7-83, cell tel. 311/283-8647, www.colombiarafting.com) or other outfitters can organize a trip here.

The **La Antigua** cave is on the road towards Barichara. **El Dorado Hostel** (Cl. 2 No. 8-55, tel. 7/723-7588, www.eldoradohostel.com) organizes an extreme trip that includes the cave plus canyoning, rappelling, and two waterfall descents. All that adventure during just five hours! This trip costs COP$80,000 including transportation.

The Medellín-based outfit **Expedición Adventure** (cell tel. 314/258-9499, www.expedicionadventure.blogspot.com, expedicionadventure@gmail.com) specializes in unique 3- to 20-day caving trips to mostly unexplored and unspoiled areas in Santander. The starting point is usually in Barbosa, a town between Tunja and Barichara.

BIKING

Colombian Bike Junkies (Cl. 12, No. 8-35, cell tel. 316/327-6101 or 313/411-5332, www.colombianbikejunkies.com), run by a pair from Seattle, Washington, and the United Kingdom, organizes downhill day-trip rides, crazy canyon adventures, multi-activity combos, and multi-day adventures. One day trip starts at 2,000 meters on the top of the Cañón del Chicamocha, going, down, down, down through beautiful countryside to the ghost town of Jordan. After a swim and lunch, there is yet one more downhill trip near Curití. Some 50 kilometers (30 miles) of downhill riding! All on top-of-the-line mountain bikes. If you want to rent a cheap-o bike for the day, go to **Bicicletería El Ring** (Cl. 7 No. 10-14, tel. 7/724-3189).

SWIMMING

On weekends and on holidays, families head to swimming holes to splash about. The atmosphere is joyous, and there's usually music and plenty of food and drink as well. (A little trash, too, unfortunately.) **Pozo Azul** is about five minutes by bus or taxi from San Gil (or a 20-minute walk). **Pescaderito** is in Curití, about a 40-minute bus ride away, and there are five swimming holes in which to cool off. During the week it's quieter.

TOURS

Your hostel or hotel can organize any activity you are interested in doing, but in case you'd like to shop around, contact the following companies. **Planeta Azul** (Parque El Gallineral, tel. 7/724-0000, www.planetaazulcolombia.com) is an agency that organizes rafting trips as well as a whole host of other activities, like bungee jumping (COP$46,000), caving (COP$40,000), rappelling (COP$40,000), paragliding (COP$60,000), and horseback riding (COP$95,000) to keep you stimulated. **Aventura Total** (Cl. 7 No. 10-27, tel. 7/723-8888, www.aventuratotal. com.co) has a good reputation as well. They offer all-inclusive packages that include rafting, caving, and other activities as well as hotel accommodations. Aventura Total often organizes activities for large school groups. **Nativox** (Cra. 11 No. 7-14 Malecón, tel. 7/723-9999, www.nativoxsangil.com) is similar to the previous two.

Accommodations

Good and affordable lodging options are plentiful in San Gil. However, for more space, fresh air, or for more luxury, consider staying in Barichara, Mesa de los Santos, or Pinchote, all close by.

One of the first hostels in town catering to international backpackers, **Macondo Hostal** (Cra. 8 No. 10-35, tel. 7/724-8001, www. macondohostel.com, COP$18,000 dorm, COP$55,000 d w/bath) remains an excellent choice. Clean dorm rooms, popular with backpackers, and private rooms, popular with older travelers, quickly fill up—make a reservation in advance! They have a hot tub, small garden, and hammocks for post-adventure relaxing. Staff are extremely knowledgeable, helpful, and great at organizing rafting, paragliding, and all other outdoor activities in the region. On the corner next door is the **Hostal Colombo Inglés** (Cra. 8 No. 9-133, tel. 7/724-3787, www.hostelcolomboingles.com, COP$18,000 dorm, COP$70,000 d), which opened in late 2013. It's small and the staff are friendly. There is no English connection here; it's just a name.

Welcome to *Sam* Gil. Native entrepreneur Sam has two lodging options in the center of town. Super-clean **Sam's VIP Hotel** (Cr. 10 No. 12-33, tel. 7/724-2746, www.samshostel. com, COP$17,000 dorm, COP$70,000 d) has a great location overlooking the plaza. The terrace is a great place for hanging out in the evenings. Plus there's a teeny pool and a sauna. His second place, with 11 rooms, is **La Mansion de Sam Hotel Boutique** (Cl. 12 No. 8-71, tel. 7/724-6044, http://hotelmansionsangil.com, COP$70,000-100,000 d) which is set in an old house just a block from the main plaza. Sam has an inviting pub that specializes in steaks, ribs, and beer. Colorful artwork by local artist "Rosenkranz" adorns the walls of the rooms. La Mansion has a lot of character, cool decoration, and big rooms, some with balconies. The only drawback is that cars sometimes park in the interior patio.

The multi-story **Hostel Santander Alemán** (Cra. 10 No. 15-07, tel. 7/724-0329, www. hostelsantanderalemantv.com, COP$20,000 dorm, COP$60,000 d) is half a block from the local bus station. It's very clean. Friendly folks, but there's nothing German about it.

If you'd like to get away from the backpacker scene but still pay close to backpacker prices, there are three clean cheapies that may fit the bill. If you stay at the **Hotel Capri** (Cl. 10 No. 9-31, tel. 7/724-4218, hotelcaprisangil@yahoo.es, COP$40,000), get a room on the third floor overlooking the street. **The Hotel Abril** (Cl. 8 at Cra. 10, tel. 7/724-8795, hotelabrilsangilss@yahoo.es, COP$45,000 pp) has 28 rooms, good fans, wireless Internet, and hot water. With just six rooms, **Posada Familiar** (Cra. 10 No. 8-55, tel. 7/724-8136, COP$45,000 pp high season) makes you feel at home. The patio is filled with flowers and plants, you can cook in the kitchen, and the owner is extremely nice.

To enjoy the peace of the countryside and charm of a colonial town but still be within easy striking distance of San Gil restaurants and activities, consider staying in the hamlet of **Pinchote**. **Hotel Boutique Wassiki** (Km. 3 Vía San Gil-Bogotá, tel. 7/724-8386, www.wassiki.com, COP$164,000-227,000 d) is an excellent upscale hotel and offers well-appointed and airy rooms, comfortable common areas, a beautiful dining room, lots of hammocks, and a pool. It's got a fine view of the valley below and is within walking distance of the idyllic Plaza Principal of Pinchote.

Food

Mostly Tex-Mex **Gringo Mike's** (Cl. 12 No. 8-35, tel. 7/724-1695, 8am-11:45am and 5pm-10pm daily, COP$18,000) is paradise for Americans who have been on the road a while. Guac and chips, barbecue burgers, black bean burgers, Philly cheese steak sandwiches, burritos, and even breakfast burritos. It's a bummer it isn't open for lunch, though. Wait staff are on the nonchalant side, and the place is full of tourists, but who cares? The margaritas are perfect!

To brush elbows with the locals try **Rogelia** (Cra. 10 No. 8-09, tel. 7/724-0823, 7am-7:30pm daily, COP$12,000) or **Maná** (Cra. 10 No. 9-42, lunch daily, COP$12,000), which is

a popular place for lunch, and inexpensive, too. Try the grilled chicken stuffed with ham and cheese, but don't expect gourmet nor charm.

The best aspect about the **Gallineral Restaurante** (Parque Gallineral, cell tel. 300/565-2653, 8am-5pm daily, COP$20,000) is its lush setting.

On a second-floor open-air terrace, **La Terraza de Sevilla Video-Bar** (Cl. 10 No. 9-09, tel. 7/724-3422, 8am-2am Mon.-Sat., COP$12,000) specializes in grilled hamburgers and hot dogs. It's the place to drink beer and watch soccer. For a coffee or drink and a friendly atmosphere, **La Habana** (Cra. 9 No. 11-68, tel. 7/724-6279, 9am-midnight Mon.-Thurs., 9am-2am Fri.-Sat., 4pm-midnight Sun.) is a good choice.

The market is small, and the atmosphere is peaceful. As you walk through the stalls, you may only hear the hushed tones of the vendors. For a huge fresh fruit juice or just plain fruit in the morning, this is the place to go.

Getting There and Around

The main **Terminal de Transportes** (Vía al Socorro, tel. 7/724-5858) for buses to the major cities, such as Bucaramanga, Tunja, and Bogotá, is five minutes out of town, on the other side of the river. The journey to Bucaramanga by bus takes 2.5 hours and costs COP$15,000. Traveling to Tunja by bus will take 3-5 hours, to Bogotá 7, and to Santa Marta or Medellín about 12 (vía Bucaramanga). Taxis to and from the main bus terminal to the town center cost COP$3,200.

A smaller bus terminal for nearby towns is on Carrera 15 at Calle 11. It serves towns such as Barichara, Charalá, Curití, and Pescadero. It doesn't have an official name, but some refer to it as the Mini Terminal. Buses to Barichara depart every half hour 6am-6:30pm and cost COP$3,800.

BARICHARA

In 1975, when it was declared a national monument, Barichara (pop. 8,000) was named the most beautiful pueblo in Colombia. Despite its popularity with weekenders and a steady stream

© ANDREW DIER

Barichara is one of the country's most beautiful pueblos.

BOYACÁ

of international visitors, it hasn't lost its charm. This old tobacco town of sloping cobblestoned streets and white-washed colonial-era homes is permanently blessed with bright blue skies and warm temperatures. Located 20 kilometers (12 miles) northwest of San Gil, the town is on a plateau that overlooks the Río Suárez. Don't skimp on your time here.

Sights

On the serene Parque Principal is the **Templo de la Inmaculada Concepción,** with two grandiose towers that soar 22 meters into the air. When lit up at night, the sandstone church is particularly striking. The church was completed around 1780. On the west side of the park is the mayor's office. Next to it is the Casa de Cultura.

Up the picturesque Calle 6, at the top of the hill is the **Capilla de Santa Bárbara,** a Romanesque-style church that is a popular place for weddings. There is a cheesy sculpture garden, **Parque de las Artes,** at the edge of the Río Suárez canyon.

There are two other colonial churches to see, the **Capilla de Jesús** (Cra. 7 at Cl. 3), next to the cemetery, and the **Capilla de San Antonio** (Cra. 4 at Cl. 5). All around town you'll see houses and walls that utilize the *tapia pisada* adobe technique, and often, on these brilliantly white walls you'll see a small patch of the mud interior left exposed on purpose, to show passersby that it's not just a modern brick construction but real *tapia pisada.*

Barichara is the birthplace of Pres. Aquileo Parra Gómez, who was the 11th president of the Estados Unidos de Colombia. His childhood home, **Casa Aquileo Parra Gómez** (Cl. 6 at Cra. 2), has been extremely well preserved and is an excellent example of typical 19th-century Barichara architecture. The site is also a handicraft workshop for the elderly, who make woven bags and other items out of the natural fiber *fique,* which are sold for a pittance. It is an excellent social program, and they seem to have a good time. They are there Monday through Thursday.

© ANDREW DIER

the Camino Real between Barichara and Guane

BOYACÁ

◖ CAMINO REAL

A must-do activity in Barichara is to take the 5.3-kilometer (3.3-mile) Camino Real path to the pueblo of Guane. It's a lovely path that zigzags down from the plateau of Barichara through farmland, affording nice views of the countryside and an excellent opportunity to burn off a few vacation calories. Parts of the path are lined with stone walls that have been there for centuries.

Before the conquest, indigenous tribes throughout what is now Colombia traded crops and goods with each other utilizing an extensive network of footpaths. These trails meandered through the countryside of present-day Santander, Boyacá, Norte de Santander, Cundinamarca, and beyond. During Spanish rule, the paths continued to be a major means of communication between colonial towns, and the networks became known as Caminos Reales.

In the late 19th century, a German, Geo von Legerke, restored the Barichara-Guane Camino Real and built a stone bridge across the Río Suárez in order to improve transportation to the mighty Río Magdalena.

The hike down takes two hours, and you don't need a guide: It's well marked, well trodden, and safe. To get to the trailhead, walk east along Carrera 10 to the Piedra de Bolívar, where you'll see the stone path leading down towards the valley.

In Guane you can check out the small **Museo Isaias Ardila Díaz** (Parque Principal, hours vary), which has three rooms, one on paleontology (fossils), the next on archaeology (mummy), and a third on colonial life in rural Santander. *Sabajón,* which is the Colombian version of eggnog, is the sweet specialty in Guane, and it is sold in various shops around the park.

If you are not up for the hike a (cute) bus departs the Parque Principal in Barichara at 6am, 9:30am, 11:30am, 2:30pm, and 5:30pm (it returns 30 minutes later from Guane).

Festivals and Events

Little Barichara proudly hosts two annual film

© SOPHIE TRAEN/123RF

Cobblestone streets in the colonial village of Guane

festivals. The **Festival Internacional de Cine de Barichara** (www.ficba.com.co) takes place in June, and the **Festival de Cine Verde** (www.festiver.org), an environmentally themed festival, is held every September.

Shopping

Barichara has always been a magnet for artists and craftspeople, and many have shops in town.

The **Fundación Escuela Taller Barichara** (Cra. 5 No. 4-26, tel. 7/726-7577, www.tallerdeoficiosbarichara.com, 8am-7pm Mon.-Thurs., 8am-10pm Fri.-Sat., 8am-4pm Sun.) is a gallery, museum, school, shop, and restaurant, all wrapped up in one. Occasional photography and painting exhibitions are held at this lovely cultural center, decorative objectives traditional from the area are always on display, ceramics and other items made by students are for sale, and anyone can take a month-long or longer course here. They offer dozens for free, and the Cruces restaurant is the best restaurant in town (it's open on weekends and holidays).

An interesting stop to make is at the **Taller de Papel de Fique** (Cl. 6 No. 2-68, no phone, 8am-3pm Mon.-Thurs.). At this workshop, craftspeople make beautiful paper out of the natural fiber of *fique*. On sale in their small store are cards, stationery, and handicrafts, all produced using that natural fiber. They are also now experimenting with other paper made from pineapple leaves. Short tours explaining the paper-making process are given, and for this there is a small charge.

One of the best-known ceramic artists in town is **Jimena Rueda** (Cra. 5 No. 2-01, cell tel. 314/400-5071). In addition to browsing her work, ask about the famous rustic handmade pottery of the Guane people. There is only one person who knows and uses this technique: **Ana Felisa Alquichire.** Doña Ana Felisa has been declared a living national cultural treasure by the Colombian presidency.

Galería Anil (Cl. 6 No. 10-46, cell tel. 311/470-1175) is the studio for local artists Jasmín and Carlos.

Accommodations

With its growth in popularity, accommodations

options to fit all budgets and styles have popped up in Barichara.

Backpackers and budget travelers have several options in Barichara. The **Color de Hormiga Hostel** (Cl. 6 No. 5-35, cell tel. 315/297-1621, http://colordehormiga.com/hostel.html, COP$45,000 d) used to house teachers from a neighboring school. It's decorated with institutional furniture that was left behind and kept the groovy tiled floors as they are. Funky! There are seven small rooms for one or two people, each with its own private bath. The kitchen is open for use by guests. The **Reserva Natural** (Vereda San José Alto, cell tel. 315/297-1621, COP$70,000 pp d), from the same owner as the Color de Hormiga Hostel, is a step up, with more luxury, more solitude, and a crazy bird show every morning while you have a healthy breakfast. Birds representing all colors of the rainbow appear like clockwork every morning to munch on pieces of banana and papaya to the delight of guests enjoying their breakfasts. This is about a 10-minute walk from town. The staff is incredibly friendly.

The **Tinto Hostel** (Cl. 6 No. 2-61, Bloque E Casa 1, tel. 7/726-7725, www.hosteltintobarichara.com) is a friendly hostel. It's in a weird, mostly residential cul de sac, about a 10-minute downhill walk from town. It seems farther away than it actually is. They are helpful with organizing outdoor adventures in the San Gil area. The funky hostel award in Barichara goes to **Casa Bakú** (Cl. 5 No. 9-69, cell tel. 301/419-2136, bakuhostal@hotmail.com). Baku, as in the capital of Azerbaijan. Like it or not, it's a social place. It's tiny. The common area, with a little homage to Bob Marley, is basically a garden with a bar and chairs. That's where they serve breakfast, which is included.

On the edge of town past the hospital, **Artepolis** (Cra. 2 at Cl. 2, cell tel. 300/203-4531) was getting going when we arrived. It is a Frenchman's idea of creating a space for creative people to come and find creative inspiration in the marvelous setting of Barichara. Its formal and serious sounding name is the Centro Internacional de Encuentro y Formación para el Arte y Cultura.

Ahh, the boutique hotel. Barichara didn't have them before; now it does! **La Nube** (Cl. 7 No. 7-39, tel. 7/726-7161, www.lanubeposada.com, COP$330,000 d) was boutique before that word entered the Colombian hotel lexicon. It's still a comfortable choice. It has seven rooms and a good restaurant (breakfast not included), and the patio is a nice place for relaxing to the soothing sound of a fountain. **Achiotte Hotel Boutique** (Cl. 5 No. 3-52, tel. 7/726-7512, COP$220,000 d) is a well-done, quiet hotel, with large rooms and common spaces filled with bamboo, flowers, and trees. You can shower here in the open air (nobody will see you!). At present the hotel has about nine rooms, which makes it really feel boutique. Along with a pool, there are plans to add several more rooms, which may change the feeling.

El Cogollo (Cra. 11 No. 7-37, cell tel. 311/202-4391, www.baricharacogollo.com, COP$280,000) is a very comfortable boutique-type hotel with eight rooms. The hotel uses construction materials and techniques from the earth, such as *tapia pisada, bahreque, adobe,* and stone. They operate the travel agency **Barichara Travel** (www.baricharaguanecito.com).

Finally, there is the peaceful **Posada Sueños de Antonio** (Cra. 9 No. 4-25, tel. 7/726-7793, www.suenosdeantonio.com, COP$120,000 d), with five spacious rooms surrounding an interior patio.

Food

The **Restaurante y Café Las Cruces** (Cra. 5 No. 4-26, tel. 7/726-7577, www.tallerdeoficiosbarichara.com, Fri.-Sun. and daily during high season, COP$28,000) is considered the top restaurant in Barichara. It's in the patio of the Fundación Escuela Taller Barichara. **Plenilunio Café** (Cl. 6 No. 7-74, tel. 7/726-7485, 6:30pm-10pm daily, COP$22,000) serves mostly Italian food but also has backpacker favorites like veggie burgers. There are just a handful of tables in this cozy spot, and most all of them are occupied by content foreign visitors on balmy Barichara evenings.

BOYACÁ

La Puerta (Cl. 6 No. 8-51, tel. 7/726-7649, www.baricharalapuerta.com, lunch and dinner daily high season, COP$22,000) is a beautiful place, candlelit at night. They serve tasty pastas and use local, organic ingredients when possible. **Castañetos** (Cl. 6 No. 10-43, tel. 7/726-7765, 6:30pm-10pm daily high season, COP$24,000) is the best pizzeria in town.

At the other end of town, near the canyon, is **Al Cuoco** (Cra. 4 No. 3B-15, cell tel. 312/527-3628, noon-9pm or 10pm daily, COP$22,000), an Italian place run by a Roman. They make their own pasta.

Locals throng to **El Balcón de Mi Pueblo** (Cl. 7 No. 5-62, cell tel. 318/280-2980, noon-5pm daily, COP$12,000) because they serve good, meaty Colombian food (*cabro, carne oreada, churrasco*) without serving up Bogotá prices! It's a cute place, up on the second floor. Another favorite is the lunch-only option **Misifú** (Cra. 6 No. 6 31, tel. 7/726-7321, noon-6pm daily, COP$12,000). Their specialty is the local specialty *carne oreada,* a dry and toothsome steak, reminiscent of beef jerky.

For a coffee or some of their world-famous (or at least pueblo-famous) *galletas de cuajada* (cheese cookies), head to **Panadería Barichara** (Cl. 5 No. 5-33, tel. 7/726-7688, 7am-1pm and 2pm-8pm daily). They've been around since 1954.

The best nightlife in town? Head to the **Mirador** bar on the west side of town overlooking the Río Suárez at around 5:30pm. Free sunsets are included with the price of your Águila beer!

Getting There

Most visitors arrive either in their own transportation or by bus to Barichara. Buses from Bogotá depart from the Autopista Norte Station. The journey to San Gil takes six hours or more, and you'll have to transfer in San Gil. It costs COP$30,000. From Bucaramanga, from the Piedecuesta terminal, a bus leaves at 4:45pm Monday-Friday. On Saturday the bus departs at 9am and on Sunday at 7:30pm. It takes three hours and costs COP$15,000. *Busetas* leave San Gil every half hour from the Terminal de Transportes Monday-Sunday starting at 6:10am, with the last bus departing at 8:15pm. The 20-kilometer (12-mile) journey takes 45 minutes.

Norte de Santander

This department in the northeast of the country borders Venezuela to the east and Santander to the south. The two main places of interest are Pamplona and Cúcuta, two very different cities. Pamplona is a charming and cool highland town that was important during the colonial era, though much of its colonial architecture has disappeared due to earthquakes and the march toward progress. To the north, the departmental capital of Cúcuta is a large, boiling hot commercial city and gateway to Venezuela. Both cities are easily accessed by road from Bucaramanga. The southernmost area of Norte de Santander and the northernmost area of Catatumbo have been plagued with guerrilla and paramilitary activity in recent years and are best avoided.

PAMPLONA

This historic and charming colonial town is a refreshing change from the *calor* (heat) of Cúcuta and Bucaramanga, set in a lush, agriculturally rich valley at 2,300 meters (7,500 feet). In addition to colonial remnants like the Casa de las Tres Marías (now Museo de Arte Moderno Eduardo Ramírez Villamizar), Pamplona is known for being the home of abstract expressionist artist Eduardo Ramírez, and for being a surprisingly lively college town, home to the Universidad de Pamplona and thousands of students.

Sights

Pamplona has its share of museums, and they are all easily visited in a day on foot. The best museum here is the **Museo de Arte Moderno Eduardo Ramírez Villamizar** (Cl. 5 No. 5-75, tel. 7/568-2999, www.mamramirezvillamizar. com, 9am-noon and 2pm-5pm Tues.-Sun., COP$3,000), prominently located on the Parque Agueda Gallardo. This museum, in a lovingly restored 16th-century house, features the work of this modernist sculptor and painter and also puts on temporary shows of modern and contemporary Colombian artists. In the courtyard, surrounding a magnolia tree, are many Ramírez sculptures. Born in Pamplona in 1922, Ramírez passed away in Bogotá in 2004.

Around the corner is the **Museo Arquidiocesano de Arte Religioso** (Cra. 5 No. 4-87, tel. 7/568-2816, 10am-noon and 3pm-5pm Wed.-Mon., COP$2,000). It houses oil paintings from masters such as Gregorio Arce y Ceballos and others, wood carvings dating back to the 17th century, and silver and gold ceremonial items.

The most interesting churches to check out include the imposing **Catedral Santa Clara** (Cl. 6 between Cras. 5-6), which dates back to 1584, and the **Ermita del Señor del Humilladero** (Cl. 2 between Cras. 7-8), which is next to the cemetery, filled with above-ground tombs. It is famous for its realistic carving Cristo del Humilladero.

The **Casa Mercado** (Cl. 6 between Cras. 4-5) stands on the previous location of a Jesuit college; this covered market was built in 1920. The **Museo Casa Colonial** (Cl. 6 No. 2-56, tel. 7/568-2043, www.casacolonialpamplona. com, 8am-noon and 2pm-6pm Mon.-Fri., free) packs quite a punch in its 17th-century abode. It includes exhibits on some of the native cultures from the area, touches on the independence movement and struggles of the early Colombian republic, and takes the visitor through to the 20th century.

Finally, the small **Museo Casa Anzoátegui** (Cra. 6 No. 7-48, 9am-noon and 2pm-5:30pm Mon.-Sat., COP$1,000) examines the life of General José Antonio Anzoátgui and the fight for independence from Spain. It was in this house that this war hero died in 1819. He was the head of Bolívar's honor guard and was promoted to general following the Batalla del Puente de Boyacá.

Accommodations and Food

(**Hostal 1549** (Cl. 8B No. 8-64, Calle los Miserables, tel. 7/568-0451, www.1549hostal. com, COP$130,000) has a big problem: Your room is so cozy that it will take an effort to get out and explore the town. Seven spacious rooms have big, comfortable beds, and many have fireplaces. The hotel has an adjacent restaurant where breakfast is served. At night locals gather to drink, but they are usually shown the door by 11pm.

Somewhat quirky, the **Hotel Ursua** (Cl. 5 No. 5-67, tel. 7/568-2470, COP$40,000 d) has a fantastic location right on the main park, and rooms, with beds that will do, come in all shapes and sizes. The restaurant serves inexpensive breakfasts and lunches.

Once home to a scribe to the Spanish authorities in the 18th century, **El Solar** (Cl. 5 No. 8-10, tel. 7/568-2010, www.elsolarhotel. com, COP$110,000 d) is one of the most popular accommodation and restaurant options in Pamplona. It has 10 rooms, and 21 beds. Breakfast at their restaurant is included, as is wireless Internet.

Pierro's Pizza (Cra. 5 No. 8B-67, tel. 7/568-0160, 5pm-11pm daily, COP$20,000) is the most popular place for pizza (as well as a whole host of other favorites), and it's run by an Italian. Other favorites include **Sal y Pimienta** (Cra. 5A No. 8B-66, cell no. 301/496-2464, 5pm-10pm daily, COP$18,000), and **Restaurante Píoko** (Cl. 5 No. 5-49 tel. 7/568-3031, 7am-9pm, COP$18,000) specializes in trout dishes.

Vegetarians will want to hunt for the hard-to-find Hare Krishna-run **Majesvara** (Cra. 3B No. 1C-26, cell 310/267-9307, 11am-2pm and 6pm-9pm Mon.-Sat., COP$8,000). If you find it try their set lunch or dinner menu.

Every town should have a place like **Stanco La Rokola** (Cl. 9 No. 5-23 Plazuela Almeida). It's a tiny nook on the Plazuela Almeida, where for about COP$2,000 you can order a shot of tequila, vodka, or rum, and then be on your merry way.

BOYACÁ

Getting There

Pamplona is reached by bus from Cúcuta. These leave on an hourly basis, and the two-hour trip costs about COP$10,000. You can also take a bus to Pamplona from Bucaramanga. It costs about COP$28,000 and takes under five hours. Pamplona's bus station is the spic and span **Terminal de Transportes** (Barrio El Camellón), about a 10-minute walk from the town center.

CÚCUTA

Midway between Bogotá and Caracas, the sizzling capital (pop. 637,000) of the Norte de Santander department straddles the border with Venezuela. Streets are lined with vendors selling cheap Venezuelan gasoline. A favorite and cheap beer served in restaurants and bars is Polar, straight from Venezuela. There is a constant stream of traffic crossing the border on the Puente Internacional in both directions. Venezuelans used to come to Cúcuta for shopping, but now it is the Colombians who are going east to load up on goods. Nonetheless, there is always a Venezuelan presence in Cúcuta, especially on weekends and holidays.

In recent years, the city has seen a large influx of persons fleeing violence in other parts of Norte de Santander and Arauca. During the 1990s, there was a bloody turf war between paramilitaries and leftist guerrillas. In 2008, in response to months of simmering tension, pop singer Juanes organized *Paz sin Fronteras* (Peace Without Borders), a concert on the border between Colombia and Venezuela, to the delight of nearly 300,000 fans. Today the city is considered a safe place to visit.

Many foreign travelers in Cúcuta are there either to cross over into Venezuela so that they can extend their visit in Colombia on their tourist visa, or they are on their way to Caracas. Despite its reputation as a hot, uninteresting city, Cúcuta is a pleasant place to explore for a couple of days.

The downtown area of the City of Trees is quite walkable, with trees lining its broad streets. There are a handful of republican period churches and buildings worth a look. And at night, particularly on weekends, restaurants, cafés, and bars in the Caobos district are pleasant gathering places for Cucuteños of all ages.

The main tourist attraction is just outside of the city in Villa del Rosario, on the way toward Venezuela. That's where Colombia's Thomas Jefferson, General Francisco de Paula Santander was born, and also is where the first constitution for Gran Colombia was drafted. Simón Bolívar officially became the country's president here.

ORIENTATION

The western boundary of Cúcuta is basically the parched Río Pamplonita and, before that, the Avenida Libertadores. A lot of the big restaurants and nightlife spots are located here, and this is where the Ciclovía is held on Sundays. The Diagonal Santander represents the boundary of the downtown towards the north. It links the Terminal de Transportes in the northwest of the city to the stadium and finally merges into the Autopista Internacional (the road that leads to San Antonio, Venezuela) in the east. All the decent hotels and most sights of interest in Cúcuta are located in the downtown area between Avenida 0 to the east and Avenida 6 to the west and Calle 8 to the north and Calle 13 to the south. Ventura Plaza Centro Comercial is a good landmark to remember. It is between Avenida 0 and the Diagonal Santander. The Aeropuerto Camilo Daza is in the northwest of the city.

Sights
CITY CENTER

All the sights in downtown Cúcuta can easily be visited on foot. There is not a tourism culture here, so obtaining basic information such as opening hours and telephone numbers is not always easy. At the beautifully restored **Biblioteca Pública Julio Pérez Ferrero** (Av. 1 No. 12-35, Barrio La Playa, tel. 7/595-5384, www.bibliocucuta.org, 8am-noon and 2pm-6pm Mon.-Fri., 9am-noon Sat.) there is always something going on: photography exhibits on

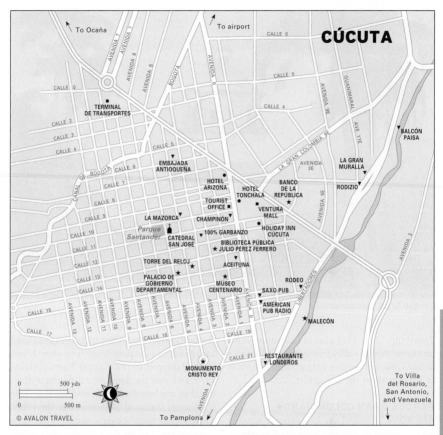

old Cúcuta, classes and workshops, concerts. The library building, declared a national monument, originally served as a hospital in the late 18th century. The library also operates the **Museo Centenario** (Cl. 14 No. 1-03, tel. 7/595-5384, www.museocentenario.com, 8am-noon and 2pm-6pm Mon.-Fri., 9am-noon Sat.), which is often the host of art exhibitions and events. It is a newish addition to the cultural scene. It is open only when there is something going on.

The **Palacio de Gobierno Departamental** (Clls. 13-14 and Avs. 4-5, not open to the public) is noteworthy for its republican, neoclassical architecture. **Torre del Reloj** (Cl. 13 and Avs. 3-4) houses a clock that plays the national

anthem on its bells at noon each day. The bells came from Italy in the early 19th century. You can ask to check it out. From the top, if you can squeeze past the bells you can get a nice view of the city with the **Monumento Cristo Rey** (Av. 4 at Cl. 19) in the distance. The Torre del Reloj is part of the **Casa de la Cultura** complex. It also hosts art exhibitions. The neoclassical **Catedral San José** (Av. 5 No. 10-53) faces the shady **Parque Santander** (Avs. 5-6 and Clls. 10-11). Finally, be sure to walk along Calle 10 or Calle 11. Canned music blares from loudspeakers on the streets all day long.

The **Banco de la República** (Diagonal Santander No. 3E-38, tel. 7/575-0131, www. banrepcultural.org/cucuta, 8am-11:30am,

© ANDREW DIER

Parque Gran Colombiano

2pm-6pm Mon.-Fri.) always has an art exhibition on view, usually featuring a Colombian artist. Concerts are also held at their theater. It is just outside of the city center.

PARQUE GRAN COLOMBIANO

The major historical site in Cúcuta is actually seven kilometers away in **Villa del Rosario** on the road towards San Antonio del Táchira, Venezuela. The **Parque Gran Colombiano** is in the middle of the busy highway that leads to the Venezuelan border. Although much of the park is green space where couples kiss under palm trees and others jog or walk their dogs, the most important historical sites within the park are the **Casa Natal del General Santander** (Km. 6 Autopista Internacional, tel. 7/570-0265, 8am-11am and 2pm-5pm Tues.-Sat., 9am-5pm Sun. and holidays, free) and the ruins of the **Templo del Congreso.** The museum tells the story of General Francisco de Paula Santander and is set in his childhood home. The Templo del Congreso is where Gran Colombia's Constitution of 1821 was drafted and where

Simón Bolívar was sworn in as president (and Santander as vice president). The church was badly damaged in the Cúcuta Earthquake of 1875, and only the dome, in a different style altogether, was rebuilt. It's unavoidable that there is a bronze statue of Bolívar inside the ruins. The congress met for over a month to draft the constitution, and on their breaks, they would rest under the shade of a huge tamarind tree. It's still there, right in front of the church.

Across the highway is the **Casa de la Bagatela,** which was the seat of the executive branch of Gran Colombia. It was named La Bagatela in honor of independence figure Antonio Nariño, who penned a revolutionary paper in Bogotá by that same name. Don't bother scurrying across the highway to the Casa de la Bagatela, as there's nothing much to see.

You can take a shared taxi or a *buseta* (small bus) bound for San Antonio del Táchira at the Ventura Plaza mall. These cost around COP\$2,500. Ask to be dropped off at the Parque Gran Colombiano. Private taxis cost about COP\$7,500 from downtown Cúcuta.

Nightlife

There are three trendy nightlife areas: the lovely and leafy Caobos neighborhood, the *malecón* (wharf) along the Río Pamplonita, and in the Centro Comercial Bolívar.

In Caobos, in the newly branded Zona E (because many spots are along the Avenida 1E) there are dozens of pub-like places where you can have a bite and/or have a brew outside on the terrace. It's not a bad atmosphere. Pubs are all more or less the same, but be on the lookout for these popular spots: **American Pub Radio** (Av. 1E No. 16-20, tel. 7/594-8398, www.americanpubradio.com); **Saxo Pub** (Cl. 16 No. 1E-13 tel. 7/571-4270, www.saxopub. com, 4pm-2am daily); and **British Pub** (Cl. 17 No. 1E-05, 5:30pm-2am Tues.-Thurs., 5:30pm-3am Fri. and Sat.).

To the east and along the banks of the Río Pamplonita, many of the restaurants in town evolve into party places as the night wears on. Another very Cúcuteño way to party is to grab your friends and pick up some booze, drive down to the Avenida de los Libertadores and park, and pump up the *vallenatos* (ballads accompanied by accordions) or, occasionally, electronica. To the north the nearby **Centro Comercial Bolívar** has a number of bars, including a couple of gay clubs, as well as clubs catering to salsa aficionados.

Recreation

On Sunday morning, head to the Avenida de los Libertadores/Paseo de los Proceres/*malecón* along the Río Pamplonita. You can work up a sweat with the locals here as they ride their bikes and jog during their mini **Ciclovía** (7am-1pm). Bike rentals aren't available, but you can always jog or people-watch.

To arrange an organized tour of points of interest in Norte de Santander contact **Crischarol Tours** (Cl. 13 No. 5-60, tel. 7/572-0407, www. crischaroltours.blogspot.com). They offer day-trip tours to Pamplona.

Accommodations

Astonishingly, Cúcuta, the sixth largest city in Colombia, did not have any international or even national chain hotels until Holiday Inn announced its arrival in late 2014. With 98 rooms, and located across from the Ventura Plaza mall, it is a much needed addition. Most downtown hotels have seemingly been around forever, the kind where you are handed the remote control in its plastic cover when you check in, and staff are dressed in outdated uniforms.

Outside of town, in Villa del Rosario, there are other hotel options. These are popular places on the weekends. Continuing onward into San Antonio, hotel options are abysmal. They are cheap, but abysmal.

It once probably seemed very flashy, but retro **Hotel Tonchalá** (Av. 0 at Cl. 10, tel. 7/575-6444, www.hoteltonchala.com, COP$209,0900 d) has kept up with the times by updating the rooms (there are about 100 of them). The hotel has a pool, gym, and sauna. It's within easy walking distance of Ventura Plaza Centro Comercial.

Staff dressed in bright pink uniforms at the **Hotel Arizona Suites** (Av. 0 No. 7-62, tel. 7/573-1884, www.hotelarizonasuites.com, COP$245,000) are so exceptionally friendly, even the most persnickety of guests will find it hard to lodge any complaint. Rooms are fine, a little on the small side, and definitely overpriced. The restaurant overlooks a small pool, and the spa area was renovated in 2012. The location is OK, not great, near two busy streets and about a 10-minute walk to sights downtown.

If you would rather be surrounded by greenery than concrete you might want to consider the **Hotel Villa Antigua** (Autopista San Antonio-Villa del Rosario, tel. 7/570-0399, www.hotelvillantigua.amawebs.com, COP$120,000 d). It is geared mostly towards Colombian families and groups as a weekend place to kick back and drink by the large pool. During the week you'll likely have the place to yourself. They have cabanas of several sizes and then spacious regular hotel rooms. Breakfast is served in an outdoor restaurant overlooking the pool, but it smells like either gas or strong floor wax. Wireless Internet is available in the lobby. The Parque Gran Colombiano is just across the

BOYACÁ

street, but you must be very careful crossing the street. This is the main drag to San Antonio, and cars and buses absolutely zoom by. At the park you can go for a morning or late afternoon walk. If you want to go into town during the day or at night, it is not an issue: Taxis are cheap and it takes about 15 minutes.

Food
The most typical food from Cúcuta includes *hayacas cucutenas,* similar to tamales; *mute,* a meaty stew; and *pastel de garbanzo* (a fried garbanzo bean pastry).

The **Embajada Antioqueña** (Cl. 6 No. 3-48, tel. 7/571-7673, 8am-10pm daily, COP$20,000) has hearty breakfasts (meaty *caldos* or broths), lunches, and dinners. It's been around for about 40 years, and the atmosphere, with tango music and Colombian classics, is quite nice. Try the baby beef or their *típica* plate with ground beef chorizo, *chicharrón* (sausage), rice, and arepa, or at lunchtime the COP$8,000 set lunch. **La Mazorca** (Av. 4 No. 9-23, tel. 7/571-1800, 7am-8pm daily, COP$18,000) is a popular chain restaurant serving the gamut of Colombian fare.

For a welcome break from meat eating, try **Champiñon** (Cl. 10 No. 0-05, tel. 7/571-1561, 8am-8:30pm Mon.-Sat., COP$12,000). This, Cúcuta's best and biggest vegetarian restaurant, opens in the morning for coffee and pastries, then offers a generous set lunch. Off the menu you can order veggie burgers, salads, and pastas. **Aceituna** (Av. 0 No. 13-135, tel. 7/583-7464, 10:30am-10pm Mon.-Sat., COP$18,000) is a long-standing Lebanese food restaurant run by a Lebanese-Colombian family.

Vegetarians, almost always prohibited from the joys of Colombian street food delights, will rejoice at the sight of *pasteles de garbanzo* purveyor **100% Garbanzo** (Cl. 11 No. 2-83, cell tel. 313/498-1712, 8am-noon and 2pm-6pm Mon.-Fri.). This snack bar is a great place to sample the bean pastry.

When darkness falls in Cúcuta, especially on the weekends, the energy shifts to the *malecón* area, about a 10-minute cab ride from downtown. That's where many of the big restaurants are located. **Londeros Sur** (Av. Libertadores No. 0E-60B, tel. 7/583-3335, www.restaurantelonderos.com, COP$25,000) is famous around town for its Argentinian steaks; **Rodizio** (Av. Libertadores No. 10-121, tel. 7/575-1719, www.rodizio.com.co, COP$30,000) for its Brazilian-style grilled meats; and **Rodeo** (Av. Libertadores No. 16-38, www.rodeogourmet.com, COP$25,000) is another very popular carnivorous option. **Balcón Paisa** (Av. Los Libertadores No. 6-40, tel. 7/575-0244, COP$22,000) is one of the most popular restaurants on the *malecón* and is huge. In addition to a vast menu of Colombian dishes, they often feature live shows. Late at night it becomes more rumba than restaurant. And for a departure, **La Gran Muralla** (Av. Libertadores No. 10-84, tel. 7/575-3946, COP$18,000) is one of the best-known Chinese places in town.

The mall, the **Ventura Plaza Centro Comercial** (between Clls. 10 and 11 at Diagonal Santander, www.venturaplaza.com.co) is usually a safe bet for a bite of fast food, if you have run out of ideas. The food court area is open until 10:30pm.

Information and Services
The **tourist office** (Cl. 10 No. 0-30, no phone, 8am-noon and 2pm-6pm Mon.-Fri., 8am-noon Sat.) has lots of brochures and maps for not only Cúcuta but also the rest of the Norte de Santander department. Staff can provide some good tips on visiting natural attractions in the area.

In case of an emergency, contact the **Policía Nacional** (tel. 7/576-0622, or 123). A major hospital in town is the **Hospital Erasmo Meoz** (Av. 11E with Cl. 4N Guaimaral, tel. 7/574-6888).

Getting There and Around
The **Terminal de Transportes** (Avs. 7-8 between Clls. 1-2) in Cúcuta is dirty, chaotic, and generally unpleasant, and is probably the main reason so many arrive in Cúcuta with a poor impression of the city. Try to get your ticket

in advance or at least find out the schedule so you don't have to be there longer than necessary. If you are waiting for a bus, it's best to wait outside on the curb, far from the claustrophobic station. There are numerous buses to Pamplona and other towns near Cúcuta. The bus to Bogotá costs around COP$70,000 and the trip takes 14 hours. To Bucaramanga it costs COP$30,000 and takes six hours, and to San Gil it costs about COP$45,000 and takes eight hours.

The airport, **Aeropuerto Camilo Daza** (Km. 5 Autopista Panamericana), is a 15-minute cab ride from downtown. **Avianca** (Cl. 13 No. 5-22, tel. 7/571-3877, www.avianca.com, 8am-noon and 2pm-6pm Mon.-Fri., 8am-noon Sat.) flies nonstop between Cúcuta and Bogotá and Medellín; **EasyFly** (tel. 7/595-5005, www.easyfly.com.co) connects Cúcuta with Bucaramanga and Medellín; and **LAN** (Col. toll-free tel. 01/800-094-9490, www.lan.com.co) flies to Bogotá.

If you are staying downtown, all attractions are within relatively easy walking distance. It's always a good policy to call a cab beforehand, and always after dark. Two reputable services are **Taxis Radio Taxi Cone** (tel. 7/582-1666) and **Radio Taxi Radio** (tel. 7/583-6828).

CROSSING INTO VENEZUELA

Crossing the border from Cúcuta into San Antonio del Táchira on the Venezuelan side is easy. *Busetas* (shared taxis) depart from in front of the Ventura Plaza mall. Expect to pay about COP$2,500 for a bus ticket. Taxis will cost upwards of COP$20,000. Be sure to get off before the bridge so you can get your passport stamped by immigration officials. Visas are not required for North Americans or European Union citizens. Hotels in San Antonio del Táchira are absolutely dismal, so it's far better to either stay in Cúcuta or continue onwards to Caracas immediately. For more information on visas you can visit the **Consulado Venezuelano** (Av. Aeropuerto Camilo Daza, Sector Corral de Piedra, Zona Industrial, Cl. 17 Esquina, tel. 7/579-1954 or 7/579-1951, 8am-10am and 2pm-3pm Mon.-Thurs., 8am-10am Fri.).

BOYACÁ

MEDELLÍN AND THE COFFEE REGION

Medellín is one of the most dynamic cities of Colombia, with a vibrant cultural scene and nightlife. However, the hallmarks of this region are the coffee plantations and tiny Paisa pueblos. This verdant countryside, with its exuberant vegetation and many shades of green, is simply spectacular.

© ANDREW DIER

HIGHLIGHTS

LOOK FOR 【 TO FIND RECOMMENDED SIGHTS, ACTIVITIES, DINING, AND LODGING.

【 Museo de Antioquia: The galleries of this art museum, a fabulous art deco building from the early 20th century, are filled with works from the best Colombian artists spanning nearly four centuries. And the terrace café is the best place for people-watching in the Centro (page 227).

【 Reserva Natural Río Claro: A jungle paradise in the Magdalena Medio is set along a canyon that was only relatively recently discovered. This private natural reserve offers caving, river rafting, and a surplus of peace (page 248).

【 Jardín: Just a few hours south of busy Medellín, the pace of life slows to a crawl in this picture-perfect coffee town of brightly colored Paisa homes. Jardín is surrounded by lush green mountains full of recreational opportunities (page 252).

【 Salamina: Life goes on much as it always has in this rather remote Paisa town known for its superb architecture and warm hospitality of its people (page 268).

【 Parque Nacional Natural Los Nevados: Dozens of hikes leading through tropical jungles afford fantastic views of snowcapped volcanoes and mountain lakes in this easily accessed national park (page 270).

【 Museo del Oro Quimbaya: This fantastic gold museum pays tribute to the original settlers of what is now the fertile coffee region: the indigenous Quimbaya people (page 277).

【 Jardín Botánico del Quindío: This is the best botanical garden in the region. You take a guided tour through a tropical forest full of *guadua* forests and dozens of species of birds. (page 279).

【 Valle de Cocora: One of the most dramatic and photographed scenes in Colombia is this valley filled with towering wax palms, Colombia's national tree. Nearby Salento offers coffee plantations and a typical Paisa pueblo experience (page 284).

MEDELLÍN

© ANDREW DIER

Jardín, a town in southern Antioquia

Medellín, the surrounding department of Antioquia, and the coffee region departments of Caldas, Risaralda, and Quindío comprise the central, mountainous section of Colombia, covering the Cordillera Central (Central Range) and Cordillera Occidental (Western Range) north of Cali. The mountains then flatten out into the Caribbean coastal lowlands. Antioquia and the coffee region lie on some of the most beautiful mountain landscapes in Colombia.

HISTORY

Despite its inaccessible terrain, Antioquia was an important province of colonial Nueva Granada due to its abundant gold deposits. It attracted settlers who panned the rivers or cultivated food for the mining camps. Santa Fe de Antioquia, founded in 1541, was the main colonial settlement.

After independence, the province continued to prosper, even attracting foreign investment in gold mining. Demographic pressure triggered a southward migration known as the *colonización antioqueña*. Waves of settlement brought Paisa families to unoccupied lands in the south of Antioquia, the coffee region, and the northern part of the Valle del Cauca.

During the early part of the 20th century, coffee was a major source of prosperity in Antioquia. Medellín grew rapidly and became the industrial powerhouse of Colombia. The last decades of the 20th century were difficult times for Antioquia, with the triple scourge of drug trafficking, paramilitary armies, and guerrillas. In the past decade, the government has made huge strides in bringing back the rule of law, and today Antioquia is one of the safest and most prosperous regions in Colombia.

PLANNING YOUR TIME

Weather-wise, anytime of the year is a good time to visit Medellín and the coffee region. There's a reason why they call Medellín the "City of Eternal Spring": The entire region has a temperate climate.

Medellín completely empties during the end of the year holidays, from December 15 to January 15, and also during Semana Santa

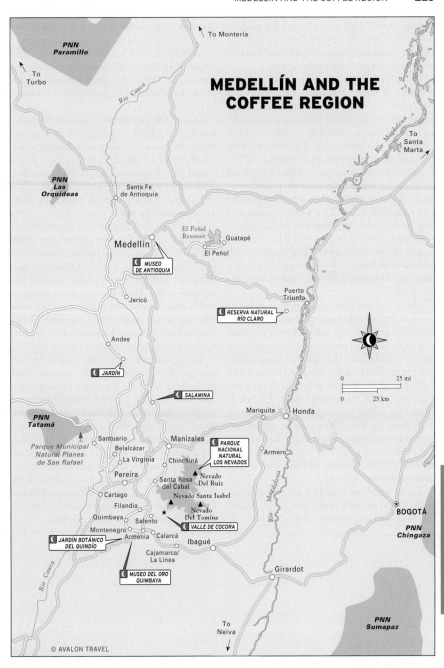

MEDELLÍN AND THE COFFEE REGION

PNN Paramillo

To Montería

To Turbo

Río Cauca

Río Magdalena

To Santa Marta

PNN Las Orquídeas

Santa Fe de Antioquia

Medellín

☾ MUSEO DE ANTIOQUIA

El Peñol Resevoir

Guatapé

El Peñol

Jericó

Puerto Triunfo

☾ RESERVA NATURAL RÍO CLARO

Andes

☾ JARDÍN

☾ SALAMINA

Mariquita Honda

PNN Tatamá

Parque Municipal Natural Planes de San Rafael

Santuario

Belalcázar

La Virginia

Manizales

Chinchiná

☾ PARQUE NACIONAL NATURAL LOS NEVADOS

Armero

Pereira

Santa Rosa del Cabal

▲ Nevado Del Ruiz

Cartago

▲ Nevado Santa Isabel

Río Magdalena

Filandia

▲ Nevado Del Tomina

Quimbaya

Salento

★

☾ VALLE DE COCORA

● BOGOTÁ

Montenegro

Armenia Calarcá

PNN Chingaza

☾ JARDÍN BOTÁNICO DEL QUINDÍO

Ibagué

Cajamarca/ La Línea

Río Cauca

☾ MUSEO DEL ORO QUIMBAYA

Girardot

To Neiva

PNN Sumapaz

0 25 mi

0 25 km

© AVALON TRAVEL

MEDELLÍN

(Easter week). This is peak time for pueblos and coffee region haciendas. During school vacations (June-July), natural parks and reserves and coffee haciendas get busy again.

Give Medellín three days. During that amount of time, you can experience "old Medellín" sights in the Centro, such as the Museo de Antioquia, as well as check out the modern Medellín icons that are the subject of great pride: the Metrocable, Biblioteca España, the café culture of cool El Poblado, and the Parque Explora. Consider spending a weekend in Medellín, when hotel rates drop, and especially if you're interested in checking out the city's nightlife scene. In a week you can add one or two other destinations in Antioquia, such as the Reserva Natural Río Claro or one of the picture-perfect Paisa pueblos, such as Jardín or Jericó. These are within about a three-hour bus ride from the Antioquian capital of Medellín.

Many visitors visit the gorgeous colonial town of Santa Fe de Antioquia to the north of Medellín as a day trip, but it's better to spend one night there, in order to enjoy strolling its quaint streets after the sun has gone down. On the banks of the mighty Río Cauca, Santa Fe is one of the hottest towns in the region. Guatape, with its famous rock, El Peñol, makes for a nice overnight on the way to or back from the Río Claro reserve, where two nights are necessary. These three destinations are popular on weekends and holidays. The stunning natural beauty of Río Claro is best enjoyed during the week.

To the south of Medellín are two picture-perfect Paisa pueblos: Jardín and Jericó. A couple of days in one of those should be enough.

You can continue from there southward into the coffee region on winding country roads.

Medellín is not a base for visiting the coffee region: The cities of Armenia, Manizales, and Pereira are. Pereira has good air connections, while the Manizales airport is often shrouded in fog.

One of the joys of this region is to book a few days at a coffee hacienda. Many tour operators will pack your days with day-trip activities. Resist! As it gets dark at 6pm every day, it would be a shame to miss spending some daylight hours strolling the grounds of the *finca* (farm), lazing in a hammock or rocking chair, or doing nothing at all.

You'll need a week or more to decompress on the coffee farm and see the region's top sights: the Valle de Cocora, the Jardín Botánico del Quindío, and Museo del Oro Quimbaya near Armenia, and one or two of the national and regional parks. There are very good transportation links between the three major cities and Salento. Roads are generally excellent. While renting a car in Colombia is not often the best option, here it makes sense.

Though you can enjoy this magnificent region just by taking a bus ride from one place to the next, there are a few spots that warrant special attention. East of Medellín toward the Río Magdalena lays the Reserva Natural Río Claro, a lush, deep canyon. The Parque Nacional Natural Los Nevados and surrounding regional parks (such as Parque Regional Natural Ucumarí) offer innumerable opportunities for day hikes and longer treks. A bit off the beaten track, Parque Municipal Natural Planes de San Rafael offers beautiful hikes in the less-visited Cordillera Occidental.

Medellín

While Medellín is the country's second in terms of population and importance, perpetually behind Bogotá, this city of around 2.7 million is the only Colombian metropolis with an urban train system. It's the first city with a cable car transportation system.

The first settlement in the region, near the present-day Poblado sector, was established in 1616. Medellín proper was founded in 1675, and was designated the capital of Antioquia in 1826.

In the 1980s, Pablo Escobar, born in nearby Rionegro, established a cocaine-trafficking empire based Medellín. In its heyday, the Medellín Cartel controlled 80 percent of the world's cocaine trade. When President Virgilio Barco cracked down on the cartel in the late 1980s, Escobar declared war on the government. He assassinated judges and political leaders, set off car bombs to intimidate public opinion, and paid a bounty for every policeman that was murdered in Medellín—a total of 657. In 1991, Medellín had a homicide rate of 380 per 100,000 inhabitants, the highest such rate on record anywhere in the world. In 1993, Escobar was killed while on the run from the law.

During the 1990s, leftist guerrillas gained strength in the poor *comunas,* or sectors, of Medellín, waging a vicious turf war with paramilitaries. At the turn of the century, the homicide rate was 160 per 100,000 inhabitants, making Medellín still one of the most dangerous places on Earth.

Shortly after assuming power in 2002, President Álvaro Uribe launched Operación Orion to wrest the poor *comunas* of Medellín from the leftist guerrillas, and violence decreased notably. By 2005, homicides were still high by international standards but a fraction of what they had been a decade before. Under the leadership of Mayor Sergio Fajardo, elected in 2004, and his successors Alonso Salazar and Aníbal Gaviria, Medellín has undergone an extraordinary transformation. In partnership with the private sector, the city has invested heavily in public works, including a new cable car transportation system, museums, and libraries. In recent years, the city has become a major tourist destination and has attracted significant foreign investment.

Medellín boasts a network of spectacular public libraries, greenspaces and plazas, and its train and cable car system. Beyond the Centro, the neighborhood of Laureles and the municipality of Envigado have their own distinct identity and atmosphere.

Orientation

Medellín is in the Valle de Aburrá, with the trickling and polluted Río Medellín dividing the city into east and west. Both the Metro (Line A) and the Avenida Regional or Autopista Sur, a busy expressway, run parallel to the river.

The main neighborhoods are **El Poblado,** including the mini-hood of Provenza, the **Centro,** and the **Carabobo Norte** area (often referred to as **Universidades**).

The El Poblado area is full of great restaurants, bars, hostels, hotels, and glitzy shopping malls. It is also full of tall brick high-rise apartment buildings, home to the well-to-do. If you arrive in Medellín from the Rionegro airport, you will descend the hill into the valley and land more or less in El Poblado. Luxury hotels and malls line the Avenida El Poblado. The Parque Lleras is the center of the Provenza neighborhood, a small, leafy, and very hip part of El Poblado. It is on the eastern side of the Avenida El Poblado. To the west, down the Calle 10, is the Parque del Poblado, and a few blocks farther is the El Poblado Metro station.

Across the river from El Poblado is the Terminal del Sur bus station and the Aeropuerto Olaya Herrera. The Cerro Nutibara (Pueblito Paisa) is north of the airport. Northwest of the Cerro Nutibara is the quiet neighborhood of Laureles, and farther west is the stadium area. The B line of the Metro connects the Centro with the stadium area.

MEDELLÍN

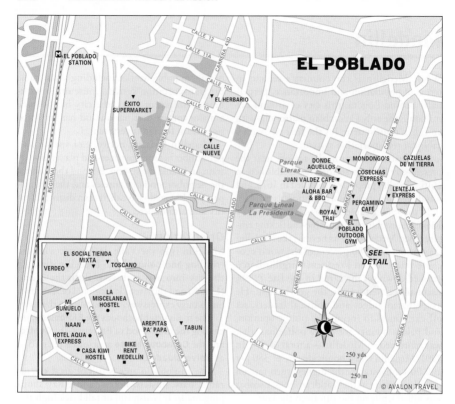

MEDELLÍN

Between El Poblado and the Centro is the Barrio Colombia and an industrial area known appropriately enough as Industriales. This is an up-and-coming area with new hotels and high-rises being built in what is known as the Ciudad del Río, where the Museo de Arte Moderno de Medellín is located. Barrio Colombia is also home to many nightspots.

The heart of the Centro is the Plaza Botero and Parque Berrío Metro station area. The Centro is between El Poblado to the south and Carabobo Norte to the north. The Avenida El Poblado, also known as Carrera 43A, connects El Poblado with El Centro. The Metro does as well.

The northern neighborhoods of Medellín are massive. To the west of the Río Medellín there are few places of interest. The Cerro Volador is a hill and landmark in the northwest of the city. To the east of the river is the Aranjuez neighborhood. The Acevedo Metro station is where you can pick up the Metrocable to the Biblioteca España and Parque Arví.

On the other side of town, in the far south, are the municipalities of Envigado and Itagüi. Envigado has some great restaurants, a busy main plaza, and the Parque El Salado. The Avenida El Poblado connects El Poblado with Envigado. Itagüi is an industrial town with little of interest for the tourist except for bars and clubs, many open until the wee hours.

Safety

As in other cities in Colombia, it is best to avoid hailing taxis on the street, particularly at night. Instead, have your hotel, or the restaurant or shop you're at, call a taxi for you. Be careful at clubs and bars, and don't accept drinks from strangers.

Neighborhoods such as La Provenza and Laureles are safe to walk about day or night. The Centro should be avoided after dark. It is not a good idea to take a carefree stroll in the northern or western neighborhoods or, especially, in the *comunas* (city sectors) on the surrounding hills, but specific sights mentioned can be visited. Not only are they clean and efficient, but the Metro, Metrocable, and Metroplús are safe.

SIGHTS

To see Medellín in full motion, visit the Centro during the week. On Saturdays, it's quieter, although the Peatonal Carabobo bustles with activity. On Sundays downtown is almost deserted except for tourists and street people. Most visits to the Centro start from the Parque Berrío Metro station. The main sights can easily be seen on foot and in a few hours.

Centro

◖ MUSEO DE ANTIOQUIA

The **Museo de Antioquia** (Cra. 52 No. 52-43, tel. 4/251-3636, www.museoantioquia.org.co, 10am-5:30pm Mon.-Sat., 10am-4:30pm Sun., COP$10,000) is one of the top art museums in the country, with an extensive permanent collection of works from Colombian artists from the 19th century to modern times. Look for the iconic painting *Horizontes* (*Horizons*) by Francisco A. Cano. It's a painting that depicts the *colonización antioqueña,* when, for a variety of reasons, families from Antioquia headed south to settle in what is now known as the coffee region. In the contemporary art rooms, you'll see *Horizontes* (1997) by Carlos Uribe. This painting presents the same bucolic scene, except this time, 84 years later, in the background, a plane is seen spraying pesticides over the countryside, in an attempt to kill coca and marijuana crops. Native son Fernando Botero has donated several of his works, over 100 of them, to the museum. There is also a small room on a series of works by Luis Caballero. The museum is in an architectural gem, an art deco-style building from the 1930s. It originally served as the Palacio

Municipal. There is a free guided tour at 2pm every day.

Carabobo Norte

One of the country's top universities is the **Universidad de Antioquia** (Cl. 67 No. 53-108, tel. 4/263-0011, www.udea.edu.co). The university was founded in 1803; however, it has only been at its current location in the Ciudad Universitaria, a few blocks west of the Centro, since 1968. There are over 37,000 students enrolled here, and the campus, full of plazas and public art, has a vibrant student energy In addition to a busy calendar of cultural events, the university has an excellent museum, **MUA** (Cl. 67 No. 53-108, Bloque 15, tel. 4/219-5180, www.udea.edu.co, 8am-5:45pm Mon.-Fri., 9am-12:45pm Sat., free), that features changing contemporary art exhibits and a permanent natural history exhibit. Access to the campus for all visitors is at the Portería del Ferrocarril entrance. Visitors must present a photo ID.

Adjacent to the university near the Metro station, the **Parque Explora** (Cra. 52 No. 73-75, tel. 4/516-8300, www.parqueexplora.org, 8:30am-5:30pm Tues.-Fri., 10am-6:30pm Sat.-Sun, COP$18,000) is one of the most iconic buildings of modern Medellín. It's a series of four futuristic red boxes. The ticket office closes 90 minutes before closing time. The **aquarium** (9am-5pm Tues.-Fri., included in admission cost) is the highlight of Explora. This is one of the largest aquariums in Latin America. Check out the tanks of Colombian marine creatures, including life in Colombian rivers such as the Amazon and Orinoco. Look for the giant pirarucú, an endangered fish that lives in the Amazon River and in its tributaries. The **Planetario Medellín** (Cra. 52 No. 71-117, tel. 4/516-8300, www.planetariomedellin.org, 8am-5pm Tues.-Wed., 8am-7pm Thurs.-Fri., 10am-6pm Sat.-Sun., COP$12,000) is across the street from the Parque Explora.

If you feel like a walk in the park, the **Jardín Botánico de Medellín** (Cra. 52 No. 73-298, tel. 4/444-5500, www.jbmed.org, 9am-5pm daily, free) is the place for you. It is across the street

MEDELLÍN

from Parque Explora. The highlight here is the Orquiderama, an open-air wood lattice-like structure where events are held. The botanical gardens are more akin to a tropical city park. It's a popular hangout for students, who will giggle as they say hello to you in English. In addition to the fantastic setting and good food of **In Situ** (inside the gardens, tel. 4/460-7007, www.botanicomedellin.org, noon-3pm Mon., noon-3pm and 7pm-10pm Tues.-Sat., COP$25,000), there are cafés and a nice gift shop.

Behind the botanical gardens is the **Esquina de las Mujeres** (Cra. 51 at Cl. 73), a small public space with busts of accomplished women from Medellín and Antioquia from the colonial era to the present day. They represent many walks of life: indigenous women, activists, social workers, and artists who all made a contribution to society. Not many locals know about this homage, which was unveiled in 2007.

Presidents, artists, and writers rest in the **Museo Cementerio de San Pedro** (Cra. 51 No.

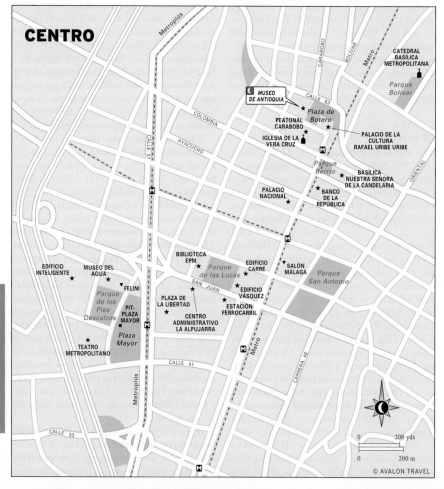

68-68, tel. 4/516-7650, www.cementeriosanpedro.org.co, 8am-5:30pm daily, free). Marble statues and elaborate tombs pay tribute to influential Antioqueños from the 19th century onward, but the reminders of the city's recent turbulent past may strike you as more interesting. One plot, near the tomb of Fidel Cano, founder of the once influential *El Espectador* newspaper, contains the tombs of several members of drug kingpin Pablo Escobar's associates and guards. (He is buried in a cemetery in the neighboring town of Itagüí.) Some tombs have stickers identifying allegiance to one of Medellín's soccer clubs, others have touching handwritten notes from wives and children left behind. There is a free tour of the cemetery on Sundays (2pm). To see the cemetery in a different light, check it out on a full moon evening (7pm-9pm). It's open to the public then and there are usually free concerts and other cultural activities going on. Check the cemetery's up-to-date webpage for a complete schedule of activities.

Cerro Nutibara

To see an authentic Paisa pueblo, go to Jardín, Jericó, or Salamina. They're just a couple of hours away and are as real as you can get. Can't do that? Then go to the **Pueblito Paisa** (Cl. 30A No. 55-64, tel. 4/235-6476, 5am-midnight daily, free), atop the Cerro de Nutibara, one of two hills that interrupt the flat landscape of the Valle de Aburrí. Here, at this rather cheesy celebration of Paisa culture, you'll be greeted by smiling folks decked out in traditional costume. There is also a small **Museo de la Ciudad.** Plenty of food and handicrafts are on sale here. Also on the hill are a sculpture park and an amphitheater. You could go just for the views: From this high point there's a good view of Colombia's second city. The hill is also a popular place for an early morning jog. The Pueblito Paisa is lit with thousands of multicolored lights at Christmastime.

Northern Medellín

The **Casa Gardeliana** (Cra. 45 No. 76-50, tel. 4/213-5965, Barrio Manrique, 9am-5pm Mon.-Sat. 10am-4pm Sun., free) has wall-to-wall tango memorabilia and some cool souvenirs. Plus a seat from the ill-fated airplane that crashed in the city and killed tango icon Carlos Gardel. Unfortunately, the museum does not tell the story of tango in Medellín in a clear manner, but it is just steps from the Metroplús Manrique station. If you are visiting downtown or the Cementerio de San Pedro, from there you can easily hitch a ride on the Metroplús.

In the neighboring barrio of Aranjuez is the **Casa Museo Pedro Nel Gómez** (Cra. 51B No. 85-24, Barrio Aranjuez, tel. 4/233-2633, free). This delightful museum houses an extensive collection of the painter's works, including several murals for which he is best known. Much of his work portrays the plight of campesinos (rural peasants), workers, and indigenous people. His house, now the museum, was designed by Gómez, and the location of it was chosen by his Italian-born wife. The hills overlooking the city here reminded her of Florence, somehow. In the new wing of the museum there is a small public library. The courtyard holds a snack bar-café. The museum is not easy to get to, and you will probably have to take a cab there. Many visitors combine this visit with a trip to the nearby Casa Gardeliana.

BIBLIOTECA ESPAÑA

When this public library was opened in the low-income neighborhood of Santo Domingo, King Juan Carlos came from Madrid for the ceremony. Spain, after all, helped to fund the project. It's one of many newly created *biblioteca parques* (public library parks) in Medellín. More than a place for books, these library parks have become community centers and sources of pride in neighborhoods that continue to struggle with poverty and violence. The **Biblioteca España** (Cra. 33B No.107A-100, tel. 4/385-7531, www.red-debibliotecas.org, 8am-7pm Mon.-Sat. and 11am-5pm Sun.) is the most famous and most visited of the 24 public libraries in the city, and, like each of them, it is stunning. The library resembles giant boulders clinging to the edge of the mountainside. It was designed by

Downtown Medellín Walking Tour

PLAZA BOTERO TO THE PLAZA DE LOS PIES DESCALZOS

Medellín's brash downtown is a compact history tour comprising stoic remnants from the colonial era, brick and mortar evidence of Medellín's rising as Colombia's most important industrial center in the early 20th century, and the vibrant public spaces, modern transportation systems, and futuristic architecture showing this proud city's 21st-century optimism.

Begin the tour at the Parque Berrío Metro station and walk five minutes north to the Plaza Botero.

PLAZA BOTERO

Most visits downtown begin under the shadows of the **Palacio de la Cultura Rafael Uribe Uribe** (Cra. 51 No. 52-03, 8am-5pm Mon.-Fri., 8am-2pm Sat., free), an occasional host of art exhibits. The **Plaza Botero** (in front of the Museo de Antioquia, Cra. 52 No. 52-43) gets its name for its 23 corpulent bronze sculptures by Fernando Botero. Passersby often pose in front of the sculptures, such as *La Mano (The Hand)* and *Eva (Eve)* for a quick snapshot. One of the most prolific, and by far the best known, of contemporary Colombian artists, Botero donated these sculptures to his hometown of Medellín. His paintings and sculptures of rotund people often portray campesino (rural) life, but many of them are also commentaries on the violence in Colombia.

PEATONAL CARABOBO

To the south, the **Peatonal Carabobo** is a pedestrian walkway that extends for eight blocks. Lined with shoe shops, five-and-dime stores, and snack bars, it's busy, loud, and colorful. (Although there is usually a police presence, be sure to watch your stuff!)

On the right-hand side is Medellín's oldest church, the brilliantly white **Iglesia de la Vera Cruz** (Cl. 51 No. 52-38, tel. 4/512-5095), which dates back to 1682. It is often filled with working-class faithful, sitting or standing in meditation and prayer. It's a refuge of quiet in this busy commercial area. The only other living testament to Spanish rule in Medellín is the white-washed **Basílica Nuestra Señora de la Candelaria** on the Parque Berrío a few blocks away.

The Belgian architect who designed the grandiose **Palacio Nacional** (Cra. 52 No. 48-45, tel. 4/513-4422) in the 1920s probably never expected that it would, over time, become the domain of around 400 tennis shoes and jeans vendors. It was originally built to house governmental offices, and today, when you walk through the corridors of this historic building, all you'll hear is the chorus of *"a la orden"* ("at your service!") from hopeful shop attendants. Towards the end of Peatonal Carabobo is **Donde Ramón,** a small kiosk in the middle of the walkway, jam-packed with antique objects like brass horse stirrups or old *carrieles* (leather handbags) from Jericó.

PARQUE DE LAS LUCES

After years of abandonment and urban decay, in 2005 the artificial forest of the **Parque de**

architect and Barranquilla native Giancarlo Mazzanti, who won a prize for this work at the VI Bienal Iberoamericana de Arquitectura y Urbanismo in Lisbon in 2008.

Getting to Santo Domingo is an attraction in itself. The neighborhood is connected to the metropolis by the Metrocable cable car system. Take the Metro towards Niquía station and transfer to the Metrocable at Acevedo.

The Santo Domingo station is the third and final stop.

When the Metrocable K line was opened in 2004, it was the first of its kind in the world: a gondola-like public transport system with a socio-economic purpose, connected to a metro. The system, consisting of gondolas, has eliminated eternal climbs up and down the mountain for low-income residents.

MEDELLÍN

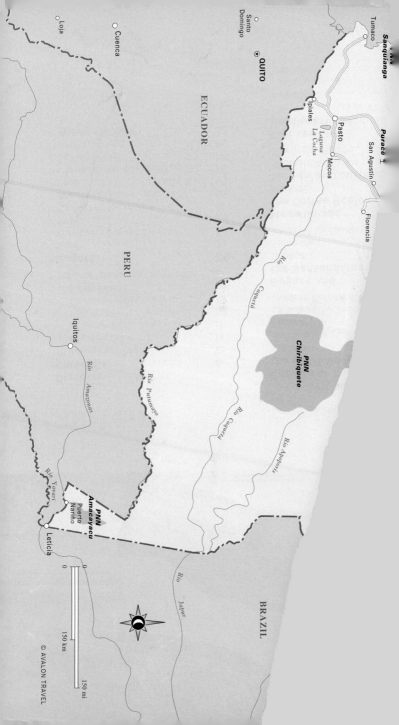

Contents

las Luces or **Plaza Cisneros** (Cl. 44 at Cra. 52) was opened in an effort to rejuvenate the area. The park, consisting of 300 illuminated posts, looks somewhat odd during the day but is spectacular at night when it shines. Check it out by car at night as it is not safe to roam about after dark. On the east side of the plaza are two historic early-20th-century brick buildings: the **Edificio Carré** and **Edificio Vásquez** (Cl. 44B No. 52-17, tel. 4/514-8200). When they were built they were the tallest buildings in Medellín. These buildings were once important warehouse facilities during the industrial boom of the early 20th century. The plaza used to be the home of the main marketplace. On the western side of the plaza is the **Biblioteca EPM** (Cra. 54 No. 44-48, tel. 4/380-7516, 8:30am-5:30pm Mon.-Sat.), a stunning public library sponsored by the electric company EPM (Empresas Públicas de Medellín), built in 2005. In addition to reading rooms, there are occasional exhibitions and cultural events held at the library.

Across from the Parque de las Luces on the southern side of Calle 44 is the **Estación Ferrocarril** (Cra. 52 No. 43-31, tel. 4/381-0733), the old main train station. There's not much to see here, except for a train engine and forgotten old tracks.

PLAZA MAYOR

To the west of the Estación Ferrocarril is the **Centro Administrativo La Alpujarra** (Cl. 44 No. 52-165), which houses the Departamento de Antioquia government offices. The sculpture *Homenaje a la Raza,* by Rodrigo Arenas Betancur, stands in the middle of the large intermediary plaza. Just beyond is the **Plaza de la Libertad** (Cra. 55 between Clls. 42-44), a complex of modern office space and interesting public space complete with urban gardens.

Cross the pedestrian bridge over the lanes of the Metroplús bus station. Metroplús is the latest addition to Medellín's transportation network. It debuted in 2013. Here is the **Plaza Mayor** (Cl. 41 No. 55-80, www.plazamayor.com.co), the city's preeminent convention and event venue; it has a fair share of nice restaurants. The **Teatro Metropolitano** (Cl. 41 No. 57-30, tel. 4/232-2858, www.teatrometropolitano.com), built from 20th-century brick, hosts concerts.

Finally, the **Plaza de los Pies Descalzos** (Cra. 58 No. 42-125) is a plaza filled with a *guadua* (Colombian bamboo) forest and fountains, where you can take off your shoes and play. It's surrounded by eateries on one side and the massive **Museo del Agua** (Cra. 57 No. 42-139, tel. 4/380-6954, 8am-6pm Tues.-Fri., 10am-7pm Sat.-Sun., COP$4,000) on the other. In the distance is a long-standing Medellín architectural icon: the **Edificio Inteligente** (Cra. 58 No. 42-125, tel. 4/380-4411). Built in the late 1950s, it has served as the headquarters of EPM, the utility company. To find out what's so smart about it, you can take a free tour of the building. They are offered Monday-Friday. Call in advance to reserve.

PARQUE ARVÍ

For some fresh, and oftentimes crisp, country air, a visit to the **Parque Arví** (Santa Elena, tel. 4/444-2979, www.parquearvi.org, 9am-5pm Tues.-Sun., free), covering 16,000 hectares (40,000 acres) of nature, hits the spot after a few days of urban exploring.

Highlights in the park include the seven well-marked nature paths, which meander through cloud forests thick with pine and eucalyptus trees, over brooks, along ancient indigenous paths, to mountain lakes and lookout points with spectacular views of the Valle de Aburra and Medellín below. Most paths, with a distance of under three kilometers (two miles), are not strenuous whatsoever. There is a longer path of over 10 kilometers (six miles) that is excellent for biking. Ask at the information booth

Getting Up the Hill

During the late 1990s to 2000s, thousands of families from rural areas in Antioquia, Córdoba, and Chocó were forced to leave their homes due to violence. Moving to Medellín to start a new life, many arrived in the low-income neighborhoods along the steep slopes of the mountains surrounding the city. But here, where many live in meager brick homes covered with corrugated zinc roofs secured only by large stones, horrific violence has followed them. First it was turf wars between guerrillas and paramilitaries in the early 2000s. Today the violence is caused by drug-trafficking gangs with links to former paramilitaries. This wave of violence has given birth to a new phenomenon: intra-urban displacement, during which families have been displaced within the city due to urban violence. For many, this is the second displacement that their families have had to endure.

City leaders have sought to improve the quality of life in the *comunas* in a variety of innovative ways. Two lines of the Metrocable gondola system have made a huge difference in allowing residents to travel to work or school in the city without having to walk up and down the mountainside. Spectacular modern public libraries have been built in many low-income communities, providing a safe and pleasant space to study, read, and connect to the Internet. These have developed into important cultural centers, with an active schedule of films, children's activities, and other cultural activities. New homes have been built and donated to 200-300 displaced families in the neighborhood, with funds from the national government under President Juan Manuel Santos.

In 2012, the city debuted its latest project, this time aimed at improving life in the Comuna 13, the most notorious of the *comunas* in the entire city. This time the project involved the creation of open-air escalators in this neighborhood. These are a series of six dual, interconnected escalators that extend down the slopes for some 384 meters (1,260 feet). The system operates from early in the morning until about 10 at night. They are monitored by city employees, and their use is free. It is the first time in the world escalators have been used in order to improve the lives of the less fortunate.

The escalators have made a difference in the lives of Comuna 13 residents, although there are some who believe that the money spent on the project (around US$6 million) could have been better used otherwise. There have been alarming reports as well that some gangs have been intimidating residents by charging them to use the escalators, under the threat of dire consequences.

Despite the high levels of violence affecting residents (never foreign tourists), the escalators have become a tourist attraction, and even appear in the city's tourism promotional materials. Celebrities and dignitaries from President Juan Manuel Santos to French fashion designer Francois Girbaud have taken a ride on the escalators.

It is indeed a strange kind of tourism, with which some may feel uncomfortable. However, if you would like to see this escalator project, you certainly can. Go during the day, and you must not wander the streets of the Comuna 13. Never remain in the neighborhood after dark. To get there, take the Metro Línea B to San Javier station. As you depart the station, in front are *colectivos* (small buses) that regularly transport passengers to the Comuna 13. It's about a 15-minute trip and costs under COP$1,500. Ask anyone which bus to take, and let the bus driver know that you'd like to go to the *escaleras eléctricas*.

From San Javier, there is also a Metrocable line (Línea J) that has three stops and travels to the top at La Aurora.

© ANDREW DIER

A trip to the Parque Arví in northern Medellín is an excellent break from the city.

upon arrival at the Arví Metrocable station for suggestions on walks to make. There are often free guided nature walks as well.

Other recreational activities are on offer in the different *nucleos* (nuclei) of the park. Understanding the nuclei and layout of the park can be confusing. Staff at the information booth at the entrance will provide you with a map and assist you in planning your visit. At the Nucleo Comfenalco, you can rent a paddle-boat on the Piedras Blancas reservoir, and there is a small hotel, as well as a butterfly pavilion. In the Nucleo Mazo there is a market.

To explore the park on bike, you can rent a bike for free with the city's Encicla program by showing an ID card. These can be rented at any of the several Encicla stations in the park, but you will be required to renew the rental at any station if you have been cycling for more than an hour. Encicla staff can provide you with a map and recommendations.

The park is a nice day trip to make, and you might consider the getting there the best part about the excursion. To get there from the city, take the Metro to the Acevedo station in the north of the city (Línea A towards Niquía). From there, transfer to the Metrocable (Línea K) to the Santo Domingo station. From there you must transfer to the Parque Arví line (Línea L, COP$4,200 one way), which has an additional cost.

The temperature can drop substantially and abruptly in the park. Pack along a light sweater and a lightweight rainproof jacket. Try to get an early start so that you can enjoy the park without rushing. There are various snack bars and restaurants throughout the park.

Southern Medellín

The Ciudad del Río area, between downtown and El Poblado near a Metro line, has developed into an up-and-coming neighborhood largely due to the arrival of the **Museo de Arte Moderno de Medellín** (MAMM, Cra. 44 No. 19A-100, tel. 4/444-2622, www.elmamm.org, 9am-5:30pm Tues.-Fri., 10am-5:30pm Sat., 10am-5pm Sun., COP$8,000). The coolest part about the MAMM is its location in an old warehouse, typical of the Barrio Colombia area. This was the home of Talleres Robledo, a steel mill that began operations in the 1930s. Exhibitions (usually two at a time) are hit or miss. The museum store, the *tienda,* is an excellent place to pick up a whimsical Medellín souvenir. Many items, like T-shirts, notepads, or cute doo-dads, are the product of local creative minds.

The **Parque El Salado** (Vereda El Vallano, Envigado, tel. 4/270-3132, www.parqueelsalado.gov.co, 9am-5pm Tues.-Sun., COP$3,000), a municipal park covering 17 hectares (42 acres) in Envigado, has trails and activities, such as a zipline, and is a good place to get some fresh air. On weekends it gets packed with families on a *paseo de olla.* Literally a soup-pot excursion, *paseo de olla* usually means *sancocho,* a hearty beef stew. Essential gear for a day out at the park includes giant aluminum pots for slowly heating a *sancocho* over a campfire. There is plenty of fresh air at this park, but from afar it may appear that there is a forest fire in the picnic area with all of the campfires. Getting to the park is easy using public transportation. From the Envigado Metro station look for a green bus with a sign that says Parque El Salado. It's about a 20-minute ride up towards the mountains.

ENTERTAINMENT AND EVENTS
Nightlife

Since 1969, **El Social Tienda Mixta** (Cra. 35 No. 8A-8, tel. 4/311-5567) has been selling the basics to local residents (soap, sugar, coffee); it's only been a recent phenomenon that it's now the hippest place to be seen at night, when it is converted into the most popular bar in Provenza! It's so popular on weekend evenings, you can forget about finding a vacant plastic chair.

Want to check out the nightlife with other party people? That's the idea behind the **Pub Crawl Medellín** (cell tel. 300/764-6145, pubcrawlmed@gmail.com, Sat. evenings, COP$30,000). In this night of shenanigans, revelers (groups of about 12) get together,

then hit several bars (enjoying courtesy shots along the way), and then wind up the night dancing to the beats at a popular dance club. Each Saturday the group explores different nightspots.

Every Thursday evening, the Medellín microbrewery **3 Cordilleras** (Cl. 30 No. 44-176, tel. 4/444-2337, www.3cordilleras.com, 5:30pm-9pm Thurs., COP$20,000) offers a tour of their brewery, during which you learn about the beer-making process. At the end of the tour, the grand finale is tasting several of their artisan beers and friendly socializing. On the final Thursday of each month, after the tour there is live music and beer.

Calle Nueve (Cl. 9 No. 43B-75, tel. 4/266-4852, 6pm-2am Mon.-Sat., no cover), in a nondescript white house, is a hipster's paradise in El Poblado. Music varies wildly from salsa to house to folk. The dim lighting and well-worn couches provide the perfect chilled-out atmosphere.

SALSA, TANGO, AND JAZZ

Medellín is no Cali, but salsa has its aficionados here. If the musical genres *son, la charanga, el guaguanco,* and *la timba* don't mean anything to you now, they might after a night at **Son Havana** (Cra. 73 No. 44-56, tel. 4/412-9644, www.sonhavana.com, 8pm-3am Wed.-Sat., cover Sat. COP$8,000) often has live performances. Nearby is **El Tíbiri** (Cra. 70 at Cl. 44B, hours vary Wed.-Sat.), an underground salsa joint on Carrera 70, which is hugely popular on the weekends. They say the walls sweat here, as after 10pm it gets packed with revelers, many of whom are university students. Friday nights are big at El Tíbiri.

The downtown **Salón Málaga** (Cra. 51 No. 45-80, tel. 4/231-2658, www.salonmalaga.com, 9am-11pm daily, no cover)—boy, has it got character. It's filled with old jukeboxes and memorabilia, and has its clientele who come in for a *tinto* (coffee) or beer during the day. The Saturday tango show at 5:30pm and oldies event on Sunday afternoons are especially popular with locals and travelers alike, but a stop here is a fine idea anytime.

Near the Parque de la Periodista, a major weekend hangout for the grungy set, there are some small bars big on personality. Tuesday nights are bordering on legendary at **Eslabón Prendido** (Cl. 53 No. 42-55, tel. 4/239-3400, 3pm-11pm Tues.-Sat., cover varies), a hole-in-the-wall salsa place that really packs them in! **El Acontista** (Cl. 53 No. 43-81, tel. 4/512-3052, noon-10pm Mon.-Thurs., noon-midnight Fri.-Sat.) is an excellent jazz club downtown. It's got a bookstore on the second floor and live music on Monday and Saturday evenings. They've got great food, too, making it an excellent stop after a day visiting the Centro.

An authentic tango spot in Envigado is **Bar Atlenal** (Cl. 38 Sur No. 37-3, tel. 4/276-5971, 3pm-2am daily). Friday night is the best time to go to see a tango performance, but to listen to some tango music from the juke box and have a beer, go any day of the week. It's an institution, with more than six decades of history. Allegiance to the soccer club Atlético Nacional is evident on the walls of the bar. Included is an homage to star player Andrés Escobar. Also in Envigado is **La Venta de Dulcinea Café Cultural** (Cl. 35 Sur No. 43-36, tel. 4/276-0208, www.laventadedulcinea.jimdo.com, 2pm-11pm Mon.-Sat.), where salsa, *milonga*, and tango nights are often held. Check the webpage for a schedule.

DANCE CLUBS

Famous **Mango's** (Cra. 42 No. 67A-151, tel. 4/277-6123, 5pm-6am daily, no cover), decked out like a Wild West saloon, is a festive club popular with foreigners and locals alike, and gets going late. **Jesús Dulce Mío-Mil Juguetes** (Cra. 38 No. 19-255, Km. 2 Vía Las Palmas, tel. 4/266-6020, www.fondadulcejesusmio.com, 7pm-3am Tues.-Sat., COP$10,000 cover) is a popular club near El Poblado. Wednesday is karaoke night.

If you go to **Fahrenheit** (Cra. 42 No. 79-125, Itagüi, tel. 4/354-6203 www.discotecafahrenheit.com, 10pm-6am Thurs.-Sat., cover varies) you should dress to impress. It's a late-night place in the neighboring town of Itagüi. Thursdays are electronica nights,

while Saturdays are for crossover, a mix of popular music with Latin tunes. Guys should expect to pay around COP$25,000 for cover, ladies *nada*.

GAY BARS AND CLUBS

There is a lively gay and youthful nightlife scene in Medellín. **Donde Aquellos** (Cra. 38 No. 9A-26, tel. 4/312-2041, cell tel. 313/624-1485, 4:30pm-2am daily) is an easy-going kind of place near the Parque Lleras in El Poblado. This friendly bar is a good place for a terrace drink. **Culture Club** (Cra. 43F No. 18-158, hours vary Thurs.-Sat., cover varies) is the hottest dance club and gets hopping at around midnight on weekends. It's a fashionable place, with chandeliers and red velvet.

Cinema and Theaters

Otraparte (Cra. 43A No. 27A Sur-11, tel. 4/448-2404, www.otraparte.org, 8am-8pm Mon.-Fri., 9am-5pm Sat.-Sun.) is a cultural center that offers a dynamic program of free concerts, films, book launches, and even free yoga classes in Envigado.

Festivals and Events

Festicamara (www.festicamara.com), an international chamber music festival, is held in March or April each year, with concerts across the city at venues like the fabulous **Orquiderama** in the Jardín Botánico.

The **Festival Internacional de Tango** (www.festivaldetangomedellin.com) takes place each year during the last week of June, commemorating the anniversary of the death of Carlos Gardel. This festival, and in fact the perseverance of tango culture in Medellín, is largely due to one man's passion and efforts. Argentine Leonardo Nieto visited Medellín in the 1960s, primarily to get to know this city where tango icon Carlos Gardel died in an airplane crash. He fell in love with the city, stayed, and created the Casa Gardelina and the Festival Internacional de Tango. During this festival, tango concerts and events take place across the city, in nightclubs, theaters, parks, and on street blocks.

MEDELLÍN

International Day of Laziness

Paisas are known throughout Colombia to be some of the most hard-working and driven people in the country. The Medellín Metro, routine 7am business meetings, the orderly pueblos in the Antioquian countryside, and even former president Álvaro Uribe, a native Paisa, are examples of this industriousness. Uribe's famous words upon taking office in 2002 were *"trabajar, trabajar, trabajar"* ("work, work, work"). Laziness is quiet simply anathema to Paisas.

But you can't be productive *all* the time. The people of **Itagüí,** an industrial town bordering Medellín, have taken that to heart. In fact, on one day each year they not only take it easy, they embrace and celebrate the virtues of slothfulness during their **Día Internacional de la Pereza** (International Day of Laziness) celebrations. On that day in August, residents rise at the leisurely hour of 10am, put out their hammocks and beds in front of their houses, and laze the day away, sometimes still in their pajamas. The day's events include a bed (on wheels) race and general goofing off. Ironically, most of the action (or inaction) of that day takes place in the Itagüí Parque del Obrero (Worker's Park).

Since 1991, Medellín has hosted an impressive **Festival Internacional de Poesía de Medellín** (www.festivaldepoesiademedellin.org), which routinely attracts poets from dozens of countries, who share their work in more than 100 venues across the city. It's held in early July.

As the leading textile manufacturing center in Colombia, Medellín is the obvious choice for the most important fashion event in the country: **Colombiamoda** (http://colombiamoda.inexmoda.org.co). It attracts designers and fashionistas from across the globe, and during this week, the Plaza Mayor becomes a fabulous model-fest.

The **Feria de las Flores** (www.feriadelasfloresmedellin.gov.co) is the most important festival of the year in Medellín, and is when the city is at its most colorful. It's a week-long celebration of Paisa culture, with horseback parades, concerts, and the highlight, the Desfile de los Silleteros. That is when flower farmers from Santa Elena show off incredibly elaborate flower arrangements in a parade through the city streets. The festival takes place in July or August each year, and it's a great time to visit the city.

At Christmastime, Medellín sparkles with light, every night. It all begins at midnight on December 1, during the **Alborada.** That's when the sights and sounds of fireworks and firecrackers envelop the entire Valle de Aburrá. On December 7, the **Alumbrado Navideño,** the city's Christmas light display, begins. The Cerro de Nutibara and the Río Medellín, along with other city sites, are illuminated with 14.5 million multi-colored lights. Sponsored by the electric company, it's an incredible sight to behold.

SPORTS AND RECREATION
Biking
The Medellín **Ciclovía** (8am-1pm Sun.) has many routes, including along the Avenida El Poblado and along the Río Medellín. On Tuesday and Thursday evenings there is a **Ciclovía Nocturna** (8pm-10pm) on two routes: along the river and around the stadium area. Not to be outdone by their neighbor, the cities of Envigado and Itagüí also have a Ciclovía on Sundays.

Encicla (office in Éxito Colombia store, Cl. 48D No. 66-61, tel. 4/436-6271, cell tel. 310/390-9314, 8am-6pm daily, www.encicla.gov.co) is Medellín's bike share program. It's free to use for those over the age of 18. Nice routes are along the Carrera 70 and around the universities. Visitors must register in person at the Encicla office, and must show their passport. Encicla bike paths follow Carreras

65 and 70, connecting with the Estadio and Universidad Metro stations. In **Parque Arví** (Santa Elena, www.parquearvi.org) there are six **Encicla en el Parque stations.** At this park, the registration procedure is less involved.

Bike Rent (Cra. 35 No. 7-14, cell tel. 310/448-3731, www.bikerent.com.co, 9am-7pm Mon., Wed., and Fri.-Sat., 9am-10pm Tues. and Thurs., 8am-1pm Sun., COP$25,000 half day, COP$35,000 full day) rents good bikes cheaply, and the prices decrease as the number of hours you rent them increases. They also have information on routes and suggestions at this convenient Provenza location.

Ciclo Barranquero (tel. 4/538-0699, cell tel. 314/806-5892, ciclobarranquero@gmail.com, COP$70,000-90,000 pp) organizes interesting day-trip bike rides for all levels of cyclists in the city and beyond, such as in the nearby pueblo of Santa Elena and in Guatape. Bikes and necessary equipment are included in the price, but transportation to the meeting point is not. **Ecoturismo Arewaro** (Cra. 72A No. 30A-21, tel. 4/444-2573, cell tel. 300/652-4327, www.ecoturismoarewaro.com, COP$46,000 pp) organizes day-trip walks and bike trips in parks and pueblos near Medellín. *Arewaro* means "gathering of friends" in the Wayúu language.

Yoga and Gyms

Atman Yoga (Tr. 37 No. 72-84, tel. 4/311-1132, www.atman-yoga.org, donations requested) holds free yoga classes every day at its main location in Laureles. They are quite popular, especially in the evenings. There are also classes at the Jardín Botánico on Tuesdays and Thursdays at 5:30pm and at other times during the week. In El Poblado there are several yoga studios, such as **108 Yoga** (Cl. 5 Sur No. 30-72, tel. 4/266-7232) and **Sati Yoga Y Meditación** (Cl. 10 No. 36-14, 2nd floor, tel. 4/352-4143, cell tel. 315/499-6625).

The gym **El Molino** (Cra. 79 No. 37-55, tel. 4/411-2714, 5am-10pm Mon.-Thurs., 5am-8pm Fri., 8am-3pm Sat., 9am-2pm Sun., COP$35,000 weekly pass) in Laureles has a large weight room, cardio machines, and a pool and sauna, and holds various classes.

You may not think of schlepping all the way to Envigado to get in a workout, but at multi-level **Dinamo Fitness** (Tr. 29S No. 32B-126, tel. 4/334-1512, www.dinamofitness.com, 5am-10pm Mon.-Thurs., 5am-2pm Sat., 8am-2pm Sun.) the price is right. A two-day pass costs COP$22,000, a ticket for six entries is COP$60,000, and a ticket for 12 entries is COP$120,000.

Many parks in Medellín have **outdoor gyms** where you can get in a free workout. These are especially popular with young men who work out on the *barras* (pull-up bars). One such gym is in the Provenza barrio (Cra. 37 at Cl. 8); another is in the Ciudad del Río behind the Museo de Arte Moderno de Medellín (Cl. 20 at Cra. 45).

Paragliding

For incredible views of both the verdant Antioquian countryside and the metropolis in the distance, check out a paragliding adventure organized by the **Aeroclub San Felix** (Km. 6 Vía San Pedro de los Milagros, tel. 4/388-1077, www.parapenteencolombia.com, 20-min. flight COP$80,000, complete course COP$1,600,000). Bus transportation to the town of San Felix is available from the Portal del Norte bus station, and the Aeroclub San Felix can also arrange transportation from El Poblado for an additional cost.

Centro Deportivo Atanasio Girardot

At the **Centro Deportivo Atanasio Girardot** (Cras. 70-74 and Clls. 48-50, tel. 4/369-9000, pool tel. 4/430-1330, ext. 146), in addition to soccer matches and the occasional big-name concert, there are running tracks, basketball courts, and swimming pools free of charge and open to the public, including visitors. To use the pools all you need is to present an ID and bring a bathing cap. They sell them on-site for under COP$20,000. The Olympic-sized pool is only open to those with a membership in the swimming league, but there are four others available to the public. The nice blue track is often packed with Paisas getting in their

© ANDREW DIER

the Estadio Atanasio Girardot complex

morning sweat. It's open to the public during the morning hours, and usually on Tuesdays and Thursday evenings it is also open 8pm-10pm. There are also jazzercise, yoga, rumba, and aerobics classes given several times a day starting at 6am. Just show up and join the fun. Call (tel. 4/369-9000, ext. 118) for class schedule information. The complex is accessible from the Estadio Metro station.

Soccer

Medellín has two professional teams, and Envigado has one. By far the most famous team, with followers across the country, is **Atlítico Nacional** (www.atlnacional.com.co). Nacional, wearing the green and white of the Antioquian flag, has been playing since 1947. It's one of the most successful teams in Colombia and has won the top division 11 times. Nacional defeated Santa Fe from Bogotá for the 2013 Liga Postobón championship, which was a very big deal. Nacional is wildly popular with young men and boys in Medellín, Antioquia, and beyond. The cheap

seats at Nacional games are always packed with kids from the barrios. The other team in town is **Deportivo Independiente Medellín** (www.dalerojo.net). This is the oldest club in Colombia and was originally called Medellín Foot Ball Club when it was established in 1913. Their colors are red and blue. Both teams play at the **Estadio Atanasio Girardot** (Cl. 48 No. 73-10, www.inder.gov.co). Tickets can be purchased at **Ticket Factory Express** (tel. 4/444-4446, www.ticketexpress.com.co).

Tours

Turibus (www.turibuscolombia.com, 9am-7:40pm daily, COP$28,000 24-hour pass) operates a hop-on, hop-off service that has seven stops in the city, including the Plaza Botero and the Cerro Nutibara/Pueblito Paisa. They also offer tours to other parts of the Antioquia department, such as to Jericó and Guatape.

While some may find it unseemly to go on a tour of Pablo Escobar's Medellín, others find it fascinating. During the three-hour **Pablo Escobar Tour** (cell tel. 317/489-2629, www.

paisaroad.com, 10am daily, COP$35,000) offered by Paisa Road, you'll see where the world's most notorious drug baron grew up, learn about the violent world of the cartels, and visit his tomb. The meeting point for the tours (offered in English) is at the Black Sheep and Casa Kiwi hostels in the Provenza area of El Poblado. If you'd like to visit Escobar's grave independently, you can take the Metro to the Sabaneta station. The **Parque Jardines Montesacro** (Cra. 42 No. 25-51, Autopista Sur Itagüi, tel. 4/374-1111, 9am-5pm daily, free) is within walking distance from there.

SHOPPING

The Provenza neighborhood and the area around Parque Lleras are home to several boutique clothing and accessories shops. **Santa Fe** (Cl. 43 No. 7 Sur-107, www.centrocomercialsantafe.com) is the largest and flashiest of Medellín's malls. It's on the Avenida El Poblado.

ACCOMMODATIONS

Accommodation options to fit every budget and taste are plentiful in Medellín. El Poblado has the most options, with luxury hotels along the Avenida El Poblado and hostels and boutiques in the walkable Provenza area, close to a smorgasbord of restaurants and bars and closeish to the El Poblado Metro station. Laureles is a quiet and green residential area with a growing number of fine options for those wanting an escape from the madding crowd. There aren't many reasons anyone would want to stay in the Centro, an area of town that feels unsafe at night. As is the case in cities in the interior of the country, on weekends Medellín empties somewhat, hotel prices fall, and vacancies increase.

Under COP$70,000

Dozens of hostels cater to more than the traditional twenty-something backpacker. Today these economical options offer comfortable private rooms for those who are looking for a friendly environment and keeping an eye on their expenses.

The **Casa Kiwi** (Cra. 36 No. 7-10, tel. 4/268-2668, www.casakiwihostel.com, COP$20,000 dorm, COP$60,000 d) is a backpacker's institution in El Poblado. A cold and *über*-cool atmosphere pervades the place at times, though, and it does have the reputation of being a party pad (loud). It's got a capacity of 60, with an array of private rooms and dorm options, plus a nice sundeck above. Nonguests can visit on Friday evenings, when there's live music on the deck.

With just one dorm room and two private rooms (with a shared bath), **La Miscelanea Hostel** (Cra. 35 No. 7-86, tel. 4/311-8635, www.lamiscelanea.co, COP$20,000 pp) is a low-key and relaxed option run by a friendly Paisa couple. This hostel in Provenza started as a restaurant/bar, and they still have occasional live music performances in their bar area. There's lots of vegetarian fare on offer, and it's open to the public. The *tienda* (store) has funky things made by Medellín's creative folk.

⬤ **Urban Buddha** (Circular 73A No. 38-55, tel. 4/413-9322, www.buddhahostel.com, COP$20,000 dorm, COP$60,000 d) is a friendly place to stay in the leafy neighborhood of Laureles. The garden out back is a peaceful urban refuge and nice place to study one's Spanish or chat with other world travelers. The Spanish owners of this hostel also run the **Secret Buddha Hostel** (Cl. 94 B Sur No. 51-121, La Estrella, tel. 4/279-5152, cell tel. 312/892-6521, www.buddhahostel.com, COP$25,000 dorm, COP$65,000 d) in the Estrella municipality, outside of Medellín. It's green and quiet out there, but you can still head into town easily on the Metro.

COP$70,000-200,000

In contrast to many Colombian cities, Medellín has a fair variety of midrange hotels. Chain hotels tend to be best, holding few surprises.

The ⬤ **Casa Hotel Asturias Medellín** (Circular 4 No. 73-124, tel. 4/260-2872, COP$89,000 d) is on a delightful corner of the tree-lined and quiet Laureles neighborhood. That's the big selling point for this small hotel.

Rooms are modern and comfortable, although not terribly huge. It's a good deal.

Well located in the Provenza neighborhood, **Acqua Hotel Express** (Cra. 35 No. 7-47, tel. 4/448-0482, cell tel. 320/788-4424, www.hotelacqua.com, COP$131,000 d) is a good value. Its 43 rooms are spic and span and comfortable.

French budget chain ◖ **Hotel Ibis** (Cl. 20 No. 44-16, tel.4/444-1554, www.ibis.com, COP$99,000 d) has modern rooms with comfortable beds at great rates, and is located in an interesting area in the Ciudad del Río, across the street from the Museo de Arte Moderno de Medellín. There's no gym, but the neighborhood is quiet, making it a decent place for a morning jog. The best views are on the hotel's south side. The hotel restaurant offers buffet meals for an additional price. On the weekends it's very quiet, and room rates drop to an unbelievable COP$79,000.

Located across from the Atanasio Girardot sports complex, the **Hotel Tryp Medellín** (Cl. 50 No. 70-24, tel. 4/604-0686, www.tryphotels.com, COP$146,000 d) has 140 large, comfortable (if spartan) rooms and an excellent rooftop terrace with a whirlpool and steam room. Guests have access to an extremely loud gym on the lobby floor. Restaurants are nonexistent in this area, except for street food, and hotel room service is iffy.

The **Hotel BH El Poblado** (Cra. 43 No. 9 Sur 35, tel. 4/604-3534, www.bhhoteles.com, COP$170,000 d) is across from the enormous Centro Comercial Santa Fe. This Colombian chain hotel with 70 rooms has huge, comfortable beds and modern rooms, and despite its location on a major street (Av. El Poblado), it's not that noisy. An included breakfast buffet is served in a pleasant open-air terrace. It's also got the world's tiniest hotel gym with about three cardio machines.

It's got a boring and frankly ugly location, but the standard-to-the-core **GHL Comfort Hotel San Diego** (Cl. 31, No. 43-90, www.ghlhoteles.com, COP$124,000 d) offers good prices and the staff is attentive. A mediocre breakfast is served on the top-floor terrace (featuring an excellent view), and amenities

include a sauna and small gym. It's close to a couple of malls and is between the Centro and El Poblado on a main road. The Ciclovía passes by in front on Sundays, making it a snap to get out and move.

Hard-core city people will be the ones interested in staying in the Centro. The **Hotel Nutibara Conference Center** (Cl. 52A No. 50-46, tel. 4/511-5111, www.hotelnutibara.com, COP$132,000 d) is the best choice. It's a faded, grand old hotel located steps from the Museo de Antioquia. With wide corridors and huge rooms with parquet floors, it retains mid-20th-century elegance and personality.

FOOD

The revitalization and resurgence of Medellín that began in the early 2000s has also led to culinary revolution, with countless new dining options popping up throughout the city. The best neighborhoods for dining are Provenza and El Poblado and the Zona M in Envigado.

Colombian

Mondongo's (Cra. 70 No. C3-43, tel. 4/411-3434, www.mondongos.com.co, 11:30am-9:30pm daily, COP$20,000) is a well-known and popular place for typical Colombian food and for drinks with friends. *Mondongo* is a tripe stew, a Colombian comfort food, In addition to the Carrera 70 location there is another Mondongo's on the busy Calle 10 in El Poblado (Cl. 10 No. 38-38, tel. 4/312-2346) that is a popular drinking hole as well. They've even got a location in Miami.

Another popular place on the Carrera 70 strip is **La Tienda** (Cra. 70 Circular 3-28, tel. 4/260-6783, 10am-2am daily). It's a festive restaurant that morphs into a late-night drinking place as Medellín evenings wear on. Their *bandeja paisa* is famous. It's a signature Antioquian dish that includes beans, rice, sausages, and pork rinds.

Along the Avenida Las Palmas above El Poblado are several large and famous grilled meat and *comida típica* restaurants. They are especially popular on weekend afternoons. **Hato Viejo** (Cl. 16 No. 28-60, Av. Las Plamas, tel.

4/268-5412 or 4/268-6811, noon-11pm daily, COP$25,000) is a popular place for a weekend lunch with the gang. On Friday nights they have live music. **San Carbón** (Cl. 15A No. 30-80, tel. 4/311-7602, www.sancarbon.com.co, noon-10pm weekdays, noon-2am on weekends, COP$29,000) often has live music Wednesday-Sunday. Specialties include barbecue pork ribs and pepper steak.

The Provenza area has a number of cute and original Colombian specialty restaurants. **Cazuelas de Mi Tierra** (Cra. 37 No. 8A-116, tel. 4/448-6810, www.cazuelasdemitierra.com, 8am-5pm Mon.-Wed., 8am-7pm Thurs.-Sat., 10am-4pm Sun., COP$20,000) has a special each day and always plenty of hangover-combating creamy *cazuelas* (stews).

Mi Buñuelo (Cl. 8 No. 35-33, tel. 4/311-5370, 6:30am-8pm Mon.-Sat., 6:30am-3pm Sun.), meanwhile, is a tribute to those unassuming, perfectly round, fried balls of dough, *buñuelos*. **Arepitas Pa' Papa** (Cra. 34 No. 7-73, tel. 4/352-2455, 11am-2:30pm and 6pm-10pm Mon.-Sat., COP$15,000) lets you create an arepa (cornmeal cake) with your favorite toppings.

 Queareparaenamorarte (tel. 4/542-0011, cell tel. 316/741-4458, 12:30pm-8:30pm Mon.-Wed., 12:30pm-10:30pm Thurs.-Sat., 12:30pm-7pm Sun., COP$25,000) is not your typical *comida típica* restaurant. Julian, owner, chef, and expert on Colombian cuisine, has traveled the country over and has brought the secrets back from grandmothers' kitchens from the Amazon to Santa Marta.

Fusion

 In Situ (Jardín Botánico, tel. 4/460-7007, www.botanicomedellin.org, noon-3pm Mon., noon-3pm and 7pm-10pm Tues.-Sat., noon-4pm Sun., COP$30,000) may have the nicest view of any eatery in Medellín. It's surrounded by a million shades of green on the grounds of the Jardín Botánico. It's an elegant place for a lunch, but if you've been sweating it visiting the city, you may feel out of place among the sharply dressed business and society crowds. In Situ has an interesting menu with items

such as apple sea bass (COP$30,000) and beef medallions in a coffee sauce with a plantain puree (COP$29,000).

Next to the Museo de Arte Moderno de Medellín is hip **Bonuar** (Cra. 44 No. 19A-100, tel. 4/235 3577, www.bonuar.com, 10am-7pm Tues.-Fri., 11am-6pm Sat., noon-4pm Sun. holidays, COP$22,000), where the burgers (including a Portobello and lentil version) are famous, but so is the brunch. It's a cool place with a nice outdoor seating area. During weekdays go in the evening when it's livelier.

A classic, old-school restaurant is **La Provincia** (Cl. 4 Sur No. 43A-179, tel. 4/311-9630, www.restaurantelaprovincia.com, noon-3pm and 7pm-midnight Mon.-Sat., COP$28,000). It is a fusion of Mediterranean cuisine (lots of seafood) with Colombian flair. Reserve a table on the romantic patio out back if you can. Try the exotic grilled fish fillet in a peanut sauce with green papaya strips.

El Herbario (Cra. 43D No. 10-30, tel. 4/311-2537, www.elherbario.com, noon-3pm and 7pm-11pm daily, COP$24,000) has an inventive menu with items such as lemongrass tuna, turmeric prawns, and artichoke risotto. Spacious and minimalistic, it can feel a little like eating in a warehouse, though. The attached store sells exotic jams and chutneys and the like.

American

Chef Ricardo Ramírez studied culinary arts in New Orleans, came back to Colombia, and immediately went to work designing the menu for the Cajun restaurant **Stella** (Cra. 44A No. 30 Sur-7, tel. 4/448-4640, 11am-11pm Tues.-Sat., 11am-3pm Sun., COP$22,000). He's got things right—there are po'boys, muffaletta sandwiches, catfish, jambalaya, and even alligator sausage. (They get the alligators from a farm near Montería.) The non-reptile crowd can try the vegetarian étouffée. Sunday brunches are often accompanied by live jazz music.

The most innovative restaurant to come Medellín's way in a long time is **Aloha Bar & BBQ** (Cra. 37A No. 8A-70, tel. 4/444-1148, 11am-11pm Mon.-Thurs., 11am-4am Fri.-Sat.,

10am-9pm Sun., COP$25,000). Run by a Hawaiian couple, this is the place for pork sliders, teriyaki ribs, and cole slaw. It's open way late on the weekends, great for a late night nosh after hitting the Parque Lleras bars.

Spanish

Cozy and chic Spanish restaurant **El Barral** (Cl. 30 Sur No. 43A-38, tel. 4/276-1212, noon-10pm Mon.-Sat., COP$30,000) specializes in paella, tapas, and sangria, and does them well.

Steak

With Colombian newspapers plastered on the walls displaying headlines of yesteryear, the Argentinian steakhouse **Lucio Carbón y Vino** (Cra. 44A No. 30 Sur-40, Envigado, tel. 4/334-4003, noon-midnight Mon.-Sat., COP$32,000) specializes in grilled steak, paired with a nice Malbec.

British

Cockers Greasy Spoon (Cl. 7 No. 35-56, Provenza, cell tel. 301/520-2668, 9am-2:30pm Tues.-Sat.) knows how to fry up an authentic British breakfast, like baked beans and bacon on toast. They make their own sausage, as well as most everything else on the menu, but the blokes who run the place admit that they don't lay the eggs. For lunch, try the fish and chips. It's a house specialty.

Thai

Authentic Asian restaurants are few and far between. **Royal Thai** (Cra. 8A No. 37A-05, tel. 4/354-2843, www.royalthaicolombia.com, COP$27,000) gets mixed reviews, and it's expensive, but hey, it's Thai.

Indian

Naan (Cra. 35 No. 7-75, tel. 4/312-6285, COP$22,000) is a small and trendy Indian place in the Provenza area.

Middle Eastern

There are a few good Lebanese and Arab food options in El Poblado and in Laureles. At **Tabun** (Cra. 33 No. 7-99, tel. 4/311-8209, www.eltabun.com, noon-10pm Mon.-Thurs., noon-11pm Fri.-Sat., noon-9pm Sun., COP$22,000), in addition to usual Arab fare, they also have a few Indian dishes. Plus belly dancers on weekends!

Fenicia (Cra. 73 No. C2-41, Av. Jardín, tel. 4/413-8566, www.feniciacomidaarabe.com, noon-8pm Mon. Thurs., noon-9pm Fri.-Sat., noon-4pm Sun., COP$15,000) is an authentic Lebanese restaurant run by a family who immigrated to Colombia years ago.

Italian

At **Crispino** (Circular 1A No. 74-04, Laureles, tel. 4/413-3266, noon-11pm Mon.-Thurs., noon-midnight Fri.-Sat., noon-5pm Sun., COP$20,000), owner Salvatore, direct from Naples, offers authentic Italian cuisine.

Whereas most restaurants in El Poblado face rather busy and noisy streets, **Toscano** (Cl. 8A No. 34-20, tel. 4/311-3094, cell tel. 314/739-6316, 10:30am-11pm Tues.-Sun., COP$13,000 lunch set menu, COP$20,000) is on a quiet street largely isolated from the neighboring riffraff. It's a delight to sit outside and have a pasta dish with a glass of wine.

Vegetarian

Most restaurants except the hard-core Colombian *parilla*-type places now offer at least one lonely vegetarian dish on their menu. No need to pity the herbivore any longer. In Provenza, make a beeline for the cool atmosphere and fantastic vegetarian food at two-story **C Verdeo** (Cra. 35 No. 8A-3, tel. 4/444-0934, www.ricoverdeo.com, noon-10pm Mon.-Wed., noon-11pm Thurs.-Sat., noon-4pm Sun., COP$18,000). This vegetarian haven discreetly set at the end of a street in the Provenza neighborhood could be the best vegetarian restaurant in Colombia. Veggie burgers go down well with an artisanal beer, but there are also Asian and Italian inspired à la carte options. Lunch menus are inventive, and are a bargain. Downstairs is more atmospheric, but if you dine upstairs, you can look out over an urban *guadua* (bamboo) forest. An organic market, **Ceres** (Cra. 35 No. 8A-3, www.ceresmercadoorganico.com) is on the second floor of Verdeo.

Lenteja Express (Cra. 35 No. 8A-76, tel. 4/311-0186, cell tel. 310/879-9136, 11am-9pm Mon.-Sat.) specializes in veggie burgers: chickpea burgers, lentil burgers, Mexican burgers.

In the Laureles area, **Pan y Vida Café** (Cra. 51D No. 67-30 Policlinica, tel. 4/583-8386, 7am-7pm Mon.-Wed., 7am-10pm Thurs.-Fri., 7am-4pm Sat., COP$12,000) serves healthy meals, often featuring the Andean super grain quinoa and organic vegetables. At lunchtime they offer a choice of two set meals. Outdoor seating is a fine idea on a pretty day. Pan y Vida is open in the mornings for coffee, juices, and pastries.

Cafés and Quick Bites

Fellini (Plaza Mayor, Cl. 41 No. 55-80, Local 105, tel. 4/444-5064, www.fellini.com.co, noon-8pm Mon.-Fri., noon-4pm Sat., COP$15,000) specializes in burgers, but they also serve sandwiches, salads, and pastas. Plan to eat here after your long day of sightseeing downtown.

The **Juan Valdez Café** (Cra. 37A No. 8A-74, 10am-9pm daily), atop the Parque Lleras, is a point of reference for the area and the place to meet up with someone for a cappuccino. It's popular with travelers and locals alike.

If you're feeling decadent, as in you'd like your latte in an actual coffee cup and served to you at a table, try **Pergamino Café** (Cra. 37 No. 8A-37, tel. 4/268-6444, 10am-9pm Mon.-Fri., 11am-9pm Sat). It's on a quietish street in the Provenza area.

Manzzino (Circular 72 No. 38-44, tel. 4/580-7000, 10am-9pm Mon.-Sat., 10am-6pm Sun.) will quickly become your fave Uruguayan neighborhood bakery café in all of Medellín, hands down. They've got apple pies, scrumptious almond cakes, quiches, and sandwiches, and you can enjoy them on a delightful terrace as you watch neighborhood folks go about their business in *tranquilo* (peaceful) and delightful Laureles.

Four in the morning and you've got the munchies? Join the legion of taxi drivers, college kids, and miscellaneous night owls at **Trigo Laurel** (Circula 1A No. 70-06, tel. 4/250-4943, 24 hours daily). It never closes, not on New Year's not on the 20 de Julio, when Colombians celebrate their independence. They specialize in baked goods, but they also serve cheap lunches. It's on a quiet corner of Carrera 70.

Fresh juices are the specialty at **Cosechas Express** (Cl. 10 No. 35-25, tel. 4/266-9139, 8am-6:30pm Mon.-Fri., 9am-4pm Sat.). There's an infinite number of possibilities here, as you can mix and match.

INFORMATION AND SERVICES
Spanish-Language Courses

Universidad EAFIT Centro de Idiomas (Cra. 49 No. 7S-50, Edificio 31, Oficina 201, tel. 4/261-9500, ext. 9439 or ext. 9669, COP$880,000 38-hr. course) offers intensive (20 hours per week) and semi-intensive (10 hours per week) Spanish classes. Their courses are certified by the Spanish Cervantes Institute. The **Universidad de Antioquia** (Cra. 52 No. 50-13, Edificio Suramericana, tel. 4/219-8332, ext. 9003, www.idiomasudea.net) offers personal language instruction at a price of COP$40,000 per hour. Group classes can also be arranged.

A language exchange called "The Lab" takes place every Wednesday at **Buena Vista Bar** (Cra. 37 No. 8A-83, cell tel. 313/788-7440, 7pm-1:30am Wed.). At this friendly gathering of Colombians, travelers, and expats, you can mingle with others and brush up on (or show off) your Spanish, Portuguese, French, Italian, German, or English skills. Afterwards, enjoy an international fiesta featuring salsa music on the bottom floor and international beats on the upstairs terrace of this cool space in the Parque Lleras area.

Tourist Information

Medellín produces the most comprehensive tourist information of any city in Colombia. In addition to tourist information booths at the bus terminals and airports, there is a large office at the **Plaza Mayor** (Cl. 41 No. 55-80, tel. 4/261-7277, 8am-noon and 2pm-6pm Mon.-Sat.). The tourism office webpage (www. medellin.travel) is up to date with information on what's going on in the city.

The main newspaper in Medellín is *El Colombiano* (www.elcolombiano.com). Other online resources for events and activities in Medellín and in the area are **Medellín Living** (www.medellinliving.com), a blog site run by expats; **Medellín Style** (www.medellinstyle. com), which has information on DJ events in town; **Plan B** (www.planb.com.co); ticket outlet **Tu Boleta** (www.tuboleta.com); and **Guia Gay Colombia** (www.guiagaycolombia.com), for information on gay and lesbian nightlife.

GETTING THERE AND AROUND

It's a snap getting to centrally located Medellín from just about anywhere in Colombia, and from Florida. And once in the Antioquian capital, getting around is pretty easy, too.

By Air

There are nonstop flights from Medellín's **Aeropuerto Internacional José María Córdova** (MDE, Rionegro, tel. 4/402-5110 or 4/562-2885) to all major cities in Colombia. The airport is simply referred to as "Rionegro." Avianca, LAN, and Viva Colombia operate domestic flights. Internationally, Avianca serves Miami, Panama City, Lima, and Madrid; American Airlines has a nonstop flight to Miami; Spirit and JetBlue to Fort Lauderdale; AeroGal and LAN to Quito; Copa to Caracas and Panama City; and Insel Air to Curaçao.

The Rionegro airport is about 45 minutes (35 km/22 miles) from downtown, depending on traffic. Taxis cost around COP$60,000 between the city and the airport.

Alternatively, there are *busetas,* small buses, that leave the airport bound for the San Diego neighborhood, which is convenient to El Poblado. These can be found as you exit the terminal towards the right. Upon arrival in Medellín, there are taxis on standby. An organized and legitimate group of young people will help place your bags in the cab, even though you may not want or need this service. They expect a COP$1,000-2,000 tip.

Traveling to the airport, there are buses (Conbuses, tel. 4/231-9681) that depart from a side street just behind the Hotel Nutibara (Cl. 52A No. 50-46, tel. 4/511-5111) in the Centro. These depart from about 4:30am until 7:20pm every day, and the trip costs COP$8,000. The buses are hard to miss: They're green and white with the word *aeropuerto* printed in all caps on the front window.

Aeropuerto Olaya Herrera (AOH, Cra. 65A No. 13-157, tel. 4/403-6781, www. aeropuertoolayaherrera.gov.co) is the super-convenient in-town airport. **EasyFly** serves Montería, Cúcuta, Bucaramanga, Apartadó, and Quibdó; **Satena** serves Bogotá, Quibdó, Apartadó, Bahía Solano, and Nuqui. **ADA** (Aerolíneas Antioqueñas) serves a whole slew of cities throughout Colombia, especially western Colombia. The Olaya Herrera terminal was built in the 1930s and is an architectural gem.

Intercity Buses

Medellín has two bus terminals: the Sur and the Norte. The **Terminal del Sur** (Cra. 65 No. 8B-91, tel. 4/444-8020 or 4/361-1186) is across from the Aeropuerto Olaya Herrera, and it serves destinations in southern Antioquia and the coffee region. The **Terminal del Norte** (Cra. 64C No. 78-580, tel. 4/444-8020 or 4/230-9595) is connected to the Caribe Metro station. It serves Santa Fe de Antioquia and Guatape, the Caribbean Coast, and Bogotá.

Metro

Medellín's **Metro** (tel. 4/444-9598, www. metrodemedellin.gov.co) is the only urban train system in the country. It's a safe and super-clean system of two lines: Línea A, which runs from Niquía (north) to La Estrella (south), and Línea B, from San Antonio in the Centro west to San Javier. The Metro line A is useful for traveling between El Centro, El Poblado, and Envigado. Metro line B has a

© ANDREW DIER

the Medellín Metro

stop at the stadium. The current Metro fare is COP$1,800; however if you think you may use the Metro, Metrocable, and Metroplús system on a regular basis, consider purchasing a refillable Tarjeta Cívica card that is valid on all three transportation networks. The cost per ride with the Tarjeta Cívica modestly drops to COP$1,600. The card can be purchased at Metro ticket booths.

Metrocable

The Metrocable public transportation system, consisting of gondola *(teleférico)* lines, was inaugurated in 2004 and consists of three lines, with two under construction. It has been internationally lauded as an innovative approach to solving the particular transportation needs of the isolated and poor *comunas* (residential sectors), built on mountainsides of the city. The three Metrocable lines are: Línea J from the San Javier Metro station to La Aurora in the west, Línea K from the Acevedo Metro station in the north to Santo Domingo, and Línea L from Santo Domingo to the Parque

Arví. The Metrocable runs 9am-10pm daily. The Metrocable Línea L from Santo Domingo to the Parque Arví operates 9am-6pm Tuesday-Sunday. When Monday is a holiday, the Línea L runs that day and does not operate the next day, Tuesday.

Metroplús Rapid Bus

The first line of the **Metroplús** (www.metroplus.gov.co) rapid bus system, with dedicated bus stops similar to those of the TransMilenio in Bogotá, debuted in 2013. There are two Metroplús lines: Línea 1 and Línea 2. Línea 1 connects the working-class neighborhood of Arjuanez in the north with the Universidad de Medellín in the southwest. Línea 2 connects the same two sectors but passes through the Centro and Plaza Mayor area. To access the system, you have to use the Tarjeta Cívica, which can be purchased at any Metro station.

Taxis

Taxis are plentiful in Medellín. Order them over the phone when possible. A few taxi companies have easy-to-remember numbers: tel. 4/444-4444, tel. 4/335-3535, and tel. 4/211-1111. Friendly **Miguel Espinosa** (cell tel. 311/378-3565) is a cabbie based around the Laureles area. You can also order reliable cabs using the smartphone app Tappsi.

Northern and Eastern Antioquia

SANTA FE DE ANTIOQUIA

Living and breathing colonial charm, this pueblo 80 kilometers (50 miles) northwest of Medellín is the best of Antioquia. The historic center of the town is compact, with landmarks of plazas, parks, and churches. Santa Fe was founded in 1541 by Jorge Robledo, a ruthless conquistador. An important center for gold mining, Santa Fe was capital of Antioquia until 1823, when it lost that title to Medellín. On the banks of the Río Cauca, its proximity to Medellín makes it an easy trip for those interested in seeing a colonial-era jewel of a pueblo.

With the average temperature a sizzling 27°C (81°F), it can be a challenge to fully enjoy strolling the lovely streets of the pueblo during the heat of the day. If you can, plan to go for the night (one weekday night will do), arriving in late afternoon. That's the nicest time to stroll the streets.

Sights

The town's narrow stone streets are adorned with charming plazas and parks and five historic churches. It's a delight to stroll the town in the late afternoon, after the heat of the day has subsided. Churches and historic buildings in Santa Fe are often built in the typical *calicanto* style, a mix of brick and stone construction materials. Historic colonial churches, with majestic facades, often face parks and are illuminated at night.

The "grandmother" of churches in Antioquia, the **Templo de Santa Bárbara** (Cl. 8 at Cra. 8, masses 7am and 6pm Mon.-Sat. 6am and 6pm Sun.), with its many baroque elements, was built towards the end of the 18th century. Next to it, in what was a Jesuit college, is the **Museo de Arte Religioso** (Cl. 11 No. 8-12, tel. 4/311-3808, 9am-5pm Sat.-Sun.,

COP$2,000), a museum that highlights paintings, sculptures, and gold and silver pieces from the Spanish New World colonies.

A nicely presented museum housed in a colonial-style house, the **Museo Juan del Corral** (Cl. 11 No. 9-77, tel. 4/853-4605, www.museojuandelcorral.com, 9am-noon and 2pm-5:30pm Mon.-Fri., 10am-5pm Sat.-Sun., free) has exhibits on the history of Santa Fe, including historical items from 1813 when Antioquia was declared free. The museum also puts on temporary exhibits of contemporary Colombian artists, and other cultural events are held here.

Six kilometers (four miles) outside of town, on an old road that leads to the town of Sopetrán on the other side of the Río Cauca, is an architectural wonder, the **Puente de Occidente,** a suspension bridge made of iron and steel. It was built towards the end of the 19th century by José María Villa, an engineer who studied in New Jersey and worked on the Brooklyn Bridge. It's a narrow bridge and has been closed to vehicular traffic, for the most part. *Mototaxis* can take you there from town, across the bridge, and back for COP$15,000. The bridge is easily reached by bike as well.

Festivals and Events

The big event in Santa Fe is the week-long **Festival de Cine de Antioquia** (www.festicineantioquia.com), a film festival held each year in early December. There is usually an international director or actor who is the guest of honor. Some free showings are held outdoors in the town's plazas and parks.

Accommodations

Medellín families converge on Santa Fe en masse on weekends, and for many the draw is

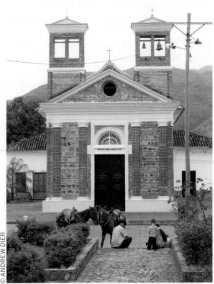

© ANDREW DIER

The historic town of Santa Fe de Antioquia makes for a pleasant overnight trip from Medellín.

to lounge by the pool at one of the hotels lining the main road leading into town. Hotels in town, however, have more charm. Hotel prices can drop substantially during the week.

In town, the 【 **Hotel Mariscal Robledo** (Cl. 10 No. 9-70, tel. 4/853-1111, cell tel. 313/760-0099, www.hotelmariscalrobledo. com, COP$120,000-170,000 d) is far and away the most comfortable hotel, and one oozing with personality. Antiques, especially with a cinematic theme, decorate the lobby and common areas. Rooms on the second floor, which have not been given a 21st-century makeover, are nonetheless comfortable, and have far more character. The pool area is luxurious.

On the boutique side, the **Hotel Casa Tenerife** (Cra. 8 No. 9-50, tel. 4/853-2261, www.hotelcasatenerife.com, COP$162,000 d) has 12 rooms, is tastefully decorated, and has a nice pool and courtyard area. It often caters to couples celebrating romantic getaways, with such details as rose petals on the bed.

On the Plaza Mayor are two options. The family-run **Hotel Caserón Plaza** (Cl. 9-41, Plaza Mayor, tel. 4/853-2040, www.hotelcaseronplaza.com.co, COP$145,000-208,000 d) has an excellent location but is overpriced for what you get. Some of the 33 rooms have air conditioning, which is a plus in Santa Fe. There is also a small pool in back, another plus. **Hostal de la Plaza Mayor** (Cra. 9 No. 9-59, tel. 4/255-7427, cell tel. 311/396-5628, http://hostalplazamayorsantafedeantioquia. blogspot.com, COP$50,000 d) is the budget option in town. Staff are friendly, but it's a little run down.

Food
There are few places in Colombia where one can dine to the soft tones of classical or jazz music. The **Restaurante Bar La Comedia** (Parque Santa Barbara, tel. 4/853-1243, noon-3pm and 6pm-10pm Wed.-Sun., COP$18,000) is one such place. Light dishes, sandwiches, and crêpes dominate the small menu, and this is also an option for late afternoon *onces,* tea time. It's diagonal to the Santa Bárbara church. **Restaurante Portón del Parque** (Cl. 10 No. 11-03, tel. 4/853-3207, noon-8pm Sun.-Thurs., noon-9:30pm Sat.-Sun., COP$20,000) is lavishly decorated with portraits and paintings by owner Olga Cecilia. In addition to typical Paisa specialties (lunch specials during the week go for under COP$10,000), the extensive menu offers seafood and international cuisine. Finally, the restaurant at the **Hotel Mariscal Robledo** (Cl. 10 No. 9-70, tel. 4/853-1111, cell tel. 313/760-0099, www.hotelmariscalrobledo.com, 8am-3pm and 7pm-10pm daily, COP$25,000) is always a good choice.

Recreation
Naturaventura (Hotel Mariscal Robledo, Cl. 10 No. 9-70, tel. 4/853-1946, naturaventura1@hotmail.com) organizes nature walks, bike trips, horseback riding, and rafting excursions. For horseback riding, contact **Guías Turantioquia** (tel. 4/853-1148), which organizes day-trip horseback riding tours in and around Santa Fe.

Shopping

Spaniards were once attracted to Santa Fe because of its gold. Today it is famous for its intricate filigree jewelry. To peruse some, visit **ORFOA** (Cl. 9 No. 6-02, tel. 4/853-2880, 9am-noon and 2pm-6pm daily) or **Dulces & Artesanías Clavellina** (Hotel Mariscal Robledo, Cl. 10 No. 9-70, tel. 4/853-2195, 9am-noon and 2pm-6pm daily). Clavellina is the symbolic flower of Santa Fe.

Guarnielería y Marroquinería (Cl. 10 No. 7-66, cell tel. 314/847-8354, noon-7pm Mon.-Fri., 10am-7pm Sat.-Sun.) sells authentic Jericó *carrieles* (shoulder bags used by Paisa cowhands) and other locally made leather handicrafts. **La Casa Solariega** (Cl. de la Amargura No. 8-09, tel. 4/853-1530, 9am-noon and 2pm-6pm daily) has an eclectic collection of handicrafts, paintings, and antiques in a typical Santa Fe house.

Information and Services

A **tourist information office** on the Plaza Mayor (Cra. 9 and Cl. 9, tel. 4/853-1022) has maps and hotel information.

Getting There and Around

There is regular bus service, several times a day, from the **Terminal de Transportes del Norte** (Cra. 64 No. 78-344, tel. 4/267-7075, www.terminalesmmedellin.com) in Medellín to Santa Fe. The journey takes two hours and takes you through a feat of modern engineering: the **Túnel Fernando Gómez Martínez,** the longest tunnel in South America. To return, walk a couple of blocks to the Medellín-Turbo highway near the market at Carrera 10 and flag down passing buses. Most of them are going to Medellín. The trip costs under COP$10,000.

MAGDALENA MEDIO
◖ Reserva Natural Río Claro

A visit to the spectacular, privately run **Reserva Natural Río Claro** (Medellín office tel. 4/268-8855, cell tel. 311/354-0119, www. rioclaroelrefugio.com) is a highlight for anyone visiting Colombia. In the steamy and remote Magdalena Medio region of Antioquia,

the reserve encompasses 450 hectares (1,100 acres) along the Río Claro canyon, a babbling, crystal-clear river. This reserve is a place to enjoy the unspoiled beauty of the river and its jungle and to disconnect from the hectic pace of urban life.

The story behind the park begins with an oft-repeated tale about a pesky jaguar. It seems that the cat was blamed for killing some livestock of a campesino in the area. In a quest to track down the guilty party (the jaguar got away unharmed), the farmer followed its tracks through the jungle, over several days, and to a spectacular canyon. When Juan Guillermo Garcés heard about the astonishing discovery, he had to see this undiscovered territory for himself. Garcés immediately knew that this was a special place, and he made a commitment to purchase the land to protect it from development, including a highway that was to pass through this pristine land.

On weekends, Río Claro receives many visitors. In addition to those staying at the reserve, many day visitors spend the afternoon at Río Claro. Don't go on a Saturday, Sunday, or holiday if you seek a peaceful commune with nature. If you visit the reserve midweek, you'll most likely have the place practically to yourself, which is heavenly.

RECREATION

Guides don't speak English, generally. There are two must-do activities at the reserve. The first is an easy rafting trip down the river (COP$20,000), during which you can see the karstic jungle, in which trees grow atop rocks. This excursion takes about two hours. The second must-do activity is a combination swim/hike trip to the **Caverna de los Guácharos** (COP$15,000 pp). This guided walk has its challenging moments: wading across the swiftly flowing river, making your way through the dark, dark cavern, climbing out of the cavern, and then making your way back across the river. *Guácharo* birds (oilbirds), living inside the cavern, act like they own the place (the cavern is, after all, named for them). They don't like it when human intruders

© ANDREW DIER

Reserva Natural Río Claro

invade their space, and they'll let you know that with their screeching. The cavern is made of marble; its stalactites and stalagmites are impressive. Waterproof shoes with good traction are recommended, as you'll be wading in water most of the time. Also, it's nice to have a headlamp so that you'll have hands free. You can take your camera, but at a certain point it will need to be kept in a water repellent bag, which the guide will have. If you're up for both trips, go on the cavern tour in the morning and go rafting in the late afternoon.

Other activities at the reserve include rock-climbing, a zip line, hanging out on the marble beach, self-guided nature walks, and tubing. These are all arranged by Río Claro staff.

ACCOMMODATIONS

The reserve has a variety of accommodations options. Contact the Río Claro office (tel. 4/268-8855, cell tel. 311/354-0119, www.rioclaroelrefugio.com) for all reservations and information. The **Hotel El Refugio** (COP$80,000) is above the reception and dining area, and is a comfortable all-wooden lodge construction. The best and most isolated is at the far end near the canyon, a 15-minute walk from the main reception area in the **Cabañas El Refugio** (COP$95,000-140,000 pp), where rooms are quite spectacular and open-air. You'll sleep well here with the sounds of the rushing water to lull you asleep. Rooms are completely open, but there are no problems with mosquitoes.

The **Hotel Río Claro** (COP$95,000 pp) is across the highway from the rest of the reserve but still along the river, and it has a big pool. These are small concrete bungalows. The hotel is popular with student groups. All meals are included in the room rates. Tell staff when you make your reservation if you have any dietary needs or special requests, like fresh fruit.

GETTING THERE

The reserve is easily reached by bus from Medellín. All buses between Medellín and Bogotá pass in front of the Río Claro entrance, where there is a small security booth. From

MEDELLÍN

Medellín, it takes around three hours, costing around COP$20,000. Be sure to tell the driver you'd like to be dropped off at the *"entrada de la Reserva Río Claro."* ("the entrance to the Río Claro Reserve").

Hacienda Napoles

The **Hacienda Napoles** (Puerto Triunfo, cell tel. 314/892-2307, www.haciendanapoles.com, 9am-6pm Tues.-Sun., COP$32,000) was a vacation home for Pablo Escobar, complete with an airstrip and exotic animals, including quite a few hippos, who apparently adapted nicely to the muggy climes of the Río Magdalena area. Today Hacienda Napoles is a theme park with giant dinosaur sculptures, some of which were built by Escobar for his children; two water parks (additional fees); hippopotami, zebras, and ostriches; an Africa museum; the remnants of Pablo Escobar's country house (now a museum); a collection of old cars that were destroyed following his death; and his private airplane landing strip.

Avoid the oppressive heat and intense sun of midday (and the crowds on weekends) by visiting early on a weekday morning. The park can easily be visited from Río Claro, which is about an hour away. When Monday is a holiday, the park closes on Tuesday rather than on Monday.

GUATAPE

The stone monolith La Piedra dominates the landscape here, but the Guatape area is more than just a big rock: It's a weekend playground chock full of recreational activities that keep the crowds from Medellín busy.

Sights

Guatape is a resort town. Aside from La Piedra, it's known for its *zócalos,* colorful designs of the friezes on the lower part of houses. Many of these honor the traditions of townspeople, such as farming and fishing, others have sheep or other animals, and still others hot rods or Pink Panther. A particularly colorful street is the **Calle del Recuerdos** near the Parque Principal.

On a serene mountainside near Guatape, beyond El Encuentro hostel on the same road is the **Monasterio Santa María de la Epifanía** (www.monjesbenedictinosguatape.org), home to around 30 Benedictine monks. Guests, up to eight at a time, are welcome to stay. Every day of the week at the 5:15pm *visperas* (vespers) service, the public is invited to hear the monks sing Gregorian chants.

Check out the **Iglesia de Piedra** in the town of El Peñol, a modern construction that resembles La Piedra, which is quite a strange sight.

La Piedra Peñol

Known simply as La Piedra, **La Piedra Peñol** (8am-6pm daily, COP$10,000) is a giant rock monolith that soars 200 meters (650 feet) into the sky from the scenic and meandering Embalse Peñol-Guatape, an important reservoir covering some 64 square kilometers (25 square miles) that is an important producer of hydro-electric energy for the country. There's been quite a rivalry between the towns of El Peñol and Guatape over the years, over which town can claim La Piedra for their own. It is located between the two, a tad closer to the Guatape side. Things digressed to a point where folks from Guatape began to paint their town's name in large letters on one prominent side of the rock. People from El Peñol were not amused, and this giant marking of territory was halted by authorities. Today all that remains of that brouhaha is what appear to be the letters "GI."

The 360-degree views from the top of La Piedra over the Guatape reservoir and Antioqiuan countryside are worth the toil of climbing up over 600 steps, in a ramshackle brick and concrete stairwell that is stuck to the rock, to the top. To celebrate your feat, you can have a drink at one of the snack bars there.

In front of La Piedra, there is a statue of the man who first climbed the monolith in 1954. Inspired by a priest, Luis Villegas López and two friends took five days to slowly climb up cracks in the rock. They had to deal with a beehive and a rainstorm along the way, adding to the challenge. It's one of the top tourist attractions in Antioquia. From the bottom of the rock, look up and notice the hundreds of bromeliads growing along the sides of it.

La Piedra can be visited several ways. You can walk from Guatape, which takes 45 minutes. (Sunscreen and water are essential.) You can bike it, although the road that winds its way up to the rock entrance is quite steep. You can take a *mototaxi* from your hotel (COP$10,000), or you can hop on a Jeep from the Parque Principal (between Cras. 28-29 and Clls. 31-32) in Guatape. It's best to make your visit during the early morning hours or late in the afternoon due to potent sun rays.

The town is surrounded by a large reservoir operated by EPM, the Medellín utility company. The reservoir was built in phases during the 1970s and was not without controversy, as the flooding of the area began without the full consent of the inhabitants. Finally all families were resettled by EPM by 1979, and the town of El Peñol gradually became covered with rising waters, with only a church steeple remaining as a reminder of the town's past.

Tours

A popular excursion is to take a **boat tour** with brothers Luis and Rodolfo Londoño (cell tel. 312/794-7150 or 312/236-5783, COP$50,000-100,000 per boat) to some of the islands of the reservoir. A standard stop on the tour is to (or rather, above) the submerged town of Viejo Peñol. It was flooded on purpose during the construction of the reservoir and nearby dam in 1978. The only real remnant of the town is a large cross rising out of the water. A small historical museum displays old photos and historical memorabilia from the old town on the waterside. These tours typically last 45 minutes to 1.5 hours.

Accommodations

During the week, prices drop significantly at most hotels, especially if you pay in cash.

[El Encuentro** (tel. 4/861-1374, cell tel. 311/619-6199, www.hostalelencuentro. com, COP$20,000 dorm, COP$65,000 d), a 12-minute walk up from town, remains one of the best options in Guatape. Run by a friendly

Californian named Greg, the hostel is on the Guatape-Peñol reservoir, and rooms are spread throughout two houses, with about 10 rooms in total. Most of these are private rooms, and some have a shared bath. A larger apartment and two dorms are available here, as well as a place for tents down by the lake. The staff at El Encuentro can organize a plethora of outdoorsy things to do: downhill mountain bike rides on their excellent bikes, hikes, and jumping off of bridges. Spanish classes can be arranged, and you can study your verbs on the nice deck.

In town is the newer **Tomate Café Hostel** (Cl. 30 No. 28-120, tel. 4/861-1100, cell tel. 312/216-1199, www.tomatecafehostel.com, COP$18,000 dorm, COP$40,000 d). It's run by a Paisa family and has four small private rooms and two dorm rooms. A strong cup of coffee is always on offer here, as well as healthy and vegetarian food in their restaurant. It's next to a disco, so on weekend nights it can get thumping. You were warned!

At **[** **Mi Casa Guatape** (tel. 4/861-0632, cell tel. 301/457-5726, www.micasaguatape. com, COP$20,000 dorm, COP$60,000 d) guests wake up, step outside with a cup of coffee in hand, and greet their neighbor, La Piedra, with a warm *Buenos días*. You can't get much closer to that big rock than from this small English-Colombian hostel. The hostel has five private rooms and one four-bed dorm as well as two kitchens for use. When not outdoors climbing La Piedra or taking out their kayak for a spin, guests can laze in hammocks on the deck, watch movies, or bond with the owners' sweet dog. Mi Casa works closely with **Adventure Activities** (cell tel. 301/411-4442), just next door, a group that organizes an intense-rock climbing excursion up one of dozens of routes up La Piedra (COP$60,000, 7 hours), as well as other outings. Owner Sean takes guests on a waterfall hike (6 km/4 miles round-trip, COP$15,000, 4 hours). It's easy to go into town from the hostel by catching a ride with a passing Jeep or with Mi Casa's preferred *mototaxi* driver. Mi Casa is about three kilometers before Guatape on the main road (25-min. walk or COP$1,500 taxi ride) and is across the street from landmark El Estadero La Mona.

There are a couple of upscale hotels in town. **Hotel Portobello** (Cl. 32 No. 28-29, tel. 4/861-0016, cell tel. 312/783-4050, www.hotelportobeloguatape.com, COP$215,000 d) has 16 rooms, and most of them have a view of the lake. You can obtain a 25 percent discount during the week if you pay in cash.

Food

Fish like massive carp and trout from the reservoir are the specialty in Guatape. Reliable fish and Colombian cuisine restaurants include **La Fogata** (Cra. 30 No. 31-32, tel. 4/861-1040, cell tel. 314/740-7282, 8am-8pm daily), on the waterfront.

Pizza and pasta are on the menu at **Rafaelos** (below Hotel Portobello on the waterfront, tel. 4/861-0016, cell tel. 310/200-9020, 11am-11pm Wed.-Sun.).

Craving a curry? **Donde Sam** (El Peñol, near church, tel. 4/851-5401, cell tel. 320/667-5870, 11am-11pm daily, COP$15,000) is worth the trip. Owner and chef Sam, from Agra, and his Colombian wife, Lina, serve up authentic Indian dishes (as well as other international cuisine). Lunches, like curry vegetables or chicken, are accompanied by a soup and salad. It's livelier at night, and sometimes they put on mood-setting music in an attempt to transport the crowd to Asia.

Sometimes exceptional hospitality can give one a sugar headache. That's what happens at Gloria Elena's generous candy tastings at **Dulces de Guatape** (Cl. 29 No. 23C-32, Barrio Villa del Carmen, tel. 4/861-0724, 7am-6pm). At this small candy factory, they make all kinds of sweets, many with *arequipe* (caramel) and some with fruits like the tart *uchuva* and guava as well as some chocolate bonbons that have peanuts and almonds.

Getting There and Around

There is frequent bus service from Medellín's north terminal to Guatape. The trip takes about two hours and costs COP$12,000. Buses depart Guatape at a bus terminal that was completed in 2013 on the waterfront. It's just one block from the main plaza. Buses returning to Medellín often fill up in a hurry on Sundays, especially during holidays. If you are relying on public transportation, book your return bus trip early. The last bus for Medellín departs at 6pm. The return fare is also COP$12,000.

Southern Antioquia

JARDÍN

Sometimes place names fit perfectly. Such is the case in the picture-perfect Antioquian town of Jardín. The main park gushes year-round with trees and flowers always in bloom, and the streets are corridors of color as well, with brightly painted houses one after another.

For many years this town has been a favorite country getaway for Paisas from Medellín. It's becoming popular with international travelers, too, but still, if you arrive during the week, you'll feel like you've stumbled upon something special. On weekends, and especially on holidays, a festive atmosphere fills the air, and the Plaza Principal buzzes with activity.

While the main selling points of Jardín are its good looks, nearby tropical forests and cloud forests, home to natural attractions such as the Caverna El Esplendor and the ProAves birdwatching reserve, provide good excuses for lacing up those hiking boots.

Sights

The **Parque Principal** is the center of life in Jardín. It's full of colorful wooden chairs, eight flower gardens, a handful of tall trees that provide welcome shade, and a constant cast of characters passing through, hanging out, or sipping a coffee. Prominent on the east side of the park is the neo-gothic cathedral the **Basílica**

© ANDREW DIER

the Parque Principal in pretty Jardín

Menor de la Inmaculada Concepción (Cra. 3 No. 10-71, mass daily 11am), a 20th-century construction, the striking interior of which is painted shades of turquoise.

The **Museo Clara Rojas** (Cra. 5 No. 9-31, tel. 6/845-5652, http://mcrpjardin.blogspot. com, 8am-noon and 2pm-6pm, COP$2,000) has 19th-century period furniture and relics from the *colonización antioqueña,* as well as a small collection of religious art, including a painting of Jesus as a child surrounded by lambs with medals hanging around their necks. The town's tourism office is behind the museum, operating the same hours as the museum.

Recreation

Walking around Jardín is a pleasant way to get to know the town and surrounding mountains. Setting out for a walk towards the surrounding western mountains, to the Alto de las Flores or Salto del Ángel, makes for a great morning. If you lose your way, ask for directions. On the east side of town, there is a charming path, the **Camino Herrera,** which

leads to the Casa de los Fundadores. In that area are several coffee plantations.

Jardín has not one, but two mini chairlifts in town. The **Cable Aereo** (8am-6pm daily, COP$5,000 round-trip) goes up to the Cristo Rey hill. The other, more rustic **La Garrucha** (8am-6pm daily, COP$4,000), goes across town. Although these are popular with tourists, they were built with a purpose in mind: so that rural farmers would have an easier way to bring their coffee and other crops to market.

Condor de los Andes (tel. 4/845-5374, cell tel. 311/746-1985, condordelosandes@ colombia.com) is a tourism operator that organizes walks, paragliding, and waterfall rappelling. Their most popular activity is a day-long **rappelling** adventure to the **Caverna El Esplendor.** This cavern in the jungle outside of town is reached on foot (about a 1.5-hour walk). Once there you rappel down a 50-meter-high (164-foot-high) waterfall into the cavern. Transportation and lunch are included in the price (COP$95,000 pp), and they usually depart Jardín at around 8am, returning

MEDELLÍN

by 4pm. The group also offers paragliding (COP$75,000, 25 mins.) and rappelling at the 53-meter-high (174-foot-high) **Cascada Escalera** (COP$55,000). Condor de los Andes has a small hostel (COP$35,000 pp) five blocks from the Parque Principal.

Those with an inner cowboy may want to take a horseback tour to the **Salto del Ángel** waterfall. Contact **John Jairo** (cell tel. 312/825-4524) to reserve your spot.

The mountains that envelop most of Jardín are protected lands encompassing some 28,000 hectares (69,000 acres). This area is called the **Reserva Cuchilla Jardín Tamesis.** Within the reserve are caverns, waterfalls, caves, and nature paths. The **park office** (Alcaldía building, 2nd floor, Cra. 3 No. 10-10, tel. 4/845-5668, cell tel. 321/758-7534, dmicuchilla@corantioquia. gov.co) offers free guided walks to these natural attractions.

BIRDING

Colombia's premier bird-watching and conservation group, **ProAves** (www.proaves.org), operates a bird-watching park, the **Reserva Natural de las Loro Orejiamarillo,** within Reserva Cuchilla Jardín Tamesis. This is where the yellow ear parrot *(Ognorhynchus icterotis)* can be seen, an endangered species in Colombia. They make their nests in the majestic *palma de cera* (wax palm) trees. Another exotic bird to look for is the *colibrí de frontino (Coeligena orina),* a species of hummingbird. In addition to birdlife, there have been spottings of pumas, the *oso de anteojos* (an Andean bear), and deer.

It is ideal to get an early start to view the parrots—as early as 5am. As the elevation is fairly high, the temperatures dip as low as 4°C (39°F). Rubber boots and warm clothing are essential.

To coordinate a visit to the bird-watching park, contact **EcoTurs** (Cra. 20 No. 36-61, Bogotá, tel. 1/287-6592, www.ecoturs.org) in advance as staff are not always at the site. This tour agency manages visits to this and all of the other ProAves reserves across the country. In Jardín, contact Joana Villa (cell tel. 312/867-1740), or contact Angela Gómez

Devils of Riosucio

Every two years in January, in the sleepy coffee- and plantain-growing town Riosucio in northern Caldas near the Antioquian town of Jardín, residents (and a growing number of visitors) go to the devil during the revelry of the **Carnaval de Riosucio.** This festival, one of the most beloved in the region, has an interesting story. It began out of a plea made by local priests for two feuding pueblos of Riosucio—the gold-mining village of Quiebralomo and La Montaña, home to a large indigenous population—to get along. In 1847 both communities were nudged to participate in that year's Three Kings Day commemoration and to set aside their differences, temporarily at least. If they didn't come together that year in peace, they would invite the wrath of the devil.

Over time, it was that last bit that resonated with the townspeople. From that year onward, groups of families, friends, and neighbors would get together and create elaborate floats and costumes, seemingly in homage to the devil over this five-day celebration. The festival is run by the República del Carnaval, which reigns over the town during that time, and the culmination of the event is the ceremonial burning of an effigy of the devil. The festival gets going on the first Friday of January with the most colorful activities taking place on Sunday.

in Bogotá (cell tel. 313/852-9158) for more information about this park in Antioquia. There is a COP$15,000 entrance fee per person for Reserva Natural de las Loro Orejiamarillo; a guide service costs COP$50,000 per group; and round-trip jeep transportation along rugged mountain roads to the reserve is a whopping COP$240,000.

La Esperanza (cell tel. 312/837-0782, COP$180,000 pp all meals incl.) is a private nature reserve run by an American, Doug Knapp, set on a mountain ridge 15 minutes from town. Sunrises, with a view to Jardín, and sunsets, looking out towards the mountains of Los Farallones del Citaró, can't be beat. A Jack of many trades, birder Knapp built three comfortable cabins complete with siesta-friendly decks and natural light pouring through the windows. He's also carved out some forest paths that meander through the property. Oh, and he cooks, too.

At La Esperanza, you don't have to go far to catch a glimpse of some spectacular birds. Knapp's colleagues have documented the presence of eight endemic birds, including the Parker's antbird, the whiskered wren, the Colombian chacalaca, and the yellow-headed manakin. More than 365 species are estimated to live in the Jardín area.

Accommodations

If you are planning to visit Jardín on a *puente* (long weekend) or during holidays, you will need to make a reservation at a hotel well in advance. On regular weekends, there is usually no problem in finding a hotel, although the best options do tend to fill up. During the week, the town is yours, and prices drop substantially (especially if you plan to pay in cash).

Although Jardín has plenty of reasonably priced hotel options, there is just one hostel. **Casa Selva y Café** (Casa del Lago Vereda La Salada, tel. 4/845-5430, cell tel. 318/518-7171, www.hostalselvaycafe.com, COP$25,000 dorm, COP$50,000-90,000 d) is a cozy countryside spot, about a 12-minute walk away from the hustle and bustle of Jardín city life. Back behind a little pond surrounded with flowers and fruit trees with pastureland and mountains behind, it is pure peace here. Alexandra, the owner, is a yoga teacher and gives classes on-site every Tuesday and Thursday, which are free for hostel guests. For nonguests the classes cost COP$20,000. The two private rooms and two dorms are spacious and clean with high ceilings and hardwood floors.

Hotel Casa Grande (Cl. 8 No. 4-33, tel. 4/845-5487, cell tel. 311/340-2207, www.hotelcasagrande.co, COP$30,000 pp) features 12 rooms, which have a capacity of 2-5 persons each. Most rooms have 2-4 beds to accommodate families. Breakfast is included in the price, and dinner can be arranged at the hotel as well.

The friendly owner, a Jardín native, can supply tourist information for the area.

Hotel Valdivia Plaza (Parque Principal, next to the Museo Clara Rojas, tel. 4/845-5055, cell tel. 316/528-1047, COP$58,000 d) has 20 rooms and is clean, but isn't bursting with personality. Splurge for a room with a private balcony overlooking the park.

Hotel Jardín (Cra. 3 No. 9-14, cell tel. 310/380-6724, COP$40,000 pp) has 11 spacious and modern apartments with a capacity of 4-8 persons each. It's a bargain. This is the most colorful house in a most colorful town, with orange, yellow, red, and blue balconies, doors, and trim. The house was restored in 2012.

A comfortable, if conservative, choice is **Comfenalco Hotel Hacienda Balandú** (Km. 1 Vía Jardín Riosucio, tel. 4/845-5561, COP$158,000 d), a hotel with all the extras: restaurant, sauna, and swimming pool. It's a tranquil 15- to 20-minute walk from town.

Food

The soft glow of candlelight at **Café Europa** (Cl. 8 No. 4-02, cell tel. 312/230-2842, 11am-3pm and 6pm-10pm Wed.-Mon.) is hard to resist for weekenders. This corner restaurant run by a German photographer and travel writer serves nice pizzas. Order a bottle of French wine (COP$35,000) and settle in. There's no rush in Jardín. The menu at **Pastelatte** (Cra. 4 No. 8-45, cell tel. 301/482-3908, noon-8:30pm Wed.-Mon., COP$14,000) features crêpes, cheesecakes, coffee, sandwiches, and pastas, and service is speedy and always with a smile. **Zodiaco** (off the main plaza in front of the Hotel El Dorado, tel. 4/845-5615, 8am-11pm daily, COP$15,000) is a *comida típica* (Colombian fare) restaurant, but it's a couple of notches fancier than most restaurants in town. At **Las Margaritas** (Cra. 3 No. 9-68, tel. 4/845-6651, 7am-9pm daily, COP$15,000), the specialty is *pollo a la Margarita* (chicken fried with a Parmesan cheese breading). This back-to-Paisa-basics place is good for a hearty breakfast. Vegetarians will appreciate a generous morning serving of *calentado* (beans and

MEDELLÍN

rice). If you want to add some juice (not a part of the typical Paisa breakfast), there is a juice stall two doors down from Las Margaritas, as well as fruit vendors in the park. The *tienda* (store) next door often has fresh Colombian pastries, such as *almojabanas* (cheese rolls) and *pandebonos* (delicious pastries made of yuca flour and cheese).

It's a weekend ritual in Jardín: spend the afternoon with family and friends at one of the *trucheras* (trout farms). One of the largest and best known of these is **La Truchería** (Km. 5 Vía Riosucio, tel. 4/845-5159, noon-6pm daily, COP$18,000). Trout is served infinite ways here: *a la mostaza* (mustard), with fine herbs, and stuffed with vegetables, to name a few. And what better way to round out the day than with a rousing paintball game!

The **Café de los Andes** (Parque Principal, Cra. 5 No. 9-73, tel. 4/845-6239, 8:30am-9pm Thurs.-Mon., 9:30am-8pm Tues.-Wed.) is the brew of choice from Jardín, and their café on the terrace of the Casa del Café is the finest spot in Jardín for a caffeine jolt. Go for an espresso; other coffee drinks are disappointingly weak. It's in the Casa del Café; if you go upstairs you might see the bean-to-bag process in action.

Dulces del Jardín (Cl. 13 No. 5-47, tel. 4/845-6584, www.dulcesdejardin.com, 8am-6pm Mon.-Sat.) is the candy-maker in town. In addition to *arequipe* (caramel) sweets, they make all-natural jams and fruit spreads (COP$6,000) from pineapple, coconut, and papaya.

Siglo XXI (Cra. 6 No. 9-18, no phone, noon-8pm daily) is a hole in the wall where you can have a beer and brush shoulders with locals. The walls of this pub are decorated with faded photos of the town and of local *futbolistas* (soccer players).

Getting There and Around

The bus company **Transportes Suroeste Antioqueño** (tel. 4/352-9049, COP$18,000) leaves Medellín each day bound for Jardín, leaving from the Terminal de Transportes Sur. There is also one bus at 6:30am that leaves

for Manizales to the south in the coffee region from Jardín. This route goes through the town of Riosucio.

JERICÓ

Jericó and Jardín are two (colorfully painted) peas in the same pod. Both are fiercely traditional Paisa pueblos, and they won't change for anybody. Although it is the closer of the two to Medellín, Jericó feels more remote, and less visited, and therein lies its charm. Set on a gentle slope of a mountain overlooking a valley dotted with cattle ranches and farms of coffee, tomato, plantain, and, cardamom, Jericó still is very much a Paisa cowboy outpost. Colombians know Jericó for two very different reasons. The first is its unique handicraft, the *carriel,* a shoulder bag made out of leather and cowhide that is a symbol of Paisa cowboy culture. The second is its homegrown saint, Laura Montoya, who was canonized in 2013.

Jericó is a pleasant place to hang one's (cowboy) hat for a night, and its sleepy streets lined with brightly colored wooden balconies and doors are a playground for shutterbugs.

Sights

The **Catedral de Nuestra Señora de las Mercedes** (Cl. 7 No. 4-34, Plaza de Bolívar, tel. 4/852-3494) is a brick construction that towers over the Parque Reyes. The cathedral is where Laura Montoya was officially declared a saint (Colombia's first) during a ceremony in May 2013. Born into poverty in 1874, Montoya was raised by her grandmother. She began her adulthood as a teacher but later decided to enter religious service. Montoya set out on a lengthy missionary mission into the jungle to witness to indigenous people. She later started a religious order that focused on marginalized peoples that has since spread to many countries. Two miracles are attributed to Montoya. At the entrance to the cathedral, there is a bronze statue of the saint alongside an indigenous child, representing Montoya's devotion to assisting impoverished communities in remote areas.

Below the cathedral is the **Museo de Arte Religioso** (Cl. 7 No. 4-34, Plaza de Bolívar, tel.

© ANDREW DIER

the colorful Paisa town of Jericó

4/852-3494, 8:30am-noon and 1:30pm-6pm Mon.-Fri., 8:30am-6pm Sat., 9am-noon and 1:30pm-5:30pm Sun., COP$2,000), in which religious art and ceremonial items from the colonial period onwards are on display. Often the museum hosts temporary art exhibitions.

The best museum in town, and probably the best outside of Medellín, is the **Museo de Jericó Antioquia** (Cl. 7 between Cras. 5-6, tel. 4/852-4045, cell tel. 311/628-8325, 8am-noon and 1:30pm-6pm Mon.-Fri., 9am-5pm Sat.-Sun., COP$2,000). This museum has several rooms, with some dedicated to archaeology (ceramics and other items from the Emberá indigenous group of western Colombia) and the rest to contemporary art from Antioquian artists. The museum also shows films during the week, and concerts featuring a range of musical genres are held on the last weekend of each month.

On the Morro El Salvador, or Cerro de Cristo Rey (called this because of the white statue of Christ on a pedestal), four blocks from the plaza, is the **Jardín Botánico Los Balsos,** a small botanical garden. For COP$8,000 round-trip you can take a *teleférico* (gondola) to the **Parque Las Nubes,** a park on a hill overlooking Jericó. The park is also known as the Parque Los Venados (Deer Park) for its many four-legged residents. Some short paths lead to a waterfall and to a grotto, and the views of the town and Antioquian countryside are sweeping. Neither the garden nor the park has an entry fee, and they are open to the public daily from sunrise to sunset.

Shopping

To find your very own *carriel* shoulder bag or other leather souvenir from Jericó, walk down Carrera 5. On the righthand side of the street are a couple of classic shops like **Guarnieleria Jericó** (Cra. 5 No. 5-35, tel. 4/852-3370, 9am-6pm daily) and **Taller de Guarnielería & Talabartería** (Cra. 5 No. 5-03, tel. 4/852-3128, cell tel. 311/716-9895, 9am-6pm daily). The classic *carriel* goes for about COP$130,000. Oddly, you probably won't see many people other than tourists actually

MEDELLÍN

using these unique handbags. *Carrieles* were used by *arrieros* (Paisa cowboys) for their horseback trips around Tierra Paisa. These bags are accordion-like, with several divisions in them for carrying items like money, a lock of hair, a knife, or a candle. Some suspect that the name *carriel* is derived from the English "carry all," while others say it comes from the French *cartier*, or handbag.

On the same street is a sweets store, **Delicias del Cardamomo** (Cra. 5 No. 2-128, tel. 4/852-5289, 9am-6pm daily) that sells cardamom candies, cardamom cookies, and plain old cardamom seeds. Cardamom is a relatively important crop in Jericó.

Accommodations

As in all Colombian pueblos, room rates drop during the week.

The best value in town is the **Casa Grande** (Cl. 7 No. 5-54, tel. 4/852-3229, cell tel. 311/329-2144, www.hotelcasagrande.freshcreator.com, COP$40,000 pp). It's a nicely renovated old house with 15 simple rooms. Rooms facing the street are preferable. **Hotel Portón Plaza** (Cl. 7 No. 3-25, tel. 4/852-3009, www.hotelportonplaza.com, COP$35,000 pp) runs a close second, although it's much larger. It is just off of the plaza. Ask for room 209 for a good view, or a second-floor room with a view over the street.

Food

On the Parque Principal there are quite a few restaurant and café options along its east side. On late afternoons, the entire length of one side of the plaza is full of folks enjoying a *tinto* (coffee) and watching the comings and goings of townspeople milling about the plaza. A meal with a view is the selling point of **El Balcón Restaurante** (Parque Principal, Cra. 4 No. 6-26, tel. 4/852-3191, cell tel. 311/784-4419, 8am-9pm daily, COP$15,000). From its perch on a balcony, you have front row seats to the action below in the plaza and a nice vista of the mountains in the distance. The Colombian dishes are filling.

Mandala (Cl. 7 No. 5-55, tel. 4/852-3331, 7am-10pm daily, COP$15,000) is as funky as it gets in Jerico. This restaurant, which serves everything from paella to Colombian comfort food, is also a hangout spot where live music is sometimes on offer. **Casa Gourmet** (Cl. 7 No. 3-16, tel. 4/852-4323, 11am-10pm daily, COP$15,000), across from the Hotel Portón Plaza, serves fast food like pizza, burgers, and crêpes. "Gourmet" is a bit of a stretch, but if you're looking for a quick meal that strays from the rigid *comida típica* fare, this will do.

Information and Services

There is a small **tourist booth** (tel. 4/852-852-3101, cell tel. 321/612-3743, www.jerico-turistico.com, 9am-6pm Thurs.-Tues.) across from the Catedral de Nuestra Señora de las Mercedes. You can get information on hotels, restaurants, and things to do. They also sell sweets, like *crema de solteras,* a typical sweet from Jericó, and cardamom candies, as well as handicrafts. The tourist office organizes walking tours of the town in Spanish on weekends. Inquire at the office or contact guide Maribel (cell tel. 313/672-0199).

Getting There and Around

There is regular bus service to Jericó from the Terminal del Sur in Medellín (COP$20,000), starting at 5am and going until 6pm. Buses arrive and depart from the **Parque Principal.** To get to Jardín from Jericó, you must take a *chiva* (rural bus) to the town of Andes or to the town of Peñalisa and transfer there to Jardín.

The Coffee Region

Blessed by lush, tropical vegetation, meticulously manicured countryside dotted with beautiful haciendas and towns, spring-like weather, and a backdrop of massive, snow-capped mountains, Colombia's coffee region is almost Eden. Nature here is a thousand shades of green: bright green bamboo groves, emerald colored forests with spots of white *yarumo* trees, dark green coffee groves, and green-blue mountains in the distance punctuated by brightly colored flowers and polychromatic butterflies and birds.

Though the main cities and many towns lack charm, dozens of well-preserved villages offer colorful balcony-clad buildings. Life in most of these towns remains untouched by tourism. A visit on market day, with bustling streets jammed with Jeeps, burdened people, and goods, is a memorable one.

And then there is coffee. It is true that Brazil and Vietnam are the world's top coffee producers, but arabica beans are grown throughout Colombia. Coffee grown in some parts of the country (such as Cauca and Nariño) is considered superior to that from this region, but here, more than anywhere else, coffee is an inseparable part of Paisa identity. While the extent of land devoted to coffee farming is diminishing, the numbers are still impressive: The department of Caldas contains over 80,000 hectares (200,000 acres) of coffee farms; Risaralda, 52,000 hectares (128,000 acres); and Quindío, 30,000 hectares (74,000 acres). Visit a coffee farm to understand the laborious production process or—even better—stay overnight.

History

In pre-Columbian times, this region was inhabited by the Quimbaya people. In 1537, Spanish conquistador Sebastián de Belalcázar conquered the region as he moved north from Ecuador towards the central Muisca region. Due to the sparse indigenous population and lack of precious metals, the region, which was governed from faraway Popayán, was largely uninhabited during most of the colonial period.

The Birth of the Coffee Economy

During the 19th century, demographic pressures spurred settlers from the northwestern province of Antioquia to migrate south, giving origin to what is known as the *colonización antioqueña*. For this reason, the coffee region is akin to Antioquia, with similar dialect, cuisine, and architecture. As the settlers made their way south, they founded towns and started farms: Salamina was established in 1825, Manizales in 1849, Filandia in 1878, and Armenia in 1889.

The region prospered enormously throughout the 20th century due to ideal conditions for producing coffee. The Colombian National Coffee Federation, owner of the Juan Valdez brand, provided technical assistance, developed infrastructure, and helped stabilize prices. High international coffee prices during the 1980s and 1990s made the region one of the most prosperous areas in the country.

The fall of global coffee prices in the past decade has forced the region to reinvent itself. Rather than produce a low-value commodity, many farmers have invested in producing high-quality strains that fetch much higher prices. Growers have also diversified, planting other crops, such as plantains, often interspersed through coffee plantations. Finally, agro- and eco-tourism has provided a much-needed new source of revenue.

MEDELLÍN

Planning Your Time

It's hard to go wrong as a tourist in the coffee region. No matter your starting point or home base, an immersion in coffee culture is easy, nearby, and rewarding. If you can, plan to spend about five days in this most pleasant part of Colombia. In that time you can stay at a coffee hacienda, visit a natural park, and tour a picture-perfect pueblo.

However, if time is short, a quick visit can be equally as rewarding. With easy transportation links to the major cities of the region and excellent tourism infrastructure to meet all budget needs, Salento has the trifecta of coffee region attractions: It's a cute pueblo, coffee farms are within minutes of the main plaza, and jungle hikes that lead through tropical forest to the Valle de Cocora are easy to organize. The town gets packed with visitors on weekends and during holidays, resulting in a more festive atmosphere, but also traffic jams.

Another option is to stay a couple of days at a hacienda. You can leisurely explore the farms and countryside, relax, and possibly go for a day trip or two to a nearby attraction. Many haciendas are high-end, like Hacienda Bambusa, Finca Villa Nora, and Hacienda San José. However, budget travelers can also enjoy the unique atmosphere of hacienda life at Hacienda Guayabal outside of Manizales, Villa Martha near Pereira, and Finca El Ocaso in Salento. Meanwhile, Hacienda Venecia has something for travelers of all budgets.

For bird-watchers, the lush region offers many parks and gardens to marvel at the hundreds of species in the area. The Reserva del Río Blanco near Manizales, Jardín Botánico del Quindío near Armenia, and the Santuario de Flora y Fauna Otún-Quimbaya near Pereira are within minutes of the city, guided walks are regularly offered, and birdlife is abundant. Outside of metropolitan areas, the Parque Municipal Natural Planes de San Rafael, which adjoins the Parque Nacional Natural Tatamá, is less known, but is a natural paradise.

Day trips to natural parks, including the Parque Nacional Natural Los Nevados, are easily organized. PNN Los Nevados is home to *páramos* (highland moors), lunar landscapes, and snowcapped volcanoes. It can be accessed from many points, and it can even be visited by car. Multiple day treks offer challenges.

If there were a Cute Pueblo Region of Colombia, this might be it. While you'll have more flexibility driving your own vehicle, it's easy to check out a pueblo or two from the region's major cities traveling by public transportation. A night or two is enough to experience the village life.

MANIZALES

The capital of the Caldas department, Manizales (pop. 393,200) is the region's mountain city. Instead of developing in a lowland valley like Armenia or Pereira, Manizales is set atop meandering mountain ridges. This location means that getting around town involves huffing and puffing up and down hills on foot, enduring rollercoaster-like bus or taxi rides along curvy roads, or taking the scenic route on the city's expanding Cable Aereo cable car network.

Above the coffee farms below at a higher altitude of 2,160 meters (7,085 feet), in Manizales good views abound. And any self-respecting sight around town has got to have a *mirador* (scenic lookout). On a clear day you can see the peaks of the Parque Nacional Natural Los Nevados in the distance, and this city serves as an excellent base to discover that rugged park of snowcapped volcanoes.

Visitors will keep busy here with many easily organized day-trip possibilities to coffee farms and natural parks. While in other cities dusk is a down time, when visitors return to their hotels or go online, in Manizales this is a good time to head out: to soak in a hot spring, to stroll the promenade along the Avenida 12 de Octubre and await a sunset, or to hang out in the Juan Valdez Café by the Torre del Cable.

ORIENTATION

The two main drags in Manizales—Avenida Santander (Carrera 23) and the Paralela (Carrera 25)—will take you to where you want

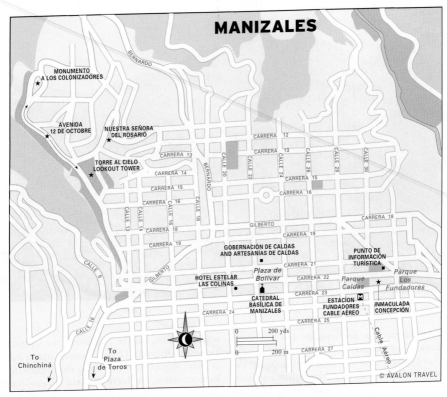

to go in town. They connect the Zona Rosa/ El Cable area with downtown and with the Avenida 12 de October, which leads to Chipre and the Monumento a los Colonizadores.

Sights

As in all the major cities in the region, the real sights are in the tropical jungles. Manizaleños can be envied for having tropical forests at their backdoor. Here you can visit a park, feel like you're far away in the jungles of Colombia, but still be within the city limits. Birds, such as the colorful *barranquero* (blue-crowned motmot; the unofficial bird of Manizales) and many varieties of trees and flowers abound. Just outside of Manizales are coffee haciendas, parks, and gardens, all easily visited from the city. In town, one day should suffice to see the urban attractions.

CENTRO

Downtown Manizales is bustling with activity during weekdays but vacates in a hurry in the evenings. There aren't many sights of interest, save for some republican period architecture and some noteworthy churches. Go on a weekend day if you can.

The **Plaza de Bolívar** (Cras. 21-22) holds an odd sculpture to honor Simón Bolívar created by Antioqueño Rodrigo Arenas Betancourt. It's known as the *Condor-Bolívar,* portraying the Liberator with a body of a condor, the national bird.

Facing the plaza, the neo-gothic **Catedral Basílica de Manizales** (Cra. 22 No. 22-15, tel. 6/883-1880, open until 6:30pm daily) is imposing. Construction began in the late 1920s and was completed in 1936. It replaced the previous cathedral on the same spot, which had

MEDELLÍN

© ANDREW DIER

Manizales is Colombia's coffee capital.

been damaged by earthquakes and had to be demolished. For 360-degree views of Manizales and beyond, climb around 500 steps up the spiral Corredor Polaco (the Polish corridor) in Colombia's tallest church tower. To climb the tower, you'll need a guide (COP$7,000). The tower is open 9am-noon and 2pm-5pm Thursday-Sunday.

Not as grandiose as the cathedral a couple of blocks away, the interior of the **Inmaculada Concepción** (Cl. 30 at Cra. 22, in the Parque Caldas, tel. 6/883-5474, 7am-noon and 2pm-6:30pm daily) is much more beautiful. The neo-gothic-style church, completed in 1909, was built with *bahareque* and *guadua,* natural materials used in construction across Colombia. The wooden rib vaulted ceiling is made of cedar, as are the columns and pews.

CHIPRE

This neighborhood to the west of downtown is known for its views and sunsets. Manizaleños like to boast how Chilean poet Pablo Neruda,

when strolling on the promenade in Chipre along the Avenida 12 de Octubre, marveled at this "sunset factory." Atop the futuristic lookout tower, **La Torre al Cielo** (10am-7pm Tues.-Sun., COP$2,000) you're guaranteed a nice vista.

At the far end of the walkway is the **Monumento a los Colonizadores** (Av. 12 de Octubre and Cra. 9, tel. 6/872-0420, ext. 22, 10am-6pm daily, free), designed by Luis Guillermo Vallejo. This monument honors the courage and sacrifice of Antioquian colonizers who settled the city, and it depicts an Antioquian family on horseback and on foot forging ahead, with cattle in tow, to this part of Colombia during the *colonización antioqueña,* when hundreds of families migrated from Medellín to settle farms in the coffee region area. Manizales residents played a role in building the monument by donating keys and the like to be melted and used in its construction. The sculpture stands atop 20 tons of *piedra de mani* (peanut stone), the namesake for the city. It was inaugurated in 2001. To get to this part

© ANDREW DIER

El Cable is a remnant of a gondola system that transported coffee over the Central Cordillera Mountains.

of the city, look for a bus with a "Chipre" sign along Avenida Santander (Cra. 23).

EL CABLE

One of the city's icons is a soaring wooden tower known as **El Cable** (52 meters/171 feet tall) that once supported the unusual gondola system that transported coffee (10 tons per hour!), other materials, and sometimes people from Manizales over the Central Cordillera. The system reached elevations of 3,700 meters (12,100 feet) and descended to the town of Mariquita (495 meters/1,625 feet). From there the coffee would be transported overland to Honda on the banks of the Río Magdalena. The rest of the journey in Colombia would take the coffee north to the port city of Barranquilla, where it would be transferred to big boats bound for North America and Europe. This system was developed in the 1920s and would last until the early 1960s.

Of the 376 towers that supported the line, this particular tower, which was in the town of Herveo, was the only one built out of wood (all the others were made of iron). They were all supposed to be made of iron, but the boat carrying one of them from Europe to Colombia was sunk by a German submarine in the Atlantic Ocean during World War I. An English engineer in Colombia, who also designed the neat **Estación del Cable,** the adjacent station for the cable transport system, designed this tower using wood found locally. The Estación del Cable, a historic building, appropriately today houses the architecture department for the Universidad Nacional.

RESERVA DEL RÍO BLANCO

An array of birds, some found only in Colombia, can be spotted during an excursion to the **Reserva del Río Blanco** (Vereda Las Palomas, tel. 6/870-3810, cell tel. 310/422-1883, www.fundegar.com, 6am-6pm daily), only three kilometers (two miles) outside of Manizales. Most hostels can arrange this day trip, charging COP$20,000 per person for a guided group hike to strategic places in the jungle apt for spotting birds. Toucans and antpittas can often be seen, but over 362 species have been identified throughout the reserve. From August until March the area receives many migratory birds from North America. Private and longer bird-watching tours are also possible.

An *oso andino* (Andean bear) that lived in captivity for most of his life was adopted and now lives in an enclosed field in the reserve near the cabins. It was decided that he would not be able to be released back into the wild.

There are comfortable lodging options available in the park in two **cabins** (tel. 6/870-3810, cell tel. 310/422-1883, US$55 pp all meals) that have a total of eight rooms. These are specifically for bird-watchers. Birding guides are offered for the additional cost of US$60 for a Spanish-speaking guide and US$90 for a guide who speaks English. The porch of the lodge is an excellent place to commune with hummingbirds, who are regular customers at the hummingbird feeders.

MEDELLÍN

Taxi transportation to the reserve costs COP$25,000 from Manizales.

RECINTO DEL PENSAMIENTO

For a walk in the park, the **Recinto del Pensamiento** (Km. 11 Vía al Magdalena, tel. 6/874-4157, www.recintodelpensamiento.com, COP$3,000) is a tranquil green space with guided nature walks, a chair lift (COP$17,000), a two-hectare orchid forest with 12,000 orchids, and a butterfly farm. The centerpiece of the park is the **Pabellón de Madera,** a large open-air event space made of *guadua* (a type of bamboo) built by a renowned Colombian architect, Simón Vélez.

ECOPARQUE LOS YARUMOS

On undisturbed mountainsides throughout Colombia, you have undoubtedly noticed the silvery-white leaves of the *yarumo blanco* tree. Should you get a closer look, you'll see that the leaves of this tree are actually green; it's a fuzzy layer on them that makes them appear white. The **Ecoparque Los Yarumos** (Cl. 61B No. 15A-01, Barrio Toscana, tel. 6/872-0420 ext. 22, 9am-6pm Tues.-Sun., free) is named for those deceptive trees. A few *yarumos* can be seen in the more than 50 hectares (125 acres) of cloud forest jungle that makes up this park. The park has nature paths, a lookout tower, and activities such as jungle zip lines. To get to the park on public transportation, you can take a bus from the Manizales city center bound for Minitas. It's about a 7- to 10-minute walk from the bus stop to the park entrance. Taxis are also cheap, costing under COP$4,000 from the El Cable area.

HOT SPRINGS

Near Manizales are two popular *termales* (hot springs). Bring your own towel and sandals for both, and visit on a weekday if you want to avoid the crowds.

Near a river, **Tierra Viva** (Km. 2 Vía Enea-Gallinazo, tel. 6/874-3089, www.termalestierraviva.com, 9am-midnight Mon.-Thurs., 9am-1am Fri.-Sun., COP$12,000-14,000) is closest to Manizales and less expensive. It

consists of one pool, some bare-bones changing rooms, and a snack bar.

Considered the better and hotter of the springs, **Termales Otoño** (Km. 5 Vía Antigua El Nevado del Ruiz, tel. 6/874-0280, http://termaleselotono.com, 7am-midnight daily, day pass COP$25,000, COP$107,000-356,000 d) is a hot spring hotel complex a 25-minute ride to the southeast of the city. It's larger, with four pools (though two of these are reserved exclusively for hotel guests).

Festivals and Events

The **Plaza de Toros** (Cra. 27 10A-07, tel. 6/883-8124, www.cormanizales.com), or bullfighting ring, takes center stage every year at Manizales's biggest bacchanal, the **Feria de Manizales** (www.feriademanizales.gov.co), a celebration of the city's founding. During the festivities there are also concerts, a ballad festival (Festival de Trova), and a Miss Coffee beauty pageant. This citywide party is held in early January.

The theater festival in Bogotá, held every two years, is the most important theatrical event in Colombia. In second place is the annual **Festival Internacional de Teatro de Manizales** (www.festivaldemanizales.com). It's always held during the first week of September and attracts theater troupes primarily from the Americas. In addition to performances in theaters throughout the city, free performances are given in parks and plazas, and an educational program for aspiring young actors takes place in schools.

Shopping

Two popular shopping malls with inexpensive food options, movie theaters, and numerous clothing and other shops are **Fundadores** (Cl. 33B No. 20-03, tel. 6/889-4318, www.centrocomercialfundadores.com, 9am-9pm daily) and **Cable Plaza** (Cra. 23 No. 65-11, tel. 6/875-6595, 9am-9pm daily).

For handicrafts, peruse the locally made wares such as woodcarvings and woven items at the **Artesanías de Caldas** (Plaza de Bolívar, Gobernación de Caldas, Cra. 21 and

Clls. 22-23, tel. 6/873-5001, www.artesani-asdecaldas.com, 8am-noon and 2pm-6pm Mon.-Sat.) downtown.

Sports and Recreation

The **Ciclovía** in Manizales takes place every Sunday from 8am to noon along the Avenida Santander (Carrera 23) and other main streets. The last Thursday of each month a **Ciclovía Nocturna** (7pm-10pm) is held. It's the nighttime version of the Ciclovía.

Once Caldas (www.oncecaldas.com.co) is the Manizales soccer club, and their stadium, the **Estadio Palogrande** (Cra. 25 No. 65-00) is in the Zona Rosa, within walking distance from many hostels and hotels. Once Caldas won the Copa Libertadores de America in 2004, defeating Boca Juniors from Buenos Aires, which was a big deal around these parts. Tickets can be purchased in the Cable Plaza Mall (Cra. 23 No. 65-11, tel. 6/875-6595, 9am-9pm daily).

Accommodations

The El Cable area in Manizales is the best place to stay, due to a large number of lodging options and its proximity to restaurants and shopping centers. It's a quiet neighborhood, bustling with international visitors, particularly on Calle 66. There is little traffic on streets here, which is nice; however, that often means that vehicles of all sorts zoom by at high speeds.

One of the long-standing budget accommodations in Manizales is **Mountain Hostels** (Cl. 66 No. 23B-91, tel. 6/887-4736, cell tel. 300/521-6120, www.mountainhostels.com.co, COP$22,000 dorm, COP$60,000 d). Spread over two houses, it has a variety of room types and a small restaurant where you can order a healthy breakfast. Rooms aren't fancy, however.

Hostal Kumanday (Cl. 66 No. 23B-40, tel. 6/887-2682, cell tel. 315/590-7294, www.kumanday.com, COP$25,000 dorm, COP$40,000 pp d) is a quiet and clean option on the same street as Mountain Hostels. There are 10 rooms and one small dorm room, and all options include breakfast (but no fruit). Staff are a little shy. Kumanday has its own, highly

recommended, tour agency that specializes in hiking in and around the Parque Nacional Natural Los Nevados. They also offer a downhill mountain-bike trip (COP$125,000 day trip, 3-person minimum) in the park.

Casa Lassio Hostal (Cl. 66 No. 23B-56, tel. 6/887-6056, cell tel. 310/443-8917, COP$23,000 dorm, COP$35,000 private room pp) has six rooms, and they also organize bike tours.

The Colombian chain Estelar (www.hotelesestelar.com) has three hotels in the Manizales area. They are among the top hotels in the city, and all have spacious and clean rooms, as well as at least one room that is accessible for people with disabilities. Weekend rates tend to be significantly lower than during the week. There are few reasons for wanting to stay in downtown Manizales, but if you do, **Hotel Estelar Las Colinas** (Cra. 22 No. 20-20, tel. 6/884-2009, COP$188,080 d) is the best option (but only on weekends, when traffic, noise, and general urban stress is manageable). The hotel's 60-some rooms are large and clean, but the restaurant and bar area is a little gloomy. A breakfast buffet is available for an additional cost.

The **Estelar El Cable** (Cra. 23C No. 64A-60, tel. 6/887-9690, COP$294,000 d) has 46 rooms over nine floors and is the upscale option in the El Cable/Zona Rosa area. Breakfast and a light dinner are often included in room rates. Rooms are spacious and clean, with pressed wood floors. A small gym offers modern cardio machines.

If you prefer birds and trees, check out Estelar's 32-room hotel at the **Recinto del Pensamiento** (Km. 11 Vía al Magdalena, tel. 6/889-7077, COP$210,000 d). Outside the city, surrounded by nature, this hotel feels a little isolated. It's a popular place for business conferences and events during the week. Rooms are spacious.

Food

For excellent down-home, regional cuisine, head to **Don Juaco** (Cl. 65 No. 23A-44, tel. 6/885-0610, cell tel. 310/830-2218, noon-10pm daily, COP$15,000), which has been serving contented diners for decades. Try the Paisa hamburger: a hamburger sandwiched in between two arepas (cornmeal cakes). Enjoy it or the popular set lunch meals on the pleasant terrace.

For delectable grilled meat dishes, **Palogrande** (Cra. 23C No. 64-18, tel. 6/885-3177, 11am-10pm daily, COP$25,000) is the place you want. Located on a quiet street, it's a rather elegant, open-air place with a nice atmosphere.

For Italian fare, there are two decent options. Try **Spago** (Cl. 59 No. 24A-10, Local 1, tel. 6/885-3328, cell tel. 321/712-3860, noon-3pm and 6pm-10pm Mon.-Sat., noon-3pm Sun., COP$25,000), which is one of the upmarket restaurants in town, with tasty thin-crust pizzas. **Il Forno** (Cra. 23 No. 73-86, tel. 6/886-8515, noon-10pm Mon.-Sat., noon-3pm Sun., COP$22,000) is a family-style chain restaurant with a great view of the city.

Vegetarian restaurants exist in Manizales, but it's difficult to track them down. **Orellana** (Cl. 50 No. 26-40, tel. 6/885-3907, noon-3pm Mon.-Sat., COP$10,000) serves healthy set lunches and is located in the Versalles neighborhood. It's near the supermarket Confamiliares de la 50. **Rushi** (Cra. 23C No. 62-73, tel. 6/881-0326, cell tel. 310/538-8387, 11am-9pm Mon.-Sat., 11am-3pm Sun., COP$12,000) is a vegetarian restaurant close to the Zona Rosa area. It offers set lunches and á la carte dishes such as paella and vegetarian fried rice.

In Colombia, you are never far from a bakery selling sweets. In Manizales there is one bakery where you can have your sweets without the guilt. At **Cero Azúcar** (Cra. 23C No. 62-42, tel. 6/881-0625, 8:30am-8pm daily), all their cakes, cookies, and ice creams are made with the natural sweetener stevia.

A fantastic place for a late afternoon cappuccino and snack is 🍵 **Juan Valdez Café** (Cra. 23B No. 64-55, tel. 6/885-9172, 10am-9pm daily). Yes, it's a chain, and there's one in any self-respecting mall in Colombia. But this one is different: Locals proudly boast that it is the largest Juan Valdez on the planet. But what

truly sets this one apart is its great location, under the shadow of the huge wooden tower that once supported the coffee cable car line that ran from Manizales to Mariquita.

Information and Services

A **Punto de Información Turística** (Cra. 22 at Cl. 31, tel. 6/873-3901, 7am-7pm daily) can be of assistance in organizing excursions to parks and coffee farms throughout Caldas. The staff are eager to help. A small **tourist office** is also located in the main hall of the Terminal de Transportes (Cra. 43 No. 65-100).

In case of an emergency, Manizales has a single emergency line: 123. To speak directly with the police, call 112.

Getting There and Around

Avianca (Cra. 23 No. 62-16, Local 110, tel. 6/886-3137, www.avianca.com, 8am-6:30pm Mon.-Fri., 8am-1pm Sat.) and **ADA** (airport tel. 6/874-6332, 5:45am-5:45pm Mon.-Fri., 8am-5:30pm Sat., 3pm-5:30pm Sun.) serve **Aeropuerto La Nubia** (tel. 6/874-5451), about 10 kilometers (six miles) southeast of downtown. But the runway is often shrouded in clouds. Because of this, the airport is closed 35 percent of the time and always at night.

There is regular and speedy **bus service** to both Armenia (COP$17,500, 2 hours) and Pereira (COP$11,000, 70 mins.). **Arauca** (www.empresaarauca.com.co) runs buses to Pereira every 15 minutes and is considered a good company. Buses bound for Cali and Medellín cost around COP$35,000-40,000 and take five hours each. Buses to Bogotá cost COP$47,000 and take about nine hours.

The **Terminal de Transportes** (Cra. 43 No. 65-100, tel. 6/878-5641, www.terminaldemanizales.com) is spacious, orderly, and clean. From there it is about a 15-minute taxi ride to the Zona Rosa area. The terminal adjoins the cable car **Cable Aereo** station. The cable car route transports passengers from the terminal (Estación Cambulos) to the Fundadores station (Cra. 23 between Clls. 31-32) in the Centro.

Public transportation is not the most organized in Manizales. Private buses are easy to use, but you'll probably have to ask someone for help to determine which bus to flag down. To get downtown from the Zona Rosa, take a bus bound for Chipre.

Taxicabs are also plentiful. **Guillermo Ortíz** (cell tel. 313/766-8376) is highly recommended. Reliable cab companies include **Taxi La Feria** (tel. 6/884-8888), **Taxi Ya** (tel. 6/878-0000), and **Taxi Express** (tel. 6/880-2000). Many hotels and hostels routinely work with one or two specific taxi drivers, but if not, they will always order a cab for you.

Walking from the Zona Rosa area, along the Avenida Santander, to downtown will take about 45 minutes.

COFFEE FARMS

The Caldas countryside is home to coffee haciendas, large and small. Hacienda Venecia and Hacienda Guayabal are two of the most highly recommended for coffee tours, as well as overnight stays. They are located near Chinchiná, only a 30-minute drive from Manizales.

Hacienda Venecia

One of the most well-known, organized, and most visited coffee farms is **Hacienda Venecia** (Vereda El Rosario, Vía a Chinchiná, cell tel. 320/636-5719, www.haciendavenecia.com, coffee tour COP$35,000, COP$70,000-250,000 d). This large working coffee plantation has been in the same family for four generations, and their coffee was the first in Colombia to receive UTZ certification for sustainable farming, in 2002. The farm is set far from the highway, providing a peaceful atmosphere. When you're there, you're surrounded by coffee plants growing everywhere you look.

If you are day-tripping, organizing an excursion to the farm for a coffee tour is easy from Manizales. In fact, you won't have to do much at all except inform the hostel or hotel where you are staying that you'd like to go. The Hacienda Venecia makes a daily pickup at the main hostels in town at around 9am.

Tours are given at 9:30am with an additional tour offered at 2:30pm, depending on demand. The 2.5-hour tour begins with a comprehensive presentation of coffee-growing in Colombia and in the world, the many different aromas of coffee, and how to differentiate between a good bean and a bad bean. (And you'll be offered a knock-your-socks-off espresso to boot.) Later, the tour heads outside through the plantation, where you'll see coffee plants at all stages in the growing process. You'll also be able to observe the soaking and drying process. At the end, in the lovely original hacienda house, it's time to roast some beans and drink another freshly roasted cup of Venecia coffee. A typical lunch, such as *ajiaco* (chicken and potato soup), is offered as well (COP$10,000) at the end of the tour. A farm tour by Jeep and private tours (both COP$50,000) can also be arranged.

There are lodging options suitable for all budgets at Venecia. In the hostel, often a lively center of activity, accommodations are basic (and bathrooms are shared) but comfortable. For more luxury and seclusion, you may want to stay at the old hacienda house.

Other activities at the farm include horseback riding (for an additional fee) or walks around the plantation on your own. This is particularly pleasant to do early in the morning, when birds (more than 116 species!) are chirping.

Hacienda Guayabal

Near Venecia, **Hacienda Guayabal** (Km. 3 Vía Chinchiná-Pereira, cell tel. 314/772-4895, www.haciendaguayabal.com, tour COP$30,000, COP$95,000 pp all meals) has a dramatic setting, with mountains and valleys covered in coffee crops and *guadua* (bamboo) completely enveloping the hacienda. This is indeed a coffee farm, and one of the pioneers in coffee farm tourism, but equally interesting is to take a nature walk through the *guaduales* (forests of Colombia's bamboo) that always spring up along water sources. This hacienda has been in Doña María Teresa's family for around 50 years.

If you come, you might as well stay, so that you can enjoy the peace and warm hospitality of this special place. While accommodations in the six rooms are not luxurious, they are more than adequate. Meals are delicious, one of the things for which Guayabal is known. Tours around the *finca* (farm) take about two hours, and you learn about the coffee process as you maneuver along the rows of orderly coffee plants. In addition, you can hike up to a spectacular lookout on a mountainside for breathtaking views of the hills, the valleys, the forests, and the farms all around. Near the guesthouse is a hut made from *guadua* with recycled floor tiles that has a small coffee bar where you can have a cup of coffee and wait for birds of every color and shape to fly up to nibble on a piece of banana. Tranquility is the watchword here; it's no wonder Guayabal is occasionally host to meditation retreats.

◖ SALAMINA

Designated as one of Colombia's most beautiful pueblos, Salamina features history, beauty, personality, and spectacular countryside; yet, for the most part, it remains off of most tourists' radar. When you visit this historic town, you'll feel as if you have stumbled upon a hidden gem. The historic center of Salamina is marked by colorful and well-preserved two-story houses with their stunning woodwork, doors, and balconies. Salamina is often called the *pueblo madre* (mother town), as it was one of the first settlements of the Antioquian colonization. It's older than Manizales.

Sights

The **Plaza de Bolívar** (Clls. 4-5 between Cras. 6-7) is the center of activity in Salamina. It's an attractive plaza with a gazebo and large fountain brought over from Germany. Carried by mules over the mountains from the coast, it took a year to arrive, in several pieces, to its final destination. The **Basílica Menor La Inmaculada Concepción** (Cl. 4 between Cras. 6-7) has an unusual architecture. The single nave worship hall is rectangular and flat with wooden beams and no columns. The church was designed by an English architect, who is said to have modeled it on the First Temple in ancient Jerusalem.

The **Casa Rodrigo Jiménez Mejía** (Cl. 4 and Cra. 6) is the most photographed house in Salamina. The colors of this exceptionally preserved house were chosen in an interesting way. An owner of the house called kids from the town to gather in the plaza and to give the owner their proposal on what colors to use for the house's exterior. The winner was a four-year-old girl, who chose bright orange, yellow, and green.

The **Casa de la Cultura** (Cra. 6 No. 6-06, tel. 6/859-5016, 8am-noon and 2pm-5pm Mon.-Fri., free) displays photos of old Salamina. It's often a hub of activity. It's also known as the Casa del Diablo, and a jovial devil wood-carving above the door greets visitors as they enter.

For decades, the **Cementerio San Esteban** (Cra. 3 between Clls. 2-4, no phone), the town cemetery, was divided into three sections: one for the rich, one for the poor, and another for so-called "N.N." bodies (non-identified corpses, or "no names"). A wall was built to divide the rich from the poor, but it was knocked down at the behest of a priest in 1976. A skull and crossbones is displayed over the cemetery entrance. There is a small neo-gothic style chapel (open occasionally) on the grounds.

In the village of **San Félix,** 30 kilometers (19 miles) east of Salamina, you can hike through serene countryside and admire a forest of *palmas de cera* (wax palms) from the hills above. Afterwards, on the village plaza, ask at the stores for a refreshing *helado de salpicón* (ice cream made from chunks of fresh fruit in frozen watermelon juice). A bus makes the round-trip (COP$10,000 each way) to San Felix twice a day, once in the early morning and again in the afternoon. It leaves from the plaza.

Festivals and Events

Salamina's **Semana Santa** (Holy Week) celebrations, which fall in either March or April, are not that well known, but it is, nonetheless, a great time to get to know this cute town. Orchids and other flowers adorn the balconies of houses, adding even more color. In addition, free classical, religious, and jazz music

© ANDREW DIER

a friendly devil in Salamina

concerts are held in churches, plazas, and even the cemetery.

San Felix is known for its **Exposición de Ganado Normando** in July, when local farmers show off their best Norman cows, with various competitions. It's an important event for ranchers throughout the region, and also a chance to see an authentic display of Paisa culture.

Halloween is a big deal in Salamina. Here it's called the **Tarde de María La Parda,** named after a local woman who is said to have sold her soul to the devil in order to obtain riches. Her ghost supposedly causes mischief in the countryside every now and then. Events for Tarde de María La Parda take place in Plaza de Bolívar, and there are costume parties at night on that day.

December 7 is a special day—or rather, night—to be in Salamina. That's when the lights are turned off in Salamina, and the streets and balconies are illuminated with handmade lanterns made by locals. This beautiful celebration is called the **Noche de las Luces,** a night to stroll the streets and enjoy the special atmosphere. Locals greet each other serving sweets, snacks, or drinks. Music fills the air and the evening culminates in a fireworks show.

Accommodations

The best place to stay in Salamina by a long shot is the ◖ **Casa de Lola Garcia** (Cl. 6 No. 7-54, tel. 6/859-5919, www.lacasadelolagarcia. com, COP$120,000 d), which opened its doors in 2012. The dream of a native Salamineño, musician Mauricio Cardona García, the carefully restored house was once the home of his grandmother, Lola García. Rooms are spacious and comfortable. If you provide Mauricio with some notice, meals at the hotel can be arranged.

Two other hotels in town, while not fancy, will do the trick if you're sticking to a budget. **Hospedaje Casa Real** (Cra. 6A No. 5-33, tel. 6/859-6355, cell tel. 311/784-2364, www. hospedajecasareal.wix.com, COP$50,000-80,000 d) has 24 rooms and is around the corner from the Plaza de Bolívar. The owners also have a *finca* with lodging facilities in the

MEDELLÍN

a campesino near Salamina

countryside. **Hotel Colonial** (Cl. 5 No. 6-74, tel. 6/859-5078, cell tel. 314/627-9124, hotel-colonial2011@hotmail.com, COP$35,000-50,000 d) is right on the square and has a variety of room options. In both of these hotels, ask to see the rooms before you check in, as their characteristics vary.

Based in Manizales, the travel agency **Rosa de los Vientos** (Centro Comercial Parque Caldas Nivel 2, Local PB45, tel. 6/883-5940, www.turismorosadelosvientos.com) can arrange a home stay (COP$25,000-35,000 pp) in one of the many historic homes in Salamina. The owner, Jackeline Rendón, is from Salamina, knows the owners well, and will match you with a good fit.

Food

Popular and atmospheric **Tierra Paisa** (no phone, 8am-9pm daily, COP$7,000), below the Hotel Colonial on the park, serves typical Colombian food, like *bandeja paisa* (a quintessential Paisa dish of beans, various meats, yuca, and potatoes), at incredibly low prices.

You can't leave Salamina without trying their specialties. One is *macana*, a hot drink made of milk, ground up cookies, cinnamon, and sugar. The other is *huevos al vapor*, a boiled egg that is methodically steamed using giant coffee urns and served in a coffee cup. For the quintessential Salamina breakfast, go for both.

Getting There and Around

There is frequent **shared taxi service** to Salamina from Manizales, costing (COP$11,000). These depart from the Terminal de Transportes (Cra. 43 No. 65-100) in Manizales.

One **bus** leaves Medellín at 7am daily bound for Salamina and other communities in the area. It departs from the **Terminal del Sur** (Cra. 65 No. 8B-91, tel. 4/444-8020 or 4/361-1186). The trip takes 4-6 hours on rural roads.

◖ PARQUE NACIONAL NATURAL LOS NEVADOS

This national park covers 583 square kilometers (225 miles) of rugged terrain along the Central

Cordillera between the cities of Manizales to the north, Ibagué to the southeast, and Pereira to the northwest. Whether you do a day trip or a multi-day trek, a visit to **Parque Nacional Natural Los Nevados** (www.parquesnacionales.gov.co) allows you to enjoy first-hand the stark beauty of the upper reaches of the Andes, far above the forest line, with its intriguing vegetation and fauna. Within the park are three snowcapped volcanoes, **Nevado del Ruiz** (5,325 meters/17,470 feet), **Nevado del Tolima** (5,215 meters/17,110 feet), and **Nevado Santa Isabel** (4,950 meters/16,240 feet), as well as myriad lakes, such as the **Laguna del Otún.**

This rugged landscape was formed by volcanic activity and later sculpted by huge masses of glaciers. At their maximum extension, these glaciers covered an area of 860 square kilometers (332 square miles). They began to recede 14,000 years ago and, according to a 2013 study by the Colombian Institute of Hydrology, Meteorology, and Environmental Studies (IDEAM), will completely disappear by 2030.

Most of the park consists of *páramo,* a unique tropical high altitude ecosystem, and super *páramo,* rocky terrain above the *páramo* and below the snow line. *Páramo* is a highland tropical ecosystem that thrives where UV radiation is higher, oxygen is scarcer, and where temperatures vary considerably from daytime to nighttime, when the mercury falls below freezing. It is the kingdom of the eerily beautiful *frailejones,* plants with statuesque tall trunks and thick yellow-greenish leaves. Other *páramo* vegetation includes shrubs, grasses, and cushion plants (*cojines*). The super *páramo* has a stark, moonlike landscape, with occasional dunes of volcanic ash. Though it's largely denuded of vegetation, bright yellow plants called *litamo real* and orange moss provide splashes of color. On a clear day, the views from the *páramo* or super *páramo* of the snowcapped volcanoes and lakes are simply stunning.

The black and white Andean condor, *vultur gryphus,* with its wingspan of up to three meters (10 feet), can sometimes be spotted gliding along the high cliffs in the park. While it

is estimated that there are over 10,000 of the birds on the continent (mostly in Argentina), there are few remaining in Colombia. Some estimates report that by the mid-1980s, there were no more than 15 left in Colombia, due in large part to poaching by cattle ranchers. In an effort to boost their numbers in Colombia, a reintroduction program was initiated in the park (and in other parts of the country) in the 1990s in conjunction with the San Diego Zoo, where newborns were hatched. Today it is estimated that there are 200-300 condors soaring above Colombia's Andean highlands. Numbers of the endangered birds in Los Nevados range 8-15. Other fauna includes spectacled bears (*oso de anteojos*), tapirs, weasels, squirrels, bats, and many species of birds.

The Nevado del Tolima and Nevado del Ruiz volcanoes are considered active, with the Ruiz presenting more activity. In 1986 it erupted, melting the glacier, which in turn created a massive mudslide that engulfed the town of Armero, burying an estimated 20,000 of the town's 29,000 residents.

ORIENTATION

The Northern Sector of the park includes the Nevado del Ruiz, with its three craters (Arenales, La Piraña, and La Olleta), and extends south to the extinct Cisne volcano and Laguna Verde. This part can be accessed by vehicle.

The Southern Sector includes everything from the Nevado Santa Isabel south to the Quindío peak, as well as Nevado del Tolima. This area has fewer visitors as access is only by foot or by horse, from Manizales, Pereira, Salento, or Ibagué.

The Northern Sector

The **Northern Sector** (turnoff to Las Brisas entry point at Km. 43 Vía Manizales-Honda, tel. 6/887-1611, www.parquesnacionales.gov.co, 8am-2pm daily high season, COP$43,500 for nonresidents, COP$28,500 for residents, COP$24,500 for students with valid student ID, COP$5,000 per vehicle) is the most visited part of the park. Until recently, day

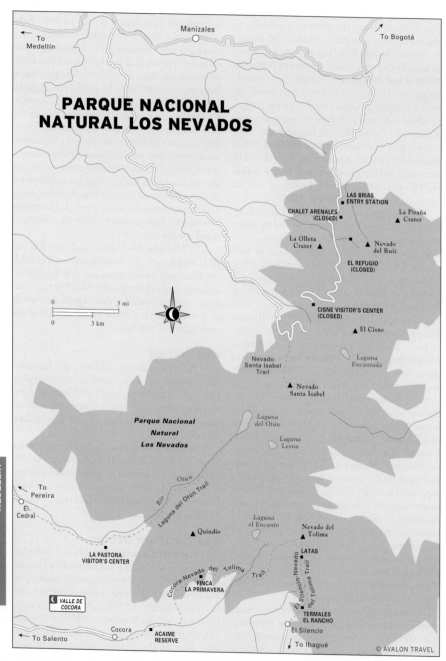

To Medellín

Manizales

To Bogotá

PARQUE NACIONAL NATURAL LOS NEVADOS

LAS BRIAS
ENTRY STATION

CHALET ARENALES
(CLOSED)

La Piraña
Crater

La Olleta
Crater

Nevado
del Ruiz

EL REFUGIO
(CLOSED)

0   3 mi

0   3 km

CISNE VISITOR'S CENTER
(CLOSED)

El Cisne

Laguna
Encantada

Nevado
Santa Isabel
Trail

Nevado
Santa Isabel

Parque Nacional

Natural

Los Nevados

Laguna
del Otún

Laguna
Leona

To
Pereira

El
Cedral

Río Otún

Laguna del Otún Trail

Laguna
el Encanto

Nevado del
Tolima

Quindío

LATAS

LA PASTORA
VISITOR'S CENTER

Cocora-Nevado del Tolima Trail

El Silencio-Nevado del Tolima Trail

VALLE DE
COCORA

FINCA
LA PRIMAVERA

TERMALES
EL RANCHO

Cocora

ACAIME
RESERVE

El Silencio

To Salento

To Ibagué

© AVALON TRAVEL

the lunar-like landscape of the Parque Nacional Natural Los Nevados

trippers could drive from Manizales right up to El Refugio, a camp at the base of the Ruiz, and climb up to the main Arenales crater (5,325 meters/17,470 feet) in a strenuous three-hour hike. The Cisne visitors center provided lodging in this sector of the park and allowed easy access to the Nevado Santa Isabel and Laguna Verde.

Due to increased activity at Ruiz, the entire Northern Sector was closed from March 2012 through early 2013. In January 2013 a small area, from the Las Brisas entry station to the Valle de las Tumbas (also known as Valle del Silencio) was reopened to visitors in organized tours and private vehicles. El Refugio at the base of the Ruiz, the Chalet Arenales camping site, and the Cisne visitors center are off limits. At the time of writing, there were no plans to reopen these facilities.

If you don't have a vehicle, the only way to visit this part of the park is on an organized day tour from Manizales. These tours leave at 6am, drive to Las Brisas park entry station, and continue on to the Valle de las Tumbas, making stops along the way to gaze at the landscape, particularly the Nevado del Ruiz and La Olleta crater (weather permitting), and to view birds and vegetation. On the way back to Manizales, the tour stops for an hour at the rundown Termales de Ruiz outside the park for a quick soak in warm sulfur-laden waters. The tours return to Manizales by 5pm. This experience will be unsatisfying for people who want to move their legs. **Ecosistemas** (Cra. 21 No. 23-21, Manizales, tel. 6/880-8300, www. ecosistemastravel.com) offers this day tour for COP$100,000 for residents and COP$120,000 for nonresidents.

If you have a vehicle (a car with 4WD is not necessary) you can drive the Brisas-Valle de las Tumbas segment but you will be required to take a guide (included in the entry price) in your vehicle.

Another possibility to view Nevado del Ruiz without entering the park is to take an early morning milk truck *(lechero)* leaving Manizales at 5am to El Sifón, northeast of the park. The trip affords beautiful views of the *páramo* and the Ruiz in the distance and a chance to share a ride with farmers from the region. At El Sifón you can catch breakfast and walk back along the road to be picked up by the truck as it returns to Manizales, where you will arrive around noon. All the major hostels in Manizales know about how to organize this excursion.

The Southern Sector

The **Southern Sector** offers numerous trekking opportunities, several of which can be done without a guide. There are no official entry stations and permits are not required, but be prepared to pay an entry fee if you bump into a ranger. If you want to be meticulous, you can pay in advance by contacting the Parques Nacionales office in Bogotá (tel. 1/353-2400, www.parquesnacionales.gov.co), sending the names of the visitors to the park, depositing the entry fee at a bank, and receiving a permit by email. However, this is a huge hassle and very few people do it.

Nevado Santa Isabel Trek

A spectacular day trek from Manizales is up to the snow line of the **Nevado Santa Isabel.** It is a long day trip, starting with a bumpy 50-kilometer (31-mile) drive to the border of the park at Conejeras and then a three-hour (5.5-kilometer/3.4-mile) hike up the canyon of the Río Campo Alegre and then to the snow line. This hike requires good physical condition as it takes you from an elevation of 4,000 meters (13,100 feet) up to 4,750 meters (15,600 feet) through *páramo* and super *páramo*. More serious mountaineers can extend the trek to the summit of the Nevado Santa Isabel (4,950 meters/16,240 feet) by camping past Conejeras and doing an early morning ascent to the top. At sunrise, the views onto the surrounding high mountain landscape, with the Nevado del Ruiz and Nevado del Tolima in the background, are magnificent. The ascent to the top requires specialized gear.

There is no public transportation to Conejeras and the trails are not clearly marked, so an organized tour from Manizales is the way to go. A recommended tour operator is **Kumanday** (Cl. 66 No. 23B-40, Manizales, tel. 6/887-2682, cell tel. 315/590-7294, kumandaycolombia@gmail.com, www.kumanday.com). The folks at **Mountain Hostels** (Cl. 66 No. 23B-137, Manizales, tel. 6/887-4736, www.mountainhostels.com.co) can also help you organize this trek.

Laguna del Otún Trek

A popular three-day trek from Pereira is to the **Laguna del Otún.** The starting point is El Cedral, a *vereda* (village) 21 kilometers (13 miles) east of Pereira at an altitude of 2,100 meters (6,900 feet). The end point of the trek at the lake is at 3,950 meters (13,000 feet). This 19-kilometer (12-mile) hike provides an incredible close-up view of the transitions from humid tropical forest to higher altitude tropical forests and the *páramo*. The trek follows the valley of the crystalline Río Otún, first through the Parque Regional Natural Ucumarí and then into the Parque Nacional Natural Los Nevados. It's not too strenuous. Most trekkers split the climb into two segments, camping at El Bosque or Jordín on the way up and spending one night at the Laguna del Otún. The return hike can be done in one day. The path is easy to follow, though quite rocky and muddy. A guide is not necessary.

The only accommodation along this route is at the **Centro de Visitantes La Pastora** (6 km/4 mi from El Cedral toward Laguna del Otún, no phone, cell tel. 312/200-7711, COP$22,000 pp) in the Parque Regional Natural Ucumarí. The dormitory-style rooms are clean and comfortable in this cozy lodge. Meals (COP$6,000-9,000) by the fireplace are excellent. It is possible to buy snacks along the way, but there is no food at the *laguna,* so bring cooking equipment and food along with tents and sleeping bags.

To get to El Cedral from Pereira, take a *chiva* (rural bus) offered by **Transportes Florida** (tel. 6/331-0488, COP$5,000, 2 hrs.), which departs from Calle 12 and Carrera 9 in Pereira. On weekdays, the bus departs at 7am, 9am, and 3pm. On weekends there is an additional bus at noon. The buses return from El Cedral approximately at 11am, 2pm, and 5pm.

The Laguna del Otún can also be visited on an organized tour in a long day trip from Pereira. This involves leaving Pereira at 5am and driving 88 kilometers (55 miles) to Potosí (3,930 meters/12,895 feet) near the park border and then hiking two hours to the lake. This is not a strenuous walk. A recommended tour operator in Pereira for this excursion is **Cattleya Ser** (Cl. 99 No. 14-78, La Florida, cell tel. 314/642-6691 or 311/380-8126, www.cattleyaser.com.co). The **Kolibrí Hostel** (tel. 6/331-3955, cell tel. 321/646-9275, www.kolibrihostel.com) in Pereira also offers guided treks to the laguna.

Nevado del Tolima and Paramillo del Quindío Treks

There are two ways to reach the classically cone-shaped Nevado del Tolima (5,215 meters/17,110 feet). The somewhat easier and more scenic route is from Vereda del Cocora near Salento, which takes four days. A more strenuous route is up from El Silencio, near Ibagué, which can be done in two days.

From **Vereda del Cocora** (2,200 meters/7,215 feet), you hike 7-8 hours (13.5 kilometers/8.4 miles) through the Valle del Cocora, up the Río Quindío canyon, through the Páramo Romerales to the Finca La Primavera at 3,680 meters (12,075 feet). There you spend the night (COP$10,000 pp) and take a simple meal. On the second day you hike 6-7 hours (12 kilometers/7.5 miles) to a campsite at 4,400 meters (14,450 feet) near the edge of the super *páramo.* On the third day, you depart the campsite at 2am and climb a further 8 kilometers (5 miles) to reach the rim of the Tolima crater at 7 or 8am, when there are incredible views to the Quindío, Santa Isabel, Cisne, and Ruiz peaks. That evening you sleep again at the Finca La Primavera and return to Vereda del Cocora on the following day. The path is not clearly marked and it is easy to lose your way (there's a reason why one part is called the Valle de los Perdidos or Valley of the Lost!), so it is best go with a guide. The ascent to the glacier requires specialized gear.

From Ibagué the starting point for the trek to Nevado del Tolima is **El Silencio,** a small *vereda* (settlement) 28 kilometers (17 miles) north of the city at the end of the beautiful Río Combeima river canyon. From El Silencio, you'll walk 2.5 kilometers (1.5 miles) along a mountain path to **El Rancho Tolima Termales** (tel. 8/266-2152, cell tel. 310/817-2526, www.ranchotolimatermales.com, 24 hours daily, COP$5,000) hot springs. From there, there are several routes up to the top of Tolima. The most direct route is via La Cueva. It is a strenuous six- to eight-hour (15-kilometer/9-mile) hike up dense tropical forest, *páramo,* and super *páramo* to **Latas,** an unmarked camp spot near some large rusting metal sheets. Water is available nearby.

From Latas, the ascent up the glacier to the rim of the volcano takes 3-4 hours and requires crampons and an ice axe. The return trip takes 5-6 hours, not including a soothing dip at the *termales.* Unless you are an experienced mountaineer, a guide is necessary.

Another less traveled but beautiful hike is to the **Paramillo del Quindío** (4,750 meters/15,585 feet), an extinct volcano that once was covered by a glacier. The 17-kilometer (10.5-mile) ascent from La Primavera Farm takes eight hours and can be done in one long day. Alternatively, you can split the hike in two, camping so as to arrive at the top of the crater in the early morning when visibility is best. There are spectacular views of the Tolima, Santa Isabel, and Ruiz volcanoes. This is a strenuous but not technically difficult climb.

Recommended guides for the Tolima and Quindío treks are **Páramo Trek** in Salento (cell tel. 311/745-3761, paramotrek@gmail.com) and **Truman David Alfonso Bejarano** in Ibagué (cell tel. 315/292-7395, trumandavid01@gmail.com), who can organize excursions from Salento or Ibagué. His blog (www.truman-adventure.blogspot.com) has detailed information about the various possible routes up to Nevado del Tolima.

Mountain Biking

There are many possible mountain-bike trips through the park, ranging from the easy (all downhill) to the fairly strenuous. **Kumanday** (Cl. 66 No. 23B-40, Manizales, tel. 6/887-2682, cell tel. 315/590-7294, kumandaycolombia@gmail.com, www.kumanday.com) offers several excursions.

ARMENIA

The defining moment for Colombia's Ciudad Milagro (Miracle City) arrived uninvited on the afternoon of January 25, 1999, when an earthquake registering 6.4 on the Richter scale shook the city. One thousand people lost their lives, nearly half the city became instantly displaced, and thousands of nearby coffee farms were destroyed. The miracle of this coffee region city can be seen in how it rapidly rebuilt and began to thrive once more.

As is the case with sister cities Pereira and Manizales, Armenia was settled in the late 19th century by Antioquian colonizers. The city is not a tourist destination itself, but you'll be astonished to see, within just a few blocks of the

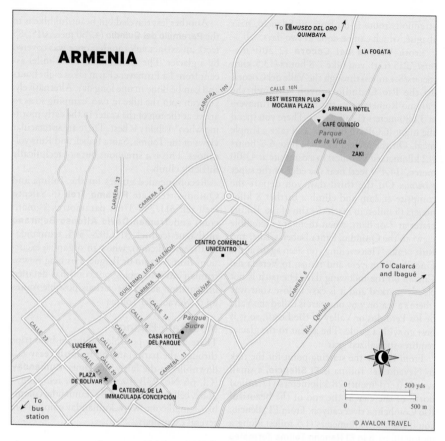

ARMENIA

To **MUSEO DEL ORO QUIMBAYA**

LA FOGATA

CALLE 10N

CARRERA 19N

BEST WESTERN PLUS
MOCAWA PLAZA

ARMENIA HOTEL

CAFÉ QUINDÍO

Parque
de la Vida

ZAKI

CARRERA 23

CARRERA 22

CENTRO COMERCIAL
UNICENTRO

GUILLERMO LEÓN VALENCIA

CARRERA 18

BOLÍVAR

CARRERA 6

CALLE 15

CALLE 13

Parque
Sucre

CASA HOTEL
DEL PARQUE

Río Quindío

To Calarcá
and Ibagué

CALLE 23

CALLE 17

LUCERNA

CALLE 19

CALLE 21

CALLE 20

CARRERA 17

PLAZA
DE BOLÍVAR

CATEDRAL DE LA
IMMACULADA CONCEPCIÓN

To
bus
station

0   500 yds
0   500 m

© AVALON TRAVEL

city center, a sea of green coffee farms. That lush countryside is the real attraction.

The city was founded in 1889 and initially named Villa Holguín to honor then-president Carlos Holguín Mallarino. It is widely believed that the city was renamed Armenia to honor victims of the 1894-1896 Hamidian massacres of ethnic Armenians living in the Ottoman Empire.

ORIENTATION

Armenia is a small city by Colombian standards, home to 294,000 residents. Although there is not much to see or do downtown, it is a compact area, and it's easy to get around on foot. The northern areas of the city are where the hotels, malls, and restaurants are to be

found. That part of town, around the Hotel Armenia, is also walkable.

Carreras run north-south and *calles* east-west. Main drags include Carreras 14 (Avenida Bolívar), 18, and 19, as well as the Avenida Centenario, which runs parallel to the Río Quindío on the eastern side of the city. Carrera 14 is pedestrian-only downtown.

Sights

Standing in downtown Armenia's **Plaza de Bolívar** (between Cras. 12-13 and Clls. 20-21) is a sculpture of Simón Bolívar (northern side of the plaza) and the love-it-or-hate-it **Monumento al Esfuerzo,** by Rodrigo Arenas Betancourt, built in the 1960s. This sculpture stands in remembrance of the sacrifices made and hardships faced by Antioquian settlers who arrived in the area seeking opportunity. The modern **Catedral de la Inmaculada Concepción** (Cra. 12 between Clls. 20-21, hours vary), completed in 1972, is a concrete, triangular-shaped building that replaced the previous cathedral, which had stood since 1927. The plaza is on the stark side.

A stroll down the **pedestrian street** from the Plaza de Bolívar to the Parque Sucre is a pleasant way to see the modern downtown at its busiest.

MUSEO DEL ORO QUIMBAYA
Even if you have visited the world-famous Museo del Oro in Bogotá, it is worth the trek to Armenia just to visit the **Museo del Oro Quimbaya** (Av. Bolívar No. 40N-80, tel. 6/749-8433, www.banrepcultural.org, 10am-5pm Tues.-Sun., free) on the outskirts of town. In contrast to the Gold Museum in Bogotá, this museum, designed by famed architect Rogelio Salmona, focuses exclusively on the Quimbaya nation, which predominated in the coffee region before the Spanish conquest. Much of the museum is devoted to ceramic and gold decorative and ceremonial items that were found in the area. Excellent explanations in English provide interesting background information on the history, ways of life, and traditions of the Quimbaya people.

Festivals and Events
Armenios celebrate their city's founding in October with their **Fiestas Cuyabras** or Fiestas de Armenia. (People from Armenia are also called Cuyabras, after a bush that produced pumpkin-like fruit that was once widespread in the region.) City parks and plazas are the stages for cultural events, a beauty pageant, and a fun Yipao (Jeep) parade. These U.S. military Jeeps (called Jeep Willys), a symbol of the region, began arriving in Colombia around 1946, after World War II.

Recreation
Several city parks and plazas are great places to enjoy the delicious Armenia climate. These include the **Parque de la Vida** (Cra. 13 at Cl. 8N) and the **Parque Sucre** (Cra. 13 at Cl. 13) downtown, which is adjacent to a delightful pedestrian street. Locals and visitors gather in the late afternoon at the **Café Quindío** in the park for *onces* (tea time).

The **Parque El Bosque** (Cl. 21 No. 22-23) is a green space that has a bust of Abraham Lincoln that was donated to the city by the Armenian community of Fresno, California, as a way of expressing their gratitude for naming the city in solidarity with the decimated Armenian nation in the early 20th century. The bullfighting ring is in this park.

Globos Colombia (cell tel. 320/667-7818, www.globoscolombia.com, COP$390,000) offers commanding views of the Zona Cafetera from a hot-air balloon. Flights usually depart 6am-6:30am and last 45 minutes. A hearty Paisa breakfast is included in the tour. Flights depart from nearby Armenia as well as near Pereira, about an hour's drive away.

Shopping
The **Centro Comercial Unicentro** (Cra. 14 No. 6-02, tel. 6/731-2667, 8am-9pm daily) along the Avenida Bolívar has the usual array of Colombian mall stores, fast food joints, an Éxito department store, a movie theater, several ATMs, and food and coffee courts (with spectacular views of the bucolic valley). **El Portal del Quindío** (Av. Bolívar 19N No. 46-057, www.elportaldelquindio.com, 8am-9pm daily) is down the road from Unicentro and offers similar shops.

Accommodations
The **Casa Quimbaya** (Cl. 16N No. 14-92, tel. 6/732-3086, cell tel. 312/590-0066, www.casaquimbaya.com, COP$20,000 dorm, COP$60,000 d) is the budget hostel option in Armenia. It is near the Universidad del Quindío. There are two dorm rooms and four private rooms. It's in an ordinary-looking house on a quiet street, very close to the action of Carrera 14.

A midrange option downtown is **Casa Hotel del Parque** (Cra. 14 No. 12-26, tel. 6/731-3166, www.casahoteldelparque.com, COP$99,000 d). It has five rooms and a great location on the Parque Sucre and the pedestrian street.

The **Armenia Hotel** (Av. Bolívar and Cl. 8N, tel. 6/746-0099, cell tel. 320/696-9111, www.armeniahotel.com.co, COP$220,000 d) has long been considered the most elegant place to stay in town. However, it has lost some of its panache over the years. It's got 129 rooms on nine floors, and a big atrium smells of eucalyptus emanating from the steam room. Rooms and bathrooms are spacious, the beds are fine, and you could go to town raiding the mini-bar. A spa, pool, and small gym are available on the premises, and guests also have privileges at a gym four blocks away.

The first U.S. hotel chain will soon be arriving in Armenia in the form of **Best Western Plus Mocawa**. It will have 97 rooms over 16 floors, a gym and spa, and a coffee bar in the lobby. Its location on the Avenida Bolívar is close to malls. It is scheduled to open in late 2013.

Food

Armenia's gastronomic center is uptown along Avenida Bolívar.

In the Centro, **Lucerna** (Cl. 20 No. 14-40, tel. 6/741-1005, 9am-7:30pm Mon.-Sat., 11am-6:30pm Sun.) is a classic. This retro-looking *salón de té* (tearoom) is always packed; you can order a meal or snack.

If you've got an appetite, head to **La Fogata** (Av. Bolívar No. 14N-39, tel. 6/749-5980, www.lafogata.com.co, noon-midnight daily, COP$28,000), a classic in Armenia. Their filet mignon is known as the best in town. Several Peruvian dishes make the menu interesting, and the loungey Café La Fogata is a popular place for a cocktail after work or before a night out dancing. Nearby, the **Café Quindío Gourmet** (Parque de la Vida, Cra. 14/Av. Bolívar 7N, tel. 6/745-4478, www.cafequindio.com.co, 11am-9:30pm Mon.-Sat., noon-4:30pm Sun.) serves coffee drinks from Armenia's preferred coffee brand, Café Quindío, and more substantial meals such as pastas and sandwiches.

Practically hidden behind a residential complex near the Armenia Hotel, **Zaki** (Cra. 13

No. 8N-39, Edificio Bambú, Local 104, tel. 6/745-1220, noon-3pm and 6pm-10pm Mon.-Thurs., noon-3pm and 6pm-11pm Fri.-Sat., COP$20,000) is a sushi joint that also serves a mish-mash of other Asian-inspired dishes. It is one of a handful of restaurants and bars in this part of town that cater to Armenia yuppies.

Natural Food Plaza (Cra. 14 No. 4-51, tel. 6/745-1597, 7:30am-6pm Mon.-Thurs., 7:30am-4pm Fri. and Sun., COP$10,000) always has a set lunch, but you can also order Paisa dishes, like tamales and *bandeja paisa*—the quintessential Paisa dish of beans, various meats, yuca, and potatoes—reinvented vegetarian-style, all to the soothing sounds of elevator music.

Many of the best-known restaurants in Armenia are on the outskirts of town, like **El Roble** (Km. 12 Vía Armenia Pereira, tel. 6/740-5120, 6:30am-9pm daily, COP$15,000), which is a sprawling 100 percent Colombian cuisine family-style restaurant.

Information and Services

Tourist offices are located at the bus station (Cl. 35 No. 20-68) and in the **Edificio de la Gobernación** (Plaza de Bolívar, tel. 6/741-7700, 8am-noon and 2pm-6pm Mon.-Sat.).

Getting There and Around

Major airlines **Avianca** (Centro Comercial Portal del Quindío, Av. Bolívar No. 19N-46, 2nd floor, tel. 6/734-5205, www.avianca.com, 10:30am-1:30pm and 2:30pm-7:30pm Mon.-Sat., 11am-1:30pm and 2:30pm-7pm Sun.) and **LAN** (Col. toll-free tel. 01/800-094-9490, www.lan.com) as well as smaller Colombian carriers **EasyFly** (tel. 6/747-9031, www.easyfly.com.co) and **Aerolíneas de Antioquia** (Col. toll-free tel. 01/800-051-4232 www.ada-aero.com) serve the **Aeropuerto Internacional El Eden** (Km. 10 Vía La Tebaida, tel. 6/747-9400). **Spirit Air** (www.spirit.com) has two weekly nonstop flights from Fort Lauderdale.

The bus terminal, the **Terminal de Transportes** (Cl. 35 No. 20-68, tel. 6/747-3355, www.terminalarmenia.com) is just south of downtown, about 13 blocks from the Plaza de Bolívar. There is frequent service to Pereira (1 hour, COP$8,000), Salento (1 hour, COP$4,000), and Manizales (4 hours, COP$17,000). Buses bound for Medellín (6.5 hours, COP$38,000) leave all day from before dawn to around midnight. While short-distance buses depart until about 10pm or later, it's better to travel earlier if possible out of safety reasons and in order to enjoy the scenery along the way.

The rapid bus system in Armenia is called the **Tinto** (www.tinto.com.co), after the ubiquitous little coffees. A line on Avenida Bolívar connects the northern part of the city with downtown. The website can be confusing, so it's best to ask someone how to get around.

VICINITY OF ARMENIA
◖ Jardín Botánico del Quindío

Just 10 minutes outside of town, the well-run **Jardín Botánico del Quindío** (Km. 3 Vía al Valle, tel. 6/742-7254, cell tel. 310/835-0236, www.jardinbotanicoquindio.org, 9am-4pm daily, English tour COP$30,000) is home to hundreds of tree and plant species, many of which are threatened. Knowledgeable volunteer guides, who are usually college students, lead visitors on a mandatory 2.5-hour tour along jungle paths, stopping every so often to point out flora that you would have overlooked had you walked through on your own. That might strike you as a major time commitment, but it really doesn't seem like it. In addition to palms (which aren't technically trees) and *guadua* (which is actually related to grass), look out for *matapalos,* a tree that wraps itself around other trees, strangling them as they fight for sunlight. It's been lovingly nicknamed the *abrazo de la suegra* (mother-in-law's hug).

In Colombia where there is tropical forest, there will be birds. The gardens are no exception, and they are home to at least 119 species. The birds are at their most active early in the morning. Some of the commonly seen species include tangers, toucans, owls, woodpeckers, the multi-colored *torito cabecirrojo* (red-headed barbet), and iconic *barranqueros* or *barranquillos* (blue-crowned motmots). These birds make

© ANDREW DIER

Jardín Botánico del Quindío

MEDELLIN

their nests in the earth. Rodent residents who frequently make cameo appearances are *ardillas* (squirrels) and cute *guatines* (Central American agoutis). By far the most photographed sector of the park is the *mariposario* (enclosed butterfly garden) in the shape of a giant butterfly, home to thousands. This is an interactive experience, in which visitors are encouraged to coax the insects to light on their fingers, arms, and shoulders. Butterflies are livelier when the sun is out.

Guides are volunteers, and although the entry price is steep, it's good form to tip the guides after the tour. Call in advance to inquire about English-speaking tours.

It's easy to get to the park using public transportation from Armenia. Just look for a bus from the Plaza de Bolívar or along Avenida Bolívar that says "Jardín Botánico."

Theme Parks

These parks are always mobbed with Colombian families on weekends and holidays.

RECUCA (Km. 5 Vía La Y-Barcelona, Vereda Callelarga, tel. 6/749-8525, www.recuca.com, 9am-3pm daily, tour with lunch COP$30,000) is a theme park, but one without rollercoasters or water rides. RECUCA stands for Recorrido de la Cultura Cafetera (Coffee Culture Experience). Upon arrival at the *finca* (farm), you'll be greeted by smiling employees dressed in traditional bean-picking garb. Then you'll explore a coffee farm, lend a hand by picking some ripe beans, and learn about the whole process. After that, you'll enjoy a big Paisa lunch (beans and rice for herbivores). If you prefer, you can just take part in a coffee-tasting session (COP$11,000). You can get to RECUCA by taking a bus bound for Barcelona from the Terminal de Transportes in Armenia (Cl. 35 No. 20-68). The bus drops you off at the park entrance. From there it is a 30-minute walk, or the guard at the entrance can order a Jeep for you (COP$5,000).

The **Parque Nacional del Café** (Km. 6 Vía Montenegro-Pueblo Tapao, tel. 6/741-7417, www.parquenacionaldelcafe.com, 9am-6pm daily, COP$22,000-55,000) is near the town of **Montenegro,** 12.5 kilometers (8 miles) west

of Armenia. While part of the park is devoted to telling the story of coffee production in Colombia, it's mostly an amusement park with rollercoasters, a chair-lift ride, horseback rides, a coffee show, a water park, and other attractions.

PANACA (Km. 7 Vía Vereda Kerman, tel. 6/758-2830, cell tel. 313/721-9211, www.panaca.com.co, 9am-6pm daily, COP$30,000-60,000) is an agricultural-themed amusement park near the town of **Quimbaya,** where visitors can see and interact with all types of farm animals and watch the occasional pig race.

Festivals and Events

In June or sometimes July, **Calarcá** puts on an event to honor what made the coffee region what it is today. A number of the usual festival events take place during the **Fiesta Nacional del Café** (www.calarca.net), but it's the **Desfile de Yipao** that steals the show. That's when Jeep Willys—U.S. military Jeeps from World War II and the Korean War that were sold to farmers in the coffee region—are laden down with people, animals, and furniture, and go on parade. There are competitions (essentially Willy beauty pageants) and a contest in which the Jeep Willys are loaded down with 1,800 kilos of cargo and race forward on two wheels only. The ubiquitous Jeep Willy has become a symbol of the region.

Accommodations and Food

With more than a century's experience growing coffee, the **Hacienda Combia** (Km. 4 Vía al Valle-Vereda La Bella, tel. 6/746-8472, cell tel. 314/682-5395, www.combia.com.co, COP$153,000 d) produces Café Inspiración, their brand of high-quality coffee. It is operated by the same owners as the Hacienda San José near Pereira. It has around 30 rooms and an infinity pool that has a fantastic view, and there are coffee tours available through the nearby fields. This hotel is not far from a highway, but you can easily block out reminders of suburbia by focusing on the fertile lands that surround you and are home to colorful birds. Its proximity to the airport (airport pickups can be arranged) and easy access make it popular for events with Colombian businesses. It also attracts foreign embassy staff living in Bogotá.

Bakkho (Cl. 41 No. 27-56, Calarcá, tel. 6/743-3331, www.bakkho.com, noon-9pm Tues., noon-10pm Wed.-Sun., COP$35,000) is considered to be the top restaurant in Quindío. Here, presentation and ambience is everything, and it's no surprise that this is where locals come to celebrate special occasions. Fare is international with many seafood dishes. Bakkho has various locations in the area, but the Calarcá location is the original.

Surrounded by 160 hectares of pineapple, cacao, banana, and citrus crops, it's hard to imagine a more relaxing place than sublime ◀ **Hacienda Bambusa** (off Vía Calarcá-Caicedonia south of Armenia, tel. 6/740-4935, cell tel. 321/313-7315, www.haciendabambusa.com, COP$160,000 pp). Its isolation is a selling point, as you feel far from everything, providing the perfect environment to disconnect. The house and much of the furniture are made of *guadua* and other traditional materials, and rooms are luxurious and tastefully decorated. There are only seven rooms, each with a private balcony or terrace. The views from those balconies are spectacular, with endless farms punctuated by *guadua* forests and mountains in the distance. Meals are prepared by the acclaimed Bakkho restaurant. It is isolated here, and it would be a shame to spend the day rushing around the area sightseeing. Here at the farm there are cacao tours to take, horses to ride, birds to watch, and massages to be enjoyed. The Armenia airport is about 40 minutes away, and taking a cab from there costs COP$45,000, although the hotel can arrange all your transportation. Bambusa offers a range of packages, some including activities and excursions, transportation to and from the airport, and all meals. They do not bump up prices during high season (nor reduce prices during low season).

Near the town of Quimbaya and off the road 800 meters past some ordinary looking houses and apartments, a spectacularly well-maintained red-and-white-painted hacienda awaits: ◀ **Finca Villa Nora** (tel. 6/741-5472, cell tel. 310/422-6335, www.quindiofincavillanora.com, COP$180,000 d with 2 meals). It's a 120-year-old house that is charming and full of character. It's built in the typical Paisa style. Amid fruit trees, flowers, coffee fields, and a huge ficus tree, at Villa Nora the air is pure, sunsets lovely, and drinks on the verandah not a bad idea. There are only seven rooms at this quiet refuge.

SALENTO

On the western edge of the Parque Nacional Natural Los Nevados, the pueblo of Salento (pop. 7,000) is one-stop shopping for those seeking a quintessential coffee region experience. The town, an enchanting pueblo, home to coffee growers and cowboys, is adorned with the trademark colorful balconies and facades of Paisa architecture. It was one of the first settlements in the region during the 19th-century Antioquian colonization. In the nearby countryside, coffee farms dominate the landscape. Here you can be a Juan Valdez, the iconic personification of Colombian coffee, during a coffee tour in which you harvest coffee beans, learn about the bean-to-bag process, and sip the freshest coffee you've ever tasted.

Within minutes of town is the Valle de Cocora, where you can play tree tag in forests of *palma de cera* (wax palm, the Colombian national tree), the skyscrapers of the palm family. Some of these can reach up to 60 meters (200 feet) high. For a more challenging hike continue on to the Reserva Acaime, a private nature reserve of tropical forest, babbling brooks, and not a few hummingbirds. From here adventurers can ascend into the *páramos* (highland moors) and, eventually, the snowcapped mountains of the Parque Natural Nacional Los Nevados.

Salento is easily accessed from between both Armenia and Pereira, and in the town and nearby countryside there are hostels, hotels, and good restaurants. It is a popular tourist destination, so if you'd like to experience Salento without the crowds, go during the week.

Sights

The **Plaza de Bolívar** or **Plaza Principal** is the center of town and center of activity. The festive pedestrian **Calle Real** (between Cl. 1 and Cl. 5) is the most photogenic street in Salento. It is lined with restaurants and souvenir shops painted in a rainbow of colors. It starts at the Plaza Principal and leads up to the **Alto de la Cruz Mirador** (scenic lookout atop the Calle Real). At the cross you can get a great bird's-eye view of the Calle Real and Salento. Farther on is another lookout with views over the surrounding jungles and valleys. But it's really about atmosphere in this Quindío town.

Coffee Tours

In the outskirts of Salento, an excellent place to learn about the coffee process from seed to cup is the **Finca El Ocaso** (Vía Salento-Vereda Palestina, cell tel. 310/451-7329, cafeelocaso@ hotmail.com, www.fincaelocasosalento.com, 8:30am-4:30pm daily, tour COP$8,000). This family-run farm with some 12 hectares (30 acres) of coffee crops produces coffee that has several international certifications, such as the German UTZ and the Rainforest Alliance. Elevation here is around 1,780 meters, a good altitude to grow coffee. Gregarious Don Elias and his wife, Gloria Luz, run the farm, and they enjoy showing their farm to visitors. It's a fairly interactive tour, lasting around 40 minutes, in which you plant a coffee seed, strap a basket to your hip to harvest some ripe, red beans, and grind the coffee pulp. Then, of course, you get to try a freshly roasted cup at the end. The *finca* (farm) also has three cozy rooms (COP$35,000-100,000), decorated with period furniture, available for rent in the traditional coffee plantation house. You can also rent the whole house (COP$420,000). If you'd like a tour in English, it's best to give the owners some advance notice. It's about an hour-long walk from town, or you can hire a Jeep Willy.

You can also check out the **Finca Don Eduardo coffee tour** (Plantation House, Alto de Coronel, Cl. 7 No. 1-04, cell tel. 316/285-2603, COP$20,000). There are two daily, at 9am and 3pm. This organic *finca* is run by the folks from Plantation House.

Recreation

For the real Paisa experience, **horseback riding** is a good way to enjoy the countryside around Salento. In the Plaza Principal there are usually horses at the ready, especially on weekends. One popular excursion is to some nearby waterfalls. **Don Álvaro** (cell tel. 311/375-1534, 3-hr. trip COP$40,000 pp) treats his horses well and is considered the best guide for this activity.

Salento, along with the neighboring countryside, is a nice place for a **bike ride.** Most hostels can arrange bike rental. Additionally, **CicloSalento** (near Plantation Hostel, Alto de Coronel, Cl. 7 No. 1-04, cell tel. 318/872-9714, COP$10,000/hr., COP$35,000/day) rents out good quality mountain bikes with helmets. Caution: The winding road leading into town from the Valle de Cocora does not have a shoulder for bikes. Vehicles tend to speed along this road, making this a dangerous stretch for cyclists and pedestrians.

Accommodations

As Salento has grown in popularity, with Paisa weekenders and international travelers, excellent accommodations options (from backpacker lodges to coffee plantations and camping options) to fit all budget types have similarly grown. Although the number of higher-end hotels in town is growing, it is often the case that small hostels and nearby coffee farms will suit your needs just fine.

One of the best hostels in the area is ◖ **Tralala** (Cra. 7 No. 6-45, cell tel. 314/850-5543, www.hostaltralalasalento.com, COP$18,000 dorm, COP$45,000 d). It's hard to miss this in-town option: It's a two-story white house with bright orange wooden trim. At Tralala there are only seven rooms, including a dormitory that sleeps six, making for a chilled-out environment for the guests. Run by a Dutchman, the hostel is spic and span and tastefully decorated. Its minimalist style provides a nice vacation for the eyes. Staff are friendly and knowledgeable, and the kitchen area is a pleasant area to hang out and chitchat with others. There's a sun deck and garden area in case relaxation is needed.

Londoner Tim was one of the first to help transform Salento from a sleepy Paisa pueblo into one of Colombia's top tourist destinations. His **Plantation House** (Alto de Coronel, Cl. 7 No. 1-04, cell tel. 316/285-2603, www.the-plantationhousesalento.com, COP$22,000 dorm, COP$55,000 d), with 24 rooms total, remains one of the top places to get to know Salento and the surrounding areas. Catering to international visitors, this hostel has two houses, one of which is over 100 years old. It's quiet and green around the hostel, and, though you'll be bound to meet other travelers like yourself, there is plenty of space to find a little solitude. Plantation House can organize bike excursions, horseback riding, and hikes to the Valle de Cocora. The owners of the Plantation House have their own organic coffee farm, **Finca Don Eduardo** (Alto de Coronel, Cl. 7 No. 1-04, cell tel. 316/285-2603, COP$15,000 dorm, COP$35,000 d), about 15 minutes outside of town, which has one private room and one dormitory. This coffee plantation is over 80 years old and set amid lush, rolling hills. It is an environmentally friendly hostel: Solar panels enable guests to have a hot shower, and a rainwater collection system provides that water.

Another excellent hostel-type option is **La Serrana Eco-farm and Hostel** (Km. 1.5 Vía Palestina Finca, cell tel. 316/296-1890, www.laserrana.com.co, COP$22,000 dorm, COP$55,000 d). It's situated on a bluff with lovely views of coffee farms in every direction. The nine rooms, of various types and sizes, are comfortable, and there is also a women-only dorm room. Camping is also available for COP$12,000. It's a peaceful place where you can enjoy sunrises and sunsets, go for a walk into town, or just hang out. La Serrana is best known for its delicious (and nutritious) family-style dinners and other meals. Vegetarians always have options, and the cooks make an effort to buy local, fresh food. La Serrana has another, smaller, lodging option, **◖ Las Camelias** (Km. 1.5 Vía Palestina Finca, cell

tel. 316/296-1890, www.laserrana.com.co, COP$70,000 d), a colonial-style house you can see from the hostel. This is geared for couples who want a little more privacy—there are only three rooms. Rooms, drenched with natural light, are spacious, with hardwood floors and fireplaces. Common space is ample with large windows, and there is a kitchen for guest use. From La Serrana it is a short distance to the Finca Ocasa coffee farm.

Centrally located **◖ Hostal Ciudad de Segorbe** (Cl. 5 No. 4-06, tel. 6/759-3794, www.hostalciudaddesegorbe.com, COP$85,000 d) is a bed and breakfast run by a Colombian and Spanish pair. The renovated house is over 100 years old and is built in the traditional Paisa style. The hostel's eight rooms have high wooden ceilings with gorgeous original geometric designs and small balconies. One room is equipped for guests with disabilities. Pictures of Spanish towns like Segorbe, the hometown of one of the owners, decorate the walls. Excellent service is provided to guests, such as transportation assistance and help with organizing sightseeing activities. There are plans to add more rooms to the hotel in the adjacent lot, which may make it less of an intimate stay, but it's still a good bet.

CAMPING

Four kilometers outside of Salento, on the banks of the Río Quindío, is **Camping Monteroca** (Valle del Río Quindío, cell tel. 315/413-6862, www.campingmonteroca.com, COP$70,000 cabin, COP$15,000 tent), a sprawling campground catering mostly to Colombian weekenders. The camp has 11 cabins, one of which is called the Hippie Hilton, and several of them have awesome waterbeds. There is a lot of space for tents here, as well. Monteroca has a restaurant and two bars. Recreational activities such as horseback riding (COP$12,000 per hour), a three-hour hike to nearby waterfalls (COP$25,000), and yoga classes are on offer as well. To get there from Salento, take a Jeep bound for Las Veredas. They leave every 15 minutes from the Plaza Principal during weekends.

MEDELLÍN

Food

Salento offers varied restaurant options, not just the standard *comida típica* fare.

Mojitería (Cl. 4 No. 5-54, cell tel. 310/409-2331, 2pm-11pm daily, COP$18,000) is a lively spot where you can grab a quick bite (appetizers, salads, soups, and pastas) or try one or two of the many mojitos on offer. At night it takes on a bar atmosphere.

It's a real treat to discover a restaurant like **La Eliana** (Cra. 2 No. 6-45, cell tel. 314/660-5987, 10am-9pm daily, COP$20,000), where great service, a cozy atmosphere, and fantastic food are the norm. This Spanish-run spot a few blocks from the center of town is the only place in this part of the woods where you can find curry dishes and gourmet pizzas on the menu. And try as they might, the friendly cocker spaniels aren't allowed to mingle with diners.

One of the best regional food restaurants is **Camino Real Parrilla Bar** (Cra. 6A No. 1-35, cell tel. 314/864-2587, 10am-midnight Sun.-Thurs., 10am-2am Fri.-Sat., COP$18,000). After a grueling climb to the Mirador, this popular place at the top of Calle Real makes for a great stop. The restaurant has outdoor seating and a huge, fairly varied menu with grilled meats, a few salads, and lots of *trucha* (trout). At night it's an *aguardiente,* a popular local drinking hangout.

Alegra (Cra. 6 No. 2-52, cell tel. 301/462-4458, 2pm-8:20pm Mon., Tues., Thurs., and Fri., 12:30pm-8:20pm Sat.-Sun., COP$18,000) is a cute place about a block from the ruckus of Calle Real. Here you can enjoy cilantro pesto pasta, a veggie burger, and a glass of wine as you listen to jazz in the background. It's run by a friendly woman from Bogotá.

Brunch (Cl. 6 No. 3-25, cell tel. 311/757-8082, 6:30am-9:30pm daily, COP$15,000), a hip little joint with graffiti and messages from hundreds of visitors from around the globe decorating the walls, is another restaurant with the international traveler in mind. They do serve brunch, but also breakfast, lunch, and dinner. The menu seems aimed squarely at Americans: Buffalo wings, Philly cheese steak sandwiches, black bean burgers, and peanut butter brownies. Menu items are assigned whimsical names like Wax Palm Pancakes. **Beta Town** (Cl. 7 No. 3-45, cell tel. 321/218-7043, 6pm-midnight daily) is a popular place for burgers, beer, and hanging out. They've even got a *tejo* field, where you can try your luck at this only-in-Colombia sport.

Information and Services

Hostels usually provide the best tourist information, but there is a city-run tourist kiosk, the **Punto de Información Turística** (10am-5pm Wed.-Mon.), in front of the Alcaldía (city offices) in the Plaza Principal.

Getting There and Around

There is frequent bus service from Pereira, Armenia, and other cities to Salento. The last bus from Armenia leaves at 8pm (under COP$4,000). From Pereira, there are four direct buses each weekday, costing under COP$6,000. There is more frequent service on weekends. As Salento is well established on the tourist route, thieves are known to prey on foreigners on late-evening buses traveling from Pereira to Salento. Keep a vigilant eye on your possessions.

Buses to Armenia (every 20 mins., COP$4,000) and Pereira (COP$6,000) depart from the the intersection of Carrera 2 at Calle 5, with the last bus departure at 6pm daily. For Filandia you have to first go to Armenia.

VALLE DE COCORA

The main attraction for most visitors to Salento is seeing the *palmas de cera* (wax palms) that shoot up towards the sky in the Valle de Cocora. These are some of the tallest palms in the world, reaching 50-60 meters high (200 feet), and they can live over 100 years. They have beautiful, smooth, cylindrical trunks with dark rings. In 1985, they were declared to be the national tree of Colombia.

The Valle de Cocora is a 15-kilometer (9-mile) section of the lower Río Quindío valley. Much of it has been turned into pastureland, but, thankfully, the palms have been preserved. The palms look particularly stunning in the denuded pastureland.

© ANDREW DIER

the picturesque Valle de Cocora and its famous wax palms

The gateway to the valley is the **Vereda de Cocora**, a stretch of restaurants specializing in trout. This *vereda* (settlement) is a major domestic tourist destination and can get incredibly crowded during holidays and weekends. Most Colombian tourists come for a late lunch and take a stroll along the main road behind the *vereda* to view the palms. However, there are two much more rewarding excursions: a leisurely 90-minute walk to **La Montaña,** a ranger station for the local environmental agency, or a more intense five-hour loop through the valley and up the Río Quindío and back via La Montaña.

For the La Montaña hike, continue down the main road beyond the Vereda de Cocoa and pass through the gate of a private farm on the right where a signpost reads "FCA. EL BOSQUE 7.6 KM." Follow a path that meanders six kilometers (four miles) up hills converted to pastureland and then along a ridge on one side of the Valle de Cocora to the ranger station. The views from the path onto the wax palms in the valley and mountainside are stunning. If you opt for the longer hike, that same spectacular scenery comes at the end of a walk that saves the valley of the palms for last, like a delicious dessert.

For the longer hike, take a right through a gate painted blue after the last building in the Vereda de Cocora. After walking about four kilometers (2.5 miles) through pasture, you'll enter the dense forest. The path crisscrosses the trickling Río Quindío. After three kilometers (two miles) you reach the **Reserva Acaime** (cell tel. 321/636-2818 or 320/788-1981, COP$4,000), a private reserve created to preserve the surrounding cloud forest. With the entrance fee, you can enjoy a complimentary cup of hot chocolate, *agua de panela* (a hot sugary drink), or coffee and watch throngs of hummingbirds of several varieties fly up to feeders. It's quite a show. You can also stay at Acaime, either in private rooms or a large dormitory (COP$40,000 pp including all meals).

From Reserva Acaime, you backtrack a kilometer and then climb a steep path to La Montaña. The last leg of the hike, back from

MEDELLÍN

La Montaña to Vereda del Cocora, provides the best and most memorable photo opportunities of the valley and hundreds upon hundreds of wax palms. Make sure your camera batteries are charged, as you'll want to take many pictures. The entire loop takes 4-5 hours. You may want to wear rubber or waterproof boots, as the path along the Río Quindío is muddy. There is no need for a guide.

To get to Vereda del Cocora from Salento, take a Jeep Willy (COP$3,500), which leave the Plaza Pincipal at 6am, 7:30am, 9:30am, and 11:30am each day.

Trek to Finca La Primavera

If you would like to do a longer expedition, you can extend the Valle de Cocora hike beyond Reserva Acaime to the **Páramo de Romerales** on the border of the Parque Nacional Natural Los Nevados and to **Finca La Primavera,** a working farm located at an altitude of 3,680 meters (12,075 feet). This excursion allows you to enjoy the transition from cloud forest to *páramo* (highland moor) but requires two days. The path from Acaime continues to **Estrella de Agua,** a research station, through the Páramo de Romerales and finally Finca Primavera, where you can bunk for COP$10,000 per person and arrange for meals. The entire hike from Vereda de Cocora to Primavera is 13.5 kilometers (8.5 miles) and takes 7-8 hours. This trek does not require camping gear; all you need is food for snacking. However, it is quite cold at Finca La Primavera, and a sleeping bag makes a difference. Hiring a guide is a good idea as the trail is poorly marked.

From Finca La Primavera, you can continue into the **Parque Nacional Natural Los Nevados,** hiking to the Nevado del Tolima (5,215 meters/17,110 feet) or the less traveled Paramillo del Quindío (4,750 meters/15,585 feet).

Recommended guides are **Páramo Trek** (cell tel. 311/745-3761, paramotrek@gmail.com) in Salento and **Truman David Alfonso Bejarano** (cell tel. 315/292-7395, trumandavid01@gmail.com) in Ibagué, who can organize excursions from Salento or Ibagué.

FILANDIA

To visit an authentic coffee town without the tourists, head to Filandia (pop. 12,000), a cute pueblo between Armenia and Pereira. Sights are few; this town is about atmosphere. The name Filandia has nothing to do with the Nordic country of Finland (which in Spanish is Finlandia).

The focal point on the **Parque Central** (between Cras. 4-5 and Clls. 6-7) is the church, the **Templo María Inmaculada** (Cra. 7), which was built in the early 20th century. From the plaza explore the charming streets of the town, including the **Calle del Tiempo Detenido** (Cl. 7 between Cras. 5-6) and the **Calle del Empedrado,** two streets of two-story houses made of *bahareque* (a natural material) adorned by colorful doors and windows. Stop by the town's oldest construction, the **Droguería Bristol** (Cra. 6 No. 5-63) along the way. A nice view of the countryside can be had near the *clínica mental* (mental hospital; Cra. 8 No. 7-55). On the street pick up one of Filandia's famous reed baskets.

On the road towards Quimbaya, just outside of town, is the wooden **Ecoparque Mirador de las Colinas Iluminadas** (10am-7pm Mon.-Fri., 10am-9pm Sat.-Sun., COP$3,000), which looks like a wooden spaceship. From the top are nice views of the countryside, and inside, looking down, is a strange mosaic of a giant blue butterfly. On the way towards the *mirador*, pop into one of the many handicraft shops, where you can browse baskets until the cows come home.

Accommodations and Food

Accommodations and restaurants in Filandia are limited. In a traditional Paisa house, the **Hostal La Posada del Compadre** (Cra. 6 No. 8-06, tel. 6/758-3054, cell tel. 313/335-9771, www.laposadadelcompadre.com, COP$60,000 d) offers a handful of rooms and ample outdoor hangout space. Rooms are large, beds are adequate, breakfast is included, and the prices are reasonable.

With a prime location on the main square, the **Hostal Tibouchina** (Cl. 6A No. 5-05, tel. 6/758-2646, COP$40,000 pp d) has seven rooms and pleasant common areas, including a large kitchen. It's on the second floor above a café/bar. The interior rooms, which lack windows, are on the stuffy side. On the other hand, if you get one of the rooms facing the street, you may hear music and the goings-on in the plaza until the wee hours on weekends.

The (**Hostal Colina de Lluvia** (Cra. 4 No. 5-15, COP$25,000 dorm, COP$60,000 d private) opened in mid-2013 and is easily the best place to stay in Filandia. Tastefully decorated rooms are spic and span with comfortable beds, and there is a small garden patio.

Candlelit tables, lounge music, and art on the walls—you won't believe your eyes when you see (**Helena Adentro** (Cra. 7 No. 8-01, cell tel. 312/873-9825, noon-2am weekends). Started by a New Zealander and a Paisa, it's by far the coolest spot in Filandia, Quindío, and perhaps this side of Medellín. Cured meats and goat cheeses come from local farmers, along with the coffee. They have their own brand of coffee but also serve coffee from other regions of Colombia, using different brewing techniques. Locals keep coming back for the inventive libations here, such as the house cocktail, the Adentro Helena (aguardiente, *lulo* juice, and lime).

The popular place for a cappuccino is **Jahn Café** (Cl. 6 No. 5-45, 7:30am-midnight Mon.-Fri., 7:30am-2am Sat.-Sun.).

Information and Services

The Filandia tourist office is in the **Casa del Artesano** (Cra. 5 at Cl. 7, 2nd floor, tel. 6/758-2172, 7am-noon and 1:30pm-4:30pm Mon.-Fri.).

Getting There and Around

Buses to Filandia leave from Armenia (COP$4,000, every 20 minutes) and Pereira (COP$5,000, hourly) all day long until around 8pm. These circulate the town picking up passengers, especially on Carrera 7.

PEREIRA AND VICINITY

In Pereira (pop. 465,000), the capital of the Risaralda department, you can get your boots muddy, see exotic birds, and experience the tropical Andean forest during the day, then later enjoy a good meal out or hit the town until late. Pereira is perfectly situated for day trips to the countryside, be it elegant haciendas or natural parks such as Santuario de Flora y Fauna Otún-Quimbaya. In town, you can easily see the major sights of interest in one day: the spectacular cathedral, the Plaza de Bolívar with its statue of a nude Simón Bolívar on horseback charging ahead, and the Museo de Arte de Pereira. Manizales, Armenia, and Salento are within one hour driving or riding of Pereira.

Sights

Downtown, in the **Plaza de Bolívar** (Clls. 19-20 and Cras. 7-8) stands a bronze sculpture by Rodrigo Arenas Betancourt depicting the Liberator Simón Bolívar on horseback charging ahead to fight the Spaniards—naked. Facing the plaza is the **Nuestra Señora de la Pobreza Catedral** (Cl. 20 No. 7-30, tel. 6/335-6545, masses every hour 6am-noon and 5pm Mon.-Sat., 6am-noon and 5pm-8pm Sun.). The cathedral was originally built in 1890, using industrial-era building techniques, and was damaged by an earthquake, needing to be almost completely reconstructed. It was rebuilt with a wooden ceiling and supports made from cumin laurel, a tree native to Colombia that is now endangered.

The **Museo de Arte de Pereira** (Av. Las Américas No. 19-88, tel. 6/317-2828, www.museodeartedepereira.com, 9am-noon and 2pm-6pm Tues.-Fri., 10am-5pm Sat.-Sun., free) is one of the best art museums in the region, and deserving of a visit. It features temporary exhibitions of contemporary Latin American artists. It's south of downtown.

In the **Parque Olaya Herrera** (between Cras. 13-14 and Clls. 19-23) is the well-preserved **Antigua Estación del Tren,** a photogenic old train station. There is a Megabus station in the park, and the park is a nice place for a morning jog.

The **Zoológico Matecaña** (Av. 30 de Agosto, tel. 6/314-2636, www.zoopereira.org, 9am-6pm daily, COP$15,000), located within screeching,

PEREIRA

howling, and roaring distance of the airport, has an extensive section on Colombian animals. It's better than many zoos in Colombia; however, big cats, including Colombian jaguars, have little space to move about.

The **Viaducto César Gavíria Trujillo** is a modern cable bridge that connects Pereira with its industrial neighbor of Dosquebradas. It's a point of reference and source of city pride. It is named for former president César Gavíria, who is from Pereira and who served as president during the early 1990s.

Recreation

For bike tours and rentals, contact **Retro Ciclas** (cell tel. 310/540-7327 or 312/437-4882, www.

mtbtourscolombia.com). One of the more popular tours is a trip to the village of Estación Pereira (COP$86,000), where in the town you'll take two different and exciting means of transportation: a *brujita,* a motorcycle-powered cart that zooms along old train tracks, and later a *garrucha,* which is a gondola-like metallic basket that transports passengers over the Río Cauca. Another trip on offer is along the Río Otún (COP$80,000) to the Santuario de Flora y Fauna Otún-Quimbaya.

Accommodations

In town, it's best to stay in the Circunvalar area. The Centro has options, but prices are comparable to hotels on the Circunvalar, where you can walk without much concern at night and there are plenty of restaurants and nightlife spots nearby.

The **(Kolibrí Hostel** (Cl. No. 16-35, tel. 6/331-3955, cell tel. 321/646-9275, www. kolibrihostel.com, COP$22,000 dorm, COP$60,000 d) is a welcome newcomer to Pereira, filling a void of budget accommodations for international clientele near the Circunvalar. In addition to a mix of private rooms and dorms, Kolibrí has two long-stay apartments. It's run by a Dutch-Colombian couple who have traveled extensively in the area to some off-the-map places, and they offer tours, such as to the village of Estación Pereira, to the Santuario de Flora y Fauna Otún-Quimbaya, and an interesting orchid tour. Bars, restaurants, and malls are within walking distance from the hostel. Great breakfasts are offered on the deck, where they also have a barbecue grill.

The **Hotel Movich** (Cra. 13 No. 15-73, tel. 6/311-3300, COP$249,000 d) is a good option if you like comfort, don't want any surprises, and want the conveniences that the Circunvalar offers. It's across the street from the Iglesia de Carmen. The pool (usually open until 9pm) and gym (open 24 hours) are quite nice. A massive breakfast buffet is included in the room rate.

A restful sleep is assured at the **Hotel Don Alfonso** (Cra. 13 No. 12-37, tel. 6/333-0909, www.donalfonsohotel.com, COP$240,000 d), a small boutique-style hotel on the main nightlife and shopping drag of the Avenida Circunvalar. It has 11 comfortable air-conditioned rooms, each with inviting beds covered by quilts.

HACIENDAS

Within minutes of the Pereira's bright lights are some gorgeous and luxurious hacienda hotels. Some of them are popular places for special events, such as weddings on the weekend and corporate seminars during the week.

Hacienda Malabar (Km. 7 Vía a Cerritos, Entrada 6, tel. 6/337-9206, www.hotelmalabar.com, COP$257,500 d) is an authentic hacienda with seven rooms, ample gardens to wander, and a pool. The wooden ceilings with their geometric designs and tile floors with Spanish Mudejar designs throughout the house are spectacular.

(Villa Martha (Km. 9 Vía a Marsella, 1 km from the main road, tel. 6/322-9994, cell tel. 310/421-5920, www.fincavillamartha.com, COP$75,000 pp with meals) offers the most affordable coffee farm experience. Here you can kick back and relax, take a dip in a pool that has "Villa Martha" written on the bottom, stroll the countryside, and take a tour of the coffee plantation. It's not luxurious, but the warm hospitality of the *finca* (farm) owners, Martha and her husband, Rafael, more than compensates. Rooms by the pool are nicer. Villa Martha doesn't allow non-guests to visit for the day.

(Castilla Casa de Huespedes (Km. 10 Vía a Cerritos, tel. 6/337-9045, cell tel. 315/499-9545, www.haciendacastilla.com, COP$281,000 d), built in the 19th century, is set amid fruit trees and has a pool to boot. The nine rooms are lovely, and staff are friendly. Once there, at this serene spot in the countryside, you'll probably not even be aware of the fact that a fried chicken restaurant is just around the corner along the highway! They make their own jam here, and a majestic cedar tree near the pool area looks even more regal when illuminated at night.

The **Hacienda San José** (Km. 4 Vía Pereira-Cerritos, Entrada 16, Cadena El Tigre, tel. 6/313-2612, www.haciendahotelsanjose.com, COP$275,000-310,000 d) was built in 1888 and has been in the Jaramillo family for generations. It's in the countryside, and the entrance to it, lined with palms, is a dramatic one. The home is spectacular, and the lovely wooden floors make a satisfying creak when you step on the planks. Service is impeccable and the restaurant, excellent. The grounds make for a nice late afternoon stroll, and you can admire an enormous and regal old *samán* tree, well into its second century of life, as you dine alfresco. Living Trips (www.livingtrips.com) manages this hotel, and they can arrange day trip excursions for you. The restaurant is open to the public, and members of the public can also come for the day and enjoy the pool. It is almost always booked on weekends and during holidays. This gorgeous hacienda is a particularly popular place for weddings on weekends. The Matecaña airport is only 10 minutes away.

Luxury hotel **Sazagua** (Km. 7 Vía Cerritos, Entrada 4, tel. 6/337-9895, www.sazagua.com, COP$446,000 d) is not technically a hacienda, as it is located in a country club type environment. Here attention to detail reigns. The 10 rooms are impeccable, the common space is inviting, the gardens are perfectly manicured (surrounded by elegant heliconia flowers, birds, and the occasional iguana), and you can lounge by the pool or enjoy a massage at the spa. Nonguests can enjoy the spa facilities for a separate charge. It's not a traditional hacienda, but it sure feels good there.

Food

Pereira makes it easy for visitors, gastronomically speaking. All the top restaurants are in more or less the same area, along and nearby the Avenida Circunvalar.

Mama Flor (Cl. 11 No. 15-12, tel. 6/335-4713, noon-10pm Mon.-Sat., noon-5pm Sun., COP$15,000) is a cute joint catering to meatlovers with mostly open-air seating and old photographs of Pereira decorating the walls. It's mostly a lunch place. Grilled beef options like tri-tip (in Colombia called *punta de anca*) are menu favorites.

The specialty at somewhat swanky **Mediterraneo** (Av. Circunvalar No. 4-47, tel. 6/331-0397, noon-2am Mon.-Thurs., noon-3am Sat., noon-1am Sun., COP$25,000) is seafood, but the menu is varied. The lighting is a little on the dark side, but the restaurant is all open-air.

Ambar Diego Panesso (Cra. 17 No. 9-50, tel. 6/344-7444, noon-3pm and 6pm-10pm Mon.-Sat., COP$30,000) serves up elaborate dishes like portobello mushrooms stuffed with apple puree and bacon bits to the Pereira elite. While vegetarian dishes are mostly nonexistent

on the menu, the kitchen will gladly take on the challenge and whip up a pasta dish for you. It's in the upscale Pinares neighborhood. Another restaurant on the elegant side is **El Mirador** (Av. Circunvalar at Cl. 4, Colina, tel. 6/331-2141, noon-2am Mon.-Sat., COP$30,000), a steakhouse that has an incredible view of the city. There's an extensive list of Argentinian wines.

The menu at **El Meson Español** (Cl. 14 No. 25-57, tel. 6/321-5636, noon-3pm and 7pm-midnight daily, COP$22,000) runs the gamut from paellas (the house specialty) to pad Thai.

Dine under a giant Italian flag at the open-air **Portobello** (Cra. 15 No. 11-55, tel. 6/325-0802, noon-3pm and 6pm-10pm Mon.-Wed., noon-3pm and 6pm-11pm Thurs.-Sat., noon-9pm Sun., COP$25,000), the top address for pasta and other Italian favorites, where pizzas are cooked in a wood-burning oven.

Diego Parrilla (Cl. 10B No. 15-09, tel. 6/333-8503, cell tel. 317/402-1980, noon-11pm Mon.-Sat daily, COP$30,000) is a popular steakhouse. It's in the pleasant Los Alpes area, not far from the Circunvalar.

For a hearty Colombian meal, like a big bowl of *ajiaco* (a filling potato-based stew), or to hang out and have a couple of beers at night, **La Ruana** (Av. Circunvalar No. 12-08, tel. 6/325-0115, 8am-2am Mon.-Sat., 8am-10pm Sun., COP$20,000) is the place to go on the Avenida Circunvalar.

Bermeo (tel. 6/333-0909, noon-3pm and 6pm-11pm daily, COP$25,000), which specializes in international cuisine, adjoins Hotel Don Alfonso. While they don't have much in the way of veggie options, they can accommodate vegetarians.

Two always reliable and reasonably priced Colombian chain restaurants that have healthy options on their menus hold prime space in the **Centro Comercial Parque Arboleda** (Circunvalar No. 5-20, www.parquearboleda.com). **Archie's** (tel. 6/317-0600, www.archiespizza.com, 8am-11pm daily, COP$22,000) has great pizzas (try the thin-crust *pizzas rústicas*) and salads. Its location on the top floor, with a breezy terrace, is a cool one. They also deliver. Directly below on the ground floor, meals at **Crepes & Waffles** (tel. 6/331-5189, www.crepesywaffles.com.co, noon-9pm Sun.-Wed., noon-10pm Thurs.-Sat., COP$25,000) serves both savory and sweet crêpes, including many vegetarian options. Desserts, such as mini-waffles with chocolate sauce and vanilla ice cream, are hard to resist.

Information and Services

In Pereira, you can call 123 for any type of emergency.

There is a small **tourist information booth** in the lobby of the Centro Cultural Lucy Tejada (Cl. 10 No. 16-60, tel. 6/311-6544, www.pereiraculturayturismo.gov.co, 8am-noon and 2pm-6:30pm Mon.-Fri.).

Getting There and Around

Excellent bus connections are available between Pereira and most major cities. The **Terminal de Transportes de Pereira** (Cl. 17 No. 23-157, tel. 6/315-2323, www.terminaldepereira.com) is relatively close to the Avenida Circunvalar area. It is clean.

The articulated bus rapid transit system, the **Megabus** (tel. 6/335-1010), has three routes and connects with 28 intra-city buses. It's not terribly convenient for those staying near the Avenida Circunvalar, unfortunately.

The **Aeropuerto Matecaña** (Av. 30 de Agosto, tel. 6/314-2765) is pint-sized, and about a 10-minute ride east from the city. It's quite convenient for those planning on staying at one of the several haciendas in that area. The two largest Colombian airliners, **Avianca** (Av. Circunvalar No. 8B-23, tel. 6/333-0990, www.avianca.com, 8am-1pm and 2:30pm-6pm Mon.-Fri., 8am-noon Sat.) and **LAN** (Cl. 19 No. 8-34, Local 102, 8am-6pm Mon.-Fri., 9am-1pm Sat.) serve Pereira. Panamanian-based **Copa** (Av. Circunvalar No. 8B-51, Edificio Bancafe, Local 103, Col. toll-free tel. 01/800-011-2600, www.copaair.com, 8am-6pm Mon.-Fri., 9am-noon Sat.) has nonstop flights to Panama City five days a week. Budget **Viva Colombia** (www.vivacolombia.co) flies nonstop between Pereira and the Caribbean cities of Cartagena (4 weekly flights) and Santa Marta (3 weekly flights).

For those looking to rent a car, **Hertz** (airport tel. 6/314-2678, www.hertz.com, 8am-6pm Mon.-Fri., 8am-noon Sat.) has an office at the airport.

VALLE DEL RÍO OTÚN

A visit to the Valle del Río Otún (Río Otún Valley) between Pereira and the Laguna del Otún is an interesting, highly enjoyable, and easy to organize introduction to Andean cloud forests. There are many possibilities for visiting the valley, from day trips out of Pereira to multi-day excursions, with very pleasant lodging facilities in the Santuario de Flora y Fauna Otún-Quimbaya and Parque Regional Natural Ucumarí.

The Río Otún flows 78 kilometers (48 miles) from the Laguna del Otún to the Río Cauca and is the main source of water for Pereira. The conservation of the upper segment of the river, from Pereira to the Laguna del Otún, has been a success story, thanks to reforestation land protection efforts.

PLANNING YOUR TIME

The Santuario de Flora y Fauna Otún-Quimbaya is 14.4 kilometers (9 miles) southeast of Pereira along the Río Otún. The Parque Regional Natural Ucumarí is 6.6 kilometers (4 miles) upriver.

You can do day trips out of Pereira to either, but don't try to do both in one day. Santuario de Flora y Fauna Otún-Quimbaya is easily accessible by public transportation, and the main nature trails can be visited in one day. However, getting to Parque Regional Natural Ucumarí involves public transportation and a two-hour hike. It can be visited on a long day trip but it is much preferable to spend a night or two at the comfortable Pastora visitor center in the midst of the Andean forest. You can combine a visit to both, visiting Santuario de Flora y Fauna Otún-Quimbaya and then spending a day or two in Parque Regional Natural Ucumarí.

December and July-August are drier months, and considered the best time for a hike to the

MEDELLÍN

© ANDREW DIER

the Río Otún

Laguna del Otún. However, during mid-December through mid-January and Semana Santa (Holy Week) in March or April the trails can be packed with hikers, as this is high season for Colombians. The hike through Parque Regional Natural Ucumarí to the Laguna del Otún is very popular then, and there can be over a hundred hikers camping each night at that mountain lake.

Santuario de Fauna y Flora Otún-Quimbaya

The **Santuario de Fauna y Flora Otún-Quimbaya** (Km. 4.5 Vía Florida-El Cedral, Vereda La Suiza, cell tel. 313/695-4305, www.parquesnacionales.gov.co, COP$5,000) covers 489 hectares (1,208 acres) of highly biodiverse Andean tropical forest at altitudes between 1,750 and 2,250 meters (5,740 and 7,380 feet). The vegetation is exuberant, and there are animal-viewing opportunities. The park is home to more than 200 species of birds, including endangered multicolored tangers and the large *pava caucana* (Cauca guan). And, although

you may not see them, you'll definitely hear the *mono aulladores* (howler monkeys). They make quite a brouhaha.

The main activities at the park are guided walks along three nature paths led by knowledgeable and enthusiastic guides from a local community ecotourism organization, the **Asociación Comunitaria Yarumo Blanco** (cell tel. 312/200-7711, yarumoblanco2009@hotmail.com). The tours cost COP$35,000 for one path, COP$70,000 for two, and COP$80,000 for all three (per group of any size). Visitors can also rent mountain bikes (COP$10,000 all day) and ride along the main road bordering the crystalline Río Otún.

The visitors center, also run by the association, offers simple but comfortable lodging (COP$32,000-42,000 pp) and meals (COP$6,000-9,000).

To get to Otún-Quimbaya from Pereira, take a bus operated by **Transportes Florida** (tel. 6/331-0488, COP$4,000, 90 mins.) from Calle 12 and Carrera 9 in Pereira. On weekdays, the bus departs at 7am, 9am, and 3pm. On weekends there is an additional bus at noon. The buses return from Otún-Quimbaya at approximately 9:30am, 11:30am, and 5:30pm.

Parque Regional Natural Ucumarí

The **Parque Regional Natural Ucumarí** is 6.6 kilometers (4 miles) southwest of Santuario Flora y Fauna Otún-Quimbaya. This regional park covers an area of 3,986 hectares (9,850 acres) of Andean tropical forest at altitudes between 1,800 and 2,600 meters (5,900 and 8,500 feet). The main path follows the Río Otún through lush cloud forests, with waterfalls feeding into the river. The park is a wonderful place to view nature, with more than 185 species of birds.

The starting point of the main path is **El Cedral,** a small *vereda* (settlement) southwest of Santuario Flora y Fauna Otún-Quimbaya. The path is a well-trod one (by humans and horses) and is often muddy and rocky. It is best to take rubber or waterproof boots. It takes about 2.5 hours to climb to the main La Pastora visitors center, six kilometers from El Cedral.

If you are on a day trip from Pereira, you can have lunch at the visitors center (COP$9,000 pp) and set off on one of three nature hikes before returning to El Cedral to catch the last bus at 5pm. Even better, you can spend a night or two in the clean and very cozy dormitory-style rooms (COP$22,000 pp). As the temperature begins to drop in the late afternoon, you can sit by the lodge's fireplace and sip hot chocolate and eat cheese (as is the custom in Colombia). There is no electricity, making a stay at La Pastora truly restful. To make a reservation, contact the ecotourism organization **Fecomar** (cell tel. 312/200-7711, fecomar.anp@hotmail.com, www.fecomar.com.co). They can arrange horses, if you would rather ride than hike up.

Past La Pastora, the path continues 13 kilometers to the **Laguna del Otún** in the **Parque Nacional Natural Los Nevados.**

To get to El Cedral take the **Transportes Florida** bus (tel. 6/331-0488, COP$5,000, 2 hrs.) from Calle 12 and Carrera 9 in Pereira. On weekdays, the bus departs at 7am, 9am, and 3pm. On weekends there is an additional bus at noon. The buses return from Santuario Flora y Fauna Otún-Quimbaya at approximately at 9am, 11am, and 5pm.

SANTA ROSA DE CABAL

The dusty town of Santa Rosa de Cabal means one thing to most Colombians: *termales* (hot springs). To get to the most well-known springs you'll have to pass through Santa Rosa de Cabal. In town, at the **Parque las Araucarias** (between Cras. 14-15 and Clls. 12-13), the main square, there are juices to be drank, *chorizo santarosano* sausages to be eaten (a specialty here), handicrafts to be bought, and people to be watched. The other point of interest is the **Santuario La Milagrosa** (Cl. 7 at Cra. 14, tel. 6/368-5201 or 6/368-5168), a generally drab modern church with a fantastic stained glass window.

Hot Springs

There are two *termales* (hot springs) near Santa Rosa de Cabal: **Termales de Santa Rosa de Cabal** (Km. 9 Vía Termales, tel. 6/364-5500,

www.termales.com.co, 9am-11:30pm daily, COP$14,000-31,000) and **Termales San Vicente** (18 km east of Santa Rosa de Cabal, tel. 6/333-3433, www.sanvicente.com.co, 8am-midnight daily, COP$19,000-60,000). Both are wildly popular with Colombian families on weekends and holidays, and are quieter during the week. Both springs offer transportation from Pereira, and entry fees drop during the week.

Built in 1945, the Termales de Santa Rosa de Cabal hot springs are closer to Santa Rosa de Cabal. There are two areas in the complex. The first area, on the left as you enter the park, was recently built and is called the **Termales Balneario.** These consist of three large pools for adults and one for children. This area is the most popular for day-trip visitors.

The oldest part of the complex, called **Termales de Hotel** (hours vary Mon.-Fri., COP$24,000), is farther on at the base of some spectacular waterfalls of cool and pure mountain waters. The highest waterfall drops some 175 meters (575 feet). If you choose to stay the night, there are three options. **La Cabaña** (COP$183,000 pp, meals incl.) is the newest and most comfortable place to stay and has 17 rooms. La Cabaña guests are allowed entry to the Termales Balneario, the Termales de Hotel, and their own small private pool. The advantage of staying at one of the hotels is that you can enjoy full use of the pools from 6am on, before the day-trip crowd begins arriving at 9am.

At both Termales Balneario and Termales de Hotel, there are additional activities on offer, such as a guided nature walk (COP$14,000) to some waterfalls—wear shoes with traction for this, the path is slippery—and spa treatments such as massages (COP$60,000, 45 mins.) and other services in a shabby-looking spa area.

The San Vicente hot springs are more remote, but the scenery of rolling hills, mountains in the distance, and farms is enchanting. Particularly scenic are the *pozos de amor,* small natural pools the size of whirlpools that perfectly fit two. The all-inclusive *pasadia* (day pass) option with transportation costs

COP$60,000. Buses leave Pereira at 8am, returning at 5pm. San Vicente also offers accommodations, with cabins and a small hotel. A cabin for two people costs COP$173,000 per person without meals.

Accommodations and Food

The bucolic countryside outside of Santa Rosa is home to many roadside, family-style restaurants. The best two are run by the same owner. On the road towards the Termales de Santa Rosa, **Mamatina** (Km. 1 Vía Termales, La Leona, tel. 6/363-4899, 9am-10pm daily, COP$18,000) specializes in trout covered with sausage, *sancocho* (a meaty stew), and grilled meats. They can also accommodate vegetarians, usually a nutritious meal of beans and rice. Next door to the restaurant is their hotel by the same name (tel. 6/363-4899), which offers clean and comfortable rooms ranging in price from COP$40,000 per person to COP$140,000 for the suite with a hot tub. Horseback riding and walks through the countryside can be arranged here.

On the way towards Termales de San Vicente is their other, newer hotel. The **⟨ Hospedaje Don Lolo** (Km. 5 Vía Termales San Vicente, cell tel. 316/698-6797, hospedajedonlol@gmail.com, COP$50,000 pp d) is a hotel on a farm with cows, pigs, fish, horses, and dogs. If you're interested, you can lend a hand milking a cow or two. Some walks through the countryside are options as well, such as to an old Indian cemetery, to a big waterfall, and through jungle to see birds and butterflies. The countryside views and fresh air are delightful. If you're lucky, you may be able to see the Nevado del Ruiz in the distance in the early morning. The **Don Lolo** (Km. 5 Vía Termales San Vicente, cell tel. 316/698-6797) restaurant just down the road has a lot of personality and is a popular stopping off point going to or returning from the Termales de San Vicente.

BELALCÁZAR

The coffee and plantain town of Belalcázar rests impossibly on a ridge, with fantastic views of the Valle de Cauca on one side and the Valle

sunny street in Belalcázar

© ANDREW DIER

del Río Risaralda on the other. Besides the incredible views, Belalcázar, an agricultural town off the tourist map, offers the visitor pure coffee region authenticity. Belalcázar has a distinct architecture, with its houses covered with colorful zinc sheets to protect against strong winds.

Built in 1954 in hopes of preventing further bloodshed during the bloody Violencia period, the 45.5-meter-high (149-foot-high) **Monumento a Cristo Rey** (Km. 1 Vía Pereira-Belalcázar, COP$3,000) has become the symbol of this town. To get to the top of the statue of Jesus, you'll have to climb 154 steps. From atop, on a clear day, you can see six Colombian departments: Caldas, Risaralda, Quindío, Valle del Cauca, Tolima, and Chocó; and both Central and Occidental mountain ranges. The other attraction in town is the **Eco Parque La Estampilla hike** (1.5 km, open daylight hours, free). It's on the northeast side of town, a 10-minute walk from the **Parque Bolívar** (Clls. 15-16 and Cras. 4-5), in which you can wander a winding path through forests of *guadua* (bamboo).

The best time to check out Belalcázar life at its most vibrant is on market day—Saturday—when farmers from the countryside converge into town to sell coffee beans, plantains, pineapples, and other crops. On this day the Parque Bolívar buzzes with activity as Jeep Willys, packed with farmers and market-goers, come and go all day long. It's quite a carnival atmosphere.

The best hotel in town is the **Hotel Balcón Colonial** (Cra. 4A No. 12-10, tel. 6/860-2433, COP$35,000 d). It's clean, cool, and basic, having just nine rooms.

Getting There

It is 45 kilometers (29 miles) from Pereira to Belalcázar. Buses leave from the Pereira Terminal de Transportes (Cl. 17 No. 23-157, Pereira, tel. 6/315-2323). **Flota Occidental** (tel. 6/321-1655) is the bus company that serves Belalcázar (COP$6,000, 1.5 hrs.).

SANTUARIO

It's worth the arduous journey to this remote village on a mountaintop in the Cordillera Occidental (Western Mountains) just to take a photo of its famous **Calle Real,** dotted with stately Paisa houses that have been done up in a rainbow of colors. Calle Real is one of the most photographed streets in Colombia.

On Saturdays, campesinos come into town to sell their coffee, cacao, sugarcane, and other crops. There is so much activity on market day in the **Plaza de Bolívar** (between Clls. 6-7 and Cras. 5-6) that you'll be tempted to find a front row seat in a café and take it all in: produce and coffee being unloaded and loaded, Jeep Willys filled with standing-room-only passengers arriving and departing, farmers drinking beer in taverns, women selling sweets in the park, and children being children. Many farmers, money in hand, whoop it up in town and stay the night.

Although Santuario is indeed picture-perfect, it's far better to continue on to the **Parque Nacional Natural Tatamá** than to spend the night in Santuario, even if you are not interested in doing any hiking or trekking. Hotels in town are not recommended.

There is regular bus transportation from the Terminal de Transportes de Pereira (Cl. 17 No. 23-157, Pereira, tel. 6/315-2323) to Santuario. **Flota Occidental** (tel. 6/321-1655) makes this two-hour trip (COP$6,000) three times a day: 6:45am, noon, and 5:20pm.

PARQUE MUNICIPAL NATURAL PLANES DE SAN RAFAEL

Located in the remote, little visited Cordillera Occidental (Western Mountains), the Tatamá Massif contains one of the world's few remaining pristine *páramos* (highland moors). The topography of the mountain range is very broken, especially the jagged **Cerro Tatamá** (4,250 meters/13,945 feet), which is the highest point in the Cordillera Occidental. The range is highly biodiverse, with an estimated 564 species of orchids and 402 species of birds. It is also home to pumas, jaguars, and *osos anteojos,* the only breed of bear in Colombia. The central part of the massif is protected by the 15,900-hectare (39,300-acre) Parque Natural Nacional Tatamá.

Access to Tatamá is through the Parque Municipal Natural Planes de San Rafael, which acts as a buffer zone on the eastern side of Tatamá near the town of Santuario, but which is an attraction in itself.

The **Parque Municipal Natural Planes de San Rafael** (10 km from Santuario, cell tel 311/719-1717, http://planesdesanrafael. blogspot.com) covers an area of 11,796 hectares (29,149 acres) of cloud forest between the altitudes of 2,000 and 2,600 meters, with significant patches of primary growth. The main activities are nature walks conducted by friendly and knowledgeable guides of a local community organization, the **Asociación de Guías e Interpretes Ambientales (GAIA),** many of whom got their start through participation in groups of youth bird-watchers.

Within the park there are four main paths. The shortest, called the **Lluvia de Semillas** (Rainfall of Seeds), allows visitors to see a forest in recuperation. It is a one-kilometer (0.6-mile) loop through land that was once used for cattle grazing and, over the past 15 years, has been slowly returning to a forest. The 9.6-kilometer (6-mile) round-trip **Cascadas** trail is a strenuous path to the border of the Parque Nacional Natural Tatamá at an elevation of 2,600 meters. It crisscrosses the Río San Rafael and culminates at a group of waterfalls. Along the way you can see a great variety of birds and large patches of primary forest. The hike takes 3.5 hours up and 2.5 hours down. The 12-kilometer (7.5-mile) **Quebrada Risaralda** hike takes six hours and can be combined into a loop with the Cascadas hike. Finally, the **Laguna Encantada** path is a nine-kilometer (5.5-mile) circuit that takes five hours and is especially good for bird-watching, with the possibility of viewing many hummingbirds. The best time for these hikes is early in the morning. Costs for these excursions are COP$25,000-35,000 per group of any size.

Parque Nacional Natural Tatamá

From Parque Municipal Natural Planes de San Rafael it is also possible to organize excursions into the **Parque Nacional Natural Tatamá** (tel. 6/368-7964, www.parquesnacionales.gov.co), located at the highest point of the Cordillera Occidental between the departments of Chocó, Risaralda, and Valle del Cauca. Though it is not officially open to ecotourism, the folks at GAIA can organize an excursion that requires at least two nights of camping. The first day involves a 12-kilometer (7.5-mile), eight-hour hike to a campground at 3,200 meters. The following day you explore the upper reaches of the Tatamá, with the unusual shrub-covered *páramo* (high tropical mountain ecosystem), craggy outcrops, and deep gorges. From the top you can see the Chocó lowlands. You return by nightfall to camp and return to Parque Municipal Natural Planes de San Rafael on the following day.

Accommodations

The clean, comfortable, and quite cozy lodge (COP$20,000 pp) at the Parque Municipal Natural Planes de San Rafael visitors center accommodates 40 people. Meals (COP$6,000-9,000) are nothing short of delicious. To reserve lodging, contact the ecotourism organization **FECOMAR** (cell tel. 312/200-7711, fecomar.anp@hotmail.com, www.fecomar.com.co) or call the park administrator (cell tel. 311/719-1717).

Getting There

To get to the Parque Municipal Natural Planes de San Rafael visitors center and lodge, pick up one of the Jeeps that leave from the main square in Santuario each day at 7am and 3pm. A taxi can also take you for COP$20,000.

IBAGUÉ

Ibagué (pop. 593,000) is the capital city of the Tolima department. It is a hot city of traffic jams that does not seduce many travelers. It is, however, a city of music and hosts several music festivals each year. It's hard to believe, but just to the west of Ibagué, a city in one of the most important tropical-fruit-producing regions in Colombia, looms the Nevado del Tolima, a snowcapped volcano in the eastern side of the Parque Nacional Natural Los Nevados. Ibagué is a great launch pad for the challenge of ascending to that mountain.

Sights

Should you have some time to spend in Ibagué, a handful of sights are worth taking a look. Shade is not an issue at the **Plaza de Bolívar** (between Cras. 2-3 and Clls. 9-10): It's full of huge, centuries-old trees.

Staff at the tourist kiosk in the plaza in front of the **Catedral Inmaculada Concepción** (Cl. 10 No. 1-129, tel. 8/263-3451, 7am-noon and 2:30pm-7:30pm daily) can suggest hiking excursions and tips on trekking up to the Nevado del Tolima. The **Banco de la República** (Cra. 3A No. 11-26, tel. 8/263-0721, 8:30am-6pm Mon.-Fri., 8:30am-1pm Sat., free) always has an exhibit in its one exhibition hall on the second floor. It's just off of **Calle Peatonal** (Cra. 3 between Clls. 10-15), which is refreshingly free from cars and motorbikes.

The **Conservatorio del Tolima** (Cra. 1 between Clls. 9-10, tel. 8/826-1852, www.

conservatoriodeltolima.edu.co, open only for concerts) is perhaps Ibagué's claim to fame and the reason it calls itself the "Capital Musical de Colombia." A few bars from the Colombian national anthem are painted on the exterior of the yellow republican-era building.

Music festivals take place in the city year-round, including the **Festival Nacional de la Musica Colombiana** (www.fundacionmusicaldecolombia.com, Mar.), the **Festival de Jazz** (May), and the **Festival Folclórico Colombiano** (www.festivalfolclorico.com, June or July).

The **Museo de Arte del Tolima** (Cra. 7 No. 5-93, tel. 8/273-2840, www.museodeartedeltolima.org, 10am-6pm daily, COP$3,000) is a small museum with a permanent collection and temporary exhibition space dedicated to contemporary Colombian artists. A leafy park in this pleasant part of town is the **Parque Centenario** (Cra. 6 between Clls. 8-10). Along with usual park goings-on, cultural events are often held in an amphitheater.

Accommodations and Food

The **Hotel Ambeima** (Cra. 3 No. 13-32, tel. 8/263-4300, www.hotelambeima.com, COP$89,000 d) is downtown on the Calle Peatonal and is a decent midrange choice.

The best hotel in town is the **Hotel Estelar Altamira** (Cra. 1A No. 45-50, tel. 8/266-6111, COP$203,000 d). There are no hostels that cater to international backpackers.

The trendy dining and drinking spot in Ibagué is 15 stories high, with a superb bird's-eye view of the city and the Parque Nacional Natural Los Nevados. **Altavista** (Cra. 2 at Cl. 11, tel. 8/277-1381, noon-midnight Mon.-Wed., noon-3am Thurs.-Sat., noon-4pm Sun., COP$25,000) has a little bit of everything: Asian-inspired dishes, tapas, and even several vegetarian options. The decor and atmosphere are all South Beach. As the sun slips behind the mountains in the distance, bartenders swing into full motion as Altavista turns into a *play* (fashionable) nightclub scene.

Getting There and Around

The **Terminal de Transportes** (Cra. 2 No. 20-86, tel. 8/261-8122, www.terminalibague.com) is in a rough part of town, so you should take a cab to and from the bus station. For the most part, Ibagué is not a walkable city, except in the center of town. From the Ibagué airport, **Aeropuerto Nacional Perales** (Vía al Aeropuerto, tel. 8/267-6096), there are nonstop flights to Bogotá and Medellín.

MEDELLÍN

CALI AND SOUTHWEST COLOMBIA

The distances between the cities in the southwest of Colombia are not great as the crow (or in this case, the condor) flies. However, Cali, Popayán, Pasto, and their environs are worlds apart. Cali is a city that melds its colonial past with visions of a modern future. In Pasto, the largest city in the Nariño department, Volcán Galeras looms in the distance. Popayán

© ANDREW DIER

HIGHLIGHTS

LOOK FOR  TO FIND RECOMMENDED SIGHTS, ACTIVITIES, DINING, AND LODGING.

COLOMBIA

PACIFIC
OCEAN

Salsa
in Cali

Tierradentro

Centro Histórico
in Popayán

San Agustín

Laguna
Verde

Laguna
La Cocha

ECUADOR

0   50 mi

0   50 km

© AVALON TRAVEL

Salsa in Cali: There is no better place to practice your moves than at one of Cali's

countless *salsatecas* (salsa clubs). But even if you have two left feet, you can still get into the spirit by taking in a salsa show, going to Salsa al Parque, or enjoying the one-of-a-kind atmosphere at an old-school salsa bar (page 308).

Laguna La Cocha: Take a boat ride from the colorful fishing village of Encano to the tiny tropical rainforest Isla de la Corota, home to Colombia's smallest national park (page 334).

Laguna Verde: The emerald-green waters of this crater lake in the Nudo de los Pastos mountains on the border with Ecuador are a fantastic sight to behold (page 334).

***Centro Histórico* in Popayán:** Explore volcanoes, coffee farms, indigenous markets, or hot springs by day, but save some energy and time to amble the streets of the White City's beautiful historic center after the sun goes down (page 341).

Tierradentro: Dozens of elaborate burial chambers lie beneath the hilltops in this important archaeological site in Cauca (page 345).

San Agustín: A visit to this incredible archaeological site, coupled with nature hikes or rafting adventures, is a highlight of any visit to Colombia. This is Colombia's Easter Island (page 348).

is the White City, historic home of presidents and poets.

In Cali, Colombia's third largest city, vestiges of the colonial past endure in the historic center. Its centerpiece is the superbly maintained 16th-century Iglesia La Merced. But Cali is best known for its warm people and its hot salsa dancing. Across the city, visitors will see Caleños at play: hanging out in the Parque San Antonio, strolling along La Loma de la Cruz artisan market, and dancing at Salsa al Parque, a free outdoor salsa party that's held once a month. This is the place to take a salsa

lesson or two, practice your fancy footwork on the dance floor, or settle back in a booth at a popular *salsateca,* enjoying the music and one-of-a-kind atmosphere.

The Valle de Cauca, just a couple hours' ride from the departmental capital, offers some unsung destinations. As you set off from the city, the flat countryside is dominated by fields of sugarcane, interrupted only by occasional *samán* trees, which look like they belong in Africa. Every once in a while, a verdant island stands out in the middle of the cane fields—a hacienda, or country estate. Buga, a Catholic

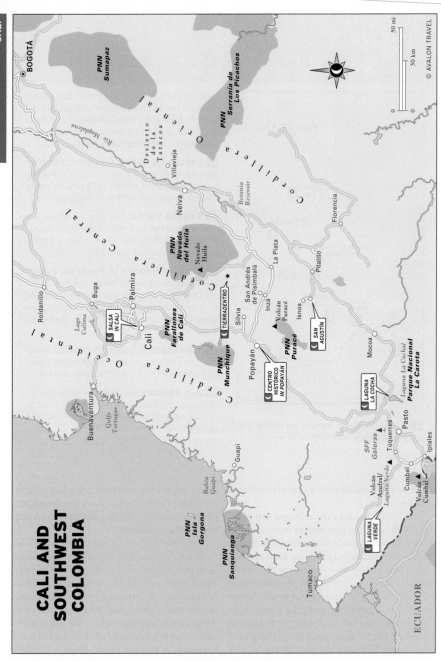

CALI AND
SOUTHWEST
COLOMBIA

© AVALON TRAVEL

BOGOTÁ

PNN
Sumapaz

PNN
Serranía de
Los Picachos

Cordillera Oriental

Río Magdalena

Desierto
de la
Tatacoa

Villavieja

Neiva

Betania
Reservir

Florencia

Cordillera Central

PNN
Nevado
del Huila

Nevado
Huila

La Plata

Pitalito

Roldanillo

Buga

Palmira

SALSA
IN CALI

TIERRADENTRO

San Andrés
de Pisimbalá

Inzá

Volcán
Puracé

Isnos

PNN
Faralones
de Cali

Lago
Calima

Cali

PNN
Munchique

Silvia

SAN
AGUSTÍN

PNN
Puracé

Mocoa

Buenaventura

Golfo
Tortuga

Popayán

CENTRO
HISTÓRICO
IN POPAYÁN

Laguna La Cochal
Parque Nacional
La Carota

LAGUNA
LA COCHA

Guapi

Bahía
Guapi

Cordillera Occidental

PNN
Isla
Gorgona

PNN
Sanquianga

Pasto

Ipiales

SFF
Galeras

Túquerres

Volcán
Azufral
Laguna Verde

Cumbal

Volcán
Cumbal

LAGUNA
VERDE

Tumaco

ECUADOR

50 mi

50 km

0

pilgrimage site, is perfectly situated near the weekend playground of Lagos Calima. In the north of the department is the sleepy town of Roldanillo, which was put on the map thanks to its famous son, abstract expressionist artist Omar Rayo. For adventurous types, this cute town is about a different art: the art of flying. Each year hundreds catch a breeze as they paraglide over the valley.

Although many travelers make a quick detour on their way to or from Ecuador to admire the neo-gothic gem of Las Lajas church, set impossibly in a narrow canyon near Ipiales, few spend the time to get to know the department of Nariño. Yet it is here that every mountain you ascend, every river you traverse, and every turn you make reveals even more jaw-dropping scenery. Jagged mountains, turquoise lakes, and sleeping volcanoes provide dramatic backdrops to the neat patchwork of potato crops that sustain many families in this agricultural region. Volcán Galeras is a sometimes ominous presence in Pasto's skyline, it doesn't stop revelers from living it up during the Carnaval de Negros y Blancos in January. Not far from the city is Laguna La Cocha, with fishing communities of brightly colored clapboard houses and wooden fishing boats.

Upstream along the Río Cauca from the Valle de Cauca is the "White City" of Popayán, home to the Universidad del Cauca. Students fill the city's cafés, bars, and its stately main plaza, the Parque Caldas. Nearby are several interesting day trips, from organic coffee farms to hot springs to indigenous markets. In the national park of Puracé, intrepid hikers trek to the rim of a snow-covered active volcano. Farther on are two of Colombia's most important and beautiful archaeological sites: Tierradentro, where dozens of ancient underground burial chambers are preserved, and San Agustín, where hundreds of well-preserved stone statues of deities and animals stand in silence.

PLANNING YOUR TIME

Three days is just enough time to get a feel for the Cali way. Try visiting the city over part of the weekend so that you can check out a salsa show or visit a *salsateca* (salsa club). Other sights of interest in Valle de Cauca can be visited out of Cali or perhaps from Buga. Roldanillo makes a nice side trip between Cali and the Coffee Region near Armenia.

It's an easy trip between Cali and Popayán, about three hours by minivan on a good road. If you'd like to check out sights near Popayán, such as the Guambiano town of Silvia, or hike to the Puracé volcano, plan for at least 3-4 days in the capital of Cauca. A circuit tour of the sights of Tierradentro, the Tatacoa desert, and San Agustín can be done out of Popayán. For that you'll need five days.

It is often slow going on the Pan-American Highway between Ipiales, through Pasto, to Popayán. (But the scenery? Simply incredible.) While Ipiales is not a great base for sightseeing, the larger city of Pasto is. You can happily spend a few days seeing the city and taking some day trips such as La Cocha or the Laguna Verde. The strenuous climb up Volcán Cumbal takes planning but is worth it.

Some of the big goings in the region are the Semana Santa processions in Popayán (Easter week), the Feria de Cali (last week of December), and the Carnaval de Negros y Blancos (January 4-7) in Pasto.

Cali

Cali's relaxed place is evident everywhere you go in this diverse city of three million. It may be the infernal heat slowing everyone down, without regard to *tinto* (coffee) intake. Here in the Valle del Cauca, where sugarcane fields go on forever, you're far removed from uptight Bogotá and over-ambitious Medellín. In a swipe at those two cities, locals like to say that, *"Cali es Cali y lo demás es loma"* ("Cali is Cali but those other cities are just hills").

While the colonial churches of La Merced and San Antonio are some of the loveliest you will see in Colombia, Cali is not a city packed with must-see sights. Yet tourists keep falling in love with the "Sultan of the Valley." Is it that late refreshing afternoon breeze? The people? Or is it the salsa?

Cali is, indeed, all about salsa. That's pretty clear once you hop in any cab in the city. The music is turned on, and there's an 80 percent chance you'll hear the driver singing along to the hypnotic rhythms of conga drums, bongos, and timbales. At the bus terminal, *muchachos* working for the bus companie break into some fancy footwork as they wait for customers. In hotels, housekeeping staff walk the corridors cheerfully singing.

Cali is the world's salsa capital. Incorporating a little salsa into your visit to Cali is a necessity if you want to get to know this seductive city, its people, and their ways.

History

Present-day Valle del Cauca was settled by the Calima people as early as 1200 BC. The first Europeans to arrive were soldiers under the command of Sebastián de Belalcázar. This Spanish conquistador served under Francisco Pizarro in the conquest of Peru, but then decided to seek his own fame by conquering most of present-day Ecuador and southwestern Colombia. In 1536, he founded Santiago de Cali, slightly north of its current location. During the colonial period and most of the

19th century, Cali was a small agricultural settlement, surrounded by haciendas, with a significant slave population.

The construction of railway links spurred economic development and in the 20th century, Valle de Cauca became sugarcane country. Cali developed rapidly, becoming a center of manufacturing. In 1971, the city hosted the Pan-American Games. That was probably Cali's heyday, before it started a long process of decay.

During the 1980s and 1990s, Cali became a global drug trafficking center and seat of the eponymous drug cartel. It is widely believed that Cali Cartel kingpins Gilberto and Miguel Rodríguez Orejuela provided key support to government authorities in their war against the Medellín Cartel, which ultimately resulted in the assassination of Pablo Escobar and breakup of his empire. For a time in the 1990s, the Cali Cartel ruled the global cocaine business unchallenged.

As a result of drug-related violence, Cali's civic leaders fled, taking investment and business elsewhere. During the 1990s and early 21st century, the city had a double scourge of urban violence and guerrilla intimidation. The FARC (Fuerzas Armadas Revolucionarias de Colombia; Revolutionary Armed Forces of Colombia) occupied much of the surrounding mountainous areas.

Currently Cali is living a renaissance of sorts, undertaking major infrastructure projects, such as the MIO mass transit system, and is beginning to attract new investments. And in 2013, Cali was the proud host of the World Games, an international sports competition.

Orientation

Nearly all of the city's tourist attractions are located in the **Centro,** in three areas in particular: **La Merced, La Ermita,** and **Plaza Cayzedo/Iglesia San Francisco.** You can visit all these areas on foot in one day. The Centro

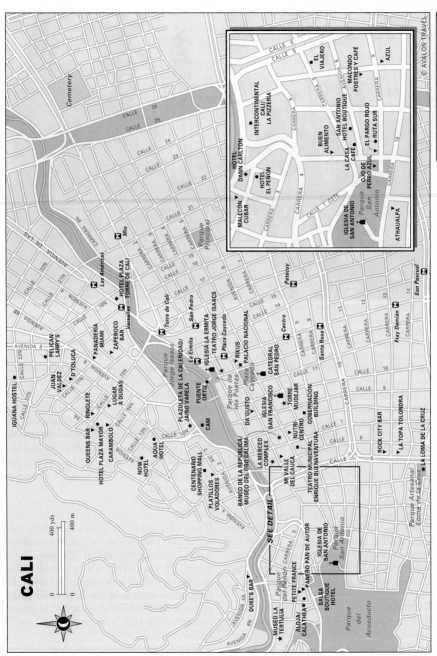

CALI

© AVALON TRAVEL

Cemetery

CALLE 26
CALLE 25
CALLE 24
CALLE 23
CALLE 22
CALLE 21

Parque Principal

Mio

Las Américas

AVENIDA DE LAS

CARRERA 3N

CALLE 22N

CALLE 21N

AVENIDA

CALLE 19N

CALLE 18N

AVENIDA 8

PELICAN LARRY'S

JUAN VALDEZ

D'TOLUCA

CALLE 17N

PANADERÍA MIAMI

ZAPEROCO BAR

HOTEL PLAZA TORRE DE CALI

Vessalles

Torre de Cali

Parque Jorge Isaacs

IGUANA HOSTEL

CALLE 5JN

RINGLETE

CALLE 9A

QUEENS BAR

HOTEL PLAZA MAYOR

CARAMBOLO

LUGAR A DUDAS

CALLE 16N

CALLE 14N

CALLE 13N

NOW HOTEL

AQUA HOTEL

AVENIDA

La Ermita

San Pedro

IGLESIA LA ERMITA

TEATRO JORGE ISAACS

Plaza Caycedo

PUENTE ORTIZ

PLAZOLETA DE LA CALENIDAD/ JAIRO VARELA

CAM

CENTENARIO SHOPPING MALL

PLATILLOS VOLADORES

AVENIDA 2

BANCO DE LA REPÚBLICA/ MUSEO DEL ORO CALIMA

LA MERCED COMPLEX

MI VALLE DEL CAUCA

TEATRO MUNICIPAL ENRIQUE BUENAVENTURA

DA'GUSTO

IGLESIA SAN FRANCISCO

TORRE MUDÉJAR

GOBERNACIÓN BUILDING

NUTRI-CENTRO

SEE DETAIL

Parque del Peñon

MUSEO LA TERTULIA

ALOJA/ CALATHEA

PETITE FRANCE

PANERO PAN DE AUTOR

SALSA BOUTIQUE HOTEL

DUKE'S BAR

AVENIDA 4A

AVENIDA 6N

AVENIDA 8N

Parque del Acueducto

Parque Artesanal Loma de la Cruz

IGLESIA DE SAN ANTONIO

Parque San Antonio

ROCK CITY BAR

LA TOPA TOLONDRA

LA LOMA DE LA CRUZ

CARRERA 1

CARRERA 3

Parque de los Poetas

RIKUS

PALACIO NACIONAL

CATEDRAL SAN PEDRO

Centro

Santa Rosa

Petecuy

San Pascual

Fray Damián

San Pascual

CARRERA 2

CARRERA 3

CARRERA 4

CARRERA 5

CARRERA 6

CARRERA 7

AVENIDA 6

CARRERA 8

CARRERA 9

CARRERA 10

CARRERA 12

CARRERA 13

CARRERA 14

CALLE 20

CALLE 19

CALLE 18

CALLE 17

CALLE 16

CALLE 15

CALLE 14

CALLE 13

CALLE 12

CALLE 11

CALLE 10

CALLE 9

CALLE 8

CALLE 7

CALLE 6

400 yds
400 m

Detail

HOTEL DANN CARLTON

INTERCONTINENTAL CALI/ LA PIZZERIA

MALECÓN CUBAR

HOTEL EL PEÑON

BUEN ALIMENTO

LA CASA

SAN ANTONIO HOTEL BOUTIQUE

EL PARGO ROJO

RUTA SUR

OJO DE PERRO ROJO

EL VIAJERO

MACONDO POSTRES Y CAFÉ

AZUL

CAFÉ

IGLESIA DE SAN ANTONIO

ATHAUALPA

Parque San Antonio

CALLE 5

CALLE 4

CALLE 3

CALLE 2

CALLE 1 OESTE

CARRERA 2

CARRERA 3

CARRERA 4

CARRERA 5

CARRERA 6

CARRERA 7

CARRERA 8

AVENIDA 6

CARRERA 9

CARRERA 10

the towering palms of the Plaza Cayzedo

is brimming with activity during weekdays. Avoid the midday heat by planning your visit in the morning or late afternoon. Avoid lingering downtown after dark.

Inviting neighborhoods such as **San Antonio, Granada,** and **El Peñon** may lack attractions but are a delight to get to know. Within a 10- to 15-minute cab ride from the Centro, these tree-lined barrios are filled with restaurants, shops, and hotels. Late-night activity on weekends tends to shift to northern areas (not far from Granada) such as Menga and Yumbo.

You may have difficulty figuring out the lay of the land in Cali, as it is not as straightforward as other cities in Colombia. The Río Cali (actually more of a stream), the Tres Cruces hill, the Torre de Cali, and the Intercontinental Cali are well-known points of reference.

Climate

The average temperature in *caliente* Cali is about 24°C (75°F); however, the average daily high is a sizzling 30°C (86°F). But 4:30pm-6:30pm, when the sun begins its descent over the western Cordillera and into the Pacific, the drop in temperature (to around 19°C/66°F), softening of the sun's rays, and a gentle breeze combine to make the weather absolutely *delicioso*. In residential areas like San Antonio, the perfect temps are a magnet drawing people outside. Plan your day accordingly: Do all your necessary emailing and online time-wasting during the heat of the day or later at night, and make that late afternoon stroll an event.

Safety

If you ask a taxi driver in Cali if a certain barrio (neighborhood) is *seguro* (safe), you may get a response along the lines of, *"¡Es seguro que te roban!"* ("It's sure that you'll be robbed!"). But don't worry—that's a common joke. Follow the general precautions of any large Colombian city, especially regarding the use of taxis and precautions to take in nightspots, and you'll be fine.

Even though pickpockets are about, walking

by day is fine in Centro (downtown), as it is always bustling with people. But be alert near sights such as Iglesia La Ermita. Walking within neighborhoods is generally safer than walking between them, such as between the Centro and Granada or San Antonio. MIO (the bus system) is a safe option.

There are community police stations (Centros de Atención Inmediata or CAI) in every neighborhood and often in parks. There is a CAI in the Parque de San Antonio, not far from the church. The national toll-free hotline for any emergency is 123. The police have an additional number, 112.

SIGHTS

All the major historical and tourist sights in Cali are found in the Centro, or downtown. The best time to visit churches is during mass; otherwise there is a good chance they'll be closed.

La Merced Complex

On June 25, 1536, the city of Santiago de Cali was founded by Sebastián de Belalcázar. He changed his mind and moved the city shortly thereafter to its present location, and a mass was held to celebrate the foundation of the city. It was on this site that the **Iglesia La Merced** (Cra. 4 at Cl. 7, tel. 2/889-2309, 6:30am-10am and 4pm-7pm daily, masses at 7am and 6pm Mon.-Sat., 9am and 6pm Sun.) was built, sometime around 1545. The oldest church in Cali, it is a lovely example of typical colonial construction of the time, with its thick, white-washed walls. The church, in the shape of a cross, has a single nave with red wooden beams. The only extravagance to be seen is the golden baroque altar with a statue of the Virgen de las Mercedes, who is the patron saint of Cali. It stands out against the austerity of this house of worship.

Adjacent to the church is the **Museo de Arte Colonial y Religioso La Merced** (Cra. 4 No. 6-117, tel. 2/888-0646, cell tel. 312/731-5948, 9am-noon and 2pm-5pm Mon.-Fri., 9am-2pm Sat., museocolonial.lamerced@gmail.com, COP$4,000 adults, COP$3,000

students, COP$2,000 children), a small museum containing Quiteño school paintings, silver objects, statues, and religious items from the colonial period. Guides, usually college students, will be happy to show you around for a small fee. The museum is located in the church's chapels of the Virgen de la Merced and Virgen de los Remedios.

The well-done **Museo Arqueológico La Merced** (Cra. 4 No. 6-59, tel. 2/885-4665, 9am-1pm and 2pm-6pm Mon.-Sat., museolamerced@une.net.co, COP$4,000 adults, COP$2,000 children) is housed in part of the Augustinian convent and has two exhibition rooms highlighting ceramics from native cultures of the region: Tolima, Quimbaya, Calima, Tierradentro, San Agustín, Tumaco, and Nariño.

MUSEO DEL ORO CALIMA

Within the Banco de la República building across the street from Iglesia La Merced is the **Museo del Oro Calima** (Cl. 7 No. 4-69, tel. 2/684-7754, www.banrepcultural.org/cali/museodelorocalima, 9am-5pm Tues.-Fri., 10am-5pm Sat., free). Cali's gold museum has a collection of more than 600 ornamental gold and utilitarian ceramics, attributed to the ancient Calima people, that have been unearthed northwest of present-day Cali.

The **Sala de Exposiciones de la Banco de la República** (Cl. 7 No. 4-69, tel. 2/684-7751, 9am-5:30pm Mon.-Fri., free) is in the same building as the Museo del Oro, and it often hosts traveling exhibits from the bank's art collection as well as special exhibits by regional artists. It's worth a peek.

IGLESIA LA ERMITA

Near the Río Cali is one of the city's most iconic landmarks: the mini, neo-gothic **Iglesia La Ermita** (Cra. 13 at Cl. 1, no phone, masses at 7am and 5pm Mon.-Fri., 10am and 5pm Sat.-Sun.). Originally built in the 16th century, the church was destroyed by earthquakes in 1787 and in 1925. There was not much left after the 18th-century tremor, except for the painting of the Señor de la Caña, another demonstration of how important sugarcane has been to the people of the Valle del Cauca. Its survival was attributed to a miracle. The three-nave church has an Italian marble altar and many stained-glass windows. The current building was completed in the 1940s, and its design is said to have been modeled after the towering Ulm Minster in Germany.

PLAZOLETA JAIRO VARELA AND BULEVAR DEL RÍO

Megaprojects to revitalize the deteriorating downtown began in 2010. In 2013 the **Plazoleta Jairo Varela** and **Bulevar del Río** were completed. The Plazoleta Jairo Varela pays homage to a beloved salsa singer and founder of the Grupo Niche. Jairo Varela passed away in Cali in 2012. It is a large outdoor cultural space to be used for concerts and other cultural activities, located near the CAM office tower (Av. 2N between Clls. 10 and 11), which is the main municipal government building. Along the river, the pedestrian walkway Bulevar del Río was also unveiled. It extends from Calle 5 to La Ermita, and within weeks of its opening became an instant hit with weekend joggers. These new projects provide an exciting contrast to some of the grandiose relics of the 19th century, such as the **Teatro Jorge Isaacs** (Cra. 3 at Cl. 12) and **Puente Ortiz** (Cra. 1 at Cl. 12).

PLAZA CAYZEDO AND AROUND

The dozens of majestic wax palms in the **Plaza Cayzedo** (Cras. 4-5 between Clls. 11-12) create a green oasis in the middle of gritty downtown Cali. Like the Plaza de Bolívar in Bogotá, Plaza Cayzedo was known as the Plaza Mayor during the colonial era, and was often the scene of lively markets that were held after mass at the San Pedro cathedral. It was also a place of open-air concerts by military bands and the occasional bullfight. In 1913, about a century following his execution, it was renamed to honor the most famous independence figure from Cali, Joaquín de Cayzedo y Cuero. Passing through the park on the brick walkways you'll encounter a colorful cross-section of Caleños, from university students to shoe-shiners to

dapper older men watching the world go by from the comfort of a park bench.

Dating to the turn of the 19th century, the brilliantly white neoclassical-style **Catedral San Pedro** (Cl. 11 No. 5-35, tel. 2/881-1378, masses at 9am, 10am, 11am, and noon Mon.-Fri., 9am and 5pm Sun.) on the southern corner of the Plaza Cayzedo has been rebuilt several times due to destruction caused by earthquakes. The most stunning building on the plaza, however, is the French neoclassical gem the **Palacio Nacional** (Cra. 4 No. 12-04), also known as the Palacio de Justicia, on the eastern side of the Plaza de Cayzedo. Completed in the early 1930s, it houses various judicial bodies of the Valle de Cauca departmental government. The Palacio Nacional is not open to the public.

The distinctive red-brick church complex of the **Iglesia San Francisco** (Cl. 10 No. 6-00, tel. 2/884-2457, masses at 7am and 5pm Mon.-Sat., 9am and 6pm Sun.) includes the **Capilla de la Inmaculada**, the **Convento de San Joaquín**, and the **Torre Mudéjar**, all built between the 17th and 19th centuries by Franciscans. The architectural star here is the Torre Mudéjar, a four-story bell tower 23 meters (75 feet) high. It is divided into four red-brick sections, each level with a different geometric design. It is considered one of the best examples of neo-Mudejar design in the Americas. The architect of the tower was supposedly a Moor who had fled Spanish authorities, seeking refuge in the convent. In return for the free lodging, he designed the bell tower.

Outside the *Centro*
MUSEO LA TERTULIA

One of the best art museums in the country is Cali's **Museo La Tertulia** (Av. Colombia No. 5 Oeste-105, tel. 2/893-2939, www.museo-latertulia.com, 10am-6pm Tues.-Sat., 2pm-6pm Sun., COP$4,000 adults, COP$2,000 students, free Sun.). Museum galleries highlight contemporary Colombian artists such as Beatriz González, Hugo Zapata, Omar Rayo, and many more. Built in the 1960s, Museo La Tertulia is perhaps the most important cultural center in Cali. The word

the Torre Mudéjar in downtown Cali

tertulia refers to a social gathering for talking and sharing ideas about culture, art, and other themes. A cinema (showings usually 7pm and 9:15pm Tues. and Sat., 4pm and 7pm Sun., COP$5,000) shows art films and hosts festivals such as EuroCine. A concert hall offers chamber music concerts and poetry readings, and the lush grounds house an amphitheater. The museum café on the terrace is a popular meeting place in the evenings.

ZOOLÓGICO DE CALI

The **Zoológico de Cali** (Cra. 2 Oeste and Cl. 14, tel. 2/488-0888, 9am-4:30pm daily, COP$14,000 adults, COP$9,000 children) is, by far, the best zoo in the country, although that may not say very much. The landscape itself would make a lovely and tranquil botanical garden. Its location straddling the Río Cali and the great diversity in flora (providing welcome shade) make it a pleasant place to spend a few hours in the morning or late afternoon. Most of the zoo is dedicated to Colombian species. The condor exhibit may be disturbing to some

visitors, as these large birds are confined in relatively small cages. American flamingos frolic nearby. Beware of swarms of families on weekends. The zoo is accessible by MIO by taking the A02 bus from the San Bosco station.

IGLESIA AND PARQUE DE SAN ANTONIO

The small white **Iglesia de San Antonio** (Cl. 1 Oeste at Cra. 10, tel. 2/893-7185), similar to Iglesia La Merced in the Centro, is beautiful in its simplicity. Its adobe walls are white, accented by the wooden beams above. The brick entrance and bell tower are also striking. The church was built in the mid-18th century, because the residents in the growing area of San Antonio wanted to worship in their own neighborhood instead of having to schlep down the hill to pray at another church. If the main doors are closed (which is often the case as the church is only open for mass), head to the back left of the church and ring (once) at the door. Clarisa nuns from the convent there may give you a quick tour. A cautionary note: Do not express any disappointment to them that this church is *just* from 1747, unlike Iglesia La Merced (which was built about two hundred years before). They are sensitive about that! On weekends couples exchange vows at this picturesque spot.

Once you've made it to the top of the hill, plan to stick around awhile: **Parque San Antonio** is the place to experience San Antonio life. You'll see hipsters with their dogs mingling with other canine lovers, couples sipping a cold beer and enjoying the view as the sun goes down, and intellectual types engrossed in books. On one side of the park are small unpretentious restaurants, bars, and ice cream shops.

LA LOMA DE LA CRUZ

While technically it's known as an *artesanías* (handicrafts) market, **La Loma de la Cruz** (Cl. 5 between Cras. 14-16, 9am-10pm daily) has such a pleasant atmosphere, especially in the early evening from Thursday through Sunday, that it is more of a tourist attraction than a shopping experience—plus, it's free. The entrance at the bottom of the *loma,* or hill, is hard to miss with the man-made waterfall cascading down and a sign that reads "Loma de la Cruz." More than 20 kiosks sell typical Colombian handicrafts, such as hand-woven handbags and the like. After perusing the handicrafts and other items for sale, you can often enjoy concerts featuring Andean music, poetry readings, dance performances, or open-air films in the small amphitheater. You can walk to the hill from the San Antonio area.

EL CERRO DE CRISTO REY

The statue of Christ on **El Cerro de Cristo Rey** (south of the Cerro de las Tres Cruces in the Los Andes neighborhood) stands 26 meters (85 feet). It was created by an Italian sculptor to celebrate 50 years of peace following the Guerra de Mil Días (the Thousand Days' War) over the turn of the 20th century. That civil war claimed around 100,000 lives in Colombia and Panama. While there is a path to the top, it is best to take a taxi (COP\$45,000). Along the way you can check out the sculpture on the

side of the mountain called *El Lamento de la Pacha Mama,* which is a tribute to indigenous peoples, and munch on an *empanada* at a roadside stall. Don't make the Cristo Rey excursion after dark.

ENTERTAINMENT AND EVENTS
◖ Salsa

In Cali, there are many ways you can get a taste of (and very likely get hooked on) salsa.

SALSA SHOWS

A good way to observe the incredibly intricate and fast footwork of Caleño salsa dancers is to go to a performance of one of the big salsa shows in town. In this cabaret-style environment, you'll be amazed at the talent and exhausted by the high energy of these dancers, often ranging in age from 4 to 40.

The most famous show of them all is **Delirio** (Parque del Amor, Cl. 69 No. 4N-88, tel. 2/893-7610, www.delirio.com.co, COP\$120,00), a sort of Cirque du Soleil—à la Cali. This group, combining dance, music, and circus, has delighted audiences all over the world. Performances go from about 8pm to well after midnight. The group is constantly updating their shows, creating segments on different themes that inspire them, such as La María and even Michael Jackson tributes. During intermission, spectators are invited to dance on the stage, but there's no pressure. Performances are usually held the last Friday of every month, and at other times during the Feria de Cali. Minors under the age of 18 are not allowed inside the big tent.

Other popular ongoing shows include **Ensálsate** (cell tel. 316/480-7822, www.en-salsate.co, COP\$90,000) which takes place the second week of each month and during the Feria de Cali at the Salón Ritz of the Hotel Dann Carlton (Cra. 2 No. 1-60, tel. 2/893-3000). It's a three-act show with a mix of music and dance with salsa, music from the Caribbean, tango, and even some hip-hop added to the mix. Tickets can be obtained at Tu Boleta (www.tuboleta.com).

SALSA AL PARQUE

On the last Saturday night of the month, go to **Salsa al Parque** (Parque de los Estudiantes), also called the Parque de Santa Librada or, most commonly, the **Parque de Jovita** (Cl. 5 at Cra. 22, fculturalatina@gmail.com, 4pm-midnight, free). This friendly and open-air freebie is known as an *audición,* which is a chance for salsa enthusiasts called *coleccionistas,* who collect salsa albums, to play their favorites for the crowd. Young and old alike, from all walks of life, gather at the park for these events, with the common denominator being a love of salsa. The event is organized by the Fundación Cultural Nuestra Cosa Latina. They usually sell CDs to defray their costs. There's nothing like it!

SALSATECAS

No matter where you go on a Saturday night, there's a good chance that you'll hear some salsa. But there are some places—*salsatecas*—where it's all about salsa and nothing more. Most are open from Wednesday until Sunday, closing at around 2am. Big *salsatecas,* like Tin Tin Deo, will have a cover.

Surrounding the Parque de la Alameda are a handful of *salsatecas,* many of them quite old-school. These are excellent places to soak up the atmosphere, enjoy the music, nurse your drink, and watch the locals dance. **El Habanero Club** (Cl. 7A No. 23A-01, tel. 2/557-5829, www.bolerohabanero.co, hours vary Wed.-Sat.) is one such place. At this fabulous small club specializing in *música Antillana* (music from the Caribbean), you may feel like you've stepped into 1940s Cuba when you open the door. International visitors are welcome here, but plan on staying awhile: the owners don't like it when gringos nurse one beer and leave. **Libaniel** (Cl. 7A No. 23-68, tel. 2/557-5157), on the opposite corner from El Habanero, is one of those established clubs where the "new" waiters have only been working there for 10 years. On Fridays and Saturdays it's "Salsa y más," and a good time to check it out. They even serve tamales to satisfy your midnight cravings. A third club on the park is another famous name, the **Portón Caldense** (Cra. 23B No. 7-32, tel. 2/557-7616, www.porton-caldense.com). It's larger than the other places previously mentioned, and similarly full of atmosphere. On Thursdays they switch gears with a tango night.

The **Casa Latina** (Cl. 7 No. 27-38, tel. 2/556-6549, garylatina1@gmail.com, no cover) is a welcoming bar with tons of personality that draws in the salsa aficionados of Cali. Owner Gary Domínguez has theme nights, usually on Saturdays, celebrating a star salsa performer. Salsa memorabilia cover the walls, and the DJ booth that Gary mans while drinking a beer is jam-packed with records. How he knows what is where is a mystery—he must have a system. You may want to contact the bar in advance to see if they have any special events coming up.

In the San Fernando neighborhood along Calle 5 are some of the best-known big salsa clubs in Cali. **Tin Tin Deo** (Cl. 5 No. 38-71B, tel. 2/514-1537, www.tintindeo.com, 7:30pm-1am Thurs., 7:30pm-3am Fri.-Sat., cover COP$10,000-COP$15,000) is a requirement on a Thursday night. At Tin Tin Deo they also dance *chichoky,* which is a new style of Cali salsa that incorporates African rhythms. Saturday night is also big here, when the music is *pachanguero,* which is sort of "party music," Cali style. Tin Tin Deo is the new *chico* on the block—it's only been around since 1985, started by some friends from the Universidad del Valle. It's always a good bet.

Conga (Cl. 5 No. 30-17, tel. 2/556-5608, 9pm-3am Thurs.-Sat., cover COP$15,000) is more of an insider's place. Fridays and Saturdays are *viejoteca* nights, which are oldies nights, with Sundays geared more toward younger folk. Finally **Zaperoco Bar** (Av. 5N No. 16-46, tel. 2/661-2040, www.zaperocobar.com, 8pm-3am Thurs.-Sat., cover COP$20,000) confidently calls itself the best rumba in Cali. It regularly hosts live acts featuring salsa, music from the Pacific, and Cuban *son* music. The long lineup of *orquestas* (bands), is planned far in advance. The service isn't as friendly as at other bars.

Other Nightlife

La Topa Tolondra (Cl. 5 No. 13-27, cell tel. 314/664-1470, 6pm-1am Wed.-Thurs., 6pm-3am Fri.-Sat.) is a cool little spot near La Loma de la Cruz, where you can have a beer with local bohemians. On the cusp between El Peñon and San Antonio is the extremely mysterious and too cool **Greco Bar** (Cra. 4 No. 2-116, cell tel. 312/854-0151, greco613-@hotmail.com, 5pm-midnight Wed.-Sat). It's in an old house, where the lighting is way dim—if you don't watch your step you'll twist your ankle fumbling down the stairs. From the outside it looks sort of abandoned, but the hipsters shooting the breeze in the hammocks out front give it away. Overlooking the park in San Antonio is **Atahualpa** (Cra. 10 No. 1-15 Oeste, tel. 2/893-7206, 1pm-midnight Thurs.-Sat.). On the first floor they sell handicrafts and on the terrace you can have a beer or two. This is a fantastic perch from which to watch San Antonio come alive as night falls. Meanwhile, the jet-setters of Cali hang out in El Peñon on Avenida 2 Oeste, a strip of fashionable restaurant/bars popular with the after-work crowd. Terrace seating is hard to come by on Thursday and Friday evenings.

ELECTRONIC

Cali has a fairly heavy electronic music scene. Clubs are not huge draws in town, but parties or raves are. Usually between June and August each year, the **Black and White Sensation Party** (www.blackandwhitesensation.com), with a big-time international and national DJ lineup, has grown to become one of the most famous rave-type parties in the country. To find out about upcoming parties, visit www.tuboleta.com or consult the Cali section of www.planb.com.co. Also be on the lookout for flyers in trendy places in Granada.

Big-time electronic music clubs, the places that stay open late, tend to congregate in the Yumbo and Menga areas to the north of Granada. **Elíptica** (Cra. 38 No. 7-161, cell tel. 311/342-2294, 10pm-4am Thurs., 10pm-6am Fri.-Sat., COP$20,000) is an electronic music club that occasionally hosts international DJs.

LGBT

Gay clubs in Cali are friendly and mixed with women and men. They tend to get hopping at around 11pm and stay open until 3am. **Queens Bar** (Av. 9A No. 15-07, tel. 2/396-5338, www.queensbarcali.com, cover COP$15,000) is one of the hottest gay clubs of the moment, with three different dance floors each with its own type of music. It's located in Granada.

Lulu Latino (Km. 2 Vía Yumbo, cover COP$15,000) is the old standard as far as gay clubs go. There are often *barra libre* (open bar) promotions. Go for the rum instead of poor quality vodka.

JAZZ AND ROCK

Near the Río Cali, **Duke's Bar** (Av. 4 Oeste No. 1-66, cell tel. 301/418-6618, 6pm-1am Wed.-Thurs., 6pm-2am Fri.-Sat.) is the place for a change of rhythm. Here it's Louis Armstrong and John Coltrane who rule. Duke's also serves meals. For all your rock needs—hard rock, glam rock, Spanish rock, you name it—head to **Rock City Bar** (Cl. 5 No. 12-57, 4pm-3am Wed.-Sat., COP$6,000 cover weekends).

TANGO

Tango lovers (of which there are many in Colombia) may feel outnumbered in this salsa town, but not at **La Matraca** (Cra. 11 No. 22-80, tel. 2/885-7113, www.lamatracacali.com, 6pm-2:30am Fri.-Sat., 3pm-11pm Sun.). On the Parque Obrero, La Matraca used to be a corner shop where you could buy staples like rice and potatoes and hear tango from the owner's collection. No more potatoes here; it's just music, dancing, and drinks. It tends to be happening on Sundays after 3pm. This neighborhood is a little rough around the edges, so it's recommended to order a cab there and back.

LOUNGES

The jet-set crowd of Cali hangs out in El Peñon on Avenida 2 Oeste, a strip of fashionable restaurant/bars popular with the after-work crowd. Terrace seating is hard to come by on Thursday and Friday evenings. In the same area but with a totally different, much more relaxed atmosphere is **Malecón Cubar** (Cl. 1 Oeste No. 1-32, tel. 2/892-2977, 3pm-2am Tues.-Sat.). Here you can groove to Caribbean sounds, drink a mojito or two, and have a meal. Drinks are a little pricey.

Cinema

All the major malls have movie theaters. **Cine Colombia** operates several of those cinemas, including the one at Chipchape (Av. 6N No. 37N-25, tel. 2/644-2463, www.cinecolombia. com). **Museo La Tertulia** (Cra. 1 Oeste No. 5-105, tel. 2/893-2941, www.museolatertulia. com) shows artsy flicks. Alternative cultural space **Lugar a Dudas** (Cl. 15 N No. 8N-41, www.lugaradudas.org, tel. 2/668-2335) also shows independent films, usually on Tuesdays and Saturdays at 7pm.

There are two beautiful historic theaters built in the early 20th century in the Centro: **Teatro Jorge Isaacs** (Cra. 3 No. 12-28, tel. 2/880-9027) and the **Teatro Municipal Enrique Buenaventura** (Cra. 5 No. 6-64, tel. 2/81-3131, www.teatromunicipal.gov.co.) Contact the theaters directly or visit www. tuboleta.com for information on upcoming performances.

Festivals and Events

The **Festival Petronio Álvarez** (www.festivalpetronioalvarez.com, mid-Aug.) is a series of outdoor concerts that celebrates Afro-Colombian music and culture. The vibrations of the drums and good vibe of the crowd at this annual festival may intoxicate you! It's named for a famous musician from the Buenaventura area on the Pacific Coast.

The **Festival Mundial de Salsa** (www. cali.gov.co, mid-Sept.) began in 2006. It is a fiercely competitive dance competition, attracting thousands of salsa dancers of all ages from around the world. The finals are usually held in the Plaza de Toros. For tickets go to www. colboletos.com.

Caleños love their *feria* (fair). During the last week of the year when other cities become virtual ghost towns, the opposite occurs in Cali: It becomes Colombia's party central

during the beloved **Feria de Cali** (www.feriadecali.com). Occurring between Christmas and New Year's, the *feria* is a celebration that crosses barriers of class and age, with parades, concerts, beauty pageants, *cabalgatas* (horseback processions), and plenty of dancing and drinking. In addition to official activities, parties and other events take over the entire city during this week.

SHOPPING

If you are hunting for some Colombian handicrafts to take back home, try **La Caleñita** (Cra. 24 No. 8-53, tel. 2/556-1172, www.lacalenita. com, 9am-6pm Mon.-Sat.). This store is all of Colombia under one roof, and it has a range of merchandise, from high-quality jewelry and woven items to general Colombian kitsch.

Malls and more malls: That's how Cali shops. There's open-air **Chipichape** (Cl. 38N 6N-35, tel. 2/659-2199, www.chipichape. com.co, 6am-midnight daily), not far from Granada, as well as smaller **Centenario** (Av. 4N No. 7N-46, tel. 2/683-9604, www.centenariocc.com, 8am-11:45pm daily), which has glorious air conditioning. To the south are newer malls like **Jardín Plaza** (Cra. 98 No. 16-200, tel. 2/324-7222, www.jardinplaza.com, 8am-11:30pm daily), which is also open-air. It's near the Universidades MIO station. Each of these *centro comerciales* (malls), or CCs, has all the big-name Colombian brands (for example, Velez shoes, La Riviera cosmetics, Totto backpacks, and Arturo Calle menswear) and expensive international stores such as Adidas, Esprit, and Lacoste. Each also has small handicrafts stores or kiosks. Food courts have a variety of options, including fast food places with fun names like Mr. Arepa and Patacontodo, serving up Colombian delights.

SPORTS AND RECREATION
El Cerro de las Tres Cruces

A weekend ritual for many Caleños is to hike up **El Cerro de las Tres Cruces** (Three Cross Hill), west of the Santa Monica neighborhood. The climb will get your blood

CALI

© ANDREW DIER

making the hike to the top of El Cerro de las Tres Cruces

pumping, and at the top and along the way, you'll have some good views of Cali, especially early in the day. The ascent will take about an hour. At the top, if you still feel energetic, you can join Cali's fit and fabulous as they work out in the makeshift outdoor gym next to the crosses. It's quite a scene up there. Bring a little cash with you to enjoy a freshly squeezed orange juice.

There is a story behind the hill's namesake crosses. According to legend, in 1837 two friars decided that they had had enough of the prostitution, plagues, fires, dengue fever, and famine in Cali, and placed the blame squarely on the Buziraco, a demon who, after having been expelled from Cartagena, made his way to Cali to this hilltop. The first cross that was set on the hill was destroyed by an earthquake (Buziraco's fault), so in 1938 it was decided to build three concrete crosses. They have withstood the test of time so far, and there have been no further reports of Buziraco's antics.

The hardest part about the walk is figuring out where to start it. Various paths lead to the top—not far from Granada—in the Altos de Normandía neighborhood or in Juanambú. If you can find your way to Avenida 10 Oeste at Calle 12N, you will be close to the path and can ask anyone you come across for directions. If you're not going with someone who knows how to get there, take a cab and request to be dropped off close to the *sendero al Cerro de las Tres Cruces* (path to Three Crosses Hill).

It's recommended to take this popular hike on weekend mornings only, when you are assured of being in good company (hundreds of others), although there is usually always a police presence along the well-marked and well-trodden path. Parts of the path are quite steep, and you may need to climb up on all fours at some points. Therefore, don't bring items that you don't need, so you can have your hands free. And bring water.

Tours

TOVYT Tours (Av. 8N No. 15A Norte-40, tel. 2/370-6800, www.tovyt.com), with an office in Granada, can organize private tours and

The Little Witches of San Cipriano

A popular day trip from Cali is to take a ride on the *brujitas*, literally "little witches," of San Cipriano. Train tracks run through the two villages of Córdoba and San Cipriano, although trains rarely pass by. Local entrepreneurs saw an opportunity here in providing a quick transportation alternative to walking the train tracks for residents to get from one village to the other. They created a wooden cart transportation system that was set upon the rails. It was originally propelled manually using long sticks. The drivers resembled witches on broomsticks flying by, hence the name *brujitas*. Nowadays, passengers–up to about 10–zip by, as the *brujitas* are powered by motorbikes (less charming but more adventurous). The teenage drivers like to go fast, so hold on and, if you see a train coming towards you, get ready to jump off. It's about a 30-minute journey from Córdoba to San Cipriano.

Upon arrival in San Cipriano, you can have a hearty seafood lunch or continue on just beyond the village to a protected area (admission COP$2,000), where you can wander down a path that leads to a refreshing swimming hole in the Río San Cipriano. Inner tubes can be rented, and you can opt to float back to Córdoba.

A spin on the *brujita* costs about COP$8,500 round-trip for tourists, less for locals. However, touts may try to charge you up to COP$80,000 for the ride. Pay for the trip only after you have returned to Córdoba.

The experience is best enjoyed in a group. These are often organized by hostels in Cali. If you would like to go on your own, though, you can take any bus bound for Buenaventura and ask the driver to let you off at Córdoba. Buses depart Cali from the Terminal para Buenaventura in the southwest of the city. Look for the metallic black sculpture of the *mariamulata* bird (the local name for a great-tailed grackle) by renowned artist Enrique Grau (Cl. 7 Oeste No. 3-03). The ride costs about COP$18,000. Be sure to make a pineapple pit stop at **Piñas del 44.** It's at kilometer 44 on the highway, and buses will often take a break here.

San Cipriano isn't the only place in Colombia with *brujitas*. Visitors to the Coffee Region can take a ride in the village of Estación Pereira along the Río Cauca near Pereira.

---

outings if you have a minimum of four people in your group. These include trips to the Hacienda El Paraíso, bird-watching tours to the Kilometer 18 area west of the city, and excursions to San Cipriano.

Rioja Travel (tel. 2/660-7092, www.riojatravel.com) offers many of the same day trips as TOVYT Tours. The agency can arrange an outing for a minimum of two people. A day trip of six hours to Lago Calima costs COP$206,000 per person; a horseback tour along the Río Pance costs COP$84,000 per person.

FHURE Travel (Cra. 94A No. 45-90, tel. 2/372-4092, www.fhuretravel.com) offers day trips to the Parque Nacional Natural Los Farallones near the town of Pance in the south of the city. This excursion costs about COP$56,000 per person.

Bird-Watching

Colombia is home to over 1,900 species of birds, 76 of which are endemic. To get a glimpse of this celebrated diversity in the Cali area, check out a bird-watching excursion offered by the organization **Mapalina** (cell tel. 318/627-7062 or 316/805-2117, www.mapalina.com, from US$100). Associated with the American Birding Association, Mapalina is a birding organization led by the nonprofit Asociación Río Cali, and it organizes birding field trips year-round to a half dozen locations near Cali, from tropical San Cipriano to the west to the Laguna Sonso in the northeast near Buga. Some of the birds you might see include the multicolored tanager, gold-ringed tanager, banded ground-cuckoo, long-wattled umbrellabird, and the unusual Andean cock-of-the-rock. Trips, almost always with an English-speaking guide, are tailor-made according to the wishes of the visitors, and can be arranged for groups of 1-10 persons. From October to April there are usually more birds in the area, as many migratory species arrive from the north. Each year in December the organization participates in a day-long bird census in a cloud forest area near Kilometer 18, west of Cali, in collaboration with the Red Nacional de Observadores de Aves de Colombia bird-watching network. Anyone is invited to participate in the census.

Gyms, Spas, and Pools
For a day of health and pampering, head to the **Intercontinental Cali** (Av. Colombia No. 2-72, tel. 2/882-3225, COP$50,000 day pass), where you can work out at the hotel's gym, splash about in the big pool, and rejuvenate at the spa. If you're in San Antonio and would like to spin, go to the minuscule **Centro de Acondicionamiento Físico Fernando Benítez** (Cl. 3 No. 5-22, cell tel. 316/281-4143, www.acondicionamientofisicofb.com, 6am-8pm Mon.-Sat., COP$15,000 day pass), which allows visitors to drop in and take a spinning class.

Acuaparque de la Caña (Cra. 8 No. 39-01, tel. 2/438-4812, www.acuaparquecali.com, 9am-6pm daily, COP$12,500 adults, COP$10,000 children) is an insanely popular place to get wet on the weekends. It's quieter during the week. It's not really a place for serious training, more of a place to cool off and people-watch. It's also got several big water flume rides. You can take MIO buses P52C, P40A, or P24B to the park.

Biking
Sunday is bike day. In Cali this recreation initiative is called **Ciclovida** (8am-1pm Sun.). Vehicular traffic is closed for some 30 kilometers with a main route extending from Calle 9 at Carretera 66 Sur to Calle 70 at Carretera 1N. It's next to impossible to find bikes to rent, but you can always jog!

Spectator Sports
There are two professional soccer teams in Cali:

Deportivo (www.deportivocali.com.co) and **América** (www.america.com.co). Deportivo, whose colors are green and white, is one of the most successful teams in the country. It is also the only team with its own stadium, the **Estadio Deportivo Cali** (Km. 8 Vía Cali-Palmira, tel. 2/688-0808). It's the largest soccer stadium in the country, with a capacity of over 50,000.

América was linked to the Cali Cartel through the now extradited brothers, who were affiliated with the club for some 15 years, Gilberto and Miguel Rodríguez Orejuela. The fact that their mascot is a red devil with pitchfork in hand is coincidental, although fits with América's reputation! América plays at the **Pascual Guerrero Stadium** (Cra. 36 No. 5B-32, tel. 2/556-6678), which is where the 1971 Panamerican Games were held. It got a big facelift just in time for the 2011 Under-20 World Cup.

The big match in town is the Clasico del Valle de Cauca between Deportivo and América. Although Deportivo leads that series, América holds the most national titles, with 13, while Deportivo has 8. Go to www.tuboleta.com for tickets and information on soccer matches.

ACCOMMODATIONS
Granada, El Peñon, and San Antonio are considered the best places to stay in Cali. These neighborhoods are safe, walkable, and offer diverse dining options. There are numerous hotels in the Centro within a few blocks of all the main tourist sights, but it's not a desirable place to be at night. The top-end hotels all provide air conditioning in their rooms; budget accommodations probably will not.

Granada
Leafy streets and proximity to restaurants and nightspots make the trendy barrio (neighborhood) of Granada a nice place to stay while in Cali. There are options for all budgets and styles. New sidewalks, refurbished streets, and speed humps began to appear in much of the area in 2013, making the area more pedestrian-friendly. The area is fine to walk about in the

evening hours, but on weekday nights it feels deserted.

UNDER COP$70,000
The hostel scene in Granada offers several options, and Granada runs neck and neck with San Antonio for backpacker business.

After a few days at the ◖ **Iguana Hostel** (Av./Cl. 9N No. 22N-22, tel. 2/660-8937, www.iguana.com.co, COP$18,000 dorm, COP$45,000 d w/bath) you'll think of the staff as new friends, such is the hospitality at this long-running hostel. Free salsa classes take place just about every evening, and the staff are full of nuggets of information, from ideas for day-trip excursions, to where to go to hear music on a Monday night, to what pizza place delivers late. The hostel is located on a steep, quiet street within easy walking distance to restaurants. There are a couple of patios to hang out in, and a fierce black and white cat guards the front gate at night. Iguana is one of the oldest hostels in Cali, but the accommodations are still fresh.

Pelican Larry's (Cl. 20N No. 6AN-44, tel. 2/420-3955, www.hostelpelicanlarry. com, COP$18,000 dorms, COP$50,000 d) has dorm rooms, private rooms with shared bath, and one private room with its own bathroom. This crash pad is close to the action of Calle Sexta.

COP$70,000-200,000
From the terrace on the 10th floor at **Aqua Hotel** (Av. 8N No. 10-91, tel. 2/667-2388, www.aquagranada.com, COP$120,000 d), you get a great view. On one side, the Iglesia Ermita peeks through two nondescript towers. You can also see the Torre de Cali skyscraper. On the other side look for Tres Cruces, Granada, and the shenanigans taking place atop the NOW Hotel. Breakfast is served in your spacious room, which has a functional kitchenette and enormous refrigerator. Aqua is on the always-busy Avenida Octava, but traffic noise does not seem to be an issue.

Granada is full of restaurants and watering holes, but the Calle Novena is not a main thoroughfare, making it a pleasant and mostly peaceful place to stay. The **Hotel Plaza Mayor** (Av. 9AN No. 14-70, tel. 2/667-0303, www. hotelplazamayorcali.com, COP$140,000 d low season, COP$175,000 d high season) is your basic nothing-special hotel, but it's a good value for Granada. Many of the rooms have kitchenettes.

OVER COP$200,000
Opened in January 2014, **Marriott Cali** (Av. 8N 9-64, tel. 1/485-1111, www.marriott.com) is the latest luxury international hotel chain to arrive in Cali, on a busy thoroughfare near the Granada neighborhood. It offers 170 rooms, a pool, restaurants, and a gym.

Catering mostly to the Bogotá jet-set, **NOW Hotel** (Av. 9AN No. 10N-74, tel. 2/488-9797, www.nowhotel.com.co, COP$297,000 d) is an island of South Beach in the middle of Granada. It has 19 luxurious rooms with interiors decorated by Bo Concept. Large beds, balconies, and DirecTV are some of the perks here. There are two restaurants in the hotel, and there are certainly worse places to be at sunset than the rooftop terrace bar. The hotel bar is a popular place for a drink, and sometimes there are parties here, especially on weekends. If you need peace and quiet for a good night's sleep, this isn't the best option.

The Torre de Cali, the tallest skyscraper in the city, is a classic point of reference, and is home to the **Hotel Plaza Torre de Cali** (Av. de las Américas No. 18N-26, tel. 2/683-3535, www.hoteltorredecali.com, COP$246,000 d), with rooms on floors 11-20. The views from the southeast side of the hotel towards the valley are unbeatable. The hotel has spruced itself up, hoping to compete with the top hotels in the city. It is in the Versailles area, about a 15-minute walk to the Zona Rosa area of Granada. Avoid walking around this part of town late at night.

El Peñon
This tidy, upscale, and somewhat boring neighborhood is home to upscale restaurants and hotels. It is sort of an island between San

Antonio and (across the Río Cali) Centenario and Granada. Unfortunately, crossing the river is a frightful experience, with pedestrian crosswalks nonexistent; you'll probably want to take a cab. To hike up the hill to San Antonio, you will also have to scamper across the Carrera 4, where cars zoom by at high speeds.

COP$70,000-200,000

If you can name your favorite salsa singer with no hesitation, the place for you might be the **Posada Salsa Boutique** (Cl. 4 Oeste No. 3A-39, tel. 2/376-0866, www.posadasalsa.com, COP$70,000 s, COP$110,000 d). Each of the six small rooms in this hotel that opened in 2010 has a different theme in homage to the great salsa stars, like the Cecilia Cruz room and the Héctor Lavoe room. You can request your favorite one. Salsa classes are offered, as you'd expect, but the best part about this hotel is its location on a quiet, tree-lined street.

Also on Calle 4 Oeste, **Aloja** (Cl. 4 Oeste No. 3A-50, tel. 2/557-0933, www.aloja.com.co, COP$120,000 apt.) has only three furnished apartments for rent, but if one is available, it's a great bargain. The three-story building is above an excellent ice cream shop, which sweetens the deal, and is a two-minute walk from a variety of neighborhood restaurants. Apartments are equipped with everything you'll probably need and come with a high-tech security system.

El Peñon Hotel (Cl. 1 Oeste No. 2-61, tel. 2/893-3625, hotelelpenon@hotmail.com, COP$156,000 d) offers rooms large enough for two people to do jumping jacks in and is reasonably priced, especially for this part of town. Rooms are carpeted.

OVER COP$200,000

Maybe it doesn't have the same cachet as it once did during its 60-odd years in Cali, but the 🄲 **Intercontinental Cali** (Av. Colombia No. 2-72, tel. 2/882-3225, www.ihg.com, COP$385,000 d), run by the Colombian Estelar group, retains its old-school elegance with all the amenities you'd expect: huge comfortable beds, a spa, multiple restaurants and bars, and a check-in counter that

must be 20 meters long. You can walk from the Intercontinental Cali to restaurants in El Peñon, but most guests prefer to cab it.

San Antonio

This neighborhood of artists and hipsters has options for all budgets, with tons of hotel and restaurant options, and also has that charm you might be seeking. All the action is centered on the Parque San Antonio, which is one of the best places to be when the sun sets. You can walk from San Antonio to the historic center in the daytime, about a 20-minute walk, if you're up for it.

UNDER COP$70,000

In an old house with lots of charm, 🄲 **La Casa Café** (Cra. 6 No. 2-13, tel. 2/893-7011, www. lacasacafecali.blogspot.com, COP$15,000 dorm, COP$30,000 d) is a friendly spot with an ideal location on a quiet street in San Antonio. Upstairs there are four rooms—one dormitory and three private rooms with shared bathrooms—and there is a small kitchen for guest use. Downstairs is a café and reading area where local bands play sometimes.

The Uruguayan hostel chain **El Viajero** (Cra. 5 No. 4-56, tel. 2/893-8342, www.hostel-sincali.com, COP$20,000 dorm, COP$37,000 d) arrived in Cali in mid-2013. This location offers the backpacking crowd a pool, a bar, free salsa classes in their dance studio, a basic breakfast, and the occasional circus performance.

COP$70,000-200,000

The 🄲 **San Antonio Hotel Boutique** (Cra. 6 No. 2-51, tel. 2/524-6364, www.hotelboutique-sanantonio.com, COP$179,000 d) is the best option in San Antonio if personalized attention and comfort are your priorities. Two of the hotel's 10 rooms have their own terrace, but anyone can enjoy the rooftop terrace. Rooms have air conditioning and comfortable beds. Guests can make free calls to the United States and Canada.

Open since October 2012, comfy 🄲 **Ruta Sur** (Cra. 9 No. 2-41, tel. 2/893-6946, www. hostalrutasurcali.blogspot.com, COP$25,000

San Antonio is Cali's most charming neighborhood.

dorm, COP$85,000 private d) offers two small dormitory rooms with triple bunkbeds (!), along with four rather luxurious private rooms (with bathrooms) where weary flashpackers (backpackers who like their comfort every once in a while) can get a sound rest 1after days on the road. At night you can laze in a hammock under the stars in an open-air interior patio. Here there are no salsa classes or bar tours on offer: It's all about comfort and rest.

FOOD

Cali lacks the international cuisine options that are found in Bogotá, but a handful of creative fusion restaurants help to fill in that void. Cali society frequents the most highly regarded restaurants in the posh neighborhoods of El Peñon and Granada. Prices for a night out are on the uptick in San Antonio, as yuppies and visitors alike crowd restaurants after soaking in the scene at the park. It's rather lonesome after dark in the Centro, but there are numerous options for a typical *valledecaucana* lunch following a morning hitting the pavement as you visit Cali's historical sights. Nothing accompanies a hearty meal in the hot city like a cool *lulada* drink made from the *lulo* fruit (a variety of orange). Tap water is fine to drink in Cali.

Centro
CAFÉS, BAKERIES, AND QUICK BITES
Vegetarians may be surprised to stumble across vegetarian options downtown. For a pastry and a coffee, or for a vegetarian buffet lunch, check out **Nutricentro** (Cra. 5 No. 7-40, tel. 2/895-9777, 10am-6pm Mon.-Sat.). It's a cheerful place near the Merced sights.

COLOMBIAN AND FUSION
Reasonable lunch options abound in the Centro. On weekends and evenings, options are fewer and less popular.

Just across the street from Iglesia La Merced is the colonial building that houses the Sociedad de Mejorasúblicas de Cali, an organization in support of public works. Discreetly facing an interior patio is ◖ **Mi Valle del Cauca** (Sociedad de Mejoras Públicas, Cra. 4 No.

6-76, tel. 2/883-6309, 11am-3pm Mon.-Fri., set lunch COP$12,000), an excellent lunch spot. It's popular with professionals on their lunch break. Try the tortilla soup and fish dishes.

There's no need to feel embarrassed about dining in a parking lot. Despite its less-than-picturesque location, **DA'gusto** (Cra. 4 No. 9-49, tel. 2/881-8697, 6am-5pm Mon.-Sun., COP$8,000) packs in the crowds day in and day out at lunchtime. Service is quick and the action in the kitchen is fast, yet friendly. *Sancocho,* a meaty stew, is a favorite, as is fried fish. Set lunches are served with juice, salad, and lots of carbs: potatoes, yuca, plantains, and rice. You can also order dishes such as beans and rice off the menu.

At the lunch counter of tiny and tidy **Rikus** (Cra. 4 No. 12-56, tel. 2/896-0795, 10am-5pm Mon.-Sat., COP$6,000) you can eat cheap Colombian fare and watch the staff furiously stir, mix, pour, and serve.

Granada
CAFÉS, BAKERIES, AND QUICK BITES
A top contender in the city for the crown of best *pandebono,* a delicious pastry made of yuca flour and cheese, is **Kuty Panadería** (Av. 6N No. 27N-03, tel. 2/661-1465, www.panaderia-kuty.com, 6am-9pm daily). Kuty also serves other fast food fare all day long. For heaps of old-style character, nothing beats ◖ **Miami** (Av. 6 No. 16N-98, tel. 2/396-5998, 7am-8pm daily). Here, right on Avenida Sexta, you can fuel up on freshly baked croissants and a *café con leche* (coffee with milk) and be endlessly entertained by the hustle and bustle of one of Cali's busiest streets. Miami even has Wi-Fi.

If you're looking to get your coffee *fuerte* (strong), go to **Juan Valdez** (Av. 9N No. 17-11, tel. 2/660-7337, www.juanvaldezcoffee.com, 10am-9pm Mon.-Thurs., 10am-midnight Fri.-Sat., 11am-9pm Sun.). This shop, the Colombian version of Starbucks, is on a fancy corner in Granada and has a wonderful terrace under the shade of acacia trees, providing the perfect setting for writing in that journal of yours or browsing on your tablet.

COLOMBIAN AND FUSION
Ringlete (Cl. 15AN No. 9N-31, tel. 2/660-1540, www.ringlete.com, noon-3pm and 6:30pm-10pm Mon.-Sat., noon-4:30pm Sun., COP$24,000) features *nueva cocina Vallecaucana* (new Valle de Cauca cuisine) in a brightly decorated restaurant in Granada. Check out the pork chops, shrimp ceviche, or seafood *cazuela* (stew).

◖ **Carambolo** (Cl. 14N No. 9N-18, tel. 2/667-5656, noon-midnight Mon.-Sat., noon-5pm Sun., COP$30,000) has a creative menu combining Mediterranean and Colombian flavors. Many dishes in this restaurant are whimsically named, such as the Shakira (stuffed eggplant combining Middle Eastern and Caribbean flavors) and the Celia Cruz—shrimp coated in coconut and *chontaduro* (fruit from a type of palm tree) and served in a *maracuya* (passion fruit) sauce. It's a popular place with Cali society and out-of-towners.

Platillos Voladores (Av. 3N No. 7-19, tel. 2/668-7750, www.platillosvoladores.com, COP$35,000, noon-3pm and 7pm-11pm Mon.-Sat.), run by chef Vicky Acosta, is consistently rated as one of Cali's top restaurants. Fusion is the watchword here: Thailand, Lebanon, Italy, France, and the Colombian Pacific are among the cuisines that Acosta works with. Menu favorites include a fresh fillet of fish from the Pacific in a caramelized *chontaduro* (a starchy fruit that grows on a variety of palm) and garlic sauce (COP$43,000), quinoa stir-fry (COP$26,000), and an exotic and spicy ostrich carpaccio (COP$23,000). Reservations are recommended.

TEX-MEX
D'Toluca (Cl. 17N No. 8N-46, tel. 2/668-9372, 11:30am-3pm and 5:30pm-11:30pm Mon.-Thurs. and Sun., 11:30am-3pm and 5:30pm-1am Fri.-Sat., COP$15,000) serves up reliable Tex-Mex cuisine and often has lunch or drink specials.

CRÊPES
Although it's a chain present in all big malls in Colombia, **Crepes & Waffles** (Av. 6AN No.

grab a veggie burger or try one of the many tempting desserts. Panero is located on a sublime tree-lined street and its terrace is an agreeable place to be for lunch or for a late afternoon tea.

INTERNATIONAL
Alain from Alsace came to Cali, loved it, and opened **Petite France** (Cra. 3A Oeste No. 3-53, tel. 2/893-3079, noon-2:30pm and 6:30pm-10:30pm Mon.-Sat., COP$24,000). This French restaurant in El Peñon is highly recommended by locals. Save room for the delicious tarte flambé.

The terrace at **La Pizzeria** (Intercontinental Hotel, Av. Colombia No. 2-72, tel. 2/886-1010, noon-11:30pm Mon.-Sun., COP$25,000) at the Intercontinental Hotel is almost always full at night, which is a good sign. The pizza is deemed by many to be the best in town. If you want to enjoy your pie and the pleasing temps of a Cali evening by dining alfresco, get there early.

San Antonio
CAFÉS, BAKERIES, AND QUICK BITES
Weary travelers and San Antonians alike flock to **Ⅽ Macondo Postres y Café** (Cra. 6 No. 3-03, tel. 2/893-1570, www.macondocafe. blogspot.com, 11:30am-11pm Mon.-Thurs., 11:30am-midnight Fri.-Sat., 4:30pm-11pm Sun.) at all hours of the day. It's one of the best places to hang out in San Antonio when you're in no rush to run to the Centro. If you're in the mood for an artisan beer or a decent coffee while you depart to Wi-Fi land, or you want a hearty meal, including the much sought-after veggie burger, Macondo is your neighborhood place. At night they show artsy movies, and there are often live jazz and blues bands performing on Saturday evenings.

COLOMBIAN AND FUSION
In a city with a surprising number of vegetarian restaurants, or at least veg-friendly options, (**Ⅽ El Buen Alimento** (Cra. 2 No. 4-53, tel. 2/375-5738, 11:30am-10pm Tues.-Thurs., 11:30am-11pm Fri.-Sat., 11:30am-9pm Sun.,

café in Granada

24N-70, tel. 2/485-4474, www.crepesywaffles. com.co, noon-10pm Sun.-Thurs., noon-11pm Fri.-Sat., COP$20,000) is a reliable friend. There are dozens of savory crêpes, all consistently good. What's important is to save room for dessert. This particular location on the Avenida Sexta is big and breezy and is between Granada and Chipichape.

El Peñon
CAFÉS, BAKERIES, AND QUICK BITES
Delicious homemade ice cream awaits you at **Calathea** (Cl. 4 Oeste No. 3A-50, tel. 2/371-0188, 11am-7pm Mon.-Sat., noon-6pm Sun.). Exotic flavors you can't get back home are constantly being invented. There's coconut-lemon, strawberries with red wine, and the native fruit *arazá* with mint.

COLOMBIAN AND FUSION
Open-air **Ⅽ Panero** (Cl. 3 Oeste No. 3A-18, tel. 2/892-3333, 9:30am-7pm Mon.-Sat., COP$12,000) serves delicious vegetarian lunches from a set menu. If you miss lunch,

COP$15,000) gives Panero in El Peñon a run for its money for the title of veggie champion. There's always a set menu option for lunch, including fresh juice, soup, and the main course, but you can also order à la carte. Veggie burgers, pastas, and vegetarian tamales—an unimaginable option for most Colombians—are plentiful. This cheerful spot in San Antonio with bright decor is even popular with devout meat-eaters.

The inspiration for **Ojo de Perro Azul** (Cra. 9 No. 1-27, tel. 2/893-6956, 5pm-10pm Tues.-Thurs., 5pm-2am Fri.-Sat., 3pm-9pm Sun., COP$15,000) was a street dog named Juancho, who had one blue eye. Ojo de Perro Azul is a laid-back place that oozes San Antonio style. The food is OK here, but the ambiance is what makes it enjoyable. It's a good place to go later in the evening, have a nibble, and have cocktails while you enjoy the music. If you're asking yourself, "Shouldn't it be Perro de Ojo Azul?," you'd be correct. The owners have a sense of humor. Sticking with the color theme, there is ⟨ **El Pargo Rojo** (Cr. 9 No. 2-09, tel. 2/893-6087, 8am-3pm Mon.-Sun., COP$18,000), or The Red Snapper. Fresh fried sea bass and *cazuelas* (seafood stews) from the waters of the Pacific are specialties at this San Antonio favorite. In the morning you can try an *arepa de huevo* (egg fried in corn meal), if you are feeling low on cholesterol. El Pargo Rojo is not open for dinner.

Going back to blue, **Azul** (Cra. 9 No. 4-02B, tel. 2/893-6057, noon-3pm and 6pm-11pm Mon.-Fri., 6pm-11pm Sat., COP$25,000) is a fusion-style restaurant, with Mediterranean, Colombian, Middle Eastern, and Asian flavors represented on the menu by chef Martha Izquierdo. Ask for the *clandestinos*—dishes that don't appear on the menu. With colorful decor, Azul is a good choice for dinner.

INFORMATION AND SERVICES
Tourist Information
The **Oficina de Turismo Municipal de Cali** (Cra. 5 No. 6-05, Oficina 102, tel. 2/885-8855, ext. 122, 8am-noon and 1:30pm-5pm Mon.-Sat.) has maps and brochures on Cali and environs. Friendly young police cadets work the booth, but their English skills are minimal.

The online entertainment and events guide **Plan B** (www.planb.com.co) has a section on Cali. Ticket companies **Tu Boleta** (www.tu-boleta.com) and **Colboletos** (www.colboletos.com) are also good resources.

Money
ATMs are not as easy to come by in San Antonio compared to other neighborhoods in the city, but you can always count on them in shopping malls. To receive a wire transfer, **Western Union** (www.westernunion.com) has several offices in Cali. Check the website for locations. **Titan Intercontinental** (Cl. 11 No. 4-48, tel. 2/898-0898, www.titan.com.co, 8am-5pm Mon.-Fri., 9am-1pm Sat.), a currency exchange office, is located in the Centro. Banks do not normally change money.

Spanish-Language Classes
All the major universities in Cali offer Spanish programs for foreigners. Check the **Universidad Javeriana Programa de Español Funcional para Extranjeros** (Cl. 18 No. 118-250, tel. 2/321-8200, ext. 510, www.javeriana-cali.edu.co) and **Universidad Santiago de Cali Programa de Lenguas Extranjeras** (Cl. 5 at Cra. 62, tel. 2/518-3000, ext. 411, www.usc.edu.co/idiomas).

Communications
INTERNET ACCESS
Wireless Internet availability is more the norm than the exception at restaurants, cafés, and big shopping malls. **Juan Valdez** (Av. 9N No. 17-11, tel. 2/660-7337, www.juanvaldezcoffee.com, 10am-9pm Mon.-Thurs., 10am-midnight Fri.-Sat., 11am-9pm Sun.) in Granada is a good place to get connected. Small Internet cafés, open until about 8pm, are plentiful too. There you can surf the Internet for hours and pay next to nothing.

MAIL SERVICES
The post office, **4-72,** has an office at the Chipichape shopping center (Av. 6 No.

35-47, Bodega 4, Local 426, tel. 2/379-7164, www.4-72.com.co, 9am-1pm and 2pm-6pm Mon.-Sat.). Other courier services such as **Servientrega** (Av. 8N No. 14N-10, Local 3, tel. 2/660-3384, 8:30am-12:30pm and 1:30pm-6pm Mon.-Sat.) have many locations in the city.

TELEPHONE
The city telephone code for Cali is 2, but you'll only need to use it if you're calling Cali from a different part of the country, or from abroad. It's generally easy to find people selling use of their cell phones, called *minutos* (minutes), for cheap on the street downtown and in *tiendas* (stores) elsewhere. Cell phone numbers must have ten digits. To report any emergency, dial 123.

NEWSPAPERS
The main daily newspaper in town is **El País** (www.elpais.com.co), although **El Tiempo** is also frequently available in drugstores, bookstores, and malls. The free monthly **Cali Cultural** (www.calicultural.net) has an extensive listing of cultural events in the city.

Health Services
Cali has excellent medical facilities. The **Fundación Valle del Lili** (Av. Simón Bolívar Cra. 98 No. 18-49, tel. 2/331-9090, appointment hotline tel. 2/680-5757, www.valledellili. org) and the **Centro Médico Imbanaco** (Cra. 38A No. 5A-100, tel. 2/682-1000, appointment hotline tel. 2/685-1000, www.imbanaco.com) are two of the top hospitals in the country.

A recommended dental office is **Orthofami** (Cl. 19 No. 4-55, tel. 2/373-4447, www.orthofami.com, 8am-6pm Mon.-Fri., 9am-1pm Sat.). The **PROFAMILIA Clinic** (Cl. 23N No. 3N-40, tel. 2/661-8032, 7am-5pm Mon.-Fri., 8am-noon Sat.), in the Versailles neighborhood, offers a wide range of sexual and reproductive health services and products at low cost for women and men.

GETTING THERE
By Air
The Cali airport, the **Aeropuerto Internacional**

Alfonso Bonilla Aragon (Palmira, tel. 2/280-1515, www.aerocali.com.co) is under an hour's drive away. A taxi ride from San Antonio to the airport will cost around COP$50,000. Minibuses from the airport to the city are usually at the ready just outside of the departure hall. They cost about COP$12,000 and take you to the Terminal de Transportes de Cali, the Cali bus station (Cl. 30N 2AN-29).

There is free wireless Internet in some areas of the airport departure hall. In the terminal, restaurants serve the usual breakfast fare; you can also get refreshed before your flight with your last *lulada* (a drink made with the juice of a *lulo*, a type of orange).

All major Colombian airlines and some international carriers serve Cali. **Avianca** (Av. 6A No. 31N-11, Local 3, tel. 2/660-7028, www.avianca.com, 8am-6pm Mon.-Fri., 9am-1pm Sat.) has numerous flights between Cali, Bogotá, and Medellín throughout the day. It also operates nonstop flights to Cartagena, Barranquilla, Pasto, and Tumaco. Internationally, Avianca flies nonstop between Cali and Madrid and Cali and Miami, and through Medellín to New York's JFK airport.

Owned by the military, **Satena** (Centro Comercial Paseo de la Quinta, Cl. 5 No. 46-83, Local 213, tel. 2/554-6919, www.satena.com) serves more exotic destinations, such as Guapi, the gateway to the island of Gorgona; Puerto Asis, bordering Ecuador in the Putumayo department; and Quibdó, the capital city of the Chocó department.

Copa Airlines (Centro Comercial Chipichape, Cl. 3N No. 6N-35, Local 318, Col. toll-free tel. 01/800-011-2600, www.copaair.com, 8am-7pm Mon.-Fri., 8am-5pm Sat., 9am-4pm Sun.) flies from Cali to Panama City, Panama, as well as to Bogotá and to the island of San Andrés in the Caribbean. **LAN Colombia** (Cl. 25N No. 6B-36, Col. toll-free tel. 01/800-094-9490, www.lan.com, 8am-6pm Mon.-Fri., 9am-1pm Sat.) flies nonstop to Bogotá and Quito, Ecuador. Discount airliner **Viva Colombia** (Cali call center tel. 2/380-8989, www.vivacolombia.co) offers daily flights between Cali and Bogotá, Medellín, Cartagena, and Santa Marta. **American Airlines** (Intercontinental Cali Hotel, Av. Colombia No. 2-72, Local 6, tel. 9/800-052-2555, www.aa.com, 8am-6pm Mon.-Fri., 9am-1pm Sat.) is the only U.S.-based airline with service to Cali. They operate daily flights out of Miami. Charter flights are offered on **TAC** (Centro Comercial Colon Plaza, Cra. 1 No. 61A-30, Local 6, tel. 2/439-4084) from Cali to Guapi, El Charco, and Timbiquí.

Ecuadorean carrier **TAME** (Cra. 4A 12-41, Oficina 118, Edificio Seguros Bolívar, tel. 2/888-9101, www.tame.com.ec, 8am-noon and 2pm-6pm Mon.-Fri., 9am-noon Sat.-Sun.) flies between popular vacation spot Esmeraldas on the Pacific Coast and Cali. **Aerogal** (www.aerogal.com.co) flies to Guayaquil.

By Bus

The organized and bustling **Terminal de Transportes** (Cl. 30N No. 2AN-29, tel. 2/668-3655, www.terminalcali.com) in Cali is a relatively quick taxi ride away from Granada. A small information booth is located in the center of it all. Attendants will be able to give you a rough idea of bus fare prices, help you organize day-trip travel, and even provide you with a Cali tourist map if you are just arriving. There is an efficient taxi stand at the main entrance (Puerta 3). If you are taking MIO to the terminal, the nearest station is Las Américas, about two blocks away.

GETTING AROUND
By Taxi

Yellow taxis are plentiful in Cali, and you will need to travel by cab often to get around, especially at night. Taxi drivers are generally helpful, chatty, and honest. However, it is always advisable to order a cab over the phone or using the smartphone app Tappsi. Staff at hotels, restaurants, and (sometimes) clubs should be happy to do this for you. **Taxi Express** (tel. 2/555-5555) has a phone number you won't forget. Another service is **Taxis y Autos de Cali** (tel. 2/664-0000). Make sure they turn on the *taximetro* (meter) when you get started, and

note that there may be small nighttime travel or telephone surcharges added on. *Taxistas* (cab drivers) don't expect tips. And they rarely have change for large bills.

A cab from Cali to the airport will cost around COP$50,000 and take under an hour. From Granada expect to pay about COP$5,000 to get to the bus terminal or to Chipichape and about COP$6,500 to get to San Antonio.

By Bus

With 82 routes and a total of 711 buses at last count, the Masivo Integrado de Occidente or **MIO** (www.mio.com.co or www.metrocali.gov.co) is Cali's public transport system. It comprises several dedicated bus lanes with stations (similar to that of the TransMilenio network in Bogotá), as well as *alimentadores*—feeder buses that connect with the articulated MIO network at various points. MIO can take you just about anywhere in the city, but the system map is not easy to figure out.

MIO is useful if you are staying in or near Granada or plan to visit the Centro or sights in the south such as shopping malls or the Universidad del Valle campus, or if you plan on going to Pance. The bright blue buses are immaculately maintained and quite safe, too. Note that if you would like to ride one of the *alimentadores* you will need to present a MIO card on-board. Those have to be bought at the MIO stations. MIO runs 5am-11pm Monday-Saturday and 6am-10pm Sundays and holidays. The current fare for a single trip to any point in the city is COP$1,600.

The first MIO buses began to operate in 2008, but private bus companies, often using old and polluting buses, were still in operation. In a noble effort to provide some order to the transportation chaos in the city, in late 2012 Cali mayor Rodrigo Guerrero implemented a gradual elimination of those private bus companies, replacing them with city-run MIO buses in order to create a single public bus system. Powerful bus company owners fought him every step of the way. The mayor faced bus strikes, hunger strikes, roadblocks, lawsuits, and threats, but he persevered. It got so nasty at one point, the mayor's transportation secretary had to seek refuge abroad due to threats. If Guerrero is successful, Cali will be the first city in Colombia with a single bus system covering almost the entire city and even extending it to the airport in Palmira. They are getting there: MIO coverage has reached 87 percent.

By Car and Motorcycle

The roads in the Valle de Cauca region are generally of high quality and the terrain is flat. So, while it's not a fantastic idea in the city, renting a car or motorbike for excursions outside of Cali (to Valle haciendas, Buga, Lago Calima, and Roldanillo) may be an option. It is not difficult, even, to drive from Cali to Armenia, for example, if you are ready to move on to the Coffee Region. Driving to Popayán or to Pasto along the Pan-American Highway is more taxing because of winding, two-lane roads. The same goes for travel westward to Buenaventura.

Hertz (Av. Colombia No. 1-14, El Peñon, tel. 2/892-0437, www.rentacarcolombia.co, 8amnoon and 2pm-6pm Mon.-Fri., 8am-3pm Sat.; airport tel. 2/666-3283, 7am-5pm Mon.-Sat.) has two offices in Cali. For motorcycle rental and tours, get in touch with Mike, the Danish owner of **Motolombia** (tel. 2/396-3949, www. motolombia.com). Though it's based in Cali, Motolombia can also hook you up with bikes in Bogotá and Medellín.

RESERVA NATURAL ANAHUAC

On lazy weekend days, Caleños descend en masse on the Río Pance, south of the city, to splash around in the cool water. Near the town of Pance, at the edge of the Parque Nacional Natural los Farallones, is **Reserva Natural Anahuac** (1 km before Pance on the Cali-Pance road, tel. 2/331-4828, www.reservanaturalanahuac.com.co, 7:30am-9:30pm daily, COP$5,000), a well-maintained private nature reserve along the Río Pance that is very accessible. It has a pleasant path that meanders through *guadua* (a type of bamboo) forests, a fishing pond, a restaurant, and, if you would like to stay the night, some cabins

(COP$22,000 pp) and a camping area. There is no need for a guide to make this excursion and it may be just the ticket on a hot day.

To get to the park, you can take MIO to the Universidades station in the south of Cali and transfer to an *alimentador* (feeder) MIO bus, the A-19, towards Pance. This ride on MIO is relaxing and pleasant as you pass through Cali suburbia and gawk at the astonishingly fierce-looking Cordillera Occidental mountains in the distance. At the intersection of the Autopista Sur with the Vía Pance is the huge, open-air **La Boquería Restaurant** (Cl. 18 No. 122-100, tel. 2/555-2199, 8am-9pm daily, COP$25,000), which serves hearty Colombian fare. Upon arrival at Anahuac, take care crossing the street: Cars and buses have little regard for pedestrians. Try to beat the crowds by returning to Cali during the early afternoon. Otherwise, finding transportation can be difficult.

HACIENDA PARAÍSO AND MUSEO DE LA CAÑA DE AZÚCAR

The **Hacienda Paraíso** (14 km from the Pan-American Highway, El Cerrito, tel. 2/514-6848, ext. 105, haciendaparaiso@inciva.gov. co, www.inciva.org, 9:30am-4:30pm Tues.-Sun., COP$5,000) is an estate near the town of Cerrito that is famous for being the home of famed Colombian poet Jorge Isaacs. His romantic novel *La María* is a love story about two adolescents—Efraín and María—set against the backdrop of an idyllic hacienda in the Valle de Cauca during the 19th century. The house is frankly rather underwhelming, but the setting amid sugarcane plantations is beautiful. The museum has period furniture and objects and some background on the famous book.

Nearby is the **Hacienda Piedechinche and Museo de la Caña de Azúcar** (El Cerrito, tel. 2/550-6076, www.museocanadeazucar.com, 9am-4pm daily, COP$5,000). This hacienda is owned by the Providencia sugar company. Here you amble through some lush and immaculately maintained grounds, seeing different examples of sugarcane mills from

© ANDREW DIER

Hacienda Paraíso

sugar-producing regions in Colombia. You can also visit the 18th-century house where the hacienda owners lived.

If you'd like to spend the night in the country, you can stay at the **Hotel Piedemonte** (cell tel. 316/555-1462, haciendaparaiso@inciva.gov.co, COP$50,000 pp d). It's on the Hacienda Paraíso grounds and has 20 chalets as well as a restaurant. During the week when there are fewer crowds at the hacienda, it is a peaceful place, and guests can lounge by natural pools and perhaps read *La María,* or go for a horseback ride.

If you do not have your own transportation, you can hire a cab for the day from Cali to the area and back, although the cost-benefit ratio may not work out. Another option is to take a bus from the Cali bus terminal (Cl. 30N No. 2AN-29) to the village of Amaime for about COP$5,000. The bus company **COODETRANS Palmira** can take you there. There are always taxis waiting at the bus stop for the arrival of buses. From here take a cab to visit both haciendas. You can negotiate with the driver to take you to both haciendas and then return you to catch a minibus back to Cali from Palmira (COP$50,000) or take you directly back to Cali (COP$80,000). The driver can drop you off in Palmira, about an hour from Cali, where transportation to Cali is easy to acquire. Buses from Buga toward Palmira can also drop you off at the roadside in the village of Amaime, a few kilometers from the sights.

Buga

The city of Guadalajara de Buga (pop. 115,000), founded in 1555, was one of the first cities established by the Spaniards in New Granada. It is best known as a place of pilgrimage. More than a million Colombian faithful come each year to pray at the Basílica Señor de los Milagros. Buga may not be chock full of attractions, but it is an excellent launching point from which to discover many lesser-known sights and breathe the fresh air of the Valle de Cauca. Plus, it's a friendly kind of place.

SIGHTS

The star attraction in town for religious pilgrims is the **Basílica Señor de los Milagros** (Cra. 14 No. 3-62, tel. 2/228-2823, www.milagrosdebuga.com, 5:30am-7:30pm daily). Built in the early 20th century, this pink church is not of architectural significance: It's known for its "Cristo Negro" or Señor de los Milagros—a charred woodcarving of Christ that is displayed in a chapel behind the altar.

Praying to the "Black Christ" is believed to provide miracles, and the story behind this icon is one of generosity, devotion, and miracles. In colonial times an indigenous woman who had converted to Christianity saved for years to purchase a crucifix. One day a man crossed her path crying because he'd go to jail if he didn't pay a debt. The woman showed her generosity to by giving him all the money she had saved. Months later, she noticed a small crucifix floating down the river towards her. She picked it up and made an altar to pray to it. The crucifix grew in size, prompting her and others to believe it had miraculous powers. After years of deterioration, the church decided to burn it and replace it with another, but it never burned, remaining charred and black—another miracle.

The shops lining the Avenida del Milagroso,

© ANDREW DIER

Buga is a major pilgrimage destination.

a pedestrian walkway leading to the church, sell all manner of basilica-related trinkets. Each September 14 there is a large procession in and around town featuring the Señor de los Milagros. It's accompanied by special masses and ceremonies in the church.

The **Parque Cabal** (between Clls. 6-7 and Cras. 14-15) is the center of this slow-paced city. Old-timers drink their *tinto* (small cups of black coffee) in corner cafés in the late afternoon, engrossed in political conversations with their friends, while lottery vendors circulate among the tables hoping to sell a couple of tickets. On the corner of Calle 6 and Carrera 15 is the **Catedral de San Pedro** (8am-noon and 2pm-6pm Mon.-Fri.), a beautifully preserved, three-nave church that was originally built in the 16th century. It is a couple of blocks west of the park.

ACCOMMODATIONS AND FOOD

The best part about the small **Buga Hostel** (Cra. 13 No. 4-83, tel. 2/236-7752, www.buga-hostel.com, COP$16,000 dorm, COP$35,000-COP$45,000 d), aside from its friendly owners, is its **Holy Water Ale Café,** where you can saddle up to the bar, try one of their home brews on tap, and chow down on sourdough pizza or the best black-bean burger this side of Austin. It's open daily for lunch and dinner. The hostel has one large dorm room and two private rooms. The hostel has a guide on staff who organizes excursions to the Sonso and Yotoco natural reserves and other sights in the Valle de Cauca. These nature hikes are open to anyone and are reasonably priced.

The **Hotel Guadalajara** (Cl. 1 No. 13-33, tel. 2/236-2611, www.hotelguadalajara.com.co, COP$200,000 d) is retro without trying to be. It's just three blocks away from Basílica Señor de los Milagros and has been around for 50 years. The pool is a good place to cool off. The hotel often has special weekend rates.

GETTING THERE

Buses depart Cali for Buga all day long. Tickets cost around COP$8,000, and the journey through the sugarcane plantations of the Valle takes under two hours. Buses will often leave you at the main highway, and from there you'll have to walk about 20 minutes or take a cab into town. Cabs are always at the ready to meet arriving buses, and this is easy to do. The pleasant open-air Buga bus station, modern and clean, is a straightforward 15-minute walk from the Buga Hostel.

VICINITY OF BUGA
Natural Reserves

There are three natural parks close to Buga where you can enjoy a day of hiking, canoeing, and bird-watching. Run by **INCIVA** (tel. 2/514-6848, www.inciva.org), an agency that promotes cultural and ecological points of interest in the Valle de Cauca department, the **Parque Natural Regional El Vínculo** (El Vínculo, cell tel. 321/831-4775, pnrelvinculo@inciva.gov.co, 8am-noon and 1pm-5pm Mon.-Fri., COP$3,000) is a center for natural exploration and education. Here you can take a short guided nature walk through the dry tropical forest for a small fee. Contact INCIVA in advance to set this up. Previously a cattle ranch, the land was donated to INCIVA by its owner in 1969 to help preserve and protect threatened wildlife and ecological diversity. You can also visit the park on weekends with a prior reservation. Parque Natural Regional El Vínculo is to the south of Buga towards Palmira, only about three kilometers away.

At the **Reserva Natural Laguna de Sonso** (tel. 2/228-1922, www.lagunasonso.tripod.com, COP$5,000) you may see many different species of waterfowl and other animals in this wetland reserve on the eastern banks of the Río Cauca to the southwest of Buga. It is a mostly marshy park, and a walk through it takes about an hour. Buses from the Buga bus station (Cl. 4 before the main highway) going towards Darien or Cali can take you there for around COP$2,000, although you will need to walk one kilometer to get to the park entrance. If you see a fisherman once you arrive at the lake, you can ask him to take you around in his canoe, for a small fee.

© ANDREW DIER

Museo Rayo

a house. If you are planning a weekend jaunt to this area, you may want to have your own transportation.

Darien is the "town" around Lake Calima. It is a cute pueblo with a few restaurants, stores, and other services. Its **Museo Arqueológico Calima** (Cl. 10 No. 12-50, tel. 2/253-3121, www.calimadarien.com, 8am-noon and 1pm-5pm Tues.-Fri., 10am-6pm Sat.-Sun., COP$3,000) has a collection of ceramics dating to 8,000 BC, and it includes artifacts from the Ilama, Yotoco, and Sonso cultures.

One of the main draws of Lago Calima is its wind- and kite-surfing opportunities. **Kite Colombia** (cell tel. 317/821-4889, www.kitecolombia.com, US$500 for a 5-day course including lodging, or US$55 for a 1-day introduction course) offers a range of kite-surfing courses and can also arrange accommodations in its lakeside hostel (US$15 dorm, US$22 d). In the mornings, try some Spanish lessons (US$200 for 20 hours).

A third option is the **Reserva Natural Bosque de Yotoco** (Km. 18 Carretera Buga-Madronal, tel. 2/228-1922, 7:30am-6pm daily, COP$5,000), where a couple of hour-long guided walks—El Corbón and El Cedro—along the Río Yotoco can be organized. This is the only way to visit the park. Contact expert guide Valentín (cell tel. 315/471-4758) to set up a tour. You can get a good view of Lago Calima from the park. This park is also accessible by bus (COP$5,000). Take one headed to Darien and ask the bus driver to let you off at Yotoco.

Lago Calima

The **Lago Calima** is the largest artificial lake in Colombia and is a favorite spot for Caleños seeking weekend rejuvenation. With winds reaching 43 knots (46 mph), it's a great place for kite-surfing and windsurfing. But other sports, such as waterskiing, boating, and swimming, are also popular. Colombian weekenders often stay in lake houses with their friends and family, but there are a handful of standard hotels if you don't have the option of renting

ROLDANILLO

Against a backdrop of mountains and the vast valley to its east, Roldanillo (pop. 35,000) is on the map for two reasons: It was the home of modernist artist Omar Rayo, and it's the undisputed paragliding capital of Colombia. This town is just two hours from Buga by bus, far away from the well-trodden tourist route.

The **Museo Rayo** (Cl. 8 No. 8-53, tel. 2/229-8623, www.museorayo.co, 9am-6pm daily, COP$5,000) is the only real sight in town, and it is well worth a visit. Omar Rayo, who was part of the Op Art, or Optical Art, movement, is known for bold and abstract paintings that often appear three-dimensional. Dedicated mostly to Rayo's paintings, drawings, and sculptures, the museum comprises five octagonal exhibition spaces, each one with a different theme. Temporary exhibits showcase other renowned Colombian artists. Rayo passed away in Roldanillo in 2010.

If you have always wanted to feel what it's like to be a condor soaring over the sugarcane fields below, **Cloud Base Colombia** (Cra. 9 No. 8-71, tel. 2/229-9106, www.

cloudbasecolombia.com) has a solution for you. This tourist agency, started in 2011 by a pair of German and Swiss paragliding fanatics, can arrange for paragliding and hang gliding lessons and excursions. If the idea of leaping off a cliff into the bright blue skies of the valley doesn't appeal to you, they can come up with some other ideas for you to pass the time. You can think of them as the Roldanillo tourist information center.

The optimal time to fly is between late December and late March, although anytime is fine. Roldanillo regularly hosts big-time paragliding competitions, such as the Paragliding World Cup Semifinal in January 2013.

The best option in town is **Casa Vieja** (Cra. 9 No. 8-71, tel. 2/229-9106, cell tel. 312/808-8841, COP$35,000 s, COP$50,000 d). It's a small hostel with a cute garden run by the guys at Cloud Base Colombia. They have 12 rooms and they know how to grill. **Balcones del Parque** (Cl. 8 No. 6-86, tel. 2/259-5151, celdosman@hotmail.com, COP$25,000 dorm, COP$70,000 d) could be very nice, as its location, overlooking the park, is fantastic.

Pasto

Many people overlook unassuming Pasto, a city of more than 400,000 people. It's seen by backpackers as a place to spend the night on the way between Ecuador and Popayán, not a destination in its own right. But Pasto, along with the stunning Nariño countryside, deserves your time and attention.

With church steeples rising out of its colonial center, Pasto is set in the verdant Valle de Atriz with the deceivingly gentle, sloping Volcán Galeras watching over it. The valley is a rich agricultural region where potatoes are king. This city even has a potato named after it—the *papa pastusa*—which is sold in every supermarket in Colombia. Pasto, the "Ciudad Sorpresa," indeed may surprise you with a number of museums and sights that will keep you intellectually stimulated for more than a couple days. Of particular interest is the extraordinary handicraft technique called *barniz de Pasto,* as well as some incredible wood carvings, an influence of Quiteño culture.

Wonderful day trips can be made from the city to La Cocha and to Laguna Verde to the south, and an overnight trip to climb Volcán Cumbal is a good plan for the adventurous.

Due to its rugged terrain and poorly patrolled border with Ecuador, Nariño, the department of which Pasto is capital, became a major corridor for drug and guerrilla activity. The areas described in this guide are safe, however.

SIGHTS
Historic Churches

The most important and only colonial-era church in the city is the **Iglesia de San Juan Bautista** (Cl. 18A No. 25-17, tel. 2/723-5440, 7:30am-11am Sun.-Fri., 3:30pm-6:30pm Sat.), in the heart of the Centro on the **Plaza Nariño.** The original construction was built in the 16th century, but an earthquake demolished that, and in 1669 the current church was built. The interior has outstanding geometric Mudejar designs on the ceiling and around the presbytery.

Statues of angels set atop the twin towers of the **Iglesia de Cristo Rey** (corner Cl. 20 and Cra. 24) beckon from blocks away. This is a stunning gothic revival church. The sanctuary is lined by 19 woodcarvings created by famous local sculptor Alfonso Zambrano and Ecuadorian woodcarvers. Above, light streams through enormous stained glass windows, creating a mystical environment.

The **Catedral de Pasto** (Cra. 26 No. 17-23, tel. 2/723-3328, 7am-11am Sun.-Fri., 3pm-7pm Sat.) was being renovated at the time of the writing of this guide. It was built in 1920. The stately red-brick church is composed of three naves.

PASTO

To Popayán and Cali

Parque Infantil

To Museo del Carnaval and La Maison del Ejecutivo

JUAN SEBASTIÁN HOTEL

RESTAURANTE CHIPICHAPE

MESTIZO PEÑA BAR

COLA DE GALLO

MUSEO TAMINANGO DE ARTES Y TRADICIONES POPULARES DE NARIÑO

CAFÉ LA CATEDRAL

CATEDRAL DE PASTO

IGLESIA DE SAN JUAN BAUTISTA

ARTESANÍAS DE COLOMBIA

PASTO TOURIST OFFICE

IGLESIA DE CRISTO REY

Río Pasto

SHIRAKABA

Plaza Nariño

VOLCAFÉ

PICANTERÍA IPIALES

Instituto Técnico Superior Industrial

OBANDO BARNIZ DE PASTO

EMBRUJO ANDINO PEÑA BAR

FERNANDO PLAZA

KOALA INN

LA MERCED

MUSEO DEL ORO NARIÑO

Parque de Santiago

Plaza del Carnaval

To LAGUNA LA COCHA

ÉXITO SHOPPING CENTER

PANAMERICAN HIGHWAY

To LAGUNA VERDE, bus station, Ipiales, and Cumbal

0   500 yds
0   500 m

© AVALON TRAVEL

CARRERA 27, CARRERA 26, CARRERA 25, CARRERA 24, CARRERA 23, CARRERA 22A, CARRERA 22, CARRERA 21, CARRERA 20, CARRERA 19, CARRERA 18

CALLE 19, CALLE 20, CALLE 21, CALLE 22, CALLE 18, CALLE 17, CALLE 16, CALLE 15, CALLE 13, CALLE 12, CALLE 11, CALLE 10

Museo Taller Alfonso Zambrano Payán

In a colonial-style house built in the 1960s, the **Museo Taller Alfonso Zambrano Payán** (Cl. 20 No. 29-78, tel. 2/731-2837, hernando-zambrano@gmail.com, 8am-noon and 2pm-4pm Mon.-Sat., free) is a tribute to Alfonso Zambrano, one of Pasto's most famous sons. Zambrano is best known in Pasto for having carved extraordinary designs for carnival floats. Each year an award was given for the best design, and he won it over and over again. Zambrano won so often that he was prohibited at a certain point from participating in the competition due to his extraordinary skill. Woodcarving and painting continue to take

place at this combination workshop/museum. And it remains a family affair: It is now operated by Zambrano's daughter, and the artist's grandsons can regularly be found at work carving designs out of cedar. The museum's small collection of pre-Columbian ceramics and Quiteño school paintings is impressive.

Museo Taminango de Artes y Tradiciones Populares de Nariño

Set in a colonial house built in the early 17th century (said to be the oldest house still standing in Pasto), the **Museo Taminango de Artes y Tradiciones Populares de Nariño** (Cl. 13 No. 27-67, tel. 2/723-5539, 8am-noon and 2pm-6pm Mon.-Fri., 9am-1pm Sat.,

© ANDREW DIER

Plaza Nariño, Pasto's main plaza

COP$2,000) is a museum dedicated to hand-icrafts. An American missionary, Catalina Morgan, who arrived in Pasto in 1934, set out to preserve the house, which had fallen into disrepair. She raised enough money to restore it and to convert it, eventually, into a cultural center. It was opened as a museum in 1989. The museum presents traditional handicrafts from Nariño, including explanations of the *barniz de Pasto* technique. This technique, developed by indigenous groups, uses the leaves and fruits of the *mopa mopa* bush, from which a resin is extracted. It is dyed in different colors using vegetables dyes, and thin sheets of it are applied to decorate wooden boxes and other objects. Adjacent to the museum is a small handicrafts store.

Museo del Oro Nariño

The **Museo del Oro Nariño** (Cl. 19 No. 21-27, tel. 2/721-9100, ext. 2624, www.banrep-cultural.org, 10am-5pm Tues.-Sat., free), in the Banco de la República building facing the Plaza Carnaval, is a small but good collection of pre-Columbian ceramics from the Nariño alti-plano (high plains) and Pacific coast. The Pasto indigenous group populated the area around Pasto and Ipiales (south of Pasto) and parts of Ecuador. The predominant group in the area was the Quillacingas, who had arrived from the Caribbean region and who were fierce warriors.

Of particular interest in the museum are the stunning *discos giratorios* (metallic discs plated with gold and copper designs) that were presumed to have been used—specifically, spun—in hypnotic religious ceremonies. In the same building you can often find temporary exhibits featuring Colombian artists.

Museo del Carnaval

To learn all about the city's *carneval* celebration, go to the **Museo del Carnaval** (Cl. 19 at Cra. 42, 8am-11:30am and 2pm-5:30pm Mon.-Fri., free). This museum, located in a former slaughterhouse, shows off what Pastuosos are most proud of: their famous Carnaval de Negros y Blancos in early January. A guide will show you the colorful floats, costumes, and masks from the annual celebration and can tell you everything you ever wanted to know about it. Visiting the museum is the next best thing to being a part of the craziness in January.

ENTERTAINMENT AND EVENTS
Nightlife
Pasto is a party town during the Carnaval de Negros y Blancos, but you can still find good times if you're not visiting in January. Thanks to its being home to the Universidad de Nariño, there are a few bars and *peñas* (Andean music bars) that you might want to check out.

Try some *hervidos* (hot alcoholic fruit drinks) at **Mestizo Peña Bar** (Cl. 18 No. 27-67, tel. 2/723-7754, 6pm-1am Thurs.-Sat.) and **Embrujo Andino Peña Bar** (Cra. 23 No. 19-58, cell tel. 313/604-4935, www.embrujoandino-bar.tk). Both are popular *peñas,* often showcasing live music.

As far as bars go, **Volcafé** (Cl. 18 No. 24-29, tel. 2/722-4301, 8am-1am Mon.-Sat.) on the Plaza Nariño is a good place for a drink in the late afternoon as you overlook the goings-on the plaza. **Cola de Gallo** (Cl. 18 No. 27-47, tel. 2/722-6194, 3pm-1am Mon.-Sat.) serves its own *café* (coffee), which is distributed nationally by Juan Valdez, and is a relaxed place for a drink later on in the evening.

Cinema
Two shopping centers have movie theaters that show mostly Hollywood blockbusters. **Royal Films** is in the Éxito shopping center (Cra. 22D No. 2-56), and **Valle de Autriz** is in the shopping mall of the same name (Cra. 42 No. 18A-94, tel. 2/731-6129, www.cinemasvalledeatriz. com.co). Movies cost around COP$5,000.

Festivals and Events
CARNAVAL DE NEGROS Y BLANCOS
January 2-6 every year, the population of sleepy Pasto explodes as up to 300,000 visitors from Colombia and beyond converge on the city during the **Carnaval de Negros y Blancos** (www. carnavaldepasto.org, Jan.), which is recognized as a world heritage tradition by UNESCO. The

celebration actually gets going on December 28, the "day of the innocents." That's a day of purification and celebration of the natural beauty of the area; many hop on their bikes on this day, cruising down the main parade route. On December 31 a parade pokes fun at politicians and other unpopular figures from the previous year (and sometimes effigies of them are burned).

On January 2 the parade of the colonies takes place, a celebration of cultures from the Nariño department, which includes a horseback procession. January 3 is a day of celebration just for children.

January 4 celebrates the arrival of the Castaneda family, who arrived in Pasto (from the Putumayo department), were welcomed with open arms, and worked to help it grow. This marks the symbolic beginning of the *negros y blancos.* January 5 is the day of the *negros,* when revelers paint themselves or others black. This day is a celebration of diversity. Finally the festival concludes with the day of the *blancos,* when fantastic floats slowly make their way along the city streets, and hundreds of thousands of onlookers are busy pelting others with white powder (a Colombian version of Holi, the Indian festival of colors).

In addition to the parades, there are concerts featuring Andean and other styles of music, and presentations of elaborately costumed stilt walkers and dancers. The *carnaval* spills over one more day to January 7, when the Cuy Festival is held, but you have to be fond of roasted guinea pig to truly enjoy this event!. The main parade route departs the stadium and ends in the Plaza de Carnaval in the Centro.

For the *carnaval,* locals strategically seek out the best spot to watch the parades, with some getting out as early as 6am. The parades—and the drinking—start at 9am on the dot. Airlines add dozens of flights during this time to Pasto, but it's still best to make plans several months in advance if you want to be a part of the fun.

SHOPPING
Fine handicrafts from the region can be picked up at **Obando Barniz de Pasto** (Cra. 25 No.

13-4, tel. 2/722-0363, 9am-6pm Mon.-Fri.), a business that has been in existence since the 1850s, which specializes in *barniz de Pasto.* **Artesanías de Colombia** (Cra. 27 No. 12-89, tel. 2/729-9433, 8am-noon and 2pm-6pm Mon.-Fri.), adjacent to the Museo Taminango, has a wide range of local handicrafts, of the highest quality, including wooden jewelry boxes employing the *enchapado en tamo* (straw marquetry) technique, in which they are decorated with thin strands of barley and wheat stems. Artesanías de Colombia is much more than a store, as it conducts numerous training programs for local artisans. On the main plaza is the combination casino/handicraft store **Shirakaba** (Cl. 18 No. 24-69, tel. 2/723-9890, 8am-6pm Mon.-Sat).

RECREATION
Santuario de Fauna y Flora Galeras
The Quillacinga people called it Urcunina, the Mountain of Fire, and when the Spaniards arrived, they renamed it **Volcán Galeras,** because the gently sloping volcano resembled the sails of ships in the Mediterranean Sea. Today, Pasto residents call it a menace, as this volcano sits right above the city, only eight kilometers away on its western side. Galeras has been one of the most active volcanoes in Colombia, and indeed the world, in recent years. There have been minor eruptions almost every year over the past decade, with the last reported in 2013. In 1993, during an international meeting of volcanologists, six scientists in the crater of the volcano were killed when it erupted.

The **Santuario de Fauna y Flora Galeras** (tel. 2/732-0493, www.parquesnacionales.gov.co) is part of the national park system, but much of the park has been closed for many years due to the volcano's activity.

Two hikes can be done, one outside the park and one inside. One hike is from the neighborhood of Anganoy to the park ranger's station, the Cabaña de Control—Urcunina. This is a leisurely walk along a slowly sloping road and takes about an hour, and it requires no guide. It starts from the neighborhood of Anganoy (Nido de Aguilas). Once there, look for the road that leads up to the park. To get to Anganoy, either take a cab (COP$4,000) or take the C7 SIT bus.

The second hike, which takes you into the park, is the 5.7-kilometer-long (3.5-mile-long) San Felipe-Laguna Telpis hike up the northern side of the volcano to the Laguna Telpis, a mountain lake. The hike begins in the village of San Felipe near the town of Yacuanquer. This hike takes three hours to the top, and at the Telpis ranger station you must pay the park entrance fee of COP$2,000. To get to the starting point you can take a taxi (COP$4,000) from Pasto.

Before setting off on any hike near Galeras, call the ranger's station (tel. 2/732-0493) to ask about the status of the trails.

ACCOMMODATIONS
€ **La Maison del Ejecutivo** (Cl. 19 No. 37-16B, tel. 2/731-0043, www.lamaisondelejecutivo.com, COP$120,000 d) is a cozy place to stay in a peaceful neighborhood a short taxi ride from the Plaza Nariño. Rooms are quite comfortable. What sets this place apart, though, is the excellent service. The French owner, Patrice, has lived in Pasto with his Colombian wife for many years. He is quite knowledgeable about tourist attractions and can give some expert travel tips. Breakfasts are generous and healthy, a rarity for hotels in Colombia. In fact, you may want to call ahead and see if you can go there for breakfast even if you're not staying there. Dinner is also served for those who wish, and given the options in town, that might be a good idea.

The **Juan Sebastián Hotel** (Cra. 29 No. 20-18, tel. 2/731-0983, COP$100,000 d) opened in 2011, is centrally located, and is a good value. It has 35 rooms, offers wireless Internet, and includes a very basic breakfast.

Fernando Plaza (Cl. 20 No. 21B-16, tel. 2/729-1432, www.hotelfernandoplaza.com, COP$124,000 d) is a business hotel in a somewhat quieter part of the Centro a few blocks from the Iglesia de Cristo Rey. It offers immaculate and comfortable rooms.

Started by an Australian many years ago but having been under other management for quite some time, the **Koala Inn** (Cl. 18 No. 22-37, tel. 2/722-1101, COP$28,000 s, COP$45,000 d) remains the only backpacker lodge in Pasto, and, although staff are pleasant, this dingy hostel just barely cuts it.

FOOD

Pasto is Colombia's *cuy* capital. *Cuy* is guinea pig meat, which is prepared by slowly barbecuing the meat for about an hour. The delicacy appears on many menus around town, but it's more of a weekend or special occasion dish, so you may have to seek it out.

Eateries popular with locals in the Centro include **Restaurante Chipichape** (Cra. 28 No. 18-78, tel. 2/722-8992, 8am-10pm Mon.-Sat., 8am-5pm Sun., COP$6,500) and **Picantería Ipiales** (Cl. 19 No. 23-37, tel. 2/723-0393, 9:30am-8:30pm Mon.-Sat., 11am-6pm Sun., COP$7,000). Similar to each other, both specialize in *lapingacho* plates. *Lapingachos* are a type of cheese-filled potato cake, made from *papa pastusa (a local potato variety),* and the meals usually contain beef, pork, or chicken surrounded by about five of these cakes. There is always some roasted *capia* (corn) on the side.

Cafeteria, bakery, and pizzeria **La Merced** (Cra. 22 No. 17-37, tel. 2/723-8830, 7am-10pm daily) has something for everyone, from typical Colombian fare to seafood to pizzas. It also has an array of sweets and baked goods.

The only strictly vegetarian restaurant is **Pan Integral** (Cra. 29 No. 20-34, no phone, 9am-6pm Mon.-Sat., COP$4,500), where a set lunch menu goes for only COP$4,500, but a nicer option is **Huerta del Chef** (Cra. 36 No. 18-114, cell tel. 301/447-0350, 7am-2:30pm Mon.-Fri., 7am-1pm Sun., COP$12,000).

The best pizza place in town is **Alina Pizza Gourmet** (Cl. 20 No. 38-07, tel. 2/731-3565, 6pm-10pm daily, COP$25,000), a hip and overpriced joint on the Avenida Los Estudiantes. It serves only pizza—including many vegetarian options—and drinks. The walls are decorated with thousands of photos and the atmosphere is friendly.

For hanging out, try **Café La Catedral** (Cra. 26 No. 16-37, tel. 2/729-8584, www.cafelacatedral.com, 8:30am-12:30pm and 3pm-8:30pm Mon.-Fri., 10am-12:30pm and 3pm-8:30pm Sat.), where you can have a coffee or light meal and watch the action in the plaza. It's a shame it isn't open on Sunday morning, though, as it's nearly impossible to find a decent cup of coffee at that time.

INFORMATION AND SERVICES

The **Pasto tourist office** (Cl. 18 No. 25-25, tel. 2/723-4962, 8am-noon and 2pm-6pm Mon.-Sat.) is right off the Plaza Nariño and across from the Iglesia de San Juan Bautista. Here you can purchase a city map (COP$2,000), pick up materials on nearby attractions, and purchase some *artesanías*. The timid staff may not volunteer information, so you may have to be persistent.

GETTING THERE AND AROUND

The **bus terminal** (Cra. 6 No. 16D-50, tel. 2/730-8955, www.terminaldepasto.com.co), about a 10-minute taxi ride from the Centro, is well-organized, with shops, cafeterias, and ATMs. From the bus terminal, *colectivos* (small, fast buses) make the journey to and from Ipiales all day long and cost around COP$7,000. Get a window seat if you make this trip along the Pan-American Highway: The scenery is breathtaking and the hairpin curves thrilling. It is a two-lane road, so accidents and road construction can cause delays. Buses going to Bogotá take around 20 hours and cost COP$80,000, while buses from Popayán take about six hours, costing COP$30,000.

Avianca (Cl. 19 No. 25-77, tel. 2/723-2320, www.avianca.com, 8am-6:30pm Mon.-Fri., 8am-1pm Sat.) serves the **Aeropuerto Antonio Nariño** (Chachagui, tel. 2/232-8141 or 2/732-8064), which is about 35 kilometers north of the city. The landing strip is dramatically set upon a plateau 50 meters above rich agricultural land, with mountains all around. Landing here in August when the winds blow can be alternately exciting and terrifying. There is regular flight service to Bogotá and Cali on Avianca and **Satena** (Cl. 18 No. 27-74, tel. 2/722-0623 or 2/733-4266, www.satena.com). A taxi into town will cost around COP$20,000. Shared *colectivos* can sometimes be found for less.

In Pasto, transportation alternatives are pretty straightforward and organized. Taxis cost COP$3,500 to anywhere in the city. As a matter of precaution, after dark order taxis by phone.

The bus system is quite good, as private bus companies have been by and large replaced by the public **SIT** network (www.ciudadsorpresa.com.co). Bus fares currently stand at COP$1,100. Unfortunately there are few signs pointing out bus stops, so you will need to ask which bus to take and from where to catch it. The vast majority of tourist sights are in the Centro, and are best visited on foot if possible.

LAGUNA LA COCHA

Only about 45 minutes outside of Pasto is **Laguna La Cocha** and the smallest park in the national park system, the **Santuario de Fauna y Flora Isla de la Corota.** This excursion is a delight. Minibuses from Pasto will take you to the lakeside fishing village of Encano, on the shores of La Cocha, and is home to about 200 families. The cheerfully painted wooden A-frames, the flowerboxes, and the colorful *lanchas* (wooden boats) waiting at the ready will remind you of someplace—but probably not Colombia! There are maybe a dozen restaurants in the Encano, all serving La Cocha trout, dozens of different ways.

From the village you can hire a boat to take you to the sanctuary on tiny **Isla de la Corota**, not far away (about a 10-minute ride). This excursion costs about COP$20,000 per boat, as the boat's owner will wait for you and take you back to the mainland. On the island, you'll have to pay an entry fee (COP$1,000) and sign in at the ranger's office. From there you'll walk through the virgin rainforest on a wooden walkway. Although the vegetation is tropical with 500 species of plants, including

ferns, bromeliads, orchids, lichen, and *siete cueros* trees, the climate is actually quite cool. It's about 2,800 meters (9,200 feet) above sea level. The highest points on the island have similar vegetation to that of *páramos* (highland moors). It's nice to go on a weekday when there are few visitors, so that you can enjoy the wonderful peace that the island brings. It's a lovely excursion, one that won't take long: the island covers only about 16 hectares (40 acres) of land.

Surrounding the lake are more than 50 private natural reserves managed by local farmers through the Asociación de Desarollo Campesino (www.adc.org.co). Many of these offer accommodations for visitors. One such reserve is **El Encanto Andino** (Vereda Santa Teresita, cell tel. 321/263-2663, www.lagunacocha.blogspot.com, COP$100,000 d incl. all meals, transportation COP$25,000 pp). Here you can take walks through the jungle, visit an orchid farm, and do some bird-watching, among other activities. Food is produced at the reserve, and it is all organic. It is difficult to get there, but the pristine environment and unique experience may make it worth the trouble. Contact the hotel for transportation assistance.

Easier to get to and more luxurious is the Swiss chalet-like **Hotel Sindamonoy** (tel. 2/721-8222, cell tel. 314/863-5186, www.hotelsindamanoy.com, COP$176,000 d) overlooking the lake. It has 23 large rooms, most with a lake view. If you are just coming for the day, you can take a boat to the hotel and have lunch at the restaurant, the best on the lake.

To get to Encano, take a *colectivo* (a small minivan) from Pasto. They leave from in front of the hospital (along Avenida Colombia) facing the big Alkosto store (not from the bus terminal). Expect to wait about 20 minutes for the car to fill up with passengers. It is a 45-minute drive and costs COP$4,000.

LAGUNA VERDE

The hike up to the sulfurous **Laguna Verde** (3,800 meters/12,500 feet), a dazzling, emerald green crater lake on the north side of the dormant **Volcán Azufral,** is easy to make from Pasto. Laguna Negra is a smaller neighboring

© ANDREW DIER

fishing community at Laguna La Cocha

lake. A sacred site for the Pasto indigenous people, the volcano is part of the Nudo de los Pastos mountain range, which serves as a natural border between Colombia and Ecuador. The vegetation in the *páramo* (highland moor) is sparse, with low shrubs, wildflowers, moss, and lichen. There is little fauna to be seen, except for the occasional *gavilan* (vulture) gliding through the air. From here on a clear day you can see as far as the Galeras volcano in Pasto.

The Nudo de los Pastos is where the great Andes mountain range coming north from Ecuador splits into two ranges in Colombia: the Cordillera Central (Central Mountain Range) and the Cordillera Occidental (Western Mountain Range). The Cordillera Central continues northwards through Pasto, Cali, much of the Coffee Region, Medellín, and eventually into the Bolívar department (province) near the Caribbean. The Cordillera Occidental rises between the Pacific Ocean and the Río Cauca and continues through the departments of Chocó and Antioquia to the Gulf of Urabá on the Caribbean coast.

The **Reserva Natural Azufral** is managed by a community organization, the **Asociación Azufral los Andariegos Túquerres** (Cra. 6A No. 16D-50, tel. 2/730-8955, cell tel. 316/713-3823). From the park ranger's cabin, it is a six-kilometer hike to Laguna Verde and Laguna Negra. Hikers are requested to register at the cabin and pay a small entry fee (COP$2,000). It is an easy, gradual ascent as it follows a dirt road all the way up the mountain. This can take 3-5 hours. It is hard to get lost, especially on weekends and holidays when there are many fellow hikers.

Weather can change on a dime, temperatures can dramatically drop, and the winds can be fierce. Wear warm clothing, bring along a waterproof windbreaker and drinking water, and pick up some fruit from the Túquerres market to keep you going. Economical breakfasts, lunches, and a hot *agua de panela* (hot drink made from raw brown sugar) or *tinto* (black coffee) can be had at the ranger's cabin. Call in advance (cell tel. 316/713-3823) to arrange for meals. The best time to make the trek

© ANDREW DIER

view from the path to Laguna Verde

is July-October or January-April when the weather is drier.

Túquerres, the nearest town to the hike's starting point, is not beautiful, but if you make the hike on a Thursday, be sure to catch the open-air **Santamaría Market** (6am-2pm). There's the usual cornucopia of fruits and vegetables, including some crazy-looking potatoes. Stray dogs hang out in the freshly slaughtered meat section. The call of *"a mil, a mil, a mil"* ("for one thousand, for one thousand") rings across the market, as increasingly anxious vendors try to sell their vegetables (and rabbits and chickens) to a dwindling number of potential customers.

Guides and Tour Agencies

Contracting a guide is not necessary for this hike, especially on weekends when there are many making the climb. Nevertheless, knowledgeable guides are available from the community-based **Asociación Azufral los Andariegos Túquerres** (Túquerres office: Cra. 13 No. 19-26, tel. 2/728-0586), the group that manages

the park. You can request a guide in advance by calling Jorge Noguera, head of the association (cell tel. 316/713-3823, COP$30,000 group). If you'd prefer an organized tour from Pasto and would like to avoid having to deal with public transportation, contact Jaime López at **Viajes Cielo & Tierra** (cell tel. 317/437-7436, www.turismopasto.com, COP$140,000-COP$200,000). This group can provide a bilingual guide for the excursion, which leaves Pasto (they can pick you up at your hotel) bright and early at 5am. Viajes Cielo & Tierra offers many other outdoor adventures and multi-day tours in the Nariño department.

Getting There

If you are making this trip independently, there is regular *colectivo* service from the Pasto bus terminal (Cra. 6A No.16D-50, tel. 2/730-8955) bound for Túquerres starting at 5am. The trip will cost about COP$8,000 and takes two hours to make. Plan to leave Pasto no later than 8am, however.

From Túquerres it is about 15 kilometers

in the Nudo de los Pastos mountain range in southern Colombia. It is 15 kilometers northwest of Cumbal (pop. 20,000), a laid-back and orderly town of broad streets.

The volcano has not seen any activity since 1930, but the Colombian Geological Service upped its level of threat from green to yellow in 2012. Indigenous people used to extract sulphur rock and snow and ice for sale in the market at Ipiales, and to make *helado de paila,* an ice cream made in large copper bowls.

To hike to the top of Volcán Cumbal, you must spend the night in the town of Cumbal and get an early morning start. It is a strenuous hike: five to six hours up and three back. The volcano has two peaks; most visitors climb the southern one. From the top, there are spectacular views of the mountainous surrounding countryside extending into Ecuador.

The path to the volcano begins in the settlement called La Origa, which is 20 minutes from town. From there it is a tough hike up. The path is not clearly marked, and it could be easy to get lost, particularly when fog rolls in over the mountains, so be sure to get a guide. A recommended guide is Fidencio Cuaical of **Turicumbes** (cell tel. 310/513-7234, turicumbes@hotmail.com, COP$60,000), a group of young, rural guides, based out of Cumbal.

If you prefer an organized excursion with transportation from Pasto, you can arrange it with **Viajes Cielo & Tierra** (tel. 2/731-3314, cell tel. 317/437-7436, www.turismopasto.com, turismocieloytierra@hotmail.com).

The best time of year to make the climb is during the dry months between July and September.

Accommodations

The **Hotel Paraíso Real** (Cl. 17 at Cra. 9, cell tel. 314/640-6046, COP$25,000 d) is really the only lodging available in Cumbal. Rooms are clean but quite basic. Surprisingly, there is wireless Internet, and the hotel adjoins a small bakery. Adjacent to the hotel is a basic restaurant where they serve trout fished from the sacred Laguna Cumbal, about six kilometers from town.

© ANDREW DIER

buckets of potatoes at the Santamaría Market in Túquerres

to the hike's starting point (the park ranger's cabin), just past the San Roque village. *Colectivos* (COP$1,000) leave from the Parque Bolívar in the morning to San Roque. (The park ranger cabin is 500 meters from there.) This is the cheapest option. However, this service is infrequent (ask a local about the bus upon arrival). Private taxis (COP$20,000-COP$40,000 round-trip) can be contracted from Túquerres to take you all the way to the park ranger's cabin and pick you up at a designated time afterwards, but it is recommended to contact Jorge Noguera, from the **Asociación Azufral los Andariegos Túquerres** (cell tel. 316/713-3823, COP$30,000), in advance to coordinate this transportation, as the association is always an honest broker. The trip up takes you past idyllic farmhouses and fields of potato crops.

VOLCÁN CUMBAL

At 4,764 meters (15,630 feet) high, the snow-dusted **Volcán Cumbal** is the highest volcano

Getting There

To get to Cumbal from Pasto, you must take a bus to Ipiales first. This costs around COP$10,000, and the trip takes two hours. At the Ipiales terminal, transfer to a minivan bound for Cumbal; the trip takes about an hour (COP$6,000).

CAFÉ DE ALBÁN

For an unforgettable experience in a Nariño coffee town, you can't beat the homestay program of **Café de Albán** (cell tel. 314/632-3765, cafealban@gmail.com or edgarivanpa@gmail.com, www.cafealban.org, COP$60,000 pp per day) in the town of San José de Albán, which is 68 kilometers northeast of Pasto, an agro-tourism project started by an American. For a few days you can live with a local family and learn the ins and outs of the coffee growing, harvesting, and roasting process. Near the town are markets to visit, hikes to hike, and opportunities to learn about handicrafts from the region. You can also volunteer by teaching English at Café de Albán's school.

IPIALES

Border towns are rarely beauties, and Ipiales, on the Pan-American Highway on the other side of Ecuador, is no exception. However, Ipiales is home to the stunning neo-gothic Santuario Nuestra Señora de las Lajas, a major pilgrimage site that is worth a look.

For meals and accommodations, the area around the Plaza La Pola is where to look. With hookahs on the tables and dishes such as prawn fettuccini on the menu, **La Terraza** (Cra. 6 No. 13-17, tel. 2/775-7677, 10am-9pm Mon.-Sat., 10am-3pm Sun., COP$18,000) might seem a little ambitious for Ipiales. It is on the second floor overlooking the Plaza La Pola. Also on the menu are shwarmas and burritos. **Los Andes** (Cra. 5 No. 14-44, tel. 2/773-4338, www.hotellosandes.com, COP$90,000 d) is one of the few good hotel options in town. Carpeted rooms are fine (there are 33) and they even have a gym.

Las Lajas

The most famous neo-gothic construction in all of Colombia, and one of the most visited pilgrimage sites for Catholics, is the **Santuario Nuestra Señora de las Lajas** (tel. 2/775-4462, 7am-6pm daily), seven kilometers from the city. It is truly a photogenic church built impossibly in the middle of a gorge and over a river. The basilica is packed with Colombian and Ecuadorean tourists on Sundays and religious holidays and, to a lesser extent, on Saturdays. Minivans head towards the basilica all day long from the bus terminal, and it costs about COP$2,000. You will need to walk down a long walkway to the cathedral. It's lined with knickknack shops and diners where you can grab a *quimbolito* pastry and a sweet, weak coffee to warm up, usually served by a lady in a *ruana* (poncho). Along the walkway you'll notice thousands plaques of prayers and thanksgiving. The pews are always packed for masses at the cathedral, and a museum (entry COP$2,000) has old photographs of prior cathedral constructions. Families often bring picnic lunches and watch their kids run around by the river, the trickling Río Guáitara. Hungry street dogs wait for scraps. The bridge leading to the cathedral is a favorite spot for photos.

For much of its history, the cathedral has been under construction. First built as a small chapel in the 18th century, its latest and stunning neo-gothic incarnation took about 33 years (until 1949) to complete. It was designed by an architect from Pasto and built by an Ecuadorean.

The sanctuary is a place of miracles, according to believers. An indigenous girl and her mother were traveling home and, during a storm, sought refuge from the rain under the protection of rocks. The girl, Rosa, who was deaf and dumb, discovered the illuminated image of Mary on the side of the canyon after a lightning bolt struck, and she astonished her mother by later uttering the words *"Mamita, la mestiza me llama"* ("Mommy, she is calling me").

After seeing the cathedral, the walk back up is steep. There are plans to build a cable car transportation system to make it all easier and make this a bigger tourism draw.

© ANDREW DIER

llama at Las Lajas

Crossing the Border

The border with Ecuador is at the town of Rumichaca about three kilometers south of the center of Ipiales. Minibuses depart from the center all day long and from the bus terminal as well. These cost about COP$1,500, or you can take a cab, which will cost COP$6,000. Leaving Colombia, you will need to fill out an entry form at the Ecuadorean side of the bridge and request either a 30- or 90-day-long permission. The border is open 5am-10pm.

Getting There

There is frequent *colectivo* (small bus) service between Pasto and Ipiales along the Pan-American Highway. It's a beautiful, if

slow-going, ride, but remember that you'll have to stay awake to enjoy the awe-inspiring scenery of mountains, valleys, and rivers. The road is two-lane and traffic is heavy, especially with big trucks. If there is a wreck on it, this 2.5-hour journey can take much longer. The trip costs about COP$8,000.

Buses to Popayán take about eight hours and cost COP$32,000; to Cali the journey takes 11 hours and costs COP$46,000. You can take a 23-hour bus ride to Bogotá for COP$107,000, but airliner **Satena** (Cra. 7 No. 16-49, tel. 2/725-6085, www.satena.com, 9am-6pm Mon.-Sat.) has a morning flight to the capital a few times a week from the tiny Ipiales airport.

Popayán

The temperate capital of the Cauca department, Popayán is the White City along the banks of the Río Cauca between the Cordilleras Central and Occidental (Central and Western Mountain Ranges). It is a dignified city, proud of its place in history as the home of presidents, poets, and priests. It retains its colonial charm despite earthquakes and modernization. Religion retains its importance in the lives of its people; during the annual Holy Week celebrations the entire city takes part in solemn processions through the streets. Idyllic churches and museums are the main places of interest in Popayán, but lingering in the Parque Caldas on

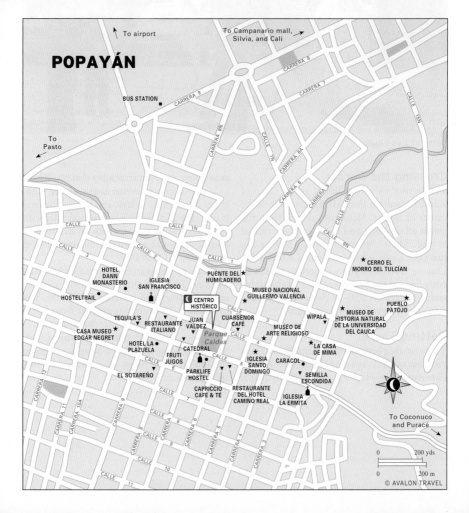

a sunny afternoon or strolling the lonely streets on a Sunday evening may be what you remember most.

Popayán is also a great base from which to explore sights nearby. Just outside of town is the Guambarino indigenous town of Silvia, famous for its colorful Tuesday market. In Coconuco, you can take a dip in the hot springs, and Parque Nacional Puracé is a nearby national park where you can hike to the rim of a volcano, the Volcán Puracé.

Farther afield in Cauca is the archaeological site of Tierradentro, and beyond that, in the Huila department, is San Agustín. These two sights can be combined in a circuit trip in three or four days from Popayán, although many tourists choose one or the other.

SIGHTS

◖ *Centro Histórico*

The **Parque Caldas** (Clls. 4-5 and Cras. 6-7) in the center of Popayán is a lovely pedestrian square and the city's main point of reference. It's a fantastic place to have a coffee (there's a Juan Valdez Café on the square) or just hang out, day or night. Your discovery of Popayán begins here.

MUSEUMS

The **Casa Museo Edgar Negret and Museo Iberoamericano de Arte Moderno de Popayán** (MIAMP, Cl. 5 No. 10-23, tel. 2/824-4546, www.museonegret.wordpress. com, 8am-noon and 2pm-6pm Wed.-Mon., COP$2,500) is in the home of Edgar Negret, a Colombian artist best known for massive abstract iron sculptures that adorn public spaces in cities throughout Colombia and in museums throughout the world. Negret donated this 18th-century house to the city in an effort to promote its rebirth following the devastating 1983 quake.

An oft-talked-about piece at the museum is a model of Negret's proposal for a monument to Simón Bolívar in Bogotá that ended up being too abstract for the Bogotanos.

The museum was the scene of excitement when, in 2011, an etching by Pablo Picasso

was stolen from Negret's private collection. Worth over US$65,000, it was recovered when the thief tried to sell it a few months later. Negret passed away in Bogotá in 2012 on his 92nd birthday.

The **Museo de Historia Natural de la Universidad del Cauca** (Cra. 2 No. 1A-25, tel. 2/820-9861, 9am-noon and 2pm-5pm daily, COP$3,000) was founded in 1936. This expansive museum on the edge of the historic center is considered the best natural history museum in Colombia and highlights the astounding variety of species, both plant and animal, that are found in Colombia. A guide will show you through.

Museo Nacional Guillermo Valencia (Cra. 6 No. 2-69, tel. 2/820-6160, 10am-noon and 2pm-5pm Tues.-Sun., COP$2,000) is an 18th-century house near the Puente del Humilladero that was the home of Popayán poet Guillermo Valencia. His son, Guillermo Leon Valencia, was president in the 1960s. The museum may not be of great interest to foreign visitors, but the house is undeniably a beauty. The **Puente Humilladero** and **Puente de la Custodia** are historic bridges next to the Museo Casa Valencia. The Puente de la Custodia dates to the 18th century.

The **Museo de Arte Religioso** (Cl. 4 No. 4-56, tel. 2/824-2759, 9am-12:30pm and 2pm-6pm Mon.-Fri, 9am-2pm Sat., COP$5,000), run by the Arquidiocesis de Popayán, has 10 rooms of religious art from the colonial era in an 18th-century neoclassical house covering Quiteño, Popayán, and Spanish styles. You'll probably be guided through by a police cadet.

CHURCHES

There are several colonial churches dating from the 17th to 18th centuries to visit in Popayán. Most of them have been restored following earthquakes over the years. The **Iglesia San Francisco** (Cl. 4 and Cra. 9, tel. 2/824-0160) is one of the most beautiful churches and dates to the late 18th century. You can ask at the church to see the mummies that were found here following the earthquake. The **Iglesia La Ermita** (Cl. 5 and Cra. 2, tel. 2/820-9725) is older, dating to the 16th century. It has some fine woodcarvings and paintings. The **Iglesia Santo Domingo** (Cl. 4 and Cra. 5, tel. 2/824-0536) is where the Good Friday procession begins every year. The neoclassical **cathedral** (Cl. 5 and Cra. 6, tel. 2/824-1710) on the Parque Caldas was completed in the early 20th century. The cathedral's official name is **Catedral Basílica de Nuestra Señora de la Asunción de Popayán,** but it is always referred to as *"la catedral."*

Cerro El Morro del Tulcán

For a quick early morning or afternoon walk and some nice views of the city, check out the **Cerro El Morro del Tulcán,** a hill to the northeast of Popayán. A statue of the city's founder, Sebastián de Belalcázar, stands on horseback on top of the hill. It is thought that this hill is actually a man-made pyramid built by pre-Columbian peoples. There have been reports of bandits at the hill, so do not go very late in the afternoon.

A corny handicraft market, the **Pueblito Patojo** (9am-6pm daily), adjoins the Cerro el Morro. Also nearby is the **Cerro de las Tres Cruces**.

ENTERTAINMENT AND EVENTS
Nightlife

For unsurpassed old-school, Popayán-style atmosphere, **El Sotareño** (Cra. 6 No.8-05, no phone, 8pm-midnight daily) can't be beat. It's a cozy mom-and-pop place where the pop plays old vinyl tunes (lots of tango) from his collection and patrons of all ages fill in the booths. For nightlife of a different sort, head to the drinking hall alongside university students at the **Campanario** shopping mall (Cra. 9 No. 24AN-21, 5pm-9pm daily), on the outskirts of town.

Festivals and Events

The most important religious site in Colombia during **Semana Santa** (Holy Week) is Popayán. During Easter week, solemn processions take place on the streets of the center, a

the White City of Popayán

© ANDREW DIER

tradition that has been fulfilled every year in the White City since 1566. This is the only time of the year that mummies discovered in the Iglesia San Francisco are displayed.

Congreso Nacional Gastronómico (www. gastronomicopopayan.org) is an annual food festival held in early September each year, mostly at the Hotel Dann Monasterio. You may be surprised to learn that Popayán is one of UNESCO's Cities of Gastronomy, along with Cheng Du, China; Ostersund, Sweden; and Jeonju, North Korea.

RECREATION
Guided Tours

Marcela from **Finca Alas y Raices** (cell tel. 320/742-3470, www.alasyraices.org) conducts walking tours of Popayán (COP$60,000) as well as day trips to Silvia and multi-day trips to San Agustín. Lorena Torres of **Kolumbien Linda Tours** (Cl. 3 No. 25-35, cell tel. 314/892-6699, www.kolumbien-linda-tours.com) specializes in German and English tours to San Agustín from Popayán (COP$250,000).

Luna Paz Tour (Cra. 11 No. 4-85, tel. 2/821-9595, www.lunapaztour.jimdo.com) organizes many interesting tours, such as to Tierradentro (COP$354,000 pp) and to Puracé (COP$120,000 pp).

The staff at **Hosteltrail** (Cra. 11 No. 4-16, tel. 2/831-7871, www.hosteltrailpopayan.com) and **Hostel Caracol** (Cl. 4 No. 2-21, tel. 2/820-7335, www.hostelcaracol.com) can arrange outings, such as a day trip to the Coconuco hot springs with an exhilarating bike ride back; a trip to the Silvia market on Tuesday; tours of the Finca Alas y Raices coffee farm; and trips to **Mamá Lombriz** (cell tel. 316/482-8655, www.mamalombriz.com), a farm on the outskirts of town where worms work!

ACCOMMODATIONS

Popayán has a fair number of accommodations options, and hostels are some of the better ones. Rooms are in short supply during Holy Week and during the Congreso Nacional Gastronómico.

UNDER COP$70,000

Relaxed is the best word to describe the ◖Hostel Caracol (Cl. 4 No. 2-21, tel. 2/820-7335, www.hostelcaracol.com, COP$48,000 d shared bath). That atmosphere has a lot to do with its easy-going staff. They are full of great suggestions on how to make the most of your visit, including how to do their "Circuito Sur," a trip that includes San Agustín, Tatacoa desert, and Tierradentro. There is free use of computers and wireless Internet. If you feel like mingling with other travelers or locals, check out their small café. ◖ **Hosteltrail** (Cra. 11 No. 4-16, tel. 2/831-7871, www.hosteltrailpopayan.com, COP$45,000 d shared bath, COP$55,000 d private bath), on the other side of the park and owned by the same Scottish couple, is a sociable place. Hosteltrail is about a 15-minute walk from the bus station.

Parklife (Cl. 5 No. 6-19, cell tel. 300/249-6240, www.parklifehostel.com, COP$18,000 dorm, COP$45,000 d) has the nicest location in Popayán. Literally right next to the *catedral*

and overlooking the Parque Caldas, it can't get much better. This is a lively and bright Spanish-Romanian-Irish-run hostel, with a pair of private "rooms with a view" that overlook the park and two dorm rooms with 8-10 beds each.

COP$70,000-200,000

La Casa de Mina (Cl. 3 No. 2-37, cell tel. 310/494-4082, www.lacasademima.com, COP$150,000 d) is a quiet and cozy bed and breakfast a few blocks from the Parque Caldas. Seven rooms overlook three courtyards. The owner, Doña Olga, lives here as well, and will make you feel right at home. **Hotel La Plazuela** (Cl. 5 No. 8-13, tel. 2/824-1084, www.hotel-laplazuela.com.co, COP$110,000 d) is a colonial-style house with a lovely large interior courtyard. The rooms are not as great as the setting, which is hard to beat. The hotel restaurant is popular with city government and university employees on their lunch break.

OVER COP$200,000

The finest option in town, although falling short of five stars, is the classic ◖**Hotel Dann Monasterio** (Cl. 4 No. 10-14, tel. 2/824-2191, www.hotelesdann.com, COP$362,000 d). It's housed in an old monastery overlooking a serene interior courtyard where you can have a coffee. It has a pool out back amid spacious, well-kept grounds.

FOOD

Five-course meals are standard at the **Restaurante del Hotel Camino Real** (Cl. 5 No. 5-59, tel. 2/824-3595, www.hotelcaminoreal.com.co, noon-3pm and 6pm-9:30pm, COP$25,000). The cuisine here is mostly French, but also on the menu are the empanadas that made Popayán famous: potato- and peanut-filled *empanadas de pipián*. It can get busy here around lunchtime.

La Semilla Escondida (Cl. 5 No. 2-28, tel. 2/820-6437, noon-3pm and 6pm-10pm Mon.-Sat.) serves healthy lunches and an economical set lunch for just COP$8,000 in a peaceful corner of town. Go for the crêpes—the owner is French, after all.

Wipala (Cra. 2 No. 2-38, tel. 2/823-3141, wipalacolectivocultural@gmail.com, 10am-9pm daily, COP$15,000) is a live music venue/gallery/restaurant surrounding a verdant patio. In the evenings it's a cool place to visit and mingle with locals as well as visitors and expats. Wipala serves some unique juices, some with coca leaf. There's also a veggie burger made out of beets, which tastes much better than it sounds. Wednesday nights are curry nights, a tradition started by the folks at Hosteltrail.

If you want Mexican food, go to a restaurant owned by a Mexican. **Tequila's** (Cl. 5 No. 9-25, tel. 2/822-2150, 5pm-9pm Wed.-Sun., COP$15,000) is a great little cantina where you can delight in the dynamic duo of enchiladas and micheladas (beer cocktail). The owners are a Popayánensa-Mexican couple who lived in Long Island for many years.

Above all, the ◖**Restaurante Italiano** (Cl. 4 No. 8-83, tel. 2/824-0607, 11am-10pm daily, COP$20,000) is consistent. Run by a Swiss woman, it's been in Popayán for years, stays open late, and serves mega portions of pasta dishes and also pizzas. Load up on your carbs here before your Puracé hike. During the day the set lunch—usually Colombian fare—is hard to beat.

Capriccio Café & Te (Cl. 5 No. 5-63, tel. 2/832-3053) looks and feels like a café should. It's a nice place to hang out, maybe have a pastry, but you may want to stick with the pros at **Juan Valdez** (Parque Caldas, Cra. 7 No. 4-36, tel. 2/839-5332) if you want a good brew. Señor Valdez has quite the location on the western side of the park.

Cuarsenor Café (Cra. 6 No. 3-85, tel. 2/834-4040, COP$6,000) is hopping all day long, packed mainly with local workers. It's a bargain breakfast spot, but it also serves hearty lunches with trout or grilled chicken. There's an adjoining bakery. **Fruti Jugos** (Cl. 5 No. 7-66, tel. 2/839-5826) serves gigantic, fresh Colombian juices out of plastic pitchers. So refreshing. You can even order aphrodisiac juices.

GETTING THERE AND AROUND

There are frequent buses to Cali (COP$15,000, 4 hours) and Pasto (5 hours, COP$25,000) from the **Terminal de Transportes** (Tr. 9 No. 4N-125, Oficina 201, tel. 2/823-1817, www.terminalpopayan.com), a modern bus station about a 15-minute walk from downtown. The **Aeropuerto Guillermo Leon Valencia** is nearby, and Popayán is served by **Avianca** (Cra. 5 No. 3-85, tel. 2/824-4505, www.avianca.com, 8am-noon and 2pm-6pm Mon.-Fri., 9am-1pm Sat.).

VICINITY OF POPAYÁN
Finca Alas y Raices

Finca Alas y Raices (Timbio, cell tel. 320/742-3470, www.alasyraices.org, COP$50,000 tour and lunch pp) is an organic coffee farm run by a Colombian and Swiss pair. They welcome visitors for tours of their farm and explanations of the coffee-producing process.

Market at Silvia

The **Market at Silvia** (Silvia, Tues. 5am-2pm) is a popular day trip destination from Popayán. It is about an hour's bus ride (COP$6,000) away. On market days starting at dawn, Guambiano indigenous people converge on the market from nearby communities to buy and sell fruits, vegetables, and textiles. There are few handicrafts to purchase. The market and the people are photogenic; however, if you would like to take close-up photos of people, it's imperative to ask for permission first. The market occurs rain or shine. To get to the market, take a bus bound for Silvia from the Terminal de Transportes. They leave every 20 minutes or so, and the trip takes about an hour.

Termales de Coconuco

For a dip in some *termales* (hot springs), **Coconuco** (cell tel. 310/543-7172, www.termalesaguatibia.com) is the place. Nestled among the hills are two springs, one *tibia* (cool-ish) and one *herviendo* (boiling hot), if sulfurous. Most of the action, especially on the weekend, takes place at the latter, as Colombian families while away the day (into evening) there. It's a gregarious scene and inevitably someone will share a box of *aguardiente*, the anise-flavored liquor of choice here. But it's a calm environment during the week. The *tibia* spring is more natural with a mud pool and an awesome water slide. It costs COP$10,000 to enter and the hot springs cost COP$4,000. The town of Coconuco is an indigenous community about 30 kilometers outside of Popayán, and a bus ride there from the terminal (Trans. 9 No. 4N-125) to town takes about one hour, costing COP$4,000. From the town you have to walk about four kilometers along a well-marked road. On clear days you can get some good views of the Puracé volcano.

Parque Nacional Natural Puracé

The **Parque Nacional Natural Puracé** (COP$20,000 non-Colombians, COP$8,500 Colombian residents, COP$4,000 children) is a national park covering some 83,000 hectares (205,100 acres) that includes two important mountainous formations within the Cordillera Central (Central Mountain Range): the Serranía de los Coconucos (Coconucos Range) and the Masizo Colombiano (Colombian Massif). It is a region of immense environmental importance that was declared a UNESCO Biosphere Reserve in 1979.

The Serranía is a six-kilometer-long chain of volcanoes, including the snow-covered Pan de Azúcar (5,000 meters/16,400 feet), Coconuco (4,600 meters/15,100 feet), Puracé (4,580 meters/15,000 feet), and Sotará (4,400 meters/14,400 feet). Puracé and Sotará are currently active. The Masizo Colombiano is a mountainous formation where five major Colombian rivers are born: Río Magdalena and Río Cauca, which flow into the Caribbean; the Río Patía, which flows into the Pacific; and the Río Caquetá and Río Putumayo, which are tributaries of the Amazon.

The park includes over 30 *lagunas* (mountain lakes), including the Laguna del Magdalena, which is the source of the Río Magdalena. Most of the park lies at an altitude greater than 2,600 meters (8,500 feet).

The primary attraction at this park is the fairly strenuous climb to the summit of the **Volcán Puracé** (7 km) in the northern part of the park. The ascent, which requires about five hours up and three down, takes you through high mountain tropical jungle and then *páramo,* a unique high mountain Andean ecosystem.

Guides are available at the Pilimbalá office, and it's a good idea to hire one. Call the Popayán parks office (tel. 2/823-1223) or the Pilimbalá office in the park (tel. 8/521-2578 or 8/521-2579) in advance to arrange for a guide. Guides usually charge around COP$35,000 for the hike up to the crater.

High season is from mid-December to mid-January, as well as during Semana Santa (Easter week) and school vacations from mid-June to mid-July. There are cabins in the park (COP$25,500-COP$35,000 pp high season), and camping is also available (COP$9,500 pp). To inquire about a reservation, contact the Pilimbalá station (tel. 8/521-2578 or 8/521-2579). A restaurant here serves all three meals for under COP$5,000 each. If you would like to request a vegetarian meal or have other dietary needs, phone the restaurant in advance (tel. 8/521-2577); ask for Señora Feliza.

GETTING THERE AND AROUND

The main Pilimbalá park ranger's station is 44 kilometers east of Popayán. From Popayán, buses depart the Terminal de Transportes (COP$5,000) bound for the community of La Plata. Buses generally leave at 6:30am, but there are often delays. The trip takes approximately 1.5 hours. Get off at the Cruce de la Mina, also known as El Crucero, and from there walk about 800 meters towards the left to the ranger's station. There are return buses coming from the opposite direction until around 5:30pm.

◖ TIERRADENTRO

From AD 500 to 900, the area of Tierradentro was settled by an agricultural society that dug magnificent decorated underground tombs, produced large stone

© ANDREW DIER

the well-preserved burial chambers of Tierradentro Archeological Park

states, and built oval buildings on artificial terraces. As in the case of San Agustín, these people disappeared without a trace. We do not even know what they called themselves. By the time of the Spanish conquest, the area was inhabited by the Paez, a Chibcha-speaking people who still inhabit the area and who are organized in *cabildos* (indigenous ruling bodies) that are recognized by the Colombian government.

Tierradentro is the site of a major indigenous necropolis that includes monumental funeral statues and hypogea (underground burial chambers). These chambers, some 12 meters wide, are decorated with intricate red and black anthropomorphic and zoomorphic geometric designs, some of which are in relief. This archaeological park was declared a UNESCO World Heritage Site in 1995.

These awe-inspiring burial chambers reveal the existence of a rich and complex society that devoted significant time and effort to preparing the way to the afterlife. There is also an intriguing symmetry to be found between these ornate underground chambers and the houses of the living above ground. Though there are some similarities between the statues and tombs of San Agustín, it is believed that these were two distinct cultures.

Sights

TIERRADENTRO ARCHEOLOGICAL PARK

Tierradentro Archeological Park (Inza, 91 km east of Popayán, www.tierradentro.info, 8am-4pm daily, COP$20,000) is a circuit of five sites set on four hills *(altos)*. If you are staying at La Portada in San Andrés de Pisimbalá, you can avoid the walk down to the main entrance of the park (30 minutes) and take the path that leads straight from the hostel to the Alto de San Andrés, one of the five sites, and continue onward towards Alto de Aguacate and the museum and park office.

It's better to start at the museum, so you can get a good introduction to the park before you tackle the sites. The sites are best visited in a counterclockwise manner. There are two museums across the street from each

© ANDREW DIER

stone carving at Tierradentro Archeological Park

other. On the Aguacate side is the archaeo-logical museum, and on the other side across from the ticket booth is the ethnographic museum. After checking out the museums and purchasing your ticket, you can continue to **Alto de Segovia,** which has some of the most impressive burial chambers. They are all very well preserved. Beyond **Alto del Duende** is **El Tablón,** which has large stone statues similar to those of San Agustín. You will follow the road to get there.

After crossing through the town, just next to La Portada is the path to the **Alto de San Andrés.** Parts of the trail—especially between Alto de San Andrés and Alto de Aguacate—are poorly marked. When in doubt, keep going left and upwards—and don't panic. You will eventually reach the top of the mountain ridge. Along the way you may run across *campesinos* (farmers) tending to their coffee and banana plantations who can point you in the right direction. Getting to the **Alto de Aguacate** is a steep climb, but the views of the country-side are breathtaking. The entire circuit can be

done in a day—a very long day. Your admission ticket is good for two days, so you could go at a slower pace and visit half the first day and the remaining half on the second day. If you are in a hurry, check out the most impressive site, the Alto de Segovia. You can also inquire about a horseback tour of the park. La Portada hotel can arrange that for you.

A good flashlight is a must to be able to get a good look at the interior paintings of the tombs and some of the elaborate artwork decorating them. Rubber boots could be use-ful if you are there during the rainy months of March-June or September-November. Also, be sure to bring water and snacks. It's a tough six-hour walk from La Portada to Alto de San Andrés, Alto del Aguacate, and down to the museum and park entrance. And that's just a little more than halfway. Near the museums you can get refreshed with a juice, water, or homemade ice cream at one of the little stores or nearby hostels.

In Alto de Segovia and Alto del Duende, a park guard will open up some of the tombs and let you in and back out. The steps can be quite steep and obviously on the dark side.

BIBLIOTECA PÚBLICA LA CASA DEL PUEBLO DE GUANACAS

After Tierradentro, you can visit the **Biblioteca Pública La Casa del Pueblo de Guanacas** (8am-6pm daily), an award-winning public li-brary in the town of Guanacas. It's made of *guadua,* a native species of bamboo, and was the idea of a couple of young locals, who pre-sented the idea of a community library to the architecture department of the Universidad Javeriana in Bogotá. Simón Hosie, an award-winning architect who involves local communi-ties intensely in the design process, took on the project, the Japanese Embassy provided fund-ing, and residents of the village, both young and old, participated in its construction. The library opened in 2004.

To get there, take a bus toward Popayán from the Tierradentro site and ask to get off at Guanacas. It's an easy walk down to the library.

Accommodations

Basic accommodations are plentiful near the official park entrance and museum, and are all located on the same road. **Hospedaje Pisimbalá** (cell tel. 311/605-4835 or 321/263-2334, COP$20,000 pp) is a neat and comfortable option, with a cool thatched roof gazebo in front. There's a good restaurant as well. **Lucerno** (no tel., COP$15,000 pp) is barebones, and the water may be cold, but the owners of this hostel, Secundino and Carmelita, are extremely friendly. It was one of the first such hostels around, and was given its name by a Swiss visitor from Lucerno. It has nine rooms. **El Refugio** (tel. 2/825-2904, hotelalbergueelrefugio@gmail.com, COP$60,000 d) is the largest and most luxurious option. It's even got a pool.

◖ La Portada (cell tel. 311/601-7884, laportadatierradentro@hotmail.com, www.laportadahotel.com, COP$30,000 d w/private bath, COP$20,000 s) is the best option. In the town of San Andrés de Pisimbalá, it is very well-run and orderly, and it's made out of *guadua,* a type of bamboo (even the shower curtain rods). Leonardo, the owner, is friendly and full of good information. His wife is an excellent cook, too.

Getting There

The trip to Tierradentro from Popayán will take you through gorgeous countryside of farms, villages, and gentle mountains shrouded in mist.

One bus a day leaves from Popayán directly to San Andrés de Pisimbalá. It leaves at 10:30am and takes four hours. From San Andrés de Pisimbalá to Popayán there is one direct bus that departs at 6am.

Another option is to take one of the buses bound for Inzá and get off at El Cruce, which is a short walk from the museum area. These leave at 5:30am, 8:30am, 10:30am, 1pm, and 3pm. It is a five-hour trip and costs COP$20,000.

From San Agustín you can take the 6am bus bound for Bogotá, then transfer in Garzón to the bus towards La Plata. From there you can take the 10:30am bus to San Andrés de Pisimbalá. That trip takes about three hours. Going from Pisimbalá to San Agustín you can take a bus at 6am. It arrives in the early afternoon. Public transportation between San Agustín and Tierradentro will require various transfers.

◖ SAN AGUSTÍN

The small colonial town of San Agustín, nestled within the folds of the southern Colombian Andes, would probably be an attractive destination in its own right. At an elevation of 1,800 meters (5,900 feet), it is set in a place of enormous natural beauty and has wonderful spring-like weather. However, its fame comes from its location near the largest pre-Columbian archaeological site south of Central America and north of Perú. From approximately AD 100-800, this region was home to an indigenous culture that produced spectacular monumental funeral statues hewn out of volcanic rock. Researchers do not know what these people called themselves, and so, lacking a better name, they have been labeled the San Agustín Culture.

To visit the main archaeological sites near San Agustín, you will need about two days. However, it makes no sense to rush your stay here, as it is an incredibly pleasant and peaceful place to visit, with several options for hiking and rafting amidst spectacular mountain landscapes.

HISTORY

The area around San Agustín was occupied as early as 3300 BC. Starting in the 1st century AD, the people of San Agustín created hundreds of monumental funeral stone statues set on large platforms. Very little is known about these people, except that they lived from agriculture and formed fairly compact settlements. By AD 800, this society had mysteriously vanished and other indigenous peoples coming from the Amazon basin occupied the area. Today, the inhabitants are predominantly mestizo.

Spanish chroniclers of the 16th century mention the statues, as did Colombian naturalist

San Agustín is Colombia's most important archaeological site.

Francisco José de Caldas in the early 19th century. However, it was not until 1913 that German ethnographer Konrad Theodor Preuss conducted the first systematic excavation. When he was finished, he carted off (probably illegally) 35 large statues that are now at the Ethnographic Museum in Dahlem on the outskirts of Berlin. Davíd Dellenback, American-born researcher and long-time resident of San Agustín, discovered on a 1992 trip to Berlin that only three of these statues are on exhibit, while the rest were piled away haphazardly in a storehouse. He found no trace of the numerous ceramic pieces that Preuss took and which were probably destroyed during the Allied bombings of World War II. Dellenback and his wife, Martha Gil, have promoted a petition, signed by more than 1,800 residents of San Agustín and nearby towns, for the German authorities to return the statues to their rightful home. Dellenback and Gil coauthored a comprehensive guide to San Agustín called *The Statues of the Pueblo Escultor*, which is available in shops in San Agustín.

Sights

The extremely well-maintained **Parque Arqueológico de San Agustín** (8am-4pm daily, COP$20,000) covers 80 hectares (200 acres) of what was one of the most important ritual areas of the San Agustín Culture. It was first established in 1937 and was declared a UNESCO World Heritage Site in 1995. The park contains over 130 statues with striking human and animal-like features, as well as carved tombs and monumental stone tables or dolmens. Your ticket also valid for Parque Arqueológico Alto de los Ídolos.

Near the entrance to the park is the **Museo Arqueológico**, which contains smaller statues, pottery, tools, and jewelry, as well as explanations on the San Agustín culture. At the time of writing, the museum was undergoing renovations. Most of the monumental stone objects are concentrated on four funeral hills designated Mesitas A, B, C, and D. The pleasant **Bosque de las Estatuas** contains a path that meanders among statues relocated from other locations in the San Agustín area. The unusual **Fuente de Lavapiés** contains bas-reliefs of human and animal figures sculpted on the rocky bed of a stream. This is the only non-funeral site in the park. On a hill behind the *fuente* is the Alto de Lavapiés, where excavations have shown human presence dating back to 3300 BC. The park is easy to navigate: plan on a couple of hours to stroll leisurely and absorb the beauty. The park is two kilometers (1.2 miles) west of town and can be reached on foot or by bus.

There are four smaller, yet definitely worthwhile sights, near the town of San Agustín: **La Chaquira**, a large bas-relief sculpted in a rock face overlooking the spectacular Río Magdalena gorge; **El Purutal**, which contains two magnificent, very well-conserved statues with original bright pigment covering; and **La Pelota** and **El Tablón**, each with additional funeral monuments.

Eight kilometers (five miles) southwest of the town of Isnos on the other side of the Magdalena, the **Parque Arqueológico Alto de los Ídolos** (8am-5pm daily, COP$20,000) is the second largest archaeological park. It includes an anthropomorphic statue that measures 4.3 meters (14 feet), along with large sarcophagi. A ticket here is also valid for Parque Arqueológico Nacional de San Agustín. The much smaller **Parque Arqueológico Alto de Las Piedras** (8am-5pm daily, free), six kilometers (four miles) north of Isnos on the road that leads to the Salto de Borodones waterfall, has statues and tombs with original pigments.

Also in the vicinity of San Agustín are several natural sights. The entire upper gorge of the **Río Magdalena** is majestic. At **El Estrecho,** the river spurts thought a 2.2-meter (7-foot) rocky funnel. On the Isnos side are two waterfalls, the 400-meter (1,300-foot) **Salto de Borodones** and 200-meter (650-foot) **Salto de Mortiño**.

Armed with a map and a willingness to ask directions, it is possible to visit all the sights on the San Agustín side by foot. This can make for a wonderful escape. However, many tourists opt for half-day or full-day horseback tours, which can cover several of these sights, including the Parque Arqueológico Alto de Ídolos. Make sure to book reliable guides that take good care of their horses through your hotel. Rates depend on the length of ride and number of people. Visiting the sites on the Isnos side by public transportation can be difficult; most people opt for day-long jeep tours that cover the Parque Arqueológico Alto de los Ídolos, Parque Alto de Las Piedras, El Estrecho, and the waterfalls.

Recreation

The upper Río Magdalena offers some of the best white-water river rafting in Colombia, set within spectacular mountain landscapes. **Magdalena Rafting** (www.magdalenarafting. com) offers numerous options, both for novices and experienced rafters, starting from short 90-minute to day-long trips.

Until recently, hiking in the Masizo Colombiano was no-go because of security. Now it is possible to ascend to the spectacular upper reaches of these mountains. One easily organized trip is to the **Laguna del Magdalena,** birthplace of the Río Magdalena, located in the Páramo de la Papas at 3,327 meters (10,915 feet). The trip takes 3-4 days and can be done on foot or by horse.

Accommodations

There are several cute and friendly accommodations options in San Agustín, and they can each provide expert advice on the area, arrange recreational activities such as horseback riding and rafting, and assist with travel needs.

El Maco (tel. 8/837-3437, cell tel. 320/375-5982, www.elmaco.ch, COP$16,000-COP$50,000 pp) is set among the hills about a 20-minute walk from town. Accommodations consist of seven small cabins, a tipi, a chalet, and an indigenous-style *maloka* (cabin) distributed throughout some pleasant gardens, home to dogs and chickens. They can organize some great horseback riding trips to archaeological spots. El Maco is run by Rene, who moved to the area from Switzerland in 1994. **La Casa de Francois** (tel. 8/837-3847, cell tel. 314/358-2930, www.lacasadefrancois. com, COP$18,000 dorm, COP$50,000 d) offers cabins, two dorm rooms with 10 beds total, and lots of hammocks to laze about after a hard day's work of archaeological exploration. The restaurant is quite good here, and reasonably priced, and they bake their own bread. It's 10 minutes from town.

Colombian-run **Huaka Yo** (Bogotá tel. 1/489-9269, cell tel. 320/846-9763, www. huakayo.com, COP$116,000 d high season) is just 200 meters from the archaeological park. It consists of a large house that has 12 rooms and six loft spaces, each with its own private bath. Huaka Yo is a five-minute bus ride from town or a 20-minute walk. They prefer that you make a deposit to their bank account to hold reservations, which means less cash you have to carry with you. The **Casa del Japones** (Cl. 8 No. 12-83, cell tel. 312/525-9552, COP$12,000 pp) is a quiet and small hostel (only eight rooms) in a cozy country house outside of town. It's an economical option, and vegetarian food is on offer. The banana pancakes exceed one's expectations.

© ANDREW DIER

horses at the ready, San Agustín

Alto de los Andaquies Hostal (cell tel. 312/444-7368 or 316/635-6006, www.anda-quies.com, COP$30,000 pp) has 15 rooms with hot water spread over three rustic houses just one kilometer from both the town and archaeological park. They produce coffee on this lush farm and other crops such as plantains, bananas, and yucca. They organize two- to four-day tours of all the major sights (COP$250,000 pp d all-inclusive).

Food

Most restaurants are on the main drag in town, the Calle 5. **Donde Richar** (Cl. 5 No. 23-45, cell tel. 312/432-6399, noon-7pm daily, COP$23,000) is famous for its grilled meats. **Tomate** (Cl. 5 No. 16-04, cell tel. 314/265-5527, 8am-3pm Thurs.-Mon., COP$8,000) is San Agustín's veggie headquarters, serving breakfast and a daily special. For pastas and pizzas go to Ugo's place, **Restaurante Italiano** (Vereda El Tablón, cell tel. 314/375-8086, 6pm-9:30pm Thurs.-Sun., COP$15,000). It's a bit outside of town, but worth the trip.

Getting There and Around

Buses from Bogotá go through Neiva. Buses from Neiva usually stop in the town of Pitalito, 138 km south, and from there you have to take a shared taxi to San Agustín (COP$5,000), about 45 minutes away.

From Popayán there are about four buses per day to Pitalito, and you'll have to get off beforehand at San Agustín (COP$35,000, 7 hours). This journey takes you through the spectacular scenery of Parque Nacional Natural Puracé.

From Tierradentro, take a bus to La Plata (COP$12,000, 2.5 hours) and change there for Pitalito (COP$22,000, 2.5 hours), where you can hop on a shared taxi for San Agustín (COP$5,000, 45 mins.).

Upon arrival in Tierradentro, you may be left at El Cruce. From there it's about a COP$5,000 truck ride into town. Once you step off in El Cruce, you may be swarmed by insistent touts who earn a commission at hotels for scoring some guests.

Bus and taxi companies have their offices at the corner of Calle 3 and Carrera 10 in the

CALI

The False Indian Ambassador

In December 1962, the high society of the dusty provincial capital of Neiva was delighted by the unannounced visit of the Indian ambassador to Colombia, Shari Lacshama Dharhamdhah. He was on a private visit to Neiva, planning to travel onward to see the archaeological sites of San Agustín. But some things about him were odd. For example, he arrived by train and without clothes befitting a high ranking diplomat. He explained that his limousine had broken down on the trip from Bogotá and that his luggage would be forwarded to Neiva. Yet, he looked Indian, spoke garbled Spanish, practiced yoga, and was a vegetarian.

News of his arrival was conveyed by a passenger sitting next to him on the train and spread like wildfire throughout Neiva, a city where nothing eventful ever happened. He was lodged in the presidential suite of Hotel Neiva Plaza (the city's most elegant hotel), presented with new clothes from Neiva's finest haberdashery, and wined and dined by leading politicians, business people, and socialites for five days.

Alas, it turned out that the ambassador was not really an international diplomat. Colombia did not even have diplomatic relations with India at that time. The man's real name was Jaime Torres and he was a high school teacher in the nearby city of Ibagué. A former schoolmate identified him and gave away his secret. He was briefly detained, but, as he had not committed any crime, he was freed. Not much is known about Torres's whereabouts after this incident, except that he eventually moved to New Haven, Connecticut.

The crazy story was made into a comedic film, *El Embajador de la India*, in 1987.

town of Tierradentro. In town, buses shuttle folks about town on a regular basis, although you can usually get where you want to go by walking.

Desierto de Tatacoa

Located next to the Río Magdalena and within view of the snowcapped Nevado del Huila, the 330-square-kilometer (127-square-mile) **Desierto de Tatacoa** makes for an unusual day trip. Technically it's not a desert, just a semiarid zone with dry tropical forest, but it feels and looks like one.

A visit to Tatacoa includes a stop at the historic town of **Villavieja,** with its 17th-century **Capilla de Santa Barbara** (Plaza Principal Villavieja, restricted hours), a church founded by the Jesuits in honor of the indigenous cacique Tocaya, who was killed by the Spaniards. The **Museo Paleontológico** (Cl. 3 No. 3-05, 7:30am-1pm Mon.-Fri., 7am-6pm Sat.-Sun., COP$2,000) provides a sample of the many fossils, dating from 3.8 million years ago, that have been found in the desert.

The dry conditions at Tatacoa make for ideal stargazing. The **Observatorio Astronómico Tatacoa** (Vereda El Cuzco, tel. 8/879-7584, cell tel. 310/465-6765, www.tatacoa-astronomia.com, 6:30am-9pm, COP$5,000), near town, provides telescopes for visitors to scan the sky in the evening hours. Camping is permitted next to the observatory. Each year in June-July, usually over a long weekend, hardcore and novice astronomers head to the desert for the annual Star Party event. There is a restaurant next to the observatory that serves mostly grilled goat or mutton.

TOURS

Chaska Tours (Hostal El Maco, Neiva, tel. 8/837-3437, cell tel. 311 /271-4802, info@chaskatours.net, COP$100,000 pp) organizes day trip tours from San Agustín to Tatacoa. There is an option to spend the night in the desert.

Neiva

The extremely hot (average highs 32-35°C/90-95°F) capital of the Huila department (province), Neiva (pop. 340,000) has few attractions for tourists. However, if you do happen to stop here, a nice place for a stroll and sitting in an outdoor café is the **Malecón Río Magdalena** (Av. Circunvalar from Cacica Gaitana monument to the Caracoli docks). This is the boardwalk along the Río Magdalena.

Neiva really gets going during the **Fiestas de San Juan y San Pablo** (June 15-June 30). The highlight is the Reinado del Bambuco, a beauty queen pageant named after *bambuco,* a traditional music of the Colombian Andes. Entrants, in flowery and frilly costumes, must dance the Sanjuanero, a famous *bambuco,* and other folk songs.

ACCOMMODATIONS

Catering to business clientele, the **Hotel Neiva Plaza** (Cl. 7 No. 4-62, tel. 8/871-0806, www.hotelneivaplaza.com, COP$189,000 s, COP$243,000 d) is in front of the Parque Santander. It has 86 spacious rooms, a gym, and a pool. It's the reliable (and overpriced) choice in Neiva.

In the Tatacoa desert, and within walking distance of the Observatorio Astronómico Tatacoa, **Posada Elvira Clever** (Vereda El Cusco, cell tel. 312/559-8576, COP$20,000

pp) has two rooms available in her small and simple zinc-roof house. There is no electricity here. In Villavieja, **La Casona** (Cl. 3 No. 3-60, tel. 8/879-7636, cell tel. 320/243-9705, http://hotellacasonavillavieja.blogspot.com, COP$50,000 d) is a small hotel in an old house located on the main park, with friendly owners. Simón Bolívar is said to have stayed here.

GETTING THERE AND AROUND

In addition to connections with the major cities of Colombia, from the **Terminal de Transportes de Neiva** (Tr. 5 No. 53-12, tel. 8/873-1232) in the south of the city, you can catch a minibus to Villavieja (COP$7,000, 1 hr.) and to San Agustín (COP$25,000, 4 hrs.). The **Aeropuerto Benito Salas** (Cra. 6 No. 32-45, tel. 8/875-8198) is in the north on the road towards Tatacoa. If you'd like to explore the region with your own wheels you can rent a vehicle at **ANT Rent A Car** (Av. 26 No. 5-12, tel. 8/872-2859, ant.rentacar@hotmail.com). It also has chauffeured cars available.

In Villavieja, *mototaxis* regularly transport visitors to the desert sights. These cost about COP$15,000 per person.

THE PACIFIC COAST

Colombia is the only country in South America with coastline on both the Atlantic and the Pacific Oceans. While the Caribbean coast is developed and populated, Colombia's Pacific coast is wild, remote, and mysterious. For the few who venture to this little-visited area, the beaches, jungles, and people are simply unforgettable.

© ANDREW DIER

HIGHLIGHTS

LOOK FOR ☾ TO FIND RECOMMENDED SIGHTS, ACTIVITIES, DINING, AND LODGING.

☾ **Estación Septiembre Sea Turtle Hatchery and Release Program:** Witnessing a release of valiant baby sea turtles fearlessly scampering across the sands into the crashing waves of the Pacific Ocean is an unforgettable experience (page 362).

☾ **Parque Nacional Natural Utría:** Jungle walks, swimming, and whale-watching are the order of the day when you stay at this beautiful national park near Nuquí (page 364).

☾ **Parque Nacional Natural Isla Gorgona:** Nature has reclaimed this island, which was once Colombia's Alcatraz. Walk through the jungle to Isla Gorgona's beautiful secluded beaches (page 368).

☾ **Santuario de Flora y Fauna Malpelo:** There's incredible diving among hammerhead sharks around this tiny rocky island almost 500 kilometers from the Colombian coast (page 371).

The Pacific coast of Colombia extends for 1,392 kilometers (865 miles), just under the length of the California coast. The departments of Chocó, Valle de Cauca, Cauca, and Nariño each share real estate on the Pacific, with Chocó boasting the largest stretch of coast. The tiny islands of Gorgona and Malpelo, both national parks, are 35 kilometers (22 miles) off

the coast of Guapi and 490 kilometers (305 miles) from Buenaventura, respectively.

The Pacific coast is populated by indigenous peoples, primarily the Emberá, who live mainly in small riverside settlements in the interior of Chocó; *colonos* or "colonists" who have arrived from Antioquia for generations; and Afro-Colombians, descendants of African slaves who make up the majority of the population (over 80 percent).

It is a sparsely populated region, but there are three major cities: Buenaventura (pop. 363,000), Colombia's most important port; Tumaco (pop. 188,000), bordering Ecuador; and Quibdó (pop. 162,000), the interior capital of the department of Chocó. Those cities are of far less interest to tourists than the coastal towns of Nuquí and Bahía Solano, where both sea and land provide countless opportunities to appreciate the natural world.

There are four national parks or protected areas on the Pacific coast. These include the Parque Nacional Natural (PNN) Utría, halfway between Bahía Solano and Nuquí; the less visited PNN Sanquianga near Tumaco; the PNN Isla Gorgona, a spectacular island park that was once a prison; and the Santuario de Fauna y Flora (SFF) Malpelo, an internationally known wildlife preserve that offers superb diving.

HISTORY

In pre-Columbian times, the region was inhabited by indigenous groups, notably the Tumaco-La Tolita people, who produced stunning goldwork. During the colonial era and into the early 20th century, the entire Pacific coast corridor was governed (or rather, not governed at all) from the city of Popayán. The main economic activity was gold mining, mostly in the Patía river valley in Nariño and the Chocó region. Afro-Colombian people, now more than 80 percent of the region's population, are descendants of slaves who were forced to work in these mines and in the haciendas of the Cauca river valley.

These slaves began arriving in New Granada from different parts of Africa starting in the 17th century. Most arrived in Cartagena and were immediately separated from their families, sold, and transported across the colony. Some slaves revolted or escaped from their owners and established communities in inaccessible areas. After the abolition of slavery in 1851, many former slaves migrated and settled along the rivers and coast of the Pacific. These communities survived intact through the 20th century but, in recent years, have been severely affected by the internal conflict. Many displaced Afro-Colombians from the Pacific have resettled in cities such as Cali.

Due to a lack of transportation links, the Pacific region has always been isolated from the rest of Colombia. While rich in biodiversity and cultural identity, cities such as Buenaventura, Quibdó, and Tumaco are underdeveloped; plagued with inadequate government services, poor infrastructure, and lack of economic opportunity. Poverty rates in urban areas often exceed 70 percent. Outside the cities, inhabitants subsist on small scale farming, fishing, and illegal gold mining and forestry.

One emerging bright spot is ecotourism, especially around Bahía Solano and Nuquí, where many enterprising Paisas from Antioquia have started tourist-related businesses. A more recent development has been the strengthening of local organizations, which are making strides in sharing the tourism peso with the broader community. The government has been promoting the region, especially for whale-watching.

SAFETY

Though most of the coastal settlements of interest to tourists are quite safe, parts of the Pacific, especially in the Nariño department bordering Ecuador and the Chocó department bordering Panama, remain major drug-trafficking corridors. The abrupt geography, dense jungle, easy water transportation routes, and lack of government border control have attracted drug traffickers, paramilitaries, and FARC guerrillas alike. With a strong and visible police and military presence, the Bahía Solano-Nuquí area is considered safe. Those towns are OK to walk around at night. The interior jungles of the Pacific provide cover for drug traffickers and illegal groups. Ask hotel staff for updated security tips.

PLANNING YOUR TIME

It requires more effort (and more money) to visit the Pacific coast than other parts of Colombia, so it would be a shame to just spend

THE PACIFIC COAST

Río Atrato

Gulfo de Cupica

Bojayá

ESTACIÓN SEPTIEMBRE SEA TURTLE HATCHERY AND RELEASE PROGRAM

El Valle

Bahía Solano

PARQUE NACIONAL NATURAL UTRÍA

Golfo de Tribugá

Nuquí

Coquí

Quibdó

Los Termales

Guachalito

Río San Juan

Ladrilleros

Buenaventura

Juanchaco

San Cipriano

Bahía Malaga

Cali

PARQUE NACIONAL NATURAL ISLA GORGONA

Río Micay

PNN Sanquianga

Guapi

Popayán

Río Patia

Río Guapi

Tumaco

0   100 mi

0   100 km

© AVALON TRAVEL

some excellent stargazing on the beach, at least in northern coastal communities. This might us the perfect place to decompress and catch up on sleep.

Three full days are sufficient to visit Parque Nacional Natural Isla Gorgona. If plan on diving or lessons, spend a full week.

Tourism picks up during humpback whale-watching season, especially during Colombian school vacations in August. The end-of-year holiday season is also a popular time, especially for Colombian families. Reserve far in advance to stay at some of the higher-end hotels during the holidays. Other times of the year are fairly quiet.

Regardless of where you go, it will rain during your stay, maybe once or twice a day. Chocó is one of the rainiest places on the planet.

What to Take

Hot and humid weather the norm (the average temperature is 28°C/82°F), so plan on getting wet each day—either on purpose or by accident. Daytime activities nearly always involve water. For walks along rivers, sandals with traction or rubber boots are very useful (flip-flops not so much). Clothes and towels take days to dry, sometimes refusing to dry altogether. Bring only lightweight clothing, packing a few more T-shirts than you usually would. And have them ready to throw in the nearest washing machine when you arrive in the city.

Bug repellent is a good idea, although, thanks to a pleasant breeze most evenings, mosquitoes are not usually a problem. There's no need to take malaria pills or any extraordinary precautions. All hotels provide mosquito netting, usually covering all windows in addition to a mosquito net over your bed.

Waste management is an issue for towns, hotels, and restaurants along the coast. Beer and soda in bottles is preferable to aluminum cans, as the glass is returnable. However, hydration is very important. Tap water isn't safe; hotels all provide filtered or boiled drinking water for guests. Bring a heavy-duty water bottle that can be refilled again and again. If you don't see filtered water readily available

just a couple of days there. Plan for about five days, split across two locations. Visit between July and October, when humpback whales travel 8,000 kilometers from Antarctica to give birth to their young in the warm waters off of the Colombian coast.

Fy into Bahía Solano and fly out of Nuquí, spending two or three days in each area, and staying within the Chocó department. Time here can be complete beach relaxation, filled with activities such as jungle hikes and canoe trips, or a combination of both.

There is not much activity at night, save for

for guest use, don't be shy to ask kitchen staff to refill your bottle with *agua filtrada* (filtered water). Bags *(bolsas)* of water are usually sold in corner stores and are preferable to plastic bottles. There is an expanding landfill in the jungle between El Valle and Bahía Solano; however, you may want to spare the rainforest by taking accumulated plastic back with you for recycling in Medellín or another large city. This is a requirement on the pristine island of Gorgona.

Binoculars are good for jungle outings and excellent for whale-watching. Take along only the most necessary electronics with you to the jungle. Extreme humidity, river crossings, sudden rain showers, and bumpy boat rides are not kind to laptops and cameras. Waterproof bags for cameras are essential, as well as sachets of silica gel to throw in camera cases.

Here on the Equator, it gets dark at around 6pm every evening year-round. There is limited electricity in this part of Colombia, with generators usually cranking on for only a few hours at night. A flashlight is good for strolls on the beach or about town. A lack of nighttime entertainment makes this a great time for reading. Pack books and magazines rather than relying on electronic gadgets. A deck of cards can also provide some evening entertainment.

Bring cash. Credit cards are not accepted at hotels. At some of the top-end places, you can make a deposit into the hotel's bank account before arriving, limiting the amount of cash you carry.

Chocó

You fly into Chocó over green mountains, part of the Cordillera Occidental, punctuated by orderly Antioquian pueblos and pastureland. But then, the jungle begins: thick, impenetrable tropical forest, of a thousand shades of green. This lowland tropical forest, with vegetation not unlike that found in the Amazon, begins to rise with undulating forested hills as you pass over the smaller Serranía del Baudó mountain range, one of the rainiest places on Earth. If you look down you will notice the tops of these low mountains shrouded in clouds. Every once in a while a milk-chocolate brown river meanders its way through the jungle westward, and tiny Afro-Colombian and Emberá communities of thatched or zinc-topped roofs spring up alongside them. Here rivers and streams are the only means of transportation, just as it has been for centuries. Just after the captain announces your "initial descent," you suddenly find yourself above the turquoise coastal waters of the Pacific. Get a window seat.

Along the Pacific coast of the Chocó department, there are four general areas that have decent tourism infrastructure: Bahía Solano, El Valle, the Parque Nacional Natural Utría, and Nuquí.

BAHÍA SOLANO

When many visitors arrive at the tiny Bahía Solano airport, after they collect their bags they head straight to the village of El Valle about 22 kilometers (14 miles) away and to the hotels on the beaches of Playa Almejal. But Ciudad Mutis, as Bahía Solano is officially named (after the famed botanist), is actually a good base for your visit—there's no need to rush off. It is one of Colombia's sport-fishing capitals, and excellent diving and whale-watching excursions can be arranged from here. The town, although the largest one in the Chocó Pacific coast, is small, and everywhere is accessible on foot.

Nice jungle walks to swimming holes fed by crystalline freshwater waterfalls are within walking distance from the town, and depending on the tides, you can also walk to the beaches of **Punta Huína** and **Playa Mecana**. These can also be easily reached by boat. During low tide, the bay becomes a soccer field; when the tide comes in, it's a place to cool off.

© ANDREW DIER

Bahía Solano

Recreation

HIKING

There are three easily done walks in or around Bahía Solano. **Punta Huína, Playa Mecana,** and the **Cascadas Cocacola** can also be reached on foot, and are all under two hours walking from town. You may want to go with a guide (hotels can arrange this) at least the first time, and find out the day's tide information before heading out. If the tide has come in, you'll have to take a boat back to the town.

The **Virgen de la Loma** path is an easy, 30-minute climb up through lush vegetation to the top of a hill with a nice view of the bay. The entrance to the trail is well-marked and is only 20 meters from the Hostal del Mar. For this you'll need no guide. About two blocks from there on the west side of town is the trail to the **Cascada Chocólatal,** which takes you along a river to a roaring waterfall. Taking about 40 minutes or so, this hike may not necessarily require a local guide, but it may be helpful, especially so you'll have someone with trained eyes to point out the occasional colorful frog, lizard, bird, or humongous spider to you. Otherwise they are quite tricky to spot. You will have to crisscross the narrow, shallow creek several times, and it can be treacherous as the rocks are slippery. You'll need to have both hands free. Wear a bathing suit so you can frolic in the cool waters of the swimming hole at the five-meter waterfall. That's your refreshing reward!

The third hike is called the **Cascada del Aeropuerto.** This hike is right across the street from the airport and leads to a towering jungle waterfall. You probably won't need a guide, but it is not impossible to become lost. Follow the stream and note that it will eventually veer to the left. It's about a half hour walk. All of these paths are maintained by a group of community members with the help of high school students who have posted signs to point the way.

SPORT-FISHING

The waters off of the Chocó coast are excellent for sport fishing. The **Posada Turística Rocas de Cabo Marzo** (tel. 4/682-7525, cell tel. 313/681-4001, bahiatebada@hotmail.com, www.posadaturisticarocasdecabomarzo.com) regularly organizes fishing adventures in the area. Species that can be found in the waters here include marlins (blue, black, and striped) and sailfish. These are considered endangered and are caught and then released. Yellowfin tuna, red snapper, wahoo, and sierra are other fish that are caught and eaten. The best time of the year for fishing is March-June. Between October and December is also a good time to fish (catch and release) for marlin and sailfish, but this is a rainy season and the waters are rough. Rental of a boat and an eight-hour day excursion costs around COP$1,600,000, with a maximum of four fishers.

Rocas de Cabo Marzo organizes catch-and-release tournaments like the **Torneo Internacional de Pesca Deportiva.** The tournament takes place far from the coastline, as much of the Chocó coast, especially around the Cabo Marzo area, is protected as a Zona Exclusiva de Pesca Artesanal del Chocó (ZEPA). That means it is limited to only local fishers using their traditional fishing methods.

THE PACIFIC COAST

This initiative is supported by Conservation International (www.conservation.org.co).

DIVING

Diving in the Pacific is much different from diving in the Caribbean. First of all, it's more expensive, due to the high price of gasoline. Secondly, the variety of fish is different: While in the Caribbean it is common to see colorful tropical fish, in the Pacific the fish are much larger. Both **Posada Turística Hostal del Mar** (tel. 4/682-7415, cell tel. 314/630-6723, hostaldelmarbahiasolano@yahoo.com) and **Posada Turística Rocas de Cabo Marzo** (tel. 4/682-7525, cell tel. 313/681-4001, bahiatebada@hotmail.com, www.posadaturisticarocasdecabomarzo.com) offer diving excursions. A popular trip is to the shipwrecked *Sebastián de Belalcázar* just to the northeast of Bahía Solano. Another good place to dive is around Cabo Marzo to the north near the Panamanian border. Rocas de Cabo Marzo charges COP\$120,000 per person (without equipment) for a diving trip to that location.

Double-check on the security situation before going to Cabo Marzo, as drug traffickers operate in the area.

Accommodations and Food

There are a handful of quite good accommodations options located near the bay. They can each help organize whale-watching and other excursions for you. **《 Posada Turística Hostal del Mar** (tel. 4/682-7415, cell tel. 314/630-6723, hostaldelmarbahiasolano@yahoo.com, COP\$50,000 pp) is run by Rodrigo Fajardo and Estrella Rojas. They are pioneers in the area in terms of community organizing and ecotourism. There are four comfortable cabins tucked in their gardens filled with orchids, vegetation, chickens, and a lazy cat, Julia. Meals, often served with their homemade *ají* (hot sauce), are taken on a picnic table in the middle of this miniature tropical paradise. Rodrigo is a certified diving instructor, and you can learn that sport in the waters of the Pacific with him or go out for a trip if you already know what you're doing. A nearby shipwreck

the port of Bahía Solano

© ANDREW DIER

Biodiversity in Chocó

This region is part of the **Chocó Biogeográfico,** one of the most biodiverse regions in the world. It comprises a wide swath of rainforest extending from Panama to Ecuador, hemmed in by the Pacific Ocean to the west and by the Andes to the east. The Colombian part of this region includes an amazing 8,000 plant species, of which 2,000 are endemic. (In comparison, all of Canada, which is hundreds of times larger, has 3,270 plant species, of which 140 are endemic.) In addition there are 838 bird species, 261 amphibian species, 188 reptile species, and 180 mammal species. The relative isolation of this region has resulted in a high level of endemism of about 25 percent. It is one of the wettest places on Earth, with annual rainfall of 10,000 millimeters (33 feet!), with some places registering up to 20,000 millimeters (66 feet). Due to the high rainfall, this biodiversity hotspot boasts one of the most dense river networks in the world, with dozens of major arteries, such as the Baudó, San Juan, and Patía. The Colombia Pacific is quite well preserved: An estimated 75 percent of the region is still covered with rainforest, and there are significant areas of mangroves.

is a popular place for underwater exploration. Both he and Estrella know the area exceptionally well and can give you pointers on how to make the most of your stay and can coordinate day trips. Estrella has a small *tienda* in the arrivals area of the airport, where she sells handicrafts made by locals.

◀ **Posada Turística Rocas de Cabo Marzo** (tel. 4/682-7525, cell tel. 313/681-4001, bahiatebada@hotmail.com, www.posadaturisticarocasdecabomarzo.com, COP$110,000 pp d, all meals incl.) is a cozy lodge-like guesthouse with five rooms. Room rates include airport pickup and drop-off, all meals, and excursions such as jungle hikes and walks to nearby beaches. Their small hotel restaurant might just be the only place in the jungle where you'll find homemade pizza. It's open daily, but just for

guests. In addition to fishing and diving expeditions, Rocas de Cabo Marzo organizes visits to the Estación Septiembre turtle hatchery program (COP$60,000), a walk to the Playa and Río Mecana (COP$100,000 for 2 people), and a specialized expedition to see poisonous frogs (as well as howler monkeys and sloths) in the jungle with an indigenous guide.

Less ecologically minded, but quite comfortable, is the **Hotel Yubarta** (tel. 4/682-7509, cell tel. 314/773-5066, COP$90,000 d). It is a multi-story building that offers 11 spacious air-conditioned rooms, a pleasant garden, and free *tinto* (coffee) all day long. Meals can be taken at the rather swanky adjacent restaurant, **Doña Aida** (7:30am-10am, noon-3pm, and 5:30pm-8:30pm Mon.-Sat., COP$18,000), which has a pleasant deck. The restaurant is open to the public.

El Marañon (Playa Mecana, cell tel. 320/671-6163, COP$35,000 pp) is a locally owned beachside lodge with just five *cabañas*. It's a five-minute boat ride here from Bahía Solano (and you can walk there during low tide). It's easy to take a hike to the Río Mecana, and they organize fishing expeditions and whale-watching trips. **Choibaná Casa** (cell tel. 310/878-1214 or 312/548-2969, www.choibana.com, COP$120,000 pp incl. meals and transportation) is a cute and colorfully painted wooden house on the beach past rowdy Playa Huína. There are just five rooms, including one spectacular hut majestically set atop a rock. It's a 20-minute boat ride from Bahía Solano.

EL VALLE

This fishing community to the south of Bahía Solano is authentic if grubby, with wooden houses lining dirt (often muddy) streets. However, just outside of town, about a 15-minute walk north is the **Playa Almejal,** a broad beach with hotels set back against the jungle. The beach is home to thousands of nervous little *cangrejos fantasmas* (ghost crabs) scurrying about. The gray sandy beaches are often covered with driftwood and other debris. But during the nearly always spectacular sunsets,

© ANDREW DIER

Playa Almejal

the pastels of the sky are perfectly reflected on the wet sands. It's a magical scene. The water is great for swimming, jumping in the waves, and surfing.

Recreation

There are some pleasant excursions to make nearby Playa Almejal. The **Cascada El Tigre** can be reached by boat or by walking (4 hrs. one way, COP$40,000 guide), and this waterfall of cool water right on a secluded cove makes for an unforgettable shower/massage. The **Río Tundó** just outside of El Valle is a great place for a jungle canoe or kayak trip. This excursion, which usually includes a two-hour hike in the verdant jungle, costs about COP$40,000 per person.

Persuasive local guides regularly make the rounds at hotels offering day-trip excursions, but don't feel pressured to sign on to any trip immediately. Excursions can by pricey due to high gasoline prices. It may be worth comparing quotes with other guests first, and negotiating a better deal.

Estación Septiembre Sea Turtle Hatchery and Release Program

From August until December, female olive Ridley sea turtles return to the beaches of the area (to the same spot where they were born) to lay up to 80 eggs. Around 40-60 days later, these eggs hatch, and baby turtles are born. At the **Estación Septiembre Sea Turtle Hatchery and Release Program** (Playa La Cuevita, 5 km south of El Valle, cell tel. 314/677-2488 or 314/675-3353), turtle eggs are collected from the beaches and protected from stray dogs, birds, and from humans. They remain in the sand until baby turtles are born. Then they are released into the ocean.

This program is run by the Fundación Natura and administered by the community-based organization the **Fundación Caguama.** (*Caguama* means sea turtle in the Emberá language.)

There are two ways to see this important work at the Estación Septiembre. You can visit for the day. (It's best to contact them in advance so they can coordinate your visit.) They request a small donation of perhaps COP$5,000. Or you can stay at one of the three simple rooms at the Estación Septiembre (Fundación Natura in Bogotá, Cra. 21 No. 39-43, tel. 1/245-5700, COP$60,000 pp all meals incl.).

A highlight of your visit to the Pacific coast might be witnessing a release of fearless newborn turtles as they scamper their way into the water. These take place at the Estación Septiembre, especially during the month of September.

Festivals and Events

There are two big annual events in Valle. During one week in July the entire community parties it up during the **Fiesta de la Virgen Carmen.** It's a week of street dances and carnival. In September is the **Festival de Viajeros Sin Maletas** (Travelers Without Luggage Festival), an environmental and conservation awareness-generation event supported by various community groups, nonprofit organizations, and international donors in celebration of the many migrating animals who visit the area each year. In addition to educational activities with children, there are theater and musical performances.

Accommodations and Food

On Playa Almejal, the **Posada Don Ai** (Playa Almejal, cell tel. 314/651-1160, COP$120,000 pp incl. meals) is a relaxed place with nine small cabins each with a porch and requisite hammock. Meals, usually fried fish, *patacones,* rice, and salad, are included in the price of your stay and are served under a breezy thatched roof dining area overlooking the Pacific. It's quite a good value. Even if you are not staying there, you can stop by for a meal. Just beyond Don Ai's on the beach is **❰ El Almejal** (tel. 4/412-5050, COP$170,000 pp). This eco-conscious lodge, with tastefully done and airy cabins, is a consistent favorite for those who want a little more comfort. Above in the jungle are the very top-end cabins. These are situated along a bird-watching trail (they organize early morning bird-watching

walks here). El Amejal has its own organic garden and sea turtle hatchery program.

The third option is the most economical, and by far the funkiest. When you first walk up from the beach, barefoot and backpack on, you'll pass through several enormous boulders, and then the **❰ Humpback Turtle** (Playa Almejal, cell tel. 312/756-3439, www.humpbackturtle.com, COP$15,000 camping pp, COP$25,000 dorm bed, COP$80,000 d) suddenly appears. Nestled at the edge of the jungle, this very colorful and rather primitive hostel, often called Donde Tyler, Donde Taylor, or Donde el Gringo Ese after the American owner Tyler, has a dorm room with six beds and four private rooms as well as a campsite. With an organic garden, composting, water conservation measures such as the use of dry toilets, and using plastic water bottles for construction materials, this is by far the most environmentally minded option in the area.

Between Playa Almejal and the town of El Valle are other options, including Villa Maga

Hang loose and kick back at the Humpback Turtle hostel.

and El Nativo. Just across from the Almejal beach, these are both run by *nativos,* as local Afro-Colombians identify themselves. **El Nativo** (cell tel. 311/639-1015, nativo58@ hotmail.com, COP$60,000 d incl. meals) has two simple cabins (four rooms in total) made from natural materials such as *guadua* (bamboo) and palm leaves. They can organize day-trip excursions for you. Nearby is Villa Maga (cell tel. 320/777-4767, www. villamaga.net, COP$45,000 pp), with a similar setup as El Nativo, although with more natural light in the A-framed cabins and little more comfortable.

Doña Rosalía (El Valle, past Internet café, no phone) is the only real restaurant in El Valle, and it's a good one. Here you are served in the dining room of Doña Rosalía's small, but immaculate, house. If you can't find it, just ask anybody around. Everybody knows Rosalía! If you have a special request—if you'd like lentils or beans instead of fish, for instance—let her know by dropping by beforehand. The hotels on Playa Almejal (Cabañas Punta Roca/Doña Betty, Don Ai, and El Almejal) all serve good seafood meals.

Tiendas (shops) in El Valle sell snacks and usually have seating if you want a cold drink or beer. A couple of bakeries offer freshly baked bread.

As for drinking spots, besides *tiendas* in El Valle where you can drink beer with the locals, the best option by far is **El Mirador.** Hard to miss, it's the only multicolored bar set on a boulder on the beach. It's between Humpback Turtle and El Almejal. It's only open on Sunday afternoons, when it gets packed with mostly locals, but visitors are more than welcome.

PARQUE NACIONAL NATURAL UTRÍA

Halfway between Bahía Solano and Nuquí, the **Parque Nacional Natural Utría** (www. parquesnacionales.gov.co, 8am-5pm daily, park entrance COP$37,500 non-Colombians, COP$14,000 Colombians and residents, COP$7,500 students with ID) has a spectacular location on the edge of the jungle but close to some great beaches. It encompasses over 54,000 hectares (135,000 acres) of tropical forest, mangroves, and waters. Several nature paths await exploration, including a wooden bridge walkway over mangroves, and you can also walk to a nearby secluded beach with a guide and arrange to be picked up later. A well-marked path through the jungle leads to El Valle in about two hours. During whale-watching season, humpbacks have been known to swim into the narrow lagoon in front of the park cabins, providing exclusive shows for park guests.

Most of the excursions require a guide. However, there are some short walks you can make near the Centro de Visitantes. One of the more unusual activities at the park is searching for glow-in-the-dark mushrooms in the evening along the nature trail, which you can do on your own. Another is a walk above the mangroves on an elevated wooden walkway.

Park facilities are managed by the local community organization Mano Cambiada. The park has three beautiful wooden cabins (separated into three inviting private rooms, each with its own bathroom), with a total capacity of over 30, and there's an open-air restaurant near the cabins. Private rooms go for about COP$192,000 per person including all meals. There is one cabin with dormitory-style accommodations. A few days at this park during the week (or off-season) when it isn't crowded with groups could be wonderfully relaxing. If the park is crowded, however, it could become quite a social scene, especially during the long evenings. Round-trip transportation from either the Bahía Solano or Nuquí airports costs COP$300,000 per person.

Other excursions include whale-watching, from June until October (COP$87,000), a two-hour jungle hike to Playa Cocalito (COP$32,000), a boat trip to Playa Blanca for snorkeling (COP$32,000), and a boat ride to the Jurubirá community, where residents live in simple wooden houses on stilts, including a walk to some hot springs (COP$93,000). Kayaks are available for free to those staying at the park.

If you are not staying at the park, it can be visited on a day trip from El Valle, Bahía Solano, or Nuquí. But that excursion gets a failing grade from many, due to its high cost (upwards of COP$125,000 per person). The standard park visit includes a chat about the national park system, a short walk, snorkeling in the lagoon in front of the Centro de Visitantes, and a boat ride to Playa Blanca (part of the park), where you can snorkel and have a greasy lunch. Playa Blanca is a party place for locals on weekends and holidays.

Accommodations and Food

It is far better to stay at the park, preferably during the week (and not during high season). Travel agency **Aviatur** (Av. 19 No. 4-62, Bogotá, tel. 1/587-5181 or 1/587-5182, www.aviaturecoturismo.com) offers package tours to PNN Utría including two nights accommodations, all meals, and transportation to and from the Nuquí airport. This costs COP$816,000 per person based on double accommodation. You can also contact **Mano Cambiada** (cell tel. 313/759-6270 or 310/348-6055, www.nuquipacifico.com).

NUQUÍ

There is not much to the town of Nuquí, except for some basic services and the airport. However, surrounding beaches and ecolodges are wonderful. Here you can head off to the jungle for hikes in search of colorful frogs, go on a whale-watching expedition, try your luck surfing, and row in dugout canoes along serpentine rivers that serve as highways between communities. Or you can blissfully relax in a hammock and while away the hours to the sound of crashing waves in the background. All hotels listed can keep you as busy or lazy as you want.

Accommodations

From locally owned accommodations in typical wooden Chocó houses to cabins on the beach to luxurious secluded resorts, the beaches near Nuquí have options for every budget. All hotels can organize hikes, whale-watching

trips, diving excursions, and other activities. **El Cantíl** (tel. 4/448-0767, www.elcantil.com, COP$717,000 pp, 2 nights, all meals and transportation incl.) is perhaps the most widely known ecolodge in the area. Run by a couple from Medellín, El Cantíl is composed of small but comfortable cabins nestled on the edge of the jungle—view of the ocean included. It is about a 35-minute boat ride from Nuquí. Whale-watching, diving, and surfing can also be arranged. Behind El Cantíl, you can take a jungle hike and go on an exotic frog safari. Beautiful nearby beaches can be explored on your own, and you'll likely be alone on the sand. The fresh seafood at the hotel restaurant is both abundant and delicious. Electricity is powered by their own hydroelectric plant.

In solitary splendor, ◀**Morromico** (45 mins. north of Nuquí, tel. 8/521-4172 or 8/522-4653, www.morromico.com, COP$200,000 pp incl. meals) is another upper-end resort, with only four rooms, a private beach, free sunsets, and freshly caught red snapper cooked in fresh coconut milk for lunch. What more could you ask for? This hotel is close to the Parque Nacional Natural Utría.

Guachalito is another favorite beach near Nuquí. One of the better lodging options there is ◀**Luna de Miel** (tel. 4/683-6152, cell tel. 314/431-2125, lunademiel@hotmail.com, COP$150,000 pp incl. meals), a simple but very comfortable lodge of two cabins. It's a peaceful place.

There are more economical and authentic locally owned options in some of the villages. **Mano Cambiada** (cell tel. 313/759-6270 or 310/348-6055, www.nuquipacifico.com) can help organize a stay.

INFORMATION AND SERVICES

In Bahía Solano there is an **ATM** at the **Banco Agrario.** (There is no ATM in El Valle, Utría, or Nuquí.) At the Banco Agrario (tel. 4/682-7522, 8am-2pm Mon.-Fri.) in Bahía Solano, you can have money wired (*giro*) to you or deposited directly into a hotel account (*consignación*). In Nuquí, at **Super Giros** (tel.

© ANDREW DIER

Over 3,000 majestic humpback whales make their way to Colombia's Pacific coast from August until October each year.

4/683-6067) you can also have money wired to you. In Nuquí there are two banks: Banco Agrario and Bancolombia.

Do not expect wireless Internet, regular cell phone service, or 24-hour electricity at your hotel along the coast. There are Internet cafés in the towns, such as Bahía Net in Bahía Solano, but connection speed is very slow.

There are **hospitals** in Bahía Solano (tel. 4/682-7016 or 4/682-7884) and in Nuquí (tel. 4/683-6003), as well as **pharmacies** in El Valle, Bahía Solano, and Nuquí. There is a significant police and military presence in these places as well. If you have access to a phone, emergencies can be reported by calling 112.

GETTING THERE AND AROUND

Two airports serve the central Chocó coast: Bahía Solano and Nuquí. Military-owned **Satena** (tel. 1/423-8530, www.satena.com), **ADA** (tel. 4/444-4232, www.ada-aero.com), and charter carrier **TAC** (tel. 4/361-0945, www.

taccolombia.com) serve both Bahía Solano and Nuquí out of the Aeropuerto Olaya Herrera in Medellín. There are also flights out of the departmental capital of Quibdó. The trip takes under an hour. Another option is with the charter airline **Selvazul** (tel. 4/362-2590, www.selvazul.net). From the Aeropuerto Olaya Herrera in Medellín this airline serves both Bahía Solano and Quibdó.

When you arrive at the Bahía Solano or Nuquí airport, most hotels will have arranged to pick you up at the airport if you have a reservation. This is the worry-free, recommended way to go. If you have not made a reservation, there are always some folks affiliated with hotels from the area at the airport to persuade visitors to stay with them.

To get to El Valle and Playa Almejal on your own from the Bahía Solano airport you can take a *mototaxi* or truck for COP$10,000-20,000 per person depending on your negotiating skills. Much of the road to El Valle, through the jungle, has been paved. It costs much less (COP$2,000 on *mototaxi*) to get to Bahía Solano from the airport, since it's only two kilometers away.

Boats leave Bahía Solano and El Valle for PNN Utría, Nuquí, and beaches beyond. As gasoline costs about three times as much as it does in the rest of Colombia, boat trips will seem expensive: at least COP$60,000 to PNN Utría, COP$80,000 to Nuquí. You can try to negotiate a better price, especially if you have a group going with you.

If comfort is an overrated commodity for you, travel between Buenaventura and Bahía Solano by boat can be arranged by hitching a ride on a cargo boat. These often depart on Fridays. Basic accommodations (bunk bed) and food are provided. The journey will take around 20 hours, costing COP$120,000. In Bahía Solano, head to the docks to inquire about these, or call Capitan César (cell tel. 314/686-3232) or the harbormaster (tel. 4/682-7064).

If you want to go to the southern coastal city of Tumaco by sea, you will probably have to hop on a boat headed to Buenaventura first. Best to contact the harbormaster or go to the Bahía Solano port in person to find out about ship departures.

Vessels bound for Panama from Bahía Solano depart weekly. To find out about the next boat, go to Bahía Solano and ask around for El Profesor Justino; everyone knows who he is. The trip usually costs about COP$100,000 and takes about four hours. If leaving the country by boat, you will need to get an exit stamp at **Migración Colombia** (www.migracioncolombia.gov.co). Request assistance from one of the local hotels in getting to Migración Colombia.

South Pacific Coast

The beaches of the South Pacific coast of Colombia in and around the port cities of Buenaventura and Tumaco have not been on the radar screen of many international visitors, but they have drawn Colombian tourists for decades. Off the coast, you'll find the island oases of Parque National Natural Isla Gorgona and the Santuario de Flora y Fauna Malpelo, where nature rules the day.

Safety

Both Buenaventura and Tumaco have been severely affected by turf battles involving rival drug trafficking gangs over the past few years. The beaches, however, are secluded and safe, and tourists are always welcomed with open arms. But do avoid the interior of the cities.

BUENAVENTURA

Buenaventura is the largest city on the coast, with a population of over 300,000, and it is Colombia's busiest port. The golden years of Buenaventura are long gone, but one of the remnants of its heydays is the elegant **Hotel Estelar Estación** (Cl. 2 No. 6-8, tel. 2/241-9512, www.sht.com.co, COP$250,000 d). It's near the Muelle Turístico, the tourist port where you can have a generous seafood meal at restaurants like **Leños y Mariscos** (Cl. 1 No. 5-08, tel. 2/241-7000) and catch a boat to the nearby beaches of Juanchaco and Ladrilleros.

The gray sandy beaches of **Juanchaco** and **Ladrilleros** have their charm, and the surf's often up in Ladrilleros. From the beachside bluffs, during whale-watching season (June-November) you can spot the humpbacks frolicking in the waters.

Lanchas (boats) make the trip to Ladrilleros from the Muelle Turístico in Buenaventura several times a day. **Asturías** (Muelle Turístico Local No. 2, tel. 2/240-4048, www.buceaencolombia.com) is one company that provides this service with boats at 10am, 1pm, and 4pm. Round-trip fares are around COP$55,000. It's a 45-minute ride to Juanchaco. Ladrilleros is a half-hour walk from Juanchaco. A 45-minute walk farther from Ladrilleros is the quiet La Barra beach. A popular hotel here, with a great view of the infinite Pacific, is the **Reserva Aguamarina** (tel. 2/246-0285, www.reservaaguamarina.com). From here you can take a walk to waterfalls and discover other remote beaches.

TUMACO

In the Nariño department, Tumaco is the second largest port on the Pacific coast. It has a population of around 170,000 and sits on the coastline border with Ecuador. Tumaco is famous for its incredibly photogenic natural stone archway on El Morro beach. It's about 10 minutes from downtown, on the same island where the airport is located. A good place to stay is **Hotel Los Corales** (tel. 2/727-2779, cell tel. 312/841-1949, www.hotelloscorales.com, COP$100,000 d), a beach hotel that boasts it has hosted not one but two Colombian superstar singers: Juanes and Carlos Vives.

Bocagrande island, home to a handful of hotels and restaurants and bars just outside of the city, is popular with local holidaymakers. A good place to stay is in one of the 25 *cabañas* at **Hotel Las Lilianas** (cell tel. 310/396-0906, COP$55,000 pp, meals included). For an extra charge of COP$20,000 the hotel arranges *lancha* transportation from and to Tumaco. The trip takes about 25 minutes. The Bocagrande island inspired a famous Colombian *bolero* song from the 1960s, *Noches de Bocagrande.* Pretty much every Colombian of a certain age knows that tune, although many mistakenly believe it is named for the Bocagrande area of Cartagena.

Tumaco is known for its excellent, fresh seafood, like *pescado sudado* (fish stew)*, langostinos al coco* (coconut shrimp)*,* and ceviche. *Piangua* (mangrove cockle), which grows in the mangroves, is a local delicacy, and is also threatened. A classic restaurant is **El Muelle** (Viaducto al Morro, tel. 2/727-2383, COP$10,000-40,000).

Getting There and Around

From Cali there are regular buses that take you to Buenaventura. This three-hour trip costs about COP$20,000. **Satena** (Col. toll-free tel. 01/800-091-2034, www.satena.com) flies to Buenaventura from Bogotá. While it

is possible to take public transportation from Pasto (4 hrs.), that road has had security problems in the past. It's best to fly. **Avianca** (Col. toll-free tel. 01/800-0953-3434, www.avianca.com) serves Tumaco from Bogotá and Cali. Cargo boats can take you from Tumaco to San Lorenzo in Ecuador. Schedules vary, so it is best to go to the port directly and inquire about this option.

◖ PARQUE NACIONAL NATURAL ISLA GORGONA

A visit to the **Parque Nacional Natural Isla Gorgona** (www.parquesnacionales.gov.co) is an unforgettable one, no matter the time of year. This 9- by 2.6-kilometer (5.6- by 1.6-mile) island about 60 kilometers (37 miles) off the coast was thought to have been originally settled by Guna indigenous peoples who lived near present-day Panama. It was named by the Spaniards after the mythical female Greek monster, Gorgon, who, among other things, wore a belt made of snakes and even had them coming out of

Parque Nacional Natural Isla Gorgona

© ANDREW DIER

Capuchin monkeys are cute—from a distance.

© ANDREW DIER

her hair. Spanish conquistador Francisco Pizarro landed on the island in 1527. He and his men were unhappy guests on the island. They didn't stay long: too many men were getting bitten by snakes. Following that, the island was mostly uninhabited.

Surrounded by sharks and crawling with snakes, it served as a prison starting in 1959, primarily for those accused of atrocities during La Violencia, when Liberals and Conservatives fought each other in cities and towns across Colombia. Many say that the prison was modeled after the Alcatraz Penitentiary in California. Once the prison was closed in 1984, the island was converted into a national park.

Water—in the form of babbling brooks, trickling streams, roaring waterfalls, dewdrops on leaves, crashing waves, and gentle rain storms—is the proof that this island is very much alive. Because of the 90 percent humidity, mist is often seen rising from the thick tropical jungle. It has its own permanent cloud lingering above its highest points.

Recreation
HIKING
Hiking excursions are included in the price of package tours with travel agency Aviatur. You are not allowed to stray far from the hotel area on your own, and all hikes must be made with a guide. Excursions can also be paid for à la carte. They cost COP$10,000-30,000 each per person.

A popular hike is a half-day trek around the edge of the island and through the jungle to Playa Palmeras, a beautiful beach on the southwestern side of the island that overlooks the smaller Isla Gorgonilla. On the way you'll have the possibility of seeing a variety of birds, snakes, monkeys, and amphibians. If you are very lucky, along the way may spot the stunning blue anole lizard, the only all-blue lizard in the world and one that exists only on this particular island. It has become threatened due to the presence of non-native iguanas. The beach is gorgeous and would be perfect except for all the flip-flops and plastic bottles—flotsam that has made its way to the island shore from all around the world. On this hike a lunch is provided and the return is via boat.

Another walk takes you to Yundigua, an area of the park with excellent snorkeling. Return from this two-hour excursion is also by boat.

You can also take a two-hour walking tour to the site of the old prison, which is an eerie experience. Nature has all but reclaimed the prison, but you can almost sense the presence of ghosts lingering on. A small museum examines the brutal conditions of prison life on the island. It is open daily and is free.

DIVING AND WHALE-WATCHING

Isla Gorgona is an excellent place for diving. There is a dive center on the island, and courses for beginners are available. You can arrange for diving classes during a week spent at Isla Gorgona. Five excursions can be arranged to one of the seven main dive sites near the island. **Aviatur** (Av. 19 No. 4-62, Bogotá, tel. 1/587-5181 or 1/587-5182, www.aviaturecoturismo.com) offers a diving package that includes six dives and just one excursion on land that costs around COP$1,500,000 per person. A PADI certification course costs about COP$1,600,000 per person. Two extra dives cost COP$215,000.

Another option can be to contract a diving trip from an independent dive company. These depart from either Buenaventura or Guapi. **Arrecifes de Pacífico** (Cra. 38 No. 8A-17, Cali, tel. 2/514-1691, cell tel. 321/642-6015) organizes four-day/three-night trips to Gorgona throughout the year. These typically depart by boat from Buenaventura. It's about an 11-hour trip to Isla Gorgona from there, and accommodations are on board the boat, which has a capacity of about 25 passengers. This trip, including six dives and one night dive with transportation, meals, and accommodations, costs around COP$1,390,000 per person (not including equipment). Diving spots include Tiburonera, Plaza de Toros, Montañita 1, Cazuelam, Parguera, El Viudo, and Remanso de la Parguera. For beginners, they recommend a short course in Cali before departing to Gorgona, where certification can be offered.

Gorgona is an excellent place for humpback whale-watching from July to October. If diving is too deep for you, within only about 20 meters of the island shore you can swim among thousands of colorful tropical fish and the occasional sea turtle. Sometimes you can hear humpback whales singing in the far-off distance.

Accommodations and Food

Travel agency **Aviatur** (Av. 19 No. 4-62, Bogotá, tel. 1/587-5181 or 1/587-5182, www.aviaturecoturismo.com) currently has a contract to operate ecotourism activities on the island. While you can visit Isla Gorgona for the day, the only way to stay on the island is to book a tour with Aviatur. A stay of three nights, including transportation from Guapi, all meals, and three excursions, costs COP$850,000 per person for two persons. During whale-watching season from mid-July through August, the package includes two whale-watching excursions and three on-land excursions and costs COP$1,002,162 per person based on double accommodations.

One area of the island has the park offices, a dozen comfortable cabins, and the pleasant open-air restaurant. All accommodations and meals (mostly seafood) are included in the package price. Call in advance if you have special dietary needs. At lunch, if it is sunny, you might be able to see dolphins frolic nearby. A band of white-headed temperamental capuchin monkeys hangs out near the settlement.

Information and Services

There is a nurse's office equipped with vials of snake bite antivenin, should it come to that. But, since the park's opening, they have never had to administer those. (A worker was once bitten by a non-poisonous snake, however.) There is also a small store with handicrafts, souvenirs, and snacks. In the evenings there is even Internet service, but you may have to wait for one of the computers. Tap water is pure coming from the freshwater of the island, and it is then filtered. You can drink it from the tap in your cabin with no worries.

Handicrafts

The main reason visitors pass through **Guapi,** an impoverished town of 30,000 and the largest town on the department of Cauca's coastline, is to catch a boat to Isla Gorgona.

If, on your way to or from Gorgona, you have some time in Guapi, be sure to check out the fantastic basketry and handicrafts at the **COOPMUJERES** handicraft store (Cra. 2 No. 10-39, cell tel. 311/385-1014, guapicoopmujeres@yahoo.es, 8am-noon and 2pm-6pm Mon.-Sat., 8am-noon Sun.), across the street from the Hotel Río Guapi. This enterprise is completely run by Afro-Colombian women artisans, many of whom are heads of their households. They specialize in woven items such as hats and basketry, using natural fibers commonly found in surrounding jungles, such as *paja tetera, chocolatillo,* and others. When the cooperative was started in 1992, the idea was met with much skepticism by men in Guapi, who doubted the women's ability to successfully run a business. Over 20 years later, it looks like they've proven the naysayers wrong.

This is one of the most ecological resorts you may ever visit. All electricity is provided by a small hydroelectric plant. For hot water, each cabin has solar power cells on its rooftop.

Getting There

The easiest and best way to get to Isla Gorgona is to organize a *lancha* (boat) with **Aviatur** (Av. 19 No. 4-62, Bogotá, tel. 1/587-5181 or 1/587-5182, www.aviaturecoturismo.com) from the coastal town of Guapi. These boats leave every Friday and Monday morning at around 11, about an hour after the arrival of the morning **Satena** (tel. 1/423-8530, www.satena.com) flight from Cali. An Aviatur representative will meet you at the Guapi airport and take you over to their office/embarkation point on a *mototaxi.* The trip to the island takes just under two hours, sometimes over rough seas. It costs COP$150,000 round-trip. If you are not able to take the Aviatur *lancha* (if you arrive on a different day, for example), you will have to rent an entire *lancha* from Guapi for about COP$500,000, which may not be so bad if you have others to share the cost.

From Buenaventura, boats heading to Bocas de Satinga can drop you off at Isla Gorgona (COP$120,000 one way). If there are four or five passengers, the boat will detour and drop you off at the island. If there are fewer passengers, the boat will radio Gorgona and rendezvous with an Aviatur speedboat, which is an adventure in its own right. Contact Aviatur about this option.

◖ SANTUARIO DE FLORA Y FAUNA MALPELO

Covering around 900,000 hectares (2.2 million acres) of protected Pacific Ocean waters and the tiny **Isla Malpelo,** the **Santuario de Flora y Fauna Malpelo** (www.parquesnacionales.gov.co, COP$85,000-159,000) was established in 1995. The area was declared a Particularly Sensitive Sea Area by the International Maritime Organization in 2002 and a UNESCO World Heritage Site in 2006. The steep volcanic rock of Isla Malpelo is nearly 500 kilometers (300 miles) from the coast of Colombia. It is administered by **Parques Nacionales** (tel. 1/353-2400, ext. 138, www.parquesnacionales.gov.co).

It is the largest no-fishing zone in the Eastern Tropical Pacific, thus making it one of the top places for diving in the world. There are 11 main dive sites, including the most important site, **La Nevera,** where it is common to see scores of hammerhead sharks. The deep waters surrounding the island are home to some of the most important coral formations in the Colombian Pacific. Mollusks and crustaceans, fish such as snapper, endangered *mero* (grouper), large populations of

Even experienced divers will be blown away by the diversity of sea life in the Santuario de Flora y Fauna Malpelo.

hammerhead sharks, whale sharks, sun ray sharks, and manta rays are found in abundance in the sanctuary. It is one of the few places in the world where the short-nosed ragged-toothed shark, a deepwater shark, has been spotted. Inhospitable to much animal life, the island is home to crabs, lizards, and geckos. Among birds, the largest colony in the world of the Nazca booby is found on Malpelo.

Malpelo is for experienced divers only. To get there you must coordinate with one of the following authorized diving tour groups:

- Out of Buenaventura: **Embarcaciones Asturías** (tel. 2/242-4620, cell tel. 313/767-2864, barcoasturias@yahoo.com)

- From Cali: **Pacific Diving** (tel. 2/558-3903, info@cascoantiguocolombia.com, seawolfaboard@gmail.com) and **Arrecifes del Pacífico** (tel. 2/514-1691, cell tel. 321/642-6015, www.arrecifesdelpacifico.com)

- Out of Panama City: **Coiba Dive Expeditions** (tel. 507/232-0216, www.coibadiveexpeditions.com) and the German group **Inula UAA Adventures** (tel. 507/667-95620, inuladiving@gmail.com, www.inula-diving.de)

The **Fundación Malpelo** (www.fundacionmalpelo.org) is a nonprofit organization working to protect this sanctuary. The island is under constant threat from illegal fishing, particularly of hammerhead sharks. In 2012 it was estimated that 200 tons of fish were illegally caught in the Colombian Pacific, mostly by boats hailing from Costa Rica, Ecuador, and from Asian countries. During Holy Week, shark fin stew is sold in Buenaventura.

SAN ANDRÉS AND PROVIDENCIA

The San Andrés Archipelago is made up of seven atolls and three major islands: San Andrés, Providencia, and Santa Catalina. San Andrés is 775 kilometers (492 miles) northeast of the Colombian mainland and only 191 kilometers (119 miles) east of Nicaragua. The islands are fairly small: San Andrés, the largest island, has an area of 26 square kilometers (10 square miles),

HIGHLIGHTS

LOOK FOR ◖ TO FIND RECOMMENDED SIGHTS, ACTIVITIES, DINING, AND LODGING.

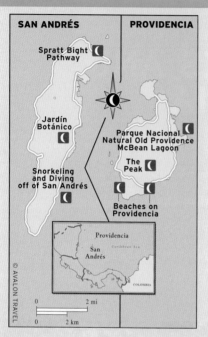

of the idyllic Johnny Cay in the distance, this beachside promenade is part boardwalk–and part catwalk (page 379).

◖ **Jardín Botánico:** This well-tended botanical garden sits on a bluff overlooking the turquoise sea. A walk among the native trees, plants, and flowers provides a pleasant break from the beach (page 380).

◖ **Snorkeling and Diving off of San Andrés:** The dozens of dive sites among thriving coral formations and steep ocean walls off of San Andrés can keep divers blissfully busy for days (page 381).

◖ **Parque Nacional Natural Old Providencia McBean Lagoon:** Paddle through the mangrove lagoons and snorkel offshore among tropical fish at this small national park (page 388).

◖ **Beaches on Providencia:** Undertake the tough field work of determining your favorite palm-lined Providencia beach. Your investigations could take several days (page 390).

◖ **The Peak:** From The Peak, the highest point on Providencia, hikers enjoy fantastic peeks from the jungle toward the deep blue sea (page 391).

◖ **Spratt Bight Pathway:** Epicenter of all goings on in San Andrés and against a backdrop

Providencia just 17 square kilometers (6.5 square miles), and Santa Catalina, attached to Providencia by a photogenic pedestrian bridge, is 1 square kilometer (247 acres) in size.

Once serving as a base for notorious English pirate Henry Morgan, Providencia—or Old Providence, as English-speaking locals call it—and its tiny tag-along neighbor of Santa Catalina are places to experience how the Caribbean used to be before tourism developed. Here visitors enjoy small bungalow-style hotels and home-cooked Creole food. The beaches are pristine and secluded and the waters are an inviting turquoise. Seafood, particularly fresh crab, is always on the menu, accompanied by cold beer.

More developed San Andrés is popular with rowdy Colombian vacationers escaping the chilly climes of the Andes. However, it has many of the same charms as Providencia. Sunbathing, snorkeling, diving, and relaxing are always the order of the day.

On both islands English and a Creole patois are spoken, in addition to Spanish.

HISTORY

Little is known of the early history of San Andrés, Providencia, and Santa Catalina. In

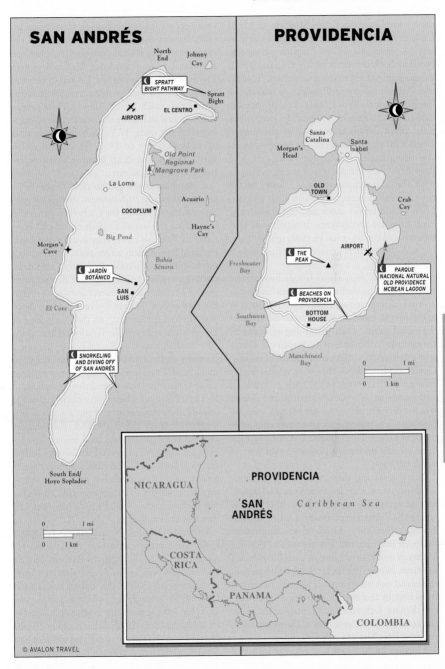

SAN ANDRÉS

North
End   Johnny
Cay

SPRATT
BIGHT PATHWAY
Spratt
Bight

AIRPORT   EL CENTRO

Old Point
Regional
Mangrove Park

La Loma

COCOPLUM   Acuario

Big Pond   Hayne's
Cay

Morgan's
Cave   Bahía
Sénora

JARDÍN
BOTÁNICO

SAN
LUIS

El Cove

SNORKELING
AND DIVING OFF
OF SAN ANDRÉS

South End/
Hoyo Soplador

0   1 mi

0   1 km

PROVIDENCIA

Santa
Catalina   Santa
Isabel
Morgan's
Head

OLD
TOWN   Crab
Cay

AIRPORT

THE
PEAK
Freshwater
Bay   PARQUE
NACIONAL NATURAL
OLD PROVIDENCE
MCBEAN LAGOON

BEACHES ON
PROVIDENCIA

Southwest
Bay   BOTTOM
HOUSE

Manchineel
Bay

0   1 mi

0   1 km

PROVIDENCIA

SAN
ANDRÉS   Caribbean Sea

NICARAGUA

COSTA
RICA

PANAMA

COLOMBIA

SAN ANDRÉS

© AVALON TRAVEL

pre-Columbian times, the Miskito people of Central America visited the islands but never settled there. In 1628, English privateers brought back information to England about the islands that led to the foundation, in 1631, of a Puritan colony on Providence Island, the English name for Providencia. This project was backed by the Providence Island Company, a joint stock company formed by prominent English Puritans who were also involved in establishing settlements in New England. The Providence settlement was contemporaneous with the Massachusetts Bay Colony. At the time, it was expected that this lush tropical Eden would be far more successful than the New England settlements. It was hoped that tobacco and cotton could be easily grown there. In 1631, 100 settlers arrived from England on the *Seaflower*.

The project was short-lived. Providence Island Company denied the settlers land ownership and required significant contribution of manpower to build the island's defenses. Rather than establishing a self-sustaining agricultural community, the colonists imported slaves and established a plantation-based economy. Correspondence from that time reveals decidedly un-Puritanical activity, such as drinking and gambling. The death knell of the colony was the decision of Providence Island Company to obtain a privateering patent and engage in outright piracy. This enraged and provoked the Spanish, the dominant power in that part of the Americas.

Wary of having their New World gold stolen from them, the Spaniards cracked down, and an attack on the islands in 1641 put an end to the Puritan experiment. During the following half century, the island was fought over by Spain and England. Pirates such as Edward Mansvelt and Henry Morgan used Providencia as a base. Nominally under the Spanish crown, the island welcomed a small number of settlers from Britain and other Caribbean islands during the late 17th and 18th centuries. In 1821, the archipelago became part of the newly independent Republic of Gran Colombia.

During the 19th century, another influx of immigrants from the British Caribbean included many former slaves, which led to the creation of the Raizal community. One settler who lived on Providence, Phillip Beekman Livingston, traveled to the United States and was ordained a Baptist minister, and he introduced that faith to the islands. He was also instrumental in freeing the islands' slaves, starting with his own, 17 years before Colombia abolished slavery in 1853. As a result of his work, the Baptist faith became a distinctive part the islands' culture.

Colombia exerted greater power over the islands in the early 20th century, delegating educational instruction to the Catholic Church and forbidding the use of English on official business. In 1953, dictator Gustavo Rojas Pinilla declared San Andrés a free port. This led to a massive influx of outsiders, mostly Colombian duty-free tourists and settlers, but also a contingent of Middle Eastern merchants, who altered the face of San Andrés forever. A dense shopping district sprouted up on the North End of San Andrés after the declaration of free port. The English-speaking Raizal people became a minority on their own island and lost control of much land. Providence, which was not declared a free trade zone, was spared this onslaught.

The 1991 Colombian constitution gave the islands some autonomy and put an end to immigration from the mainland. Providencia enacted strict zoning and land ownership regulations that have preserved the island's Raizal identity. Both the Colombian and Nicaraguan governments have declared interest in opening these waters to oil exploration, prompting a grass roots "Old Providence, not Oil Providence" campaign.

In recent decades, Nicaragua has contested Colombian jurisdiction over the islands, renouncing the 1928 Esguerra-Barcenas treaty and filing a suit at the International Court of Justice. In 2001, the court reaffirmed Colombian sovereignty over the islands and atolls but left the maritime border up in the air. In 2012, the court decided that roughly 70,000 square kilometers of sea north and south of San Andrés, which had previously been Colombian,

© ANDREW DIER

iguana in San Andrés

were in fact Nicaraguan. Colombians and islanders were shocked, especially because of the loss of traditional fishing areas. Two large atolls became enclaves in the Nicaraguan maritime area. The court decision cannot be appealed, but Colombian president Juan Manuel Santos has declared that it will not abide by the decision until Nicaragua ensures the Raizal fishers have access to their traditional fishing areas.

THE LAND

The archipelago covers 280,000 square kilometers of marine area (it was 350,000 before the 2012 International Court decision). It includes three major islands and seven atolls, and well-preserved coral reefs, particularly the barrier reef surrounding Providence and Santa Catalina, home to more than 80 species of corals and 200 species of fish.

The islands were once covered by forest. Though much has been cleared, especially in San Andrés, significant tracts of forest remain, with cedars, cotton trees, stinking toes, birch gums, and other indigenous trees. The abundance of fruit-bearing trees and plants includes breadfruit, tamarind, mango, and guava, though much of the fruit that is consumed on the islands is imported from Colombia and Central America. There are several large, well-preserved mangrove lagoons, notably the McBean Lagoon in Providencia.

The islands support a wide range of reptiles, including snakes, iguanas, geckos, and lizards, including the blue or green lizard. Other land animals include crabs, especially the black and shankey crabs, which effect massive migrations to and from the sea to spawn. Coralina (www.coralina.gov.co), the archipelago's environmental agency, recruits army personnel to block traffic on Providencia's roads to protect these migrating crabs. Four species of protected sea turtles nest here. Approximately 100 bird species have been identified on the islands, but only 18 are resident. The island's only non-human land mammals are bats. Dolphins and whales are sighted occasionally.

Despite obvious environmental degradation, especially in San Andrés, the archipelago remains one of the best preserved corners of the Caribbean. In 2000, the 300,000 square kilometers of the Seaflower Biosphere Reserve became part of UNESCO's "Man and the Biosphere" program, which aims to preserve both biological and ethnic diversity, combining conservation with sustainable use by local communities. The 2012 International Court decision transferred about 45 percent of the biosphere to Nicaragua. Islanders hope that Nicaragua will continue to preserve this priceless marine nature reserve.

PLANNING YOUR TIME

High tourist seasons on both islands are during the Christmas and New Year's holidays. It may be hard to find a hotel from mid-December until mid-January. During this time, as throngs of Colombian families and a growing number of Brazilians and Argentinians take over San Andrés. Also popular are Easter week and school vacations, between mid-June and August. May and September are quiet. Because it's more difficult to reach, Providencia never feels crowded.

The average temperature is 27°C (81°F). During the dry season between January and April, water rationing can be necessary, especially in Providencia, where it rains as little as five days per month. The rainy season extends from June until November, when it can rain 20-24 days per month. October is the rainiest month and is also when hurricanes occasionally churn up the warm Caribbean waters. March and April are some of the best months for snorkeling and diving because the waters are calm. December and January are windy, making snorkeling and diving challenging. Strong winds can prompt airlines to cancel flights into and out of Providencia.

San Andrés is a possible long weekend getaway from mainland Colombia. However, most opt to stay 5-7 days. Week-long all-inclusive plans are popular. A visit to Providencia from San Andrés can be a budget buster, but it is well worth the expense if you are interested in getting away from it all. A jaunt to Providencia involves an extra flight, and hotels and restaurants are generally more expensive than in San Andrés, which itself is already more expensive than the mainland. If you want to do some serious diving, plan for at least a week, say three days in San Andrés and four days in Providencia.

San Andrés

Surrounded by a large barrier reef, San Andrés is Colombia's Caribbean playground. Here the waters are of seven shades of blue, the sandy beaches are white, and coco locos, the official island cocktail, are always served. Days here are spent lazing on the beach, island hopping, snorkeling and diving, and enjoying fresh seafood. For many Colombians, the deals at the many duty-free stores are too good to pass up—that's one reason why they visit the island in the first place.

San Andrés has a population of about 75,000, about two-thirds of which are of mainland Colombian origin. The rest are English- and Creole-speaking Raizales, many of whom have origins as Jamaican slaves. There is also a community of "Turcos" or "Arabes," whose roots can be traced to mostly Lebanon and Syria. Their presence on the island is not an insignificant one, as demonstrated by a brilliantly white modern mosque that stands prominently in the commercial center.

Orientation

The island of San Andrés resembles a seahorse floating gently eastward in the western Caribbean Sea. It is only about 13 kilometers (8 miles) long from top to bottom and 3 kilometers (2 miles) wide, and has a total area of 26 square kilometers (10 square miles). The Circunvalar ring road more or less circles the entire island.

© ANDREW DIER

The beach at Spratt Bight is full of activity.

The "town" of San Andrés is usually called the Centro or the North End. It is in the snout of the seahorse, in the northeast. This is the center of activity and where the majority of the island's restaurants, hotels, and shops (nearly all of which are owned and operated by mainland Colombians) are found. About 1.6 kilometers (1 mile) of the main drag here, Avenida Colombia, is the *paseo peatonal* or *malecón,* the Spratt Bight Pathway, a delightful pedestrian promenade along the Spratt Bight beach. About two kilometers northwest of the Centro is the airport. The west side is quieter, with a handful of points of interest, hotels, and restaurants. The coastline on the west side is all coral; there are no beaches. At the southernmost point of the island is the Hoyo Soplador blow hole. Continuing counterclockwise, the town of San Luis extends along the southeastern edge of the island. This area has some good beaches, hotels, and restaurants, and is much more laid-back than the Centro.

The middle part of the island, called **La**

Loma (The Hill), is the highest point on the island. The main point of reference here is the stately white First Baptist Church. This is home to the largest community of Raizal people.

SIGHTS
◖ Spratt Bight Pathway
For many, their first stop in San Andrés after checking in to their hotel is the **Spratt Bight Pathway** (Centro). This pedestrian walkway is the liveliest stretch on the island, lined with restaurants, hotels, and souvenir shops on one side. On the ocean side of the pathway is the island's most popular beach, **Spratt Bight,** which looks out toward the enticing Johnny Cay in the distance.

Casa Museo Isleña
Casa Museo Isleña (Km. 5 Av. Circunvalar, tel. 8/512-3419, 8:30am-5pm daily, COP$8,000) is a reconstruction of a typical island wooden house that provides a glimpse into island life in the 19th century. After a required guided tour (15 minutes), your cheerful young guide will tell you "now let's dance!" Reggae dancing is a rather strange component of the museum experience, but then again, it's hard to say no. Those smiling guides are a persuasive lot.

Cueva de Morgan (Morgan's Cave)
It would seem that all caves hidden along the coasts of San Andrés and Providencia are reputed to hold hidden treasures stashed away by notorious pirates. On the western side of San Andrés is **Cueva de Morgan** (Morgan's Cave, tel. 8/513-2946, 9am-6pm daily, COP$10,000), a sort of theme park where Welsh privateer/pirate Captain Henry Morgan allegedly stored some of his loot (but there's no evidence to prove this). There isn't much to see at the cave itself. That's why the park owners added on some reconstructions of traditional wooden island cabins that serve as mini-museums on island culture and ways of life. You visit these on a guided tour that is included in the cost. One is an art gallery where local dancers often perform to calypso beats. All in all, it's a tourist trap.

Hoyo Soplador

At the **Hoyo Soplador** on the island's southern tip, the attraction is a hole in the coral where, when the tide and winds are right, water sprays up, reaching heights of more than 10 meters. It can't compare to Old Faithful, but then again, can you order a coco loco in Yellowstone?

Jardín Botánico

The **Jardín Botánico** (Vía Harmony Hill in front of Hotel Sol Caribe Campo, tel. 8/513-3390, www.caribe.unal.edu.co, 8:30am-5pm Mon.-Fri., 10am-4pm Sat.-Sun., COP$5,000) is easily the most peaceful place on San Andrés. In this lovely botanical garden run by the Universidad Nacional, you can stroll along several paths and view trees and plants that grow in San Andrés. From the five-story lookout tower, you can take in an impressive view of the island and its barrier reefs. Guided tours, included in the price of admission, are technically required, but if you are in a hurry or arrive in the late afternoon, you can request to amble the trails unaccompanied.

First Baptist Church

The white, clapboard **First Baptist Church** (La Loma, no phone, services 7:30pm Thurs. and 10:30am Sun., COP$3,000 donation requested) was built in 1844 and rebuilt before the turn of the 20th century using wood imported from Alabama. It was the first Baptist church established on the island. A guide will give you a little history of the church and allow you to climb up to the bell tower for a commanding view of the island. The Sunday worship service can last several hours. Church members dress up for services, and you'll often see a smattering of tourists in the balcony on Sundays. The church is an excellent place to hear gospel music.

Paradise Farm

Job Saas, a local Raizal man, operates **Paradise Farm** (Cove Seaside, Km. 11 Polly Higgs Rd., tel. 8/513-0798, cell tel. 315/770-3904, donations accepted). Saas decided to transform the former standard family farm into one with a focus on conservation and the environment.

breadfruit at Jardín Botánico

Here you can see animals, such as iguanas and turtles, and plants that are threatened due to overdevelopment on San Andrés. Saas uses the same farming techniques that his family has used for decades. It is a great initiative on this island where environmental awareness is lacking. He welcomes visitors to the farm, and, if you are lucky, you can hear his band play.

Big Pond

Managed by a Rastafarian community, the **Big Pond** (La Loma, no phone, no set visiting hours, donations requested) is a pond on the top of La Loma, home to a few domesticated alligators. When called, they will swim close to the shore, where they are fed a diet of white bread. The alligators live in harmony with turtles, and herons watch the action from a tree nearby. Upon arrival, ask for Fernando. There is no set entry fee.

ENTERTAINMENT AND EVENTS
Nightlife

The nightlife scene on San Andrés is big and brash. The most famous nightspots are near Spratt Bight. Clubs generally open from Thursday to Saturday during off-season but every night during high season. Things get cranking around 10pm. The perennial top discos are **Coco Loco** (Av. Colombia, tel. 8/513-1047), **Extasis** (Hotel Sol Caribe, tel. 8/512-3043), and **Blue Deep** (Sunrise Hotel). **Aquarius** (Av. Colombia between Bahía Sardina and Hotel Toné, tel. 8/512-5933) is more of a bar scene during the afternoon and early evening, turning into a dancing spot later on. You'll feel like you're in Ibiza at the **Majia Restaurante Italiano y Cocktail Bar** (Av. Colombia, cell tel. 318/860-5234, www.majiasanandres.com), where chill-out music and mojitos go along with a beachside view. Guest DJs usually spin on weekends.

RECREATION
Beaches

Some of the best beaches on the island include **Spratt Bight,** near the Centro in front of the pedestrian walkway; **San Luis,** near Chammey Marina; **Cocoplum**; **Bahía Sonora** (near Rocky Cay) beaches; and the **Parque Regional Johnny Cay.**

Out of all of these, the Johnny Cay beaches are probably the best. **Johnny Cay** is the island that beckons off the Spratt Bight beach. During peak tourist seasons, on weekends, and on holidays, though, it gets crazy packed.

To get to Johnny Cay, you must take a boat, called a *lancha* in Spanish, from Spratt Bight, It is a quick 15-minute ride there. There are always boats owned by individuals (not organized tour companies) at the ready at the Spratt Bight beach. To arrange a trip, your negotiating skills will be put to the test. Hiring an individual boat can cost up to COP$200,000. The inexpensive option is to take a day tour (COP$20,000). These leave from Spratt Bight by 9:30am every day of the year, and the boats return at around 4pm.

In the late afternoon, the island clears out, but you can stay until almost 6 when the last boats leave. It's nice to be one of the last visitors on the island as the sun begins its descent. There are no accommodations options on the island. While there, take a walk around the entire island, where flocks of birds are likely the only company you'll have. It takes about 15 minutes.

◖ Snorkeling and Diving

San Andrés is surrounded by a well-preserved coral reef teeming with marine life that makes it a diver's and snorkeler's paradise. On the eastern edge is the windward barrier, 15 kilometers long and 60-80 meters wide, with significant live coral communities. Beyond the reef, the shelf ends abruptly with a vertical wall that drops hundreds of meters. To the west, the windward barrier protects a large marine lagoon that has seagrass cover. The reef on the western, leeward side is a bit less well preserved due to tourism and boat traffic, but it also has beautiful patches of coral and significant marine life. In all, the waters surrounding San Andrés include more than 40 species of corals and 131 species of fish. It is common to see

a diving lesson

large schools of brightly colored jacks, tangs, grunts, and snapper, as well as barracudas, groupers, and parrotfish. Other marine creatures include turtles, stingrays, moray eels, octopus, squid, and lobster.

A unique feature of San Andrés is that the dives are very close to shore, which means a 10- to 30-minute boat ride maximum. The water is warm and has excellent visibility year round. The best conditions for diving are January to May, with stronger winds in June and July. Popular dive sites are: The Pyramids, a shallow 4-meter dive with striking anemones and fish; Nirvana, a reef at about 15 meters, teeming with marine life; Trampa Tortuga, a reef at about 15 meters with great visibility; and Blue Wall, on the eastern edge of the windward barrier, which starts at 6 meters and drops to 300 meters with magnificent corals and large tube sponges.

Most dive operators also offer short (three hours) introductory courses for beginners, costing around COP$155,000 per person, which allow you to do an easy dive without being certified. There are also many opportunities to do full introductory and advanced courses with certification. A three-day Open Water Diver certification course typically costs around COP$800,000.

Recommended diving operators on San Andrés include **Banda** (Hotel Lord Pierre, tel. 8/513-1080, www.bandadiveshop.com), **Blue Life** (Hotel Sunrise Beach, Local 112/113, tel. 8/512-5318, www.bluelifedive.com), **Sharky's Surf Shop** (Sunset Hotel, Km. 13 Carretera Circunvalar, tel. 8/512-0651, www.sharkydiveshop.com), and **Karibik** (Av. Newball 1-248, Edificio Galeon, tel. 8/512-0101, www.karibikdiver.com). Diving excursions typically include two dives and cost COP$170,000. Night diving trips can be arranged by most dive shops.

Other Water Sports

Samuel Raigosa, better known as Chamey, is the **kite-surfing** guru of San Andrés, and those at **Chamey's Náutica** (Km. 4 Vía San Luis, tel. 8/513-2077, cell tel. 317/752-4965) is a park with two components: on the water side there is a restaurant and features include a waterslide, a trampoline, snorkeling, and Aquanaut suits that you can rent to walk on the floor of the ocean. Across the road are some houses made entirely of coconuts, fruit orchards, dozens of lizards and turtles to gawk at, and a cave to enter. South of the West View is **La Piscina Natural** (cell tel. 318/363-6014, COP$5,000), a low-key spot for snorkeling that attracts fewer crowds.

Tours

The locally run **Coonative Brothers** (Spratt Bight Beach, tel. 8/512-1923) company offers tours to some of the best known beaches and swimming spots. A standard day tour costs COP$20,000 and leaves at 9:30 every morning. That includes a 1.5-hour stop at **El Acuario/La Piscina/Haynes Cay,** where you can wade and swim in waters labeled "seven shades of blue." Animal lovers may find the attraction of "swimming with the manta rays" to be disturbing. On busy tourist days, the manta rays are handled over and over again, being lifted out of the water for snapshots with smiling tourists. They are fed a steady diet of white sandwich bread. For the sake of the rays, it's best to avoid participating in this activity. The rest of the day is spent on **Johnny Cay,** where you can buy lunch and drinks, and rent snorkeling equipment. (If you go to Johnny Cay, don't pay for a guide. There is no need.). You can just show up at the beach at around 9am to join the tour.

Local boaters affiliated with Coonative Brothers also offer full-day tours with more stops, including a visit to the San Andrés mangroves for COP$60,000 per person. There is a minimum of 10 passengers for these tours. If you would like to go out on a private trip to one of those locations, that can cost up to COP$200,000, depending on your negotiating skills. Inquire at the Coonative Brothers' beach kiosk.

Another option to get out on the water is to take a glass-bottom boat tour. During this tour, you make several stops to coral reefs, to sunken

kite-boarding in San Andrés

are experts on kite-surfing. A one-hour class costs COP$70,000.

The group **Ecofiwi Turismo Ecológico** (Vía San Luis, Mango Tree sector, tel. 8/513-0565, cell tel. 316/567-4988 or 316/624-3396, 9am-4pm daily) offers **kayak tours** of the mangroves in the Old Point Regional Mangrove Park led by local guides. The kayaks are completely transparent, providing kayakers with up-close views of sea life such as upside down jellyfish, sea cucumbers, seagrass beds, and also birds such as frigatebirds, pelicans, herons, and migratory birds. Snorkeling is also part of the tour (equipment included). The two-hour tour costs COP$50,000, and that cost includes a snack of a crab empanada and a juice or something of the like, plus a CD of photos from the trip. There are no additional costs. The group also offers **artisanal fishing tours,** during which the visitor goes fishing with local Raizal fishers. A half-day fishing tour costs COP$200,000 and an entire day is COP$300,000.

The **West View** (tel. 8/513-0341, cell tel. 312/308-8942, 9am-6pm daily, COP$8,000) ships, and to exotic islands. You'll be able to get in the water and snorkel several times to observe sealife. For information regarding these tours contact **San Andrés Unlimited** (Tom Hooker Road No. 8-75, South End, tel. 8/513-0035, tel. 8/513-0129, cell tel. 316/889-8701, or 310/625-2938). A 1-hour 45-minute tour costs around COP$45,000 per person.

ACCOMMODATIONS

On this island where tourism is king, lodging options are plentiful, except during high season (mid-December to mid-January, Holy Week, and, to a lesser extent, during school vacations from June to July). Top-end hotels and low-end hostels are not as common as mid- to upper-range all-inclusive hotels. Colombian chain Decameron has five properties on the island and is building its largest hotel yet near the airport, expected to be ready in 2015. There are no familiar international hotel chains on the island.

You will probably want to stay on or near the beach on the eastern side of the island, including in quiet San Luis. From here, you can hop on public transportation or hail a cab if you want to go to town, or rent a motorbike, golf cart, jeep (*mulita*), or bicycle. The busy downtown (North End) of San Andrés can feel claustrophobic, but you'll always be within walking distance of restaurants and services, and you can often find some good deals in this area. Waterfront hotels here have pools, not beaches. Stay near the airport if you prefer more seclusion but still want to be close to the action in the city center.

The western side of the island has coral coastline instead of beaches, and the few hotels cater mostly to divers, so this side feels more isolated.

In the interior of the island are some *posadas nativas,* guesthouses owned and operated by locals, many with deep roots on the island. Staying at a *posada nativa* is the best way to get to know the local culture. For a list of guesthouse options, you can visit the webpage of the program of *posadas nativas* sponsored by the Colombian Ministry of Tourism and Ministry of Rural Affairs: www.posadasturisticasdecolombia.com.

In the North End, boutique hotel ☾ **Casa Harb** (Cl. 11 No. 10-83, tel. 8/512-6348, www.casaharb.com, COP$800,000 d) is by far the most luxurious place to stay in San Andrés. The five suites, the lobby, dining area, and spa area are thoughtfully decorated with fantastic art and furniture from Morocco to Malaysia, personally chosen by owner Jak Harb. The **Hostal Mar y Mar** (Av. Colombia No. 1-32, cell tel. 317/401-6906, COP$150,000 d), in the same part of the island, is a squeaky clean and friendly little place that opened in 2012. There are only four rooms and meals are not included. It's two blocks from the beach. Noise from airplane take-offs may be a nuisance in the mornings for some.

Although it may look retro-Miami Beach, brilliantly white **Casablanca** (Av. Colombia No. 3-59, tel. 8/512-4115, www.hotelcasablancasanandres.com, COP$391,000 d low season, COP$659,000 d high season) is an upscale option facing the beachfront pedestrian walkway. Of the 91 spacious rooms it offers, 10 of them are *cabañas.* There is a small pool and, more importantly, a pool bar, **Coco's.** The hotel has three on-site restaurants.

The Decameron chain seems to be on a mission to take over San Andrés. They currently operate five hotels on San Andrés. Close to town is their boutique hotel, **Decameron Los Delfines** (Av. Colombia No. 1B-86, tel. 8/512-7816, Bogotá tel. 1/628-0000, www.decameron.co, COP$310,000 d). It has 39 very comfortable rooms and a pool. As is the case with all Decameron hotels, all meals are included. Fortunately, you are permitted to dine at other Decameron hotels on the island. This hotel does not have a beach.

The small hotels in the busy downtown are far more reasonably priced than those with a view to the sea and are just a few blocks away. The most popular choice for backpackers is the five-floor **El Viajero** (Av. 20 de Julio No. 3A-122, tel. 8/512-7497, www.elviajerohostels.com, COP$52,000 dorm, COP$132,000-200,000 d), which is part of a Uruguayan chain. It has several air-conditioned gender-separated dorms, as well as private rooms. The top floor bar serves cold beer and assorted rum drinks, and there are several common areas with wireless Internet and computers. A paltry breakfast is included, and a kitchen is provided for guests' use. Staff aren't overly friendly, but they can arrange excursions.

It's surprising just how peaceful the **Posada Mary May** (Av. 20 de Julio No. 3-74, tel. 8/512-5669, COP$60,000-110,000 d) is. Every morning you can pick up a cup of coffee in the lovely courtyard that is shaded by a huge avocado tree. On the downside, beds (usually three per room) are on the soft side in the spacious rooms, wireless Internet is sporadic, and in general the place could use an update. Around the corner, **Cli's Place** (Av. 20 de Julio No. 3-47, tel. 8/512-0591, luciamhj@hotmail. com, COP$160,000 d), owned by Cletotilde Henry, has four double rooms in the main house as well as a *cabaña* that accommodates seven people. You will feel at home here, although the price is high. **Casa D'Lulú** (Av. Antioquia No. 2-18, tel. 8/512-2919, laposadadelulu.sanandresyprovidencia@hotmail.com, COP$150,000 d) has 10 rooms and three large studio apartments.

Brightly colored **Cocoplum Hotel** (Vía San Luis No. 43-49, tel. 8/513-2121, www.cocoplumhotel.com, COP$240,000-420,000 d) in the San Luis area has the most important feature for a beach hotel: It is actually on the beach, with rooms that are steps from the water. Rooms are comfortable and spacious with kitchens. The restaurant and bar face the water, and quite often the only thing you hear is the palm branches rustling in the wind. Food is not fantastic, so don't go for the all-meals-included plan.

Ground Road Native Place (Circunvalar No. 54-88, before the health clinic, San Luis, tel. 8/513-3887, cell tel. 313/776-6036, edupeterson1@hotmail.com, COP$50,000 pp) is a small, comfortable *posada nativa* with five spacious rooms with air conditioning and wireless Internet in San Luis. It's in the home of Edula and George Peterson and is just a three-minute walk to the beach.

An option in La Loma is **Coconut Paradise Lodge** (Claymount No. 50-05, La Loma, tel. 8/513-2926, oldm26@hotmail.com, COP$50,000 pp with breakfast), a beautiful turn-of-the-20th century wooden home with six rooms. It's a great place to stay if you are interested in learning about Raizal culture. It's close to the botanical gardens and the San Luis beaches. Try for the top floor room, which has great views and a delicious breeze.

On the quiet west side of the island, for those interested in diving, **Sunset Hotel** (Km. 13 Circunvalar, tel. 8/513-0433, 0420, www.sunsethotelspa.com, COP$196,000 low season, COP$320,000 d high season) is a great option. It has 16 bright and basic rooms that surround a small pool. While there is no beach, the hotel's dive shop, Sharky's, offers diving lessons and organizes diving excursions. You can go snorkeling in the waters across the street. Week-long diving packages may be a good option. And as its name indicates, great sunsets are included at no extra cost. You can also rent bikes here.

FOOD

Seafood is on every menu in every restaurant in San Andrés. Fish, lobster, crab, and conch are likely to come from the waters off of San Andrés and Providencia. However, *langostinos* (prawns) and *camarones* (shrimp) often come from either the Pacific or from the Cartagena area on the mainland. A Caribbean specialty you'll likely find only on San Andrés, Providencia, and Jamaica is the rundown or *rondón*. It is a filling to-the-max stew that has fish or conch, pig's tail, dumplings, yuca, and other ingredients slowly cooked in coconut milk. All restaurants are beach casual, and most of the larger ones accept credit cards.

Cafés, Bakeries, and Quick Bites

Part of the Casablanca Hotel, the groovy turquoise **Sea Watch Café** (Av. Colombia, 6am-11pm daily, COP$18,000) is as close as it comes in Colombia to a New York-style coffee shop. Here you can have a leisurely breakfast as you watch the tourists file by on the walkway out front. They also offer pizza, hamburgers, ceviche, pasta, and desserts.

From the outside, (**Coffee Break** (Av. Colombia No. 3-59, in front of Parque de la Barracuda, tel. 8/512-1275, www.coffeebreak.com.co, 7am-11pm daily) often appears empty or even closed. But when you go inside, it's almost always packed with visitors and locals alike sipping on Vietnamese coffee, munching on nachos, or smearing cream cheese on their toasted bagels. Customers here take their time (likely because of the air conditioning!). A bakery/café popular with locals is **Bread Fruit** (Av. Francisco Newball No. 4-169, outside the Sunrise Hotel, tel. 8/512-6044, 7:30am-8:30pm Mon.-Sat.). It's named after the breadfruit tree, which is typical to the area. (There is no breadfruit on the menu.)

Finally, Miss Carmen is a familiar face on the Spratt Bight walkway, where she has been selling her homemade empanadas, ceviche, and cakes for years. Her stand doesn't really have a name, but you can call it **La Mesa Grande de Carmen** (Av. Colombia pathway).

Seafood

North of downtown, the (**Fisherman's Place** (Cra. 9 No. 1-10 Spratt Bight, tel. 8/512-2774, noon-4pm daily, COP$20,000) is a restaurant run by a cooperative of local fishers. It overlooks the water and is near the airport, and is always packed. Try the Rondón Típico Especial. Ask anyone in town what's the best seafood place on the island and a solid majority will mention **La Regatta** (tel. 8/512-0437, www.restaurantelaregatta.com, noon-11pm daily, COP$40,000) next to the Club Náutico. It is open-air and juts out onto the water. For a sampling of the finest of San Andrés seafood, try their Fiesta Náutica, which has lobster tails, prawns, and crab. Just far enough for a little peace and quiet from the Centro, **Niko's Seafood Restaurant** (Av. Colombia No. 1-93, tel. 8/512-7535, 11am-11pm daily, COP$30,000) is what a family-run seafood place should be: over the water, not fancy-schmancy, and no lounge music. Lobster is the house specialty.

Seafood, Sustainably

To protect their sustainability, some seafood should be avoided during certain times of the year, and some should be avoided completely.

Langosta (lobster), pargo (snapper), and caracol pala (conch) are the three most fished species around San Andrés and Providencia, and are very often found on restaurant menus. It is recommended to avoid ordering conch from June to October (but due to overfishing it's wise to avoid conch entirely), lobster from April until June, and cangrejo negro (black crab) from April to July.

Other threatened species include Atlantic blue fin tuna, tarpon, lebranche mullet, robalo blanco (white sea bass), mero guasa (goliath grouper), cherna (Nassau grouper), and the masked hamlet, which is only found in the waters off Providencia.

Although the namesake for (**Miss Celia** (Av. Newball and Av. Raizal, tel. 8/513-1062, restaurantemisscelia@gmail.com, noon-10pm daily, COP$30,000) passed away not too long ago, the restaurant continues the Raizal cuisine tradition in this cute, colorful, and authentic spot. Located in front of the Club Naútico, Miss Celia is surrounded by gardens and flowers, and the sounds of reggae and other local music add to the atmosphere. They recommend to their foreign guests to only order *rondón* at lunchtime, as they may not be able to handle it at night (it's a heavy dish).

(**Donde Francesca** (El Pirata Beach, San Luis, tel. 8/513-0163, cell tel. 315/770-1315, restaurantedondefrancesca@gmail.com, 7:30am-8:30pm daily, COP$35,000) is colorful and has great food. The menu includes *langosta tempura* (tempura lobster, COP$50,000) and *pulpo reducción al balsámico* (balsamic octopus, COP$34,000). In-the-know locals make a weekly visit to (**Restaurante Lidia** (Ground Rd. No. 64-65, San Luis, tel. 8/513-2192) a ritual. It's only open on Sundays and on holiday Mondays. This place gets great reviews from local foodies. Lidia's crab empanadas are recommended.

The **Restaurante Punta Sur** (Km. 15.8, South End, tel. 8/513-0003, 10am-6pm daily, COP$30,000) is close to the Hoyo Soplador. Sitting on the terrace when the waves come crashing in, it feels like you might be taken out to sea. With a small pool and deck area, it's a nice place to enjoy an afternoon. This family restaurant is a great place for some fresh seafood or drinks. *Arroz con camarones* (rice with shrimp) and grilled lobster are a couple of the more popular menu items.

International

Margherita e Carbonara (Av. Colombia No. 1-93, tel. 8/512-1050, 11am-11pm daily, COP$30,000) gets packed at night during high season due to its prized location near the big hotels. It's a boisterous family-style place where the pastas aren't bad.

Majia Restaurante Italiano y Cocktail Bar (Av. Colombia, cell tel. 318/860-52344, www.majia.co, COP$25,000) is a good choice for some authentic Italian pastas. It's run by a couple from Florence. **Mr. Panino** (Edificio Bread Fruit Local 106-7, tel. 8/512-3481, www.misterpaninosanandres.com, 10:30am-10pm Mon.-Sat., 11am-4pm Sun., COP$30,000) is a reliable, somewhat upscale Italian restaurant, popular at both lunch and dinner. It's nice to sit on the high wooden tables in the back. Try their *risotto con langostinos,* a prawn risotto that's a generous plate to share.

Although there is a strong Lebanese influence on the island, Middle Eastern food is hard to come by in San Andrés. **Hansa Pier** (Av. Colombia next to Tres Casitas hotel, cell tel. 313/758-4604, noon-10pm daily, COP$20,000) has a great waterfront location in town, but the falafels and shwarma are nothing to write home about.

It may have an unfortunate name, but the **Gourmet Shop Assho** (Av. Newball in front of Parque de la Barracuda, tel. 8/512-9843, 12:30pm-midnight Mon.-Sat., 6pm-11:30pm Sun., COP$30,000) is an excellent choice for a break from the seafood platter. The salads,

pasta, and other dishes are good, and on every table there is a big bottle of imported spicy Asian chili sauce. With gourmet food items and wine for sale along the walls, and thousands of empty wine bottles decorating the ceiling, it's a cozy place. For something quick, you can try the hole in the wall (literally) **Gourmet Shop To Go** (Av. Newball in front of Parque de la Barracuda, tel. 8/512-9843, 11am-3pm daily, COP$15,000) in the same building.

Markets

Super Todo (Av. 20 de Julio No. 3-41, tel. 8/512-6366, 8am-8pm daily) is the largest supermarket on San Andrés. It's in the Centro.

INFORMATION AND SERVICES

A humongous **tourist office** (Av. Newball, 8am-noon and 2pm-6pm daily) was opened in 2012. It's located between downtown and San Luis, across from Club Náutico. Tourism bureau staff are on hand at a tourist information kiosk where Avenida Colombia intersects with Avenida 20 de Julio (8am-7pm daily).

GETTING THERE AND AROUND

San Andrés is served by all the major Colombian airlines. In addition to their counters at the airport, most of them have ticket offices in the Centro. Copa has nonstop flights to Panama City. Air Transat (www.airtransat.com) operates charter flights between Canada and San Andrés. The **Aeropuerto Gustavo Rojas Pinillas** (Centro, tel. 8/512-3415) is very close to many hotels. Cabs to the airport cost COP$10,000. Satena operates flights to Providencia from San Andrés.

Public buses serve the entire island. These cost about COP$2,000 each way. To get to San Luis, you can take the bus from the Parque de la Barracuda just south of the Centro.

Renting a car is possible, but it's not recommended because parking is scarce, distances are not far, and, more importantly, there are more fun options. Most visitors rent heavy-duty, gas-powered golf carts referred to as *mulas* (literally, mules) for the day instead. **Millennium Rent A Car** (Av. Newball, in front of the Parque La Barracuda, tel. 8/512-3114) rents golf carts (COP$70,000 day) and *mulas* (COP$150,000 day). **Rent A Car Esmeralda** (Av. Colombia, in front of Buxo del Caribe, tel. 8/512-8116 or 8/512-1934) offers the same prices. Although you can rent both golf carts and *mulas* for multiple days, their use is prohibited after 6pm.

To take a day tour of the entire island, you can rent a van with the professional and knowledgeable driver **José Figueroa** (cell tel. 316/317-2020). Taxis are plentiful in the Centro.

Bikes can be rented at **Bicycle Rental Shop** (Cra. 1B, Sector Punta Hansa, in front of Edificio Hansa Reef, cell tel. 318/328-1790 or 321/242-9328, 8am-6pm daily, COP$45,000/ day).

Providencia and Santa Catalina

Secluded palm-lined beaches, gorgeous turquoise Caribbean waters, mellow locals, fresh seafood, and rum drinks make it easy to become smitten with Providencia and tough to leave.

Located about 90 kilometers (56 miles) north of San Andrés, these islands are the easygoing cousins of hyperactive San Andrés. Of volcanic origin, Providencia and Santa Catalina are older islands than San Andrés, and are smaller in area and population than it, having a total area of about 18 square kilometers (7 square miles) and a population of only 5,000. Only 300 people live on minuscule Santa Catalina, an island known as the "Island of Treasures," which was once home to an English fort.

Orientation

The two islands of Providencia and Santa Catalina combined are about seven kilometers long and four kilometers wide (four miles by 2.5 miles). The harbor area of Providencia is called Santa Isabel and is the center of island activity. Other settlements on the island are usually referred to by the names of their beaches or bays. The main ones are on the western side of the island: Manchineel Bay (Bahía Manzanillo), on the southern end, which has some excellent beaches; Southwest Bay (Bahía Suroeste); and Freshwater Bay (Aguadulce), home to many hotels and restaurants. A ring road encircles the entire island of Providencia.

◖ PARQUE NACIONAL NATURAL OLD PROVIDENCE MCBEAN LAGOON

The **Parque Nacional Natural Old Providence McBean Lagoon** (office Jones Point, east of airport, tel. 8/514-8885 or 8/514-9003, www.parquesnacionales.gov.co, 8am-12:30pm and 2pm-6pm daily, COP$14,000 non-Colombians, COP$8,500 Colombians, COP$4,000 students) is a small national park on the northeast coast of the island. It occupies about 1,485 hectares/3,670 acres (1,390 hectares/3,435 acres of that is in the sea). Here you can observe five different ecosystems: coral reefs, sea grass beds, mangroves, dry tropical forests, and volcanic keys.

Crab Cay (Cayo Cangrejo) is one of the main attractions of the park, and it's an easy place for some splashing about in the incredibly clear, warm waters. This is a great place for some easy snorkeling, and, in addition to tropical fish, you may see manta rays or sea turtles. A short five-minute nature path on this minuscule island takes you to the top of the island. A snack bar on Crab Cay sells water, soft drinks, beer, coco locos, and snacks like ceviche. They are there every day until around 1pm.

Boat tours, organized by all hotels and dive shops, motor around the coast of Providencia, stopping at beaches and at Crab Cay for snorkeling or swimming. These tours depart the hotels at around 9am each morning and cost

© ANDREW DIER

sailing race in Providencia

about COP$35,000 per person. Once you disembark at Crab Cay, you'll have to pay the park entry fee of COP$14,000. Following the stop at Crab Cay, the boats go to Southwest Bay for a seafood lunch, not included in the price of the tour.

Otherwise you can hire a boat for yourself at around COP$350,000 total. Upon arrival at the island, you'll be required to pay the park entry fee. All hotels can arrange this more exclusive option.

The park's **Iron Wood Hill Trail** is a three-kilometer (1.8-mile) round-trip nature trail along which you can explore the tropical dry forest landscape, and will see different types of lizards, birds, and flora. There are nice views from here of the coastline. You are required to go with a local guide arranged by the parks office (Jones Point, east of airport, tel. 8/514-8885 or 8/514-9003, www.parquesnacionales. gov.co, 8am-12:30pm and 2pm-6pm daily, COP$25,000 pp plus park entry fee).

An additional activity is to hire a **kayak** and row to Crab Cay or through the park's McBean

Lagoon mangroves. Passing through the mangroves you'll enter the **Oyster's Creek Lagoon,** where you'll see several species of birds, like blue and white herons and pelicans, as well as crabs, fish, and some unusual jellyfish. This is an interesting trip. Try to go early in the morning or late in the afternoon, as the sun can be brutal. Kayaks can be rented at the Posada Coco Bay (Maracaibo sector on the northeastern side of the island, tel. 8/514-8226, cell tel. 311/804-0373, www.posadacocobay.com, COP$30,000). A kayak with a guide costs COP$50,000, and for snorkeling equipment tack on another COP$10,000.

ENTERTAINMENT AND EVENTS
Nightlife

In Manchineel Bay, follow the reggae music down the beach and you'll discover **Roland Roots Bar** (Manchineel Bay, tel. 8/514-8417, hours vary), which will easily become one of your favorites. It is set back among coconut palms and is the perfect place to spend a lazy, sunny day in Providencia. Or go at night, when you can order your rum drink to go and walk to the beach and stargaze, or hang out by a bonfire. Roland's competition is **Richard's Place** on the beach in Southwest Bay. Both of these spots often light up bonfires on the beach on weekend nights. Both also serve food, like fried fish.

Festival del Chub

In early January of each year, the Parque Nacional Natural Old Providence McBean organizes the **Festival del Chub** (tel. 8/514-8885 or 8/514-9003). Chub is a plentiful but not very popular fish for consumption. The purpose of the festival is to encourage fishers and consumers to choose chub instead of other fish like red snapper, the stocks of which have been depleted throughout the Caribbean. There is one area of the island, Rocky Point (Punta Rocosa), where chub is widely eaten, and that is where the festival is held. In addition to an all-chub seafood festival, where you can try chub burgers and chub ceviche, there is also a sailing race from Southwest Bay to Manzanillo. It's fun to hang out at **Roland Roots Bar** (Manchineel Bay, tel. 8/514-8417) in the morning to watch the sailors ready their boats for the race. This colorful festival usually takes place on a Saturday.

RECREATION
Beaches

The best beaches on Providencia can be found generally on the western side of the island. From Manchineel Bay (Bahía Manzanillo) on the southern end to Allan or Almond Bay in the northwest, they are each worth exploring, if you have the time. On these beaches, the waters are calm, the sand golden, and there's always a refreshing breeze.

Manchineel Bay, home to Roland Roots Bar, is an exotic beach where you can relax under the shade of a palm tree. Be careful of falling coconuts. In **Southwest Bay (Suroeste),** there are a couple of hotels and restaurants nearby, and you can sometimes see horses cooling off in the water or people riding them along the shoreline. The beaches of **Freshwater**

beach in Providencia

© ANDREW DIER

Bay are very convenient to several hotels and restaurants.

The beach at **Allan Bay** (or **Almond Bay**) is more remote. It's notable for its large octopus sculpture on the side of the road (can't miss it) and nicely done walkway down to the beach from the ring road. The beach area is a public park, and there is a snack bar and stand where you can purchase handicrafts. You'll have to either drive to this beach or hitch a ride on a taxi.

A couple of coves on Santa Catalina have some secluded beaches on the path to Morgan's Head, and there is decent snorkeling nearby.

Snorkeling and Diving

Providencia, which is surrounded by a 32-kilometer-long large barrier reef, is a fantastic place to dive or to learn to dive. The water temperature is always warm, and water visibility is usually 25-35 meters (82-115 feet).

Popular diving sites are **Felipe's Place,** made up of several ledges with significant coral and marine life; **Turtle Rock,** a large rock at 20 meters covered with black coral; **Tete's Place,** teeming with fish; **Confusion,** with corals and sponges at 20-40 meters; and **Nick's Place,** a deep crack in the island's shelf that starts at 18 meters and drops to 40 meters. Good snorkeling can be done near **Cayo Cangrejo,** at the small islands of **Basalt** and **Palm Cays,** and around **Morgan's Head** in Santa Catalina, among other places.

Enjoy the Reef (Southwest Bay, cell tel. 312/325-8207) has snorkeling and diving tours for very small groups, and snorkeling tours for children.

The **Hotel Sirius** (Southwest Bay, tel. 8/514-8213, www.siriushotel.net) is serious about diving and offers a PADI certification (COP$850,000) that includes four immersions over open water during a period of five days. They also offer a mini-course (COP$185,000), which includes a double immersion excursion. Hotel Sirius's diving courses have an excellent reputation.

Hiking
THE PEAK

The Peak (El Pico) is the highest point (360 meters/1,181 feet) on Providencia, and from this mountaintop the 360-degree views are stunning. This hike takes about 1.5 hours to the top and under an hour down. The path to The Peak begins in the middle of the island and meanders along relatively well-marked trails through tropical rainforest and tropical dry forest. You'll likely come across lizards, cotton trees, and maybe a friendly dog who will follow you up to the top and back.

From the top you'll be able to see the barrier reef that extends for 32 kilometers off of the east coast of the island. This reef is the second longest in the Caribbean and is part of the Parque Nacional Natural Old Providence McBean Lagoon.

To get to the starting point, go to the Bottom House (Casa Baja) neighborhood in the southeastern corner of the island just to the east of Manchineel Bay. Although you may come across a sign pointing towards The Peak, roads are not marked very well, so you will probably have to ask for directions to get to the starting point.

At the beginning of the walk, follow a path straight ahead, veering towards the right, and five minutes later go towards the right before a two-story house. You'll then go left (not to the right of the concrete well). From here on, you will pass a small garden, then follow a rocky creek straight on, fording it back and forth several times. You'll go through a gate and eventually veer to the left as you begin climbing up the hill. After you cross over a wooden bridge the path becomes steep; hold on to the wooden handrails. Occasional signs identify some of the trees or fauna you might see along the way.

During rainy seasons, the path can become muddy and slippery. Make sure to bring a bottle of water with you. Guides are not necessary for this walk, but it's not impossible to get lost. All hotels can contract a guide for you, and this usually costs around COP$50,000.

SANTA CATALINA

From atop Santa Catalina island, English colonists and privateers once ruled, keeping their eyes peeled for potential enemies—usually the Spanish Armada or competing Dutch pirates. Today you can see some remains from 17th-century English rule at **Fort Warwick.** It is adjacent to a big rock called **Morgan's Head.** If you look hard enough, it resembles the head of Henry Morgan, the notorious Welsh pirate and admiral of the English Royal Navy who marauded the Spanish New World colonies during the mid-17th century Morgan captured Santa Catalina from the Spaniards in 1670. Morgan's Head is next to **Morgan's Cave,** where the pirate supposedly hid his loot. You can go snorkeling inside the cave along with the occasional shark. Crossing the bridge, particularly at night, you may be able to spot manta rays gracefully swimming about. Start this hike at the colorful pedestrian bridge that connects Providencia with Santa Catalina in the Santa Isabel area. Once on Santa Catalina, take a left and follow the path.

Tours

Paradise Tours (Freshwater Bay, tel. 8/514-8283, cell tel. 311/605-0750, paradisetourscontact@gmail.com) is your one-stop shop, offering tours around the island, snorkeling excursions, diving excursions, and fishing excursions. One of their popular tours is the **Reefs and Snorkeling Tour** (3-4 hours, min. 4 people, COP$85,000), during which you boat to coral reefs around the island, exploring the underwater cities that exist just below the surface. Snorkeling equipment on this tour is extra.

A double immersion diving excursion offered by the same agency costs COP$140,000, not including diving equipment, and lasts four hours. A full-day trip to El Faro reef, nine kilometers off of the island, costs COP$110,000. It's an excellent place for snorkeling in warm, crystalline waters.

On land, Paradise Tours offers several hiking options, such as to The Peak, where you can see coral reefs in the not so far distance; to Manchineel Hill, where you might see wild orchids on your way; and to the Iron Wood Hill in the Parque Nacional Natural Old Providence McBean Lagoon. These cost COP$85,000.

A popular excursion is to take a boat tour around the island. The tours, departing at around 9am and returning at 3pm, make several stops, including Crab Cay and Santa Catalina. Any hotel can assist you in arranging one, and the boats make the rounds to pick up tourists at various hotels. These tours cost around COP$35,000 per person and usually leave from Freshwater Bay. If you prefer, you can rent a boat for just yourself and your crew, but that will cost more, up to COP$350,000. But in this option, you can decide when and where to go.

ACCOMMODATIONS

Located directly over the lapping waters on the eastern side of Providencia, █ **Posada Coco Bay** (Maracaibo, tel. 8/514-8903 or 8/514-8226, posadacocobay@gmail.com, www.posadacocobay.com, COP$180,000 d) is a small guesthouse with five comfortable rooms, three of which are on the water side. The other two (more spacious) options are across the street. You can go snorkeling just outside the hotel, and you can rent kayaks here, but there is no beach. You will have to rent a golf cart or *mula* to get to island restaurants and beaches.

By far the most luxurious option on Providencia is at **Deep Blue** (Maracaibo Bay, tel. 8/514-8423, www.hoteldeepblue.com, COP$600,000 d). It has 13 luxurious rooms sloping up a hill. A deck with a small pool provides spectacular views of the water. There is no beach, and unless you plan on dining exclusively at their elegant restaurant, you will need to find transportation to get to other restaurants and beaches on the island.

The **Hotel Old Providence** (Santa Isabel, tel. 8/514-8691 or 8/514-8094, COP$100,000 d) is the only option in the "town" area of Santa Isabel. It's close to Santa Catalina and offers basic comfortable rooms with air conditioning. Breakfast is not provided.

If you'd like to stay in Santa Catalina, close to the colorful pedestrian bridge is the guesthouse **Posada Villa Santa Catalina** (Santa Catalina, tel. 8/514-8398, cell tel. 311/257-3054, villasdesantacatalina@yahoo.com, www.villasantacatalina.com, COP$50,000 pp d). It's a comfortable and clean option and has air conditioning in the room. A small beach is about a 10-minute walk away.

Somewhat far from everything is the **Posada Refugio de la Luna** (Bluff, eastern side, tel. 8/514-8460, providenciarefugiodelaluna@gmail.com, COP$170,000 d), a guesthouse with just one very comfortable and spacious room. Carmeni, the owner, is a papier-mâché artist and has her studio upstairs in the house.

The Colombian all-inclusive chain **Decameron** (Bogotá office tel. 1/219-3030, www.decameron.co) has an affiliation with four locally owned and operated guesthouses in Providencia. These are all about the same high quality: clean, comfortable, and with air conditioning. Decameron requires that you make all of your travel arrangements with them in a tourist package. In exchange for getting the rights to make reservations at these hotels Decameron helped rebuild these family-run guesthouses after Hurricane Beta damaged them and the island in 2005.

There are three Decameron affiliated hotels in Freshwater Bay. The least expensive option is simply called **Relax** (Freshwater Bay, tel. 8/514-8087, COP$80,000 pp). It has a small pool, hot water, and eight rooms, and is near a couple of restaurants and stores. It is across the road from the beach. **Miss Elma** (Freshwater Bay, tel. 8/514-8229, COP$180,000 d) has just four rooms and a restaurant on the beach, with each room overlooking the sea. **Hotel Posada del Mar** (Freshwater Bay, tel. 8/514-8052, posadadelmar@latinmail.com, www.posadadelmarprovidencia.com, COP$190,000 pp d) is a 24-room hotel with air conditioning and a pool. Oddly, instead of a beach, a grassy lawn overlooks the water. Not all rooms have a sea view.

Cabañas Miss Mary (Southwest Bay, tel. 8/514-8454, hotelmissmary@yahoo.com, COP$180,000 d) is beachside in the southwest with five beach-view rooms and three others. The restaurant is pretty good.

Hotel Sirius (Southwest Bay, tel. 8/514-8213, www.siriushotel.net, COP$250,000 d) is a beachside hotel that specializes in diving and snorkeling excursions. (But you don't have to be a diver to enjoy your stay here.) It offers some huge rooms, and the friendly manager will make every effort to ensure you have a pleasant stay in Providencia.

FOOD

Providencia is practically synonymous with fresh Caribbean seafood. A Providencia specialty is black crab. These fast-moving crabs live on the interior mountains and descend to the sea en masse once a year to lay their eggs in April or May. Many restaurants in Providencia do not accept credit cards. Hotel restaurants are open every day, while others often close on Sundays.

The **Deep Blue Hotel Restaurant** (Maracaibo Bay, tel. 8/514-8423, noon-3pm and 6pm-10pm daily, COP$35,000) is the most elegant and pricey restaurant on the island. However, menu items are innovative and beautifully presented, and the service is excellent. It's a perfect place for a romantic "last night in Providencia" meal, particularly under the stars on the dock. **Caribbean Place** (Freshwater Bay, tel. 8/514-8698, noon-3pm and 6pm-10pm Mon.-Sat., COP$25,000) is one of the best seafood places in Providencia. Try the delicious fish in ginger butter sauce or coconut shrimp, and for dessert, the coconut pie. Cheerfully decorated, it is a great choice for both lunch and dinner.

The Canadian owner of **Café Studio** (Southwest Bay on ring road, tel. 8/514-9076, 11am-10pm Mon.-Sat., COP$25,000) is likely to be found in this excellent restaurant's busy kitchen. It is a favorite not only for lunch and dinner, but also for afternoon coffee and their trademark cappuccino pie. Café Studio has a varied menu, with pastas, interesting seafood dishes, and salads.

◖**Old Providence Taste** (Old Town Bay, to the west of Santa Isabel, tel. 8/514-9028, 11:30am-3pm Mon.-Sat., COP$18,000), on the beach to the west of Santa Isabel, is run by a local sustainable seafood and farming co-op. Each day they offer a different menu, depending on what fishers and farmers bring in. It's the best deal on the island. They can also organize visits to farms and excursions with local fishers.

The **Miss Mary Hotel** (Southwest Bay, tel. 8/514-8454, noon-3pm and 6pm-9pm daily, COP$20,000) has an open-air restaurant overlooking the beach. It's a nice place for lunch.

For a pizza night, try **Blue Coral** (Freshwater Bay, tel. 8/514-8718, 11am-3pm and 6pm-9pm Mon.-Sat., COP$20,000). Though not out of this world, the pizzas and pastas here can taste exotic after several days of seafood.

For a midafternoon ice cream fix head to **Donde Puchi** (Santa Isabel, hours vary). **Miss Lucy's** (Southwest Bay, on the ring road, no phone, open daily) is a general store, but they also serve inexpensive meals, including *rondón*. It's a friendly, local hangout.

Kalaloo Point Café-Boutique (near Halley View lookout, eastern side of the island, tel. 8/514-8592) is a cute café and shop in a wooden house where you can have a cup of coffee or cool off with a Frenchy's frozen fruit bar. In the store they sell tropical dresses by a Colombian designer and various knick-knacks. There's also a small library.

A small **grocery store** (open-11pm daily) is in Freshwater Bay below the Hotel Pirata Morgan.

INFORMATION AND SERVICES

There is a **tourist office** (Santa Isabel, tel. 8/514-8054, ext. 12, www.providencia.gov. co, 8am-noon and 2pm-6pm Mon.-Fri.) in the town area near the port. They may be able to assist with accommodations, including *posadas nativas* (guesthouses owned and operated by locals), and give you some maps. A bank, ATM, and Internet café are in the town. Since 2013, there is free wireless Internet on the island.

In case of an emergency the police can be reached at 112 or 8/514-8000. For medical emergencies, call 125.

GETTING THERE AND AROUND

There are two ways to travel to Providencia: by plane or by fast catamaran boat service from San Andrés. There are three daily flights on **Satena** (Centro Comercial New Point, Local 206, San Andrés, tel. 8/512-1403; Aeropuerto El Embrujo, Providencia, tel. 8/514-9257, www.satena.com). Charter flights are usually organized by Decameron (Colombian toll-free tel. 01/800-051-0765, www.decameron.co) from San Andrés to Providencia. All flights are on small propeller planes, and there are strict weight limitations. Passengers are only allowed 10 kilograms (22 pounds) in their checked baggage, and each passenger is required to be weighed upon check in along with their carry-on bag, which makes for an amusing photo op. The average weight per passenger cannot exceed 80 kilograms (176 pounds), including luggage. The flight takes about 25 minutes. The airport in Providencia is called **Aeropuerto El Embrujo** (tel. 8/514-8176, ext. 6528). It is on the northeast side of the island near the Parque Nacional Natural Old Providence McBean Lagoon.

The **Catamaran Sensation** (tel. 8/512-5124, www.elsensation.com, COP$65,000 one-way) provides fast boat service (three hours) between San Andrés and Providencia. It provides service on Sunday, Wednesday, and Friday during low season. There is greater frecuency during high season. Boats leave San Andrés at 7:30am from the Casa de la Cultura near the Hotel Arena Blanca and leave Providencia from the docks in Santa Isabel at 3:30pm. The catamaran service, while cheaper than air travel, often gets ghastly reviews due to the rough seas and resulting seasickness among the passengers. When the winds are strong and the waters are choppy between the two islands, especially between June and July and again in December and January, the ride can be extremely rough, requiring boat attendants to constantly circulate among the passengers to distribute sea sickness bags. This is especially true on the San Andrés to Providencia leg. Waters are normally calmer the other way around.

Taxis are expensive in Providencia, costing around COP$20,000 no matter where you go.

Mototaxis (motorcycle taxis) are much cheaper and you can find them almost anywhere. You can also flag down passing vehicles and hitchhike (paying a small fee). As in San Andrés, you can rent golf carts and *mulas* (gasoline-powered golf carts) in Providencia. All hotels can arrange this for you. They cost around COP$120,000 for one day.

THE AMAZON AND LOS LLANOS

The Amazon and Los Llanos cover the eastern two-thirds of the country, a vast territory with very little population. Topographically they are the same: low-lying undulating terrain that is periodically flooded. But because of soil and climate, they have evolved different vegetation: dense rainforest in the Amazon and lush tropical savannahs in Los Llanos. The main draw in

HIGHLIGHTS

LOOK FOR ◖ TO FIND RECOMMENDED SIGHTS, ACTIVITIES, DINING, AND LODGING.

◖ **San Martín de Amacayacu:** Experience life in this Ticuna village in the brimming-with-vitality Parque National Natural Amacayacu (page 414).

◖ **Puerto Nariño:** No freeways, no traffic jams, no honking horns: In this eco-minded indigenous town overlooking the Río Loretoyaco, life is peaceful and the air is always pure (page 414).

◖ **Lago Tarapoto:** Pink dolphins perform for you in their natural habitat, and you can finally overcome your long-held piranha-phobia by taking a dip in this serene lake surrounded by lush jungle near Puerto Nariño (page 415).

◖ **Río Yavarí:** Spend a few days under the immense Amazon rainforest canopy at a spectacular eco-lodge (page 417).

◖ **Caño Cristales:** Nature shows its psychedelic side at this stream of vibrant colors in the vast Llanos (page 423).

◖ **Hacienda La Aurora:** Take a safari on horseback through this enormous cattle ranch cum nature reserve in the heart of the Llanos and be astounded by the abundant wildlife. If you're lucky(!), you may even come across an anaconda (page 425).

both the Amazon and Los Llanos is the unique natural landscapes and the magnificent wildlife inhabiting them.

A trip to the Amazon is a highlight not only to any visit to Colombia, but a highlight in any person's life. The survival of this vast ecosystem, the preservation of which is by no means assured, is of great importance to humanity. Learning about its variety of plants and animals, how it acts to stabilize the world's climate, how indigenous people managed to make a home there for thousands of years without disturbing its balance, and how modern civilization is threatening to destroy it is fascinating. Long after an introduction to Amazonia,

one can't help reflecting on its significance for all of humanity.

This vast terrain of undulating hills and savannahs, with large patches of forest, abounds with wildlife: *chigüiros* (capybaras), deer, armadillos, sloths, anteaters, monkeys, anacondas, and an infinity of birds. Sadly, advancing human settlement and hunting have decimated much of it, but at places like Hacienda La Aurora you can view this wondrous wildlife in all its glory.

The Llanos is synonymous with cattle ranching and the cowboy way of life. If you are not squeamish, viewing traditional cattle-ranching activities, such as herding and

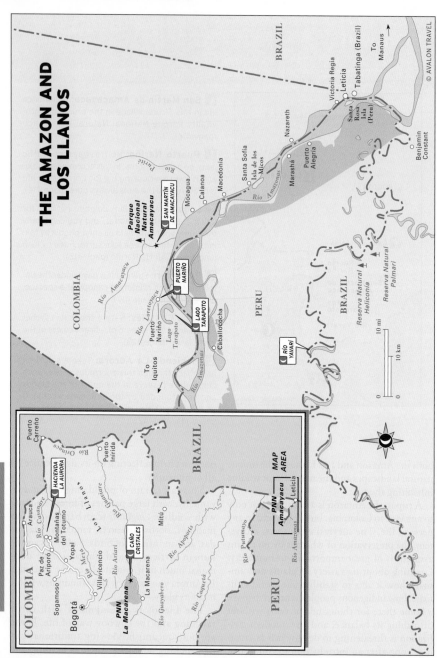

THE AMAZON AND LOS LLANOS

© AVALON TRAVEL

branding calves, as they have been done for centuries by *llaneros* (plainsmen), is an essential Llanos experience. Finally, the Llanos is home to a natural wonder not to be found anywhere else in the world: the vivid red, purple, yellow, and green streams of Caño Cristales in the southern extreme of the remote Serranía de la Macarena.

PLANNING YOUR TIME

Traveling in the Amazon and Los Llanos entails long-distance travel, mostly point to point from Bogotá by airplane, and is therefore more expensive. To visit the Amazon, at least five days are required, and more if you want to spend some time in a nature reserve in the rainforest. The destinations in Los Llanos—Caño Cristales and Hacienda La Aurora—could be

done in three days, though ideally you would want to spend more time there.

Though the Amazon rainforest covers about one-third of the country east of the Andes and south of the Río Guaviare, the only real option to visit it is from the Amazon port city of Leticia, which has a multitude of options and ecotourism operators. The rest of the Colombian Amazon simply does not have even the minimum infrastructure to accommodate an independent traveler, and the region may be unsafe.

The great eastern plains of Colombia, Los Llanos, which comprise a further third of the country east of the Andes and north of the Río Guaviare, are the least explored region of the country. The reason is simply a lack of infrastructure, along with, until recently, security concerns.

The Amazon

Covering an expanse of 8.2 million square kilometers (3.2 million square miles), the Amazon rainforest is the largest humid tropical forest in the world. Rainforests are important because of the enormous biodiversity that they sustain. And among rainforests, the New World rainforests are the most biodiverse. In fact, the Amazon jungle is home to one-tenth of all species on Earth, though it occupies only 1.6 percent of the world's surface. It holds more than 40,000 plant species, 3,000 fish species, 1,300 bird species, 428 mammal species, and 380 reptile species. By contrast, all of Canada, which occupies a surface larger than the Amazon rainforest, has 3,270 plant species, 1,100 fish species, 838 bird species, 188 reptile species, and 180 mammal species. Rainforests are also important as the world's main "lungs," sucking in vast amounts of carbon dioxide through photosynthesis. Their ongoing destruction means the loss of invaluable biodiversity and increased warming.

The formation of the Amazon basin started about 180 million years ago, in the Jurassic era, when the westerly drifting American

Continental Plate (South America) collided with the Nazca Plate (under the Pacific Ocean), forming the Andes. Water flowing eastward down the mountains accumulated in a vast freshwater lake that was hemmed in on the east by old mountainous formations (now the Guyana and Brazilian highlands). Large amounts of sediments were deposited, forming the basis for the Amazon's undulated topography. Around 28 million years ago, the water broke through the eastern mountain barrier and started flowing east into the Atlantic, forming the Amazon drainage basin.

The Amazon River (Río Amazonas), which measures about 6,400 kilometers (4,000 miles) in length, is fed by more than 1,000 tributaries. Though Colombia only has 180 kilometers (112 miles) on the Amazon river itself, several of its major rivers originate and flow through the Colombian Amazon region into the mighty river, including the Putumayo and the Caquetá. It is estimated that one-fifth of all the water that runs off the Earth's surface flows through this basin. The gradient is very slight: Leticia, which is more than 2,000 kilometers (1,200

a rainy trip on the Amazon

© ANDREW DIER

miles) from the mouth of the river, stands at an elevation of 96 meters (315 feet). During the annual flood, lasting from November to April, the river can rise up to 50 meters (165 feet), submerging large sections of the jungle. Average river velocity is 1.5 kilometers per hour (0.9 miles per hour), though it increases slightly with the flooding.

The topography of the Amazon consists of two distinct but intermingled areas: *terra firme,* the undulated lands that are above the highest flood point (which comprise two-thirds of the surface of the basin), and *varzea,* floodplains along the main rivers, which can extend up to 50 kilometers (30 miles) from the river. *Varzea,* rich in sediments transported by the rivers, is where most human activity is concentrated.

There are two distinct types of rivers in the Amazon region: the predominant white rivers, which carry sediments down from the Andes, and the black rivers, which originate in the Guyanese and Brazilian highlands that were long ago denuded of soil due to erosion. As these waters travel through the flooded forest,

they pick up pigments that give them their characteristic black color. *Igapó* is the name given to jungles flooded by black-water rivers. The largest of the black rivers, and the largest tributary of the Amazon, is the Río Negro, called Río Guainía in Colombia. It flows into the Amazon at Manaus, creating the extraordinary *encontro das aguas,* where white and black waters flow side by side for several kilometers until they mix.

The forest itself has a complex, layered structure. Towering trees, held up by complex buttresses at the base of the trunks, soar 40 meters (130 feet) high, forming the jungle's canopy. Occasionally, trees known as *emergentes* rise above the canopy to a height of 60 meters (200 feet). According to a Ticuna myth, a giant fallen ceiba tree is the origin of the Amazon River. The canopy, flooded by sunlight, is full of plant and animal life. If you don't suffer from vertigo, a climb up to the canopy is an unforgettable experience. Below the canopy, shade tolerant species of trees and plants comprise the underbrush (*sotobosque*) and support

Explorers in the Amazon

The first Europeans to travel to the Amazon were Spanish conquistadors Gonzalo Pizarro (half brother of Francisco Pizarro, the infamous conqueror of Peru) and Francisco de Orellana, who, in 1541, headed down the Río Napo in present-day Ecuador to search for the mythical "Land of Cinnamon." Pizarro, frustrated, turned back after one year. Orellana followed the course of the Napo, eventually floating down the entire course of the Amazon to its mouth in the Atlantic. Reportedly, he was attacked by women warriors and hence the region came to be named after the Amazons of Greek mythology.

During the colonial period, the Spaniards largely ignored the region as there were no ready sources of riches. French naturalist Charles Marie de la Condamine was the first European scientific explorer to visit the region. In 1743, he traversed the entire basin, discovering, among other things, quinine and latex (for rubber). Another notable explorer was Alexander von Humboldt, who visited the Casiquiare Canal, which links the Río Orinoco and Río Negro, in 1800. It is located in southern Venezuela.

many epiphytes (plants that live on others), such as orchids and bromeliads. Large networks of vines entangle the growth.

The waters of the Amazon are home to more than 1,500 species of fish, including the endangered pirarucú, one of the largest freshwater fishes on Earth, and notorious meat-eating piranha. They are also home to dolphins, both pink and gray. Pink dolphins evolved separately and have horizontal neck mobility that allows them to navigate the flooded forest easily, while gray dolphins are distant relations of the seafaring kind. Other aquatic mammals include manatees and *nutrias* (otters). There are dozens of species of turtles, alligators, lizards, snakes, and frogs. Land-faring mammals include deer, anteaters, armadillos, tapirs, jaguars, ocelots, and pumas, though sighting of these large cats is quite rare. The trees support sloths, squirrels, and many species of moneys and bats. With more than 3,000 species of birds, the Amazon is truly a bird-watcher's paradise. During the floods, a canoe ride through the partially submerged trees will allow you to spot a variety of birds, including herons, kingfishers, ducks, woodpeckers, oropendulas, kiskadees, and hawks. Finally, there are innumerable insects, including giant leaf-cutting ants, as well as centipedes and scorpions.

To truly get a sense of the place, you need to get into the jungle, either by doing a trek or taking canoe rides in the flooded jungle. Then, the small details that make up this wonderland will come into focus: a ray of sun shining through the canopy; a massive, 40-meter-high ceiba tree; a vine that has wound itself around a tree like a boa constrictor; an orange mushroom popping up from a fallen tree, accelerating its final stage of decay; a single bright blue butterfly that crosses your path momentarily and then flutters away; a leaf as big as your head floating down to the ground; a whimsical song from a bird somewhere above in the canopy.

History

During the 20th century, settlement has been mostly limited to a swath of jungle in the Caquetá and Putumayo departments near the Andes. There, oil and plentiful land have attracted settlers from the interior of the country. However, the sheer inaccessibility of most of the Colombian jungle has spared the type of development seen in Brazil. During the drug wars of the 1990s and early 2000s, coca cultivation spread deeper into the jungle in the departments of Caquetá, Putumayo, Guaviare, and Vaupés, bringing along the FARC, and Leticia became a center for drug trafficking. At present much of the Amazonian drug business appears to have shifted to the Peruvian side of the river.

Climate

It is always muggy in the Amazon, and rarely is there a breeze to provide some relief to the heat. The border town of Leticia reports an average 85 percent humidity year-round with an average temperature of 25.8°C (78.4°F). The region has one dry season, between June and August, and one rainy season, between January and May. In August it can rain as little as 10 days per month. During the dry season, rivers shrink, creating beaches, and trees and shrubs appear in parts of the jungle that during the rainy season are hidden under water.

During the rainy season, water falls from the skies and pours down from the Andes into the mighty river, and canoes become the only means of getting from point A to point B in the jungle. You can glide in canoes through the treetops, an unforgettable experience. Ponchos, rubber boots, and insect repellent are especially critical during the rainy season.

Environmental Threats

Unfortunately, this diverse ecosystem is under severe threat. Over the past 40 years, 20 percent of the Amazon jungle has been destroyed. If strong measures are not taken, half of what remains could be destroyed within the next few decades. The main causes of the destruction (in order of importance) are cattle ranching, agriculture, dams, and illegal mining. The main means for its destruction are roads. Without these, human encroachment is limited to the borders of navigable rivers. Voracious, short-sighted development in Brazil, where road development has been greatest, is the main cause of the destruction of this wonderland. Though the Brazilian authorities tout decreasing levels of deforestation, the roads crisscrossing the jungle have made irreparable damage inevitable. Significant deforestation has also occurred along the Andes piedmont, especially in the headwaters of the Caquetá and Putumayo

rivers in Colombia, where illegal coca cultivation has been one of the main culprits.

There is alarming evidence that, as deforestation progresses, the Amazon ecosystem is breaking down and will be unable to sustain itself. With deforestation comes lower evaporation and rainfall. As the forest dries up, it may become prone to fires (which it is not currently), changing the overall dynamics. The Amazon has not yet reached that scary "tipping point" after which it cannot sustain itself, but vastly reduced measured rainfall points in that direction.

Though the Colombian section of the Amazon rainforest represents only 10 percent of the total, it is the best preserved, due to a dearth of roads, and also the most likely to be preserved thanks to enlightened policies. From 1986 to 1990, President Virgilio Barco transferred 163,000 square kilometers (63,000 square miles—twice the surface of Austria or 15 percent of Colombia) to national parks and indigenous *resguardos* (land collectively owned by indigenous groups) and protected areas. Predio Putumayo, the largest *resguardo,* measures 59,000 square kilometers (23,000 square miles), the size of Costa Rica. Subsequent governments have continued to expand the protected areas, and now at least 65 percent of all the Colombia Amazon is a protected area, either through the system of national parks or through indigenous *resguardos.*

The 1991 constitution enshrined significant rights for Colombia's indigenous peoples, adding further protections. Though the threat of illegal logging and mining is ever present, particularly due to the presence of valuable rare earth minerals, Colombia seems to have taken successful steps to preserve a large section of one of the world's most important ecosystems.

In 2013, the Colombian government took a positive step by more than doubling the size of its Parque Nacional Natural Serranía de Chiribiquete, in the Amazon departments of Caquetá and Guaviare, to over 28,000 square kilometers (11,000 square miles). It is the largest national park in Colombia.

The Peruvian Amazon Company

The Colombian section of the Amazon was largely untouched until the mid-19th century, when quinine and then rubber extraction attracted Colombian and Peruvian adventurers. Vast tracts of land with rubber trees and plentiful indigenous labor seemed like a perfect combination to make a fortune. In 1901, Julio César Arana, a Peruvian *cauchero* (rubber baron), founded the Casa Arana, a company that operated a ruthless system of rubber extraction based on torture and slavery. The company, later known as the Peruvian Amazon Company headquartered in London, operated out of La Chorrera on the Río Putumayo. A visiting American, W. E. Hardenburg, witnessed the horrors and in 1909 published a damning article in the British magazine *Truth*. This prompted the British government to order an inquiry, which uncovered the terrible conditions. In 1912, Parliament opened an investigation, which cleared the British Board of Directors of all responsibility in the atrocities. At the same time they determined that over 32,000 Huitoto people had been murdered or worked to death during a five-year period. Huitoto leaders estimate that over 80,000 were killed between 1912 and 1929.

The Peruvian Amazon Company was liquidated in 1916, but, incredibly, Arana continued operations through the 1930s. It was not until 2012 that the Colombian government formally apologized to the indigenous people for these atrocities in a letter by President Santos at a ceremony in La Chorrera commemorating the 100th anniversary of the genocide.

LETICIA

Visitors come to Leticia to experience the jungle. This border town of 40,000 doesn't have much in the way of charm, and it's clogged with buzzing motorbikes, but, alas, all is not lost here. It has improved since the 1970s and 1980s when it was synonymous with cocaine and exotic animal trafficking. During that anything-goes time, poor native villagers would catch monkeys (to be sent to labs and zoos) in exchange for clothes, and unknown and fierce-looking men would routinely zoom up and down the river in speedboats to unknown destinations.

Today, without a doubt, ecotourism is the future for Leticia, and more and more Colombians and visitors from abroad are discovering the area, for better or for worse. There was a 300 percent increase in visitors to Leticia between 2002 and 2006.

A handful of sights worth checking out in town and along the Kilometers road will keep you occupied for a couple of days, and there are comfortable accommodations options. But best of all, it is close to the jungle and the Río Amazonas is always at the ready to take you there.

It is possible to book package tours that include all the sights and take care of your accommodations. However, a growing number of visitors explore the jungle independently. Leticia is an excellent base for that.

ORIENTATION

Leticia, the capital city of the Amazonas department of Colombia, is the southernmost city in the country, and it sits on the northern side of the Río Amazonas at the convergence of Colombia with Brazil and Peru. It is 1,100 kilometers (700 miles) southeast of Bogotá. It borders the grubby Brazilian town of Tabatinga to the east, and Isla de Santa Rosa (Peru) is an island in the river to Leticia's south. Just to the north of the city the town abruptly ends and the rainforest takes over—no suburbs here. The closest Colombian town of any significance is Puerto Nariño, 87 kilometers (54 miles) to the northwest.

Leticia is laid out on a grid that is easy to figure out. The airport is north of town on the Avenida Vásquez Cobo, which turns into Carrera 10, one of the main drags in town. *Carreras* run north-south with *calles* going from

© ANDREW DIER

breakdancers in Leticia

east to west. The *malecón,* from where all boats depart, is on the eastern side of town at the end of Calle 8. Carretera Los Kilómetros, also called Vía a Tarapaca, leads to Mundo Amazónico and the Reserva Natural Tanimboca. There are some Huitoto settlements beyond those attractions, and then the road abruptly stops, surrendering to the jungle.

Sights

Occupying just one (air-conditioned!) room in the red **Banco de la República** building, the **Museo Etnográfico de Leticia** (Cra. 11 No. 9-43, tel. 8/592-7783, 8:30am-6pm Mon.-Fri., 9am-1pm Sat., www.banrepcultural.org/leticia, free) provides a good introduction to the traditions and ways of life of some of the main indigenous people who live in the Colombian Amazon region, including the Ticunas, the Huitotos, and the Yukunas. Colorful feather crowns made of *guacamaya* (macaw) feathers and descriptions of *chagras* (islands of small vegetable plots in the middle of the jungle) and *malocas* (community

houses) are part of the exhibit. Explanations are provided in both Spanish and English. Sometimes art exhibits and other events are held in the building as well.

The **Parque Santander** (between Cras. 10-11 and Clls. 10-11) is a quiet place where unoccupied locals go for a brief reprieve from the intense midday sun. That is, it's quiet until around 5:30 each evening, when thousands of *loros* (parrots) gather in the trees. It's a cacophonous racket. At 6pm on the dot, the Colombian national anthem blares from the loudspeakers from the military base facing the park. People stop what they are doing and stand at attention. The birds, however, have no such respect. They won't quiet down for anyone! The *loros* have not always been here and are not native to the area. Some say that eccentric American hotel owner, anaconda wrestler, and convicted drug trafficker Mike Tsalickis released them in the park during his final days in Leticia in the 1980s.

The **Muelle Turístico** (Cra. 11 at Cl. 8), also known as the *malecón,* is a busy bus station on water. It once faced a broad channel into the Amazon, but the current has brought sediments, creating a new island in front called, paradoxically, Isla de la Fantasía (it's a grubby neighborhood). During dry season, the channel closes for navigation and passengers must tramp across the island to embark. The port is seedy and grimy but 100 percent authentic. It's a real clash of cultures here, as tourists await their river tours while villagers, hailing from the very places the tourists will visit, arrive in the city to stock up on supplies. For any trip along the Amazon, including to the Peruvian town of Santa Rosa, you'll leave from here.

If you are interested in learning more about some of the medicinal plants, fruits, and trees you will see in the Amazon, a visit to the **Mundo Amazónico** (Km. 7.7 Vía a Tarapacá, tel. 8/592-6087, www.mundoamazonico.com, 8am-2pm daily, four-trail tour COP$36,000, one-trail tour COP$10,000) is a must. In the park you can take a walk among exotic fruit trees (like *copoazú*) found in the area, learn about indigenous farming techniques, see some medicinal plants found in the rainforest, and see unusual fish, reptiles, and amphibians in the aquarium and terrarium area. On this last tour you can observe the prehistoric-looking *mata-mata* turtle. Each guided tour takes 30-45 minutes. However, if you are in a hurry, you can request to take just one tour or do a fast trek around the park. Rafael Clavijo, the owner of the park, is a dedicated environmentalist, is knowledgeable about the flora and fauna of the Amazon, and speaks English. It is easy to take public transportation to the park. Look for a green Kilometer 11 bus (not towards Lagos) departing from the Parque Orellana (Cra. 11 between Clls. 7-8) across from the Hotel Anaconda. The bus costs only COP$2,000. (The trip costs COP$15,000 by *moto-taxi*.) Tell the bus driver you'd like to be dropped off at Mundo Amazónico. It is a pleasant 10- to 15-minute walk from the road to the park entrance. You can inquire about day-trip excursions on offer.

The **Reserva Natural Tanimboca** (Carretera Los Kilómetros/Vía a Tarapaca, office Cra. 10

Border Disputes

During the 19th and early 20th centuries, the border between Ecuador, Peru, and Colombia was a matter of dispute. In 1922, Colombia and Peru signed the Salomón-Lozano Treaty, settling their common border at the expense of Ecuador. In 1932, a group of Peruvian civilians and some soldiers occupied Leticia. It is not clear whether the Peruvian government supported this attack. The occupation of Leticia led to a war in which both countries scrambled to get troops to this remote area. In 1932, Peru took the remote town of Tarapacá. In 1933, Colombia sent a fleet up the Amazon (including two new warships purchased from France), retook Tarapacá, and captured the Peruvian town of Güeppi. As troops from both countries were preparing for a major confrontation, the League of Nations brokered a truce on May 24, 1932. This was the first time that the League, precursor to the United Nations, actively intervened in a dispute between two countries. On June 19, Peru returned Leticia to Colombia.

No. 11-69, tel. 8/592-7679, www.tanimboca. com) is a nature reserve and lodge and is the best place close to Leticia where you can gain a real appreciation for the Amazonian jungle. Once there you can marvel at the stunning *maloca* (community house) that they have built, check out the serpentarium, take a jungle walk, kayak, and experience the jungle from above by canopying. They also have some truly spectacular accommodations options. Spend the night 12 meters (40 feet) high in one of their three treehouses in the *dosel* (canopy). Up above it's just you in the canopy, and thousands upon thousands of chatty jungle creatures. Although you may not be interested in long-term rental, these small thatched houses are comfortable and come equipped with a toilet. (You can also sleep in a hammock in the *maloca*.) Included in your treehouse stay is a nocturnal jungle walk. Local cuisine, mostly grilled fish, is served at their restaurant. Tanimboca also organizes excellent multi-day tours of the Amazon region.

The reserve is on the Kilometers road, about 15 minutes from town. It is accessible by the Kilometers public bus, which leaves from across the Hotel Anaconda.

Across the Peruvian border is privately owned **Reserva Natural Marashá** (Cra. 10 No. 7-55, tel. 8/592-5622, www.reservamarasha.com, COP$225,000 pp, all meals and activities included). It offers a range of ecotourism activities and is 25 kilometers (15 miles) from Leticia, so it can be easily visited as a day trip. The standard day trip includes excursions in kayaks or canoes and various nature walks. Lunch and transportation from Leticia and back is also included. Seven cabins can lodge 2-15 people. Conveniently located near Leticia, Marashá is a good alternative to more remote reserves in the Río Yavarí area.

Festivals and Events

From around the 15th of July to the 20th, the **Festival de Confraternidad Amazónica** has been going strong since 1987 and is a celebration of Amazonian culture and friendship between the three neighboring countries of Colombia, Brazil, and Peru.

You have to like events that celebrate fish, especially ugly three-meter-long ones! The **Festival Pirarucú de Oro** takes place over three days at the end of November and beginning of December. It is more formally known as the **Festival Internacional de Música Popular Amazonense.** Named in honor of the enormous pirarucú river fish, this is actually a cultural festival with numerous musical and dance performances.

Shopping

The **Mercado Municipal** (Cl. 8 at Cra. 12, 7am-3pm daily) is a good place to pick up rubber boots or other gear for any jungle trip. (Many reserves and travel agencies can either rent or loan you a pair, so find out beforehand.) As you're trying on rubber boots, make sure they are easy to take off. Always shake out your socks, shoes, and boots before putting them on in the jungle. In the food section of the market, you can pick up some fruit or a dirt cheap meal.

The **Museo Uirapuru** (Cl. 8 No. 10-35, tel. 8/592-7056, 9am-noon and 3pm-7pm Mon.-Sat., 9am-noon Sun.) is more a handicraft store than museum, although you can take a look at various river creatures in aquariums and snakes in jars in the back. Traditional medicines are also sold here.

Recreation

TOURS

Tour companies based in Leticia or Bogotá offer a wide range of tour packages, from day trips to week-long packages. Hotels and hostels can organize these packages as well, or at least refer you to a tour agency.

One-day tours leaving from Leticia are a popular option for exploring the Amazon. These tours hit all the major sights: Victoria Regia, Isla de los Micos, Macedonia, Puerto Alegría, and Lago Tarapoto along the river from Leticia to Puerto Nariño. These cost around COP$170,000 each, depending on how many people are in the tour group. Tours leave Leticia at about 7am, returning at 5:30pm. You can also do a half-day tour, which does not include Puerto Nariño. This will cost around COP$60,000-80,000 depending on your negotiating skills.

A three-day tour may be a good option if you have limited time and would rather not have to worry about organizing things on your own. Before booking a package tour, find out where you'll be overnighting. Some tours may have you spending several nights in Leticia. It's OK to spend a night or two in dusty Leticia, but to get a real taste of the Amazon you really need to get to the jungle!

Ecodestinos (Cl. 8 No. 7-99, Local 2, Leticia, tel. 8/592-4816; Cra. 70H No. 127A-72, Bogotá, tel. 1/608-8031, www.ecodestinos.com.co) is affiliated with Aviatur, one of the top travel agencies in Colombia, popular with Colombian tourists. They offer various package tours of the Amazon. Their "Amazonas Selva y Río" tour starts at COP$598,000 per person and includes two nights accommodations in Leticia, all meals, and tours to Puerto Nariño, Lago Tarapoto, Parque Amacayacu, and Ticuna villages. The Ecodestinos website has an extensive listing of their offers, and these can be booked online. There are also some day-trip excursions, such as kayak tours (COP$75,000 pp) near Leticia, for those who are traveling independently.

Yurupary Amazonastours (Cl. 8 No. 7-26, tel. 8/592-4743, www.hotelyurupary.com) is affiliated with the Hotel Yurupary. A four-day, three-night package including a stay at their lodge on the Peru side of the Río Yavarí starts at COP$640,000 per person. In addition, they offer full-day tours on the river that cost about COP$117,000 (for groups of four or more) and half-day tours (COP$99,000) by land to a Huitoto community that include a nature walk.

Tanimboca (www.tanimboca.org, tel. 8/592-7679) is affiliated with the Reserva Natural Tanimboca in the jungle just outside of Leticia. Package tours with Tanimboca include jungle walks, a couple of nights in their fabulous treehouses at their reserve, and overnight visits to Puerto Nariño and to the Marashá reserve in Peru. They offer mostly private or small group tours. For a stay of five days and four nights, including activities, expect to pay around COP$1,300,000 per person. They can also arrange private one-day tours on the river. Tanimboca is a highly recommended and reputable agency.

Accommodations

Surprisingly, there are very good accommodations options, for all budgets, in Leticia. All of these are owned and managed by Colombians from other parts of the country or by Europeans.

Apaporis Hostel (Cra. 10 No. 6-17, cell tel. 312/522-0446 or 311/886-5996, COP$20,000 dorm, COP$35,000 d) is a small, sparkling clean hostel on a quiet street. It has one dormitory room, two private rooms, a kitchen, and a garden (including a small organic vegetable garden) out back. It's owned by Elizabeth, a young Colombian entrepreneur. The largest hostel you probably ever have seen just might be **Mahatu Jungle Guesthouse** (Cl. 7 No. 1-40, tel. 8/592-7384, cell tel.

311/539-1265, www.mahatu.org, COP$25,000 dorm, COP$60,000 d), literally straddling the Brazilian border. It's run by the affable Gustavo Alvarado, and you feel like you're in the country here. It is a peaceful, green place with dorm accommodations and private rooms spread out on a huge property that has a pool and two lakes! You can even take out a paddleboat for a quick spin. There's no shortage of hammocks around here. It's about a 15-minute walk into town from the hostel.

Run by a Swiss-Colombian couple, **La Jangada Hospedaje** (Cra. 9 No. 8-106, cell tel. 311/498-5447, http://la-jangada-hostel.minihostels.com, COP$25,000 dorm, COP$70,000 d) is a friendly hostel option in town. They have an extensive program of day trips from which to choose.

Waira (Cra. 10 No. 7-36, tel. 8/592-4428, www.wairahotel.com.co, COP$148,000 d) is a midrange option that caters to Colombian tourists. It looks swanky from the outside, but its 41 rooms are on the small side. Wireless Internet and air conditioning are available. The **Hotel Anaconda** (Cra. 15 No. 93-75, tel. 8/218-0125, www.hotelanaconda.com.co, COP$160,000 pp) was one of the first hotels in Leticia and has been in operation for years. The 50 air-conditioned rooms are large, there is wireless Internet in the lobby, and a restaurant is on-site. It's no longer the swank hotel it may have once been, but it's in the heart of town and they have a big pool and a poolside bar! If you're not staying here and want to cool off you can get a day pass that costs COP$12,000. Note that per person room rates decrease as the number of guests increases.

An excellent choice in Leticia is the friendly and professionally run **Amazon B&B** (Cl. 12 No. 9-30, tel. 8/592-4981, www.theamazonbb. com, COP$216,000 d). It's on a quiet street away from the bustle of the city but within easy walking distance to restaurants and services at the same time. It's a popular place for a good rest before and/or after a few days in the jungle. There's no air conditioning in the six *cabañas* (they have fans), but they are modern and tastefully decorated. Breakfast is included.

They also offer Spanish classes and can arrange all sorts of excursions for you. **Hospedaje Los Delfines** (Cra. 9 No. 12-81, tel. 8/592-7488, COP$70,000 d) has wireless Internet, but there's no air conditioning, and breakfast is not included.

The crème de la crème of hotels in Leticia is the all-inclusive **Decameron Decalodge Tikuna** (Cra. 11 No. 6-11, tel. 8/592-6600, www.decameron.com, COP$520,000 d). It's a spacious place with a very good open-air restaurant (open to non-guests) where you dine under a gigantic green anaconda-like snake. There's even a vegetarian menu. Facilities are nice here: a swimming pool, a *maloca* (community house), and tastefully done *cabañas* complete with comfy beds and hammocks. The hotel organizes excursions and activities, so you don't have to plan anything! Internet is expensive here.

The **Omshanty Jungle Lodge** (Km. 11 Vía Leticia-Tarapacá, cell tel. 311/489-8985, www.omshanty.com, COP$15,000 dorm, COP$55,000 d) is north of Leticia and offers clean dorm-style accommodations as well as private rooms. It's really in the jungle! You can cook meals in their kitchen, and there are some small mom-and-pop restaurants across the street. Efficient and inexpensive public transportation is available. The lodge can also organize stays in nearby indigenous communities. The lodge is just before the Reserva Natural Tanimboca.

Food

Leticia is not a culinary capital, but it is the place to sample some unusual Amazonian dishes. The standard Amazon meal includes fried fish, cassava, rice, *patacones* (fried plantains), and perhaps a small salad. Pirarucú is the king of fish around here. It is one of the largest fish in the world, reaching up to three meters (10 feet) long and 350 kilograms (770 pounds). This fish is threatened, and regional governments have banned its fishing and consumption from November to March. You may not see it in the wild, although it does pop up to the surface to breathe every 15 minutes. You

have a reasonably good chance, however, of hearing it. It makes a deep bellowing sound that echoes across the river. A particular dish popular here is the *patarasca,* which is two types of fish, usually *dorado* and *pintado,* grilled with herbs and vegetables in banana leaves. This is accompanied by a juice such as *copoazú* or the ever-popular Brazilian beer.

C El Cielo (Cl. 7 No. 6-50, cell tel. 312/351-0427, 4pm-11pm Mon., Wed., and Fri., 11am-5pm Sun., COP$20,000) has the most interesting menu in town: Amazon fusion. They make pizza dough out of cassava flour, and Amazonian ants and *mojojoy* (worms) may appear as ingredients in some dishes on the menu. There are vegetarian dishes like crêpes and lasagnas as well, and the cocktails are fine.

With dusty handicrafts from the Amazon adorning its walls, **Tierras Amazónicas** (Cl. 8 No. 7-50, hours vary Tues.-Sun., COP$20,000) strives to be Leticia's version of the famous Andrés Carne de Res in Bogotá. Some of the unusual dishes you can order here include *chicharrón de pirarucú,* which are sort of like fish nuggets, and pirarucú steamed in banana leaf. Big lemonades (to complement the big food portions) here hit the spot. There's not much for vegetarians here. Sometimes they have live music to satisfy both Brazilian and Colombian tastes.

El Abuelo (Cra. 11 at Cl. 7, no phone, set lunches COP$12,000) is a popular place with locals. It serves up the usual seafood dishes. **El Sabor** (Cl. 8 No. 9-25, tel. 8/592-4774, set lunch COP$12,000) has inexpensive and tasty set lunches.

The only place in town where you'll find burritos, cheesy crêpes, and other fast food is **Amektiar** (Cl. 9 No. 8-15, tel. 8/592-6094, 4pm-midnight). Across from Parque Santander, **Casa del Pan** (Cl. 11 No. 10-20, 6:30am-11pm Mon.-Sat.) is Leticia's version of Starbucks, a place for breakfast and a carb fix after a day in the jungle. It also serves refreshing lemonades and juices. At **Barbacoas** (Cra. 10 No. 8-28, daily) you can pick up a coffee and light breakfast in the morning, and at night have a beer and watch locals play pool.

Supermercado Hiper Kosto (Cl. 8 No. 9-31, tel. 8/592-8067) is a very basic grocery store where you can stock up on jungle provisions.

Information and Services

VISAS AND OFFICIALDOM

To travel to Tabatinga, Brazil, or Santa Rosa, Peru, for the day, or for stops at Peruvian villages on the way to Puerto Nariño, there is no need for immigration formalities, but it's a good idea to carry your passport with you just in case.

If you are traveling on to destinations in the interior of Brazil or Peru from Leticia, you must obtain an exit stamp at the Migración Colombia office at Aeropuerto Internacional Vásquez Cobo (3 km north of town, tel. 8/592-4562). There is a **Migración Colombia** (Cl. 9 No. 9-62, tel. 8/592-6001) office in town, but it does not provide entry or exit stamps for visitors. This office mainly provides services for Colombian citizens or non-Colombian residents.

Once you get your passport stamped at the airport, if you're continuing on to Manaus, Brazil, you will need to present your papers at the Brazilian **Policía Federal** (650 Av. Da Amizade, Tabatinga, 7am-noon and 2pm-6pm Mon.-Fri.), near the Tabatinga hospital. If continuing to Peru, get your Peruvian entry stamp at the police office in Isla de Santa Rosa, which is on the main path through town.

At the **Brazilian Consulate** (Cra. 10 No. 10-10, Piso 2, Leticia, 8am-2pm Mon.-Fri., tel. 8/592-7530), you can obtain a visa for Brazil, which is necessary for U.S. and Canadian citizens. Again, this is only necessary if you are planning to stay overnight in Brazil. You must have a yellow fever vaccination card and an onward airline ticket ready to present. Processing time is two to three 2-3 days. For U.S. citizens, the visa costs a hefty COP$430,000.

No visa is required to visit Peru for under 90 days. The **Peruvian Consulate** (Cl. 11 No. 5-32, Leticia, tel. 8/592-3947, www.embajadadelperu.org.co, 8am-2pm Mon.-Fri.) can assist with further information.

HEALTH AND MEDICAL SERVICES

The Colombian health authorities recommend getting a yellow fever vaccination 10 days before arriving in the area. The World Health Organization yellow health card, nonetheless, is not regularly checked at the airport. Malaria is very rare, but to be on the safe side, consider taking anti-malarial pills starting before your visit and up until four weeks after departure from the Amazon area. These can easily be purchased in pharmacies across Colombia without prescription.

The major hospital in town is the **Hospital San Rafael** (Cra. 10 No. 13-78, tel. 8/592-7074). The **Clínica Amazonas** (Cra. 6 No. 6-05, tel. 8/592-5579) is open 24 hours a day, as is the **IPS Indígena Trapecio Amazónico** (Cra. 9 No. 9-62). A dental clinic in town is the **Centro Odontológico del Amazonas** (Cra. 10 No. 12-109, tel. 8/592-5953).

For whatever ails you, go to **Productos Naturales del Trapecio Amazónico** (Cl. 8 No. 9-87, tel. 8/592-4796, 9am-6pm Mon.-Sat.) and you're bound to find a remedy. Traditional remedies to cure a laundry list of maladies, from impotence to arthritis and obesity, are available, and the knowledgeable staff can suggest certain medicinal therapies for you.

EMERGENCIES

Report emergencies to the local **Policía Nacional** (Cra. 11 No. 12-30, emergency line 112 or 8/892-5060).

TOURIST INFORMATION

For information on the area, the **Fondo de Promoción Ecoturística del Amazonas** (Cl. 8 No. 9-75, tel. 8/592-4162, www.fondodepromocionamazonas.com) may be of help. It is near the Museo Uirapuru.

MONEY

There are several Colombian banks in Leticia with ATMs. These include: **Banco de Bogotá** (Cra. 10 No. 10-108), **BBVA** (Cl. 7 No. 10-12, tel. 8/592-4975), **Banco Agrario** (Cl. 8 No. 10-66, tel. 8/100-0000), and **Bancolombia** (Cra. 11 No. 9-52, tel. 8/592-6067). Generally, banking hours are 8am-11:30am and 2pm-4pm on weekdays. Each of these has ATMs. This is the best (if not only) place in the region to get cash. As you venture further afield from Leticia, credit cards are rarely accepted and ATMs are nonexistent. Colombian currency is accepted in the entire Amazon region near Leticia, including in Brazil and Peru.

INTERNET ACCESS
Leticia has a few Internet cafes, but don't expect rapid connections. **Amazon Technology** (Cra. 10 No. 7-85, 8:30am-noon and 3pm-9pm Mon.-Sat., 3pm-9pm Sun.) is a comfortable place to check email.

LAUNDRY
There is a **laundry service** (Cra. 10 No. 9-32) that will have your clothes ready (and dry!) within one day.

Getting There And Around
All major national carriers serve the Leticia airport, **Aeropuerto Internacional General Alfredo Vásquez Cobo** (3 km north of town). **Avianca** resumed service in November 2013 with flights from Bogotá. **Copa** (Cl. 7 No. 10-36, tel. 8/592-7838, 8am-12:30pm Mon.-Fri., 9am-1pm Sat., www.copaair.com) and **LAN** (Colombian toll-free tel. 01/800-094-9490, www.lan.com) offer daily flights from Bogotá. **Satena** (Cra. 11 No. 9-42, Local 1, cell tel. 312/457-6291, Colombian toll-free tel. 01/800-091-2034, www.satena.com) flies from Leticia to La Chorrera (with connections to Araracuara and San Vincente del Caguán), La Pedrera, and Tarapaca. Flights to those supremely exotic destinations are usually once a week. Viva Colombia will launch flights to Leticia (out of Medellín) in the near future. There are no international flights from Leticia. Taxis to and from the airport should cost under COP$10,000.

All river transportation to **Puerto Nariño, Caballococha** (Peru), and to points in between departs from the **Muelle Turístico** (Tourist Wharf) in Leticia. To Puerto Nariño there are daily boats at 6am, 8am, 10am, and 2pm. The trip takes two hours and costs COP$29,000 per person. By paying extra, it is possible to arrange for these boats to leave you off at stops along the way to Puerto Nariño, such as Isla de los Micos, and be picked up by a later boat. Tickets for these boats can be obtained at the port in the Malecón Plaza Local 101. This little shopping area is on the lefthand side when facing the port. There are three agencies with offices there: **Transportes Amazónicos** (tel. 8/592-5999, cell tel. 313/347-8091), **Líneas Amazonas II** (tel. 8/592-6711, cell tel. 311/532-0633), and **Expreso Unidos Tres Fronteras** (tel. 8/592-4687, cell tel. 311/452-6809). It's best to go in person to the offices. It's organized and straightforward.

The boats to and from **Manaus** depart from the main port in **Tabatinga**. Slow cargo boats depart frequently, take three days, and cost COP$210,000 if you sleep in a hammock or COP$1,100,000 for a two-person cabin with air conditioning. These usually leave on Wednesdays and Saturdays at around 2 or 3 in the afternoon. These prices include food on board. If you plan to sleep in a hammock (which you must purchase in town beforehand), try to get on board early (up to four hours) to stake out a good place. In fact, you can board the boat as soon as you buy a ticket, even a day before departure. Stock up on snacks and water, as the food, which is included in the price, is not that great. A good book and a deck of cards will come in handy. There aren't any mosquitoes to bother you while snoozing in your hammock at night, but every once in a while a flying beetle may annoy you. You will be searched, presumably for drugs, once you board the boat. The reverse journey can also be made (from Manaus to Leticia), but it will take six days.

Weekly fast boats (30 hours) depart on Friday and cost COP$430,000. So as not to miss your boat, remember that Tabatinga is one hour later than Leticia. Be sure to get your departure stamp at the Leticia airport! You can also take a flight from Tabatinga to Manaus.

To Iquitos, **Transtur** (Rua Marechal Mallet No. 349, tel. 97/8113-5239, iquitostours@

hotmail.com) and **Golfinho** (Av. Marechal Mallet No. 306, tel. 97/3412-3186) have offices in Tabatinga. Boats leave six days a week from Tabatinga, stopping at the Peruvian town of Santa Rosa, across from Leticia, for immigration purposes. The trip takes nine hours and costs COP$140,000. Departure time is 3:30am or 5:30am, depending on the boat company. There are also boats, usually twice in the afternoon, to the Peruvian town of **Caballococha**, where you can catch a flight to Iquitos.

Leticia is a small town; you can walk everywhere you'd like to go. Some hotels have bikes you can rent to explore the town and beyond. *Moto-taxis* (motorcycle taxis) and *motocarros* (three-wheeled *moto-taxis*) are plentiful. Sights along Kilometer 11 can be reached by public bus or *moto-taxi*. Sights down the river can be reached by taking a *lancha* from the port.

ALONG THE RÍO AMAZONAS

Several sights provide excellent photo ops along the Río Amazonas westward from Leticia to the Parque Amacayacu. These are usually visited as part of a package one-day tour offered by all hotels and travel agencies. Most of these tours continue past Amacayacu to Puerto Nariño and the Lago Tarapoto. That is the easiest way to visit them, but it's a rather "touristy" proposition.

For greater flexibility and to avoid feeling part of the herd you can also charter your own boat for around COP$300,000, but you'll have to be specific about where you want to go in order to negotiate a good price. Head to the *malecón* (wharf) and ask any of the boat captains lingering about for this option.

When on the water, keep your eyes peeled for dolphins, both gray and pink, and pelicans above. Every once in a while, you'll pass a fisherman in a *peque peque* dugout canoe, just barely above water. When it rains you'll see them furiously scooping out water with their hands so as not to sink!

Victoria Regia

Seven kilometers (four miles) and about a 15-minute boat ride west from Leticia, **Victoria Regia** (COP$5,000 admission) is a private reserve that is usually the first stop on the river. You can view large circular *Victoria amazonica* lily pads and their lovely white lotus flowers floating atop the water. These are some of the largest water plants in the world, and the leaves can measure up to 1.5 meters (5 feet) in diameter, with roots extending 7 meters (23 feet) below the water's surface. They say that these plants are so strong they can support the weight of a one-year old child. It's not recommended, however, to test this theory on your offspring. You can also marvel at a magnificent old ceiba tree farther along on the park walkway. Ceibas are some of the tallest trees in the world. This is also your chance to get that quintessential Amazon photo with a colorful *guacamaya* (macaw) or two on your shoulders.

Puerto Alegría

On the Peruvian side of the river farther along is the community of **Puerto Alegría.** Here the attraction is exotic animals. When tourist boats show up at the community dozens of times each day, local women and children greet the tourists with all sorts of animals in hand: alligators, sloths, turtles. For a contribution you can be photographed holding several of the animals. Tourists are told that the animals are released into the wild after a period of time, but that seems hard to believe. Even if that is the case, they must have a hard time adjusting to their natural habitat after years in captivity, being held by humans day in and day out. You may find it disturbing how these creatures are used for human entertainment here.

Isla de los Micos

The **Isla de los Micos** (Monkey Island) is the most popular tourist attraction on the river. It's about 40 kilometers (25 miles) west of Leticia. At this island, owned by the Colombian hotel chain Decameron, elevated walkways meander through the jungle, and with just a morsel of fruit in your hand, you'll make the monkeys go bananas. They'll proceed to climb all over you in hopes of a snack, as if you were a tree. The monkeys are not native to the island, rather

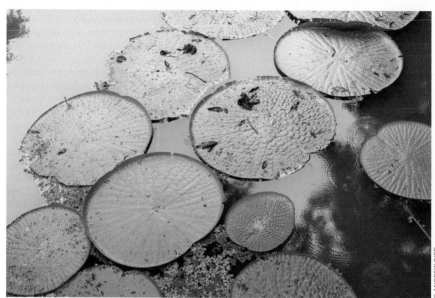

lily pads at Victoria Regia

they were brought there by controversial hotel owner and entrepreneur Mike Tsalickis in the 1970s. Up to 12,000 supposedly lived there at one point. Some even were used for medical experiments. It is a tourist trap, but it's hard to deny that kids love it.

Macedonia

The Ticuna village of **Macedonia** is a regular stop for tourist boats. When visitors arrive, they are invited in to the *maloca* (community house), where an authentic ceremonial dance is performed. Tourists are led onto the middle of the dance floor to the beat of a turtle shell drum. Around the *maloca* you can peruse an array of handicrafts at stalls set up by local women. A specialty is *palo de sangre* wood carvings. Although touristy, it is nice that the community manages all the activities here, and all the income goes directly to them.

Reserva Calanoa

Tucked away on the bank of the Amazon, west of the Macedonia community and just before the community of Makagua and the Parque Nacional Natural Amacayacu, is (**Reserva Calanoa** (Río Amazonas, 60 km/37 miles west of Leticia, cell tel. 311/842-4392, www.calanoaamazonas.com, COP$230,000 pp). Most people speeding by in their boats do not notice it. That's OK, because here the emphasis is on appreciation of the natural surroundings, of indigenous cultures, and learning: about art, photography, cooking, and flora and fauna. Activities offered (most are included in the overall price) include day and nighttime canoe trips, bird- and dolphin-watching, and canoe trips, by day and by night. It is a project of a Canadian-Colombian couple, Diego and Marlene Samper. Diego is an accomplished photographer. Calanoa offers one-of-a-kind tours, for example an annual workshop on natural fibers in February. During that week, participants learn the art of weaving *palma de caraná* leaves that form the stunning *maloca* rooftops that you have seen at every stop in the Amazon.

Reserva Calanoa has four beautifully done

THE AMAZON

© ANDREW DIER

Life abounds in the Parque Nacional Natural Amacayacu.

cabins made of all natural materials, and a lovely dining and relaxing area overlooks the river. The lodgings are called the Hotel de Selva. There is a strong emphasis here on working with and supporting neighboring indigenous communities, such as in the settlement of Mocagua, where Calanoa is undertaking a mural painting project in order to preserve and celebrate indigenous culture.

Parque Nacional Natural Amacayacu

The prime, unspoiled plot of land known as Parque Nacional Natural Amacayacu covers some 300,000 hectares (740,000 acres). It has its southern border on the banks of the Amazon between the Río Amacayacu ("River of Hammocks") and the Río Matamata and extends northward to the Río Cotuhe. It was declared a national park in 1975. The park is characterized by undulating hills, swamps, and an intricate network of streams. The highest point in the park reaches 200 meters (650 feet) above sea level. It is estimated that in the park

there are more than 5,000 plant species, 150 mammal species (including pink dolphins, tapirs, jaguars, manatees, nutrias, and numerous primates), 500 species of birds, about 100 species of fish, and the list goes on. Resident animals such as squirrel monkeys, sloths, wild boars, and jaguars are hard to spot in the park, and in the jungle in general.

Each year much of the park is flooded during the rainy months of April and May. In 2012 it was a particularly wet wet season, resulting in extensive damage to park structures. The park has since been closed to tourism, although the Ticuna settlement of San Martín can be visited.

If you are traveling by boat up the spectacular and serpentine Amacayacu (this can apply to any jungle cruise you take in the region), insist that the captain completely cut the engine at least once or twice during the journey, so that you can enjoy the incredible sounds of the jungle. When you float along in silence, hearing nothing but the calls of distant monkeys, shrieks of birds, or the constant hum of legions of frogs and insects, it is a magical experience.

It makes you think, that, despite the tsunami of evidence to the contrary, just maybe we can, for the first time in the history of humanity, turn things around and save this remarkable ecosystem. Boat drivers are usually in a hurry, so you'll have to ask them something like: *"Podemos parar aquí sin motor un minutico por favor?"* ("Would it be possible to stop here without the motor for a moment, please?").

Deep within the Parque Amacayacu, a dedicated team of animal lovers is rehabilitating monkeys that have been rescued from poor conditions in captivity. **Fundación Maikuchiga** (Leoncio Sánchez, cell tel. 313/397-1981, www. maikuchiga.org) is a group that rescues and cares for dozens of primates, like woolly monkeys, red howlers, and brown capuchins, who have been injured, orphaned, or rescued from poor conditions in captivity in the Colombian Amazon. Dr. Sara Bennett is the "mother of the monkeys" and runs the show here. She has been in Colombia for many years, originally arriving to conduct research on Amazonian trees. One of her greatest accomplishments has been in convincing local tribes to no longer hunt woolly monkeys, in order to protect their survival. Her aim is to promote the protection and awareness of these species, and generally to promote conservation efforts. You can visit the foundation to get to know their work, and they are always in need of financial support. Maikuchiga can be reached on foot from San Martín during dry months.

🞔 SAN MARTÍN DE AMACAYACU

Up the Río Amacayacu, within the PNN Amacayacu, is the Ticuna community of **San Martín**. The community has organized itself to receive tourists and offers walks, canoe rides, and other activities. Friendly and knowledgeable community elder Victor Ángel Pereira (cell tel. 310/769-7305) will receive you and get you organized. Entrance to the community costs COP$5,000, and this is an interesting day-trip excursion from either Leticia or Puerto Nariño. There is a handicrafts store where local girls sell beautiful handwoven *mochilas* (handbags), bark scrolls from the *yanchama* tree on which scenes of jungle animals are painted using all natural

dyes, and jewelry. You can also do a homestay with a local family for only about COP$10,000 per night in a hammock.

The 🞔 **Casa de Gregorio** (cell tel. 310/279-8147, heike_van_gils@hotmail.com) is a lodge run by a Ticuna-Dutch couple, Heike and José Gregorio. She arrived in San Martín as a doctoral student in agriculture sciences at the Universidad Nacional in 2004, and he is a Ticuna community leader. Through their **Small World Foundation** (www.smallworld-foundation.org), they work to improve the lives of the residents of this indigenous community, by installing toilets, starting a kindergarten, and purchasing rainwater tanks. A stay at the Casa de Gregorio provides visitors with a unique opportunity to discover the jungle and get to know Ticuna culture. A new, deluxe cabin was finished in 2013, and that costs COP$120,000 for a double in a luxurious king bed. There are two other simple double rooms and a small cabin, with a total capacity of 10. Lodging for two costs COP$80,000, and there are additional costs for meals, the community entry fee of COP$5,000, and for guides. Although it is possible to come for a day trip, this is not a recommended option. To get a taste of village life, it's best to not rush things and stay at least three or four days. To get there, you take a boat for about 1.5 hours from Leticia for COP$24,000. These depart at 8am, 10am, and 2pm. Ask to be dropped off at Bocana Amacayacu (not the Parque Amacayacu). The return trip costs COP$29,000. You will need to arrange with Casa de Gregorio transportation from Bocana Amacayacu to San Martín. That costs COP$30,000. You can also take a *peque-peque* canoe from Puerto Nariño or walk from there to San Martín. You can also walk from Puerto Nariño in tours organized by various hotels and agencies there. That expedition (you'll need a guide; ask Heike) takes three hours.

🞔 PUERTO NARIÑO

When you disembark at the village of Puerto Nariño, atop a sloping hill overlooking the Río Loretoyacú, you'll wonder: Where are the motorbikes? Here in idyllic Puerto Nariño, there

© ANDREW DIER

an artisan at the Ticuna community of San Martín

are no roads and no motorized vehicles whatsoever. Environmentally minded and forward-thinking town council members decided many years ago that they wanted Puerto Nariño to chart a different path than almost all other towns in Colombia (and for that matter in the world), and for their efforts, this town was named the first tourism sustainable town in the country. Here "roads" are actually palm-lined sidewalks that connect all the neighborhoods of this community together. Puerto Nariño is so peaceful, you'll probably want to linger a while.

Sights

To get a bird's-eye view of Puerto Nariño and the rivers and jungle beyond, climb up the steps to the **Mirador Nai-pata** (COP$7,000, closes at 6pm). You pick up an entry ticket in the adjacent house. The tall treehouse (which is what *nai-pata* means in Ticuna) is the perfect place to be at dusk.

The **Centro de Interpretación Ambiental Natütama** (cell tel. 312/410-1925, www. natutama.org, 8am-12:30pm and 2pm-5pm,

donations encouraged) is run by the conservation and education nonprofit Natütama. At their center, you can watch some excellent videos about two important river species: the pink dolphin and the manatee. While the pink dolphin is celebrated in indigenous mythology, the unfortunate manatee is not. Thus it has been hunted to the brink of extinction. The focus of this organization is conservation awareness among the community, and in large part due to their educational outreach activities, the number of manatees in the Puerto Nariño area has grown from 11 in 2002 to 24 in 2012. They also sell handicrafts and T-shirts, the proceeds of which help them carry out their activities. Natütama means, in Ticuna, the "world below the water."

Recreation
LAGO TARAPOTO

Lago El Correo and **Lago Tarapoto** are about a 20-minute boat ride from Puerto Nariño, and this area is a good place for dolphin spotting (both pink and gray), swimming, piranha

a bird's-eye view of Puerto Nariño

fishing, and nature hikes. Lago Tarapoto is connected with the Amazon, so by swimming in its serene waters you can truthfully say that you swam in the Amazon. The Lago Tarapoto at 37 square kilometers (14 square miles) is much larger than the adjacent Lago El Correo, which is closer to Puerto Nariño. There are several spots in this area where you can see *renacos,* also known as *el arbol que camina* (the tree that walks), a tree with a jumble of above-ground roots. To get to the lake you'll have to go with a guide on a boat. The tourist office in Puerto Nariño or any hotel can help organize a visit to these lakes and surrounding flooded jungles. This excursion, pleasant to make in the late afternoon, will cost COP$50,000 per person.

Festivals and Events

The **Festival Autóctono de Danza, Murga y Cuento** takes place at the end of December through early January each year, and is a celebration of indigenous culture and identity. Each night the town gathers around the basketball court for evenings of storytelling, dance, and the requisite beauty pageant. Interestingly, an important component of the pageant is a demonstration of the girls' knowledge of their native tongue.

Accommodations and Food

Hospedaje Wone (Cra. 1 No. 4-14, cell tel. 314/266-5496 or 320/878-5785, wonenemico@hotmail.com, COP$20,000 d) is a pleasant, locally owned place, with potted plants and flowers throughout, that has three rooms. It's near the port. A bathroom is outside in the back. They lost everything recently during the disastrous 2012 rainy season. After rebuilding, they are crossing their fingers that nature will be on their side for a while.

A cozy and inexpensive option in Puerto Nariño is **⦗ Malocas Napu** (Cl. 4 No. 5-72, cell. tel. 314/437-6075 or 313/800-2771, www.malocanapu.com, COP$35,000 d, pp). There are eight rooms here in two *malocas* (community houses). Bathrooms are separate. They can take you on fun excursions to Lago Tarapoto, including a little piranha fishing on a dugout canoe, if you are so inclined, and also show you the flooded jungle. Napu works closely with the travel agency Ecodestinos.

Friendly **Hotel Lomas del Paiyü** (Cl. 7 No. 2-26, cell tel. 313/268-4400, www.hotellomas-delpaiyu.turismo.co, COP$50,000-70,000 d) offers 22 clean, if a little stuffy, rooms. The top end option in town is the **Hotel Casa Selva** (Cra. 2 No. 6-72, cell tel. 311/280-7319, Bogotá tel. 1/657-1468, www.casaselvahotel.com, COP$150,000 d). The rooms are immaculate and it is undeniably comfortable, but the atmosphere is rather businesslike.

If you'd like to get away from the hustle and bustle of Puerto Nariño but still be within walking distance of it, the (**Alto del Águila Cabañas del Fraile** (cell tel. 314/234-7292, 314/201-3154, or 311/502-8592, altodelaguila@hotmail.com, COP$25,000 pp with private bath) is your best bet. It's actually quite fun, too, with resident monkeys monkeying about always making things interesting. Cabins are clean and cheerful, the kitchen area is a comfortable place to have a *tinto* and read, and you can take a kayak out for a spin on the river for free. The owner is indeed a Franciscan missionary, a straight-talking one at that, and he's a joy to meet.

The best restaurant in town is the **Restaurante Las Margaritas.** They specialize in the usual fish dishes but can also whip up vegetarian fare. Another friendly spot is **Delicias Amazónicas Metane** (Cra. 2 between Clls. 6-7). Set lunches go down well with a *copoazú* juice as you watch everybody walk by on the pathway in front. The small grocery store **Mercaselva** (Cra. 2 and Cl. 5, 6:30am-8:30pm daily) also makes OK pizzas. Order yours a few hours in advance.

Information and Services

The helpful **tourist office** (Cra. 1 at Cl. 5, Palacio Municipal, no phone, 7am-noon and 2pm-5:45pm Mon.-Fri.) can help you organize excursions with official tour guides. There are no ATMs in Puerto Nariño. There are a couple of Internet cafés, but the connections are very slow.

Getting There and Around

It takes just under two hours on a public boat to make the 87-kilometer (54-mile) river journey from Leticia to Puerto Nariño without stopping. Tickets (COP$24,000 one way) for this trip can be purchased at the Leticia *malecón*. Look for the office at Malecón Plaza Local 101, to the left of the *malecón*. Three companies provide this service: **Transportes Amazónicos** (tel. 8/592-5999), **Líneas Amazonas II** (tel. 8/592-6711), and **Expresos Unidos Tres Fronteras** (tel. 8/592-4687). There are usually three boats per day starting at 8am, 10am, and 2pm.

When leaving Puerto Nariño bound for Leticia, make sure you reserve your spot a day or so in advance. You can do this at the office on stilts along the walkway to the docks. Boats leave Puerto Nariño at 7:30am, 11am, 2pm, and 4pm. You can also take a boat to Caballococha, Peru, from Puerto Nariño. Ask at the office about this option.

(RÍO YAVARÍ

The **Río Yavarí** (Rio Javari in Brazil) begins in Peru and serves as a border between Brazil and Peru. Its waters flow some 1,050 kilometers (650 miles) before it meets the Amazon in Brazil. About a six-hour journey from Leticia by boat (three hours when the jungle is flooded), this part of the Amazon basin is unspoiled, isolated, and is home to two excellent private natural reserves where you will be immersed in the jungle. Spend at least three days or up to a week at one of the Yavarí nature reserves (they are both excellent) to gain a real appreciation for jungle life. The longer you stay the more wildlife you are apt to see: pink dolphins, alligators, snakes, and dozens of birds. Although this region is technically in Brazil, it very well may be one of the highlights of your trip to Colombia.

Reserva Natural Palmarí

Located on a bluff overlooking the river, the **Reserva Natural Palmarí** (office Cra. 10 No. 93-72, Apt. 602, Bogotá, tel. 1/610-3514, www.palmari.org or www.travesiassas.com, COP$256,000) is a pioneer in ecotourism in

© ANDREW DIER

beautiful mushroom in the jungle

this part of the Amazon. Once you arrive, you will be paired with a guide who will accompany you throughout your stay. You won't be grouped together with others. Activities offered include jungle walks (including nighttime), treks, canopying, kayaking, canoe rides, and visits to nearby indigenous communities. Usually guests spend one night in the jungle. Near Reserva Natural Palmarí you can admire massive ceiba trees, also called *lupuna* trees. These noble giants reach up to 70 meters (230 feet) high and have witnessed a lot in their over 400 years of life! Ticuna Indians believe that these trees are what started life and created the river.

The reserve, first and foremost, has a strong commitment to the environment and to the community. The rooftops are made from a durable, recycled material imported from Canada. That is because of the growing scarcity of the native palm trees. Palmarí works together on sustainable agriculture and ecotourism projects as well as environmental education with local communities, and has been instrumental in the construction of schools in several villages.

Mucho credit is due to gregarious Axel, the German-Colombian owner of the reserve, for being a forward-thinking eco-example.

Palmarí has a range of accommodations options, and if you are traveling in a group, this is an excellent choice. Palmarí is a favorite for Colombian school field trips, but you'll be warned about that possibility when you make a reservation. You can sleep in a hammock, in a communal lodge, or in private rooms. Food is delicious and varied, and, yes, there is cold beer. You can also get online as well, although this might be the perfect time for an Internet diet. There are two great places at Palmarí to spend the late afternoon hours as you watch the sun go down: the lookout tower and the swing set. Although it is possible (and adventurous) to get to Palmarí on your own, they will arrange your transportation directly from Leticia.

To get to Palmari from Leticia, you can take public transportation along the river, which will require multiple transfers, or you can let Palmarí take care of everything and go direct (COP$150,000 pp one way).

view from the lookout tower at the Reserva Natural Palmarí

Reserva Natural Heliconia

In Brazil, 109 kilometers (68 miles) southeast of Leticia, the **Reserva Natural Heliconia** (office Cl. 13 No. 11-74, Leticia, tel. 8/592-5773, cell tel. 311/508-5666, www.amazonheliconia.com, COP$1,600,000 pp d for 4 days/3 nights incl. transportation) is a fantastic lodge and nature reserve hidden in the dense Amazonian jungle on a tributary of the Río Yavarí, which flows into the Río Amazonas. And that makes it all the more exotic, like a bird of paradise flower (for which it is named) growing in the middle of a sea of green in the jungle. Ideally, plan on spending at least three nights here, as anything less than that will feel rushed.

Activities here (included in the price except for canopying) include nature walks, birdwatching, pink dolphin-watching, canoeing above the inundated forest, fishing, and canopying. You'll usually have two outings each day, and sometimes in the evenings you can explore the jungle at night, panning the darkness with your flashlight as you look for red eyes of jungle beasts looking back at you. It's an unsettling feeling to be immersed in the pitch black jungle against a backdrop of chirping insects, frogs, and birds. Another nocturnal activity is to take a canoe ride in search of alligators (or, if there are no gators, simply enjoying the sounds of the jungle and the millions of stars above).

The comfortable cabins at this reserve are made of all natural materials. Cabins come in different sizes, such as for two guests or families, and they have an area for larger groups. At night you don't even realize there are others around, such is the privacy.

A hospitable local Brazilian family takes care of all the day-to-day details. There's no Internet access or cell phone coverage, and electricity comes on only for a few hours in the evening. Meals are taken in an open-air thatched roof *maloca* in the center. Food is basic and does not vary much, usually fried fish, rice, and plantains. The friendly kitchen staff can, however, accommodate vegetarians if provided with some advance notice.

Los Llanos

The vast plains of eastern Colombia known as Los Llanos or Llanos Orientales (Eastern Plains) are lush tropical grasslands teeming with wildlife. They comprise the lands west of the Andes and north of the Amazon rainforest, and extend well into Venezuela. While this part of Colombia comprises around 25 percent of the total area in the country, it is home to only about 3 percent of the population. The border between the Amazon and the Llanos is roughly at the Río Guaviare, a tributary of the Río Orinoco, but the transition is gradual.

Elevations in the Llanos rarely exceed 300 meters (1,000 feet), and the land gradually descends from the Andes piedmont in the west towards the Río Orinoco to the east. The plains are drained by a multitude of large rivers, such as the Guaviare, Vichada, and Meta Rivers, that flow down from the Andes. The savannahs are covered with long-stemmed and carpet grasses in the drier areas and swamp grasses in low-lying humid areas. There are also thick patches of forest throughout the plains and along the rivers (known as gallery forests).

The climate is marked by two clear seasons: the *invierno,* or rainy season, which lasts from April to November, and the *verano,* or dry season, from December to March. During the rainy season, the rivers overflow and large parts of the Llanos are flooded. During the dry season, the land becomes parched.

The Llanos are literally full of wildlife, with more than 100 species of mammals and 1,300 species of birds, including many migratory birds. Mammals include several species of deer and rabbit, anteaters, armadillos, tapirs, otters, jaguars, pumas, and *chigüiros* (capybaras), the world's largest rodent. The plains are also home to the giant anaconda and to one of the most endangered species on earth, the Orinoco crocodile, which reaches up to seven meters (23 feet) long. Unfortunately, human settlement and hunting have vastly decreased the wildlife.

History

At the time of the Spanish conquest, the Llanos were inhabited by several indigenous people, including the Guahibos, Achaguas, and Jiraras. The first European to explore the region was German conquistador Nikolaus Federmann, who set off in 1538 from Venezuela and crossed these plains on his way to the Muisca highlands of El Dorado in the Cordillera Oriental (Eastern Range of the Andes). Gonzalo Jiménez de Quesada, the founder of Bogotá, was granted dominion over a large part of the Llanos but took little interest due to the apparent lack of treasures and sparse population. Starting in the second half of the 16th century, Jesuits set up missions to convert the indigenous people and established large cattle ranches. During the wars of independence, Venezuelan *llaneros* (plainsmen) were an important element in Bolívar's army and played a key role in the expedition that crossed the plains, climbed the Andes, and finally defeated the Spanish army at the Batalla de Puente de Boyacá on August 7, 1819.

Thanks to its lush grasslands, historically the Llanos have been an important cattle-ranching region in Colombia. To this day, the Llanos are synonymous with cowboy culture. Most of human habitation takes place along a narrow fringe of land bordering the Andes, in cities such as Villavicencio and Yopal.

In the 1980s oil was discovered, first in the far eastern department of Arauca and then in Casanare, and today, the area is Colombia's most important oil-producing region, with several pipelines linking the oil fields to the Caribbean port of Coveñas, from where it is exported. The lucrative oil industry became a tempting target for guerrilla insurgencies operating in the area. In the 1980s, the guerrilla group ELN (the National Liberation Army) extorted large amounts of money from the oil companies and their contractors and launched a bombing campaign of the pipelines. The

© ANDREW DIER

chigüiros (capybaras)

region for big agriculture, with large multinationals such as Cargill setting up massive plantations of African palm, soy, maize, and rubber, especially in the northeast Vichada region. A source of concern to environmentalists is the fact that the Llanos, unlike the Amazon, does not have many protected areas and could succumb to unchecked development.

Today the region is still suffering sporadic violence caused by illegal groups, especially in Arauca and parts of Caquetá. The current governor of Meta, elected in 2011, is Alan Jara, who was kidnapped by the FARC in 2001 and was held for nearly eight years.

VILLAVICENCIO

The capital of the department of Meta is only 80 kilometers (50 miles) southeast of Bogotá and is a gateway to the vast Llanos. Villavicencio does not have much in the way of tourist attractions; it does, however, attract Bogotanos en masse in search of sun and a swimming pool. It's also a base from which to visit Caño Cristales.

Centers of activity (aside from shopping malls) in Villavicencio are parks like **Parque los Fundadores** (Av. 40 and Vía a Bogotá), which has an enormous sculpture by Rodrigo Arenas Betancourt, and the **Plaza Los Libertadores** (Cl. 39 between Cras. 32-33), over which the cathedral, the late-19th-century **Catedral Metropolitana Nuestra Señora del Carmen,** stands. Near the Plaza Los Libertadores are some pleasant pedestrian side streets, the result of an urban renewal project.

Festivals and Events

Joropo is the music and dance of the Llanos. With European origins (it is said that it is related to Spanish flamenco), it's a dance of fast and fancy footwork, accompanied by folk music that utilizes the harp and guitar and other instruments. The **Torneo Internacional del Joropo** is a showcase of this particularly Llanos art form, and the festival has taken place in Villavicencio since 1960. Over a thousand dance pairs bedecked in traditional costume, including many children, participate. In

780-kilometer (485-mile) Caño Limón-Coveñas pipeline, which transports oil from oil fields in Arauca owned by California-based Occidental Oil, was bombed an incredible 170 times in 2001 alone. With Plan Colombia came money to defend this infrastructure, and bombings had dropped to only 17 by 2004.

The FARC (Fuerzas Armadas Revolucionarias de Colombia; Revolutionary Armed Forces of Colombia) has been present in the region since the 1960s. From 1998 to 2002 their position was strengthened when President Pastrana granted them as part of a peace process a large demilitarized zone the size of Switzerland in the Meta and Caquetá departments. The FARC managed this zone like a mini-state, using it to grow and process coca, smuggle arms, and hold kidnap victims. They even built roads and a recreation center for FARC commanders.

As a result of the guerrilla presence, agricultural output from the Llanos was depressed for many years. With increased security in the mid-2000s, the Llanos emerged as an important

Los Llanos for Beginners

For a taste of the Llanos, head eastward from Villavicencio to **Lagos de Menegua** (17 km east of Puerto López, cell tel. 315/326-6068, tel. 1/616-0439, www.lagosdemenegua.com, COP$154,000 pp d). This family-friendly resort set in the grassy hills of the Llanos has 24 rooms and a large swimming pool. Here you can take a horseback ride through the ranch, take a jungle walk, and see some of the wildlife that is abundant here: alligators, cute *chigüiros* (capybaras), monkeys, and many varieties of birds. While there are some walks you can make on your own, the resort offers guided walks on horseback (COP$35,000 pp), Jeep tours of the savannah (COP$25,000), and nighttime excursions to see alligators (COP$50,000 pp). *Colectivos* bound for Puerto Gaitán leave from the bus stations in both Bogotá (COP$37,000) and Villavicencio (COP$15,000). Tell the driver you'd like to be dropped off at kilometer 17 between Puerto López and Puerto Gaitán. It's just past Puerto López, where an obelisk marks the geographic center of Colombia, and the Río Meta.

addition to the dancing, there are rodeo events and, of course, a beauty pageant. It's held over four days in late June.

Cowboy culture in the Llanos is not limited to men. Proof of that is the **Concurso Mundial de la Mujer Vaquera** (www.mundialmujervaquera.com), a competition in which cowgirls show their skills in a series of events held at the Parque Las Malocas in Villavicencio in late March every year. *Llaneras* are well represented and get the support of the hometown crowd, but it is an international event: The 2013 winner hailed from Mexico.

The **Encuentro Mundial del Coleo** (www.mundialcoleo.com.co) is for men, and they demonstrate their *coleo* skills. *Coleo* is a *llanero* cowboy technique to recapture stray bulls so that they can be branded. The cowboys do this by galloping on horseback and thrusting the bulls to the ground by pulling their tails. Animal rights sympathizers should skip this event! The competition takes place at the Parque Las Malocas in October of every year.

Accommodations and Food

Those en route to Caño Cristales in La Macarena may need to spend a night in Villavo, as locals call it. One of the best hotels in town is the [**GHL Hotel Villavicencio** (Cra. 39C No. 19C-15, www.ghlhoteles.com, COP$240,000 d). It is on the backside of a small shopping mall (Villa Centro) that has a Yumbo supermarket. Rooms are spacious, the restaurant is pretty good, and on the top floor is a pool, with a fantastic view of the Llanos.

A budget option is **Mochilero's Hostel** (www.mochileroshostel.com, COP$24,000 dorm, COP$50,000 d), which opened in 2012 and has six rooms (with fan). It's close to shopping malls and restaurants.

When it comes to local cuisine, *llaneros* like their beef, and open-air steakhouses are, have always been, and always will be the rage in Villavo. The specialty here is *mamona,* which is grilled veal. Ingredients of this dish aren't complex: a one-year-old calf, salt, and beer.

El Amarradero del Mico (Vía Vanguardia Restrepo, cell tel. 313/829-6228, noon-midnight daily, COP$22,000) is a popular open-air restaurant on the outskirts of town featuring something for all manner of carnivores. For a departure from the local specialties, try **Pizza Nostra** (Av. 40 No. 25A-47, tel. 8/668-4000, noon-11pm daily, COP$18,000) for pizzas, pastas, and hamburgers.

At the Unicentro mall there is a food court with a decent Italian restaurant and a Juan Valdez Café. **Oliva Mediterranea** (Unicentro shopping mall, Av. 40 No. 26C-10, 3rd floor, tel. 8/668-2020, noon-9pm daily, COP$18,000) makes a noble effort to make you think you're not in a food court. On the menu are Italian dishes, pizzas, and salads.

La Estaca Club (Cra. 40 No. 57, no phone, 6pm-2am Mon.-Wed., 6pm-3am Thurs.-Sat., 6pm-10pm Sun., COP$15,000) is a popular pub-like gathering place with a pleasant terrace where you can eat soul food such as buffalo wings and have a couple of beers.

Information and Services

There are **tourist information stands** at the airport (Vereda Vanguardia vía Restrepo) and at the bus terminal (Cra. 1 No. 15-05) and one at Llanocentro shopping mall. They generally keep the hours of 8am-5pm daily.

Getting There and Around

There's really no need to fly to Villavicencio from Bogotá, unless you seek comfort, are averse to the assertive motoring style of Colombian bus drivers, or are in a hurry, as there are **buses** (Flota la Macarena, tel. 1/421-5556, www.flotalamacarena.com, 2 hrs., COP$20,000) between the two cities practically 24 hours a day. From Villavicencio's **Terminal de Transportes de Villavicencio** (Cra. 1 No. 15-05, Anillo Vial, no phone) there's no shortage of *colectivo* (smaller bus) service to Bogotá, but expect at least another frustrating hour in the Bogotá traffic during much of the day. *Colectivos* going to Puerto López cost about COP$14,000. It's a good road.

Airlines **LAN** (Colombian toll-free tel. 01/800-094-9490, www.lan.com) and **Satena** (Cra. 31 No. 39-37, 2nd floor, tel. 8/662-1260, www.satena.com) operate flights to the **Aeropuerto Vanguardia** (Vereda Vanguardia Vía Restrepo, tel. 8/670-9610) in Villavicencio from Bogotá. It's about a 45-minute long flight. There are connection flights to La Macarena, usually via small charter planes.

◖ CAÑO CRISTALES

Taking a flight (or two) to a remote corner of Colombia with a troubled past just to see some river algae may not, on the surface, sound like a wise investment of precious vacation time. But, here in the remote Llanos, you'll be rewarded as

the colorful pools of Caño Cristales

© ANDREW DIER

you trek through the stark lowland hills of the Serranía de la Macarena, with its unusual dry tropical vegetation, and behold the vibrant purple, fuchsia, goldenrod, and green *Macarenia clavigera* plants swaying in the gushing streams of **Caño Cristales.**

The Serranía de la Macarena (Macarena Range) is a 120-kilometer-long, 30-kilometer-wide (75-mile-long, 19-mile wide) mountain range 70 kilometers (43 miles) south of Villavicencio and 45 kilometers (28 miles) east of the Andes. The range, which is entirely contained within the 629,280-hectare (1.6 million-acre) **Parque Nacional Natural Sierra de la Macarena,** is the highly eroded remnant of mountains that once towered on the supercontinent of Panagea, before the South American plate separated from the African plate and drifted westward to its present location, crashing into the Nazca plate and creating the Andes. These ancient outcrops, which form the Guyana Shield, dot the northwest Amazon basin in Colombia, Venezuela, and Guyana.

The Macarena is also unique in that it is at

THE AMAZON

the confluence of three highly distinct ecosystems: the Amazon to the south, the Llanos to the north, and the Andes mountain rainforests to the west. A large number of endemic plants evolved in this isolated mountain range, including the striking *Macarenia clavigera,* which draws tourists from all over Colombia and from abroad.

Caño Cristales is a stream that flows from west to east in the very southern part of the sierra and flows into the Río Guayabero, a tributary of the Río Guaviare. In its upper reaches, it has three branches that join to form the Caño Cristales stream proper. The surrounding landscape is quite dry and rocky, covered with unusual *Vellozia macarenensis* plants, which have evolved to survive the dry climate and bush fires. These plants produce beautiful white flowers that add to the beauty of the stark environs.

The small town of **La Macarena** on the Río Guayabero is the gateway to Caño Cristales. It was part of the demilitarized zone granted to the FARC as part of the 1998-2002 peace process. Evincing little respect for nature, the FARC destroyed the park facilities, chased away the staff, and built a road right through the park, sparking squatters to take illegal possession of lands within the park. The town of La Macarena is now home to a 4,000-strong army base, one of the largest in Colombia. The areas in the vicinity of the town, including all the sights described in this section, are safe to visit. Tourism has given this isolated community new life. A highly successful nature guide training program for high school students has given youths in the town the opportunity to gain a living through ecotourism. Six thousand visitors came to Caño Cristales in 2012, and each year more and more are coming.

To visit Caño Cristales, you need a minimum of one full day and two nights, but staying a day or two longer is definitely worthwhile. The best time of the year to visit is during the rainy season, from May until November, when you can marvel at the *Macarenia clavigera* in bloom.

Recreation
HIKING
All excursions require a guide. Visitors are asked to avoid using sunscreen or mosquito repellent, as it can damage the *Macarenia clavigera.* Therefore, make sure to bring a wide-brimmed sun hat and wear lightweight, long-sleeve shirts and pants to protect your skin. Wear shoes that have good traction on slippery rocks and that you don't mind getting wet.

The most popular trek is a half-day excursion that involves a pleasant 20-minute boat ride up the Río Guayabero from the town of La Macarena, a six-kilometer (3.7-mile) truck ride, and a two-kilometer (1.2 mile) hike to Caño Cristales. There, you'll admire the multicolored stream as it gushes through pools and waterfalls. At the end you get to cool off in the Piscina del Turista, a natural pool, and have a waterside lunch.

Another longer, all-day excursion takes you to the upper part of Caño Cristales, where you'll visit the three different branches of the river. The vegetation here is much denser, and the *Macarenia clavigera* also take on yellow and green hues. This excursion involves wading across the stream numerous times. If it has been raining, the level and force of the water increases considerably, making for an exhilarating experience. Depending on the level of the water and physical conditions of the trip, you may visit one, two, or all three of the branches.

Two other half-day excursions also involve a ride up the Río Guayabero to visit **Cristalitos,** a smaller stream that is Caño Cristales in miniature, or to **El Mirador,** a hike to the top of a hill that offers sweeping views of the Río Guayabero and surrounding countryside.

Another excursion, which can only be done in the dry months of December through April, is 20 kilometers (12 miles) up to the **Raudal del Guayabero** to admire the white-water rapids, ancient indigenous petroglyphs, and interesting rock formations known as **Ciudad de Piedra.**

TOURS
The easiest way to visit Caño Cristales is to buy a packaged tour. Two well-reputed local

operators, **Ecoturísmo Sierra de la Macarena** (Av. Alfonso López No. 40-28, Villavicencio, tel. 8/664-3364, cell tel. 314/325-3522, www.ecoturismomacarena.com) and **Cristales Aventura Tours** (La Macarena, cell tel. 313/294-9452, cristalesaventuratours@hotmail.com) offer two- to five-night packages from Villavicencio. Expect to pay around COP$1,300,000 per person for a four-day trip. This includes air transportation out of Villavicencio, accomodations in La Macarena, and tours to Caño Cristales. The tours include transportation from Villavicencio in small charter planes, local transportation, food, and accommodations. These operators hire guides from UNIGMA, an association of young, local guides that have received specialized training since high school. You can also buy these tours from tourist operators elsewhere in the country, but these will simply take a margin and send you with the two local operators.

It is quite feasible, and cheaper, to organize your Caño Cristales trip on your own by arranging air transportation, local transportation, accommodations, and food. For all hikes in and around Caño Cristales you are required to hire a guide from UNIGMA (cell tel. 320/856-7571, guiasunigma@hotmail.com, http://canocristalesguiasdeturismo.wordpress.com, COP$100,000 per day for a group of up to 7 people).

Accommodations and Food
Hotels and restaurants in La Macarena, all economically priced, are nothing special. 【 **Centro Vacacional Punto Verde** (Parque Principal, cell tel. 310/341-8899, cvpuntoverde@hotmail.com, COP$40,000 pp incl. all meals) is the best option by far, with nine rooms spread out behind an ample and leafy common area, including a small pool. Breakfast is included, and the restaurant, the Punta Verde, is the best in town. It's open to hotel guests and non-guests. Let them know ahead of time if you require vegetarian meals.

Casa Hotel (Parque Principal, cell tel. 313/292-9925 or 314/279-2764, COP$35,000

pp) has 21 rooms, some with air conditioning. **La Cascada** (Cl. 5 No. 7-35, tel. 8/560-3132, cell tel. 313/294-9452, cristalesaventuratours@hotmail.com, COP$80,000 d) has 32 smallish rooms over two floors.

Information
The group of local guides, UNIGMA, operates a **tourist information office** at the tiny Aeropuerto Javier Noreña Valencia (5-min. walk from Parque Principal). It's the most buzzing place in La Macarena and is open daily 8am-5pm.

Getting There and Around
To **Aeropuerto Javier Noreña Valencia** in La Macarena, there are flights from Bogotá via **Satena** (tel. 1/423-8530, Colombian toll-free tel. 01/800-091-2034, www.satena.com) Sundays at 2:11pm and on Fridays at 10:54am. There are charter flights from Villavicencio on small charter planes (and, on occasion, old DC-3s). Contact **Ecoturismo Sierra de la Macarena** (Av. Alfonso López No. 40-28, Villavicencio, tel. 8/664-3364, www.ecoturismomacarena.com) or **Cristales Aventura Tours** to buy a seat on these flights. Travel by land to La Macarena, while theoretically possible, is not advisable due to safety concerns.

La Macarena is a small town and you can get everywhere on foot. Boats up the Río Guayabero to Caño Cristales, Cristalitos, and El Mirador will cost COP$60,000-70,000 per group of up to 10 people and COP$250,000 to the Raudal del Guayabero.

【 HACIENDA LA AURORA
Hacienda La Aurora (near the town of Paz de Ariporo, Casanare, cell tel. 310/580-5395, www.juansolito.com), 180 kilometers (112 miles) northwest of Yopal in the department of Casanare and about double that from Villavicencio, is in many ways a typical extensive cattle-ranching farm of the Llanos. It was once part of the immense 430,000-hectare (1.1 million-acre) Jesuit hacienda that was subdivided over time. The hacienda measures 17,000 hectares (42,000 acres) and has 6,000 head of

cattle. However, in one aspect it differs radically from other haciendas in the Llanos: Since the Barragán family, the current owners, purchased it in the 1970s, they have not allowed any hunting of animals, even if that means if jaguars and pumas attack and eat their cattle. This prohibition on hunting comes from the family's deep-seated conviction that cattle ranching must be a sustainable activity and that it must coexist peaceful with the Llanos' abundant biodiversity.

As a result, the hacienda abounds with wildlife that mixes with cattle herds and is not afraid of humans. As you travel through the farm, on the back of a specially outfitted safari truck, on horseback, or on foot, there is wildlife everywhere you look: herds of absurdly cute looking *chigüiros* (the world's largest rodents, also known as capybaras), deer, foxes, anteaters, armadillos, sloths, monkeys, tortoises, and caimans. Even non-bird-watchers will be amazed by what they see: huge ungainly *garzón soldados* (jabirus), bright red ibises, families of borrowing owls, incredibly exotic plumed hoatzins, parakeets, macaws,

and toucans. In the dry season, it is not unusual to see anacondas on the banks of the Río Ariporo or in watering holes. There are also water buffalo and herds of wild horses roaming about. Finally, pumas and jaguars can also be spotted (albeit through wildlife cameras installed in strategic points on the farm). There is most definitely nowhere in Colombia where you can see this much wildlife in its natural setting.

Hacienda La Aurora is also very much a working cattle farm. The herds are spread out throughout the hacienda. There is a main hacienda house, which is the center of operations. When cattle-ranching activities need to be done, such as taming horses, branding calves, or rounding up cattle for sale, *vaqueros* (cowboys) move to one of several smaller peripheral camps called *fundos* to do these activities. Viewing the traditional cattle-ranching ways of the Llanos is a fascinating part of a visit to La Aurora.

Haciendas such as this used to be the norm in the Llanos. However, many have been subdivided into smaller, more modern ranches with

double-striped thick knee bird

fenced pastures. Others have been converted into large African palm, corn, soy, or rubber plantations. La Aurora's administrators complain that it is increasingly difficult to find personnel willing to do what they call the "work of the Llano"—cattle ranching the traditional way—as wages in the oil industry are much better and the work is less taxing.

To fully enjoy a visit to Hacienda La Aurora, stay at least two full days. Accommodations at La Aurora are at the Ecolodge Juan Solito, which borders the ranch. Visits are easier in the dry season (Nov.-Mar.), when getting around the farm is not difficult and wildlife congregates around the water holes. However, a visit in the rainy season is also interesting. The ground often gets drenched, but is not impossible to visit the ranch and spot animals. Also, in the rainy season it is possible to do boat excursions.

Recreation

All visitors pay a fixed price of COP$120,000 per person per day for all activities on the ranch. In return, all activities are tailored to your wishes and you are accompanied by a dedicated guide. Easily arranged activities include photo safaris on the back of a truck specially outfitted with benches, visits to view the traditional cattle-ranching activities of the hacienda, excursions on horseback, nature hikes, and canoe trips up the Río Ariporo (only in the rainy season). You can also swim in the Ariparo, though you must be careful of stingrays, electric eels, piranhas (a minor threat), and anacondas, but they are on the riverbank. Maybe just skip the swimming!

If you have a particular interest, such as specialized bird-watching or photographing specific wildlife, these activities can be arranged at no additional cost.

Accommodations and Food

Lodging and food is provided at the **Ecolodge Juan Solito** (near Paz de Ariporo, Casanare, cell tel. 320/342-6409, www.juansolito.com, COP$180,000 pp including all meals) just across the Río Ariporo on the south side of the Hacienda La Aurora. Juan Solito is owned

by incredibly friendly and attentive Nelson Barragán, of the family that owns the hacienda. There are seven simple and comfortable rooms at the lodge. Meals are taken with the lodge staff on long benches in a thatched-roof dining room overlooking the river. Vegetarian fare can be arranged with advance notice. Sometimes, when there is a large group of guests, local musicians and dancers perform traditional *joropo* music and dance, with Nelson playing the harp.

Getting There

This Llanos adventure begins in **Yopal**, the orderly and pleasant capital city of Casanare. Due to the presence of large multinational oil companies in the area, there are several flights every day between Bogotá and the Yopal airport, **Aeropuerto Alcaravan-EYP** (Cl. 40 No. 19-20, tel. 8/635-8352). **LAN** (tel. 01/800-094-9490, www.lan.com) and **Avianca** (Cl. 10 No. 22-22, tel. 8/634-8406, www.avianca.com, 8am-noon and 2pm-6pm Mon.-Fri., 8:30am-12:30pm Sat.) offer various nonstops between the two cities. **EasyFly** (Col. toll-free tel. 01/800-012-3279, www.easyfly.com.co) serves both Bogotá and Bucaramanga from Yopal.

From Yopal, the easiest way to get to La Aurora is by contracting transportation directly with them. For COP$380,000 (each way) they will pick you up (maximum four passengers) at the Yopal airport or bus station and take you directly to the farm.

If you'd like to save some money and don't mind a little adventure, you can take public transportation to the farm entrance. From the **Terminal de Transportes de Yopal** (Cra. 23 between Clls. 25-26) take a bus to Paz de Aviporo (COP$17,000, 1.25 hours; frequent departures). From there, take a slow bus to Montañas de Totumo (COP$22,000; 6am, 12:30pm, and 3pm). The 12:30 bus continues on along a road that passes in front of the entrance of Ecolodge Juan Solito. Tell the bus driver to leave you at "Finca La Vigia," where there is a sign that says "Reserva Casanare." Confirm with the ecolodge for a pickup at Montañas de Totumo (the 6am and 3pm buses) or at the entrance to the farm (12:30pm bus).

BACKGROUND

The Land

Colombia covers a land area of 1.14 million square kilometers (440,000 square miles), roughly the size of Texas and California combined, making it the fourth largest South American country in area after Brazil, Argentina, and Peru. It is located in the north-west corner of South America, with seacoast on both the Pacific and the Atlantic, and bordering Venezuela, Brazil, Peru, Ecuador, and Panama. The Amazonian departments of Putumayo, Caquetá, Amazonas, and Vaupás in the south of the country straddle the Equator.

For a country of its size, it has an astonishing variety of landscapes, including the dense rainforests of the Amazon and the Pacific Coast, the vast grassland plains of the Llanos, the lofty Andes Mountains, and the Caribbean islands of San Andrés and Providencia. Colombia's mountainous regions themselves hold a succession of vertically layered landscapes: tropical rainforests at their base, followed by cloud forests at higher elevations, topped by the unique tropical high mountain *páramo* (highland moor) above 3,500 meters. The country boasts several peaks higher than 5,000 meters, including Nevado del Ruiz (5,325 meters/17,470 feet) and Pico Cristóbal Colón (5,776 meters/18,950 feet).

GEOGRAPHY
Región Andina

This central part of Colombia is dominated by the Andes mountain range. This region, which is referred to as the Región Andina or simply *el interior* (the interior) is the heartland of the country. It covers roughly 25 percent of the surface of the country and is home to 60 percent of the Colombian population.

The Andes mountain range, 8,000 kilometers (5,000 miles) long, runs the entire length of South America. The Andes are relatively young mountains, and some of the loftiest in the world after the Himalayas, resulting from the collision of the westward-moving South American plate with the Nazca and Antarctic plates starting 145 million years ago. The heavier Nazca and Antarctic plates to the west subducted under the lighter and more rigid South American plate, propelling it upwards and forming the Andes. In Colombia, as a result of a complex pattern of tectonic collisions, three parallel ranges were formed. At the Masizo Colombiano (Colombian Massif), a mountain range 175 kilometers north of the border with Ecuador, the Andes split into the Cordillera Occidental (Western Range), Cordillera Central (Central Range), and Cordillera Oriental (Eastern Range).

The Cordillera Occidental is the lowest and least populated of the three ranges. It runs roughly 750 kilometers parallel to the Pacific Coast and ends 150 kilometers from the Caribbean Sea. Its highest point is the Cerro de Tatamá (4,250 meters/13,945 feet). Of Colombia's three ranges, it has the least human intervention and is home to some of the world's only pristine high mountain *páramos* ecosystems, notably that covering the Cerro de Tatamá.

The Central Cordillera is the highest of the three ranges and is the continuation in Colombia of the main Andes range. It runs roughly 800 kilometers and tapers off in the northern Caribbean plains, 200 kilometers form the Caribbean coast. Like the Andes in Ecuador, it is dotted with volcanoes. North of the Masizo Colombiano is the Serranía de los Coconucos (Coconucos Range), a range of 15 volcanoes including the Volcán del Puracé (Puracé Volcano, 4,580 meters/15,025 feet). Farther north, the Cordillera Central reaches its maximum elevation at the massive Nevado del Huila (5,750 meters/15,585 feet). Farther north is a large complex formed by the Nevado del Tolima (5,215 meters/17,110 feet), Nevado Santa Isabel (4,950 meters/16,240 feet), and Nevado del Ruiz (5,325 meters/17,470 feet). In its northern part, the Cordillera Central broadens to form the uneven highland that comprises the mountainous heartland of Antioquia with Medellín as its capital.

Several of the volcanoes of the Cordillera Central have seen recent activity, notably Volcán Galeras (4,276 meters/14,029 feet), near the southern city of Pasto, which last erupted in 2005, forcing evacuation of nearby settlements. Volcán Galeras is currently closed to visitors because of the threat of volcanic activity. In 1985, the Nevado del Ruiz erupted unexpectedly, creating a landslide that engulfed the town of Armero, killing more than 20,000 people. Since 2012, the Nevado del Ruiz has seen some activity, which has restricted access to the northern part of the Parque Nacional Natural Los Nevados.

The Cordillera Oriental, which like the Cordillera Occidental is non-volcanic, extends more than 1,100 kilometers to the border with Venezuela. The range broadens to form a broad high plateau called the Altiplano Cundiboyacense, which extends 200 kilometers north of Bogotá. This is an area of broad valleys with the extremely rich soil of sedimentary deposits. It is not one continuous plane, but rather a series of valleys. The Sabana de Bogotá, or Bogotá High Plateau, where Bogotá is located, is one particularly broad valley. North of the altiplano is the soaring Sierra Nevada del Cocuy, a mountain range with 11 glacier-covered peaks, including Ritacuba Blanco (5,380 meters/17,650 feet). North of El Cocuy, the Cordillera Oriental loses altitude and splits in two: A smaller western segment forms the Serranía de Perijá on the border between Colombia and Venezuela, and a larger

Colombia is a mountainous country.

branch continues into Venezuela to form the Venezuelan Andes.

The 1,500-kilometer-long Río Magdalena flows along a broad valley that separates the Cordillera Central and the Cordillera Oriental, making it the main commercial waterway of Colombia. Due to heavy sedimentation, it is now only navigable when waters rise during the rainy seasons in the central part of the country (Apr.-May and Oct.-Nov.). The Río Cauca, which flows parallel to the Magdalena along the much narrower valley between the Cordillera Central and the Cordillera Occidental, is the main tributary of the Magdalena. They join in northern Colombia and flow into the Caribbean.

Andean Colombia is a seismically volatile area, and the country has suffered some major earthquakes in the past. The most deadly measured 7.5 on the Richter Scale and occurred in Cúcuta in 1875. It killed 10,000 and completely destroyed the city. In recent years, around 600 were killed in the Pacific port city of Tumaco during a quake and tsunami

in 1979; 300 perished in the 1983 Holy Week earthquake in Popáyan; and over 1,100 died in the Armenia quake of 1999.

Caribe

Colombia's Caribbean Coast runs 1,760 kilometers from the border of Panama to Venezuela, just longer than the California coast. However, the term Caribe or Región Caribe refers to much more than the narrow strip of coast; it encompasses basically all of Colombia north of the Andes, including a vast area of plains. This region covers 15 percent of the surface of Colombia and is home to 20 percent of the population.

The terrain is mostly low-lying and undulating. Near the border with Panama, the land is covered by dense tropical forests, similar to those of the Pacific Coast. Farther east is the Golfo de Urabá (Gulf of Urabá), a large, shallow bay. Between the Golfo de Urabá and Cartagena is the Golfo de Morrosquillo, a broad inlet that is 50 kilometers wide. Off the shore of the Golfo de Morrosquillo are two small archipelagos, the Islas de San Bernardo (San Bernardo Islands) and the Islas del Rosario (Rosario Islands), with beautiful coral reefs. Inland to the south is a large area of savannahs in the departments of Córdoba and Sucre largely devoted to cattle ranching. This area was once covered by dry tropical forests, which have been largely felled.

The bay of Cartagena, farther east, is a magnificent deep bay that caught the attention of the Spaniards early on. To the southeast of Cartagena is the lower valley of the Magdalena and Cauca rivers, a vast expanse of low-lying lagoons and lands prone to seasonal flooding. The Río Magdalena flows into the Caribbean east of Cartagena at the port city of Barranquilla. Farther to the east along the coast is a major mountain range, the Sierra Nevada de Santa Marta. It was formed by the collision of the South American plate and the Caribbean plate to the north and is entirely independent of the Andes. This mountain is home to Colombia's two highest peaks, the twin Pico Cristóbal Colón and Pico Bolívar (5,776 meters/18,950 feet), and is considered the highest coastal mountain range in the world. The Sierra Nevada de Santa Marta contains the same range of vertically layered landscapes as the Andes, from low-lying tropical forest through cloud forest, Andean forests, *páramo*, and glaciers. There are eight peaks with elevations greater than 5,000 meters.

Northeast of the Sierra Nevada de Santa Marta is La Guajira peninsula, an arid peninsula jutting into the Caribbean. Punta Gallinas, at the tip of La Guajira, is the northernmost point in South America. There are a few low-lying mountain ranges in La Guajira, such as the Serranía de la Macuira (864 meters/2,835 feet), which is covered with rainforest. The Sierra Nevada de Santa Marta and Serranía de la Macuira are biological islands, and their upper reaches are home to numerous endemic species that evolved in isolation.

Pacífico

The Pacific Coast of Colombia extends 1,329 kilometers from Ecuador to Panama, about the same length as the coast of California. The term Pacífico, as it relates to Colombia, designates all the land—jungle to be more accurate—that lies between the Pacific Ocean and the Cordillera Occidental. This region covers 6 percent of Colombia and is home to about 2 percent of the population.

The topography of this region is mostly flat, with the low-lying coastal Serranía del Baudó (1,810 meters/5,940 feet) providing a mountainous backdrop to the coastal plain and forming an inland basin that is drained by the mighty Río Atrato, which flows northwards into the Caribbean Sea. The coast has a number of bays and inlets, notably the Ensenada de Utría (Utría Inlet), visited by humpback whales traveling every winter from the Antarctic Sea to give birth in the warm waters of the Colombian Pacific. South of Buenaventura, the coast has extensive mangroves, much of which are well-preserved. Offshore are two islands: Isla Gorgona is 35 kilometers off the coast on the continental shelf, and tiny Malpelo is 490 kilometers off the coast. Both of these islands are likely of volcanic origin.

The Colombian Pacific region is one of the wettest places on Earth, with average annual rainfall of 10,000 millimeters (33 feet). Due to the enormous amount of precipitation, the region has a dense river network with dozens of major arteries, such as the Río Baudó, Río San Juan, and Río Patía.

Los Llanos

The Llanos, Colombia's vast eastern plains, cover an area of 250,000 square kilometers, roughly 25 percent of Colombia's territory. The plains are hemmed in to the west by Cordillera Oriental and to the south by the Amazon rainforest, and extend far into Venezuela. Though the transition between the Amazon and the Llanos is gradual, the Río Guaviare, which flows from west to east at a longitude that is roughly midway between the northern and southern tips of Colombia, is considered the demarcation line between these two areas. The Llanos are home to about 1.5 million inhabitants, or about 3 percent of the population, making it the region with the second lowest population density—after the Amazon region—in the country.

After the genesis of the Andes, water flowing eastward down the mountains accumulated in a vast freshwater lake that was confined on the east by old mountainous formations (now the Guyana and Brazilian highlands). Large amounts of sediments were deposited, forming the basis for the Llanos' undulating topography. Near the Andes, elevations can reach 300 meters and, moving east, slowly decrease in altitude until they reach the north-flowing Río Orinoco, which forms the border between Colombia and Venezuela.

The only significant mountain range in Los Llanos is the Serranía de la Macarena (Macarena Range), a 120-kilometer-long, 30-kilometer-wide range that is 45 kilometers east of the Andes just of the Río Guayabero, a tributary of the Río Guaviare. This range is part of the Guyana Shield complex of ancient, highly eroded remnants of mountains that existed long before the formation of the Andes.

The Llanos are drained by a multitude of large rivers, such as the Río Guaviare, Río Vichada, and Río Meta, which flow down from the Andes and meander towards the east. All the rivers of the Llanos are tributaries of the Orinoco—for this reason, this region is also often called La Orinoquía.

Amazon

The Amazon region of Colombia comprises 400,000 million kilometers, or roughly 35 percent of Colombia's territory, including all the territory east of the Andes and south of the Río Guaviare. The Colombian portion covers only 10 percent of the entire Amazon drainage basin. Total population in the Amazon region is 1.1 million, or 2 percent of the country's population. It is the most sparsely populated area in the country.

Like the Llanos, the Amazon has an undulating terrain, interrupted occasionally with ancient, low-lying mountainous formations of the Guyana Shield, such as the Serranía de Chiribiquete, a series of highly eroded tabletop mountains. The Amazon consists of two distinct but intermingled areas: *terra firme*, the undulated lands that are above the highest flood point, and *varzea*, floodplains along the main rivers, which can extend 50 kilometers from the river.

There are two types of rivers in the Amazon: the predominant white rivers, which carry sediments down from the Andes; and the black rivers, which originate within the rainforest in the Guyana Shield formations that were long ago denuded of soil due to erosion. As these waters travel though the flooded forest, they pick up pigments that give them their characteristic black color. *Igapo* is the name given to jungles flooded by black water rivers. Most of the rivers of the Colombian Amazon are white, such as the massive Río Putumayo, Río Caquetá, Río Apaporis, and Río Vaupés, all of which are more than 1,000 kilometers long. The main black river in Colombia is the Río Guainía, which does originate in the Andes, and which is the headwater of the largest black river of the Amazon—the Río Negro—which flows into the milky Amazon at Manaus, in Brazil.

CLIMATE

Colombia has a typically tropical climate, with no change of seasons. Climate is related primarily to elevation, and there are defined annual precipitation patterns.

In the mountainous areas, temperature decreases approximately six degrees Celsius per every 1,000 meters of elevation (three degrees Fahrenheit per every 1,000 feet). The common designations for the altitudinal zones are as follows: *tierra caliente* (hot lands) is anywhere below 1,000 meters of elevation; *tierra templada* (temperate lands) is anywhere between 1,000 and 2000 meters; and *tierra fría* (cold land) is anywhere above 2,000 meters. Roughly 80 percent of the country is *tierra caliente*, 10 percent is *tierra templada,* and 7 percent is *tierra fría*.

Cartagena, which is at sea level, has an average temperature of 27.5°C (81.5°F); Medellín, which is at 1,600 meters (5,250 feet), has an average temperature of 22°C (71.5°F); and the capital city of Bogotá, which is built at 2,625 meters (8,612 feet), has an average temperature of 13.5°C (56°F).

Precipitation patterns vary throughout the country. In the Andean region, there are generally two periods of *verano* (dry season, literally "summer"), from December to March and from June to September, and two periods of *invierno* (rainy season, literally "winter"), in April and May and from October to November. In the Caribbean Coast, the dry period is from December to April and the rainy season is from May to November. In the Pacific it rains almost the entire year, but there is a slight dry spell from December to March. In the Llanos, there are two very marked seasons: a very dry *verano* from November to March and a very wet *invierno* from April to October. In the Amazon, it rains almost the entire year, but there is a slight dry spell from August to October.

Extreme weather in Colombia is rare, but the country is susceptible to weather phenomena such as El Niño or La Niña, when temperatures in the Pacific Ocean rise or fall, respectively. More than 400 people died during devastating flooding and mudslides that occurred throughout much of the country during a particularly strong Niña in 2010-2011.

San Andrés and Providencia are occasionally, and the Caribbean mainland of Colombia rarely, in the path of Atlantic hurricanes August through October. The last storm of significance was Hurricane Beta in 2005. It caused considerable damage in Providencia.

Flora and Fauna

When it comes to biodiversity, Colombia is a place of superlatives. Though representing only 0.2 percent of the Earth's surface, it is home to about 10 percent of all the species in the world. The country has an estimated 55,000 plant species, including 3,500 species of orchids. Only Brazil, with seven times the land surface, has as many plant species. Colombia is the country with the greatest number of bird species in the world—about 1,800. It's also home to about 3,200 fish, 750 amphibian species, 500 reptile, and 450 mammal species. No wonder Colombia was designated as one of 17 so-called megadiverse countries, a select club of countries that are home to an outsized proportion of the world's biodiversity. Other megadiverse countries include Australia, Brazil, China, Democratic Republic of Congo, Indonesia, Madagascar, Mexico, the United States, and South Africa.

This enormous biodiversity is the result of Colombia's location in the tropics, where year-round sunlight and high precipitation are conducive to plant growth, plus the country's mountainous topography with numerous climatic zones and microclimates that have created biological islands where species have evolved in relative isolation. Furthermore, the recent Ice Ages were not as severe in this part of the world and as a result many ancient species were preserved. Finally, Colombia's location on the crossroads between Central and South America has further enriched the country's biodiversity.

RAINFOREST

Rainforests are among the most complex ecosystems on Earth. They have a layered structure with towering trees that soar 30-40 meters high to form the forest's canopy. Some of the most common rainforest trees are the ceiba, mahogany, myrtle, laurel, acacia, and rubber trees. Occasionally, particularly high trees known as *emergentes* pierce the canopy, reaching as high up as 60 meters (200 feet). Below the canopy is the *sotobosque*, a middle layer of smaller trees and palms that vie for the sunlight filtering in through the canopy. In the canopy and *sotobosque* there are many epiphytes (plants such as orchids and bromeliads) that have adapted to live on top of trees so as to be nearer to the sunlight. Near the ground live

Colombian Fruits

Colombia is a land bursting with exotic fruit. Sold from the back of pickup trucks by farmers on the roadside, overflowing at stalls in colorful markets in every town and village, lined up in neat rows in the produce section at fancy grocery stores and at juice stands—just about anywhere you go, delicious fruit is in reach.

You know pineapple, papaya, mangos, and bananas, but be sure to try these tropical delights that you may not have encountered outside of Colombia.

· **Pitahaya** (dragon fruit): Looking like a yellow grenade, *pitahayas* have a sweet white meat inside.

· **Guanábana** (soursop): By far the most weird-looking fruit, soursop resemble prehistoric dinosaur eggs. Inside the large green spiky fruit is a milky and slimy flesh. *Guanábana* is great in juices and desserts.

· **Granadilla:** Crack open this orangey-yellow fruit and slurp down the slimy gray contents, seeds and all. It's delicious.

· **Higo** (prickly pear): This green fruit comes from cactus plants and has sweet, if tough, orange-colored meat.

· **Chirimoya** (cherimoya): This green fruit that resembles a smooth artichoke is covered with a smooth, silky skin and filled with delectable, sweet pulp.

· **Níspero** (sapodilla): A fruit with a deep brown color that tastes like a prepared sweet.

· **Mangostino** (mangosteen): Crack open a deep purple mangosteen and enjoy the sweet segments inside. They're full of antioxidants.

· **Uchuva** (Cape gooseberry): Known in English as Cape gooseberries, these tart yellow berries are a cousin of the tomato and are tasty on their own or in salads, but are often used in jams and sweets.

· **Mamoncillo:** Tough-skinned grapes (don't eat the skin), mamoncillos are usually only sold at street markets.

---

plants that require little sunlight, including ferns, grasses, and many types of fungi. The two main rainforests in Colombia, the Amazon and the Chocó, have the same layered structure, though they have some differences in their flora and fauna.

The Amazon Rainforest is home to a large number of vertebrates. Over millennia, a large number of canopy-dwelling species evolved. Monkeys, such as the large and extremely agile spider monkey, the woolly monkey, and the howler monkey, evolved prehensile tails that allowed them to move easily from branch to branch. Anteaters, such as the tamandua and the *oso mielero* (giant anteater), and the incredibly cute *kinkajú* (kinkajou) also developed prehensile tails. Other inhabitants of the canopy include sloths, such as the adorable-looking three-toed sloth, whose strategy is not agility but passivity: It eats tree

vegetation and is covered with algae which gradually turn it green to allow for good camouflage. The canopy is also home to myriad bats and many birds, including exotic eagles, curassows, toucans, woodpeckers, cotingas, and macaws.

Notable is the majestic harpy eagle, with powerful claws and the ability to fly unencumbered through the canopy. It preys on monkeys and sloths, which it kills with the force of its claws. The *tigrillo* (tiger cat) is a small and extremely endangered species. It has a long tail that helps with its balance as it moves from tree to tree.

On the ground, large vertebrates include the extremely endangered tapir, an ancient mammal species that can grow two meters long (over six feet) and weigh 300 kilograms (660 pounds). It is equally at ease on land as in the water. Other land mammals include the giant armadillo, giant anteater, deer, and boars, such as the *saíno* and *pecarí.* Smaller mammals include the *guatín* and *borugo,* both rodents. These animals are often prey to the puma and jaguar, both of which inhabit the Amazon but are difficult to observe in the wild.

The rivers of the Amazon are home to more than 1,500 species of fish, including endangered *pirarucú,* one of the largest freshwater fishes on Earth. There are also dolphins, both pink and gray. The former evolved separately from the ocean-going dolphins when the Amazon was an inland sea. The Amazonian gray dolphins are sea dolphins that adapted to living in freshwater. Other aquatic mammals include the highly endangered manatee and otters.

The Chocó Rainforest is particularly rich in palms, of which 120 species have been identified. In fact, it is sometimes referred to as the "Land of the Palms." The forest also abounds in cycads, ancient plants that have a stout trunk and crowns of hard, stiff leaves. Chocó is also notable for more than 40 species of brightly colored poisonous frogs, known locally as *ranas kokois.* These small frogs are covered with a deadly poison and have evolved stunning coloring, from bright orange to red, gold, and blue. They are active in the day and therefore relatively easy to spot. Of Colombia's 1,800 species of birds, more than 1,000 have been identified in the Chocó, including a large number of hummingbirds. Offshore, the Pacific welcomes the annual migration of Antarctic humpback whales. The beaches of the Pacific Coast are popular nesting areas for sea turtles, in particular the *tortuga golfina* (olive ridley) and *tortuga carey* (hawksbill) sea turtles. On the island of Gorgona 35 kilometers from the mainland, an unusual—and quite stunning—species of lizard is the blue anole lizard. Highly threatened, it is found only on Gorgona.

CLOUD FOREST

Rainforests that grow at higher altitudes on the flanks of the Andes are known as montane rainforests or cloud forests because they are often enveloped in mist that results from the condensation of warm air against chillier mountain currents. Unlike the lowland rainforest, cloud forests only have two layers, the canopy and ground layer. Generally, the vegetation is less dense than the lowland rainforest. However, it is home to many palms, ferns, and epiphytes, particularly orchids.

The type of cloud forest vegetation is dictated by altitude. *Selva subandina* (sub-Andean forest) vegetation grows between the altitudes of 1,000-2,300 meters (3,300-7,500 feet), where temperature varies 16-23°C (61-73°F). Plant species include the distinctive Dr. Seuss-like white *yarumo* with its oversized leaves, as well as cedar, oak, and mahogany trees. Many palms grow here, including the svelte wax palm and *tagua,* which produces a nut that resembles ivory. Ferns include the striking *palma boba* or tree fern. Colombia's premier crop, coffee, is grown at this elevation.

At elevations between 2,300-3,600 meters (7,500-12,000 feet), the vegetation is described as *selva Andina* (Andean forest). This vegetation is even less dense and at higher elevations the trees are smaller. The vegetation bears some resemblance to landscapes in the northern and southern hemispheres. *Selva Andina* includes many oak, *encenillo, sietecuero* (glory bush), and pine trees.

Mammals include the spectacled or Andean bear, the only species of bear in South America, the mountain (or woolly) tapir, anteaters, armadillos, sloths, boars, foxes, and *olingos,* a small arboreal carnivore of the raccoon family. In 2013, the *olinguito* (small *olingo*), an incredibly cute-looking animal, was declared a new species. Other unusual animals include the slow-moving *guagua loba* and *guatín,* both of which are rodents. In addition, numerous species of monkeys inhabit the cloud forest, including noisy troops of howler monkeys. Birds include many types of *barranqueros* (motmots), including the spectacular blue-crowned motmot. Other common birds include *tángaras* (tanagers), woodpeckers, warblers, parrots, owls, and ducks, including the beautiful white and black torrent duck.

PÁRAMOS

Páramos are a unique tropical highland ecosystem that thrives above 3,500 meters (11,500 feet), where UV radiation is higher, oxygen is scarcer, and where temperatures vary from minus 2 to 10 degrees Celsius (28-50°F). Due to frequent mist and precipitation, *páramos* are often saturated with water and have many lakes. They are true "water factories" that provide water to many of Colombia's cities, notably Bogotá. Though *páramos* exist throughout the New World tropics, most are located in Colombia. The Parque Nacional Natural Sumapaz, south of Bogotá, is the world's largest *páramo*.

Páramo vegetation includes more than 50 species of *frailejón* (genus *Espeletia*), eerily beautiful plants that have imposing tall trunks and thick yellow-greenish leaves. Other *páramo* vegetation includes shrubs, grasses, and *cojines* (cushion plants). Mammals include the spectacled bear, *páramo* tapir, weasels, squirrels, and bats. The *páramo* is the realm of the majestic black and white Andean condor, which has a wingspan of up to three meters (10 feet). The condor, whose numbers had declined to the point of extinction, are found in the national parks of the Sierra Nevada de Santa Marta, Sierra Nevada del Cocuy, and Los Nevados. The *páramo* lakes welcome many types of ducks, including the Andean duck, as well as smaller birds.

TROPICAL DRY FORESTS

Tropical dry forests exist in areas where there is a prolonged dry season. The vegetation includes deciduous trees that lose their leaves during the dry season, allowing them to conserve water. Trees on moister sites and those with access to ground water tend to be evergreen. Before Columbus, this ecosystem covered much of the Colombian Caribbean coast. However, much of it was cut down for cattle ranching. Pockets still exist east of the Golfo de Morrosquillo and at the base of the Sierra Nevada de Santa Marta. Tropical dry forests are the most endangered tropical ecosystem in the world.

© ANDREW DIER

This unusual *frailejón*, a type of cactus, grows in Colombia's *páramos*.

Though less biologically diverse than rainforests, tropical dry forests are home to a wide variety of wildlife. They were once the stomping ground of the now highly endangered *marimonda*, or white-fronted spider monkey.

TROPICAL GRASSLANDS

Los Llanos (The Plains) of Colombia are covered with lush tropical grasslands. Vegetation includes long-stemmed and carpet grasses in the drier areas and swamp grasses in low-lying humid areas. There are also thick patches of forest throughout the plains and along the rivers (known as gallery forests). These plains are teeming with wildlife, including deer, anteaters, armadillos, tapirs, otters, jaguars, pumas, and *chigüiros* (also known as capybaras), the world's largest rodent. The Llanos are also home to the giant anaconda and to one of the most endangered species on Earth, the Orinoco crocodile, which reaches up to seven meters (23 feet) long.

© ANDREW DIER

hawk

History

BEFORE COLUMBUS

Located at the juncture between Central and South America, what is now Colombia was a necessary transit point for the migration of people who settled South America. However, as these peoples left few physical traces of their passage, little is known of them. The oldest human objects found in Colombia, utensils discovered near Bogotá, are dated from 14,000 BC. With the expansion of agriculture and sedentary life throughout the territory of present-day Colombia around 1000 BC, various indigenous cultures started producing stunning ceramic and gold work, as well as some monumental remains. These remains provide rich material evidence of their development. Nonetheless, there are significant gaps in the understanding of the history of these early peoples.

From around 700 BC, the area of San Agustín, near the origin of the Río Magdalena in southern Colombia, was settled by people who practiced agriculture and produced pottery. Starting in the 1st century AD, the people of San Agustín created hundreds of monumental stone statues set on large platforms, which comprise the largest pre-Columbian archaeological site extant between Mesoamerica and Peru. By AD 800, this society had disappeared.

In the northwestern plains of Colombia, south of present-day Cartagena, starting in the 1st century AD, the Sinú people constructed a large complex of mounds in the shape of fish bones that regulated flooding, allowing cultivation in flooded and dry seasons. During rainy seasons, the water flooded the lower cavities, allowing for cultivation on the mounds; during dry season, cultivation took place in the cavities that had been enriched by the flood waters. These monumental formations are still visible from the sky. By the time of the Spanish conquest, these people no longer inhabited the area.

From AD 500 to 900, the area of Tierradentro, west of San Agustín, was settled by an agricultural society that dug magnificent decorated underground tombs, produced large stone statues, and built oval-shaped buildings on artificial terraces. As in the case of the San Agustín and the Sinú people, it is not known what happened to these people.

At the time of the conquest, present-day Colombia was populated by a large number of distinct agricultural societies that often maintained peaceful trading relations among themselves. The two largest groups were the Muisca people, who lived in the altiplano (highlands) of the Cordillera Oriental, and the Tayrona, who lived on the slopes of the Sierra Nevada de Santa Marta. Other groups included the Quimbaya, who settled the area of the present-day Coffee Region; the Calima, in present-day Valle del Cauca; and the Nariños, in the mountainous areas of southwest Colombia.

These indigenous societies were mostly organized at the village level with loose association with other villages. Only the Muisca and the Tayrona had a more developed political organization. Though these were all agricultural societies, they also engaged in hunting, fishing, and mining and produced sophisticated ceramics and gold work. Each group specialized in what their environment had to offer and engaged in overland trade. For example, the Muiscas produced textiles and salt, which they traded for gold, cotton, tobacco, and shells with other groups.

The Muiscas, a Chibcha-speaking people, were the largest group, with an estimated 600,000 inhabitants at the time of the Spanish conquest. They settled the Cordillera Oriental in AD 300 and occupied a large territory that comprises most of the highland areas of the present-day departments of Cundinamarca and Boyacá. At the time of the conquest, they were organized into two large confederations: one in the south headed by the Zipa, whose capital was Bacatá near present-day Bogotá; and another headed by the Zaque, whose capital was at Hunza, the location of present-day Tunja. The Muiscas had a highly homogeneous culture, skilled in weaving, ceramics, and gold work. Their cosmography placed significant importance on high Andean lakes, several of which were sacred, including Guatavita, Siecha, and Iguaque.

The Tayrona, who settled the slopes of the Sierra Nevada de Santa Marta, were also a Chibcha-speaking people. They had a more urban society, with towns that included temples and ceremonial plazas built on stone terraces, and practiced farming on terraces carved out of the mountains. There are an estimated 200 Tayrona sites, of which Ciudad Perdida (Lost City), built at 1,100 meters in the Sierra Nevada de Santa Marta, is the largest and best known. Many of these towns, including El Pueblito in the Parque Nacional Natural Tayrona, were occupied at the time of the Spanish conquest. The Kogis, Arhuacos, Kankuamos, and Wiwas, current inhabitants of the sierra, are their descendants and consider many places in the sierra sacred.

THE SPANISH CONQUEST (1499-1550)

As elsewhere in the New World, the arrival of Europeans was an unmitigated disaster for the Native American societies. Though there were pockets of resistance, on the whole the indigenous people were unable to push back the small number of armed Spanish conquistadors. Harsh conditions after the conquest and the spread of European diseases, such as measles and smallpox, to which the indigenous people had no immunity, killed off millions of indigenous people. The Spanish conquest of present-day Colombia took about 50 years and was largely completed by the 1550s.

In 1499, the first European set foot on present-day Colombia in the northern Guajira peninsula. In 1510, a first, unsuccessful colony was established in the Gulf of Urabá near the current border with Panama. In 1526, the Spanish established Santa Marta, their first permanent foothold, from where they tried, unsuccessfully, to subdue the Tayronas. In 1533, they established Cartagena, which was to become a major colonial port.

In 1536, Gonzalo Jiménez de Quesada set off south from Santa Marta to conquer the fabled lands of El Dorado in the Andean heartland. After a year of grueling travel up the swampy Río Magdalena valley, 200 surviving members of Jiménez de Quesada's 800 original troops arrived in the Muisca lands near present-day Bogotá. After a short interlude of courteous relations, the Spaniards' greed led them to obliterate the Muisca towns and temples. They found significant amounts of gold, especially in the town of Hunza, but they were, by and large, disappointed. In 1538, Jiménez de Quesada founded Santa Fe de Bogotá as the capital of this new territory, which he called Nueva Granada—New Granada—after his birthplace.

Sebastián de Belalcázar, a lieutenant of Francisco Pizarro, led a second major expedition that arrived in the Muisca lands from the south. Having conquered the Inca city of Quito, Belalcázar and his army traveled north, conquering a vast swath of land from present-day Ecuador to the *sábana* (high plateau) of Bogotá. Along the way, he founded several cities, including Popayán and Cali in 1536. He arrived shortly after Quesada had founded Bogotá. Incredibly, a third conquistador, the German Nikolaus Federmann, arrived in Bogotá at the same time, having traveled from Venezuela via the Llanos. Rather than fight for supremacy, the three conquistadors decided to take their rival claims to arbitration at the Spanish Court. In an unexpected turn of events, none of the three obtained title to the Muisca lands. When Bogotá became the administrative capital of New Granada, they came under the sway of the Spanish Crown. Other expeditions swept across the Caribbean coast, through current-day Antioquia and the Santanderes.

COLONIAL NUEVA GRANADA (1550-1810)

For most of its colonial history, Nueva Granada, as colonial Colombia was called,

was an appendage of the Viceroyalty of Peru. In 1717, Spain decided to establish a viceroyalty in Nueva Granada but changed its mind six years later because the benefits did not justify the cost. In 1739, the viceroyalty was reestablished, with Santa Fe de Bogotá as its capital. It was an unwieldy territory, encompassing present-day Colombia, Venezuela, Ecuador, and Panama. To make it more manageable, Venezuela and Panama were ruled by captain-generals and Ecuador by a president. At the local level, the viceroyalty was divided into *provincias* (provinces), each with a local assembly called a *cabildo*.

Settlement in Nueva Granada occurred primarily in three areas: where there were significant indigenous populations to exploit, as in the case of Tunja in the former Muisca territory; where there were gold deposits, as in Cauca, Antioquia, and Santander; and along trade routes, for example at Honda and Mompóx on the Río Magdalena. Cartagena was the main port of call for the biennial convoys of gold and silver sent to Spain. Bogotá lived off of the official bureaucracy and sustained a fair number of artisans. Present-day Antioquia and Santander supported small-scale farming to provide provisions to the gold mining camps. Nueva Granada was one of the least economically dynamic of Spain's New World possessions. The mountainous topography and high transportation costs meant that agricultural production was primarily for local consumption and gold was the only significant export.

Colonial society was composed of a small Spanish and Creole (descendants of Spanish settlers) elite governing a large mestizo (mixed indigenous-white) population. The Spanish had initially preserved indigenous communal lands known as *resguardos*, but the demographic collapse of the native population and intermarriage meant that, unlike in Peru or Mexico, there were relatively few people who were fully indigenous. There were also black slaves who were forced mostly to work in the mines and haciendas (plantations). Society was overwhelmingly Catholic and Spanish-speaking.

Culturally, Nueva Granada was also

Colombia's National Parks

From undisturbed coral reefs to the Amazonian jungle to snow-covered mountain ranges, Colombia's national park system is indeed a treasure and making the effort to visit them is worthwhile for any visitor. The country's system of natural parks and protected areas covers more than 14 million hectares: around 13.4 percent of the country! It includes 42 Parques Nacionales Naturales (National Natural Parks), which are major areas of ecological interest that have remained largely untouched by human intervention; and 10 Santuarios de Flora y Fauna (Flora and Fauna Sanctuaries), areas that are devoted to the preservation of specific ecosystems. Of the 42 parks, 24 are open for tourism. The rest are officially off limits, mostly due to security reasons or in order to respect the territory of indigenous communities.

In 1960, PNN Cueva de los Guácharos, in the southwest, was the first park to be established. The number of parks steadily increased, especially from 1986 to 1990 when President Virgilio Barco doubled the extension of parks from roughly 5 million hectares to 10 million hectares. In the past few years, the government has again been increasing the number and extension of parks. In 2013 President Juan Manuel Santos doubled the size of the PNN Serranía de Chiribiquete to its present 2.8 million hectares, or three times the size of Yellowstone National Park.

Charged with the considerable task of administering this huge system are a mere 430 rangers: roughly one person for every 33,000 hectares. Rangers face a great challenge in protecting the parks against threats related to human encroachment, particularly cattle ranching and the planting of illicit crops. There are other threats as well, such as illegal mining and logging. Paradoxically, what has preserved many of the parks until now has been the lack of security due to Colombia's internal conflict. As security conditions improve, there will be increasing pressure on these natural habitats. The Parks Service is actively engaging with the communities that live near the parks and is transferring the operation of much of the ecotourism infrastructure to community-based organizations as part of an effort to enlist local communities in the preservation of the land.

Entry permits and entry fees are only required in a handful of highly visited parks, such as PNN Tayrona, PNN Gorgona, PNN Cocuy, and PNN Los Nevados. At these, you will automatically be charged if you book lodging in advance, or if not, upon arrival. If you want to be meticulous, you can obtain the entry permit and pay entry fees in advance by contacting the **Parques Nacionales** (tel. 1/353-2400, www.parquesnacionales.gov.co) in Bogotá.

---

somewhat of a backwater. Though there was a modest flourishing of the arts, Bogotá could not compete with the magnificent architectural and artistic production of Quito, Lima, or Mexico City. The only truly notable event of learning that took place was the late 18th-century Expedición Botánica (Botanical Expedition), headed by Spanish naturalist José Celestino Mutis, the personal doctor to one of the viceroys. The aim of the expedition was to survey all the species of Nueva Granada—that was a rather tall order given that Colombia is home to 10 percent of the world's species! However, the expedition did some remarkable research and produced beautiful prints of the fauna and flora.

The late colonial period saw unrest in Nueva Granada. Starting in 1781, a revolt known as the Rebelión de los Comuneros took place in the province of Socorro (north of Bogotá) in present-day Santander as a result of an attempt by colonial authorities to levy higher taxes. It was not an anti-royalist movement, however, as its slogan indicates: ¡Viva el Rey, Muera el Mal Gobierno! ("Long live the king, down with bad government!"). Rather it was a protest against unfair taxes, not much different from the Boston Tea Party. However, it gave the Spanish government a fright. A rebel army, led by José Antonio Galán, marched on Bogotá. Negotiations put an end to the assault, and later the authorities ruthlessly persecuted the leaders of the revolt.

THE STRUGGLES FOR INDEPENDENCE (1810-1821)

Though there was some ill feeling against the colonial government, as the Rebelión de los Comuneros attests, as well as rivalry between the Spanish- and American-born elites, it was an external event, the Napoleonic invasion of Spain, that set off the chain of events that led to independence of Nueva Granada and the rest of the Spanish dominion in the New World.

In 1808, Napoleon invaded Spain, took King Ferdinand VII prisoner, and tried to impose his own brother, Joseph, as king of Spain. The Spaniards revolted, establishing a Central Junta in Seville to govern during the king's temporary absence from power. Faced with the issue of whether to recognize the new Central Junta in Spain, the colonial elites decided to take matters in their own hands and establish juntas of their own. The first such junta in Nueva Granada was established in Caracas in April 1810. Cartagena followed suit in May and Bogotá on July 20, 1810. According to popular myth, the revolt in Bogotá was the result of the failure of a prominent Spaniard merchant to lend a flower vase to a pair of Creoles.

Though they pledged alliance to Ferdinand VII, once the local elites had tasted power, there was no going back. Spanish authorities were expelled, and in 1811, a government of sorts, under the loose mantle of the Provincias Unidas de Nueva Granada (United Provinces of New Granada), was established with its capital at Tunja. Bogotá and the adjoining province of Cundinamarca stayed aloof from the confederation, arguing that it was too weak to resist the Spanish. Subsequently, various provinces of Nueva Granada declared outright independence, starting with Venezuela and Cartagena in 1811 and Cundinamarca in 1813.

Several cities remained loyal to the crown, namely Santa Marta and deeply conservative Pasto in the south. From 1812-1814 there was a senseless civil war between the Provincias Unidas and Cundinamarca—that is why this period is called the Patria Boba, or Foolish Fatherland. Ultimately, the Provincias Unidas prevailed with the help of a young Venezuelan captain by the name of Simón Bolívar.

After the restoration of Ferdinand VII, Spain attempted to retake its wayward colonies, with a military expedition and reign of terror known as the Reconquista—the Reconquest. The Spanish forces took Cartagena by siege in 1815 and took control of Bogotá in May 1816. However, in 1819, a revolutionary army composed of Venezuelans, Nueva Granadans, and European mercenaries headed by Bolívar arrived across the Llanos from Venezuela and decisively defeated the Spanish army in the Batalla del Puente de Boyacá—the Battle of the Boyacá Bridge—on August 7, near Tunja. The rest of the country fell quickly to the revolutionary army. With support from Nueva Granada, Bolívar defeated the Spanish in Venezuela in 1821. Panama, which had remained under Spanish control, declared independence in 1821. Finally, Bolívar dispatched Antonio José de Sucre to take Quito in 1822, bringing an end to the Spanish rule of Nueva Granada.

GRAN COLOMBIA: A FLAWED UNION (1821-1830)

Shortly after the Battle of Boyacá, the Congress of Angostura, a city on the Río Orinoco in Venezuela, proclaimed the union of Nueva Granada, Venezuela, and Ecuador under the name of the República de Colombia. Historians refer to this entity as Gran Colombia. In 1821, while the fight for independence was still raging in parts of Venezuela and Ecuador, a constitutional congress met in Cúcuta. An ongoing debate about whether a centralist or federalist scheme was preferable resulted in a curious compromise: the República de Colombia assumed a highly centralist form, considered necessary to finish the battle for independence, but left the issue of federalism open to review after 10 years. The document was generally liberal, enshrining individual liberties and providing for the manumission of slaves, meaning that the children of slaves were born free.

Bolívar, who was born in Venezuela, was named president. Francisco de Paula Santander, who was born near Cúcuta in Nueva Granada, was named vice president. Santander had fought alongside Bolívar in the battles for independence of Nueva Granada and was seen as an able administrator. While Bolívar continued south to liberate Ecuador and Peru, Santander assumed the reins of power in Bogotá. He charted a generally liberal course, instituting public education and a curriculum that included avant garde thinkers such as Jeremy Bentham. However, the highly centralist structure was unsavory to elites in Venezuela and Ecuador, who disliked rule from Bogotá. Shortly after the Congress of Cúcuta, revolt broke out in Venezuela and Ecuador. In 1826, Bolívar returned from Bolivia and Peru, hoping for the adoption in Gran Colombia of the Bolivian Constitution, an unusual document he drafted that called for a presidency for life.

There had been a growing distance between Bolívar and Santander: Bolívar saw Santander as an overzealous Liberal reformer while Santander disliked Bolívar's authoritarian tendencies. In 1828, after a failed constitutional congress that met in Ocaña in eastern Colombia, Bolívar assumed dictatorial powers. He rolled back many of Santander's liberal reforms. In September 1828 there was an attempt on Bolívar's life in Bogotá. This was famously foiled by his companion, Manuela Sáenz. The last years of Gran Colombia were marked by revolts in various parts of the country and a war with Peru. In 1830, a further constitutional assembly was convened in Bogotá, but by that point Gran Colombia had ceased to exist: Venezuela and Ecuador had seceded. In March 1830, a physically ill Bolívar decided to leave for voluntary exile in Europe and died on his way in Santa Marta.

CIVIL WARS AND CONSTITUTIONS (1830-1902)

After the separation of Venezuela and Ecuador, what is now Colombia adopted the name República de Nueva Granada. In 1832, it adopted a new constitution that corrected many of the errors of the excessively centralist constitution of Gran Colombia. There was a semblance of stability with the orderly succession of elected presidents. The elimination of some monasteries in Pasto sparked a short civil conflict known as the Guerra de los Supremos, which lasted 1839-1842. During this war, Conservative and Liberal factions coalesced for the first time, establishing the foundation of Colombia's two-party system. Generally, the Conservative Party supported the Catholic church, favored centralization, and followed the ideas of Bolívar. The Liberal Party supported federalism and free trade and identified with the ideas of Santander.

The country's rugged topography meant that Nueva Granada was not very integrated into the world economy. Gold, extracted mostly in Antioquia, was the main export. Most of the country eked out its subsistence from agriculture, with trade restricted within regions. This period saw some economic development, such as steam navigation on the Magdalena and Cauca rivers, and a contract for the construction of the trans-isthmanian railroad in Panama, which had yet to secede.

Mid-century saw the rise of a new class of leaders who had grown up wholly under republican governments. They ushered in a period of liberal reform. In 1851, Congress abolished slavery. In 1853, a new constitution established universal male suffrage, religious tolerance, and direct election of provincial governors. The government reduced tariffs and Nueva Granada experienced a short export-oriented tobacco boom.

Conflicts between radical reformers within the Liberal Party, moderates, and Conservatives led to unrest in various provinces. In 1859, discontented Liberals under Tomás Cipriano de Mosquera revolted, leading to generalized civil war in which the Liberals were ultimately victorious. Once in power, they pushed radical reform. Mosquera expropriated all non-religious church property, partly in vengeance against church support of the Conservatives in the previous civil war.

The 1863 constitution was one of the world's

© ANDREW DIER

a plaque in Mompóx, denoting Simón Bolívar's presence

most audacious federalist experiments. The country was renamed the Estados Unidos de Colombia (United States of Colombia), comprising nine states. The president had a two-year term and was not immediately re-electable. All powers that were not explicitly assigned to the central government were the responsibility of the states. Many of the states engaged in true progressive policies, such as establishing public education and promoting the construction of railroads. This period coincided with agricultural booms in quinine, cotton, and indigo that, for the first time, brought limited prosperity. This period saw the establishment of the Universidad Nacional (National University) and the country's first bank.

In 1880 and then in 1884, a coalition of Conservatives and moderate Liberals, who were dissatisfied with the radical policies, elected Rafael Núñez as president. Núñez tried to strengthen the power of the central government, sparking a Liberal revolt. The Conservatives were ultimately victorious and, in 1886, enacted a new centralist constitution

that lasted through most of the 20th century. The country was rechristened República de Colombia, the name it has conserved since then. During the period 1886 through 1904, known as the Regeneración, the Conservative Party held sway, rolling back many of the previous reforms, especially anticlerical measures and unrestricted male suffrage. The Liberal Party, excluded from power, revolted in 1899. The ensuing Guerra de los Mil Días (Thousand Days' War), which raged through 1902, was a terribly bloody conflict. It is not clear how many died in the war, but some historians put the figure as high as 100,000, or an incredible 2.5 percent of the country's population of four million at the time.

One year after the end of the war, Panama seceded. During the late 19th century, there had been resentment in Panama about the distribution of revenues from the transit trade that mostly were sent to Bogotá. However, in 1902 the local Panamanian elites had become alarmed at the lackadaisical attitude of the government in Bogotá regarding the construction of an interoceanic canal. After the failure of the French to build a canal, Colombia had entered into negotiations with the United States. In the closing days of the Guerra de los Mil Días, Colombia and the United States signed the Hay-Terran Treaty, which called for the construction of the canal, surrendering control over a strip of land on either side of the canal to the United States. The Americans threatened that if the treaty were not ratified, they would dig the canal in Nicaragua. Arguing that the treaty undermined Colombian sovereignty, the congress in Bogotá unanimously rejected the treaty with the United States in August 1903. That was a big mistake: A few months later, Panama seceded with the support of the United States.

PEACE AND REFORM (1902-1946)

Under the leadership of moderate Conservative Rafael Reyes, who was president 1904-1909, Colombia entered a period of peace and stability. Reyes focused on creating a professional, nonpartisan army. He gave representation to Liberals in government, enacted a protective tariff to spur domestic industry, and pushed public works. During his administration, Bogotá was finally connected by railway to the Río Magdalena. He reestablished relations with the United States, signing a treaty that provided Colombia with an indemnity for the loss of Panama. During the 1920s and 1930s, Colombia was governed by a succession of Conservative Party presidents. Though there was often electoral fraud, constitutional reform that guaranteed minority representation ensured peace.

Expanding world demand for coffee spurred production across Colombia, especially in southern Antioquia and what is now known as the Coffee Region, creating a new class of independent farmers. Improved transportation, especially the completion of the railways from Cali to Buenaventura on the Pacific Coast and from Medellín to the Río Magdalena, was key to the growth of coffee exports. In the Magdalena Medio region and in Norte

de Santander, U.S. companies explored and started producing petroleum. Medellín became a center of textile manufacturing. With its broken geography, air transportation developed rapidly. The Sociedad Colombo Alemana de Transportes Aéreos (Colombian German Air Transportation Society) or SCADTA, the predecessor of Avianca, was founded in Barranquilla in 1919, and is reputedly the second oldest commercial aviation company in the world (the oldest is KLM).

In 1930, a split Conservative ticket allowed the Liberals to win the elections. After being out of power for 50 years, the Liberal Party was happy to regain control of the state apparatus. This led to strife with Conservatives long accustomed to power—presaging the intense interparty violence that was to erupt 14 years later.

From 1932-1933, Colombia and Peru fought a brief war in the Amazon over the control of the port city of Leticia. The League of Nations brokered a truce, the first time that this body, which was a precursor to the United Nations, actively intervened in a dispute between two countries.

Starting in 1934, Liberal president Alfonso López Pumarejo undertook major social and labor reforms, with some similarities to Roosevelt's New Deal. His policies included agrarian reform, encouragement and protection of labor unions, and increased spending on education. He reduced the Catholic church's sway over education and eliminated the literacy requirement for male voters. Many of these reforms simply returned the country to policies that had been enacted by Liberals in the 1850s, 80 years prior. In opposition to these policies, a new radical right, with a confrontational style and strains of fascism and anti-Semitism, arose under the leadership of Laureano Gómez.

During World War II, Colombia closely allied itself with the United States and eventually declared war on the Axis powers in retaliation for German attacks on Colombian merchant ships in the Caribbean Sea. The government concentrated those of German-descent in a hotel in Fusagasugá near Bogotá and removed all German influence from SCADTA.

LA VIOLENCIA (1946-1953)

In the 1946 elections, the Liberal Party split its ticket between establishment-backed Gabriel Turbay and newcomer Jorge Eliécer Gaitán. Gaitán was a self-made man who had scaled the ladders of power within the Liberal Party despite the opposition of the traditional Liberal elite. He had a vaguely populist platform and much charisma. The moderate Conservative Mariano Ospina won a plurality of votes and was elected to the presidency. As in 1930, the transfer of power from Liberals to Conservatives and bureaucratic re-accommodation led to outbursts of violence.

On April 9, 1948, a deranged youth killed former presidential candidate Gaitán as he left his office in downtown Bogotá. His assassination sparked riots and bloodshed throughout the country, with severe destruction in the capital. The disturbance in Bogotá, known as El Bogotazo, occurred during the 9th Inter-American Conference, which had brought together leaders from all over the hemisphere. Young Fidel Castro happened to be in Bogotá that day, though he had no part in the upheaval.

The assassination of Gaitán fueled the violence that had started in 1946. Over the course of 10 years, an estimated 100,000-200,000 people died in what was laconically labeled La Violencia (The Violence). This conflict was comparable in destruction of human life with the Guerra de los Mil Días, the last civil war of the 19th century. The killing took place throughout the country, often in small towns and rural areas. Mostly it involved loyalists of the predominant party settling scores or intimidating members of the opposite party to extract land or economic gain. In some cases, the violence was sheer banditry. Numerous, horrific mass murders took place. The police often took sides with the Conservatives or simply turned a blind eye. In response, some Liberals resorted to armed resistance, giving birth to Colombia's first guerrilla armies. The Liberal Party boycotted the 1950 elections, and radical Conservative Laureano Gómez was elected president. His government pursued authoritarian and highly partisan policies, further exacerbating the violence.

DICTATORSHIP (1953-1957)

In 1953, with the purported aim of bringing an end to fighting between Liberals and Conservatives, the Colombian army, under the command of General Gustavo Rojas Pinilla, staged a coup. Rojas was able to reduce, but not halt, the violence, by curtailing police support of the Conservatives and by negotiating an amnesty with Liberal guerrillas. In 1954, Rojas was elected for a four-term period by a hand-picked assembly. Incidentally, it was this, non-democratically elected assembly that finally got around to extending suffrage to women, making Colombia one of the last countries in Latin America to do so. Rojas tried to build a populist regime with the support of organized labor, modeled after Perón in Argentina. His daughter, María Eugenia Rojas, though no Evita, was put in charge of social welfare programs. Though a majority of Colombians supported him at first, his repressive policies and press censorship ended up alienating the political elites.

THE NATIONAL FRONT (1957-1974)

In May 1957, under the leadership of Liberals and Conservatives, the country went on an extended general strike to oppose the dictatorship. Remarkably, Rojas voluntarily surrendered power and went into exile in Spain. As a way to put an end to La Violencia, Liberal and Conservative Party leaders proposed alternating presidential power for four consecutive terms while divvying up the bureaucracy on a 50-50 basis. The proposal, labeled the National Front, was ratified by a nationwide referendum and was in effect 1958-1974.

The National Front dramatically reduced the level of violence. After years of fighting, both factions were ready to give up their arms. During this period, thanks to competent economic management, the economy prospered and incomes rose. The government adopted import substitution policies that gave rise to a number of new industries, including automobiles.

By institutionalizing the power of the two traditional parties, the National Front had the unintended consequence of squeezing out other political movements, especially from the left. As a result, during the 1960s a number of leftist guerrilla groups appeared. Some were simply the continuation, under a new name, of the Liberal guerrillas formed during La Violencia. The Fuerzas Armadas Revolucionarias de Colombia (FARC) was a rural, peasant-based group espousing Soviet Marxism. The Ejército de Liberación Nacional (ELN) was a smaller group inspired by the Cuban revolution. The even smaller Ejército Popular de Liberación (EPL) was a Maoist-inspired group. The Movimiento 19 de Abril (M-19) was a more urban group formed by middle-class intellectuals after alleged electoral fraud deprived the populist ANAPO Party (Alianza Nacional Popular; created by ex-dictator Rojas) of power. During the 1970s and 1980s, the M-19 staged flashy coups, such as stealing Bolívar's sword (and promising to return it once the revolution had been achieved) in 1974 and seizing control of the Dominican Republic Embassy in Bogotá in 1980.

UNDER SIEGE (1974-1991)
The Drug Trade and the Rise of Illegal Armed Groups

Due to its relative proximity to the United States, treacherous geography, and weak government institutions, Colombia has been an ideal place for cultivation, production, and shipment of illegal drugs, primarily to the United States. During the 1970s, Colombia experienced a short-lived marijuana boom centered around the Sierra Nevada de Santa Marta. Eradication efforts by Colombian authorities and competition from homegrown marijuana produced in the U.S. quickly brought this boom to an end.

During the late 1970s, cocaine replaced marijuana as the main illegal drug. Though most of the coca cultivation at the time was in Peru and Bolivia, Colombian drug dealers based in Medellín started the business of picking up coca paste in Peru and Bolivia, processing it into cocaine in Colombia, and exporting the drug to the United States, where they even controlled some distribution at the local level. At its heyday in the mid-1980s, Pablo Escobar's Medellín Cartel controlled 80 percent of the world's cocaine trade. The rival Cali Cartel, controlled by the Rodríguez brothers, emerged in the 1980s and started to contest the supremacy of the Medellín Cartel, leading to a bloody feud.

During the 1980s and 1990s, coca cultivation shifted from Peru and Bolivia to Colombia, mainly to the Amazon regions of Putumayo, Caquetá, Meta, and Guaviare. Initially, leftist guerrillas such as the FARC protected the fields from the authorities in return for payment from the cartels. Eventually, they started processing and trafficking the drugs themselves. Though the guerrillas had other sources of income, such as kidnapping and extortion, especially of oil companies operating in the Llanos, the drug trade was a key factor in their growth. With these sources of income, they no longer needed popular support and morphed into criminal organizations. By the mid-1980s, the FARC had grown into a 4,000-strong army that controlled large portions of territory, especially in the south of the country.

During the 1980s and 1990s, the price of land was depressed as a result of the threat from the guerrillas. Using their vast wealth and power of intimidation, drug traffickers purchased vast swaths of land, mostly in the Caribbean coast of Colombia, at bargain prices. To defend their properties from extortion, they allied themselves with traditional landowners to create paramilitary groups. These groups often operated with the direct or tacit support of the army.

Colombian campesinos (small farmers), caught in the middle of the conflict between guerrillas and paramilitaries, suffered disproportionately. They were accused by both guerrillas and paramilitaries of sympathizing with the enemy, and the government was not there to protect them. The paramilitaries were particularly ruthless, often ordering entire villages to abandon their lands or massacring them. The conflict between guerrillas and paramilitaries is at the source of the mass displacement of people in Colombia. According to the Office of the United Nations High Commissioner for Refugees, the number of displaced people in Colombia ranges 3.9-5.3 million, making it the country with the most internal refugees in the world.

Peace Negotiations with the FARC and M-19

In 1982, President Belisario Betancur was elected with the promise of negotiating peace with the guerrillas. The negotiations with the guerrillas got nowhere, but the FARC did establish a political party, the Unión Patriótica (UP), which successfully participated in the 1986 presidential elections and 1988 local elections, managing to win some mayoralties. The paramilitaries and local elites did not want the political arm of the FARC to wield local power. As a result, the UP was subjected to a brutal persecution by the paramilitaries, who killed more than 1,000 party members. In the midst of this violence, Colombia suffered one of its worst natural disasters: the eruption of the Nevado del Ruiz in November 1985, which produced a massive mudslide that engulfed the town of Armero, killing more than 20,000 people.

In 1985, the M-19 brazenly seized the Palacio de Justicia in Bogotá. The Colombian army responded with a heavy hand, and in the ensuing battle, half of Colombia's Supreme Court justices had been killed. Many people, including many cafeteria employees, disappeared in the army take-over, and there is speculation that they were executed and buried in a mass grave in the south of Bogotá. Weakened by this fiasco, leaders of the M-19 took up President Virgilio Barco's offer to negotiate peace. The government set down clear rules, including a ceasefire on the part of the M-19,

before talks could proceed. Unlike the FARC, the M-19 was still an ideological movement. The leaders of the M-19 saw that by participating in civil life they could probably gain more than by fighting. And they were right: In 2011 the people of Bogotá elected Gustavo Petro, a former M-19 guerrilla, as their mayor. On March 19, 1990, Barco and the M-19's young leader, Carlos Pizarro, signed a peace agreement, the only major successful peace agreement to date between the authorities and a major guerrilla group.

The Rise and Fall of the Medellín Cartel

Initially, the Colombian establishment turned a blind eye to the rise of the drug cartels and even took a favorable view of the paramilitaries, who were seen as an antidote to the scourge of the guerrillas. For a time, Escobar was active in politics and cultivated a Robin Hood image, funding public works such as parks and housing projects. Rather than stick to his business, as the Cali Cartel did, Escobar started to threaten any official who tried to check his power. In 1984, he had Rodrigo Lara Bonilla, the Minister of Justice, assassinated. When the government subsequently cracked down, Escobar declared outright war. He assassinated judges and political leaders, set off car bombs to intimidate public opinion, and paid a reward for every policeman that was murdered in Medellín—a total of 657. To kill an enemy, he planted a bomb in an Avianca flight from Bogotá to Cali, killing all passengers on board. The Medellín Cartel planted dozens of massive bombs in Bogotá and throughout the country, terrorizing the country's population. The cartel is allegedly responsible for the assassination of three presidential candidates in 1990: Luis Carlos Galán, the staunchly antimafia candidate of the Liberal Party; Carlos Pizarro, the candidate of the newly demobilized M-19; and Bernardo Jaramillo, candidate of the Unión Patriótica.

There was really only one thing that Escobar feared—extradition to the United States. Through bribery and intimidation, he managed to get extradition outlawed, and he negotiated a lopsided deal with the government of César Gaviria: In return for his surrender, he was allowed to control the jail where he was locked up. From the luxurious confines of La Catedral, as the prison was named, he continued to run his empire. In 1992 there was an outcry when it became known that he had interrogated and executed enemies within the jail. When he got wind that the government planned to transfer him to another prison, he fled. In December 1993, government intelligence intercepted a phone call he made to this family, located him in Medellín, and killed him on a rooftop as he attempted to flee. It is widely believed that the Cali Cartel actively aided the authorities in the manhunt.

A New Constitution

The 1990s started on a positive footing with the enactment of a new constitution in 1991. The Constitutional Assembly that drafted the charter was drawn from all segments of the political spectrum, including the recently demobilized M-19. The new constitution was very progressive, devolving considerable power to local communities and recognizing the rights of indigenous and Afro-Colombian communities to govern their communities and ancestral lands. The charter created a powerful new Constitutional Court, which has become a stalwart defender of basic rights, as well as an independent accusatory justice system, headed by a powerful attorney general, which was created to reduce impunity.

COLOMBIA ON THE BRINK (1992-2002)
The Unchecked Growth of New Cartels, Paramilitaries, and Guerrillas

Drug cultivation and production increased significantly during the 1990s. The overall land dedicated to coca cultivation rose from 60,000 hectares in 1992 to 165,000 hectares in 2002. As a result of the government's successful crackdown first on the Medellín Cartel and then on the Cali Cartel, drug

production split into smaller, more nimble criminal organizations. During the 1990s, the paramilitaries became stand-alone organizations that engaged in drug trafficking, expanding to more than 30,000 men in 2002. They created a national structure called the Autodefensas Unidas de Colombia, or AUC, under the leadership of Carlos Castaño. The AUC coordinated activities with local military commanders and committed atrocious crimes, often massacring scores of so-called sympathizers of guerrillas.

At the same time, the guerrillas expanded significantly during the 1990s. Strengthened by hefty revenues from kidnapping, extortion, and drug trafficking, they grew to more than 50,000 mostly peasant fighters in 2002. Their strategy was dictated primarily by military and economic considerations and they had little to no public support. At their heyday, the FARC covered the entire country, attacking military garrisons and even threatening major urban centers such as Cali. They performed increasingly large operations, such as attacking Mitú, the capital of the department of Vaupés, in 1998 or kidnapping 12 members of the Assembly of Valle del Cauca in Cali in 2002. The FARC commanders moved around the countryside unchecked. In the territories they controlled, they ruled over civilians, often committing heinous crimes. In 2002, they attacked a church in the town of Bojayá in Chocó, killing more than 100 unarmed civilians, including many children, who had sought refuge there.

Plan Colombia

The increasing growth of drug exports from Colombia to the United States in the 1990s became a source of concern for the U.S. government. From 1994 to 1998, the U.S. was reluctant to provide support to Colombia because the president at the time, Ernesto Samper, was tainted by accusations of having received campaign money from drug traffickers, and because of evidence about human rights abuses by the Colombian army. When Andrés Pastrana was elected president in 1998, the Colombian and U.S. administrations designed a strategy to curb drug production and counteract the insurgency called Plan Colombia. This strategy had both military and social components, and was to be financed jointly by the U.S. and Colombia. Ultimately, the United States provided Colombia, which was becoming one of its strongest and most loyal of allies in Latin America, with more than US$7 billion, heavily weighted towards military aid, especially for training and for providing aerial mobility to Colombian troops. While the impact of Plan Colombia was not immediately visible, over time it changed the balance of power in favor of the government, allowing the Colombian army to regain the upper arm in the following years.

Flawed Peace Negotiations with the FARC

President Pastrana embarked on what is now widely believed to have been an ill-conceived, hurried peace process with the FARC. He had met Manuel Marulanda, the head of the FARC, before his inauguration in 1998 and

was convinced that he could bring about a quick peace. Without a clear framework, in November 1998 he acceded to the FARC's request to grant them a demilitarized zone the size of Switzerland in the eastern departments of Meta and Caquetá. In hindsight, it seems clear that the FARC had no interest or need to negotiate as they were at the peak of their military power. Rather, the FARC commanders saw the grant of the demilitarized zone as an opportunity to strengthen their organization.

From the beginning, it became clear that the FARC did not take the peace process seriously. Marulanda failed to show up at the inaugural ceremony of the peace process, leaving a forlorn Pastrana sitting alone on the stage next to a now famous *silla vacilla* (empty seat). They ran the demilitarized zone as a mini-state, nicknamed Farclandia, using it to smuggle arms, hold kidnap prisoners, and process cocaine. During the peace negotiations, the FARC continued their attacks on the military and civilians. In February 2002, after the FARC kidnapped Eduardo Gechem, senator and president of the

protest for peace in Bogotá

© ANDREW DIER

Senate Peace Commission, Pastrana declared the end of this ill-advised demilitarized zone and sent in the Colombian Army.

A Failed State?

In 2002, the Colombian Army was battling more than 50,000 guerrillas and 30,000 paramilitaries, with an estimated 6,000 child soldiers. The insurgents controlled approximately 75 percent of the country's territory. An estimated 100,000 antipersonnel mines covered 30 of 32 departments. More than 2.5 million people had been internally displaced between 1985 and 2003, with 300,000 people displaced in 2002 alone. Not surprisingly, prestigious publications such as *Foreign Policy* described Colombia at the time as failed state.

REGAINING ITS FOOTING (2002-PRESENT)
Álvaro Uribe's Assault on the Guerrillas

In the 2002 elections, fed-up Colombians overwhelmingly elected Álvaro Uribe, a former governor of Antioquia who promised to take the fight to the guerrillas. Uribe had a real grudge against the FARC, who had assassinated his father. The FARC were not fans of his, either. In a brazen show of defiance, during Uribe's inauguration ceremony in Bogotá on August 7, 2002, the guerrilla group fired various rockets aimed at the presidential palace, during a post-swearing in reception. Several rockets struck the exterior of the palace, causing minor damage (attendees were unaware of the attack), but many more fell on the humble dwellings in barrios nearby, killing 21.

During his first term, Uribe embarked on a policy of Seguridad Democrática, or Democratic Security, based on strengthening the army, eradicating illicit crops to deprive the guerrillas of revenues, and creating a controversial network of civilian collaborators who were paid for providing tips that led to successful operations against the insurgents. The government increased military expenditure and decreed taxes on the rich totaling US$4 billion to finance the cost of the war. Colombian military personnel grew from 300,000 in 2002 to 400,000 in 2007.

From 2002 to 2003, the army evicted the FARC from the central part of the country around Bogotá and Medellín, although that did not prevent them from causing terror in the cities. In February 2003, a car bomb attributed to the FARC exploded in the parking lot of the exclusive social club El Nogal, killing more than 30 people—mostly employees. From 2004 to 2006, the army pressed the FARC in its stronghold in the southern part of the country. Aerial spraying of coca crops brought down cultivated areas from 165,000 hectares in 2002 to 76,000 in 2006.

In 2006, Uribe was reelected by a landslide, after Congress amended the constitution to allow for immediate presidential reelection. There is clear evidence that the government effectively bribed two congressmen whose vote was necessary for passage of the measure. Uribe interpreted the election results as a mandate to continue single-mindedly pursuing the guerrillas. The FARC came under severe stress, with thousands of guerrillas deserting and, for the first time, subjected to effective strikes against top commanders. No longer safe in their traditional jungle strongholds in Colombia, many FARC operatives crossed the border into Venezuela and Ecuador, causing tension between Colombia and the governments of those countries.

In early 2008, the Colombian military bombed and killed leading FARC commander Raúl Reyes in a camp in Ecuador, causing a diplomatic crisis with that country. Later that year, the military executed Operación Jaque (Operation Checkmate), a dramatic rescue operation in which they duped the FARC into handing over their most important hostages. The hostages released included three U.S. defense contractors and Ingrid Betancur, a French-Colombian independent presidential candidate who was kidnapped by the FARC during the 2002 presidential election as she proceeded by land, against the advice of the military, towards the capital of the former FARC demilitarized zone. In 2008, Manuel

Marulanda, founder of the FARC, died a natural death. At that time, it was estimated that the FARC forces had plummeted to about 9,000 fighters, half of what they had been eight years before.

The Colombian army has been implicated in serious human rights abuses. Pressure from top brass to show results in the war against the guerrillas and the possibility of obtaining extended vacation time led several garrisons to execute civilians and present them as guerrillas killed in combat. In 2008, it was discovered that numerous young poor men from the city of Soacha, duped by false promises of work, had been taken to rural areas, assassinated by the army, and presented as guerrillas killed in anti-insurgency operations. This macabre episode—referred to as the scandal of *falsos positives* (false positives)—was done under the watch of Minister of Defense Juan Manuel Santos, who was later elected president of Colombia.

Peace Process with the AUC

From 2003 to 2008, the Uribe government pursued a controversial peace process with the right wing paramilitaries, the Autodefensas Unidas de Colombia. As part of that process, an estimated 28,000 paramilitary fighters demobilized, including most of the high level commanders. In 2005, the Colombian Congress passed a Justice and Peace Law to provide a legal framework for the process. Unlike previous peace laws that simply granted an amnesty to the insurgents, this law provided for reduced sentences for paramilitaries who had committed serious crimes in exchange for full confessions and reparation of victims. Domestic and international observers were extremely skeptical about the process, worrying that the paramilitaries would use their power to pressure for lenient terms. These misgivings were justified by evidence that they used their power of coercion to influence the results of the 2006 parliamentary elections, a scandal referred to as *parapolítica*. Many congresspersons, including a first cousin of Uribe, ended up in prison.

It soon became clear that the paramilitary commanders were not sincere in their commitment to peace. Many refused to confess crimes and transferred their assets to front men. Covertly, they continued their drug-trafficking operations. The government placed scant importance on the truth and reparation elements of the Justice and Peace Law, severely underfunding the effort to redress crimes committed against more than 150,000 victims who had signed up as part of the process. Through 2008, the paramilitaries had confessed to a mere 2,700 crimes, a fraction of the estimated total, and refused to hand over assets. Fed up with their lack of cooperation, in 2008 Uribe extradited 14 top ranking paramilitary commanders to the United States, where they were likely to face long sentences. However, the extradition severely hampered the effort to obtain truth and reparation for the victims of their crimes.

The difficulty in redressing the crimes against victims has been further hampered by the growth of the dozens of small *bacrim (bandas criminals,* or illegal armed groups) who have taken territorial control of former paramilitary areas, intimidating victims who have returned to their rightful lands under the peace process. Many of these *bacrim* inherited the structures of the former AUC groups and employed former paramilitaries.

Social and Economic Transformation

During the past decade, Colombia has made some remarkable strides in improving social and economic conditions. Due to improved security conditions, investment, both domestic and international has boomed, totaling almost US$80 billion from 2003 to 2012. Economic growth has averaged 4.7 percent 2002-2012, a significant increase over the prior decades. The number of people below poverty, as measured by the ability to buy a wide basket of basic goods and services, has declined from 59.7 percent in 2002 to 32.7 percent in 2012. In Colombia's 13 largest cities, which represent 45 percent of the population, poverty has fallen to 18.9 percent. In terms of basic needs, most urban areas are well served in terms of education, health, electricity, water, and sewage.

However, there is a wide gap between the cities and rural areas, where 30 percent of the country's population lives. As of 2012, rural poverty stood at 46.8 percent. Though income inequality has been slowly falling, Colombia still has one of the most unequal distributions of income in the world.

Peace with the FARC?

In the 2010 elections, Uribe's former minister of defense, Juan Manuel Santos, was elected by a large majority. Santos continued to pursue an aggressive strategy against the FARC. Army operations killed Alfonso Cano, the new leader of the FARC, as well as Víctor Julio Suárez Rojas, the guerrillas' military strategist. As evidenced in the diary of Dutch FARC member Tanya Nijmeijer, found by the Colombian Army after an attack on a rebel camp, morale within the FARC had sunk to an all-time low.

At the same time, Santos recognized the need to address non-military facets of the violence. In 2011, Congress passed a comprehensive Victims and Land Restitutions Law, to redress the weaknesses of Uribe's Justice and Peace Law. This law provides a comprehensive framework to redress the crimes committed against all victims of violence since 1985.

After a year of secret negotiations, Santos announced the start of peace dialogues with the FARC in October 2012 in Cuba. These have proceeded at a slow pace, surprisingly without any halt to military actions. Former president Uribe and his allies have been very vocal against this initiative, claiming that a military defeat of the FARC is the only sensible path forward. At the time of writing, it was not clear whether the guerrillas were sincere in their desire for peace.

Government and Economy

GOVERNMENT

Under the 1991 constitution, Colombia is organized as a republic, with three branches of power—the executive, the legislative, and the judicial. The country is divided into 32 *departamentos* (departments or provinces) and the Distrito Capital (Capital District), where Bogotá is located. The departments are in turn divided into *municipios* (municipalities). These *municipios* include towns and rural areas.

The president of the republic, who is both head of state and head of government, is elected for a four-year term. With the exception of the military dictatorship of Gen. Gustavo Rojas Pinilla 1953-1957, presidents has been elected by the people since 1914. In 2005, then-president Álvaro Uribe succeeded in changing the constitution to allow for one immediate presidential re-election. In 2009, he attempted to get the constitution changed once more to allow for a second reelection but was thwarted by the powerful Constitutional Court, which decreed that this change would break the

necessary checks and balances of the constitutional framework.

Presidential elections will be held in May 2014 and 2018. If no candidate receives more than 50 percent of the votes, there will be a run-off election. Inauguration of the president takes place on August 7, the anniversary of the Batalla del Puente de Boyacá, which sealed Colombia's independence from Spain.

The legislative branch is made up of a bicameral legislature: the Senado (102 members) and the Cámara de Representantes (162 members). These representatives are elected every four years. Senators are voted for on a nationwide basis, while representatives are chosen for each department and the Distrito Capital. In addition, two seats in the Senate are reserved for indigenous representation. In the Cámara de Representantes, there are seats reserved for indigenous and Afro-Colombian communities as well as for Colombians who live abroad.

All Colombians over the age of 18—with the exception of active duty military and police as well as those who are incarcerated—have the right to vote in all elections. Women only gained the right to vote in 1954.

Political Parties

Historically Colombia has had a two-party system: the Conservative Party and the Liberal Party. The Conservative Party has traditionally been aligned with the Catholic Church and has favored a more centralized government, and followed the ideas of Simón Bolívar. The Liberal Party favored a federal system of governing, has opposed church intervention in government affairs, and was aligned with the ideas of Gen. Francisco Paula Santander.

The hegemony of the two largest political parties came to a halt in the 2002 presidential election of rightist candidate Álvaro Uribe, who registered his own independent movement and then established a new party called El Partido de la Unidad. Since then, traditional parties have lost some influence. A third party, the Polo Democrático, became a relatively strong force in the early 2000s, capturing the mayorship of Bogotá, but has since faded, leaving no clear representative of the left.

Colombia is known for its coffee production.

The Partido Verde (Green Party) ran strong in the 2010 elections, with former mayor Antanas Mockus becoming the main rival against eventual winner Juan Manuel Santos. This party has little to do with the global Green Party movement. Political parties today have become personality oriented, and many candidates have been known to shop around for a party—or create their own—rather than adhere to the traditional parties.

ECONOMY

Colombia has a thriving market economy based primarily on oil, mining, agriculture, and manufacturing. The country's GDP in 2013 was US$226 billion and per capita GDP was US$10,100, placing it as a middle-income country. Growth over the past decade has been a robust 4.7 percent. Inflation has averaged 3.8 percent in the past five years and unemployment has hovered around 10 percent.

During the colonial period and up until the early 20th century, small-scale gold mining and subsistence agriculture were the mainstays of Colombia's economy. Starting in the 1920s, coffee production spread throughout the country and rapidly became Colombia's major export good. Coffee production is of the mild arabica variety and is produced at elevations of 1,000 to 1,900 meters, mostly by small farmers. During most of the 20th century, Colombia emphasized increasing the volume of production, using the Café de Colombia name and mythical coffee farmer Juan Valdez and his donkey Paquita to brand it. A severe global slump in coffee prices during the past decade has led to a reassessment of this strategy and an increasing focus on specialty coffees. Today, coffee represents only 3 percent of all Colombian exports.

Colombia's wide range of climates, from hot on the coast to temperate in the mountains, means that the country produces a wide range of products. Until recently, sugar cane production, fresh flowers, and bananas were the only major export-driven agribusiness. However, improvements in security in recent years have resulted in a boom in large scale agricultural projects in

© ANDREW DIER

palm oil, rubber, and soy. Cattle ranching occupies an estimated 25 percent of the country's land. Commercial forestry is relatively underdeveloped, though there is considerable illegal logging, especially on the Pacific Coast.

In recent decades, oil production and mining have become major economic activities. The main center of oil production is the Llanos, the eastern plains of Colombia, with oil pipelines extending from there over the Cordillera Oriental to Caribbean ports. Oil currently represents roughly half of all Colombian exports. There is also significant natural gas, which is used mostly for residential use. Large-scale mining has been focused on coal and nickel, with large deposits in the Caribbean coastal region. With the improvement of security conditions in the past decade, many international firms, such as Anglogold Ashanti, have requested concessions for large-scale gold mining, often with opposition from the community. Illegal gold mining, often conducted with large machinery, is a severe threat to fragile ecosystems, especially in the Pacific Coast rainforest.

During the post-war period, Colombia pursued an import substitution policy, fostering the growth of domestic industries such as automobiles, appliances and petrochemical goods.

Since the early 1990s, the government has been gradually opening the economy to foreign competition and tearing down tariffs. In recent years, the country has signed free trade agreements with the United States and the European Union. Today, the country has a fairly diversified industrial sector. The country is self-sufficient in energy, with hydropower supplying the bulk of electricity needs.

Until recently, tourism was minimal because of widespread insecurity and a negative image. Things started to change in the mid-2000s, and the annual number of international visitors has increased almost threefold from 600,000 in 2000 to 1.7 million in 2012. While Bogotá and Cartagena still receive the bulk of visitors, almost the entire country has opened up for tourism, though there are still pockets of no-go zones. This boom in tourism has fostered a growth of community and ecotourism options, often with the support from government. The network of *posadas nativas* (guesthouses owned and operated by locals) is one initiative to foment tourism at the community level, particularly among Afro-Colombians. In recent years, Parques Nacionales has transferred local operation of ecotourism facilities in the parks to community-based associations.

People and Culture

DEMOGRAPHY

Colombia was estimated to have had a population of a little over 47 million in 2013 and has the third highest population in Latin America, behind Brazil and Mexico and slightly higher than Argentina. Around four million Colombians live outside of Colombia, mostly in the United States, Venezuela, Spain, and Ecuador. The population growth rate has fallen significantly in the past two decades and is now 1.1 percent. The population of the country is relatively young, with a median age of 28.6 years. Average life expectancy is 75 years.

Sixty percent of the Colombian population lives in the highland Andean interior of the country, where the three largest cities are located: Bogotá (7.7 million), Medellín (3.4 million), and Cali (3.1 million).

It is increasingly an urban country, with around 75 percent of the population living in urban areas. This trend began during La Violencia and accelerated in the 1970s and 1980s. At least 3.9 million persons have been internally displaced due to the armed conflict in Colombia, leaving their homes in rural areas and seeking safety and economic opportunity in large cities.

Most of the population (over 86 percent) is either mestizo (having both Amerindian and white ancestry) or white. People of African (10.4 percent) and indigenous or Amerindian

Gay Rights in Colombia

In a country still struggling with armed conflict and basic human rights, it might come as a surprise that gay and lesbian rights have not been pushed aside. Colombia has some of the most progressive laws regarding the rights of LGBT people in the western hemisphere. Since 2007, same-sex partners have enjoyed full civil union rights with a wide range of benefits, such as immigration, inheritance, and social security rights.

However, when it comes to marriage, it's a little more complicated. In 2011, the top judicial body, the Colombian Constitutional Court, ordered Congress to regulate marriage rights by mid-2013. Congress dithered, leaving the issue up in the air. Since then, scores of same-sex couples have gotten married despite the vehement opposition of the country's Procurador (inspector general), although the country's powerful attorney general has sided with same-sex couples in this legal battle. This limbo has left a bad taste in the mouths of just about everyone: gay rights advocates, the Catholic Church, and powerful conservative politicians.

(over 3.4 percent) origin make up the rest of the Colombian population. There is a tiny Romani or Roma population of well under 1 percent of the population, but nonetheless they are a protected group in the constitution.

There are more than 80 indigenous groups, with some of the largest being the Wayúu, who make up the majority in the La Guajira department; the Nasa, from Cauca; the Emberá, who live in the isolated jungles of the Chocó department, and the Pastos, in Nariño. Departments in the Amazon region have the highest percentages of indigenous residents. In Vaupés, for example, 66 percent of the population is of indigenous background. Many indigenous people live on *resguardos*, areas that are collectively owned and administered by the communities.

Afro-Colombians, descendants of slaves who arrived primarily via Spanish slave trade centers in the Caribbean, mostly live along both Pacific and Caribbean coasts and in the San Andrés Archipelago. Chocó has the highest percentage of Afro-Colombians (83 percent), followed by San Andrés and Providencia (57 percent), Bolívar (28 percent), Valle del Cauca (22 percent), and Cauca (22 percent). Cali, Cartagena, and Buenaventura have particularly large Afro-Colombian populations. In the Americas, Colombia has the third highest number of citizens of African origin, behind Brazil and the United States.

While Colombia has not attracted large numbers of immigrants, there have been periods in which the country opened its doors to newcomers. In the early 20th century, immigrants from the Middle East, specifically from Lebanon, Syria, and Palestine arrived, settling mostly along the Caribbean Coast, especially in the cities of Barranquilla, Santa Marta, Cartagena, and Maicao in La Guajira. From 1920 to 1950, a sizable number of Sephardic and Ashkenazi Jews immigrated. Colombia has not had a large immigration from Asia, although in the early 20th century there was a small immigration of Japanese to the Cali area.

RELIGION

Over 90 percent of Colombians identify as Roman Catholics, and it has been the dominant religion since the arrival of the Spaniards. The numbers of evangelical Christians, called simply *cristianos*, continue to grow, and there are other Christian congregations, including Mormons and Jehovah's Witnesses, but their numbers are small. In San Andrés and Providencia, the native Raizal population—of African descent—is mostly Baptist.

The Jewish community—estimated at around 5,000 families—is concentrated in the large cities, such as Bogotá, Medellín, Cali, and Barranquilla. There are significant Muslim communities, especially along the Caribbean Coast, and there are mosques in Barranquilla,

Happy Monday!

Colombians enjoy a long list of holidays (over 20). With a few exceptions, such as the Independence celebrations on July 20 and August 7, Christmas, and New Year's Day, holidays are celebrated on the following Monday, creating a *puente* (literally bridge, or three-day weekend).

During Easter week and between Christmas Day and New Year's, interior cities such as Bogotá and Medellín become ghost towns as locals head to the nearest beach or to the countryside. Conversely, beach resorts, natural reserves and parks, and pueblos fill up. Along with that, room rates and air tickets can increase substantially.

The following is a list of Colombian holidays, but be sure to check a Colombian calendar for precise dates. Holidays marked with an asterisk are always celebrated on the Monday following the date of the holiday.

- Año Nuevo (New Year's Day): January 1
- Día de los Reyes Magos (Epiphany)*: January 6
- Día de San José (Saint Joseph's Day)*: March 19
- Jueves Santo (Maundy Thursday): Thursday before Easter Sunday
- Viernes Santo (Good Friday): Friday before Easter Sunday
- Día de Trabajo (International Workers' Day): May 1
- Ascensión (Ascension)*: Six weeks and one day after Easter Sunday
- Corpus Christi*: Nine weeks and one day after Easter Sunday
- Sagrado Corazón (Sacred Heart)*: Ten weeks and one day after Easter Sunday
- San Pedro y San Pablo (Saint Peter and Saint Paul)*: June 29
- Día de la Independencia (Independence Day): July 20
- Batalla de Boyacá (Battle of Boyacá): August 7
- La Asunción (Assumption of Mary)*: August 15
- Día de la Raza (equivalent of Columbus Day)*: October 12
- Todos Los Santos (All Saint's Day)*: November 1
- Día de la Independencia de Cartagena (Cartagena Independence Day)*: November 11
- La Inmaculada Concepción (Immaculate Conception): December 8
- Navidad (Christmas): December 25

Santa Marta, Valledupar, Maicao (La Guajira), San Andrés, and Bogotá.

Semana Santa—Holy or Easter Week—is the most important religious festival in the country, and Catholics in every village, town, and city commemorate the week with a series of processions and masses. The colonial cities of Popayán, Mompox, Tunja, and Pamplona are known for their elaborate Semana Santa processions. Popayán and Mompox in particular attract pilgrims and tourists from Colombia and beyond. In cities such as Bogotá, Cali, and Cartagena, there are multitudinous processions to mountaintop religious sites, such as Monserrate, the Cerro de la Cruz, and El Monasterio de la Popa, respectively.

LANGUAGE

Spanish is the official language in Colombia. In the San Andrés Archipelago, English is spoken by Raizal natives who arrived from former English colonies after the abolition of slavery.

According to the Ministry of Culture, there are at least 68 native languages, which are spoken by around 850,000 people. These include 65 indigenous languages, two Afro-Colombian languages, and Romani, which is spoken by the small Roma population.

Three indigenous languages have over 50,000 speakers: Wayúu, primarily spoken in La Guajira; Páez, primarily spoken in Cauca; and Emberá, primarily spoken in Chocó.

ESSENTIALS

Getting There

BY AIR

Most visitors to Colombia arrive by air at the **Aeropuerto Internacional El Dorado** in Bogotá, with some carrying on from there to other destinations in the country. There are also nonstop international flights to the **Aeropuerto Internacional José María Córdova** in Medellín and to the airports in Cali, Cartagena, Barranquilla, and Armenia.

From North America

Avianca (www.avianca.com) has nonstop flights between Bogotá and Miami, Fort Lauderdale, Orlando, Washington, and New York-JFK. From Miami there are also nonstops to Medellín, Cali, Barranquilla, and Cartagena.

American (www.american.com) flies between Miami and Dallas and Bogotá; Miami and Medellín; and Cali and Medellín. **Delta** (www.delta.com) flies from Atlanta and New York-JFK to Bogotá. **United** (www.united.com) has flights from Newark and Houston to Bogotá.

Jet Blue (www.jetblue.com) has service between Orlando and Fort Lauderdale and Bogotá, Cartagena and New York, and Medellín and Fort Lauderdale. **Spirit** (www.

the airport shuttle in Acandí

spirit.com) has flights from Fort Lauderdale to Bogotá, Medellín, Cartagena, and Armenia.

Air Canada (www.aircanada.com) operates nonstops from Toronto to Bogotá.

From Europe

Avianca (www.avianca.com) has service to Bogotá and Medellín from Madrid and Barcelona. **Air France** (www.airfrance.com) flies from Paris to Bogotá. **Iberia** (www.iberia.com) serves Bogotá from Madrid. **Lufthansa** (www.lufthansa.com) offers service between Bogotá and Frankfurt.

From Latin America

Avianca (www.avianca.com) flies to many capitals in Latin America, including Buenos Aires, São Paulo, Rio de Janeiro, Valencia, Caracas, Lima, Santiago, and La Paz in South America; Cancún, Guatemala City, Mexico City, San José, San Juan, San Salvador, and Panama City in Central America; and Havana, Santo Domingo, Punta Cana, Aruba, and Curaçao in the Caribbean. Aerolíneas Argentinas,

AeroGal, Aeromexico, Air Insel, Conviasa, Copa, Cubana, LAN, Gol TAM, TACA, and Tiara Air Aruba also have connections to Colombia.

BY CAR OR MOTORCYCLE

A growing number of travelers drive into Colombia in their own car or with a rented vehicle. The most common point of entry is at the city of Ipiales on the Pan-American Highway: the Rumichaca border crossing with Ecuador at Ipiales (Tulcán on the Ecuador side). This entry point is open 5am-10pm daily.

On the Venezuelan side, the border at Cúcuta and San Antonio del Táchira is open 24 hours a day. Although there are other border crossings with Venezuela, this is the recommended overland point of entry.

BY BUS

Frequent buses that depart Quito bound for Cali (20 hours) or Bogotá (30 hours). You can also take a taxi from the town of Tulcán to the border at Ipiales and from there take an onward bus to Pasto, Popayán, Cali, or beyond. In Quito contact **Líneas de los Andes** (www. lineasdelosandes.com.co).

BY BOAT

It is possible to enter the country from Panama, usually via the San Blas islands. **Blue Sailing** (U.S. tel. 203/660-8654, www.bluesailing.net) offers sailboat trips between various points in Panama to Cartagena. The trip usually takes about 45 hours and costs around US$500. Sometimes, particularly during the windy season between November and March, boats stop in Sapzurro, Colombia, near the border. **San Blas Adventures** (contact@sanblasadventures.com, www.sanblasadventures.com) offers multi-day sailboat tours to the San Blas islands that usually depart from Cartí and end up in the Panamanian border village of La Miel. From there you can walk over the border to Sapzurro and take a *lancha* (boat) from there on to Capurganá. There are regular morning boats from Capurganá to both Acandí and Turbo. During the windy season, especially between December and February, this trip can be quite rough.

It is also possible to hitch a ride on a cargo boat from Ecuador to Tumaco or Buenaventura; however, service is irregular.

Getting Around

BY AIR

Air travel is an excellent, quick, and, thanks to the arrival of discount airliners such as VivaColombia, an often economical way to travel within Colombia. Flying is, without a doubt, the best option for those for whom the idea of 16 hours in a bus is not very appealing. Airlines have generally excellent track records and maintain modern fleets.

Bogotá is the major hub in the country, with domestic **Avianca** (tel. 1/401-3434, www.avianca.com) flights departing from the Puente Aereo (not from the main terminal of the adjacent international airport). All other domestic carriers: **LAN Colombia** (Colombian toll-free tel. 01/800-094-9490, www.lan.com), **Viva Colombia** (tel. 1/489-7989, www.vivacolombia.com.co), **EasyFly** (tel. 1/414-8111, www.easyfly.com.co), **Satena** (Colombian toll-free tel. 01/800-091-2034, www.satena.com), and **Copa** (tel. 01/800-011-0808, www.copaair.com) do depart from the new domestic wing of the international airport.

For some destinations (namely Leticia in Amazonia), the Pacific Coast destinations of Bahía Solano and Nuquí, La Macarena (Caño Cristales) in Los Llanos, and San Andrés and Providencia in the Caribbean, the only viable way to get there is by air.

If you plan to fly to Caribbean destinations such as Cartagena, San Andrés, Providencia, and Santa Marta during high tourist season, be sure to purchase your ticket well in advance, as seats quickly sell out and prices go through the roof. If your destination is Cartagena or Santa Marta, be sure to check fares to Barranquilla. These may be less expensive, and that city is only about an hour away. Similarly, if you plan to go to the Carnaval de Barranquilla in February, check fares to both Cartagena and Santa Marta. If you are flying to the Coffee Region, inquire about flights to Pereira, Armenia, and Manizales, as the distances between these cities are short. The Manizales airport, however, is often closed due to inclement weather.

Medellín has two airports: **Aeropuerto Internacional José María Córdova** (in Rionegro) and **Aeropuerto Olaya Herrera.** All international flights and most large airplane flights depart from Rionegro, a town about an hour away from Medellín. The airport is simply referred to as "Rionegro." **Satena** (Colombian toll-free tel. 01/800-091-2034, www.satena.com) and **Aerolíneas Antioqueñas-ADA** (Colombian toll-free tel. 01/800-051-4232, www.ada-aero.com) use the Olaya Herrera airport, which is conveniently located in town. This is a hub for flights to remote communities in the western and Pacific Region, including Acandí and Capurganá near the Panamanian border.

There are often strict weight restrictions for flights to Providencia from San Andrés and generally on small planes, such as on the military-owned Satena airline.

BY BUS

The vast majority of Colombians travel by bus. This is the money-saving choice and often the only option for getting to smaller communities. There are different types of buses, from large coaches for long-distance travel to *colectivos* for shorter distances. *Colectivos* (minivans) are often much quicker, although you won't have much leg room. There are also shared taxi options between many towns.

When you arrive at a bus station with guidebook in hand and backpack on, you will be swarmed by touts barking out city names to you, desperately seeking your business on their bus. You can go with the flow and follow them, or, if you prefer a little more control and calm, you can instead walk past them to the ticket booths. Forge ahead and shake your head while saying *"gracias."*

Be alert and aware of your surroundings and of your possessions when you arrive at bus stations, are waiting in the bus terminal, and are onboard buses. Try to avoid flashing around expensive gadgets and cameras while onboard. During pit stops along the way, be sure to keep your valuables with you at all times. Don't feel obliged to tell anyone your life story, where you are off to, or where you are staying. At the same time, most Colombians are extremely friendly and are simply just curious about foreigners visiting their country.

During most bus rides of more than a few hours' length, you will be subjected to violent films that the bus companies apparently find appropriate to be shown to small children. Earplugs, eyemasks, and even sleeping pills available at most pharmacies for those superlong journeys may come in handy, but make sure your possessions are well-guarded.

Bus drivers like to drive as fast as possible, and generally have few qualms about overtaking cars even on hairpin curves. You're better off not paying too much attention to the driving—it will do you no good! Large buses tend to be safer than smaller ones, although they may not go as fast.

During major holidays, purchase bus tickets in advance if you can, as buses can quickly fill up.

Buses may be stopped by police, and you may be required to show or temporarily hand over your passport (keep it handy). Sometimes all the passengers may be asked to disembark from the bus so that the police can search it for illegal drugs or other contraband. Young males may be given a pat-down. Even if it annoys you, it is always best to keep one's cool and remain courteous with police officers who are just doing their job.

Within cities, traveling by bus is often the easiest way to get around. Many cities, such as Medellín, Cali, Armenia, Bucaramanga, Pereira, Barranquilla, and (soon) Cartagena, have adopted the Bogotá rapid bus system model of the TransMilenio.

BY CAR, MOTORCYCLE, OR BICYCLE

Driving in Colombia is generally a poor idea for tourists. Roads are often in a poor state and are almost always just two lanes, speed limits and basic driving norms are not respected, driving through large towns and cities can be supremely stressful, signage is poor, sudden mudslides can close roads for hours on end during rainy seasons, and roads can be unsafe at night.

One exception is the Coffee Region. Here the roads are excellent, often four lanes, distances are short, and traffic is manageable. If you are planning on spending some time visiting coffee farms and idyllic towns, this might be a good option.

Another region where renting a car may make sense is in Boyacá. Here the countryside is beautiful and traffic is manageable.

There are car rental offices in all the major airports in the country. **Hertz** (tel. 1/756-0600, www.rentacarcolombia.co) and the national **Colombia Car Rental** (U.S. tel. 913/368-0091, www.colombiacarsrental.com) are two with various offices nationwide.

Touring Colombia on motorcycle is an increasingly popular option. One of the best motorcycle travel agencies in the country is **Motolombia** (tel. 2/392-9172, www.motolombia.com), based in Cali. Many motorcyclists take the Pan-American Highway through Colombia to Ecuador to continue on a once-in-a-lifetime South American bike tour.

Bicyclists will not get much respect on Colombian roads, and there are rarely any bike lanes of significance. In Santander and in Boyacá the scenery is absolutely spectacular, but, especially in Santander, it is often quite mountainous. In the Valle de Cauca, around Buga and towards Roldanillo, the roads are good and flat! Staff at **Colombian Bike Junkies** (cell tel. 316/327-6101, www.colombianbikejunkies.com), based in San Gil, are experts on biking throughout the country.

Every Sunday in cities across Colombia thousands of cyclists (joggers, skaters, and dog walkers, too) head to the city streets for some fresh air and exercise. This is the **Ciclovía**, an initiative that began in Bogotá, when city streets are closed to traffic. Except in Bogotá, it may be difficult to find a bike rental place, but you can still head out for a jog. *Ciclorutas* (bike paths) are being built in the major cities as well, and Bogotá has an extensive *cicloruta*

network. Again, cyclists don't get much respect from motorists, so be careful!

BY BOAT

In some remote locations in Colombia the most common way to get around is by *lancha* or boat. Many of the isolated villages and beaches and the Parque Nacional Natural Utría along the Pacific Coast are accessed only by boat from either Bahía Solano or Nuquí. The same goes for Isla Gorgona. To get to this island park, you normally have to take a boat from Guapi or from Buenaventura. All hotels or travel agencies can organize these trips for you.

Although there are some flights from Medellín to the Darien Gap village of Capurganá, it is often more convenient to either fly to the town of Acandí and take a boat onward to Capurganá or take a boat from the grubby town of Turbo. Waters can be rough, especially from November to March.

In the Amazon region, the only way to get from Leticia to attractions nearby, including Puerto Nariño and the ecolodges on the Río Yavarí, is by a boat on the Amazon, which is a memorable experience. All boats leave from the *malecón* (wharf) in Leticia.

The island resorts off of the coast of Cartagena are accessed only by boat from the Muelle Turístico near the Old City. If visiting Mompox from Cartagena, you'll need to take a ferry from the town of Magangué along the mighty Río Magdalena.

Visas and Officialdom

PASSPORTS AND VISAS

U.S. and Canadian citizens do not need a passport for visits to Colombia of under 90 days. Upon arrival, specify if you plan to spend more than 60 days in the country, as immigration officials may automatically stamp a 60-day permission (instead of 90). You could be asked to show a return ticket.

There is an exit tax of about US$66, divided into two categories (the Tasa Aeroportuaria and the Timbre Aeroportuario), that must be paid in cash in Colombian pesos or U.S. dollars upon departure from Colombian airports. Those who stay fewer than 30 days may be eligible for an exemption of one of the taxes. If you are exempt from one of the taxes, you may be sent at the airport to the airport authority office for an exemption stamp. Sometimes the taxes are included in the price of the airline ticket.

To renew a tourist visa, you must go to an office of **Migración Colombia** (www.migracioncolombia.gov.co) to request an extension of another 90 days. Some travelers prefer to make a "visa run" to Cúcuta, get their Colombian exit stamp, cross into Venezuela, and return the same day.

CUSTOMS

Upon arrival in Colombia, bags will be spot checked by customs authorities. Duty-free items up to a value of US$1,500 can be brought in to Colombia. Firearms are not allowed into the country, and many animal and vegetable products are not allowed. If you are carrying over US$10,000 in cash you must declare it.

Departing Colombia, expect thorough security checks with police looking for illegal drugs. They also may look for pre-Columbian art and exotic animals.

EMBASSIES AND CONSULATES

The **United States Embassy** (Cl. 24 Bis No. 48-50, Gate One, tel. 1/275-4900, http://bogota.usembassy.gov) is in Bogotá. In case of an emergency, contact the U.S. Citizen Services Hotline (tel. 1/275-2000). Non-emergency calls are answered at the American Citizen Services Section from Monday through Thursday 2pm-4pm. To be informed of security developments or emergencies during your visit, you can enroll in the Smart Traveler Enrollment Program (STEP) on the U.S. Embassy website. In Barranquilla, there is a **Consular Agency Office** (Cl. 77B No. 57-141, Suite 511, tel. 5/369-0419, 8am-noon Mon.-Fri.).

The **Canadian Embassy** (Cra. 7 No. 114-33, Piso 14, tel. (57-1) 657-9800, www.canadainternational.gc.ca/colombia-colombie) is in Bogotá. There is a **Canadian Consular Office** (Bocagrande Edificio Centro Ejecutivo Oficina 1103, Cra. 3, No. 8-129, tel. 5/665-5838) in Cartagena. For emergencies, Canadian citizens can call the emergency hotline in Canada collect (Can. tel. 613/996-8885).

Tips for Travelers

ACCESS FOR TRAVELERS WITH DISABILITIES

Only international and some national hotel chains offer rooms (usually just one or two) that are wheelchair accessible. Hostels and small hotels in secondary cities or towns will not. Airport and airline staff will usually bend over backwards to help those with disabilities, if you ask.

Getting around cities and towns is complicated, as good sidewalks and ramps are the exception, not the rule. Motorists do not stop—or even slow down—for pedestrians.

WOMEN TRAVELING ALONE

Along the Caribbean and Pacific coasts especially, women traveling alone should expect to be on the receiving end of flirts and various friendly offers by men and curiosity by everyone. In other parts of the country this is not as prevalent. Women should be extra cautious in taxis and buses. Always order taxis by phone and avoid taking them alone at night. While incidents are unlikely, it is not a fantastic idea to go out for a jog, a walk on a remote beach, or a hike through the jungle on your own. Walking about small towns at night alone may elicit looks or comments. Don't feel obliged to reveal your life story, where you are staying, or where you are going to inquisitive strangers. There have been incidents in the past with single women travelers in remote areas of La Guajira.

gay pride flag in Bogotá's Plaza de Bolívar

GAY AND LESBIAN TRAVELERS

In urban areas, especially in Bogotá, there is wide acceptance (or at least tolerance) of gays and lesbians, except for perhaps some of the poor neighborhoods. But public displays of affection between same-sex couples will generally get stares everywhere.

There is a huge gay community in Bogotá (with the epicenter of gay life the Chapinero area) and gay nightlife scenes in all the other major cities. Bars and clubs are usually quite mixed with gay men and lesbians.

It may be more of an annoyance than anything else, but cab drivers will routinely ask foreign men what they think of Colombian women and will suggest that they should "get" one. (Some will offer to help.) A word or two about the beauty of women from Medellín or Cali is usually a good response.

Gay men should be cautious in nightclubs and on online dating service sites, as persuasive thieves may use their seduction skills to get the chance to steal stuff back at your hotel room! Always keep an eye on your drinks at nightclubs, don't accept drinks or sips from strangers, and don't take cabs off the street, especially in front of clubs late at night.

Same-sex couples should not hesitate to insist on *matrimonial* (double) beds at hotels. Most hotels in the cities and even in smaller towns and rural areas are becoming more clued in on this.

Health and Safety

VACCINATIONS

There are no vaccination requirements for travel to Colombia. However, for certain regions, such as Amazonia and the Sierra Nevada de Santa Marta, it is officially recommended to carry proof of vaccination against yellow fever. You may be required to show this upon entry to the Parque Nacional Natural Tayrona. If traveling onwards to Brazil, you may be required to present proof of yellow fever vaccination. The yellow fever vaccination may not be recommended for persons who are HIV positive, for pregnant women, for children, or for others with weakened immune systems.

The Centers for Disease Control (CDC) recommends that travelers to Colombia get up-to-date on the following vaccines: measles-mumps-rubella (MMR), diphtheria-tetanus-pertussis, varicella (chickenpox), polio, and the yearly flu shot.

MEDICAL SERVICES

Colombia has excellent hospitals in its major cities. Sixteen hospitals in Colombia (in Bogotá, Medellín, Bucaramanga, and Cali) were listed in the *América Economía* magazine listing of the top 40 hospitals of Latin America. Four hospitals were in the top 10. Those were the **Fundación Santa Fe de Bogotá** (www.fsfb.org.co), the **Fundación Valle del Lili** (www.valledellili.org) in Cali, the **Fundación Cardioinfantil** (www.cardioinfantil.org) in Bogotá, and the **Fundación Cardiovascular de Colombia** (www.fcv.org) in Floridablanca, near Bucaramanga. For sexual and reproductive health issues, **Profamilia** (www.profamilia.org.co) has a large network of clinics that provide walk-in and low-cost services throughout the country.

Aerosanidad SAS (tel. 1/439-7080, 24-hour hotline tel. 1/266-2247 or tel. 1/439-7080, www.aerosanidadsas.com) provides transportation services for ill or injured persons in remote locations of Colombia to medical facilities in the large cities.

Travel insurance is a good idea to purchase before arriving in Colombia, especially if you plan on doing a lot of outdoor adventures. One recommended provider of travel insurance is **Assist Card** (www.assist-card.com). Before taking a paragliding ride or white-water rafting trip inquire to see whether insurance is included in the price of the trip—it should be.

DISEASES AND ILLNESSES
Malaria, Yellow Fever, and Dengue Fever

In low-lying, tropical areas of Colombia, mosquito-borne illnesses such as malaria, dengue fever, and yellow fever are not uncommon.

Malaria is a concern in the entire Amazon region and in lowland areas of Antioquia, Chocó, Córdoba, Nariño, and Bolívar. There is low to no malarial risk in Cartagena and in areas above 1,600 meters. The Colombian Ministry of Health estimates that there are around 63,000 annual cases of malaria in the country, 20 of which result in death. Most at risk are children under the age of 15. Malaria symptoms include fever, headache, chills, vomiting, fatigue, and difficulty breathing. Treatment involves the administration of various antimalarial drugs.

Yellow fever is another disease that is transmitted by mosquitoes. Early symptoms of yellow fever are similar to those of malaria and dengue fever: fever and chills, flu-like symptoms, and yellow-colored skin and eyes (jaundice). Every year there are around 20 cases of yellow fever reported in Colombia. It is most commonly contracted in low-lying areas, such as around the Sierra Nevada de Santa Marta, along the Río Magdalena, and in the Amazon region. There's no specific treatment for yellow fever, but it could involve blood transfusions, dialysis for kidney failure, and intravenous fluids.

The number of cases of dengue fever in Colombia has grown from 5.2 cases per

100,000 residents in the 1990s to around 18.1 cases per 100,000 in the 2000s. It is another mosquito-borne illness. The most common symptoms of dengue fever are fever; headaches; muscle, bone, and joint pain; and pain behind the eyes. It is fatal in less than 1 percent of the cases. Treatment usually involves rest and hydration and the administration of pain relievers for headache and muscle pain.

PREVENTION

Use mosquito nets over beds when visiting tropical areas of Colombia. Examine them well before using, and if you notice large holes in the nets request another one. Mosquitos tend to be at their worst at dawn, dusk, and in the evenings. Wear lightweight, long-sleeved, and light-colored shirts, long pants, and socks and keep some insect repellent handy.

DEET is considered effective in preventing mosquito bites, but there are other, less-toxic alternatives.

If you go to the Amazon region, especially during rainy seasons, take an antimalarial prophylaxis starting 15 days before arrival, continuing 15 days after departing the region. According to the CDC, the recommended chemo prophylaxis for visitors to malarial regions of Colombia is atovaquone-proguanil, doxycycline, or mefloquine. These drugs are available at most pharmacies in Colombia with no prescription necessary.

Altitude Sickness

The high altitudes of the Andes, including in Bogotá (2,625 meters/8,612 feet), can be a problem for some. If arriving directly in Bogotá, or if you are embarking on treks in the Sierra Nevada del Cocuy or in Los Nevados, where the highest peaks reach 5,300 meters (over 17,000 feet), for the first couple of days take it easy and avoid drinking alcohol. Make mountain ascents gradually if possible. You can also take the drug acetazolamide to help speed up your acclimatization. Drinking coca tea or chewing on coca leaves may help prevent *soroche,* as altitude sickness is called in Colombia.

Traveler's Diarrhea

Stomach flu or traveler's diarrhea is a common malady when traveling through Colombia. These are usually caused by food contamination resulting from the presence of E. coli bacteria. Undercooked meats, raw vegetables, dairy products, and ice are some of the main culprits. If you get a case of traveler's diarrhea, be sure to drink lots of clear liquids and perhaps an oral rehydration solution of salt, sugar, and water.

Tap Water

Tap water is fine to drink in Colombia's major cities, but you should drink bottled, purified, or boiled water in the Amazon, in the Pacific coast, in the Darien Gap region, in La Guajira, and in San Andrés and Providencia. If the idea of buying plastic bottles of water upsets you, look for *bolsitas* (bags) of water. They come in a variety of sizes and use less plastic.

CRIME

Colombia is safe to visit, and the majority of visitors have a wonderful experience in the country. But these remain uncertain times as guerrilla groups continue to fight the military, smaller groups of former paramilitaries (*bacrim*) operate in cities and towns across the country as small drug lords, and dangerous gangs rule many urban areas. It isn't always safe all the time.

The threat of kidnapping no longer terrorizes Colombians as it did in the 1990s when Colombia earned the unwanted distinction of kidnapping capital of the world, but it continues to be a source of income for illegal armed groups.

While kidnapping of foreigners has decreased dramatically, it still happens. In June 2013, a former U.S. Navy Seal, Kevin Scott Sutay, was kidnapped by the FARC as he was trekking (against the advice of the Colombian police and others) through the Amazonian rainforest towards Ecuador. In 2012, a pair of German brothers who were driving across Colombia in their four-wheel-drive vehicle were kidnapped in the Catatumbo region in the eastern department of Cesar by the ELN

Colombian police

guerrilla group, who accused them of being spies. A Norwegian was kidnapped in 2013 as he was attempting to cross through the Darien Gap into Panama on foot. A Spanish couple, touring the deserts of La Guajira in their own vehicle, were kidnapped by common criminals near Cabo de la Vela in May 2013 and rescued by the police about a month later.

The areas where these foreigners were kidnapped, with the exception of Cabo de la Vela, are known to be volatile regions where tourists would be wise to contract local drivers. While it is a good idea to get informed on the security situation of areas in Colombia before traveling by checking the U.S. Embassy website (http://bogota.usembassy.gov), some areas are widely known to be iffy for visitors due to the presence of illegal and armed groups. These areas include much of the Amazon region, including the departments of Putumayo, Caquetá, Guaviare, Vaupés, and Amazonas except for around Leticia and Puerto Nariño; the southern Llanos (visiting Caño Cristales by plane is OK); the

department of Arauca; the Catatumbo region of Cesar and Norte de Santander; most of the Chocó department, with the exceptions of Quibdó and the coastal tourist areas of Bahía Solano and Nuquí; the Darien Gap region, including the Los Katios park (Capurganá and Sapzurro are considered safe); and parts of Cauca near Santander de Quilichao.

Around tourist attractions in large cities, there is a strong police presence. This is especially true in the Old City of Cartagena and in the Centro Histórico of Bogotá. Street crime and homelessness are problems in poor neighborhoods and downtown areas of all the major cities after dark.

Particularly in Bogotá, but in other large cities as well, countless locals and visitors alike have been victims of the taxi crime of *paseo milonario* (the millionaire's ride). This occurs when you take a cab off the street, and within minutes the driver makes a sudden turn or invents an excuse that he needs to stop. At that point, usually two others will jump into the cab on either side of the victim and will threaten him or her at knife or gunpoint. The victim will then be driven to several ATMs in the city and forced to withdraw large amounts of cash. This crime tragically claimed the life of an American Drug Enforcement Agency agent in 2013 in Bogotá. Largely due to this crime, which soiled Colombia's reputation abroad, authorities have redoubled their efforts to prevent this crime and prosecute the perpetrators.

Prevention is the key to avoiding becoming a victim. Always order a cab by phone or by the popular and free smartphone application Tappsi (available in most cities). When you order a cab, or have one ordered for you, be sure to jot down the *placas* (license plate numbers). The operator will give these to you. When the cab arrives, confirm the *placas*. It is especially important to order a cab at night and when leaving upscale restaurants, shopping areas, and nightclubs.

Another crime to be aware of is poisoning. Poisoning most often occurs in nightclubs, when someone will either poison your drink or offer you a drink that has been poisoned. They will then easily persuade the victim to leave the club with them, and will force him or her to withdraw large sums of money from ATMs or will rob the victim of possessions. Although this is commonly called *burundanga* poisoning, after a flower called the *borrachero* whose seeds, when consumed, can render one helpless and in a zombie-like trance, the drug used by most criminals is not from the flower but a potent cocktail of drugs including the antianxiety drug lorazepam.

Information and Services

MONEY
Currency
Colombia's official currency is the peso, which is abbreviated as COP. Prices in Colombia are marked with a dollar sign, but remember that you're seeing the price in Colombian pesos. COP$1,000,000 isn't enough to buy a house in Colombia, but it will usually cover a few nights in a nice hotel!

Bills in Colombia are in denominations of $1,000, $2,000, $5,000, $10,000, $20,000, $50,000, and $100,000. Coins in Colombia got a makeover in 2012, so you may see two different versions of the same coin amount. Coins in Colombia are in denominations of $50, $100, $200, $500, and $1,000. The equivalent of cents is *centavos* in Colombian Spanish.

The exchange rate for Colombian pesos fluctuates. The best way to make a quick (though imprecise) conversion to U.S. dollars is to take half of the amount and move the decimal three places to the left. Thus, think of COP$10,000 to be around US$5, and COP$20,000 to be US$10.

Most banks in Colombia do not exchange money. For that, you'll have to go to a exchange bank, located in all major cities. There are money changers on the streets of Cartagena, but the street is not the best place for safe and honest transactions!

Travelers checks are not worth the hassle of carrying around anymore, as they are hard to cash. Dollars are rarely accepted, save for high-end hotels or in San Andrés. To have cash wired to you from abroad, look for a Western Union office. These are located only in major cities.

Counterfeit bills are a problem in Colombia, and unsuspecting international visitors are often the recipient of them. Bar staff, taxi drivers, and street vendors are the most common culprits of this. It's good to always have a stash of small bills as a preventative measure. Tattered and torn bills will also be passed off to you, which could pose a problem. Try not to accept those.

Consignaciones
Consignaciones (bank transfers) are a common way to pay for hotel reservations (especially in remote areas such as in Amazonia or in Chocó),

tour packages or guides, or entry to national parks. Frankly it's usually a pain to make these deposits in person, as the world of banking can be confusing for non-Colombians. On the plus side, making a deposit directly into the hotel's bank account provides some peace of mind as it will diminish the need to carry with you large amounts of cash. To make a *consignación* you will need to know the recipient's bank account and whether that is a *corriente* (checking) or *ahorros* (savings) account, and you will need to show some identification and probably have to provide a fingerprint. Be sure to hold on to the receipt to be able to notify the recipient of your deposit.

ATMs

The best way to get cash is to use your bank ATM card. These are almost universally accepted at *cajeros automáticos* (ATMs) in the country. *Cajeros* are almost everywhere except in the smallest of towns or in remote areas. Withdrawal fees are relatively expensive, although they vary. You can usually take out up to around COP$300,000-500,000 (the equivalent of around US$150-250) per transaction. Many banks place limits on how much one can withdraw in a day (COP$1,000,000).

Credit and Debit Cards

Credit and debit card use is becoming more and more prevalent in Colombia; however, online credit card transactions are still not so common except for the major airlines and some of the event ticket companies, such as www.tuboleta.com or www.colboletos.com. When you use your plastic, you will be asked if it's *credito* (credit) or *debito* (debit). If using a *tarjeta de credito* (credit card) you will be asked something like, *"¿Cuantas cuotas?"* or *"¿Numero de cuotas?"* ("How many installments?"). Most visitors prefer one *cuota* (*"Una, por favor"*). But you can have even your dinner bill paid in up to 24 installments! If using a *tarjeta de debito*, you'll be asked if it is a *corriente* (checking) or *ahorros* (savings) account.

Tipping

In most sit-down restaurants, a 10 percent service charge is automatically included in the bill. Wait staff are required to ask you, *"¿Desea incluir el servicio?"* ("Would you like to include the service in the bill?"). Many times restaurant staff neglect to ask tourists about the service inclusion. Of course if you find the service to be exceptional, you can leave a little extra in cash. Tipping is not expected in bars, nor is it expected at cafés, although tip jars are becoming more common in larger cities.

It is not customary to tip taxi drivers. But if you feel the driver was a good one, driving safely and was honest, or if he or she made an additional stop for you, waited for you, or was just pleasant, you can always round up the bill (instead of COP$6,200 give the driver COP$7,000 and say *"Quédese con las vueltas por favor"* ("Keep the change"). Note that sometimes a tip is already included in the fare for non-Colombian visitors!

In hotels, usually a tip of COP$5,000 will suffice for porters who help with luggage, unless you have lots of stuff. Tips are not expected, but are certainly welcome, for housekeeping staff.

RESOURCES

Spanish Phrasebook

Knowing some Spanish is essential to visit Colombia, as relatively few people outside the major cities speak English. Colombian Spanish is said to be one of the clearest in Latin America. However, there are many regional differences.

Spanish commonly uses 30 letters—the familiar English 26, plus four straightforward additions: ch, ll, ñ, and rr, which are explained in "Consonants," below.

PRONUNCIATION

Once you learn them, Spanish pronunciation rules—in contrast to English—don't change. Spanish vowels generally sound softer than in English. (*Note:* The capitalized syllables below receive stronger accents.)

Vowels

a like ah, as in "hah": *agua* AH-gooah (water), *pan* PAHN (bread), and *casa* CAH-sah (house)

e like ay, as in "may:" *mesa* MAY-sah (table), *tela* TAY-lah (cloth), and *de* DAY (of, from)

i like ee, as in "need": *diez* dee-AYZ (ten), *comida* ko-MEE-dah (meal), and *fin* FEEN (end)

o like oh, as in "go": *peso* PAY-soh (weight), *ocho* OH-choh (eight), and *poco* POH-koh (a bit)

u like oo, as in "cool": *uno* OO-noh (one), *cuarto* KOOAHR-toh (room), and *usted* oos-TAYD (you); when it follows a "q" the **u** is silent; when it follows an "h" or has an umlaut, it's pronounced like "w"

Consonants

b, d, f, k, l, m, n, p, q, s, t, v, w, x, y, z, and **ch** pronounced almost as in English; **h** occurs, but is silent—not pronounced at all

c like k as in "keep": *cuarto* KOOAR-toh (room), casa KAH-sah (house); when it precedes "e" or "i," pronounce **c** like s, as in "sit": *cerveza* sayr-VAY-sah (beer), *encima* ayn-SEE-mah (atop)

g like g as in "gift" when it precedes "a," "o," "u," or a consonant: *gato* GAH-toh (cat), *hago* AH-goh (I do, make); otherwise, pronounce **g** like h as in "hat": *giro* HEE-roh (money order), *gente* HAYN-tay (people)

j like h, as in "has": *Jueves* HOOAY-vays (Thursday), *mejor* may-HOR (better)

ll like y, as in "yes": *toalla* toh-AH-yah (towel), *ellos* AY-yohs (they, them)

ñ like ny, as in "canyon": *año* AH-nyo (year), *señor* SAY-nyor (Mr., sir)

r is lightly trilled, with tongue at the roof of your mouth like a very light English d, as in "ready": *pero* PAY-roh (but), *tres* TRAYS (three), *cuatro* KOOAH-troh (four)

rr like a Spanish r, but with much more emphasis and trill. Let your tongue flap. Practice with *burro* (donkey), *carretera* (highway), and Carrillo (proper name), then really let go with *ferrocarril* (railroad)

Note: The single small but common exception to all of the above is the pronunciation of Spanish **y** when it's being used as the Spanish word for "and," as in "Ron y Kathy." In such case, pronounce it like the English ee, as in "keep": Ron "ee" Kathy (Ron and Kathy).

Accent

The rule for accents, the relative stress given to syllables within a given word, is straightforward. If a word ends in a vowel, an n, or an s, accent the next-to-last syllable; if not, accent the last syllable.

Pronounce *gracias* GRAH-seeahs (thank you), *orden* OHR-dayn (order), and *carretera* kah-ray-TAY-rah (highway) with stress on the next-to-last syllable.

Otherwise, accent the last syllable: *venir* vay-NEER (to come), *ferrocarril* fay-roh-cah-REEL (railroad), and *edad* ay-DAHD (age).

Exceptions to the accent rule are always marked with an accent sign: (á, é, í, ó, or ú), such as *teléfono* tay-LAY-foh-noh (telephone), *jabón* hah-BON (soap), and *rápido* RAH-pee-doh (rapid).

BASIC AND COURTEOUS EXPRESSIONS

Colombians use many courteous formalities. Whenever approaching anyone for information or some other reason, do not forget the appropriate salutation—good morning, good evening, etc. Standing alone, the greeting *hola* (hello) can sound brusque.

Hello. *Hola.*
Good morning. *Buenos días.*
Good afternoon. *Buenas tardes.*
Good evening. *Buenas noches.*
How are you? Colombians have many ways of saying this: *¿Cómo estás/como está? ¿Qué hubo/Qu'hubo? ¿Cómo va/vas? ¿Que tal?*
Very well, thank you. *Muy bien, gracias.*
Okay; good. *Bien.*
Not okay; bad. *Mal.*
So-so. *Más o menos.*
And you? *¿Y Usted?*
Thank you. *Gracias.*
Thank you very much. *Muchas gracias.*
You're very kind. *Muy amable.*
You're welcome. *De nada.*
Goodbye. *Adiós.*
See you later. *Hasta luego. Chao.*
please *por favor;* (slang) *por fa*
yes *sí*
no *no*

I don't know. *No sé.*
Just a moment, please. *Un momento, por favor.*
Excuse me, please (when you're trying to get attention). *Disculpe.*
Excuse me (when you've made a mistake). *Perdón. Que pena.*
I'm sorry. *Lo siento.*
Pleased to meet you. *Mucho gusto.*
How do you say... in Spanish? *¿Cómo se dice... en español?*
What is your name? *¿Cómo se llama (Usted)? ¿Cómo te llamas?*
Do you speak English? *¿Habla (Usted) inglés? ¿Hablas inglés?*
Does anyone here speak English? *¿Hay alguien que hable inglés?*
I don't speak Spanish well. *No hablo bien el español.*
Please speak more slowly. *Por favor hable más despacio.*
I don't understand. *No entiendo.*
Please write it down. *Por favor escríbalo.*
My name is... *Me llamo... Mi nombre es...*
I would like... *Quisiera... Quiero...*
Let's go to... *Vamos a...*
That's fine. *Está bien.*
All right. *Listo.*
cool, awesome *chévere, rico, super*
Oh my god! *¡Dios mío!*
That's crazy! *¡Qué locura!*
You're crazy! *¡Estás loca/o!*

TERMS OF ADDRESS

When in doubt, use the formal *Usted* (you) as a form of address.

I *yo*
you (formal) *Usted*
you (familiar) *tú*
he/him *él*
she/her *ella*
we/us *nosotros*
you (plural) *Ustedes*
they/them *ellas* (all females); *ellos* (all males or mixed gender)
Mr., sir *señor*
Mrs., madam *señora*
miss, young lady *señorita*

wife *esposa*
husband *esposo*
friend *amigo/a*
girlfriend/boyfriend *novia* (female); *novio* (male)
partner *pareja*
daughter; son *hija; hijo*
brother; sister *hermano; hermana*
mother; father *madre; padre*
grandfather; grandmother *abuelo; abuela*

TRANSPORTATION

Where is...? *¿Dónde está...?*
How far is it to...? *¿A cuánto queda...?*
from... to... *de... a...*
How many blocks? *¿Cuántas cuadras?*
Where (Which) is the way to...? *¿Cuál es el camino a...? ¿Por dónde es...?*
bus station *la terminal de buses/terminal de transporte*
bus stop *la parada*
Where is this bus going? *¿A dónde va este bús?*
boat *el barco, la lancha*
dock *el muelle*
airport *el aeropuerto*
I'd like a ticket to... *Quisiera un pasaje a...*
roundtrip *ida y vuelta*
reservation *reserva*
baggage *equipaje*
next flight *el próximo vuelo*
Stop here, please. *Pare aquí, por favor.*
the entrance *la entrada*
the exit *la salida*
(very) near; far *(muy) cerca; lejos*
to; toward *a*
by; through *por*
from *de*
right *la derecha*
left *la izquierda*
straight ahead *derecho*
in front *en frente*
beside *al lado*
behind *atrás*
corner *la esquina*
stoplight *la semáforo*
turn *una vuelta*
here *aquí*

somewhere around here *por aquí*
there *allí*
somewhere around there *por allá*
road *camino*
street *calle, carrera*
avenue *avenida*
block *la cuadra*
highway *carretera*
kilometer *kilómetro*
bridge; toll *puente; peaje*
address *dirección*
north; south *norte; sur*
east; west *oriente (este); occidente (oeste)*

ACCOMMODATIONS

hotel *hotel*
Is there a room available? *¿Hay un cuarto disponible?*
May I (may we) see it? *¿Puedo (podemos) verlo?*
How much is it? *¿Cuánto cuesta?*
Is there something cheaper? *¿Hay algo más económico?*
single room *un cuarto sencillo*
double room *un cuarto doble*
double bed *cama matrimonial*
single bed *cama sencilla*
with private bath *con baño propio*
television *televisor*
window *ventana*
view *vista*
hot water *agua caliente*
shower *ducha*
towels *toallas*
soap *jabón*
toilet paper *papel higiénico*
pillow *almohada*
blanket *cobija*
sheets *sábanas*
air-conditioned *aire acondicionado*
fan *ventilador*
swimming pool *piscina*
gym *gimnasio*
bike *bicicleta*
key *llave*
suitcase *maleta*
backpack *mochila*
lock *candado*

safe *caja de seguridad*
manager *gerente*
maid *empleada*
clean *limpio*
dirty *sucio*
broken *roto*
(not) included *(no) incluido*

FOOD

I'm hungry. *Tengo hambre.*
I'm thirsty. *Tengo sed.*
Table for two, please. *Una mesa para dos, por favor.*
menu *carta*
order *orden*
glass *vaso*
glass of water *vaso con agua*
fork *tenedor*
knife *cuchillo*
spoon *cuchara*
napkin *servilleta*
soft drink *gaseosa*
coffee *café, tinto*
tea *té*
drinking water *agua potable*
bottled carbonated water *agua con gas*
bottled uncarbonated water *agua sin gas*
beer *cerveza*
wine *vino*
glass of wine *copa de vino*
red wine *vino tinto*
white wine *vino blanco*
milk *leche*
juice *jugo*
cream *crema*
sugar *azúcar*
cheese *queso*
breakfast *desayuno*
lunch *almuerzo*
daily lunch special *menú del día*
dinner *comida*
the check *la cuenta*
eggs *huevos*
bread *pan*
salad *ensalada*
lettuce *lechuga*
tomato *tomate*
onion *cebolla*

garlic *ajo*
hot sauce *ají*
fruit *fruta*
mango *mango*
watermelon *patilla*
papaya *papaya*
banana *banano*
apple *manzana*
orange *naranja*
lime *limón*
passionfruit *maracuyá*
guava *guayaba*
grape *uva*
fish *pescado*
shellfish *mariscos*
shrimp *camarones*
(without) meat *(sin) carne*
chicken *pollo*
pork *cerdo*
beef *carne de res*
bacon; ham *tocino; jamón*
fried *frito*
roasted *asado*
Do you have vegetarian options? *¿Tienen opciones vegetarianas?*
I'm vegetarian. *Soy vegetarian(o).*
I don't eat... *No como...*
to share *para compartir*
Check, please. *La cuenta, por favor.*
Is the service included? *¿Está incluido el servicio?*
tip *propina*
large *grande*
small *pequeño*

SHOPPING

cash *efectivo*
money *dinero*
credit card *tarjeta de crédito*
debit card *tarjeta de débito*
money exchange office *casa de cambio*
What is the exchange rate? *¿Cuál es la tasa de cambio?*
How much is the commission? *¿Cuánto es la comisión?*
Do you accept credit cards? *¿Aceptan tarjetas de crédito?*

credit card installments *cuotas*
money order *giro*
How much does it cost? *¿Cuánto cuesta?*
expensive *caro*
cheap *barato; económico*
more *más*
less *menos*
a little *un poco*
too much *demasiado*
value added tax *IVA*
discount *descuento*

HEALTH

Help me please. *Ayúdeme por favor.*
I am ill. *Estoy enferma/o.*
Call a doctor. *Llame un doctor.*
Take me to... *Lléveme a...*
hospital *hospital, clínica*
drugstore *farmacia*
pain *dolor*
fever *fiebre*
headache *dolor de cabeza*
stomach ache *dolor de estómago*
burn *quemadura*
cramp *calambre*
nausea *náusea*
vomiting *vomitar*
medicine *medicina*
antibiotic *antibiótico*
pill *pastilla, pepa*
aspirin *aspirina*
ointment; cream *ungüento; crema*
bandage (big) *venda*
bandage (small) *cura*
cotton *algodón*
sanitary napkin *toalla sanitaria*
birth control pills *pastillas anticonceptivas*
condoms *condones*
toothbrush *cepillo de dientes*
dental floss *hilo dental*
toothpaste *crema dental*
dentist *dentista*
toothache *dolor de muelas*
vaccination *vacuna*

COMMUNICATIONS

Wi-fi *wifi*
cell phone *celular*

username *usuario*
password *contraseña*
laptop computer *portátil*
prepaid cellphone *celular prepago*
post office *4-72*
phone call *llamada*
letter *carta*
stamp *estampilla*
postcard *postal*
package; box *paquete; caja*

AT THE BORDER

border *frontera*
customs *aduana*
immigration *migración*
inspection *inspección*
ID card *cédula*
passport *pasaporte*
profession *profesión*
vacation *vacaciones*
I'm a tourist. *Soy turista.*
student *estudiante*
marital status *estado civil*
single *soltero*
married; divorced *casado; divorciado*
widowed *viudado*
insurance *seguro*
title *título*
driver's license *pase de conducir*

AT THE GAS STATION

gas station *estación de gasolina*
gasoline *gasolina*
full, please *lleno, por favor*
tire *llanta*
air *aire*
water *agua*
oil (change) *(cambio de) aceite*
My... doesn't work. *Mi... no funciona.*
battery *batería*
tow truck *grúa*
repair shop *taller*

VERBS

Verbs are the key to getting along in Spanish. They employ mostly predictable forms and come in three classes, which end in *ar, er,* and *ir,* respectively:

to buy *comprar*
I buy, you (he, she, it) buys *compro, compra*
we buy, you (they) buy *compramos, compran*

to eat *comer*
I eat, you (he, she, it) eats *como, come*
we eat, you (they) eat *comemos, comen*

to climb *subir*
I climb, you (he, she, it) climbs *subo, sube*
we climb, you (they) climb *subimos, suben*

Here are more (with irregularities indicated):

to do or make *hacer* (regular except for *hago*, I do or make)
to go *ir* (very irregular: *voy, va, vamos, van*)
to walk *caminar*
to wait *esperar*
to love *amar*
to work *trabajar*
to want *querer* (irregular: *quiero, quiere, queremos, quieren*)
to need *necesitar*
to read *leer*
to write *escribir*
to send *enviar*
to repair *reparar*
to wash *lavar*
to stop *parar*
to get off (the bus) *bajar*
to arrive *llegar*
to stay (remain) *quedar*
to stay (lodge) *hospedar*
to rent *alquilar*
to leave *salir* (regular except for *salgo*, I leave)
to look at *mirar*
to look for *buscar*
to give *dar* (regular except for *doy*, I give)
to give (as a present or to order something) *regalar*
to carry *llevar*
to have *tener* (irregular: *tengo, tiene, tenemos, tienen*)
to come *venir* (irregular: *vengo, viene, venimos, vienen*)

Spanish has two forms of "to be":

to be *estar* (regular except for *estoy*, I am)
to be *ser* (very irregular: *soy, es, somos, son*)

Use *estar* when speaking of location or a temporary state of being: "I am at home." *"Estoy en casa."* "I'm happy." *"Estoy contenta/o."* Use *ser* for a permanent state of being: "I am a lawyer." *"Soy abogada/o."*

NUMBERS

zero *cero*
one *uno*
two *dos*
three *tres*
four *cuatro*
five *cinco*
six *seis*
seven *siete*
eight *ocho*
nine *nueve*
10 *diez*
11 *once*
12 *doce*
13 *trece*
14 *catorce*
15 *quince*
16 *dieciseis*
17 *diecisiete*
18 *dieciocho*
19 *diecinueve*
20 *veinte*
21 *veinte y uno* or *veintiuno*
30 *treinta*
40 *cuarenta*
50 *cincuenta*
60 *sesenta*
70 *setenta*
80 *ochenta*
90 *noventa*
100 *cien*
101 *ciento y uno*
200 *doscientos*
500 *quinientos*
1,000 *mil*
10,000 *diez mil*
100,000 *cien mil*

1,000,000 *millón*
one half *medio*
one third *un tercio*
one fourth *un cuarto*

TIME
What time is it? *¿Qué hora es?*
It's one o'clock. *Es la una.*
It's three in the afternoon. *Son las tres de la tarde.*
It's 4 a.m. *Son las cuatro de la mañana.*
six-thirty *seis y media*
quarter till eleven *un cuarto para las once*
quarter past five *las cinco y cuarto*
hour *una hora*
late *tarde*

DAYS AND MONTHS
Monday *lunes*
Tuesday *martes*
Wednesday *miércoles*
Thursday *jueves*
Friday *viernes*
Saturday *sábado*

Sunday *domingo*
today *hoy*
tomorrow *mañana*
yesterday *ayer*
day before yesterday *antier*
January *enero*
February *febrero*
March *marzo*
April *abril*
May *mayo*
June *junio*
July *julio*
August *agosto*
September *septiembre*
October *octubre*
November *noviembre*
December *diciembre*
week *una semana*
month *un mes*
after *después*
before *antes*
holiday *festivo*
long weekend *puente*

Suggested Reading

HISTORY
Bushnell, David. *The Making of Modern Colombia: A Nation in Spite of Itself.* Berkeley, CA: University of California Press, 1993. Mandatory reading for students of Colombian history. Bushnell, an American, is considered the "Father of the Colombianists".

Hemming, John. *The Search for El Dorado.* London: Joseph, 1978. Written by a former director of the Royal Geographical Society, this book explores the Spanish gold obsession in the New World. It's a great companion to any visit to the Gold Museum in Bogotá.

Lynch, John. *Simón Bolívar: A Life.* New Haven, CT: Yale University Press, 2007. This biography of the Liberator is considered one of the best ever written in English, and is the result of a lifetime of research by renowned English historian John Lynch.

Palacios, Marco. *Between Legitimacy and Violence: A History of Colombia, 1875-2002.* Durham, NC: Duke University Press Books, 2006. Written by a Bogotano academic who was a former head of the Universidad Nacional, this book covers Colombia's economic, political, cultural, and social history from the late 19th century to the complexities of the late 20th century, and drug-related violence.

THE DRUG WAR AND ARMED CONFLICTS
Bowden, Mark. *Killing Pablo: The Hunt for the World's Greatest Outlaw.* New York: Grove Press, 2001. This account of U.S. and Colombian efforts to halt drug trafficking and

terrorism committed by drug lord Pablo Escobar was originally reported in a 31-part series in *The Philadelphia Inquirer.*

Dudley, Steven. *Walking Ghosts: Murder and Guerrilla Politics in Colombia.* New York: Routledge Press, 2004. Essential reading for anyone interested in understanding the modern Colombian conflict, this book is written by an expert on investigating organized crime in the Americas.

Gonsalves, Marc, Tom Howes, Keith Stansell, and Gary Brozek. *Out of Captivity: Surviving 1,967 Days in the Colombian Jungle.* New York: Harper Collins, 2009. Accounts of three American military contractors who were held, along with former presidential candidate Ingrid Betancourt, by FARC guerrillas for over five years in the Colombian jungle.

Leech, Garry. *Beyond Bogotá: Diary of a Drug War Journalist in Colombia.* Boston: Beacon Press, 2009. The basis for this book is the author's 11 hours spent as a hostage of the FARC.

Otis, John. *Law of the Jungle: The Hunt for Colombian Guerrillas, American Hostages, and Buried Treasure.* New York: Harper, 2010. This is a thrilling account of the operation to rescue Ingrid Betancourt and American government contractors held by the FARC. It's been called a flip-side to *Out of Captivity.*

NATURAL HISTORY

Hilty, Steven L., William L. Brown, and Guy Tudor. *A Guide to the Birds of Colombia.* Princeton, NJ: Princeton University Press, 1986. This massive 996-page field guide to bird-rich Colombia is a must for any serious bird-watcher.

McMullan, Miles, Thomas M. Donegan, and Alonso Quevedo. *Field Guide to the Birds of Colombia.* Bogotá: Fundación ProAves, 2010. This pocket-sized field guide published by ProAves, a respected bird conservation society, is a more manageable alternative to Hilty's guide.

ETHNOGRAPHY

Davis, Wade. *One River: Explorations and Discoveries in the Amazon Rain Forest.* New York: Simon & Schuster, 1997. From the author of *The Serpent and the Rainbow,* this is a rich description of the peoples of the Amazonian rain forest, and the result of Davis' time in the country alongside famed explorer Richard Evan Schultes.

Reichel-Dolmatoff, Gerardo. *Colombia: Ancient Peoples & Places.* London: Thames and Hudson, 1965. A thorough anthropological investigation of the indigenous cultures across Colombia by an Austrian-born anthropologist who emigrated to Colombia during World War II.

----. *The Shaman and the Jaguar: A Study of Narcotic Drugs Among the Indians of Colombia.* Philadelphia: Temple University Press, 1975. An examination of shamanic drug culture in Colombia, particularly among indigenous tribes from the Amazon jungle region.

ARCHITECTURE

Escovar, Alberto, Diego Obregón, and Rodolfo Segovia. *Guías Elarqa de Arquitectura.* Bogotá: Ediciones Gamma, 2005. Useful guides for anyone wishing to learn more about the architecture of Bogotá, Cartagena, and Medellín.

TRAVEL

Lamus, María Cristina. *333 Sitios de Colombia Que Ver Antes de Morir.* Bogotá: Editorial Planeta Colombiana, 2010. Colombian version of *1,000 Places to See Before You Die* (only available in Spanish).

Mann, Mark. *The Gringo Trail.* West Sussex: Summersdale Publishers, 2010. A darkly comic tale of backpacking around South America.

Nicholl, Charles. *The Fruit Palace*. New York: St. Martin's Press, 1994. A wild romp that follows the seedy cocaine trail from Bogotá bars to Medillín to the Sierra Nevada and a fruit stand called the Fruit Palace during the wild 1980s. The English author was jailed in Colombia for drug smuggling as he conducted research for the book.

PHOTOGRAPHY AND ILLUSTRATED BOOKS

Often only available in Colombia, coffee table books by Colombian publishers Villegas Editores and the Banco de Occidente are gorgeous, well-done, and often in English. Save room in your suitcase for one or two.

Cobo Borda, Juan Gustavo, Gustavo Morales Lizcano, and César David Martínez. *Colombia en Flor*. Bogotá: Villegas Editores, 2009. This book features fantastic photographs of flowers you will see in Colombia.

Davis, Wade and Richard Evans Schultes. *The Lost Amazon: The Photographic Journey of Richard Evans Schultes*. Bogotá: Villegas Editores, 2009. A fantastic journey deep into the Amazonian jungle by famed explorer Richard Evans Schultes.

Díaz, Hernán. *Cartagena Forever*. Bogotá: Villegas Editores, 2002. A tiny little book of stunning black-and-white images of the Cartagena of yesteryear, by one of Colombia's most accomplished photographers.

Díaz, Merlano, Juan Manuel and Fernando Gast Harders. *El Chocó Biogeográfico de Colombia*. Banco de Occidente Credencial Cali, 2009. A spectacular trip through the unique and biodiverse Chocó region.

Freeman, Benjamin and Murray Cooper. *Birds in Colombia*. Bogotá: Villegas Editores, 2011. Dazzling photographs of native bird species found in Colombia, a veritable birding paradise.

Hurtado García, Andrés. *Unseen Colombia*. Bogotá: Villegas Editores, 2004. Photos and descriptions of the many off-the-beaten-track destinations in the country.

Montaña, Antonio and Hans Doering. *The Taste of Colombia*. Bogotá: Villegas Editores, 1994. A thorough survey of Colombian cuisine by region, with recipes included.

Ortiz Valdivieso, Pedro and César David Martínez. *Orquídeas Especies de Colombia*. Bogotá: Villegas Editores, 2010. Jaw-dropping photos of orchids, from the unusual to the sublime, found in the forests of Colombia.

Rivera Ospina, David. *La Amazonía de Colombia*. Cali: Banco de Occidente Credencial, 2008. An excellent souvenir of your visit to the Amazon region.

----. *La Orinoquía de Colombia*. Cali: Banco de Occidente Credencial, 2005. One of the least visited areas of Colombia is the Río Orinoco basin in the Llanos and Amazon regions.

Various. *Colombia Natural Parks*. Bogotá: Villegas Editores, 2006. Gorgeous photos from all of Colombia's spectacular national parks.

Villegas, Liliana. *Coffees of Colombia*. Bogotá: Villegas Editores, 2012. Everything you'd like to know about Colombian coffee in one charming and compact book.

Villegas, Marcelo. *Guadua Arquitectura y Diseño*. Bogotá: Villegas Editores, 2003. Profiles of minimalistic and modern constructions throughout Colombia all made from guadua.

FICTION

Caballero, Antonio. *Sin Remedio*. Bogotá: Alfaguara, 2006. A novel about a struggling poet in 1970s Bogotá by one of Colombia's best-known columnists.

Espinosa, Germán. *La Tejedora de Coronas*. Bogotá: Alfaguara, 2002. This novel contains the remembrances of Genovevea Alcocer, who, during the 18th century, leaves her native Cartagena to travel the world. Considered one of the most beautiful books of Latin American literature from the 20th century.

Franco, Jorge. *Rosario Tijeras*. New York: Siete Cuentos, 1999. An acclaimed suspense novel that takes place in violent Medellín in the 1980s.

García Márquez, Gabriel. *Innocent Eréndira and Other Stories*. New York: Harper, 2005. A collection of short stories, including a memorable tale of poor Eréndira and her awful grandmother.

----. *Love in the Time of Cholera*. New York: Alfred A. Knopf, 1988. A Colombian love and lovesickness story set in a fictitious version of Cartagena.

----. *One Hundred Years of Solitude*. New York: Harper, 2006. One of the Nobel Prize-winning author's classic novels, this book tells the story of the Buendía family from the fictitious town of Macondo.

Isaacs, Jorge. *María*. Rockville, Wildside Press, 2007. Considered one of the most important Latin American romantic novels of the 19th century, this love story takes place among the sugar cane fields near Cali.

Sánchez Baute, Alonso. *Líbranos del Bien*. Bogotá: Alfaguara, 2008. The incredible account of how two friends from the Caribbean coastal city of Valledupar became powerful adversaries.

Vallejo, Fernando. *Our Lady of the Assassins*. London: Serpent's Tail, 2001. A novel that takes place in Medellín, about a gay writer who returns to his violent hometown, where he falls in love with a young contract killer.

Internet and Digital Resources

ACCOMMODATIONS
Hostel Trail
www.hosteltrail.com
Run by a Scottish couple living in Popayán, this is an excellent resource on hostels throughout South America.

Posadas Turísticas de Colombia
www.posadasturisticasdecolombia.gov.co
Find information on interesting accommodations alternatives, like home stays.

BIRDING
ProAves
www.proaves.org
Excellent website for the largest birding organization in the country.

CARTAGENA
This is Cartagena

www.tic.com
Experience Cartagena like a local.

ECO-TOURISM
Parques Nacionales Naturales de Colombia
www.parquesnacionales.gov.co
Colombia's national parks website has information on all of the natural parks and protected areas in the country.

Aviatur Ecoturismo
www.aviaturecoturismo.com
Package tours of the Amazon, PNN Tayrona, PNN Isla Gorgona, and more are available from one of Colombia's most respected travel agencies.

Fundación Malpelo
www.fundacionmalpelo.org

This nonprofit organization works to protect Colombia's vast maritime territory, including the Santuario de Flora y Fauna Malpelo.

Fundación Natura
www.natura.org.co
The Fundación Natura operates several interesting eco-tourism reserves in the country.

EMBASSIES AND VISAS
U.S. Embassy in Colombia
http://bogota.usembassy.gov
The Citizen Services page often has security information for visitors, and is where you can register your visit in case of an emergency.

Colombian Ministry of Foreign Relations
www.cancilleria.gov.co
Offers information on visas and other travel information.

ENTERTAINMENT, CULTURE, AND EVENTS
Vive In
www.vive.in
Updated information on restaurants, entertainment, and cultural events in Bogotá.

Plan B
www.planb.com.co
Competitor of Vive In, Plan B offers information on what's going on in Bogotá, Medellín, and Cali.

Tu Boleta
www.tuboleta.com
The top event ticket distributor in the country, Tu Boleta is a good way to learn about concerts, theater, parties, and sporting events throughout Colombia.

Banco de la República
www.banrepcultural.org
Information on upcoming cultural activities

sponsored by the Banco de la República in 28 cities in the country.

HISTORY AND HUMAN RIGHTS ISSUES
CIA World Factbook Colombia
www.cia.gov
Background information on Colombia from those in the know.

Centro de Memoria Histórica
www.centrodememoriahistorica.gov.co
Excellent website on the human toll of the Colombian conflict.

International Crisis Group
www.crisisgroup.org
In-depth analysis of the human rights situation in Colombia.

Colombia Diversa
www.colombiadiversa.org
Covers LGBT rights in Colombia.

LANGUAGE COURSES
Spanish in Colombia
www.spanishincolombia.gov.co
Official government website on places to study Spanish in Colombia.

MEDELLÍN
Medellín Living
www.medellinliving.com
This website run by expats is an excellent purveyor of insider information on the City of Eternal Spring.

NEWS AND MEDIA
El Tiempo
www.eltiempo.com
El Tiempo is the country's leading newspaper.

El Espectador
www.elespectador.com.co
This is Colombia's second national newspaper.

Revista Semana
www.semana.com
Semana is the top news magazine in Colombia.

La Silla Vacia
www.sillavacia.com
Political insiders dish about current events.

Colombia Reports
http://colombiareports.co
Colombian news in English.

The City Paper Bogotá
www.thecitypaperbogota.com
Website of the capital city's English-language monthly.

Colombia Calling
www.richardmccoll.com/colombia-calling
Weekly online radio program on all things Colombia from an expat perspective.

TRANSPORTATION
Moovit
This app will help you figure out public transportation in Bogotá.

Tappsi
To order a safe taxi in Colombia's large cities, first upload this excellent app.

SITP
www.sitp.gov.co
This is the official website of the ever-improving (yet confusing) public bus transportation system in Bogotá.

TRAVEL INFORMATION
Colombia Travel
www.colombia.travel
This is the official travel information website of Proexport, Colombia's tourism and investment promotion agency.

Pueblos Patrimoniales
www.pueblospatrimoniodecolombia.travel
Find a pueblo that suits your needs at this informative website.

VOLUNTEERING
Conexión Colombia
www.conexioncolombia.com
This website is one-stop shopping for the nonprofit sector in Colombia. Find out how you can help, here.

Index

List of Maps

Acknowledgments

Mil gracias to: Dylan Misrachi, Alejandro Maldonado, Camilo Polo, Marcela Manrique, Marco Chiandetti, Alberto Dante, Eric Sánchez, Nery Luz Hoyos, Martha Rubio and Fabio Jiménez, Rainbow Nelson, Elena Posada, Marcela Sánchez, Jay Speller, Alex Zuluaga, Jorge Barbosa, Paola Lenis, Johana Granados, Matthew Freiberg, everyone at Iguana Hostel in Cali, Los Pinos folks in Minca, Claudia of Hostal Ruta Sur in Cali, Heike van Gils, Victor Sepulveda, Jade Gosling, Felipe Escobar, Rodrigo Andrés Fajardo, Tyler Stacy, Stefan Schnur, Tim Harbour, Tony Clark and Kim Macphee, Richard Emblin and María Claudia Peña, Richard McColl, Diego Duarte, Alexa and Daniel from Kolibrí in Pereira, Don Ai in El Valle, Ryan H. from Medellín, Javier Gamba, Patrice Chambragne, Carolina, Julia, and Diana Barco, Paulino Gamboa, Martin Climent, Mauricio Quintero, Juan Guillermo Garcés, Ximena Arosemena and everyone at the Reserva Natural Río Claro, Julio Suárez, Greg Shiffer, Alexandra Gómez, Guillermo Valderrama, Luzlilian Gómez, Juanita Saenz, Marta Royo, Shaun from Macondo in San Gil, Douglass Knapp, Max Hartshorne, Mary Luz Parra, Diana and Pepe Gómez, Juan Pablo Echeverri of Hacienda Venecia, Irene Torres, Jorge Torres and the staff of Hacienda Guayabal, Daniel Maxian, Karla Miliani, Finca Villa Martha, Jackeline Rendón, Mauricio Cardona, Héctor Buitrago, Hemmo Misker, Fibas Jardín Botánico del Desierto--Villa de Leyva, Jorge Raul Díaz, Nelson Barragán and everyone at Hacienda La Aurora, Goran Mihajlovic, Rafael Clavijo, Axel H. Antoine-Feill S., Kelly Brooks, Yaneth Caballero, Chris Hardyment, Alonso Sánchez, Gustavo Osorio, and Jorge Navas.

Thanks to everyone at Avalon Travel, especially Leah Gordon, Domini Dragoone, Mike Morgenfeld, and Grace Fujimoto. For their moral support, canines Tiga and Lumi, and finally, and most of all, to my partner Vio for his good sense, good humor, and incredible patience.